THE "CORN STALK" MILITIA

OF KENTUCKY

1792 - 1811

A brief statutory history of the militia and records of commissions of officers in the organization from the beginning of statehood to the commencement of the War of 1812

By

G. Glenn Clift

Assistant Secretary
of the
Kentucky Historical Society

Frankfort, Kentucky
Kentucky Historical Society
1957

This volume was reproduced from
an 1982 edition located in the
publishers private library,
Greenville, South Carolina

Please direct all Correspondence & Orders to:

**Southern Historical Press, Inc.
P.O. Box 1267
375 W Broad Street
Greenville, S.C. 29602-1267**

Originally published: Frankfort, KY 1957
New Material Copyright: Southern Historical Press, Inc. 1982
ISBN: 978-0-89308-318-2
Printed in the United States of America

CONTENTS

Preface iii

Organization of the Militia, 1792 viii

Organization of the Militia, 1793–1796 ix

Organization of the Militia, 1797–1798 x

Organization of the Militia, 1799–1804 xi

Organization of the Militia, 1805–1811 xiii

Arrangement of the Militia by Counties xv

Commissioned Officers, 1792 1

Commissioned Officers, 1793–1796 15

Commissioned Officers, 1797–1798 28

Commissioned Officers, 1799–1804 55

Commissioned Officers, 1805–1811 155

Index 207

PUBLISHER'S PREFACE

Southern Historical Press wishes to thank General William R. Buster, Director of the Kentucky Historical Society, and Dr. James C. Klotter, General Editor, Kentucky Historical Society, for their kindness in allowing us to reprint this extremely valuable book.

The copy used for the production of this reprinted edition has been taken from the Library of the Kentucky Historical Society, and has been reduced in page size from an 8½"×11" to a 6"×9" page size. Southern Historical Press has also had the index to this book retyped in three columns for a 6"×9" page size, which has allowed us to cut the index from 58 pages to 25 pages, and which provides a cost savings to the customer.

The Rev. Silas Emmett Lucas, Jr.
Southern Historical Press, Inc.

PREFACE

The need for and urgency of an effective military establishment in frontier Kentucky was first voiced in the new Commonwealth's Constitution. Faced with Indian attacks and the exposed situation of the country, the framers of the Constitution, many of them veterans of the Revolutionary War, immediately caused to be written into the document a provision that "The freemen of this Commonwealth shall be armed and disciplined for its defense..."

The military background and farsightedness of Colonel Isaac Shelby, the new state's first governor, further enhanced the prompt organization of a defense system. On June 24, 1792, only twenty days after the first General Assembly met was approved "An Act to arrange this State into Divisions, Brigades, Regiments, Battalions and Companies, and for other purposes." This act, passed in conformity with the then recently enacted Federal law for the better arrangement of the militia of the various states, provided for two Divisions, four Brigades and fifteen Regiments, as shown by a table following. [1] Four days later approval of "An Act for regulating the Militia of this Commonwealth" provided for the general discipline of the defense force. [2]

This law was soon repealed, however, when it was early discovered that it was "inadequate to answer the purpose intended." This was the first of many and frequent laws and legislative changes concerning the militia from 1792 until the organization died out after the Constitution of 1849-50 was put into force. The repealing act, approved December 10, 1792, provided first that many in public life be exempted from militia service. These included the Judges of the Supreme Courts, Speakers of the two houses of General Assembly, the Treasurer, Auditor, Attorney-General, Secretary, Register of the Land Office, Inspectors of Tobacco, all professors and tutors of public seminaries of learning, the Public Printer and his office staff, Ministers, keepers of the public jails and public hospitals, persons concerned at iron or lead works and persons employed in repairing or manufacturing fire-arms. All other free male persons between the ages of 18 and 45 were liable for militia duty. Commanding officers of companies were required to enroll all men subject to duty within the company's bounds, including all who settled or resided within the bounds for a space of ten days and all those who from time to time arrived at the age of 18. No person not an inhabitant of the State for three months was liable for militia duty.

All appointments of officers according to this law were made in the manner prescribed by the Constitution, or nominated and appointed by the governor with the advice and consent of the Senate. However, no officer not a resident of the State one year "next before his appointment" could be commissioned. (When the Constitution of 1799 took effect on June 1, 1800, all military appointments by the governor alone terminated at the end of the subsequent session of the General Assembly.) [3]

The governor was granted power to make alterations in the bounds of Divisions, Brigades and Regiments and to appoint officers for new Regiments thus

---

1. Acts passed at the First Session of the General Assembly... Lexington, Ky., 1792, Chap. xxviii, p. 37-8.
2. Ibid, Chap. xix, p. 28-31.
3. Garrard, Governor James, Executive Journal, 1800-1804, Part 2, p. 9.

created or laid off. [4]

This law, which further outlined the duties of officers, provided election procedures for vacancies, defined tours of duty, etc., was found defective and amended December 18, 1794, as to pay, dates of regimental musters, Courts Martial, etc.,[5] and a further change was approved at the January session of 1798. Thereafter, with increased population and militia boundaries constantly subject to change by formation of new counties, new legislation was frequent. The General Assembly at the November, 1798, session passed still another act concerning the militia which fully repealed all former laws on the subject. This last act was amended by one passed in 1799, and both were again amended by one which was approved in 1800, following Governor Garrard's complete reorganization of the militia into five Divisions, twelve Brigades and fifty-one Regiments.

In 1801 an act was passed to amend and reduce into one the several acts concerning the militia and this again repealed all former laws on the subject. One amendment to this act was made in 1804, then again in 1806 an act was passed which "utterly repealled and annulled all former laws concerning the militia." [6]

The act of 1806 was the first concerted effort to build a strong militia. It exempted Negroes, mulattoes and Indians from armed service and excused conscientious objectors provided they pay an equivalent for personal service. The governor retained his power to lay off Divisions, Brigades and Regiments and to change their boundaries as he saw fit. Commanding officers of the respective Regiments were empowered to appoint the regimental staff; Brigadier Generals could appoint their Brigade Majors; Major Generals were to choose their aides and Captains to select and appoint the non-commissioned officers in their companies. A majority of the field officers and Captains in each Regiment nominated the commissioned officers in each company, to be commissioned by the governor.

The governor was also empowered for the first time to raise companies of grenadiers, light infantry, cavalry, riflemen and artillery.

Regimental musters were ordered for October of each year; battalion musters were to be held in May and at least four company musters in each year were to be held between the last day of May and the last day of September.

It was from these fall musters of these first days of the defense system that the old state militia commonly became known as the "Corn Stalk Militia." The troops as a rule had no arms for musters and drills and often used corn stalks in the place of guns. (Bennett H. Young's A History of Jessamine County, Kentucky... Louisville, 1898, p. 95. In this work Mr. Young also described an early muster in Jessamine County.)

---

4. Acts passed at the Second Session of the General Assembly... Lexington [1792?], Chap. v, p. 5-15.
5. Acts passed at the First Session of the Third General Assembly... Lexington [1794?], Chap. viii, p. 7-11.
6. Littell, William, The Statute Law of Kentucky... v. 1, p. 87.

The act of 1806, which was ordered published and distributed to every general, field and staff officer and each company to be read at muster once each year, also specified a schedule of pay and fines. Pay of certain of the militiamen beginning this year was: [7]

"Adjutant General	$100 per annum
Brigade Inspector	$2 per day
Division Judge Advocate	$2 per day
Brigade Judge Advocate	$2 per day
Regimental Judge Advocate	$2 per day
Provost Martials	$1 per day
Adjutants of Regiments	$2 per day
Drum and Fife Majors and Clarinetists	$2 per day
Expresses	$1 per day"

Uniforms were first prescribed for all parades, reviews, field days and all actual service. A general or general staff officer was required to appear with a coat of blue, lapels of buff, gold epaulets and buff under clothes, with boots, spurs, a cocked hat, cockade and small sword or hanger; field officers and field staff observed the same uniform, except that their coats were turned up and lapelled with red and that they wore silver epaulets; the captains, subalterns and regimental staff were to "uniform themselves as the reputation of the service will materially by affected by a conformity to a regulation so essential in a military view; provided that for good cause shewn, the courts shall not fine the subalterns for not appearing in uniform; their trimmings to be the same with the field officers, except no epaulets shall be necessary, except the officers of the dragoons, rifle, infantry, and artillery corps, who may wear and adopt their own uniforms..." [8]

This act was amended in 1807 to provide for four company musters in each year, from June through September; to install the Adjutant General in the State House "in some room not appropriated for other purposes" and increase his salary to $150 per year, and stipulated stricter discipline and heavier fines for neglect of duty. [9]

The militia law was further amended in 1810 [10] and again in the December session of 1810. [11] These amendments attempted to solve many problems arising in the various units and as in previous laws and amendments failed.

Accordingly on January 12, 1812, "An Act to Revise and Amend the Militia

---

7. Acts passed at the First Session of the 15th General Assembly... Frankfort, 1807, p. 33-56.
8. Ibid.
9. Littell, op. cit., v. 3, Chap. dxxiii, p. 517-24.
10. Acts passed at the First Session of the 18th General Assembly... Frankfort, 1810, Chap. cxliv, p. 83-86.
11. Acts passed at the First Session of the 19th General Assembly... Frankfort, 1811, Chap. cclxxix, p. 128-31.

Laws" was approved, "repealing every former law, rule and regulation, heretofore enacted or adopted by the authorities of this state relative thereto."

This 42-page act, the last affecting the militia treated in the present study, was a more determined attempt, spurred by rumors of war with Great Britain, to provide for a powerful, well organized striking force. Duties of all commanding officers were more clearly defined, fines for unmilitary conduct increased, additional military courts set up, enrollment and classification of companies outlined, pay increases made and regiments of cavalry authorized. Changes were made in the uniform, substituting a round black hat, cockade, plume, and small - sword or hanger for Generals and general staff officers. Lieutenant Colonels, Majors and Brigade Inspectors were to wear a coat of blue, lapels of red, silver epaulets, white waistcoat, and blue pantaloons, boots, spurs a round black hat, cockade, plume, and small-sword or hanger. Captains, subalterns and regimental staff officers (except surgeons, chaplains and surgeon's mates) wore a coat of blue, lapels of red, epaulets of silver, and white underclothes, a round black hat with cockade, plume and sword or hanger. Officers of the dragoons, artillery, light infantry and rifle corps wore the uniforms of their respective corps.

Difficulties of long standing with the Shakers, prohibited by their religious doctrines from bearing arms, received attention in this law which provided "That when any man belonging to any society who hold community of property shall be fined by virtue of this act and refuseth or is not able to pay said fine, it shall be the duty of the sheriff, or other proper officer, to call on the agent or superintendent of the common stock or firm of said society or compact, for said fine or fines; and in case said agent shall refuse to pay or be absent, it shall be the duty of the sheriff or officer aforesaid, to execute and sell so much property belonging to said stock as shall be sufficient to satisfy said fine or fines and costs." [12]

Records of officers commissioned for the militia during this period have not heretofore been published. In 1891 the then Adjutant General issued his Report of the Adjutant General of the State of Kentucky, Soldiers of the War of 1812 which represented an attempt to list all militiamen active in that war from 1812 until 1814. This work has been supplemented from time to time by publication in the Register of the Kentucky Historical Society of fugitive lists of men who served from certain of the present counties.

This study attempts to bring together in one publication the name, rank and date of commission, unit to which assigned and county in which unit was laid off of every duly elected and commissioned officer of whom record exists from the beginning of statehood to the period when the above described publication begins its lists near the close of 1811.

Sources for the records of commissions are such as to break the lists into

---

12. Acts passed at the First Session of the 20th General Assembly... Frankfort, 1812, p 7-52.

five periods:　　　　　　　Part 1:　1792
　　　　　　　　　　　　　Part 2:　1793-1796
　　　　　　　　　　　　　Part 3:　1797-1798
　　　　　　　　　　　　　Part 4:　1799-1804
　　　　　　　　　　　　　Part 5:　1805-1811

　　　The names, ranks, units, etc., from 1792 to 1799 generally were entered in the Executive Journals of Governor Shelby and Governor Garrard. From the latter date to August, 1804, they were kept only in a manuscript volume of 374 pages (owned by the Society and not before published) titled: Company Officers, 1799-1804... comprehending a register of commissions issued to Captains, Lieutenants and Ensigns. After 1804 records of commissions of company officers had to be taken from manuscript papers, styled "Nominations of Officers," in the official papers of the governors, also in the Society. However, the last named papers for reasons undetermined cover only the years 1808 - 1811 and supply nominations and commissions for the first through thirtieth Regiments only. From 1808 until 1811, therefore, it was possible to find only the names, ranks and dates of commissions of the general officers.

　　　To enable the researcher to go to the original of any commission sources for all periods of the lists are here described, by period:

　　　Part 1: 1792.　Executive Journal, Governor Isaac Shelby, June 4 - December, 1792, MS, p. 1-24.

　　　Part 2: 1793 - 1796.　Executive Journal, Governor Isaac Shelby, April 5, 1793 - May 23, 1796, MS, p. 25-80.
　　　　　　　　　　　　　Executive Journal, Governor James Garrard, June 1 - December, 1796, MS, p. 81-100.

　　　Part 3: 1797 - 1798.　Executive Journal, Governor James Garrard, January 2, 1797 - December 17, 1798, MS, p. 102-186.

　　　Part 4: 1799 - 1804.　Executive Journal, Governor James Garrard, January 2, December 23, 1799, MS, p. 196-[214].
　　　　　　　　　　　　　Ibid, April 1, 1799 - December 20, 1804 (Part 2), for general officers.
　　　　　　　　　　　　　Company Officers [April 8] 1799 - [August] 1804, A Record of the Official Proceedings of the Executive: Part the Fifth, commencing with August, 1799, and comprehending A Register of commissions issued to Captains, Lieutenants and Ensigns. MS, 374 p.
　　　　　　　　　　　　　Governors' Executive Papers, "Nominations of Officers,"MSS, for August - December, 1804.

　　　Part 5: 1805 - 1811.　Executive Journal, Governor James Garrard, Part 2 for general officers to March 18, 1808.
　　　　　　　　　　　　　Executive Journal, Governor Charles Scott, September 1, 1808 - December 31, 1811, MS, p. 1-222.

Governors' Executive Papers, Governor Christopher Greenup, 1804 - 1808, Section 1, Box 7, Jackets 38 - 46, for company officers. MSS.

Ibid, Governor Charles Scott, 1808, Section 1, Box 8, for company officers. MSS.

It should be noted that in extracting records from the above named sources no attempt was made to record reasons for commissions, i.e., to replace officers who had died, moved from the bounds of the unit or who refused to qualify. Too it should be emphasized that the spelling of the original record has been used throughout even though obviously in error. In instances of doubt as to a name the spelling as it appears in the tax records of the county has been added in parenthesis.

For the convenience of local historians and others interested in the geographical make-up of the militia of 1792 - 1811 tables of the five periods have been prepared from data in the Executive Journals. It must be remembered that in many instances boundary lines of Regiments included parts of counties not indicated in the tables. For example the 21st Regiment is designated as the Campbell County unit through 1804 yet a check of Pendleton County tax lists shows that many appointments made in the 21st in 1804 were from the latter county.

Kentucky Militia

Organization in 1792*

DIVISIONS	BRIGADES	REGIMENTS	
1st (All of Kentucky lying south of the Kentucky River)	1st	1st	Jefferson and Shelby
		2nd	Nelson
		3rd	Nelson and Logan
		4th	Washington
	2nd	5th	Mercer
		6th	Lincoln
		7th	Madison
2nd (All of Kentucky lying north of the Kentucky River)	3rd	8th]	
		9th]	Fayette
		10th]	
		11th	Woodford
	4th	12th	Scott
		13th]	Bourbon
		14th]	
		15th	Mason

* Provided for by Act of the General Assembly, approved June 24, 1792. See Acts... 1792, p. 37f.

Kentucky Militia

Organization in 1793 - 1796*

DIVISIONS	BRIGADES	REGIMENTS		
1st	1st	1st	Jefferson.	By Act of June 24, 1792.
		2nd	Nelson.	By Act of June 24, 1792.
		3rd	Nelson & Logan.	By Act of June 24, 1792.
		4th	Washington.	By Act of June 24, 1792.
		18th	Shelby.	December 21, 1792.
	2nd	5th	Mercer.	By Act of June 24, 1792.
		6th	Lincoln.	By Act of June 24, 1792.
		7th]	Madison.	By Act of June 24, 1792.
		19th]		Laid off Mar. 2, 1795.
		16th	Green.	May 15, 1793.
2nd	3rd	8th]		
		9th]	Fayette.	By Act of June 24, 1792.
		10th]		
		11th	Woodford.	By Act of June 24, 1792.
		17th	Clark.	Created 1792/93.
	4th	12th	Scott.	By Act of June 24, 1792.
		13th]	Bourbon.	By Act of June 24, 1792.
		14th]		
		15th	Mason.	By Act of June 24, 1792.
		20th	Harrison.	December 16, 1795.
		21st	Campbell.	December 21, 1795.

* Regiments laid off or designated during this period were assigned to Brigades by the compiler on the basis of existing Brigades and locations of the new counties formed. Throughout the term of the first governor it was a practice to indicate creation of new Regiments only by entry in the <u>Executive Journal</u> of the names and ranks of officers commissioned for the new unit. When there was doubt as to the county in which the new Regiment was formed a check was made against the tax lists of the county. In most all instances after the four - year term of the first governor the recording secretaries noted the Brigade to which a new Regiment was attached. Only three of the sixty-one Regiments formed to the close of the 1799 - 1804 period failed to be assigned to a Brigade in the <u>Executive Journals</u> and of the eighty-six active at the close of the final period only two had to be checked against the tax lists. All such assignments by the compiler agree with a table (MS) forming the first two pages of a manuscript volume of 274 pages titled <u>Commissioned Officers, War of 1812 - 1816</u>.

Kentucky Militia

Organization in 1797 - 1798

DIVISIONS	BRIGADES	REGIMENTS		
1st	1st	1st	Jefferson.	By Act of June 24, 1792.
		2nd ⎤	Nelson.	By Act of June 24, 1792.
		27th ⎦		Laid off Apr. 1, 1797.
		3rd	Hardin.	Designated Feb. 23, 1797.
		4th	Washington.	By Act of June 24, 1792.
		18th	Shelby.	Designated Dec. 21, 1794.
	2nd	5th	Mercer.	By Act of June 24, 1792.
		6th	Lincoln.	By Act of June 24, 1792.
		7th ⎤	Madison.	By Act of June 24, 1792.
		19th ⎦		Laid off Mar. 2, 1795.
		16th	Green.	Designated May 15, 1793.
		22nd	Franklin.	Laid off Jan. 16, 1797.
		23rd	Logan.	Laid off Feb. 23, 1797.
		24th	Christian.	Laid off Feb. 23, 1797.
		25th	Warren.	Laid off Feb. 23, 1797.
		26th	Garrard.	Laid off Feb. 23, 1797.
2nd	3rd	8th ⎤		
		9th ⎥	Fayette.	By Act of June 24, 1792.
		10th ⎦		
		11th	Woodford.	By Act of June 24, 1792.
		17th	Clark.	First commissions 1792/93.
	4th	12th	Scott.	By Act of June 24, 1792.
		13th ⎤	Bourbon.	By Act of June 24, 1792.
		14th ⎦		
		20th	Harrison.	First commissions Dec.16,1795.
		21st	Campbell.	First commissions Dec.21,1795.
		31st	Montgomery.	Laid off Feb. 8, 1798.
	5th (First commissions on Jan.30, 1798)	15th ⎤	Mason.	By Act of June 24, 1792.
		29th ⎦		Laid off Jan. 22, 1798.
		28th	Mason & Bracken.	Laid off Jan. 22, 1798.
		30th	Fleming.	Laid off Jan. 22, 1798.

Kentucky Militia

Organization 1799 - 1804

DIVISIONS	BRIGADES	REGIMENTS		
1st Laid off Dec.13,1799	10th Laid off Dec.13,1799	16th 25th] 61st] 45th 46th 52nd*	Green. Warren. Barren. Cumberland. Adair.	First commissions May 15, 1793. Laid off Feb. 23, 1797. Created Dec. 10, 1804. Laid off Dec. 22, 1799. Laid off Dec. 24, 1799. Laid off Dec. 17, 1801.
	11th Laid off Dec.13,1799	23rd 24th] 55th] 39th 40th 41st	Logan. Livingston. Christian. Muhlenberg. Henderson.	Laid off Feb. 23, 1797. First commissions July 1, 1799. Laid off Dec. 15, 1802. Laid off Dec. 13, 1799. Laid off Dec. 15, 1799. Laid off Dec. 16, 1799.
2nd Laid off Dec.13,1799	9th Laid off Dec.13,1799	7th] 19th] 35th] 26th] 57th]	Madison. Garrard.	By Act of June 24, 1792. Laid off Mar. 2, 1795. Laid off Nov. 29, 1799. Laid off Feb. 23, 1797. Laid off Mar. 3, 1803.
	8th Laid off Dec.13,1799	6th 5th] 43rd] 44th 53rd* 54th*	Lincoln. Mercer. Pulaski. Wayne. Knox.	By Act of June 24, 1792. By Act of June 24, 1792. Laid off Dec. 17, 1799. Laid off Dec. 20, 1799. Laid off Dec. 10, 1802. Laid off Dec. 10, 1802.
3rd Laid off Dec.13,1799	7th Laid off Dec.13,1799	15th] 29th] 28th 30th] 58th] 56th	Mason. Bracken & Mason. Fleming. Floyd.	By Act of June 24, 1792. First commissions Jan.22,1798. Laid off Jan. 22, 1798. Laid off Jan. 22, 1798. Laid off Dec. 9, 1803. Laid off Dec. 17, 1802.
	6th Laid off Dec.13,1799	12th 13th] 14th] 47th]	Scott. Bourbon.	By Act of June 24, 1792. By Act of June 24, 1792. By Act of June 24, 1792. Laid off Apr. 10, 1800.

* Assigned to Brigades by the compiler on basis of location of parent counties.

Kentucky Militia

Organization 1799 - 1804, page 2

DIVISIONS	BRIGADES	REGIMENTS		
4th Laid off Dec.13,1799	1st Laid off Dec.13,1799	2nd] 27th] 60th 4th] 50th] 32nd	Nelson. Hardin. Washington. Bullitt.	By Act of June 24, 1792. Laid off Apr. 1, 1797. Laid off Dec. 10, 1804. By Act of June 24, 1792. Laid off Dec. 18, 1800. First commissions July 12,1799.
	12th Laid off Dec.10,1804	3rd 49th 59th 60th	Hardin. Ohio. Breckinridge. Hardin.	By Act of June 24, 1792. Laid off Dec. 13, 1800 to in- clude Breckinridge; divided to include Ohio only Dec. 10, 1804. Laid off Dec. 10, 1804. Laid off Dec. 10, 1804.
5th Laid off Dec.13,1799	5th Laid off Dec.13,1799	8th 17th] 36th] 31st] 34th]	Fayette. Clark. Montgomery.	By Act of June 24, 1792. First commissions 1792/93. Laid off Dec. 5, 1799. Laid off Feb. 8, 1798. Laid off Nov. 28, 1799.
	3rd Laid off Dec.13,1799	9th 10th] 42nd] 11th	Jessamine. Fayette. Woodford.	First commissions June 21,1799. By Act of June 24, 1792. Laid off Dec. 16, 1799. By Act of June 24, 1792.
6th Formed Dec.19,1804	2nd Laid off Dec.13,1799	1st] 33rd] 18th] 37th] 38th	Jefferson. Shelby. Henry.	By Act of June 24, 1792. Laid off Nov. 21, 1799. First commissions Dec.21,1794. Laid off Dec. 5, 1799. Laid off Dec. 11, 1799.
	4th Laid off Dec.13,1799	20th 22nd 48th 51st 21st	Harrison. Franklin. Campbell & Boone. Gallatin. Campbell.	First commissions Dec.16,1795. Laid off Jan. 16, 1797. Laid off Dec. 13, 1800. Laid off Dec. 20, 1800. First commissions Dec.21,1795.

Kentucky Militia

Organization 1805 - 1811

DIVISIONS	BRIGADES	REGIMENTS		
1st	11th Regrouped Feb.17, 1808	23rd 39th] 72nd] 66th	Logan. Christian. Butler.	Laid off Feb. 23, 1797. Laid off Feb. 13, 1799. Laid off Feb. 17, 1808. Laid off Dec. 16, 1806.
	17th Formed Feb. 18, 1808.	40th] 82nd] 41st 76th	Muhlenberg. Henderson. Hopkins.	Laid off Dec. 15, 1799. Laid off Jan. 11, 1811. Laid off Dec. 16, 1799. Laid off Jan. 30, 1809.
	19th Formed Jan. 12, 1811.	24th 55th 83rd 84th	Livingston. Livingston & Caldwell. Union. Caldwell.	First commissions July 1, 1799. Laid off Dec. 15, 1802. Laid off Jan. 11, 1811. Laid off Jan. 11, 1811.
2nd	9th Regrouped Jan.27, 1808 and Jan. 11, 1811.	26th] 57th] 63rd 79th	Garrard. Lincoln. Rockcastle.	Laid off Feb. 23, 1797. Laid off Mar. 3, 1803. Laid off May 9, 1806. Formed Jan. 23, 1810.
	13th Formed Dec.24, 1806; regrouped Jan. 11, 1811.	7th] 19th] 35th] 78th	Madison. Estill.	By Act of June 24, 1792. Laid off Mar. 2, 1795. Laid off Nov. 29, 1799. Formed Jan. 22, 1810.
	18th Formed Jan. 11, 1811.	54th] 75th] 68th] 80th]	Knox. Clay.	Laid off Dec. 10, 1802. Laid off Jan. 21, 1809. Laid off Dec. 17, 1806. Created Jan. 11, 1811.
3rd Regrouped Dec. 27, 1806.	6th	12th] 77th] 14th] 71st] 22nd	Scott. Bourbon. Franklin.	By Act of June 24, 1792. Laid off Feb. 11, 1809. By Act of June 24, 1792. Laid off Dec. 27, 1806. Laid off Jan. 16, 1797.
	15th Formed Dec. 27, 1806.	13th 34th 47th 65th	Nicholas. Montgomery. Bourbon. Bath.	First commissions Dec.27,1806. Laid off Dec. 28, 1799. Laid off Apr. 10, 1800. Laid off Dec. 16, 1806.

Kentucky Militia

Organization 1805 - 1811, page 2

DIVISIONS	BRIGADES	REGIMENTS		
4th	1st Regrouped Jan. 27, 1808	2nd] 27th] Nelson. 62nd] 32nd Bullitt.		By Act of June 24, 1792. Laid off Apr. 1, 1797. Laid off Dec. 20, 1805. First commissions July 12,1799
4th	12th	3rd] 60th] Hardin. 49th Ohio. 59th Breckinridge. 73rd Daveiss.		By Act of June 24, 1792. Laid off Dec. 10, 1804. Designated Dec. 10, 1804. Laid off Dec. 10, 1804. Laid off Feb. 17, 1808.
5th	3rd	9th Jessamine. 10th] Fayette. 42nd] 11th Woodford.		First commissions June 21,1799 By Act of June 24, 1792. Laid off Dec. 16, 1799. By Act of June 24, 1792.
5th	5th	8th Fayette. 17th] Clark. 36th] 31st Montgomery.		By Act of June 24, 1792. First commissions 1792/93. Laid off Dec. 5, 1799. Laid off Feb. 8, 1798.
6th	2nd	1st] Jefferson. 33rd] 18th] 37th] Shelby. 85th] 38th Henry. Squadron of Cavalry.		By Act of June 24, 1792. Laid off Nov. 21, 1799. First commissions Dec.21,1794. Laid off Dec. 5, 1799. Laid off Jan. 18, 1811. Laid off Dec. 11, 1799. Constituted Jan. 18, 1811.
6th	4th	20th] Harrison. 86th] 21st Pendleton. 48th Campbell. 51st Gallatin. 67th Boone.		First commissions Dec.16,1795. Laid off Jan. 29, 1811. Designated Dec. 17, 1806. Designated Dec. 17, 1806. Laid off Dec. 20, 1800. Laid off Dec. 17, 1806.
7th	7th	15th] 29th] Mason. 69th]		By Act of June 24, 1792. Laid off Jan. 22, 1798. Created Dec. 27, 1806.
Formed Dec. 27, 1806.	14th Formed Dec. 27, 1806.	30th] Fleming. 58th] 56th Floyd. 70th Greenup.		Laid off Jan. 22, 1798. Laid off Dec. 9, 1803. Laid off Dec. 17, 1802. Laid off Dec. 27, 1806.

Kentucky Militia

Organization 1805 - 1811, page 3

DIVISIONS	BRIGADES	REGIMENTS		
8th Formed Jan. 27, 1808.	8th Regrouped Jan. 27, 1808.	4th] 50th] 5th] 43rd]	Washington. Mercer.	By Act of June 24, 1792. Laid off Dec. 18, 1800. By Act of June 24, 1792. Laid off Dec. 17, 1799.
	16th Formed Jan. 27, 1808.	6th 44th 53rd 74th	Lincoln. Pulaski. Wayne. Casey.	By Act of June 24, 1792. Laid off Dec. 20, 1799. Laid off Dec. 10, 1802. Laid off Dec. 28, 1808.
9th Formed Jan. 12, 1811.	10th Regrouped Jan. 12, 1811.	16th 46th] 81st] 52nd	Green. Cumberland. Adair.	First commissions May 15, 1793. Laid off Dec. 24, 1799. Laid off Jan. 11, 1811. Laid off Dec. 17, 1801.
	20th Formed Jan. 12, 1811.	25th] 61st] 45th 64th	Warren. Barren. Allen.	Laid off Feb. 23, 1797. Created Dec. 10, 1804. Laid off Dec. 22, 1799. Laid off May 9, 1806.

As noted on page 157 commissions entered from that page to page 206 are in one alphabetical sequence, for reasons noted on page 157. For the convenience of county historians, faced with the task of ferreting out officers of a given county, the following table is appended.

Kentucky Militia, 1792 - 1811

Arrangement by Counties

COUNTY	REGIMENT	DATE OF FORMATION
Adair.....................	52nd....	Laid off Dec. 17, 1801.
Allen.....................	64th....	Laid off May 9, 1806. See also Mason (69th).
Barren....................	45th....	Laid off Dec. 22, 1799.
Bath......................	65th.... 34th....	Laid off Dec. 16, 1806. On creation of county, Jan. 15, 1811. (See also Montgomery.)

Kentucky Militia, 1792 - 1811

Arrangement by counties, page 2

COUNTY	REGIMENT	DATE OF FORMATION
Boone................	67th....	Laid off Dec. 17, 1806. (See also Campbell and Boone.)
Bourbon..............	13th....	By Act of June 24, 1792. Nicholas after Dec. 27, 1806.
	14th....	By Act of June 24, 1792.
	47th....	Laid off Apr. 10, 1800.
	71st....	Laid off Dec. 27, 1806.
Bracken..............	28th....	Laid off Dec. 27, 1806. (See also Mason and Bracken.)
Breckinridge.........	59th....	Laid off Dec. 10, 1804. (See also Ohio and Breckinridge.)
Bullitt..............	32nd....	First commissions July 12, 1799.
Butler...............	66th....	Laid off Dec. 16, 1806.
Caldwell.............	55th....	Laid off Dec. 24, 1809.
	84th....	Created Jan. 11, 1811. (See also Livingston.)
Campbell.............	21st....	First commissions Dec. 21, 1795. Pendleton after Dec. 17, 1806.
Campbell and Boone...	48th....	Laid off Dec. 13, 1800. Campbell only after Dec. 17, 1806.
Casey................	74th....	Laid off Dec. 28, 1808.
Christian............	24th....	Laid off Feb. 23, 1797. Livingston after July 1, 1799.
	39th....	Laid off Dec. 13, 1799.
	72nd....	Laid off Feb. 17, 1808.
Clark................	17th....	First commissions 1792/93.
	36th....	Laid off Dec. 5, 1799.
Clay.................	68th....	Laid off Dec. 17, 1806.
	80th....	Created Jan. 11, 1811.
Cumberland...........	46th....	Laid off Dec. 24, 1799.
	81st....	Created Jan. 11, 1811.

Kentucky Militia, 1792 - 1811

Arrangement by counties, page 3

COUNTY	REGIMENT	DATE OF FORMATION
Daveiss...............	73rd....	Laid off Feb. 17, 1808.
Estill................	78th....	Formed Jan. 22, 1810.
Fayette...............	8th....	By Act of June 24, 1792.
	9th....	By Act of June 24, 1792. Jessamine after June 21, 1799.
	10th....	By Act of June 24, 1792.
	42nd....	Laid off Dec. 16, 1799.
Fleming...............	30th....	Laid off Jan. 22, 1798.
	58th....	Laid off Dec. 9, 1803.
Floyd.................	56th....	Laid off Dec. 17, 1802.
Franklin..............	22nd....	Laid off Jan. 16, 1797.
Gallatin..............	51st....	Laid off Dec. 20, 1800.
Garrard...............	26th....	Laid off Feb. 23, 1797.
	57th....	Laid off Mar. 3, 1803.
Green.................	16th....	First commissions May 15, 1793.
Greenup...............	70th....	Laid off Dec. 27, 1806.
Hardin................	3rd....	Laid off Feb. 23, 1797.
	60th....	Laid off Dec. 10, 1804. (See also Nelson and Logan.)
Harrison..............	20th....	First commissions Dec. 16, 1795.
	86th....	Created Jan. 29, 1811.
Henderson.............	41st....	Laid off Dec. 16, 1799.
Henry.................	38th....	Laid off Dec. 11, 1799.
Hopkins...............	76th....	Laid off Jan. 30, 1809.
Jefferson.............	1st....	By Act of June 24, 1792. Jefferson and Shelby to Dec. 21, 1794.
	33rd....	Laid off Nov. 21, 1799.

Kentucky Militia, 1792 - 1811

Arrangement by counties, page 4

COUNTY	REGIMENT	DATE OF FORMATION
Jessamine..................	9th....	First commissions June 21, 1799. (See also Fayette, 9th.)
Knox......................	54th....	Laid off Dec. 10, 1802.
	75th....	Laid off Jan. 21, 1809.
Lewis. See Mason (69th)		
Lincoln...................	6th....	By Act of June 24, 1792.
	63rd....	Laid off May 9, 1806.
Livingston................	24th....	Laid off Dec. 24, 1809.
	55th....	Laid off Dec. 15, 1802. Caldwell after Dec. 24, 1809. (See also Christian.)
Logan.....................	23rd....	Laid off Feb. 23, 1797.
Madison...................	7th....	By Act of June 24, 1792.
	19th....	Laid off Mar. 2, 1795.
	35th....	Laid off Nov. 29, 1799.
Mason.....................	15th....	By Act of June 24, 1792.
	28th....	Laid off Jan. 22, 1798. Mason and Bracken to Dec. 27, 1806, then Bracken only.
	29th....	Laid off Jan. 22, 1798.
	69th....	Created Dec. 27, 1806. Later Lewis and part of Allen.
Mercer....................	5th....	By Act of June 24, 1792.
	43rd....	Laid off Dec. 17, 1799.
Montgomery................	31st....	Laid off Feb. 8, 1798.
	34th....	Laid off Nov. 28, 1799. Bath after Jan. 15, 1811.
Muhlenberg................	40th....	Laid off Dec. 15, 1799.
	82nd....	Created Jan. 11, 1811.
Nelson....................	2nd....	By Act of June 24, 1792.
	27th....	Laid off Apr. 1, 1797.
	62nd....	Laid off Dec. 20, 1805.

Kentucky Militia, 1792 - 1811

Arrangement by counties, page 5

COUNTY	REGIMENT	DATE OF FORMATION
Nelson and Logan..........	3rd....	By Act of June 24, 1792. Hardin after Feb. 23, 1797.
Nicholas..................	13th....	Laid off Dec. 27, 1806. (See also Bourbon, 13th.)
Ohio......................	49th....	Laid off Dec. 10, 1804.
Ohio and Breckinridge......	49th....	Laid off Dec. 13, 1800. Ohio only after Dec. 10, 1804.
Pendleton.................	21st....	Laid off Dec. 17, 1806. (See also Campbell, 21st.)
Pulaski...................	44th....	Laid off Dec. 20, 1799.
Rockcastle................	79th....	Formed Jan. 23, 1810.
Scott.....................	12th....	By Act of June 24, 1792.
	77th....	Laid off Feb. 11, 1809.
Shelby....................	18th....	First commissions Dec. 21, 1794.
	37th....	Laid off Dec. 5, 1799.
	85th....	Created Jan. 18, 1811. (See also Jefferson, 1st.)
Union.....................	83rd....	Created Jan. 11, 1811.
Warren....................	25th....	Laid off Feb. 23, 1797.
	61st....	Created Dec. 10, 1804.
Washington................	4th....	By Act of June 24, 1792.
	50th....	Laid off Dec. 18, 1800.
Wayne.....................	53rd....	Laid off Dec. 10, 1802.
Woodford..................	11th....	By Act of June 24, 1792.

KENTUCKY MILITIA, 1792-1811 - by REGIMENTS

No. - County	No. - County
1st - Jefferson	48 - Campbell, Boone
2 - Nelson	49 - Ohio, Breckinridge
3 - Hardin, Nelson, Logan	50 - Washington
4 - Washington	51 - Gallatin
5 - Mercer	52 - Adair
6 - Lincoln	53 - Wayne
7 - Madison	54 - Knox
8 - Fayette	55 - Livingston, Caldwell
9 - Fayette, Jessamine	56 - Floyd
10 - Fayette	57 - Garrard
11 - Woodford	58 - Fleming
12 - Scott	59 - Breckinridge
13 - Bourbon, Nicholas	60 - Hardin
14 - Bourbon	61 - Warren
15 - Mason	62 - Nelson
16 - Green	63 - Lincoln
17 - Clark	64 - Allen
18 - Shelby	65 - Bath
19 - Madison	66 - Butler
20 - Harrison	67 - Boone
21 - Pendleton, Campbell	68 - Clay
22 - Franklin	69 - Lewis, Mason
23 - Logan	70 - Greenup
24 - Christian, Livingston	71 - Bourbon
25 - Warren	72 - Christian
26 - Garrard	73 - Daveiss
27 - Nelson	74 - Casey
28 - Bracken, Mason	75 - Knox
29 - Mason	76 - Hopkins
30 - Fleming	77 - Scott
31 - Montgomery	78 - Estill
32 - Bullitt	79 - Rockcastle
33 - Jefferson	80 - Clay
34 - Montgomery, Bath	81 - Cumberland
35 - Madison	82 - Muhlenberg
36 - Clark	83 - Union
37 - Shelby	84 - Caldwell
38 - Henry	85 - Shelby
39 - Christian	86 - Harrison
40 - Muhlenberg	
41 - Henderson	
42 - Fayette	
43 - Mercer	
44 - Pulaski	
45 - Barren	
46 - Cumberland	
47 - Bourbon	

COMMISSIONED OFFICERS, 1792

[By Act of General Assembly, June 24, 1792]

General Officers

Barbee, Joshua............	Inspector (Major), 2nd Brigade...	September, 1792
Breckinridge, Robert.....	Brigadier General, 1st Brigade...	December 19, 1792
Cravens, Jesse............	Aide-de-Camp to General Benjamin Logan (Major)................	December 18, 1792
Hardin, John..............	Brigadier General, 1st Brigade...	June 25, 1792
Harrison, Benjamin.......	Brigadier General, 4th Brigade...	June 24, 1792
Henry, William............	Inspector (Major), 4th Brigade...	September, 1792
Kennedy, Thomas...........	Brigadier General, 2nd Brigade...	Disqualified
Lemon, James..............	Inspector (Major), 4th Brigade...	September, 1792
Logan, Benjamin...........	Major General, 1st Division......	June 25, 1792
Moore, Peter..............	Inspector (Major), 3rd Brigade...	December 12, and December 22, 1792
Ormsby, Stephen...........	Aide-de-Camp to General Benjamin Logan (Major)................	December 18, 1792
Parker, Alexander........	Inspector (Major), 3rd Brigade...	September, 1792
Scott, Charles............	Major General, 2nd Division......	June 25, 1792
Thomas, Edward............	Inspector (Major), 1st Brigade...	September, 1792
Todd, Robert..............	Brigadier General, 3rd Brigade...	June 24, 1792

Company Officers

Bourbon County Regiments

Allen, John...............	Paymaster, 14th Regiment.........	December 12, 1792
Arnold, William...........	Captain, 14th Regiment...........	August 9, 1792
Baker, William............	Captain, 13th Regiment...........	August 9, 1792
Bartlett, William........	Captain, 13th Regiment...........	August 9, 1792
Black, Alexander.........	Lieutenant, 14th Regiment........	August 9, 1792
Blare, John...............	Captain, 14th Regiment...........	August 9, 1792
Brady, William............	Ensign, 13th Regiment............	August 9, 1792
Bready, William...........	Ensign, 13th Regiment............	August 9, 1792
Brenton, William.........	Ensign, 14th Regiment............	August 9, 1792
Byrd, John................	Captain, 13th Regiment...........	August 9, 1792
Colvin, Joseph............	Captain, 14th Regiment...........	August 9, 1792
Conn, Thomas..............	Quartermaster, 13th Regiment.....	December 12, 1792
Couchman, Mely............	Lieutenant, 14th Regiment........	August 9, 1792
Craig, John...............	Ensign, 14th Regiment............	August 9, 1792
Cutright, Samuel.........	Captain, 14th Regiment...........	August 9, 1792
Dennison, James...........	Ensign, 14th Regiment............	August 9, 1792
Dougherty, Robert........	Adjutant, 14th Regiment..........	December 12, 1792
Duncan, James.............	Quartermaster, 14th Regiment.....	December 12, 1792
Duncan, John..............	Ensign, 13th Regiment............	August 9, 1792
Elgin, Samuel.............	Ensign, 13th Regiment............	August 9, 1792

COMMISSIONED OFFICERS, 1792

Fitte, John	Captain, 13th Regiment	August 9, 1792
Fletcher, Thomas	1st Major, 13th Regiment	July 3, 1792
Friend, Charles	Lieutenant, 14th Regiment	August 9, 1792
Furnis, James	Lieutenant, 13th Regiment	August 9, 1792
Gathins, Henry (?)	Lieutenant, 13th Regiment	August 9, 1792
Griffin, Thomas	Lieutenant, 13th Regiment	August 9, 1792
Hall, Horatio	Lieutenant Colonel, Commandant 14th Regiment	July 8, 1792
Hall, James	Captain, 14th Regiment	August 9, 1792
Hamilton, John	Lieutenant, 13th Regiment	August 9, 1792
Hamilton, Robert	Ensign, 14th Regiment	August 9, 1792
Hamilton, Thomas	Lieutenant, 14th Regiment	August 9, 1792
Harrison, Robert	2nd Major, 13th Regiment	No date. (June or July, 1792)
Harrison, Robert	Captain, 13th Regiment	August 9, 1792
Hawkins (no first name)	Ensign, 13th Regiment	August 9, 1792
Hornback, John	Lieutenant, 14th Regiment	August 9, 1792
Hughes, David	Captain, 14th Regiment	August 9, 1792
Irwin, William	Ensign, 14th Regiment	August 9, 1792
Jones, John	Ensign, 13th Regiment	August 9, 1792
Jones, Thomas	Lieutenant Colonel, Commandant 13th Regiment	July 10, 1792
Kennedy, Joseph	Lieutenant, 14th Regiment	August 9, 1792
Kirk, Vincent	Ensign, 14th Regiment	August 9, 1792
Kirkpatrick, Joseph	Lieutenant, 14th Regiment	August 9, 1792
Kizer, Jacob	Lieutenant, 13th Regiment	August 9, 1792
McClenehan, Thomas	Captain, 13th Regiment	August 9, 1792
McDaniel, Francis	Lieutenant, 14th Regiment	August 9, 1792
McDanniel, John	Lieutenant, 13th Regiment	August 9, 1792
McIntire, John	2nd Major, 14th Regiment	July 3, 1792
Martin, Henry	Ensign, 14th Regiment	August 9, 1792
Matthews, William	Ensign, 14th Regiment	August 9, 1792
Miller, John	Lieutenant, 13th Regiment	August 9, 1792
Miller, John	2nd Major, 13th Regiment	July 10, 1792
Montur, Robert	Lieutenant, 13th Regiment	August 9, 1792
Moore, William	Captain, 14th Regiment	August 9, 1792
Philips, Elijah	Captain, 14th Regiment	August 9, 1792
Pickens, Aaron	Ensign, 13th Regiment	August 9, 1792
Pullon, John	Ensign, 14th Regiment	August 9, 1792
Rawlings, Nathan	Captain, 13th Regiment	August 9, 1792
Reader, Thomas	Paymaster, 13th Regiment	December 12, 1792
Robertson, Joseph	Adjutant, 13th Regiment	December 12, 1792
Robinson, Joseph	Captain, 13th Regiment	August 9, 1792
Rogers, Thomas	Lieutenant, 14th Regiment	August 9, 1792
Scott, George	Captain, 14th Regiment	August 9, 1792
Scott, James	Lieutenant, 13th Regiment	August 9, 1792
Sherron, Peter	Ensign, 14th Regiment	August 9, 1792
Shortridge, George	Captain, 14th Regiment	August 9, 1792
Sites, John	Lieutenant, 14th Regiment	August 9, 1792
Smith, Charles	Major, 13th Regiment	December 12, 1792
Sorency (no first name)	Captain, 14th Regiment	August 9, 1792

Spears, Jacob............	Captain, 13th Regiment...........	August 9, 1792
Stinson, John............	Ensign, 13th Regiment............	August 9, 1792
Summit, George...........	Ensign, 13th Regiment............	August 9, 1792
Tharp, Samuel............	Captain, 13th Regiment...........	August 9, 1792
Thompson, William........	Lieutenant, 14th Regiment........	August 9, 1792
Trimble, John............	Ensign, 14th Regiment............	August 9, 1792
Vanmetre, Morgan.........	Lieutenant, 13th Regiment........	August 9, 1792
Wallace, John............	Lieutenant, 14th Regiment........	August 9, 1792
Ward, Benjamin...........	Captain, 14th Regiment...........	August 9, 1792
Wells, Francis...........	Ensign, 13th Regiment............	August 9, 1792
Wilmot, Robert...........	1st Major, 13th Regiment.........	June 9, 1792
Wilmot, Robert...........	Lieutenant Colonel, Commandant 13th Regiment.................	December 17, 1792
Wilson, Israel...........	Ensign, 14th Regiment............	August 9, 1792
Worley, A.	Captain, 13th Regiment...........	August 9, 1792

Fayette County Regiments

Allison, William.........	Captain, 9th Regiment............	November 9, 1792
Anderson, George.........	Lieutenant, Infantry Company, 9th Regiment..................	August 9, 1792
Baxter, Thomas...........	Ensign, 8th Regiment.............	August 9, 1792
Beaty, Cornelius.........	Captain, Infantry Company, 9th Regiment..................	August 9, 1792
Beaty, Cornelius.........	Major, 9th Regiment..............	August, 1792
Berry, William...........	Lieutenant, 9th Regiment.........	August 9, 1792
Boswell, William.........	Ensign, 8th Regiment.............	August 9, 1792
Brock, Harry.............	Adjutant, 9th Regiment...........	December 12, 1792
Brock, Henry.............	Captain, 9th Regiment............	August 9, 1792
Brown, Elijah............	Ensign, 9th Regiment.............	August 9, 1792
Bullock, Lewis...........	Adjutant, 10th Regiment..........	December 12, 1792
Bullock, Nathaniel.......	Ensign, 8th Regiment.............	August 9, 1792
Bush, Philip.............	Captain, 8th Regiment............	August 9, 1792
Calloway, Edmond.........	Ensign, 8th Regiment.............	August 9, 1792
Campbell, Robert.........	Ensign, 9th Regiment.............	August 9, 1792
Campbell, William........	Captain, 8th Regiment............	August 9, 1792
Campbell, William........	Captain, 10th Regiment...........	August 9, 1792
Chinn, Elijah............	Lieutenant, 8th Regiment.........	August 9, 1792
Clark, Bennet............	Lieutenant, 8th Regiment.........	August 9, 1792
Cock, John...............	Captain, 9th Regiment............	November 9, 1792
Cowherd, James...........	Adjutant, 8th Regiment...........	December 12, 1792
Curtner, Henry...........	Ensign, 9th Regiment.............	August 9, 1792
Custed, Arnold...........	Lieutenant, 10th Regiment........	August 9, 1792
Dedman, Richard..........	Captain, 9th Regiment............	August 9, 1792
Dickison, Archer.........	Lieutenant, 9th Regiment.........	August 9, 1792
Dickison, Mastin.........	Captain, 9th Regiment............	August 9, 1792
Dudley, William..........	Captain, 8th Regiment............	August 9, 1792
Dullum, Francis..........	Quartermaster, 9th Regiment......	December 12, 1792
Dunn, James..............	Lieutenant, 9th Regiment.........	August 9, 1792
Faulkner, Joseph.........	Lieutenant, 9th Regiment.........	August 9, 1792

COMMISSIONED OFFICERS, 1792

Frazer, George............	Captain, 9th Regiment............	August 9, 1792
Gilkison, William........	Lieutenant, 10th Regiment........	August 9, 1792
Grant, William...........	Captain, 10th Regiment...........	August 9, 1792
Hall, Moses..............	Captain, 9th Regiment............	August 9, 1792
Hampton, David...........	Lieutenant, 8th Regiment.........	August 9, 1792
Hawkins, John............	Lieutenant, 9th Regiment.........	August 9, 1792
Hickman, James...........	Captain, 8th Regiment............	August 9, 1792
Hickman, Richard.........	Captain, 8th Regiment............	August 9, 1792
Hogan, James.............	Captain, 9th Regiment............	August 9, 1792
Howard, Benjamin.........	Paymaster, 10th Regiment.........	December 12, 1792
Huff, John...............	Ensign, 9th Regiment.............	August 9, 1792
Hume, Gerrand............	Captain, 8th Regiment............	August 9, 1792
Johnston, Martin.........	Ensign, 8th Regiment.............	August 9, 1792
Johnston, Silas..........	Lieutenant, 9th Regiment.........	August 9, 1792
Jones, Thomas............	Ensign, 8th Regiment.............	August 9, 1792
Kirtner, Christopher.....	Lieutenant, 9th Regiment.........	November 9, 1792
Kizer, Jacob.............	Lieutenant, 9th Regiment.........	August 9, 1792
Landers, Jacob...........	Lieutenant, 8th Regiment.........	August 9, 1792
Lewis, William...........	Captain, 9th Regiment............	August 9, 1792
McConnell, John..........	Lieutenant, 10th Regiment........	August 9, 1792
McCoy, Kenneth...........	Lieutenant, Troop of Horse, 9th Regiment...................	August 9, 1792
McDowell, James..........	1st Major, 10th Regiment.........	June 27, 1792
McDowell, John...........	2nd Major, 10th Regiment.........	No date. (June or July, 1792)
McKinny, John............	Ensign, 9th Regiment.............	August 9, 1792
McMillian, William.......	Lieutenant, 8th Regiment.........	August 9, 1792
McMillion, James.........	1st Major, 8th Regiment..........	July, 1792
McMillion, Robert........	Captain, 8th Regiment............	August 9, 1792
McMurdie, Francis........	Captain, 10th Regiment...........	August 9, 1792
McMurtry, James..........	Captain, 10th Regiment...........	August 9, 1792
Marshall, Henry..........	Ensign, Troop of Horse, 9th Regiment...................	August 9, 1792
Martin, James............	Lieutenant, 9th Regiment.........	August 9, 1792
Martin, John.............	2nd Major, 8th Regiment..........	June 27, 1792
Meredith, Samuel.........	Quartermaster, 10th Regiment.....	December 12, 1792
Miller, James............	Captain, 10th Regiment...........	August 9, 1792
Mitchell, Daniel.........	Captain, 9th Regiment............	August 9, 1792
Mitchell, Richard........	Ensign, 8th Regiment.............	August 9, 1792
Mitchell, William........	Captain, 10th Regiment...........	August 9, 1792
Moore, William...........	Lieutenant, 10th Regiment........	August 9, 1792
Morrison, John...........	1st Major, 9th Regiment..........	July 4, 1792
Moss, John...............	Ensign, 9th Regiment.............	August 9, 1792
Muldrough, Hugh..........	Lieutenant, 10th Regiment........	August 9, 1792
Overton, Waller..........	Paymaster, 8th Regiment..........	December 12, 1792
Patterson, Ezekiel.......	Lieutenant, 10th Regiment........	August 9, 1792
Payne, Edward............	Captain, 10th Regiment...........	August 9, 1792
Porter, Nathaniel........	Ensign, 9th Regiment.............	August 9, 1792
Price, Bird..............	Lieutenant, 8th Regiment.........	August 9, 1792
Price, Evan..............	Lieutenant, 9th Regiment.........	August 9, 1792
Price, John..............	Lieutenant, 8th Regiment.........	August 9, 1792

COMMISSIONED OFFICERS, 1792

Price, William............	2nd Major, 9th Regiment..........	July 1, 1792
Ramsey, George...........	Captain, 9th Regiment............	August 9, 1792
Ray, John................	Ensign, 8th Regiment.............	August 9, 1792
Ritchie, John............	Lieutenant, 10th Regiment........	August 9, 1792
Russell, William.........	Lieutenant Colonel, Commandant 10th Regiment.................	July 3, 1792
Sanders, Charles.........	Ensign, 9th Regiment.............	August 9, 1792
Saunders, Nathaniel......	Lieutenant, 9th Regiment.........	August 9, 1792
Scholl, Joseph...........	Lieutenant, 8th Regiment.........	August 9, 1792
Shears, Charles..........	Lieutenant, 9th Regiment.........	August 9, 1792
Sheley, David............	Captain, 10th Regiment...........	August 9, 1792
Shores, Richard..........	Lieutenant, 10th Regiment........	August 9, 1792
Simpson, Samuel..........	Lieutenant, 10th Regiment........	August 9, 1792
Smith, John..............	Captain, 9th Regiment............	August 9, 1792
South, John..............	Captain, 8th Regiment............	August 9, 1792
South, John..............	Major, 8th Regiment..............	November, 1792
Stephens, James..........	Captain, 8th Regiment............	August 9, 1792
Stout, David.............	Captain, Troop of Horse, 9th Regiment...................	August 9, 1792
Taylor, George...........	Captain, 10th Regiment...........	August 9, 1792
Thompson, Clifton........	Lieutenant, 10th Regiment........	August 9, 1792
Thompson, Hugh...........	Captain, 10th Regiment...........	August 9, 1792
Thompson, William........	Ensign, 9th Regiment.............	August 9, 1792
Todd, Levi...............	Lieutenant Colonel, Commandant 8th Regiment..................	June 26, 1792
Trotter, James...........	Lieutenant Colonel, Commandant 9th Regiment..................	June 28, 1792
Venable, Abraham.........	Captain, 9th Regiment............	August 9, 1792
Wallace, John............	Ensign, 8th Regiment.............	August 9, 1792
Ward, George.............	Ensign, 9th Regiment.............	August 9, 1792
Whiteside, William.......	Lieutenant, 8th Regiment.........	August 9, 1792
Wilkins, Charles.........	Paymaster, 9th Regiment..........	December 12, 1792
Wilson, Nathaniel........	Quartermaster, 8th Regiment......	December 12, 1792
Wright, Israel...........	Ensign, Infantry Company, 9th Regiment...................	August 9, 1792
Zimmerman, Frederick.....	Ensign, 9th Regiment.............	August 9, 1792

Jefferson and Shelby County Regiment

Allen, James.............	Lieutenant, 1st Regiment.........	August 9, 1792
Amos, Thomas.............	Lieutenant, 1st Regiment.........	August 9, 1792
Ashby, Fielding..........	Lieutenant, 1st Regiment.........	August 9, 1792
Ballard, James...........	Lieutenant, 1st Regiment.........	August 9, 1792
Bartholomew, Joseph......	Lieutenant, 1st Regiment.........	August 9, 1792
Bartlett, Frederick......	Ensign, 1st Regiment.............	August 9, 1792
Boone, William...........	Ensign, 1st Regiment.............	August 9, 1792
Brenton, John............	Ensign, 1st Regiment.............	August 9, 1792
Burks, John..............	Captain, 1st Regiment............	August 9, 1792
Christie, William........	Adjutant, 1st Regiment...........	December 12, 1792
Collins, Zebulon.........	Ensign, 1st Regiment.............	August 9, 1792

COMMISSIONED OFFICERS, 1792

Croghan, William.........	Paymaster, 1st Regiment..........	December 12, 1792
Crookes, William.........	Lieutenant, 1st Regiment.........	August 9, 1792
Denny, James.............	Quartermaster, 1st Regiment......	December 12, 1792
Finley, George...........	Lieutenant, 1st Regiment.........	August 9, 1792
Floyd, Robert............	Captain, 1st Regiment............	August 9, 1792
Gardener, Thomas.........	Ensign, 1st Regiment.............	August 9, 1792
Giger, Frederick.........	Captain, 1st Regiment............	August 9, 1792
Greathouse, Isaac........	Captain, 1st Regiment............	August 9, 1792
Gregory, Richard.........	Lieutenant, 1st Regiment.........	August 9, 1792
Hall, William............	Lieutenant, 1st Regiment.........	August 9, 1792
Harrison, John...........	Captain, 1st Regiment............	August 9, 1792
Hill, Hardy..............	Captain, 1st Regiment............	August 9, 1792
Hunter, Joseph...........	Lieutenant, 1st Regiment.........	August 9, 1792
Linn, William............	Captain, 1st Regiment............	August 9, 1792
Nash, Harmon.............	Captain, 1st Regiment............	August 9, 1792
Philips, David...........	Ensign, 1st Regiment.............	August 9, 1792
Pollard, Bland Williams..	Captain, 1st Regiment............	August 9, 1792
Quertermus, Elisha.......	Lieutenant, 1st Regiment.........	August 9, 1792
Rickar, John.............	Lieutenant, 1st Regiment.........	August 9, 1792
Rose, Mathias............	Ensign, 1st Regiment.............	August 9, 1792
Rub, John (?)............	Ensign, 1st Regiment.............	August 9, 1792
Scott, Andrew............	Captain, 1st Regiment............	August 9, 1792
Shrader, Jacob...........	Ensign, 1st Regiment.............	August 9, 1792
Smith, Jacob.............	Ensign, 1st Regiment.............	August 9, 1792
Sparks, Daniel...........	Captain, 1st Regiment............	August 9, 1792
Sullivan, William........	Ensign, 1st Regiment.............	August 9, 1792
Thruston, John...........	Lieutenant Colonel, Commandant 1st Regiment...................	July 5, 1792
Tramcand, William (?)....	Ensign, 1st Regiment.............	August 9, 1792
Tuly, Charles............	Lieutenant, 1st Regiment.........	August 9, 1792
Vaughan, John............	Lieutenant, 1st Regiment.........	August 9, 1792
Warford, David...........	Captain, 1st Regiment............	August 9, 1792
Wells, Samuel............	2nd Major, 1st Regiment..........	July 11, 1792
Wheat, Jacob.............	Ensign, 1st Regiment.............	August 9, 1792
Whitacre, Aquilla........	1st Major, 1st Regiment..........	July 8, 1792
Winchester, William......	Captain, 1st Regiment............	August 9, 1792
Winlock, Joseph..........	Captain, 1st Regiment............	August 9, 1792

Lincoln County Regiment

Arnold, Humphrey.........	Ensign, 6th Regiment.............	August 9, 1792
Blain, James.............	Adjutant, 6th Regiment...........	December 12, 1792
Blain, John..............	Quartermaster, 6th Regiment......	December 12, 1792
Bryant, John.............	Paymaster, 6th Regiment..........	December 12, 1792
Campbell, William........	Captain, 6th Regiment............	August 9, 1792
Carpenter, Conrod........	Lieutenant, 6th Regiment.........	August 9, 1792
Crockett, Anthony........	1st Major, 6th Regiment..........	June 29, 1792
Davis, Thomas............	Ensign, 6th Regiment.............	August 9, 1792
Embree, Joshua...........	Ensign, 6th Regiment.............	August 9, 1792
Faris, James.............	Captain, 6th Regiment............	August 9, 1792

COMMISSIONED OFFICERS, 1792

Faris, Johnston..........	Ensign, 6th Regiment..............	August 9, 1792
Foreman, David...........	Ensign, 6th Regiment..............	August 9, 1792
Givens, Robert...........	Captain, 6th Regiment.............	August 9, 1792
Glover, Joseph...........	Ensign, 6th Regiment..............	August 9, 1792
Hardgrove, James.........	Ensign, 6th Regiment..............	August 9, 1792
Hill, William............	Lieutenant, 6th Regiment..........	August 9, 1792
Horine, George...........	Captain, 6th Regiment.............	August 9, 1792
Huston, Nathan...........	2nd Major, 6th Regiment...........	No date. (June or July, 1792)
Jennings, William........	Ensign, 6th Regiment..............	August 9, 1792
Lewis, Joseph............	Lieutenant, 6th Regiment..........	August 9, 1792
Logan, Jonathan..........	Lieutenant, 6th Regiment..........	August 9, 1792
McClure, William.........	Captain, 6th Regiment.............	August 9, 1792
McKinny, John............	Lieutenant, 6th Regiment..........	August 9, 1792
Miller, Abram............	Lieutenant, 6th Regiment..........	August 9, 1792
Montgomery, Robert.......	Captain, 6th Regiment.............	August 9, 1792
Montgomery, Samuel.......	Lieutenant, 6th Regiment..........	August 9, 1792
Moore, Samuel............	Captain, 6th Regiment.............	August 9, 1792
Murrell, George..........	Captain, 6th Regiment.............	August 9, 1792
Patton, James............	Ensign, 6th Regiment..............	August 9, 1792
Pollard, Absolem.........	Captain, 6th Regiment.............	August 9, 1792
Pope, Elemander..........	Lieutenant, 6th Regiment..........	August 9, 1792
Ray, James...............	2nd Major, 6th Regiment...........	June 28, 1792
Reynolds, Charles........	Lieutenant, 6th Regiment..........	August 9, 1792
Richardson, Jesse........	Captain, 6th Regiment.............	August 9, 1792
Shackleford, Edward......	Lieutenant, 6th Regiment..........	August 9, 1792
Shackleford, Zachariah...	Captain, 6th Regiment.............	August 9, 1792
Shook, John..............	Ensign, 6th Regiment..............	August 9, 1792
Steene, William..........	Ensign, 6th Regiment..............	August 9, 1792
Stephenson, Robert.......	Lieutenant, 6th Regiment..........	August 9, 1792
Sutton, James............	Lieutenant, 6th Regiment..........	August 9, 1792
Thompson, William, Jr....	Lieutenant, 6th Regiment..........	August 9, 1792
Tincle, George...........	Ensign, 6th Regiment..............	August 9, 1792
Todd, Thomas.............	Lieutenant Colonel, Commandant 6th Regiment...................	July 7, 1792
Wade, Pierce.............	Ensign, 6th Regiment..............	August 9, 1792
Whitley, William.........	1st Major, 6th Regiment...........	June 28, 1792
Wilkinson, John..........	Captain, 6th Regiment.............	August 9, 1792
Worthington, Edward......	Captain, 6th Regiment.............	August 9, 1792

Madison County Regiment

Adams, Matthew...........	Captain, 7th Regiment.............	August 9, 1792
Alcorn, John.............	Lieutenant, 7th Regiment..........	August 9, 1792
Bailey, John.............	Ensign, 7th Regiment..............	August 9, 1792
Bennet, Hardy............	Ensign, 7th Regiment..............	August 9, 1792
Boyles, Alex.............	Ensign, 7th Regiment..............	August 9, 1792
Burton, Abraham..........	Ensign, 7th Regiment..............	August 9, 1792
Butler, Thomas...........	Ensign, 7th Regiment..............	August 9, 1792
Carson, (Lindsey)........	Ensign, 7th Regiment..............	August 9, 1792

COMMISSIONED OFFICERS, 1792

Cochran, James............	Lieutenant, 7th Regiment.........	August 9, 1792
Cooper, Benjamin.........	Captain, 7th Regiment............	August 9, 1792
Crews, Thomas............	Ensign, 7th Regiment.............	August 9, 1792
Davis, Zachariah.........	Ensign, 7th Regiment.............	August 9, 1792
Debriel, Charles.........	Captain, 7th Regiment............	August 9, 1792
Donelson, Robert.........	Captain, 7th Regiment............	August 9, 1792
Dooley, Moses............	Captain, 7th Regiment............	August 9, 1792
East, North..............	Lieutenant, 7th Regiment.........	August 9, 1792
Estill, Samuel...........	2nd Major, 7th Regiment..........	July 4, 1792
Finley, James............	Lieutenant, 7th Regiment.........	August 9, 1792
Gentry, David............	Ensign, 7th Regiment.............	August 9, 1792
Gordon, Richard..........	Ensign, 7th Regiment.............	August 9, 1792
Hale, Frederick..........	Lieutenant, 7th Regiment.........	August 9, 1792
Hane, Drew...............	Lieutenant, 7th Regiment.........	August 9, 1792
Kavenaugh, William.......	Captain, 7th Regiment............	August 9, 1792
Kennedy, Andrew..........	Paymaster, 7th Regiment..........	December 12, 1792
Kennedy, David...........	Captain, 7th Regiment............	August 9, 1792
Kennedy, Joseph..........	1st Major, 7th Regiment..........	July 5, 1792
Kerly, William...........	Quartermaster, 7th Regiment......	December 12, 1792
Knox, Robert.............	Lieutenant, 7th Regiment.........	August 9, 1792
Landham, Thomas..........	Lieutenant, 7th Regiment.........	August 9, 1792
Logsdon, Joseph..........	Captain, 7th Regiment............	August 9, 1792
McAlister, James.........	Captain, 7th Regiment............	August 9, 1792
Martin, Azariah..........	Captain, 7th Regiment............	August 9, 1792
Maxfield, David..........	Ensign, 7th Regiment.............	August 9, 1792
Miller, John.............	Lieutenant Colonel, Commandant 7th Regiment...................	June 30, 1792
Moore, Williams..........	Ensign, 7th Regiment.............	August 9, 1792
Morrison, William........	Captain, 7th Regiment............	August 9, 1792
Pierce, William..........	Ensign, 7th Regiment.............	August 9, 1792
Portwood, Page...........	Lieutenant, 7th Regiment.........	August 9, 1792
Searcy, Asa..............	Lieutenant, 7th Regiment.........	August 9, 1792
Shackleford, James.......	Captain, 7th Regiment............	August 9, 1792
South, Samuel............	Captain, 7th Regiment............	August 9, 1792
Symes, Randall...........	Ensign, 7th Regiment.............	August 9, 1792
Terrell, Edmund..........	Captain, 7th Regiment............	August 9, 1792
Terrill, Edmund..........	Adjutant, 7th Regiment...........	December 12, 1792
Tuder, Valentine.........	Ensign, 7th Regiment.............	August 9, 1792
Turner, Edward...........	Lieutenant, 7th Regiment.........	August 9, 1792
Turner, John.............	Lieutenant, 7th Regiment.........	August 9, 1792
Weldon, John.............	Lieutenant, 7th Regiment.........	August 9, 1792
Williams, Daniel.........	Lieutenant, 7th Regiment.........	August 9, 1792
Williams, John...........	Lieutenant, 7th Regiment.........	August 9, 1792
Wilson, John.............	Captain, 7th Regiment............	August 9, 1792

Mason County Regiment

Bailey, Henry............	Lieutenant, 15th Regiment........	August 9, 1792
Baker, Joshua............	Captain, 15th Regiment...........	August 9, 1792
Baltimore, Philip........	Ensign, 15th Regiment............	August 9, 1792

COMMISSIONED OFFICERS, 1792

Bennet, William..........	Lieutenant, 15th Regiment.........	August 9, 1792
Brevard, Adam............	Lieutenant, 15th Regiment........	August 9, 1792
Brooks, William..........	Captain, 15th Regiment...........	August 9, 1792
Cartes, John.............	Lieutenant, 15th Regiment........	August 9, 1792
Dishay, John.............	Ensign, 15th Regiment............	August 9, 1792
Drake, Isaac.............	Ensign, 15th Regiment............	August 9, 1792
Evans, Nathan............	Lieutenant, 15th Regiment........	August 9, 1792
Finch, John..............	Captain, 15th Regiment...........	August 9, 1792
Fitzgerald, Thomas.......	Ensign, 15th Regiment............	August 9, 1792
Fotch, Nathan............	Lieutenant, 15th Regiment........	August 9, 1792
Fox, Arthur..............	Paymaster, 15th Regiment.........	December 12, 1792
Fry, Jacob...............	Ensign, 15th Regiment............	August 9, 1792
Gonns, Thomas (?)........	Ensign, 15th Regiment............	August 9, 1792
Hancock, Joseph..........	Lieutenant, 15th Regiment........	August 9, 1792
Harman, James............	Ensign, 15th Regiment............	August 9, 1792
Helm, Meredith...........	Captain, 15th Regiment...........	August 9, 1792
Helm, William............	Lieutenant, 15th Regiment........	August 9, 1792
Kenton, Simon............	Captain, 15th Regiment...........	August 9, 1792
Kenton, Simon............	1st Major, 15th Regiment.........	July 1, 1792
Kirling, Thomas..........	Lieutenant, 15th Regiment........	August 9, 1792
Lee, Henry...............	Lieutenant Colonel, Commandant 15th Regiment.................	July 4, 1792
Lewis, George............	Captain, 15th Regiment...........	August 9, 1792
McDole, John.............	Lieutenant, 15th Regiment........	August 9, 1792
Michie, Daniel...........	Captain, 15th Regiment...........	August 9, 1792
Rains, John..............	Lieutenant, 15th Regiment........	August 9, 1792
Records, Spencer.........	Captain, 15th Regiment...........	August 9, 1792
Ricketts, Richard........	Lieutenant, 15th Regiment........	August 9, 1792
Ross, William............	Lieutenant, 15th Regiment........	August 9, 1792
Smith, Samuel............	Captain, 15th Regiment...........	August 9, 1792
Smith, Samuel............	Adjutant, 15th Regiment..........	December 12, 1792
Stephenson, Mills........	Ensign, 15th Regiment............	August 9, 1792
Stockdon, George.........	2nd Major, 15th Regiment.........	July 2, 1792
Strickling, David........	Ensign, 15th Regiment............	August 9, 1792
Survell, Benjamin (?)....	Ensign, 15th Regiment............	August 9, 1792
Taylor, Francis..........	Quartermaster, 15th Regiment.....	December 12, 1792
Walker, Alexander........	Ensign, 15th Regiment............	August 9, 1792
Ward, James..............	Captain, 15th Regiment...........	August 9, 1792
Warney, Jonathan (?).....	Ensign, 15th Regiment............	August 9, 1792
Whiteman, Benjamin.......	Captain, 15th Regiment...........	August 9, 1792
Williams, Lawrence.......	Captain, 15th Regiment...........	August 9, 1792
Wilson, James............	Ensign, 15th Regiment............	August 9, 1792
Woods, Moses.............	Captain, 15th Regiment...........	August 9, 1792

Mercer County Regiment

Armstrong, Robert........	Captain, 5th Regiment............	August 9, 1792
Arnold, John.............	Captain, 5th Regiment............	August 9, 1792
Arnold, Stephen..........	Lieutenant, 5th Regiment.........	August 9, 1792
Barbee, Daniel...........	Captain, 5th Regiment............	August 9, 1792

COMMISSIONED OFFICERS, 1792

Barbee, Thomas............	Lieutenant Colonel, Commandant 5th Regiment...................	June 29, 1792
Buchanan, James...........	Ensign, 5th Regiment.............	August 9, 1792
Clements, Jeremiah.......	Lieutenant, 5th Regiment.........	August 9, 1792
Cochran, John.............	Captain, 5th Regiment............	August 9, 1792
Cook, John................	Captain, 5th Regiment............	August 9, 1792
Davis, Joseph.............	Captain, 5th Regiment............	August 9, 1792
Faris, Elijah.............	Lieutenant, 5th Regiment.........	August 9, 1792
Hale, Job.................	Captain, 5th Regiment............	August 9, 1792
Harbenson, John...........	Captain, 5th Regiment............	August 9, 1792
Harrison, John............	Captain, 5th Regiment............	August 9, 1792
Hill, Robert..............	Ensign, 5th Regiment.............	August 9, 1792
Hutton, Samuel............	Ensign, 5th Regiment.............	August 9, 1792
Lamb, William.............	Ensign, 5th Regiment.............	August 9, 1792
McAfee, John..............	Lieutenant, 5th Regiment.........	August 9, 1792
Miles, John...............	Lieutenant, 5th Regiment.........	August 9, 1792
Rains, James..............	Lieutenant, 5th Regiment.........	August 9, 1792
Robards, Joseph...........	Quartermaster, 5th Regiment......	December 12, 1792
Robertson, John...........	Ensign, 5th Regiment.............	August 9, 1792
Rose, Lewis...............	Captain, 5th Regiment............	August 9, 1792
Smith, Jesse..............	Lieutenant, 5th Regiment.........	August 9, 1792
Spilman, Charles..........	Lieutenant, 5th Regiment.........	August 9, 1792
Strong, Walter E.(Waller?)	Ensign, 5th Regiment.............	August 9, 1792
Strong, Waller Edward....	Paymaster, 5th Regiment..........	December 12, 1792
Veanoy, Anderson..........	Adjutant, 5th Regiment...........	December 12, 1792
Voress, Cornelius.........	Ensign, 5th Regiment.............	August 9, 1792
Walker, Philip............	Ensign, 5th Regiment.............	August 9, 1792
Watts, Peter..............	Ensign, 5th Regiment.............	August 9, 1792
Woods, Samuel.............	Lieutenant, 5th Regiment.........	August 9, 1792
Yocum, Jesse..............	Ensign, 5th Regiment.............	August 9, 1792
Young, Henry..............	Lieutenant, 5th Regiment.........	August 9, 1792

Nelson County Regiment

Bealer, Christopher......	Captain, 2nd Regiment............	August 9, 1792
Bowman, William...........	Captain, 2nd Regiment............	August 9, 1792
Brownfield, William......	Lieutenant, 2nd Regiment.........	August 9, 1792
Chapman, Thomas...........	Lieutenant, 2nd Regiment.........	August 9, 1792
Cleaver, Stephen..........	Lieutenant, 2nd Regiment.........	August 9, 1792
Cox, Phenis...............	Captain, 2nd Regiment............	August 9, 1792
Craven, Jeremiah..........	Ensign, 2nd Regiment.............	August 9, 1792
Duncan, John..............	Captain, 2nd Regiment............	August 9, 1792
Freck, Joseph.............	Lieutenant, 2nd Regiment.........	August 9, 1792
Goodman, Samuel...........	Ensign, 2nd Regiment.............	August 9, 1792
Guthrie, Adam.............	2nd Major, 2nd Regiment..........	July 9, 1792
Hagen, Ignatius...........	Ensign, 2nd Regiment.............	August 9, 1792
Harrison, Cuthbert.......	Paymaster, 2nd Regiment..........	December 12, 1792
Inlow, Isham..............	Ensign, 2nd Regiment.............	August 9, 1792
Kirkpatrick, Moses.......	Lieutenant, 2nd Regiment.........	August 9, 1792

COMMISSIONED OFFICERS, 1792

Lewis, Jasper............	Lieutenant Colonel, Commandant 2nd Regiment...................	July 9, 1792
Masterson, Charles.......	Captain, 2nd Regiment............	August 9, 1792
Masterson, Jeremiah......	Lieutenant, 2nd Regiment.........	August 9, 1792
Mastison, John...........	Ensign, 2nd Regiment.............	August 9, 1792
Miller, Adam.............	Lieutenant, 2nd Regiment.........	August 9, 1792
Miller, Samuel...........	Lieutenant, 2nd Regiment.........	August 9, 1792
Miller, William..........	Ensign, 2nd Regiment.............	August 9, 1792
Morehead, Charles........	Adjutant, 2nd Regiment...........	December 12, 1792
Robertson, John..........	1st Major, 2nd Regiment..........	July 6, 1792
Robinson, John...........	Lieutenant, 2nd Regiment.........	August 9, 1792
Skaggs, James............	Ensign, 2nd Regiment.............	August 9, 1792
Skaggs, William..........	Captain, 2nd Regiment............	August 9, 1792
Snider, Jacob............	Captain, 2nd Regiment............	August 9, 1792
Stephens, Richard........	Quartermaster, 2nd Regiment......	December 12, 1792
Thomas, John.............	Captain, 2nd Regiment............	August 9, 1792
Vertrice, Joseph.........	Ensign, 2nd Regiment.............	August 9, 1792
Vitito, Samuel...........	Ensign, 2nd Regiment.............	August 9, 1792
Waters, Conrad...........	Captain, 2nd Regiment............	August 9, 1792
Waters, John.............	Lieutenant, 2nd Regiment.........	August 9, 1792
Williams, Edward.........	Captain, 2nd Regiment............	August 9, 1792
Wilson, George...........	Ensign, 2nd Regiment.............	August 9, 1792

Nelson and Logan Regiment

Brown, John P.	Ensign, 3rd Regiment.............	August 9, 1792
Brown, Patrick...........	Lieutenant Colonel, Commandant 3rd Regiment...................	July 6, 1792
Bruce, George............	Captain, 3rd Regiment............	August 9, 1792
Calhoon, George..........	Captain, 3rd Regiment............	August 9, 1792
Case, William............	Ensign, 3rd Regiment.............	August 9, 1792
Chinoweth, William.......	Lieutenant, 3rd Regiment.........	August 9, 1792
Colvin, Luke.............	Ensign, 3rd Regiment.............	August 9, 1792
Connell, James...........	Lieutenant, 3rd Regiment.........	August 9, 1792
Cox, James...............	Captain, 3rd Regiment............	August 9, 1792
Dotson, William..........	Ensign, 3rd Regiment.............	August 9, 1792
Dozier, John.............	Captain, 3rd Regiment............	August 9, 1792
Duncan, Samuel...........	Lieutenant, 3rd Regiment.........	August 9, 1792
Dunn, Vincent............	Lieutenant, 3rd Regiment.........	August 9, 1792
Foreman, Joseph..........	Captain, 3rd Regiment............	August 9, 1792
Froman, John.............	Lieutenant, 3rd Regiment.........	August 9, 1792
Grabell, Joseph..........	Lieutenant, 3rd Regiment.........	August 9, 1792
Gray, Presly.............	Captain, 3rd Regiment............	August 9, 1792
Harrell, Moses...........	Captain, 3rd Regiment............	August 9, 1792
Heady, James.............	Captain, 3rd Regiment............	August 9, 1792
Johnston, Ephraim........	Lieutenant, 3rd Regiment.........	August 9, 1792
Keith, William...........	Ensign, 3rd Regiment.............	August 9, 1792
Kennedy, Charles.........	Lieutenant, 3rd Regiment.........	August 9, 1792
Kirkpatrick, Joseph......	1st Major, 3rd Regiment..........	July 13, 1792
McCowan, Alexander.......	Lieutenant, 3rd Regiment.........	August 9, 1792

COMMISSIONED OFFICERS, 1792

Marks, George............	Lieutenant, 3rd Regiment.........	August 9, 1792
Mauldin, Morton..........	2nd Major, 3rd Regiment..........	July 12, 1792
Miller, Adam.............	Adjutant, 3rd Regiment...........	December 12, 1792
Milligan, Joseph.........	Ensign, 3rd Regiment.............	August 9, 1792
Morton, Samuel...........	Captain, 3rd Regiment............	August 9, 1792
Nall, John...............	Ensign, 3rd Regiment.............	August 9, 1792
Polke, Charles...........	Ensign, 3rd Regiment.............	August 9, 1792
Purcell, James...........	Ensign, 3rd Regiment.............	August 9, 1792
Rogers, William..........	Captain, 3rd Regiment............	August 9, 1792
Rollins, Stephen.........	Quartermaster, 3rd Regiment......	December 12, 1792
Samuel, James............	Captain, 3rd Regiment............	August 9, 1792
Samuel, Robert...........	Lieutenant, 3rd Regiment.........	August 9, 1792
Simmons, William.........	Ensign, 3rd Regiment.............	August 9, 1792
Spencer, Spears..........	Lieutenant, 3rd Regiment.........	August 9, 1792
Thomas, John.............	Paymaster, 3rd Regiment..........	December 12, 1792
Troutman, Jacob..........	Ensign, 3rd Regiment.............	August 9, 1792
Wakefield, John..........	Captain, 3rd Regiment............	August 9, 1792
Williams, Jarrod.........	Captain, 3rd Regiment............	August 9, 1792
Williams, John...........	Ensign, 3rd Regiment.............	August 9, 1792
Wilson, John.............	Ensign, 3rd Regiment.............	August 9, 1792
Woods, James.............	Lieutenant, 3rd Regiment.........	August 9, 1792

Scott County Regiment

Bell, James..............	Ensign, 12th Regiment............	August 9, 1792
Bradly, Thomas...........	Ensign, 12th Regiment............	August 9, 1792
Brenham, Thomas..........	Lieutenant, 12th Regiment........	August 9, 1792
Collins, Bartlett........	1st Major, 12th Regiment.........	July 7, 1792
Craig, Toliver, Jr.	Lieutenant, 12th Regiment........	August 9, 1792
Ewin, John...............	Ensign, 12th Regiment............	August 9, 1792
Flournoy, Daniel.........	Paymaster, 12th Regiment.........	December 12, 1792
Gath, John...............	Captain, 12th Regiment...........	August 9, 1792
Gholson, Francis.........	Ensign, 12th Regiment............	August 9, 1792
Grant, John..............	2nd Major, 12th Regiment.........	July 7, 1792
Gregor (Gregory?), Stephen	Lieutenant, 12th Regiment........	August 9, 1792
Griffith, Josiah.........	Ensign, 12th Regiment............	August 9, 1792
Griffith, Robert.........	Lieutenant, 12th Regiment........	August 9, 1792
Hamilton, Alexander......	Ensign, 12th Regiment............	August 9, 1792
Henry, William...........	2nd Major, 12th Regiment.........	No date. (June or July,1792)
Hunter, John.............	Adjutant, 12th Regiment..........	December 12, 1792
Johnson, Robert..........	Lieutenant Colonel, Commandant 12th Regiment...................	June 27, 1792
Jones, James.............	Captain, 12th Regiment...........	August 9, 1792
Kelly, Griffin...........	Ensign, 12th Regiment............	August 9, 1792
Kelly, William...........	Lieutenant, 12th Regiment........	August 9, 1792
Lee, Ambrose.............	Ensign, 12th Regiment............	August 9, 1792
Lindsay, John V.	Lieutenant, 12th Regiment........	August 9, 1792
McClelland, Abram........	Lieutenant, 12th Regiment........	August 9, 1792
McClure, James...........	Lieutenant, 12th Regiment........	August 9, 1792

COMMISSIONED OFFICERS, 1792 13

McElhatten, William......	Captain, 12th Regiment...........	August 9, 1792
Payne, John..............	Captain, 12th Regiment...........	August 9, 1792
Shannon, George..........	Captain, 12th Regiment...........	August 9, 1792
Shepherd, Samuel.........	Lieutenant, 12th Regiment........	August 9, 1792
Stucker, Jacob...........	Captain, 12th Regiment...........	August 9, 1792
Thompson, Rhodes.........	Captain, 12th Regiment...........	August 9, 1792
Trotter, William.........	Captain, 12th Regiment...........	August 9, 1792
Vaughter, William........	Quartermaster, 12th Regiment.....	December 12, 1792
Walls, William...........	Ensign, 12th Regiment............	August 9, 1792
Wood, Thomas.............	Captain, 12th Regiment...........	August 9, 1792

Washington County Regiment

Abel, Robert.............	Quartermaster, 4th Regiment......	December 12, 1792
Bennet, Benjamin.........	Ensign, 4th Regiment.............	August 9, 1792
Briscoe, Jeremiah........	Captain, 4th Regiment............	August 9, 1792
Caldwell, David..........	2nd Major, 4th Regiment..........	July 8, 1792
Caldwell, John...........	Lieutenant Colonel, Commandant 4th Regiment...................	July 1, 1792
Carlisle, James..........	Ensign, 4th Regiment.............	August 9, 1792
Cunningham, John.........	Captain, 4th Regiment............	August 9, 1792
Davis, John..............	Ensign, 4th Regiment.............	August 9, 1792
Ewing, Charles...........	Captain, 4th Regiment............	August 9, 1792
Ewing, George............	Captain, 4th Regiment............	August 9, 1792
Gibbs, Benjamin..........	Adjutant, 4th Regiment...........	December 12, 1792
Hardin, John.............	Ensign, 4th Regiment.............	August 9, 1792
Hayden, Charles..........	Lieutenant, 4th Regiment.........	August 9, 1792
Hayden, John.............	Lieutenant, 4th Regiment.........	August 9, 1792
Hayden, Wilford..........	Ensign, 4th Regiment.............	August 9, 1792
Helms, John..............	Paymaster, 4th Regiment..........	December 12, 1792
Lincoln, Mordacai........	Ensign, 4th Regiment.............	August 9, 1792
Mock, Daniel.............	Captain, 4th Regiment............	August 9, 1792
Muldrough, John..........	Captain, 4th Regiment............	August 9, 1792
Myers, William...........	Lieutenant, 4th Regiment.........	August 9, 1792
Philips, William.........	Ensign, 4th Regiment.............	August 9, 1792
Right, William...........	Lieutenant, 4th Regiment.........	August 9, 1792
Russell, Charles.........	Lieutenant, 4th Regiment.........	August 9, 1792
Sandusky, John...........	Ensign, 4th Regiment.............	August 9, 1792
Smock, Henry.............	Captain, 4th Regiment............	August 9, 1792
Swearingen, Charles......	Lieutenant, 4th Regiment.........	August 9, 1792
Thomas, Hardin...........	Lieutenant, 4th Regiment.........	August 9, 1792
Walton, Matthew..........	1st Major, 4th Regiment..........	June 30, 1792
Wapshot, Graves..........	Captain, 4th Regiment............	August 9, 1792
Washburn, John...........	Lieutenant, 4th Regiment.........	August 9, 1792

Woodford County Regiment

Allen, John..............	Ensign, 11th Regiment............	August 9, 1792
Arnold, James............	Lieutenant, 11th Regiment........	August 9, 1792

COMMISSIONED OFFICERS, 1792

Ashford, Thomas..........	Ensign, 11th Regiment............	August 9, 1792
Bartlett, Anthony........	Captain, 11th Regiment...........	August 9, 1792
Berry, Benjamin..........	Captain, 11th Regiment...........	August 9, 1792
Bledsoe, Benjamin........	Lieutenant, 11th Regiment........	August 9, 1792
Calmes, Marquis..........	1st Major, 11th Regiment.........	Resigned
Christopher, William.....	Captain, 11th Regiment...........	August 9, 1792
Connolly, Arthur.........	Captain, 11th Regiment...........	August 9, 1792
Fox, Richard.............	Ensign, 11th Regiment............	August 9, 1792
Fox, Richard.............	Quartermaster, 11th Regiment.....	December 12, 1792
Francisco, John..........	Lieutenant, 11th Regiment........	August 9, 1792
Gist, Thomas.............	Captain, 11th Regiment...........	August 9, 1792
Gullion, Jeremiah........	Ensign, 11th Regiment............	August 9, 1792
Harris, Jordan...........	2nd Major, 11th Regiment.........	July 6, 1792
Haydon, Benjamin.........	Lieutenant, 11th Regiment........	August 9, 1792
Haydon, Ezekiel..........	Captain, 11th Regiment...........	August 9, 1792
Haydon, James............	Lieutenant, 11th Regiment........	August 9, 1792
Hedges, Jonathan.........	Lieutenant, 11th Regiment........	August 9, 1792
Howard, Edwin............	Ensign, 11th Regiment............	August 9, 1792
Moffett, George..........	Ensign, 11th Regiment............	August 9, 1792
Montgomery, William......	Ensign, 11th Regiment............	August 9, 1792
Mosby, John..............	Lieutenant, 11th Regiment........	August 9, 1792
Pemberton, Bennet........	Major, 11th Regiment.............	(August 9, 1792)
Sample, John.............	Ensign, 11th Regiment............	August 9, 1792
Spencer, Edward..........	Lieutenant, 11th Regiment........	August 9, 1792
Steel, William...........	Lieutenant Colonel, Commandant, 11th Regiment.................	July 3, 1792
Stewart, James...........	Lieutenant, 11th Regiment........	August 9, 1792
Taylor, Richard..........	Adjutant, 11th Regiment..........	December 12, 1792
Thomas, William..........	Captain, 11th Regiment...........	August 9, 1792
Trabue, Daniel...........	Captain, 11th Regiment...........	August 9, 1792
Twyman, Reuben...........	Captain, 11th Regiment...........	August 9, 1792
Vaughan, John............	Ensign, 11th Regiment............	August 9, 1792
Wooldrige, Jonah.........	Lieutenant, 11th Regiment........	August 9, 1792
Woolfolk, Sowell.........	Major, 11th Regiment.............	December 18, 1792
Young, Richard...........	Paymaster, 11th Regiment.........	December 12, 1792

COMMISSIONED OFFICERS, 1793 - 1796   15

General Officers

Barbee, Thomas............	Brigadier General, 2nd Brigade...	December 19, 1793
Breckinridge, Robert.....	Major General, 1st Division......	December 21, 1794
Harrison, Benjamin.......	Brigadier General, 4th Brigade...	July 10, 1792
	(Appointed December 19, 1793)	
Lemon, James.............	Brigade Inspector, 4th Brigade...	December 3, 1794
Scott, Charles...........	Major General, 2nd Division......	June 5, 1792
	(Appointed December 19, 1793)	
Todd, Robert.............	Brigadier General, 3rd Brigade...	July 1, 1792
	(Appointed December 19, 1793)	

Company Officers

Bourbon County Regiments

Alexander, Aaron.........	Captain, 1st Battalion, 14th Regiment......................	August 22, 1796
Black, Alexander.........	Captain, 1st Battalion, 14th Regiment......................	August 22, 1796
Browning, Jesse..........	Lieutenant, 13th Regiment........	November 27, 1796
Bryan, Alexander.........	Ensign, 1st Battalion, 14th Regiment......................	August 22, 1796
Bryan, Andrew............	Lieutenant, 1st Battalion, 14th Regiment......................	August 22, 1796
Clarkson, Charles........	Captain, 13th Regiment...........	November 27, 1796
Conn, John...............	Captain, 13th Regiment...........	November 27, 1796
Cragg, John..............	Lieutenant, 1st Battalion, 14th Regiment......................	August 22, 1796
Donaldson, John..........	Captain, 2nd Battalion, 14th Regiment......................	August 22, 1796
Ellis, Henry.............	Lieutenant, 1st Battalion, 14th Regiment......................	August 22, 1796
Ewalt, Henry.............	Captain, 13th Regiment...........	November 27, 1796
Fisher, Solomon..........	Lieutenant, 2nd Battalion, 14th Regiment......................	August 22, 1796
Funk, Adam...............	Lieutenant, 2nd Battalion, 14th Regiment......................	August 22, 1796
Giltner, Francis.........	Lieutenant, 13th Regiment........	November 27, 1796
Hall, Horatio............	Lieutenant Colonel, Commandant 14th Regiment.................	July 8, 1792
	(Appointed December 20, 1793)	
Hambleton, Joseph........	Lieutenant, 1st Battalion, 14th Regiment......................	August 22, 1796
Hambleton, Robert........	Ensign, 1st Battalion, 14th Regiment	August 22, 1796
Harrison, Robert.........	Major, 13th Regiment.............	December 20, 1793
Hildreth, Joseph.........	Ensign, 13th Regiment............	November 27, 1796
Johnston, William........	Lieutenant, 13th Regiment........	November 27, 1796
Kemp, Reuben.............	Ensign, 13th Regiment............	November 27, 1796
Laughlin, William........	Lieutenant, 14th Regiment........	November 4, 1793

COMMISSIONED OFFICERS, 1793 - 1796

Lyon, Hezekiah............	Captain, 13th Regiment............	November 27, 1796
McConnel, Edward..........	Captain, 13th Regiment............	November 27, 1796
McCune, George............	Captain, 2nd Battalion, 14th Regiment.......................	August 22, 1796
McDonald, James...........	Lieutenant, 2nd Battalion, 14th Regiment.......................	August 22, 1796
McGlaughlin, George.......	Ensign, 13th Regiment.............	November 27, 1796
McKitrick, James..........	Ensign, 14th Regiment.............	November 4, 1793
Mitchell, Moses...........	Captain, 1st Battalion, 14th Regiment.......................	August 22, 1796
Mitchell, William.........	Captain, 1st Battalion, 14th Regiment.......................	August 22, 1796
Mooney, John..............	Lieutenant, 13th Regiment.........	November 27, 1796
Moore, William............	Captain, 14th Regiment............	November 4, 1793
Nellis, William...........	Ensign, 1st Battalion, 14th Regiment.......................	August 22, 1796
Norton, James.............	Ensign, 1st Battalion, 14th Regiment.......................	August 22, 1796
Petty, Ebenezer...........	Captain, 2nd Battalion, 14th Regiment.......................	August 22, 1796
Pullen, James.............	Ensign, 2nd Battalion, 14th Regiment.......................	August 22, 1796
Robertson, Robert.........	Ensign, 13th Regiment.............	November 27, 1796
Scott, George.............	Major, 14th Regiment..............	August 29, 1795
Scott, George.............	Lieutenant Colonel, Commandant 14th Regiment..................	August 22, 1796
Shortridge, George........	Major, 14th Regiment..............	September 28, 1795
Swearingham, Joseph.......	Ensign, 2nd Battalion, 14th Regiment.......................	August 22, 1796
Tillett, James............	Ensign, 2nd Battalion, 14th Regiment.......................	August 22, 1796
Trimble, Robert...........	Captain, 1st Battalion, 14th Regiment.......................	August 22, 1796
Trotter, Joseph...........	Lieutenant, 1st Battalion, 14th Regiment.......................	August 22, 1796
Tucker, Leonard...........	Lieutenant, 13th Regiment.........	November 27, 1796
Wallace, John.............	Captain, 2nd Battalion, 14th Regiment.......................	August 22, 1796
Ward, Benjamin............	Major, 14th Regiment..............	August 22, 1796

Campbell County Regiment

[First commissions December 21, 1795]

Bartel, John..............	Adjutant, 21st Regiment...........	December 7, 1796
Campbell, William.........	Ensign, 21st Regiment.............	November 4, 1796
Corn, George..............	Captain, 21st Regiment............	October 12, 1796
Craig, John H.	Major, 21st Regiment..............	December 21, 1795
Emmitt, Alexander.........	Ensign, 21st Regiment.............	December 7, 1796
Garnett, Edward...........	Ensign, 21st Regiment.............	October 12, 1796

COMMISSIONED OFFICERS, 1793 - 1796

Grant, Squire............	Lieutenant Colonel, Commandant 21st Regiment..................	December 21, 1795
Graves, Bartel...........	Captain, 21st Regiment...........	December 7, 1796
Graves, William..........	Lieutenant, 21st Regiment........	October 12, 1796
Harsley, Elijah..........	Ensign, 21st Regiment............	October 12, 1796
Johnston, James..........	Lieutenant, 21st Regiment........	November 4, 1796
Kelley, George...........	Captain, 21st Regiment...........	November 4, 1796
Kelly, Nathan............	Captain, 21st Regiment...........	October 12, 1796
Little, James............	Major, 21st Regiment.............	December 21, 1795
Lucust, Jesse............	Lieutenant, 21st Regiment........	December 7, 1796
Marklin, Thomas..........	Lieutenant, 21st Regiment........	October 12, 1796
Puits (Pruitt?), John....	Lieutenant, 21st Regiment........	October 12, 1796
Webb, Edward.............	Captain, 21st Regiment...........	October 12, 1796

Clark County Regiment

[First commissions, 1792/1793]

Adams, Simon.............	Captain, 17th Regiment...........	November 4, 1793
Anderson, Abihew.........	Ensign, 17th Regiment............	November 4, 1793
Blackburn, Joseph........	Captain, 17th Regiment...........	November 4, 1793
Browning, James..........	Ensign, 17th Regiment............	October 23, 1794
Bryan, Anderson..........	Lieutenant, 17th Regiment........	November 4, 1793
Dale, John...............	Ensign, 17th Regiment............	October 23, 1794
Downing, Samuel..........	Captain, 17th Regiment...........	July 1, 1795
Hathaway, David..........	Ensign, 17th Regiment............	November 4, 1793
Holder, John.............	Lieutenant Colonel, Commandant 17th Regiment..................	January, 1793, or December, 1792
Hughes, David............	Captain, 17th Regiment...........	July 1, 1795
Humble, Uriah............	Lieutenant, 17th Regiment........	November 4, 1793
Johnston, Martin.........	Lieutenant, 17th Regiment........	October 23, 1794
Judy, John...............	Ensign, 17th Regiment............	July 1, 1795
Kelso, Henry.............	Lieutenant, 17th Regiment........	July 1, 1795
McClung, Matthew.........	Lieutenant, 17th Regiment........	November 4, 1793
McGary, Robert...........	Lieutenant, 17th Regiment........	July 1, 1795
McMilian, William........	Captain, 17th Regiment...........	June 10, 1796
Magill, James............	Captain, 17th Regiment...........	November 4, 1793
Maupin, James............	Ensign, 17th Regiment............	July 1, 1795
Minor, Thomas............	Captain, 17th Regiment...........	November 4, 1793
Morton, John.............	Captain, 17th Regiment...........	October 23, 1794
Oakly, William...........	Ensign, 17th Regiment............	November 4, 1793
Ray, John................	Lieutenant, 17th Regiment........	October 23, 1794
Ritcher, Alexander.......	Lieutenant, 17th Regiment........	June 10, 1796
Ritcher, George..........	Ensign, 17th Regiment............	June 10, 1796
Robertson, Jesse.........	Ensign, 17th Regiment............	October 23, 1794
Rodgers, William.........	Captain, 17th Regiment...........	November 4, 1793
Spurgen, Isaac...........	Ensign, 17th Regiment............	November 4, 1793
Strode, Jeremiah.........	Ensign, 17th Regiment............	October 23, 1794
Sudduth, William.........	Major, 17th Regiment.............	August 5, 1796

COMMISSIONED OFFICERS, 1793 - 1796

Tinsley, William.........	Lieutenant, 17th Regiment........	October 23, 1794
Wade, James..............	Lieutenant, 17th Regiment........	November 4, 1793
Wilson, Daniel...........	Ensign, 17th Regiment............	November 4, 1793
Yarbrough, John..........	Ensign, 17th Regiment............	November 4, 1793
Yates, Benjamin..........	Lieutenant, 17th Regiment........	November 4, 1793

Fayette County Regiments

Adams, Absalom...........	Ensign, 8th Regiment.............	November 22, 1796
Alexander, James.........	Lieutenant, 10th Regiment........	April 10, 1793
Baxter, Thomas...........	Lieutenant, 8th Regiment.........	April 24, 1795
Beaty, Cornelius.........	Major, 9th Regiment..............	August 10, 1792
	(Appointed December 20, 1793)	
Boston, Reuben...........	Ensign, 9th Regiment.............	June 26, 1795
Coger, James.............	Cornet, 9th Regiment.............	June 1, 1793
Crispin, Hugh............	Captain, 9th Regiment............	June 26, 1795
Dangerfield, William.....	Cornet, Troop of Horse, 9th Regiment......................	June 20, 1796
Darnaby, John............	Lieutenant, 8th Regiment.........	April 24, 1795
Dennison, William........	Ensign, 8th Regiment.............	April 24, 1795
Dennison, William........	Lieutenant, 8th Regiment.........	October 10, 1795
Dickey, Adam.............	Ensign, 9th Regiment.............	June 26, 1793
Dornaby, Edward..........	Ensign, 8th Regiment.............	November 10, 1796
Ellis, Hezekiah..........	Ensign, 8th Regiment.............	July 21, 1793
Evans, Hamilton..........	Captain, 9th Regiment............	November 4, 1796
Freeman, Elijah..........	Lieutenant, 9th Regiment.........	October 11, 1793
Graves, John.............	Lieutenant, 8th Regiment.........	November 10, 1796
Gray, Patrick............	Captain, 9th Regiment............	June 26, 1793
Hardy, John D.	Lieutenant, 9th Regiment.........	November 4, 1796
Hunt, John William.......	Lieutenant, Troop of Light Horse, 9th Regiment...................	June 20, 1796
Jones, Joseph............	Ensign, 10th Regiment............	April 10, 1793
Jones, Robert............	Lieutenant, 10th Regiment........	April 10, 1793
Logan, Hugh..............	Lieutenant, 8th Regiment.........	September 12, 1794
Love, Thomas.............	Lieutenant, Light Infantry Company, 9th Regiment..........	July 20, 1793
McConnell, John..........	Ensign, 10th Regiment............	April 10, 1793
McDowell, James..........	Major, 10th Regiment... (Appointed December 20, 1793) Commission dated...............	June 27, 1792
McDowell, John...........	Major, 10th Regiment... (Appointed December 20, 1793) Commission dated...............	June 20, 1792
McKee (no first name)....	Ensign, 9th Regiment.............	June 26, 1795
McKee, Archibald.........	Ensign, 8th Regiment.............	September 12, 1794
McKee, Archibald.........	Captain, 8th Regiment............	April 24, 1795
McKiney, John............	Captain, 9th Regiment............	June 26, 1793
Marshall, Henry..........	Captain, Troop of Cavalry, 9th Regiment.......................	June 1, 1793
Mitchell, Richard........	Lieutenant, 8th Regiment.........	July 21, 1793
Mitchem, Dudley..........	Captain, 8th Regiment............	February 25, 1794
Moss, John...............	Lieutenant, 9th Regiment.........	June 26, 1795

COMMISSIONED OFFICERS, 1793 - 1796

Neal, Archibald..........	Captain, 8th Regiment............	April 1, 1793
Parker, Thomas...........	Ensign, 8th Regiment.............	September 12, 1794
Parrish, James...........	Captain, 8th Regiment............	November 10, 1796
Porter, William..........	Ensign, 8th Regiment.............	October 23, 1795
Price, Samuel............	Captain, Troop of Light Horse, 9th Regiment...................	June 20, 1796
Price, William...........	Major, 9th Regiment..............	July 1, 1792
	(Appointed December 20, 1793)	
Price, William...........	Lieutenant Colonel, Commandant 9th Regiment...................	May 1, 1795
Rice, John...............	Captain, 8th Regiment............	July 21, 1793
Russell, William.........	Lieutenant Colonel, Commandant 10th Regiment..................	July 2, 1792
	(Appointed December 20, 1793)	
Scholl, Isaac............	Ensign, 8th Regiment.............	April 24, 1795
Scott, Benjamin..........	Lieutenant, 9th Regiment.........	June 26, 1793
Shores, Richard..........	Captain, 10th Regiment...........	April 9, 1793
Simpson, John............	Captain, 10th Regiment...........	April 10, 1793
Stewart, James H.	Lieutenant, 9th Regiment.........	August 20, 1794
Thurman, Fielding........	Ensign, 8th Regiment.............	March 8, 1794
Turner, Fielding Lewis...	Ensign, 8th Regiment.............	October 10, 1795
Valindingham, George.....	Lieutenant, 8th Regiment.........	April 1, 1793
Valindingham, George.....	Captain, 8th Regiment............	April 24, 1795
Walker, Charles..........	Ensign, 9th Regiment.............	November 4, 1796
Ward, George.............	Lieutenant, 9th Regiment.........	October 11, 1793
West, Lewis..............	Ensign, 9th Regiment.............	August 20, 1794
Wilson, Samuel...........	Captain, 8th Regiment............	April 2, 1793
Winn, Thomas.............	Lieutenant, 8th Regiment.........	November 7, 1796
Young, Minor.............	Lieutenant, 9th Regiment.........	June 26, 1793

Green County Regiment

[First commissions December 18, 1792, and May 15, 1793]

Abbott, Samuel...........	Ensign, 16th Regiment............	May 15, 1793
Barnet, Andrew...........	Ensign, 16th Regiment............	May 15, 1793
Barnett (no first name)..	Paymaster, 16th Regiment.........	December 18, 1792
Barnett, Andrew..........	Lieutenant, 16th Regiment........	May 31, 1793
Barbee, Elias............	1st Major, 16th Regiment.........	December 18, 1792
Belcher, John............	Captain, 16th Regiment...........	December 11, 1796
Briant, John.............	Lieutenant, 16th Regiment........	June 15, 1795
Burks, Nicholas..........	Lieutenant, 16th Regiment........	May 15, 1793
Burks, Samuel............	Adjutant, 16th Regiment..........	December 18, 1792
Butler, John.............	Captain, 16th Regiment...........	December 11, 1796
Cannon, John.............	Lieutenant, 16th Regiment........	December 11, 1796
Casey, William...........	Lieutenant Colonel, Commandant 16th Regiment..................	December 18, 1792
Davis, Norton............	Lieutenant, 16th Regiment........	December 11, 1796
Dobson, James............	Ensign, 16th Regiment............	December 11, 1796
Durham, James............	Ensign, 16th Regiment............	December 11, 1796

COMMISSIONED OFFICERS, 1793 - 1796

Fought, George............	Ensign, 16th Regiment............	May 15, 1793
Geaham, Jeremiah.........	Ensign, 16th Regiment............	December 11, 1796
Goldsby, James............	Captain, 16th Regiment...........	December 11, 1796
Headspeath, Charles......	Captain, 16th Regiment...........	December 11, 1796
Junip (Jump?), Peter.....	Lieutenant, 16th Regiment........	December 11, 1796
McCartey, Elijah.........	Lieutenant, 16th Regiment........	December 11, 1796
McFarland, Alexander.....	Captain, 16th Regiment...........	May 15, 1793
McHenry, Isaac...........	Lieutenant, 16th Regiment........	May 15, 1793
Mitchel, Adam............	Lieutenant, 16th Regiment........	December 11, 1796
Mitchel, John............	Ensign, 16th Regiment............	December 11, 1796
Montgomery, Nathan.......	2nd Major, 16th Regiment.........	December 18, 1792
Ray, Joseph..............	Ensign, 16th Regiment............	June 15, 1795
Reynick, Henry...........	Captain, 16th Regiment...........	May 15, 1793
Reynolds, John...........	Ensign, 16th Regiment............	May 15, 1793
Sanders, Hanary..........	Lieutenant, 16th Regiment........	December 11, 1796
Scaggs, William..........	Captain, 16th Regiment...........	May 31, 1793
Selby, Thomas............	Captain, 16th Regiment...........	December 11, 1796
Shields, James...........	Captain, 16th Regiment...........	May 15, 1793
Shivly, Jacob............	Ensign, 16th Regiment............	December 11, 1796
Skaggs, David............	Lieutenant, 16th Regiment........	May 15, 1793
Skaggs, Frederick........	Lieutenant, 16th Regiment........	May 15, 1793
Smith, Lawrence..........	Captain, 16th Regiment...........	December 11, 1796
Sparks, James............	Ensign, 16th Regiment............	December 11, 1796
Thurman, Richard.........	Captain, 16th Regiment...........	May 15, 1793
Walls, John..............	Quartermaster, 16th Regiment.....	December 18, 1792

Harrison County Regiment

[First commissions December 16, 1795]

Hinkson, William.........	Major, 20th Regiment.............	December 16, 1795
Rawlings, Nathan.........	Lieutenant Colonel, Commandant 20th Regiment.................	December 16, 1795

Jefferson County Regiment

Buckner, Nicholas........	Paymaster, 1st Regiment..........	June 15, 1795
Funk, John, Jr.	Ensign, 1st Regiment.............	November 27, 1796
Geiger, Frederick........	Major, 1st Regiment..............	December 16, 1795
Giger, Jacob.............	Ensign, 1st Regiment.............	November 27, 1796
Kuykendal, Moses.........	Captain, 1st Regiment............	November 27, 1796
Lynn, William............	Major, 1st Regiment..............	December 16, 1795
Miller, Samuel...........	Ensign, 1st Regiment.............	November 27, 1796
Querey, Charles..........	Captain, 1st Regiment............	November 27, 1796
Ross, Philip.............	Lieutenant, 1st Regiment.........	November 27, 1796
Taylor, Thompson.........	Lieutenant, 1st Regiment.........	November 27, 1796
Tyler, Robert............	Ensign, 1st Regiment.............	May 10, 1793
Wells, Samuel............	Major, 1st Regiment..............	July 11, 1792 (Appointed December 20, 1793)
Wells, Yelverton Peyton..	Captain, 1st Regiment............	November 27, 1796

Lincoln County Regiment

Burdet, Joseph............	Captain, 6th Regiment............	April 1, 1793
Campbell, William........	Major, 6th Regiment..............	June 19, 1793
Clark, Christopher.......	Ensign, 6th Regiment.............	December 1, 1793
Elliott, Alexander.......	Lieutenant, 6th Regiment.........	April 1, 1793
Ewing, Urban.............	Captain, 6th Regiment............	December 1, 1793
		and March 15, 1794
Faris, Johnston..........	Lieutenant, 6th Regiment.........	July 27, 1795
Ford, Charles............	Ensign, 6th Regiment.............	July 27, 1795
Harling, George..........	Lieutenant, 6th Regiment.........	April 23, 1794
Horine, Jacob............	Ensign, 6th Regiment.............	April 23, 1794
Horine, Michael..........	Captain, 6th Regiment............	April 23, 1794
Huston, Nathan...........	Major, 6th Regiment..............	July 5, 1792
	(Appointed December 20, 1793)	
Jennings, William........	Lieutenant, 6th Regiment.........	July 27, 1795
Kerr, Armstrong..........	Ensign, 6th Regiment.............	July 27, 1795
Lawson, David............	Ensign, 6th Regiment.............	July 27, 1795
McKinney, John...........	Captain, 6th Regiment............	April 1, 1793
		and March 15, 1794
Nash, William............	Lieutenant, 6th Regiment.........	April 1, 1793
Payne, Reuben............	Lieutenant, 6th Regiment.........	April 23, 1794
Pope, Elimander..........	Captain, 6th Regiment............	November 20, 1793
Reybourn, Robert.........	Captain, 6th Regiment............	April 23, 1794
Richardson, Jesse........	Captain, 6th Regiment............	July 27, 1795
Shackleford, Richard.....	Captain, 6th Regiment............	April 23, 1794
Weid, Peace..............	Lieutenant, 6th Regiment.........	July 27, 1795
Whiles, Thomas...........	Adjutant, 6th Regiment...........	May 21, 1793
Whitley, William.........	Lieutenant Colonel, Commandant 6th Regiment...................	June 1, 1793
Wilkinson, John..........	Captain, 6th Regiment............	November 20, 1793

Madison County Regiments

[19th Regiment laid off March 2, 1795]

Alcorn, John.............	Captain, 19th Regiment...........	May 20, 1795
Anderson, John...........	Lieutenant, 19th Regiment........	August 18, 1796
Baker, Joseph............	Ensign, 7th Regiment.............	June 10, 1795
Barker, Elias............	Captain, 7th Regiment............	June 10, 1795
Baxter, Edmund...........	Captain, 7th Regiment............	April 1, 1796
Bennett, Hardiman........	Captain, 19th Regiment...........	May 20, 1795
Blackwell, Benjamin......	Ensign, 7th Regiment.............	July 29, 1795
Bone, John...............	Captain, 19th Regiment...........	May 20, 1795
Boyston, William.........	Lieutenant, 19th Regiment........	May 20, 1795
Brock, Thomas............	Lieutenant, 19th Regiment........	August 18, 1796
Brooks, Lynch............	Lieutenant, 7th Regiment.........	April 1, 1796
Brown, Beverly...........	Captain, 19th Regiment...........	May 20, 1795
Calloway, Richard........	Captain, 7th Regiment............	June 10, 1795
Chiles, James............	Ensign, 19th Regiment............	August 18, 1796

COMMISSIONED OFFICERS, 1793 - 1796

Cochran, Samuel	Captain, 19th Regiment	May 20, 1795
Collins, Barby	Lieutenant, 7th Regiment	June 10, 1795
Crawford, Edward	Ensign, 19th Regiment	May 20, 1795
Crews, Thomas	Captain, 7th Regiment	August 13, 1793
Denny, George	Captain, 19th Regiment	August 18, 1796
Depriest, John	Ensign, 19th Regiment	August 18, 1796
Dunham, John	Lieutenant, 7th Regiment	June 10, 1795
Durbin, Edward	Ensign, 7th Regiment	June 10, 1795
East, James	Ensign, 19th Regiment	May 20, 1795
Estill, Samuel	Lieutenant Colonel, Commandant 19th Regiment	March 2, 1795
Finnell, James	Captain, 19th Regiment	October 26, 1796
Fort, Frederick	Captain, 7th Regiment	June 10, 1795
Fowler, Thomas	Ensign, 7th Regiment	August 13, 1793
Goggins, John	Captain, 19th Regiment	May 20, 1795
Hackett, Peter	Ensign, 7th Regiment	April 1, 1796
Highat, William	Ensign, 19th Regiment	October 26, 1796
Hunter, John	Lieutenant, 19th Regiment	May 20, 1795
Hutcheson, Lawrence	Lieutenant, 19th Regiment	October 26, 1796
Jameson, Robert	Lieutenant, 7th Regiment	June 10, 1795
Johnston, James	Captain, 7th Regiment	August 13, 1793
Kavenaugh, William	Major, 7th Regiment	March 2, 1795
Lynch, David	Ensign, 7th Regiment	June 10, 1795
McMillion, James	Ensign, 19th Regiment	October 26, 1796
McNeley, George	Lieutenant, 19th Regiment	October 26, 1796
McQueen, John	Lieutenant, 7th Regiment	June 10, 1795
Moore, David	Lieutenant, 19th Regiment	May 20, 1795
Morrison, William	Major, 19th Regiment	March 2, 1795
Mullens, Gabriel	Lieutenant, 7th Regiment	June 10, 1795
Nickleson, William	Lieutenant, 19th Regiment	October 26, 1796
Paisley, James	Ensign, 7th Regiment	June 10, 1795
Pearce, William	Lieutenant, 19th Regiment	May 20, 1795
Phelps, John	Captain, 19th Regiment	August 18, 1796
Proctor, Nicholas	Captain, 7th Regiment	June 10, 1795
Pullers, Lofty	Ensign, 19th Regiment	May 20, 1795
Redman, George	Captain, 7th Regiment	April 1, 1796
Shackleford, Edward	Captain, 19th Regiment	October 26, 1796
Small, John	Ensign, 19th Regiment	May 20, 1795
South, Samuel	Major, 7th Regiment	March 2, 1795
Stepp, Elijah	Lieutenant, 19th Regiment	May 20, 1795
Terrill, Edmund	Major, 19th Regiment	March 2, 1795
White, James	Lieutenant, 7th Regiment	July 29, 1795
Wilkinson, John	Captain, 7th Regiment	July 4, 1795
Williams, Frederick	Ensign, 7th Regiment	June 10, 1795
Wilson, Israel	Lieutenant, 19th Regiment	August 18, 1796

Mason County Regiment

Armstrong, Joshua	Ensign, 15th Regiment	September 3, 1794
Barrow, George	Ensign, 15th Regiment	November 11, 1796

COMMISSIONED OFFICERS, 1793 - 1796   23

Bilderbec, Ephraim.......	Captain, 15th Regiment...........	November 11, 1796
Briant, John..............	Ensign, 15th Regiment............	September 3, 1794
Brinson, Thomas...........	Ensign, 15th Regiment............	November 11, 1796
Butler, William...........	Captain, 15th Regiment...........	September 3, 1794
Davis, David..............	Major, 15th Regiment.............	August 4, 1796
Deshea, Joseph............	Captain, 15th Regiment...........	November 11, 1796
Drake, Jacob..............	Lieutenant, 15th Regiment........	November 11, 1796
Drake, Reune..............	Captain, 15th Regiment...........	November 11, 1796
Early, David..............	Ensign, 15th Regiment............	November 11, 1796
Evans, Gabriel............	Lieutenant, 15th Regiment........	November 11, 1796
Fought, George............	Captain, 15th Regiment...........	September 3, 1794
Fulton, Hugh..............	Captain, 15th Regiment...........	November 11, 1796
Green, John...............	Ensign, 15th Regiment............	November 11, 1796
Hardester, Uriah..........	Ensign, 15th Regiment............	March 13, 1793
Harman, Mathias...........	Captain, 15th Regiment...........	August 16, 1796
Harrison, John............	Ensign, 15th Regiment............	November 11, 1796
Hoard, Elias..............	Ensign, 15th Regiment............	November 11, 1796
Jones, Benjamin...........	Ensign, 15th Regiment............	November 11, 1796
Jones, Thomas.............	Captain, 15th Regiment...........	September 11, 1793
Jump, Peter...............	Ensign, 15th Regiment............	September 3, 1794
Kelly, Nathaniel..........	Captain, 15th Regiment...........	March 13, 1793
Kenton, Simon.............	Major, 15th Regiment.............	August 1, 1793
Kirkpatrick, Moses........	Captain, 15th Regiment...........	September 3, 1794
McCullough, John..........	Ensign, 15th Regiment............	November 11, 1796
McFarlin, John............	Ensign, 15th Regiment............	September 3, 1794
Mais, Mathew..............	Lieutenant, 15th Regiment........	September 3, 1794
Meshawn, Daniel...........	Lieutenant, 15th Regiment........	November 11, 1796
Payne, Duvall.............	Captain, 15th Regiment...........	November 11, 1796
Pepper, Jesse.............	Ensign, 15th Regiment............	November 11, 1796
Pepper, William...........	Lieutenant, 15th Regiment........	November 11, 1796
Rigdon, John..............	Lieutenant, 15th Regiment........	November 11, 1796
Scott, John...............	Ensign, 15th Regiment............	November 11, 1796
Seisam, Benjamin (?)......	Lieutenant, 15th Regiment........	September 3, 1794
Shackleford, John.........	Lieutenant, 15th Regiment........	November 11, 1796
Spencer, John.............	Lieutenant, 15th Regiment........	March 13, 1793
Spilman, James............	Captain, 15th Regiment...........	September 3, 1794
Steward, Robert...........	Lieutenant, 15th Regiment........	November 11, 1796
Strutten, Solomon.........	Lieutenant, 15th Regiment........	August 16, 1796
Sweet, Benjamin...........	Captain, 15th Regiment...........	November 11, 1796
Sypoald, Jasper...........	Captain, 15th Regiment...........	November 11, 1796
Whiteman, Benjamin........	Captain, 15th Regiment...........	November 11, 1796
Wood, Abner...............	Lieutenant, 15th Regiment........	November 11, 1796
Wood, David...............	Lieutenant, 15th Regiment........	November 11, 1796
Wood, John................	Lieutenant, 15th Regiment........	November 11, 1796

Mercer County Regiment

Adair, John...............	Lieutenant Colonel, Commandant 5th Regiment..................	December 19, 1793
Brenton, James............	Lieutenant, 5th Regiment.........	June 20, 1793

COMMISSIONED OFFICERS, 1793 - 1796

Grider, Henry............	Captain, 5th Regiment............	June 20, 1793
Steen, John..............	Captain, 5th Regiment............	April 1, 1793
Taylor, John.............	Ensign, 5th Regiment.............	June 20, 1793

Nelson County Regiment

Dunn, Vincent............	Captain, 2nd Regiment............	February 18, 1795
Floyd, John..............	Ensign, 2nd Regiment.............	July 20, 1793
Floyd, John..............	Lieutenant, 2nd Regiment.........	February 18, 1795
Snyder, John.............	Ensign, 2nd Regiment.............	February 18, 1795

Nelson and Logan Regiment

Baird, Robert............	Captain, 3rd Regiment............	May 15, 1793
Boyles, David............	Ensign, 3rd Regiment.............	December 16, 1796
Caits, Joshua...........	Captain, 3rd Regiment............	May 15, 1793
Calloway, Chesly.........	Ensign, 3rd Regiment.............	May 15, 1793
Chapman, Thomas..........	Lieutenant, 3rd Regiment.........	May 15, 1793
Collins, William.........	Lieutenant, 3rd Regiment.........	December 16, 1796
Cox, Phenix..............	Captain, 3rd Regiment............	May 15, 1793
Dromgoole, Alexander.....	Captain, Light Horse Company, 3rd Regiment..................	January 3, 1794
Ewing, Chatham...........	Lieutenant, 3rd Regiment.........	December 16, 1795
Ewing, Young.............	Captain, 3rd Regiment............	May 15, 1793
Gaits, William...........	Lieutenant, 3rd Regiment.........	May 15, 1793
Glover, John.............	Lieutenant, 3rd Regiment.........	May 15, 1793
Graves, Dennis...........	Ensign, 3rd Regiment.............	May 15, 1793
Hardin, Abraham..........	Ensign, 3rd Regiment.............	May 15, 1793
Helm, George.............	Paymaster, 3rd Regiment..........	December 19, 1796
Holmes, Elias............	Ensign, 3rd Regiment.............	May 15, 1793
Howard, Elisha...........	Captain, 3rd Regiment............	May 15, 1793
Linder, Jacob............	Major, 3rd Regiment..............	December 19, 1796
McCombs, John............	Captain, 3rd Regiment............	May 15, 1793
Neal, John...............	Lieutenant, 3rd Regiment.........	May 15, 1793
Thomas, John.............	Colonel, 3rd Regiment............	December 19, 1796
Wilson, George...........	Ensign, 3rd Regiment.............	May 15, 1793
Wilson, Samuel...........	Ensign, 3rd Regiment.............	December 16, 1795
Withrons, John (?).......	Captain, 3rd Regiment............	March 3, 1795

Scott County Regiment

Allen, James.............	Ensign, 12th Regiment............	May 1, 1793
Boyd, Joseph.............	Lieutenant, 12th Regiment........	May 24, 1795
Bradley, Bensa...........	Ensign, 12th Regiment............	November 29, 1794
Burbridge, George........	Lieutenant, 12th Regiment........	July 15, 1795
Campbell, William........	Ensign, 12th Regiment............	March 25, 1796
Connolly, James..........	Captain, 12th Regiment...........	July 15, 1795
Davis, William...........	Ensign, 12th Regiment............	June 22, 1795

COMMISSIONED OFFICERS, 1793 - 1796   25

Dehaven, Edward..........	Lieutenant, 12th Regiment........	November 29, 1794
Ely, Henry...............	Lieutenant, 12th Regiment........	March 25, 1796
Ewing, John..............	Lieutenant, 12th Regiment........	May 10, 1794
Fegland (Ficklin?), John.	Ensign, 12th Regiment............	July 15, 1795
Flournoy, Francis........	Lieutenant, 12th Regiment........	May 14, 1793
Flournoy, John J.	Lieutenant, 12th Regiment........	May 14, 1793
Flournoy, Mathew.........	Captain, 12th Regiment...........	June 22, 1795
Gevill, John.............	Lieutenant, 12th Regiment........	May 10, 1794
Gevill, John.............	Captain, 12th Regiment...........	March 25, 1796
Gholson, Francis.........	Captain, 12th Regiment...........	May 10, 1794
Grant, Squire............	Captain, 12th Regiment...........	May 24, 1795
Hall, John, Jr.	Captain, 12th Regiment...........	May 1, 1793
Harling, George..........	Lieutenant, 12th Regiment........	June 22, 1795
Harwood, John............	Ensign, 12th Regiment............	November 10, 1793
Henry, William...........	Major, 12th Regiment.............	August 20, 1794
Hunter, John.............	Captain, 12th Regiment...........	November 10, 1793
Hunter, Robert...........	Lieutenant, 12th Regiment........	November 10, 1793
Hunter, Robert...........	Quartermaster, 12th Regiment.....	December 9, 1796
Huston, Anthony..........	Lieutenant, 12th Regiment........	November 29, 1794
Lambert, Daniel..........	Ensign, 12th Regiment............	July 15, 1795
Lindsay, Henry...........	Captain, 12th Regiment...........	May 10, 1794
Lindsey, Joseph..........	Ensign, 12th Regiment............	May 10, 1794
McCressky, James.........	Captain, 12th Regiment...........	November 29, 1794
Nichols, William.........	Adjutant, 12th Regiment..........	December 9, 1796
Payne, John..............	Major, 1st Battalion, 12th Regiment	December 9, 1796
Sanders, Robert..........	Lieutenant Colonel, Commandant 12th Regiment..................	August 21, 1796
Smith, Rhodes............	Lieutenant, 12th Regiment........	July 15, 1795
Thomas, Elisha...........	Ensign, 12th Regiment............	May 10, 1794
Thrasher, Stephen........	Ensign, 12th Regiment............	May 24, 1795

Shelby County Regiment

Ballard, Bland............	Major, 18th Regiment.............	December 21, 1794
Boone, John..............	Cornet, Troop of Cavalry, 18th Regiment......................	June 24, 1795
Butler, William..........	Captain, Troop of Cavalry, 18th Regiment......................	June 24, 1795
Matlock, Absolem.........	2nd Lieutenant, Troop of Cavalry, 18th Regiment.................	June 24, 1795
Ryland, Nicholas.........	1st Lieutenant, Troop of Cavalry, 18th Regiment.................	June 24, 1795
Whittaker, Aquilla.......	Lieutenant Colonel, Commandant 18th Regiment..................	December 22, 1794
Winlock, Joseph..........	Major, 18th Regiment.............	December 23, 1794

Washington County Regiment

Barlow, Cornelius........	Lieutenant, 4th Regiment.........	August 20, 1794

COMMISSIONED OFFICERS, 1793 - 1796

Caldwell, David..........	Major, 4th Regiment..............	July 17, 1792
		(Appointed December 20, 1793)
Call (also spelled Cull), Thomas...	Ensign, 4th Regiment....	March 3, 1795
Catlin, James............	Ensign, 4th Regiment.............	December 19, 1795
Cull (also Call), Thomas.	Ensign, 4th Regiment.............	August 20, 1794
Hammitt, John............	Lieutenant, 4th Regiment.........	December 19, 1795
Lincoln, Mordecai........	Captain, 4th Regiment............	August 20, 1794
McDaniel, Richard........	Captain, 4th Regiment............	August 20, 1794
Marshall, James..........	Lieutenant, 4th Regiment.........	August 20, 1794
Marshall, William........	Lieutenant, 4th Regiment.........	March 3, 1795
Mudd, Francis............	Ensign, 4th Regiment.............	August 20, 1794
Purdy, Edmund............	Captain, 4th Regiment............	August 20, 1794
Robins, Aaron............	Ensign, 4th Regiment.............	August 20, 1794
Wapshot, James...........	Major, 4th Regiment..............	December 17, 1796
Washburn, Phillip........	Captain, 4th Regiment............	December 19, 1795

Woodford County Regiment

Bean, George.............	Ensign, 11th Regiment............	October 20, 1796
Beatty, Otho.............	Lieutenant, Light Infantry Company, 11th Regiment.........	October 11, 1796
Bohannon, George.........	Captain, 11th Regiment...........	November 10, 1796
Briscoe, Hezekiah........	Ensign, 11th Regiment............	November 30, 1796
Brooking, Samuel.........	Ensign, 11th Regiment............	December 21, 1793
Brown, William...........	Ensign, 11th Regiment............	July 15, 1796
Burbridge, Rowland.......	Captain, 11th Regiment...........	February 11, 1795
Burton, Jeremiah.........	Ensign, 11th Regiment............	November 20, 1796
Calmes, Marquis..........	Lieutenant Colonel, Commandant 11th Regiment.................	December 20, 1793
Cole, Richard............	Lieutenant, 11th Regiment........	November 10, 1796
Collins, Joel............	Captain, 11th Regiment...........	May 2, 1794
Fields, Henry............	Captain, 11th Regiment...........	October 26, 1796
Francisco, John..........	Captain, 11th Regiment...........	October 11, 1793
Gano, Richard M.	Captain, Light Infantry Company, 11th Regiment.........	October 11, 1796
Graham, William..........	Lieutenant, 11th Regiment........	July 15, 1796
Harman, Abraham..........	Ensign, 11th Regiment............	October 11, 1793
Hayden, Ezekiel..........	Captain, 11th Regiment...........	May 15, 1793
Haydon, Benjamin.........	Lieutenant, 11th Regiment........	July 15, 1796
Holman, Isaac............	Ensign, 11th Regiment............	October 26, 1796
Jarvis, Franklin.........	Ensign, 11th Regiment............	October 26, 1796
Lee, Willis..............	Ensign, Light Infantry Company, 11th Regiment.........	October 11, 1796
Lizenbry, William........	Ensign, 11th Regiment............	October 26, 1796
Martin, John.............	Lieutenant, 11th Regiment........	October 11, 1793
Mitchel, Joseph F.	Captain, 11th Regiment...........	July 15, 1796
Mosby, John..............	Captain, 11th Regiment...........	October 26, 1796
Raybourn, James..........	Lieutenant, 11th Regiment........	October 10, 1795
Richards, Phillip........	Ensign, 11th Regiment............	October 10, 1795
Ross, Zachariah..........	Ensign, 11th Regiment............	May 15, 1793

Searcy, Edmund...........	Lieutenant, 11th Regiment........	October 11, 1793
Searcy, Edmund...........	Captain, 11th Regiment...........	October 26, 1796
Singleton, Jaconiar......	Captain, 11th Regiment...........	October 26, 1796
Spencer, Edward..........	Captain, 11th Regiment...........	October 11, 1793
Stewart, James...........	Captain, 11th Regiment...........	October 11, 1793
Stucker, Philip..........	Ensign, 11th Regiment............	July 18, 1795
Stucker, Philip..........	Lieutenant, 11th Regiment........	October 26, 1796
Taylor, Joseph...........	Lieutenant, 11th Regiment........	October 11, 1793
Thompson, Anthony........	Lieutenant, 11th Regiment........	December 21, 1793
Trabue, Daniel...........	Major, 11th Regiment.............	December 21, 1795
Utterback, Lewis.........	Ensign, 11th Regiment............	October 11, 1793
Utterback, Martin........	Lieutenant, 11th Regiment........	October 26, 1796
Witterback, Martin. See Martin Utterback.		
Wooldridge, Elisha.......	Ensign, 11th Regiment............	October 11, 1793
Wooldridge, Elisha.......	Lieutenant, 11th Regiment........	October 26, 1796

General Officers

Adair, John..............	Brigadier General, 2nd Brigade...	February 25, 1797
Lee, Henry...............	Brigadier General, 5th Brigade...	January 30, 1798
Ward, William............	Brigade Inspector, 5th Brigade...	January 31, 1798

Company Officers

Bourbon County Regiments

Archer, James............	Ensign, 14th Regiment............	July 4, 1798
Baker, James.............	Ensign, 13th Regiment............	February 23, 1797
Baker, William...........	Major, 2nd Battalion, 13th Regiment.......................	February 23, 1797
Berry, Robert............	Lieutenant, 14th Regiment........	July 4, 1798
Black, Samuel............	Captain, 14th Regiment...........	August 22, 1797
Blackberry, William......	Lieutenant, 13th Regiment........	May 25, 1798
Blount, Andrew...........	Lieutenant, 14th Regiment........	August 22, 1797
Brady, William...........	Captain, 13th Regiment...........	February 23, 1797
Breckinridge, Robert.....	Lieutenant, 14th Regiment........	November 1, 1796
Briant, Alexander........	Ensign, 14th Regiment............	August 22, 1797
Briant, Andrew...........	Lieutenant, 14th Regiment........	August 22, 1797
Bukhannan, Henry.........	Captain, 14th Regiment...........	December 20, 1798
Caldwell, William........	Ensign, 14th Regiment............	July 4, 1798
Chinn, William Ball......	Captain, Rifle Company, 13th Regiment..................	October 8, 1798
Clarkson, Charles........	Major, 2nd Battalion, 13th Regiment.......................	December 21, 1798
Clarkston, David.........	Paymaster, 13th Regiment.........	January 25, 1798
Cowin, Hugh..............	Lieutenant, 14th Regiment........	April 3, 1798
Croutch, James...........	Captain, 14th Regiment...........	July 4, 1798
Fisher, Solomon..........	Captain, 14th Regiment...........	March 5, 1797
Friend, Elijah...........	Ensign of Cavalry, 14th Regiment.	August 22, 1797
Furman, James............	Lieutenant, 14th Regiment........	July 4, 1798
Gregg, James.............	Ensign, 13th Regiment............	May 25, 1798
Hall, Adam...............	Lieutenant, 14th Regiment........	April 3, 1798
Hawkins, Samuel..........	Lieutenant, 13th Regiment........	February 23, 1797
Hibler, Samuel...........	Ensign, 14th Regiment............	August 22, 1797
Hughes, William..........	Lieutenant, 13th Regiment........	May 25, 1798
Ireland, David...........	Captain, 14th Regiment...........	August 22, 1797
Jackson, Thomas..........	Ensign, 14th Regiment............	August 22, 1797
Jay, Francis.............	Lieutenant, 14th Regiment........	July 4, 1798
Jones, Moses.............	Lieutenant, 13th Regiment........	February 23, 1797
Junifer, John............	Captain, 13th Regiment...........	February 23, 1797
Kenney, John.............	Captain, 14th Regiment...........	August 22, 1797
Lindsey, George..........	Captain, 14th Regiment...........	March 12, 1797
Lips, Jacob..............	Lieutenant, 13th Regiment........	February 23, 1797
Litton, John.............	Ensign, 14th Regiment............	August 22, 1797
Louir, Christian.........	Ensign, 14th Regiment............	April 3, 1798
Lyon, John...............	Captain, 13th Regiment...........	November 28, 1797

COMMISSIONED OFFICERS, 1797 - 1798

McDaniel, John............	Captain, 13th Regiment............	November 29, 1797
McDaniel, Rowland........	Ensign, 13th Regiment............	November 29, 1797
McIntire, Robert.........	Captain, 13th Regiment............	May 25, 1798
Martin, William..........	Lieutenant, 14th Regiment........	August 22, 1797
Mitchell, Thomas.........	Captain, 14th Regiment............	April 3, 1798
Moore, Samuel............	Captain, 14th Regiment............	July 4, 1798
Neasbit, Robert..........	Ensign, 13th Regiment............	February 23, 1797
Nelson, John.............	Ensign, 14th Regiment............	July 4, 1798
Norman, Ezekiel..........	Ensign, 13th Regiment............	November 28, 1797
Phelps, John.............	Lieutenant, Cavalry Company, 14th Regiment..................	July 4, 1798
Phillips, Elijah.........	Surgeon, 13th Regiment............	January 25, 1798
Porter, Andrew...........	Lieutenant, 14th Regiment........	November 1, 1796
Roberts, William.........	Ensign, 14th Regiment............	August 22, 1797
Ruddle, John.............	Captain, 13th Regiment............	February 23, 1797
Scott, Elijah............	Captain of Cavalry, 14th Regiment	August 22, 1797
Scott, John..............	Lieutenant, 14th Regiment........	August 22, 1797
Scott, Robert............	Ensign, 14th Regiment............	July 4, 1798
Scroggins, John..........	Ensign, Rifle Company, 13th Regiment...................	October 8, 1798
Smith, John..............	Quartermaster, 13th Regiment.....	January 25, 1798
Stephenson, William......	Captain, 14th Regiment............	July 4, 1798
Sweaney, James...........	Captain, Cavalry Company, 14th Regiment..................	July 4, 1798
Sweaney, John............	Lieutenant, 14th Regiment........	July 4, 1798
Swinney, James...........	Lieutenant of Cavalry, 14th Regiment..................	August 22, 1797
Talbot, Hugh.............	Ensign, 13th Regiment............	February 23, 1797
Thompson, Thomas A.	Captain, 13th Regiment............	February 23, 1797
Tillett, Giles...........	Ensign, 14th Regiment............	March 5, 1797
Tillett, James...........	Lieutenant, 14th Regiment........	March 5; 1797
Timmerson, John..........	Ensign, 14th Regiment............	August 22, 1797
Trimble, James...........	Lieutenant, 14th Regiment........	August 22, 1797
Tucker, Leonard..........	Lieutenant, 13th Regiment........	November 29, 1797
Whealy, John.............	Lieutenant, 14th Regiment........	July 4, 1798
Williams, Roger..........	Lieutenant, Rifle Company, 13th Regiment...................	October 8, 1798
Wright, James............	Ensign, 14th Regiment............	April 3, 1798

Campbell County Regiment

Anderson, William........	Lieutenant, 21st Regiment........	September 1, 1797
Ashcraft, Jediah.........	Lieutenant, 21st Regiment........	July 12, 1797
Ashcraft, Jediah.........	Captain, 21st Regiment............	October 8, 1798
Black, George............	Lieutenant, 21st Regiment........	June 7, 1798
Brackin, Jesse...........	Lieutenant, 21st Regiment........	September 20, 1797
Childers, Robert.........	Lieutenant, 21st Regiment........	October 8, 1798
Colvin, John.............	Lieutenant, 21st Regiment........	September 1, 1797
Conner, Frederic.........	Captain, 21st Regiment............	September 20, 1797
Flournoy, John J.	Judge Advocate, 21st Regiment....	September 20, 1797

COMMISSIONED OFFICERS, 1797 - 1798

Fowler, Edmond..........	Lieutenant, 21st Regiment........	September 20, 1797
Glave, Matthew..........	Captain, 21st Regiment..........	October 8, 1798
Hume, Gerard.............	Captain, 21st Regiment..........	July 12, 1797
Kilger, Robert...........	Ensign, 21st Regiment............	September 20, 1797
Linn, Nathan.............	Ensign, 21st Regiment............	June 7, 1798
McClanaghan, Elijah......	Ensign, 21st Regiment............	October 8, 1798
McCray, William..........	Ensign, 21st Regiment............	September 20, 1797
McLaughlin, Charles......	Ensign, 21st Regiment............	September 1, 1797
Martin, William..........	Lieutenant, 21st Regiment........	September 20, 1797
Morgan, Willis...........	Ensign, 21st Regiment............	September 1, 1797
Peary, William...........	Captain, 21st Regiment..........	September 1, 1797
Reed, Archibald H.	Captain, 21st Regiment..........	June 7, 1798
Rifle, John..............	Lieutenant, 21st Regiment........	October 8, 1798
Rush, Peter..............	Captain, 21st Regiment..........	September 20, 1797
Sandford, Thomas.........	Major, 21st Regiment............	May 24, 1798
Scott, Thomas............	Ensign, 21st Regiment............	September 20, 1797
Sharp, Richard...........	Lieutenant, 21st Regiment........	October 8, 1798
Swords, Donald...........	Ensign, 21st Regiment............	October 8, 1798
Thrasher, William........	Lieutenant, 21st Regiment........	September 20, 1797
Wilkinson, Abner.........	Captain, 21st Regiment..........	May 24, 1798

Christian County Regiment

[Laid off February 23, 1797]

Arthur, Thomas...........	Captain, 24th Regiment..........	August 9, 1798
Bell, George.............	Captain, 24th Regiment..........	November 9, 1797
Coleman, Robert..........	2nd Lieutenant of Cavalry, 24th Regiment..................	November 17, 1797
Crawthers (Caruthers), William...	Ensign, 24th Regiment.....	November 28, 1797
Davidson, David..........	Lieutenant, 24th Regiment........	November 28, 1797
Dillingham, Vachel, Jr...	Captain of Cavalry, 24th Regiment	November 17, 1797
Doom, Jacob..............	Ensign, 24th Regiment............	November 28, 1797
Ewing, Young.............	Major, 24th Regiment............	February 23, 1797
Garrison, James..........	Ensign, 24th Regiment............	August 9, 1798
Gibb, Samuel.............	Captain, 24th Regiment..........	August 9, 1798
Gillihan, William........	Captain, 24th Regiment..........	November 28, 1797
Gorden, John.............	Ensign, 24th Regiment............	August 9, 1798
Gordon, John.............	Ensign, 24th Regiment............	November 9, 1797
Grant, Charles...........	Lieutenant, 24th Regiment........	November 28, 1797
Grayson, Thomas..........	Lieutenant, 24th Regiment........	May 14, 1797
Grisom, Thomas...........	Lieutenant, 24th Regiment........	August 9, 1798
Hawkins, Josiah..........	Ensign, 24th Regiment............	November 28, 1797
Hayes, Robert............	Lieutenant, 24th Regiment........	November 9, 1797
Hayes, Robert............	Lieutenant, 24th Regiment........	August 9, 1798
Hodge, Samuel............	Lieutenant, 24th Regiment........	August 9, 1798
Johnson, Hugh............	Cornet, Cavalry, 24th Regiment...	November 17, 1797
Kinchloe, Lewis..........	Captain, 24th Regiment..........	August 9, 1798
Logan, Robert A.	Ensign, 24th Regiment............	August 9, 1798
McFaddin, Samuel.........	Lieutenant, 24th Regiment........	August 9, 1798

COMMISSIONED OFFICERS, 1797 - 1798   31

Roberts, Joseph..........	Lieutenant, 24th Regiment........	November 9, 1797
Robertson, George........	Captain, 24th Regiment..........	November 28, 1797
Robertson, John..........	Lieutenant, 24th Regiment........	November 28, 1797
Shelby, Moses............	Lieutenant Colonel, Commandant 24th Regiment..................	February 23, 1797
Smith, David.............	Major, 24th Regiment.............	February 23, 1797
Stewart, Abraham.........	Captain, 24th Regiment..........	November 9, 1797
Stewart, Abraham.........	Captain, 24th Regiment..........	August 9, 1798
Vaughan, George..........	Ensign, 24th Regiment............	November 9, 1797
Vaughan, George..........	Ensign, 24th Regiment............	August 9, 1798
Vaughan, Joseph..........	Captain, 24th Regiment..........	November 9, 1797
Vaughan, Joseph..........	Captain, 24th Regiment..........	August 9, 1798
Wallis, William..........	Ensign, 24th Regiment............	November 9, 1797
Ward, Thomas.............	Ensign, 24th Regiment............	August 9, 1798
Whitley, Elijah..........	Lieutenant, 24th Regiment........	August 9, 1798
Williams, John...........	Captain,24th Regiment............	November 28, 1797
Young, Ezekiel...........	1st Lieutenant, Cavalry, 24th Regiment..................	November 17, 1797

Clark County Regiment

Christy, Ambrose.........	Captain, Rifle Company, 17th Regiment..................	June 14, 1798
Crabtree, Isaac..........	Captain, Rifle Company, 17th Regiment..................	January 1, 1798
Dooley, John.............	Captain, 17th Regiment...........	August 7, 1798
Douglas, High............	Lieutenant, 17th Regiment........	May 1, 1797
Goosey, Peter............	Ensign, 17th Regiment............	August 7, 1798
Grigsby, Lewis...........	Lieutenant, 17th Regiment........	May 1, 1797
Hardy, Andrew............	Lieutenant, 17th Regiment........	August 7, 1798
Higgins, Robert..........	Captain, Troop of Horse, 17th Regiment......................	November 1, 1796
Kelly (no first name)....	Ensign, 17th Regiment............	November 20, 1798
Knight, John.............	Ensign, 17th Regiment............	November 29, 1797
Lyle, Daniel.............	Ensign, Rifle Company, 17th Regiment......................	June 14, 1798
Martin, Job..............	Lieutenant, Rifle Company, 17th Regiment......................	June 14, 1798
Martin, John.............	Lieutenant, 17th Regiment........	October 15, 1798
Moore, Harry.............	Lieutenant, Troop of Horse, 17th Regiment..................	November 1, 1796
Price, Francis...........	Cornet, Troop of Horse, 17th Regiment......................	November 1, 1796
Strode, Stephen..........	Lieutenant, 17th Regiment........	October 29, 1798
Young, James.............	Captain, 17th Regiment...........	May 1, 1797

Fayette County Regiments

Adams, Absalom...........	Lieutenant, 8th Regiment.........	January 2, 1798

COMMISSIONED OFFICERS, 1797 - 1798

Alexander, James	Captain, 10th Regiment	April 3, 1798
Barns, Heriah	Ensign, 9th Regiment	December 3, 1798
Brown, John	Ensign, 10th Regiment	April 3, 1798
Browning, Abner	Lieutenant, 10th Regiment	November 8, 1798
Bryan, Morgan	Captain, 10th Regiment	November 8, 1798
Bryant, George	Ensign, 8th Regiment	October 1, 1798
Bullock, Edmond	Quartermaster, 8th Regiment	October 25, 1797
Chinn, Christopher	Captain, 10th Regiment	October 27, 1798
Chinn, William	Lieutenant, 10th Regiment	April 3, 1798
Chinn, William	Adjutant, 10th Regiment	November 27, 1798
Croathers, James	Ensign, 10th Regiment	April 3, 1798
Darnaby, Edward	Lieutenant, 8th Regiment	July 9, 1798
Davenport, William	Captain, 8th Regiment	March 26, 1798
Dudly, Robert	Ensign, 8th Regiment	May 11, 1798
Dudly, Robert	Lieutenant, 8th Regiment	October 1, 1798
Dudly, William	Major, 2nd Battalion, 8th Regiment	July 30, 1798
Ellis, Littlebury	Lieutenant, 8th Regiment	October 2, 1798
Fitzgerald, Jesse	Lieutenant, 10th Regiment	April 3, 1798
Fucher (Fousher?), Robert	Captain, 10th Regiment	June 27, 1798
Gibson, John	Ensign, 8th Regiment	October 16, 1797
Goodnight, Peter	Lieutenant, 10th Regiment	February 5, 1798
Graves, Benjamin	Captain, Rifle Company, 8th Regiment	November 22, 1798
Graves, John C.	Captain, 8th Regiment	July 9, 1798
Hamilton, John	Lieutenant, 10th Regiment	October 27, 1798
Hanback, William	Ensign, 8th Regiment	July 9, 1798
Hardin, John	Lieutenant, 8th Regiment	January 8, 1798
Irwin, Robert	Captain, 8th Regiment	October 16, 1797
Jones, John	Lieutenant, 8th Regiment	October 16, 1797
Kindred, Bartholomew	Lieutenant, 9th Regiment	January 1, 1798
McMurtry, Joseph	Major, 10th Regiment	October 3, 1797
Masterson, Moses	Lieutenant, 10th Regiment	July 20, 1798
Mays, Robert	Lieutenant, 8th Regiment	October 16, 1797
Meredith, Samuel	Quartermaster, 10th Regiment	November 27, 1798
Moore, William	Captain, 10th Regiment	February 5, 1798
Muldrow, Hugh	Captain, 10th Regiment	April 3, 1798
Oliver, Joseph	Lieutenant of Artillery, 9th Regiment	November 25, 1797
Patterson, Ezekiel	Captain, 10th Regiment	February 5, 1798
Patterson, Robert	Ensign, 10th Regiment	October 27, 1798
Patterson, Samuel	Ensign, 10th Regiment	October 20, 1798
Payne, Edward	Paymaster, 10th Regiment	November 27, 1798
Pollard, Braxton	Ensign, 10th Regiment	February 5, 1798
Pollard, Braxton	Captain, 10th Regiment	October 20, 1798
Porter, Ephraim	Captain, 9th Regiment	December 3, 1798
Porter, William	Lieutenant, 10th Regiment	April 3, 1798
Porter, William	Captain, 8th Regiment	October 1, 1798
Porter, William, Jr.	Lieutenant, 8th Regiment	May 11, 1798
Randolph, Moses	Ensign, 10th Regiment	February 5, 1798
Rayburn, Joseph	Lieutenant, 10th Regiment	February 5, 1798

Reaves, James............	Captain, 8th Regiment............	January 8, 1798
Richardson, Joseph.......	Ensign, 8th Regiment.............	January 8, 1798
Ridgley, Frederick.......	Surgeon, 8th Regiment............	October 25, 1797
Ring, William............	Ensign, Artillery, 9th Regiment..	November 25, 1797
Rodgers, George..........	Ensign, 10th Regiment............	February 5, 1798
Rodgers, George..........	Lieutenant, Rifle Company, 8th Regiment...................	November 22, 1798
Russel, Robert...........	Captain, 10th Regiment...........	April 10, 1798
Scott, Samuel............	Ensign, 9th Regiment.............	October 20, 1798
Shock, John..............	Lieutenant, 10th Regiment........	October 20, 1798
Sidner, Peter............	Ensign, 10th Regiment............	November 8, 1798
Smith, Martin............	Ensign, Rifle Company, 8th Regiment......................	November 22, 1798
Smyth, Samuel............	Lieutenant, 9th Regiment.........	September 21, 1797
Spangler, John...........	Captain, 9th Regiment............	September 21, 1797
Stephens, Seth...........	Ensign, 10th Regiment............	July 20, 1798
Stephenson, William......	Ensign, 10th Regiment............	April 10, 1798
Stone, James.............	Ensign, 10th Regiment............	April 3, 1798
Swinney, John............	Lieutenant, 9th Regiment.........	December 20, 1798
Thompson, Hugh...........	Captain, 10th Regiment...........	April 3, 1798
Tyler, Charles...........	Ensign, 10th Regiment............	April 3, 1798
Tyler, Charles...........	Captain, 10th Regiment...........	April 3, 1798
Warfield, Walter.........	Surgeon's Mate, 8th Regiment.....	October 25, 1797
Weagly, Abraham..........	Lieutenant, 10th Regiment........	April 3, 1798
Webb, Charles............	Captain, 8th Regiment............	January 2, 1798
West, William............	Captain of Artillery, 9th Regiment	November 25, 1797
White, Jeremiah..........	Ensign, 8th Regiment.............	January 2, 1798
Wilson, Charles..........	Ensign, 8th Regiment.............	October 16, 1797
Winn, Thomas.............	Captain, 8th Regiment............	October 16, 1797
Wood, James..............	Captain, 10th Regiment...........	July 20, 1798

Fleming County Regiment

[Laid off January 22, 1798]

Cassady, Michael.........	Captain, 30th Regiment...........	November 13, 1798
Evans, Gabriel...........	Adjutant, 30th Regiment..........	November 13, 1798
Fitch, Elisha............	Captain, 30th Regiment...........	August 7, 1798
Howson, John.............	Paymaster, 30th Regiment.........	November 13, 1798
Jones, Thomas............	Major, 30th Regiment.............	January 24, 1798
Keith, John..............	Cornet, Cavalry, 30th Regiment...	October 1, 1798
Kennon, William..........	1st Lieutenant, 30th Regiment....	October 1, 1798
Kennon, William..........	Quartermaster, 30th Regiment.....	November 13, 1798
McCulloch, Alexander.....	2nd Lieutenant of Cavalry, 30th Regiment..................	October 1, 1798
McIntire, Joseph.........	Captain of Cavalry, 30th Regiment	October 1, 1798
Marshon, Daniel..........	Lieutenant, 30th Regiment........	November 13, 1798
Payne, Duval.............	Colonel, 30th Regiment...........	January 24, 1798
Plummer, Abraham.........	Lieutenant, 30th Regiment........	August 7, 1798
Plummer, William.........	Ensign, 30th Regiment............	August 7, 1798

COMMISSIONED OFFICERS, 1797 - 1798

Scott, Moses.............	Ensign, 30th Regiment............	November 13, 1798
		(i.e., November 11, 1796)
Shackleford, John........	Major, 30th Regiment.............	January 24, 1798
Steel, Jacob.............	1st Lieutenant of Cavalry, 30th Regiment..................	October 1, 1798
Thompson, Andrew.........	Ensign, 30th Regiment............	November 13, 1798

Franklin County Regiment

[Laid off January 16, 1797]

Arnold, John.............	Captain, 22nd Regiment...........	April 1, 1797
Arnold, Stephen..........	Captain, 22nd Regiment...........	April 2, 1797
Banks, James.............	Ensign, 22nd Regiment............	July 18, 1798
Barns, William...........	Ensign, 22nd Regiment............	March 13, 1797
Beatty, Otho.............	Captain, Infantry Company, 22nd Regiment.................	June 14, 1797
Bennett, John............	Lieutenant, 22nd Regiment........	April 2, 1797
Bledsoe, Jacob...........	Ensign, 22nd Regiment............	September 19, 1797
Brown, Jesse.............	Lieutenant, 22nd Regiment........	August 2, 1797
Caldwell, Phillips.......	Captain, 22nd Regiment...........	April 13, 1798
Craig, Elijah............	2nd Lieutenant of Artillery, 22nd Regiment.................	March 22, 1798
Crockett, Anthony........	Major, 1st Battalion, 22nd Regiment.......................	February 9, 1797
Crockett, William........	Ensign, 22nd Regiment............	April 2, 1797
Crutchfield, John........	Ensign, Frankfort Company, 22nd Regiment.................	March 13, 1797
Fenwick, William.........	Captain, 22nd Regiment...........	April 20, 1798
Gano, Daniel.............	Captain of Artillery, 22nd Regiment.......................	March 22, 1798
Gano, Isaac E.	Surgeon, 22nd Regiment...........	April 1, 1797
Gist, Thomas.............	Major, 2nd Battalion, 22nd Regiment.......................	February 9, 1797
Graham, William..........	Captain, 22nd Regiment...........	July 18, 1798
Grant, Loudovic (?)......	Lieutenant, 22nd Regiment........	September 19, 1797
Grimes, John.............	Captain, 22nd Regiment...........	July 12, 1798
Hatton, Robert...........	Captain, 22nd Regiment...........	March 13, 1797
Hutton, Joseph...........	Lieutenant, 22nd Regiment........	April 1, 1797
Kennedy, Benjamin........	Captain, 22nd Regiment...........	August 15, 1797
Kerr, Peter..............	Ensign, 22nd Regiment............	April 1, 1797
Lafon, Nicholas..........	Quartermaster, 22nd Regiment.....	April 1, 1797
Lee, Willis..............	Lieutenant, Infantry Company, 22nd Regiment.................	June 14, 1797
Lillard, Thomas..........	Captain, 22nd Regiment...........	April 1, 1797
Mears, Samuel............	Ensign, 22nd Regiment............	April 1, 1797
Newberry, Henry..........	Surgeon's Mate, 22nd Regiment....	March 1, 1798
Pemberton, Bennett.......	Lieutenant Colonel, Commandant 22nd Regiment.................	January 16, 1797

COMMISSIONED OFFICERS, 1797 - 1798

Renwick, John............	Lieutenant, Frankfort Company, 22nd Regiment..................	March 13, 1797
Richardson, John.........	Ensign, Infantry Company, 22nd Regiment......................	June 14, 1797
Robins, Thomas...........	1st Lieutenant of Artillery, 22nd Regiment..................	March 22, 1798
Ross, Zachariah..........	Lieutenant, 22nd Regiment........	March 13, 1797
Sargeant, William........	Ensign, 22nd Regiment............	August 15, 1797
Scott, John M.	Captain, Frankfort Company, 22nd Regiment......................	March 13, 1797
Scott, John M.	Captain, 22nd Regiment...........	August 5, 1797
Scott, John M.	Major, 2nd Battalion, 22nd Regiment......................	March 22, 1798
Searcy, Berry............	Lieutenant, 22nd Regiment........	April 1, 1797
Sheats, Henry............	Lieutenant, 22nd Regiment........	April 20, 1798
Slaughter, George........	Ensign, 22nd Regiment............	April 1, 1797
Smith, James.............	Lieutenant, 22nd Regiment........	August 15, 1797
Voorheis, Peter G.	Adjutant, 22nd Regiment..........	April 1, 1797
Weisiger, Daniel.........	Paymaster, 22nd Regiment.........	April 1, 1797

Garrard County Regiment

[Laid off February 23, 1797]

Alcorn, John.............	Captain, 1st Battalion, 26th Regiment......................	September 20, 1797
Blakey, Pleasant.........	Cornet, Troop of Horse, 26th Regiment......................	December 10, 1798
Blanton, John............	Ensign, 1st Battalion, 26th Regiment......................	September 20, 1797
Blanton, John............	Lieutenant, 26th Regiment........	April 3, 1798
Brown, Beverly...........	Captain, 2nd Battalion, 26th Regiment......................	September 20, 1797
Bryant, John.............	Paymaster, 26th Regiment.........	September 20, 1797
Bryant, William..........	Captain, 2nd Battalion, 26th Regiment......................	September 20, 1797
Bufford, Thomas..........	Lieutenant, Troop of Horse, 26th Regiment..................	December 10, 1798
Burditt, Enoch...........	Ensign, 2nd Battalion, 26th Regiment......................	September 20, 1797
Burditt, Joseph L.	Captain, 2nd Battalion, 26th Regiment......................	September 20, 1797
Campbell, William........	Major, 26th Regiment.............	March 1, 1797
Clark, Thomas............	Lieutenant, 1st Battalion, 26th Regiment..................	September 20, 1797
Cunningham, Right........	Ensign, 1st Battalion, 26th Regiment......................	September 20, 1797
Davis, James.............	Lieutenant, 26th Regiment........	April 3, 1798
Dismukes, Joseph.........	Lieutenant, 2nd Battalion, 26th Regiment..................	September 20, 1797

COMMISSIONED OFFICERS, 1797 - 1798

East, James.............	Ensign, 2nd Battalion, 26th Regiment......................	September 20, 1797
Finnel, James...........	Captain, 1st Battalion, 26th Regiment......................	September 20, 1797
Folkner, John...........	Lieutenant, 1st Battalion, 26th Regiment.................	September 20, 1797
Graham, Luke............	Lieutenant, 2nd Battalion, 26th Regiment.................	September 20, 1797
Grider, Henry...........	Captain, 2nd Battalion, 26th Regiment......................	September 20, 1797
Grider, Tobias..........	Lieutenant, 2nd Battalion, 26th Regiment.................	September 20, 1797
Harrison, John..........	Major, 26th Regiment...........	March 1, 1797
Hiat, Benjamin..........	Ensign, 1st Battalion, 26th Regiment......................	September 20, 1797
Houghman, True..........	Ensign, 2nd Battalion, 26th Regiment......................	September 20, 1797
Hutcheson, Laurence.....	Lieutenant, 1st Battalion, 26th Regiment.................	September 20, 1797
Hutcheson, Laurence.....	Captain, 26th Regiment..........	April 3, 1798
Jennings, Augustine.....	Ensign, 26th Regiment...........	April 3, 1798
Jennings, William.......	Lieutenant, 1st Battalion, 26th Regiment.................	September 20, 1797
Jennings, William.......	Captain, 26th Regiment..........	April 3, 1798
Kennady, David..........	Captain, 1st Battalion, 26th Regiment......................	September 20, 1797
Kerns, Alexander........	Quartermaster, 26th Regiment.....	September 20, 1797
Letcher, Benjamin.......	Captain, Troop of Horse, 26th Regiment.................	December 10, 1798
Lewis, John.............	Lieutenant, 2nd Battalion, 26th Regiment.................	September 20, 1797
Littlepage, Epps........	Ensign, 26th Regiment...........	April 3, 1798
McMullen, James.........	Ensign, 1st Battalion, 26th Regiment......................	September 20, 1797
Nicholson, William......	Lieutenant, 1st Battalion, 26th Regiment.................	September 20, 1797
Pope, Alexander.........	Captain, 1st Battalion, 26th Regiment......................	September 20, 1797
Renshaw, Samuel.........	Adjutant, 26th Regiment.........	September 20, 1797
Shackleford, Edward.....	Captain, 1st Battalion, 26th Regiment......................	September 20, 1797
Smith, James............	Ensign, 2nd Battalion, 26th Regiment......................	September 20, 1797
Smith, William..........	Captain, 2nd Battalion, 26th Regiment......................	September 20, 1797
Taylor, John............	Ensign, 2nd Battalion, 26th Regiment......................	September 20, 1797
Terril, Edmond..........	Lieutenant Colonel, Commandant 26th Regiment.................	March 1, 1797
West, Joseph............	Lieutenant, 2nd Battalion, 26th Regiment.................	September 20, 1797

Green County Regiment

Barbee, Elias............	Colonel, 16th Regiment..........	February 23, 1797
Barnett, William.........	Major, 16th Regiment.............	January 8, 1798
Burks, Nicholas..........	Captain, 16th Regiment..........	September 20, 1798
Chisum, George...........	Lieutenant, 16th Regiment.......	April 30, 1798
Dixon, Henry.............	Lieutenant, 16th Regiment.......	September 20, 1798
Hamilton, Ferdinand......	Captain, 16th Regiment..........	April 30, 1798
King, John E.	Adjutant, 16th Regiment.........	September 20, 1798
McCandles, John..........	Ensign, 16th Regiment............	September 20, 1798
Miliken, James...........	Ensign, 16th Regiment............	April 30, 1798
Mitchel, Adam............	Captain, 16th Regiment..........	April 30, 1798
Rhea, Robert.............	Ensign, 16th Regiment............	April 30, 1798
Skaggs, David............	Lieutenant, 16th Regiment.......	April 30, 1798
Skaggs, Solomon..........	Ensign, 16th Regiment............	April 30, 1798
Smith, William...........	Lieutenant, 16th Regiment.......	April 30, 1798
Spears, George...........	Lieutenant, 16th Regiment.......	April 30, 1798
Thomas, Elisha...........	Captain, 16th Regiment..........	April 30, 1798
Weas, Philip.............	Ensign, 16th Regiment............	April 30, 1798

Hardin County Regiment

[First commissions February 14, 1797]

Ashcraft, Daniel.........	Ensign, 3rd Regiment.............	November 13, 1798
Bennett, John............	Ensign, 3rd Regiment.............	November 13, 1798
Boyworth (Bozorth), Jonathan...	Captain, 3rd Regiment.......	November 13, 1798
Cisna, William...........	Lieutenant, 3rd Regiment........	October 10, 1797
Cleaver, Stephen.........	Major, 2nd Battalion, 3rd Regiment......................	October 10, 1797
Critchlow, James.........	Lieutenant, 3rd Regiment........	October 10, 1797
Crow, Joshua.............	Captain, 3rd Regiment...........	November 13, 1798
Cummins, John............	Ensign, 3rd Regiment.............	October 10, 1797
Field, Henry.............	Ensign, 3rd Regiment.............	November 13, 1798
Funkhouser, Christley....	Captain, 3rd Regiment...........	February 14, 1797
Glen, John...............	Lieutenant, 3rd Regiment........	October 10, 1797
Harges, Isaac............	Captain, 3rd Regiment...........	October 10, 1797
Linder, Isaac............	Ensign, 3rd Regiment.............	October 10, 1797
Logsdon, Thomas..........	Captain, 3rd Regiment...........	October 10, 1797
Miller, Nicholas.........	Captain, 3rd Regiment...........	October 10, 1797
Miller, William..........	Lieutenant, 3rd Regiment........	October 10, 1797
Money, Joseph............	Ensign, 3rd Regiment.............	October 10, 1797
Odum, Willis.............	Captain, 3rd Regiment...........	November 13, 1798
Smith, Daniel............	Lieutenant, 3rd Regiment........	November 13, 1798
Walker, John.............	Captain, 3rd Regiment...........	October 10, 1797
Westfall, Cornelius......	Lieutenant, 3rd Regiment........	November 13, 1798

COMMISSIONED OFFICERS, 1797 - 1798

Harrison County Regiment

Barret, Peter............	Ensign, 20th Regiment............	April 17, 1797
Boswell, William E.	Captain, 20th Regiment...........	April 17, 1797
Boswell, William E.	Paymaster, 20th Regiment.........	February 12, 1798
Boswell, William E.	Major, 1st Battalion, 20th Regiment......................	December 20, 1798
Campbell, William........	Lieutenant, 20th Regiment........	April 17, 1797
Caulk, Richard...........	Captain, 20th Regiment...........	April 17, 1797
Deam, John...............	Captain, 20th Regiment...........	April 17, 1797
Fuice (Foose), Joseph....	Lieutenant, 20th Regiment........	April 17, 1797
Goodridge, Elisha........	Lieutenant, 20th Regiment........	January 24, 1798
Goodwin, B.	Ensign, 20th Regiment............	April 17, 1797
Gouch, Thomas............	Ensign, 20th Regiment............	April 17, 1797
Harris, Hosea............	Ensign, 20th Regiment............	January 24, 1798
Harrison, William........	Lieutenant, 20th Regiment........	November 13, 1798
Hinkston, William........	Lieutenant Colonel, Commandant 20th Regiment..................	December 20, 1798
Hutcheson, Archibald.....	Captain, 20th Regiment...........	April 17, 1797
Hutcheson, John..........	Ensign, 20th Regiment............	April 17, 1797
McCandles, William.......	Captain, 20th Regiment...........	January 24, 1798
McClure (no first name)..	Lieutenant, 20th Regiment........	April 17, 1797
Massey, John.............	Lieutenant, 20th Regiment........	April 17, 1797
Miller, James............	Captain, 20th Regiment...........	April 17, 1797
Mounts, Thomas...........	Captain, 20th Regiment...........	April 17, 1797
Neisbit, Robert..........	Ensign, 20th Regiment............	April 17, 1797
Porter, Andrew...........	Lieutenant, 20th Regiment........	April 17, 1797
Porter, Andrew...........	Captain, 20th Regiment...........	January 24, 1798
Rankin, David............	Captain, 20th Regiment...........	April 17, 1797
Rardon, Moses............	Captain, 20th Regiment...........	April 17, 1797
Sloane, Thomas...........	Ensign, 20th Regiment............	April 17, 1797
Stewart, Jesse...........	Ensign, 20th Regiment............	July 12, 1797
Thompson, Abraham........	Lieutenant, 20th Regiment........	April 17, 1797
Thompson, Abraham........	Adjutant, 20th Regiment..........	July 12, 1797
Tittle, John.............	Major, 20th Regiment.............	July 12, 1797
Van Hook, Samuel.........	Lieutenant, 20th Regiment........	April 17, 1797
Veach, Thomas............	Lieutenant, 20th Regiment........	April 17, 1797
Ward, Andrew.............	Lieutenant, 20th Regiment........	January 24, 1798

Jefferson County Regiment

Adkins, Josiah...........	Ensign, 1st Regiment.............	July 12, 1798
Applegate, Benjamin......	Lieutenant, 1st Regiment.........	September 22, 1798
Armstrong, Archibald.....	Cornet, Cavalry Company, 1st Regiment......................	September 22, 1798
Batman, Henry............	Ensign, 1st Regiment.............	July 12, 1798
Bringman, Martin.........	Lieutenant, Rifle Company, 1st Regiment......................	November 27, 1798
Brown, John..............	Lieutenant, 1st Regiment.........	July 12, 1798
Buckner, Nicholas........	Lieutenant, 1st Regiment.........	September 1, 1798

COMMISSIONED OFFICERS, 1797 - 1798

Chambers, William........	Captain, 1st Regiment............	November 27, 1798
Chenoweth, James.........	Ensign, 1st Regiment.............	September 22, 1798
Christy, William........	Captain of Cavalry, 1st Regiment.	September 22, 1798
Edwards, William........	Ensign, 1st Regiment.............	September 22, 1798
Floyd, Davis............	2nd Lieutenant of Cavalry, 1st Regiment...................	September 22, 1798
Fowler, Joshua..........	Lieutenant, 1st Regiment.........	July 12, 1798
Gaphney, John...........	1st Lieutenant of Cavalry, 1st Regiment...................	September 22, 1798
Johnston, Gabriel J. ...	Captain, 1st Regiment............	July 12, 1798
Kinnason, John..........	Lieutenant, 1st Regiment.........	July 12, 1798
Linn, Asahel............	Ensign, 1st Regiment.............	July 12, 1798
Nash, Harman............	Captain, 1st Regiment............	September 22, 1798
Nelson, John............	Lieutenant, 1st Regiment.........	July 12, 1798
Nelson, John............	Adjutant, 1st Regiment...........	September 22, 1798
Phillips, Richard.......	Captain, 1st Regiment............	July 12, 1798
Prince, Thomas..........	Lieutenant, 1st Regiment.........	July 12, 1798
Pumroy, Thomas..........	Ensign, Rifle Company, 1st Regiment.......................	November 27, 1798
Slegar, David...........	Lieutenant, 1st Regiment.........	July 12, 1798
Smith, William..........	Lieutenant, 1st Regiment.........	September 22, 1798
Wise, David.............	Captain, 1st Regiment............	July 12, 1798
Young, William..........	Captain, 1st Regiment............	September 22, 1798

Lincoln County Regiment

Artkus, Jacob...........	Lieutenant, 6th Regiment.........	September 23, 1797
Berry, Joseph...........	Lieutenant, 6th Regiment.........	September 19, 1797
Blair, John.............	Captain, 6th Regiment............	September 19, 1797
Carter, Charles.........	Captain, 6th Regiment............	November 24, 1797
Carter, Jesse...........	Lieutenant, 6th Regiment.........	November 24, 1797
Collier, Moses..........	Ensign, 6th Regiment.............	October 2, 1797
Cook, Anthony...........	Ensign, 6th Regiment.............	December 1, 1797
Davidson, Samuel........	Captain, 6th Regiment............	September 19, 1797
Garven, Isaac...........	Captain, 6th Regiment............	September 19, 1797
Glover, Abner...........	Lieutenant, 6th Regiment.........	September 19, 1797
Griffith, John..........	Lieutenant, 6th Regiment.........	October 2, 1797
Grifhum, Uriah..........	Lieutenant, 6th Regiment.........	December 1, 1797
Hite, Thomas............	Ensign, 6th Regiment.............	October 4, 1798
Horine, Jacob...........	Captain, 6th Regiment............	September 23, 1797
Hutchin, John...........	Lieutenant, 6th Regiment.........	September 19, 1797
Jasper, John............	Ensign, 6th Regiment.............	October 4, 1798
Jenney, Nathaniel.......	Lieutenant, 6th Regiment.........	March 17, 1798
Kiney, Michael..........	Captain, 6th Regiment............	March 17, 1798
Lewis, Joseph Frasis....	Captain, 6th Regiment............	January 1, 1797
Logan, Hugh.............	Ensign, 6th Regiment.............	April 24, 1798
McFeran, James..........	Lieutenant, 6th Regiment.........	October 4, 1798
McKinzy, Colin (?)......	Lieutenant, 6th Regiment.........	September 19, 1797
McLane, Thomas..........	Ensign, 6th Regiment.............	December 27, 1797
McLaughlin, Thomas......	Captain, 6th Regiment............	December 1, 1797

COMMISSIONED OFFICERS, 1797 - 1798

Moore, Jonathan..........	Ensign, 6th Regiment.............	September 19, 1797
Morris, Adam.............	Ensign, 6th Regiment.............	September 19, 1797
Owsley, Thomas...........	Lieutenant, 6th Regiment.........	December 27, 1797
Paxton, John.............	Captain, 6th Regiment............	April 24, 1798
Payne, Reuben............	Captain, 6th Regiment............	September 19, 1797
Portman, John............	Captain, 6th Regiment............	October 4, 1798
Ralls, Hardy.............	Captain, 6th Regiment............	December 27, 1797
Richardson, Jesse........	Major, 6th Regiment..............	September 19, 1797
Russel, Andrew...........	Ensign, 6th Regiment.............	September 19, 1797
Shackleford, William.....	Lieutenant, 6th Regiment.........	September 23, 1797
Stephenson, David........	Lieutenant, 6th Regiment.........	April 24, 1798
Waid, Pearce.............	Captain, 6th Regiment............	October 4, 1798
Warren, Thomas...........	Captain, 6th Regiment............	October 2, 1797
Wood, John...............	Lieutenant, 6th Regiment.........	October 4, 1798
Wright, John.............	Ensign, 6th Regiment.............	September 23, 1797

Logan County Regiment

[Laid off February 23, 1797]

Allen, Beverly Anthony...	Surgeon, 23rd Regiment...........	November 1, 1798
Ashmore, Samuel..........	Ensign, 23rd Regiment............	August 12, 1797
Baily, James.............	Lieutenant, 23rd Regiment........	August 11, 1797
Bell, Robert.............	Captain, 23rd Regiment...........	August 12, 1797
Briant, Absalom..........	Captain, 23rd Regiment...........	August 14, 1797
Caldwell, Samuel.........	Major, 23rd Regiment.............	February 23, 1797
Cambell, William.........	Lieutenant, 23rd Regiment........	August 14, 1797
Dickey, John.............	Captain, 23rd Regiment...........	November 29, 1797
Edger, William...........	Ensign, 23rd Regiment............	August 13, 1797
Elms, David..............	Ensign, 23rd Regiment............	November 25, 1797
Elms, Thomas.............	Lieutenant, 23rd Regiment........	November 25, 1797
Ewing, Chatham...........	Captain, 23rd Regiment...........	August 10, 1797
Ewing, Elijah............	Lieutenant, 23rd Regiment........	November 26, 1797
Ewing, Finis.............	Captain, Rifle Company, 23rd Regiment.....................	July 29, 1797
Ewing, Robert............	Lieutenant Colonel, Commandant 23rd Regiment.................	February 23, 1797
Ewing, Urbin.............	Adjutant, 23rd Regiment..........	February 9, 1798
Funk, Christopher........	Captain, 23rd Regiment...........	November 25, 1797
Gilbert, John............	Cornet, Troop of Horse, 23rd Regiment.....................	December 3, 1798
Gordon, Samuel...........	1st Lieutenant, Cavalry, 23rd Regiment.....................	June 22, 1797
Goreham, Thomas..........	Lieutenant, 23rd Regiment........	August 10, 1797
Graves, Anthony..........	Ensign, 23rd Regiment............	August 10, 1797
Grayson, Reuben..........	Captain, 23rd Regiment...........	August 13, 1797
Hans, Jacoby.............	Ensign, 23rd Regiment............	November 27, 1797
Hargrove, Willis.........	Lieutenant, 23rd Regiment........	November 27, 1797
Harrison, William........	Quartermaster, 23rd Regiment.....	November 1, 1798
Hayden, James............	Lieutenant, 23rd Regiment........	August 12, 1797

COMMISSIONED OFFICERS, 1797 - 1798

Jones, William	Adjutant, 23rd Regiment	November 1, 1798
Love, James	Captain, 23rd Regiment	November 27, 1797
McCutchen, Hugh	Ensign, Rifle Company, 23rd Regiment	July 29, 1797
McDaniel, James	Ensign, 23rd Regiment	August 14, 1797
McGoodwin, Daniel	Lieutenant, Rifle Company, 23rd Regiment	July 29, 1797
McLean, Charles	Captain, 23rd Regiment	November 26, 1797
McLean, Ephraim	Major, 2nd Battalion, 23rd Regiment	January 1, 1798
Maulding, Moreton	Major, 23rd Regiment	February 23, 1797
Maulding, Richard	Captain of Cavalry, 23rd Regiment	June 22, 1797
Newman, Isaac	Lieutenant, 23rd Regiment	November 30, 1797
Ray, James	Captain, 23rd Regiment	November 30, 1797
Rhodes, David	Ensign, 23rd Regiment	November 30, 1797
Robertson, James	Lieutenant, 23rd Regiment	November 29, 1797
Ross, Henry	Ensign, 23rd Regiment	November 29, 1797
Russell, Handly	Cornet, Cavalry, 23rd Regiment	June 22, 1797
Russell, Handly	2nd Lieutenant, Troop of Horse, 23rd Regiment	December 3, 1798
Stewart, Charles	Paymaster, 23rd Regiment	November 1, 1798
Swift, John	2nd Lieutenant of Cavalry, 23rd Regiment	June 22, 1797
Tate, Stephen	Ensign, 23rd Regiment	August 11, 1797
Taylor, Tekler	Ensign, 23rd Regiment	November 26, 1797
Webb, Jesse	Captain, 23rd Regiment	August 11, 1797
White, Alexander	Lieutenant, 23rd Regiment	August 13, 1797

Madison County Regiments

Anderson, William	Lieutenant, 7th Regiment	June 12, 1798
Baker, Joseph	Ensign, 7th Regiment	June 12, 1797
Bales, Alexander	Lieutenant, 19th Regiment	May 14, 1797
Barkley, Robert	Lieutenant, 7th Regiment	October 17, 1798
Benton, Richard	Lieutenant, 7th Regiment	November 1, 1798
Brock, Thomas	Captain, 19th Regiment	July 22, 1798
Brutin, Davis	Lieutenant, 7th Regiment	October 15, 1798
Burgen, Thomas	Lieutenant, 7th Regiment	July 29, 1798
Caldwell, Robert	Captain, 19th Regiment	July 15, 1798
Callaway, Richard	Major, 1st Battalion, 7th Regiment	April 13, 1798
Chinault, William	Lieutenant, 7th Regiment	June 5, 1798
Clay, Green	Lieutenant Colonel, Commandant 7th Regiment	February 1, 1798
Cox, James	Ensign, 7th Regiment	March 24, 1798
Crews, Jeremiah	Captain, 7th Regiment	October 17, 1798
Culwell, William	Lieutenant, 7th Regiment	June 12, 1797
Davis, John	Captain, 19th Regiment	May 14, 1797
Duncan, Robert	Ensign, 19th Regiment	May 14, 1797

COMMISSIONED OFFICERS, 1797 - 1798

Durbin, Edward..........	Captain, 7th Regiment............	February 10, 1797
Durbin, Joseph..........	Lieutenant, 7th Regiment........	February 10, 1797
Goggins, John...........	Major, 19th Regiment............	February 2, 1798
Goodman, Philip.........	Lieutenant, 7th Regiment........	July 9, 1798
Hackett, Peter..........	Lieutenant, 7th Regiment........	April 13, 1798
Hendrickson, John.......	Ensign, 7th Regiment............	October 17, 1798
Houston, David..........	Ensign, 19th Regiment...........	August 7, 1798
Houston, John...........	Captain, 19th Regiment..........	August 7, 1798
Hubbard, Dirrett........	Ensign, 7th Regiment............	June 12, 1798
Jameson, Joseph.........	Ensign, 7th Regiment............	February 10, 1797
Jameson, Joseph.........	Lieutenant, 7th Regiment........	June 12, 1797
Jameson, Robert.........	Captain, 7th Regiment...........	February 10, 1797
Johnson, Matthew........	Ensign, 7th Regiment............	February 10, 1797
Jones, Humphrey.........	Lieutenant, 7th Regiment........	July 9, 1798
Jones, Humphrey.........	Captain, 7th Regiment...........	October 15, 1798
Kavanaugh, William......	Captain, 7th Regiment...........	June 25, 1798
Kavenaugh, William......	Lieutenant, 7th Regiment........	June 12, 1797
Kennedy, Andrew.........	Major, 19th Regiment............	February 12, 1798
Kerley, William.........	Adjutant, 7th Regiment..........	April 13, 1798
Lynch, David............	Lieutenant, 7th Regiment........	February 10, 1797
McCormic, James.........	Quartermaster, 19th Regiment....	August 15, 1798
McQueen, John...........	Captain, 7th Regiment...........	February 10, 1797
Maupin, Daniel..........	Captain, 7th Regiment...........	June 12, 1798
Miller, Robert..........	Lieutenant, 7th Regiment........	June 25, 1798
Moreen, John............	Adjutant, 19th Regiment.........	August 7, 1798
Morrison, William.......	Lieutenant Colonel, Commandant 19th Regiment.................	February 2, 1798
Morrison, William Mitchell...	Major, 19th Regiment..........	August 7, 1798
Mullins, Gabriel........	Captain, 7th Regiment...........	June 12, 1797
Noland, William.........	Lieutenant, 7th Regiment........	February 10, 1797
Proctor, John...........	Lieutenant, 7th Regiment........	February 10, 1797
Proctor, Paige..........	Captain, 7th Regiment...........	June 12, 1797
Quick, Alexander........	Ensign, 7th Regiment............	November 1, 1798
Richerson, Daniel.......	Lieutenant, 7th Regiment........	March 24, 1798
Roberts, Elisha.........	Ensign, 7th Regiment............	June 12, 1797
Sebastian, William......	Ensign, 7th Regiment............	June 12, 1797
Selfe, John.............	Ensign, 19th Regiment...........	July 22, 1798
Smith, Thomas...........	Lieutenant, 19th Regiment.......	July 22, 1798
Teder, Valentine........	Lieutenant, 7th Regiment........	February 10, 1797
Thorpe, Zach.	Ensign, 7th Regiment............	July 9, 1798
Towns, Oswald...........	Captain, 7th Regiment...........	February 10, 1797
Townsend, Thomas........	Captain, 7th Regiment...........	July 9, 1798
Turner, Thomas..........	Captain, 7th Regiment...........	June 12, 1797
Turpin, Champion........	Ensign, 7th Regiment............	February 10, 1797
White, John.............	Ensign, 7th Regiment............	February 10, 1797
Williams, John..........	Captain, 7th Regiment...........	March 24, 1798
Wills, Alexander........	Ensign, 7th Regiment............	April 13, 1798

COMMISSIONED OFFICERS, 1797 - 1798   43

Mason County Regiments

[29th Regiment laid off January 22, 1798]

Aldridge, John............	Lieutenant, 15th Regiment........	January 21, 1797
Anderson, Matthew........	Ensign, 15th Regiment............	January 21, 1797
Applegate, Richard.......	Captain, 15th Regiment...........	January 21, 1797
Ashcraft, Jacob..........	Lieutenant, 15th Regiment........	August 25, 1797
Baker, Joshua............	Lieutenant Colonel, Commandant 15th Regiment.................	January 31, 1798
Baldwin, Samuel..........	Captain, Infantry Company, 15th Regiment......................	August 28, 1798
Bell, David..............	Cornet, Cavalry, 15th Regiment...	November 13, 1798
Bertly (Bartley), James..	Lieutenant, 15th Regiment........	October 23, 1797
Blanchard, John..........	Captain, 15th Regiment...........	January 21, 1797
Botts, Richard...........	Lieutenant, 15th Regiment........	December 4, 1797
Bright, Edward...........	Ensign, 15th Regiment............	April 25, 1797
Brown, John..............	Captain, 15th Regiment...........	October 16, 1797
Brown, Joseph............	Ensign, 15th Regiment............	January 21, 1797
Buchannan, Alexander.....	Lieutenant, 15th Regiment........	January 21, 1797
Bullock, Lewis...........	Major, 2nd Battalion, 15th Regiment......................	January 30, 1798
Butts, Aron..............	Ensign, 15th Regiment............	January 21, 1797
Chiles, David............	Captain, 15th Regiment...........	January 21, 1797
Colglaizer, Christopher..	Lieutenant, 15th Regiment........	December 4, 1797
Colvill, William.........	Lieutenant, 15th Regiment........	May 22, 1797
Cornwell, John...........	Lieutenant, 15th Regiment........	April 16, 1797
Corwine, Amos............	Ensign, 15th Regiment............	April 5, 1797
Craig, John..............	Ensign, 15th Regiment............	January 21, 1797
Cristy, James............	Captain, 15th Regiment...........	May 22, 1797
Davis, David.............	Ensign, 15th Regiment............	April 16, 1797
Davison, Josiah..........	Captain, 15th Regiment...........	January 21, 1797
Desha, Joseph............	Major, 29th Regiment.............	January 23, 1798
Downing, Joseph..........	Lieutenant, 15th Regiment........	April 15, 1797
Downing, Timothy.........	Captain, 15th Regiment...........	April 15, 1797
Downing, Timothy.........	Major, 1st Battalion, 15th Regiment......................	November 8, 1798
Drummin, Samuel..........	Captain, 15th Regiment...........	January 21, 1797
Duke, Basil..............	1st Lieutenant of Cavalry, 15th Regiment.................	June 15, 1797
Fee, James...............	Ensign, 15th Regiment............	January 21, 1797
Fields, Thomas...........	Ensign, Infantry Company, 15th Regiment......................	August 28, 1798
Flora, Abijah............	Lieutenant, 29th Regiment........	June 12, 1798
Fulton, Hugh.............	Major, 29th Regiment.............	January 23, 1798
Gallager, Edward.........	Captain, 15th Regiment...........	December 4, 1797
Gilkerson, James.........	Ensign, 15th Regiment............	May 22, 1797
Grayham, Henry R.	Lieutenant, Infantry Company, 15th Regiment.................	August 28, 1798
Harris, Edward...........	Cornet of Cavalry, 15th Regiment......................	June 15, 1797

COMMISSIONED OFFICERS, 1797 - 1798

Harris, Edward............	2nd Lieutenant of Cavalry, 15th Regiment......................	November 13, 1798
Harris, Edward, Jr.	Captain, 15th Regiment...........	January 21, 1797
Harris, George...........	Captain, 15th Regiment...........	August 28, 1798
Haskin, George...........	Lieutenant, 15th Regiment........	January 21, 1797
Helms, William...........	Captain, 15th Regiment...........	January 21, 1797
Horn, Elijah.............	Ensign, 15th Regiment............	August 28, 1798
Hunt, John...............	Captain, 15th Regiment...........	January 1, 1797
Johnston, David..........	Captain, 15th Regiment...........	January 21, 1797
Jones, Jacob.............	Captain, 15th Regiment...........	August 25, 1797
Lansdale, James..........	Lieutenant, 15th Regiment........	January 21, 1797
Leech, Benjamin..........	Ensign, 15th Regiment............	August 25, 1797
Looney, David............	Ensign, 15th Regiment............	October 23, 1797
Mannon, John.............	Captain, 15th Regiment...........	January 21, 1797
Meranda, George..........	Ensign, 15th Regiment............	January 21, 1797
Meranda, Isaac...........	Lieutenant, 15th Regiment........	January 21, 1797
Miller, Robert...........	Ensign, 15th Regiment............	August 28, 1798
Moss, James W.	Lieutenant, 15th Regiment........	January 21, 1797
Nichols, Thomas..........	Captain, 15th Regiment...........	December 4, 1797
Parker, Henry............	Captain, 15th Regiment...........	January 21, 1797
Parks, Arthur............	Ensign, 15th Regiment............	May 22, 1797
Patten, James............	Ensign, 15th Regiment............	December 4, 1797
Pickett, John............	Captain, 15th Regiment...........	November 13, 1798
Pratter, Enos............	Lieutenant, 15th Regiment........	April 25, 1797
Putnam, James............	Ensign, 15th Regiment............	December 4, 1797
Rankins, Benjamin........	Ensign, 15th Regiment............	January 21, 1797
Rayman, William..........	Captain, 29th Regiment...........	June 12, 1798
Reed, William............	Captain, 29th Regiment...........	May 6, 1798
Ritter, Richard..........	Captain, 15th Regiment...........	January 21, 1797
Robb, Robert.............	Captain, 15th Regiment...........	October 23, 1797
Roberts, John............	Lieutenant, 15th Regiment........	May 22, 1797
Small, James.............	Ensign, 29th Regiment............	June 12, 1798
Smith, Samuel............	Colonel, 29th Regiment...........	January 23, 1798
Soward, Richard..........	Lieutenant, 15th Regiment........	November 13, 1798
Stansel, Henry...........	Lieutenant, 15th Regiment........	November 13, 1798 (i. e., December 8, 1796)
Stewart, Robert..........	Lieutenant, 15th Regiment........	January 21, 1797
Stewart, William.........	Lieutenant, 15th Regiment........	August 28, 1798
Stith, Baldwin...........	2nd Lieutenant of Cavalry, 15th Regiment.................	June 15, 1797
Stith, Baldwin B.	1st Lieutenant of Cavalry, 15th Regiment.................	November 13, 1798
Stratton, Aron...........	Captain, 15th Regiment...........	April 16, 1797
Thomas, Jacob............	Captain, 15th Regiment...........	October 16, 1797
Thomas, Thruston.........	Lieutenant, 15th Regiment........	January 21, 1797
Thomas, Thruston.........	Captain, 15th Regiment...........	August 28, 1798
Voshell, Daniel..........	Lieutenant, 15th Regiment........	August 28, 1798
Walker, James............	Ensign, 15th Regiment............	November 13, 1798
Watson, John.............	Lieutenant, 15th Regiment........	January 21, 1797
Whips, James.............	Lieutenant, 15th Regiment........	September 12, 1797
Wood, Abner..............	Captain, 15th Regiment...........	April 25, 1797

COMMISSIONED OFFICERS, 1797 - 1798

Wood, Andrew............ Lieutenant, 15th Regiment........ October 16, 1797

Mason and Bracken Regiment

[Laid off January 22, 1798]

Aldridge, John...........	Lieutenant, 28th Regiment........	July 24, 1798 (re-commissioned)
Anderson, Matthew........	Lieutenant, 28th Regiment........	May 10, 1798
Anderson, Stokes.........	Ensign, 28th Regiment............	May 10, 1798
Beckly, Peter............	Ensign, 28th Regiment............	May 29, 1798
Blanchard, John..........	Quartermaster, 28th Regiment.....	February 12, 1798
Brashears, Thomas........	Captain, 28th Regiment...........	July 24, 1798
Chiles, David............	Major, 28th Regiment.............	January 22, 1798
Collins, Solom...........	Ensign, 28th Regiment............	May 6, 1798
Craig, Lewis.............	Ensign, Infantry Company, 28th Regiment..................	July 5, 1798
Craig, Whitfield.........	Paymaster, 28th Regiment.........	February 12, 1798
Doniphan, Anderson.......	Surgeon, 28th Regiment...........	February 12, 1798
Fee, James...............	Ensign, 28th Regiment............	July 24, 1798 (re-commissioned)
Fee, John................	Major, 28th Regiment.............	January 22, 1798
Gates, William...........	Lieutenant, 28th Regiment........	May 6, 1798
Harman, Samuel...........	Lieutenant, 28th Regiment........	May 29, 1798
Hook, John...............	Captain, 28th Regiment...........	April 20, 1798
Howard, Thomas...........	Captain, 28th Regiment...........	May 10, 1798
Irwin, James.............	Ensign, 28th Regiment............	July 12, 1798
Lancaster, Henry.........	Ensign, 28th Regiment............	May 10, 1798
Mannon, John.............	Captain, 28th Regiment...........	May 10, 1798
(Renewal of commission in the 15th Regiment, dated January 27, 1797)		
Moor, Benjamin...........	Lieutenant, Infantry Company, 28th Regiment.................	July 5, 1798
Morford, John............	Captain, 28th Regiment...........	May 29, 1798
Morris, Nathaniel G. ...	Adjutant, 28th Regiment..........	February 12, 1798
Pepper, Jesse............	Captain, 28th Regiment...........	May 6, 1798
Slack, Jacob.............	Captain, 28th Regiment...........	May 10, 1798
Thomas, John.............	Lieutenant, 28th Regiment........	May 10, 1798
Thomas, Philemon.........	Colonel, 28th Regiment...........	January 22, 1798
Thomas, Rowland..........	Captain, Infantry Company, 28th Regiment......................	July 5, 1798
Weatherington, John......	Captain, 28th Regiment...........	July 12, 1798
Whips, James.............	Lieutenant, 28th Regiment........	July 24, 1798 (re-commissioned)
Woodward, Joel...........	Lieutenant, 28th Regiment........	July 12, 1798

Mercer County Regiment

Allin, Thomas............	Major, 5th Regiment..............	March 30, 1797
Barlow, Aron.............	Ensign, 5th Regiment.............	January 19, 1798

COMMISSIONED OFFICERS, 1797 - 1798

Bilbo, Archibald..........	Lieutenant, 5th Regiment..........	July 16, 1798
Brown, Jeremiah...........	Lieutenant, 5th Regiment..........	June 21, 1798
Buchannan, Alexander.....	Captain, 5th Regiment............	June 21, 1798
Buchannan, James.........	Ensign, 5th Regiment.............	June 1, 1798
Bush, Philip.............	Captain, Troop of Light Horse, 5th Regiment....................	February 20, 1797
Curry, Robert............	Lieutenant, 5th Regiment..........	June 21, 1798
Daviess, Samuel..........	Lieutenant, 5th Regiment..........	January 19, 1798
Durham, Thomas...........	Lieutenant, 5th Regiment..........	January 19, 1798
Fisher, Joseph...........	Lieutenant, 5th Regiment..........	January 19, 1798
Gates, James.............	Ensign, 5th Regiment.............	January 19, 1798
Graham, Joseph...........	Lieutenant, 5th Regiment..........	June 20, 1798
Hale, Armstrong..........	Lieutenant, 5th Regiment..........	June 20, 1798
Haplittle, William.......	Cornet, Troop of Light Horse, 5th Regiment....................	February 20, 1797
Hungate, Charles.........	Ensign, 5th Regiment.............	June 20, 1798
Law, Laurence............	Lieutenant, 5th Regiment..........	June 21, 1798
Little, John.............	Captain, 5th Regiment............	July 16, 1798
McAffee, John............	Ensign, 5th Regiment.............	June 20, 1798
McAffee, John............	Lieutenant, 5th Regiment..........	June 1, 1798
McDaniel, William........	Captain, 5th Regiment............	June 20, 1798
McDowell, William........	Major, 5th Regiment..............	March 29, 1797
Mahan, John..............	Captain, 5th Regiment............	January 19, 1798
Palmer, Henry............	1st Lieutenant, Troop of Light Horse, 5th Regiment............	February 20, 1797
Rains, James.............	Captain, 5th Regiment............	January 19, 1798
Ray, James...............	Colonel, 5th Regiment............	March 29, 1797
Robertson, George........	Captain, 5th Regiment............	June 20, 1798
Rowland, Robert..........	Ensign, 5th Regiment.............	July 16, 1798
Strong, Walter E.	2nd Lieutenant, Troop of Light Horse, 5th Regiment............	February 20, 1797
Turner, Charles..........	Lieutenant, 5th Regiment..........	June 21, 1798
Vanarsdall, Lucas........	Captain, 5th Regiment............	June 1, 1798
Walker, Philip...........	Ensign, 5th Regiment.............	January 19, 1798
Watts, Peter.............	Captain, 5th Regiment............	January 19, 1798
Woods, Samuel............	Captain, 5th Regiment............	June 1, 1798

Montgomery County Regiment

[Laid off February 8, 1798]

Anderson, Abihu..........	Lieutenant, 31st Regiment........	May 8, 1798
Black, David.............	Captain, 31st Regiment..........	May 25, 1798
Burcham, Samuel..........	Captain, 31st Regiment..........	May 25, 1798
Cheatam, Lewis...........	Ensign, 31st Regiment............	May 25, 1798
Davis, Jeremiah..........	Cornet of Cavalry, 31st Regiment.	July 16, 1798
Downing, Samuel..........	Major, 2nd Battalion, 31st Regiment......................	February 8, 1798
Farrow, William..........	Captain, 31st Regiment..........	April 8, 1798
Fleming, William.........	Ensign, 31st Regiment............	May 25, 1798

COMMISSIONED OFFICERS, 1797 - 1798   47

Harrison, Micajah........	Captain of Cavalry, 31st Regiment......................	July 16, 1798
Hathaway, David..........	Lieutenant, 31st Regiment........	April 8, 1798
Herriford, John..........	Ensign, 31st Regiment............	May 27, 1798
Judy, John...............	Lieutenant, 31st Regiment........	July 9, 1798
Kirkly, Beverly..........	Ensign, 31st Regiment............	May 8, 1798
Langston, Jacob..........	Lieutenant, 31st Regiment........	May 29, 1798
Lasey, James.............	Lieutenant, 31st Regiment........	July 16, 1798
Litten, Caleb............	Lieutenant, 31st Regiment........	May 27, 1798
McClung, Matthew.........	Captain, 31st Regiment...........	May 25, 1798
Mockbee, John............	Captain, 31st Regiment...........	May 27, 1798
Montgomery, Isaac........	Ensign, 31st Regiment............	May 29, 1798
Moore, Thomas............	Lieutenant, 31st Regiment........	May 21, 1798
Nickel, John.............	Ensign, 31st Regiment............	July 16, 1798
Nickel, Thomas...........	Captain, 31st Regiment...........	July 16, 1798
Paton, Daniel............	Captain, 31st Regiment...........	May 8, 1798
Paul, Michael............	Ensign, 31st Regiment............	April 8, 1798
Poage, James.............	Lieutenant Colonel, Commandant 31st Regiment...................	February 8, 1798
Pritchett, John..........	Ensign, 31st Regiment............	May 21, 1798
Rodgers, William.........	Captain, 31st Regiment...........	October 2, 1798 (i.e., November 4, 1793)
Rogers, William..........	Captain, 31st Regiment...........	May 29, 1798 (i.e., November 4, 1793)
Simpson, Joseph..........	Lieutenant of Cavalry, 31st Regiment.......................	July 16, 1798
Smith, Enoch.............	Lieutenant, 31st Regiment........	May 25, 1798
Stafford, William........	Lieutenant, 31st Regiment........	May 25, 1798
Swearingham, Andrew......	Major, 1st Battalion, 31st Regiment.......................	February 8, 1798
Terrel, John.............	Ensign, 31st Regiment............	July 9, 1798
Wilcox, David............	Captain, 31st Regiment...........	July 9, 1798
Wilson, John.............	Ensign, 31st Regiment............	September 26, 1798
Wilson, Uriah............	Lieutenant, 31st Regiment........	September 26, 1798
Yarborrough, John........	Adjutant, 31st Regiment..........	December 22, 1798

Nelson County Regiments

[27th Regiment laid off April 1, 1797]

Ash, Peter...............	Ensign, 27th Regiment............	June 20, 1798
Baird, Alexander.........	Lieutenant, 27th Regiment........	March 1, 1798
Bell, Peter..............	Ensign, 2nd Regiment.............	November 30, 1797
Bland, Elijah............	Captain, 27th Regiment...........	March 1, 1798
Bland, John..............	Captain, 2nd Regiment............	February 20, 1797
Bowles, Wilfred..........	Ensign, 2nd Regiment.............	November 30, 1797
Bowman, William..........	Captain, 2nd Regiment............	November 30, 1797
Brashears, Thomas........	Captain, 2nd Regiment............	November 1, 1797
Brown, Nathaniel.........	Ensign, 27th Regiment............	June 20, 1798
Bullock, John............	Major, 2nd Battalion, 27th Regiment	April 1, 1797

COMMISSIONED OFFICERS, 1797 - 1798

Case, William............	Captain, 27th Regiment...........	March 1, 1798
Chalfunt, Abner..........	Ensign, 27th Regiment............	February 28, 1798
Chenowith, William.......	Captain, 2nd Regiment............	November 1, 1797
Cleaver, Jacob...........	Ensign, 2nd Regiment.............	November 30, 1797
Coombe, Asa..............	Ensign, 2nd Regiment.............	February 21, 1797
Coombe, Edward...........	Lieutenant, 2nd Regiment.........	February 21, 1797
Cotton, Zachariah........	Lieutenant, 27th Regiment........	March 1, 1798
Cox, James...............	Major, 1st Battalion, 27th Regiment......................	April 1, 1797
Crist, Jacob.............	Lieutenant, 27th Regiment........	June 20, 1798
Davee, James (?).........	Ensign, 2nd Regiment.............	February 20, 1797
Davis, James D.	Cornet, Troop of Horse, 27th Regiment......................	December 22, 1798
Decker, Luke.............	Ensign, 27th Regiment............	June 20, 1798
Dozier, John.............	Captain, Troop of Horse, 27th Regiment......................	December 22, 1798
Drake, John..............	Ensign, 27th Regiment............	March 1, 1798
Froman, John.............	Captain, 27th Regiment...........	March 1, 1798
Fulkerson, Jacob.........	Lieutenant, 27th Regiment........	February 28, 1798
Gohagan, Anthony.........	Adjutant, 27th Regiment..........	February 2, 1798
Grabel, David............	Ensign, 2nd Regiment.............	November 1, 1797
Grabel, Joseph...........	Captain, 27th Regiment...........	February 28, 1798
Greathouse, Herman.......	Captain, 27th Regiment...........	February 28, 1798
Guthrie, Adam............	Colonel, 27th Regiment...........	April 1, 1797
Hann, Christian..........	Captain, Light Infantry Company, 2nd Regiment...................	November 16, 1798
Harned, Edward...........	Lieutenant, 2nd Regiment.........	February 10, 1797
Howston, John............	Captain, 2nd Regiment............	November 30, 1797
Huston (no first name)...	Lieutenant, Troop of Horse, 27th Regiment..................	December 22, 1798
Huston, James............	Lieutenant, Light Infantry Company, 2nd Regiment..........	November 16, 1798
Irwin, James.............	Captain, 2nd Regiment............	February 10, 1797
Jourden, William.........	Captain, 2nd Regiment............	November 30, 1797
Leaman, Robert...........	Lieutenant, 2nd Regiment.........	November 30, 1797
Love, James..............	Captain, 27th Regiment...........	March 1, 1798
McArty (McCarthy?), Jonathan...	Captain, 27th Regiment......	February 28, 1798
McCambron, James.........	Lieutenant, 2nd Regiment.........	November 30, 1797
McClane, Duncan..........	Adjutant, 2nd Regiment...........	February 2, 1798
Marks, George............	Captain, 2nd Regiment............	February 20, 1797
May, Edmond..............	Ensign, 27th Regiment............	March 1, 1798
Miller, Samuel...........	Captain, 2nd Regiment............	November 30, 1797
Minor, Nicholas..........	Paymaster, 27th Regiment.........	February 2, 1798
Morehead, Charles........	Major, 2nd Regiment..............	April 1, 1797
Morton, Francis..........	Ensign, 2nd Regiment.............	May 31, 1798
Nalle, John..............	Ensign, 2nd Regiment.............	February 20, 1797
Nalle, John, Jr.	Lieutenant, 2nd Regiment.........	February 20, 1797
O'Neal, George...........	Ensign, 27th Regiment............	February 28, 1798
Polke, Charles...........	Captain, 2nd Regiment............	February 21, 1797
Shain, Francis...........	Lieutenant, 2nd Regiment.........	November 1, 1797
Shroud, William..........	Ensign, 2nd Regiment.............	February 10, 1797

COMMISSIONED OFFICERS, 1797 - 1798   49

Slaughter, James, Jr. ...	Quartermaster, 2nd Regiment......	February 2, 1798
Slaughter, Robert, Sr. ...	Paymaster, 2nd Regiment..........	February 2, 1798
Snellen, William.........	Lieutenant, 2nd Regiment.........	November 30, 1797
Spencer, Sharp...........	Ensign, 27th Regiment............	March 1, 1798
Stephens, Richard........	Quartermaster, 27th Regiment.....	February 2, 1798
Sweets, Thomas...........	Ensign, 2nd Regiment.............	April 3, 1798
Taylor, Isaac............	Lieutenant, 27th Regiment........	February 28, 1798
Waller, Mathias..........	Lieutenant, 2nd Regiment.........	November 1, 1797
Watson, James............	Lieutenant, 2nd Regiment.........	February 15, 1797
Whetherson, John.........	Captain, 2nd Regiment............	November 30, 1797
White, Jacob.............	Ensign, Light Infantry Company, 2nd Regiment...................	November 16, 1798
Wilson, John.............	Captain, 27th Regiment...........	June 20, 1798
Wortham, Charles.........	Ensign, 2nd Regiment.............	May 7, 1798

Scott County Regiment

Boswell, George..........	Ensign, Infantry Company, 12th Regiment......................	January 16, 1798
Boswell, George G.	Captain, Rifle Company, 2nd Battalion, 12th Regiment.......	June 24, 1798
Branham, William.........	Ensign, 12th Regiment............	June 22, 1797
Burk, Richard............	Ensign, 12th Regiment............	January 6, 1798
Cole, Jesse..............	Lieutenant, 12th Regiment........	June 22, 1797
Craig, William...........	Captain, 12th Regiment...........	January 6, 1798
Crighton, Henry..........	Lieutenant, 12th Regiment........	April 19, 1797
Emmerson, Thomas.........	Lieutenant, Rifle Company, 2nd Battalion, 12th Regiment.......	June 24, 1798
Henderson, John..........	Ensign, Rifle Company, 12th Regiment......................	November 13, 1798
Henry, William...........	Lieutenant Colonel, Commandant 12th Regiment.................	February 8, 1798
Hobdy, John..............	Ensign, Rifle Company, 1st Battalion, 12th Regiment.......	June 25, 1798
Hunter, John.............	Captain, Infantry Company, 12th Regiment......................	January 16, 1798
Johnson, Adam............	Captain, 12th Regiment...........	April 30, 1798
Johnson, James...........	Captain, Rifle Company, 1st Battalion, 12th Regiment.......	June 25, 1798
Latimore, David..........	Surgeon, 12th Regiment...........	November 24, 1798
Lowry, Samuel............	Captain, 12th Regiment...........	January 6, 1798
Nuckles, Lewis...........	Captain, 12th Regiment...........	June 22, 1797
Rozel, Stephen...........	Ensign, 12th Regiment............	January 15, 1798
Scandland, Benjamin......	Ensign, Rifle Company, 2nd Battalion, 12th Regiment.......	June 24, 1798
Sugget, James............	Lieutenant, Rifle Company, 1st Battalion, 12th Regiment.......	June 25, 1798
Taurence, David..........	Ensign, 12th Regiment............	April 19, 1797
Thompson, John...........	Major, 12th Regiment.............	February 12, 1798
Tilford, David...........	Captain, 12th Regiment...........	April 30, 1798

COMMISSIONED OFFICERS, 1797 - 1798

Triplett, Hedgman........	Captain, 12th Regiment...........	June 22, 1797
Trotter, James...........	Ensign, 12th Regiment............	June 22, 1797
Ward, William............	Captain, 12th Regiment...........	April 10, 1798
Weathers, John...........	Lieutenant, 12th Regiment........	April 10, 1798
West, Lynn...............	Ensign, 12th Regiment............	July 16, 1798
White, John..............	Lieutenant, 12th Regiment........	June 22, 1797
Wood, Edmund.............	Lieutenant, 12th Regiment........	January 6, 1798

Shelby County Regiment*

Adams, Simon.............	Captain of Infantry, 18th Regiment......................	January 1, 1798
Aken, John...............	Lieutenant (?), 18th Regiment....	January 4, 1797
Ashby, Beady.............	Ensign, 18th Regiment............	October 5, 1798
Ashby, Silas.............	Captain, 18th Regiment...........	September 27, 1797
Ballard, James...........	Captain, 18th Regiment...........	November 1, 1796
Bedle, Jonathan..........	Lieutenant, 18th Regiment........	September 1, 1797
Bilderback, Jacob........	Lieutenant, 18th Regiment........	December 4, 1796
Boon, John...............	Captain (?), 18th Regiment.......	December 1, 1796
Bowman, Aron.............	Ensign, 18th Regiment............	June 16, 1798
Bradshaw, John...........	1st Lieutenant of Cavalry, 18th Regiment......................	April 17, 1798
Buskirk, Thomas..........	Adjutant, 18th Regiment..........	November 5, 1798
Carr, Absalom............	Captain, 18th Regiment...........	December 14, 1796
Carr, Elijah.............	Lieutenant, 18th Regiment........	July 8, 1798
Cash, Warren.............	Lieutenant, 18th Regiment........	April 25, 1797
Connaway, Hugh...........	Lieutenant, 18th Regiment........	September 27, 1797
Davis, John..............	Captain, 18th Regiment...........	December 4, 1796
Gragg, David.............	Lieutenant, 18th Regiment........	November 8, 1796
Gragg, David.............	Captain,18th Regiment............	April 25, 1797
Hall, William............	Captain, 18th Regiment...........	January 4, 1797
Hattey, Samuel...........	Lieutenant of Infantry, 18th Regiment......................	January 1, 1798
Hogland, Moses...........	Lieutenant, 18th Regiment........	September 27, 1797
Holmes, Andrew...........	Captain, 18th Regiment...........	November 8, 1796
Holmes, Andrew...........	Quartermaster, 18th Regiment.....	November 5, 1798
Howe, John...............	Adjutant, 18th Regiment..........	September 1, 1797
Hubbs, Jacob.............	Lieutenant, 18th Regiment........	April 2, 1798
Jacobs, Samuel...........	Lieutenant, 18th Regiment........	January 4, 1797
Johns, Henry.............	Ensign, 18th Regiment............	April 25, 1797
Johnson, John............	Ensign, 18th Regiment............	September 1, 1797
Knight, John.............	Surgeon, 18th Regiment...........	November 5, 1798
Lawding, Thomas..........	Captain, 18th Regiment...........	December 8, 1796
Lawson, John.............	Lieutenant, 18th Regiment........	June 16, 1798

* Commissions in the 18th Regiment dated 1796 were issued February 15, 1797. To facilitate locating the original record [in Governor James Garrard's Executive Journal, 1797-1799] it was thought best to leave these earlier commissions in this 1797 - 1798 grouping.

COMMISSIONED OFFICERS, 1797 - 1798   51

Long, Anderson............	Lieutenant, 18th Regiment........	September 26, 1798
McClure, William..........	Captain, 18th Regiment...........	December 1, 1796
McCormic, Peter P.	Captain, 18th Regiment...........	September 1, 1797
McDavitt, James...........	2nd Lieutenant of Cavalry, 18th Regiment......................	April 17, 1798
McGaughey, John...........	Captain, 18th Regiment...........	September 27, 1797
Martin, Thomas............	Lieutenant, 18th Regiment........	April 14, 1797
Meek, Jeremiah............	Lieutenant, 18th Regiment........	December 8, 1796
Merefield, Alexander.....	Ensign, 18th Regiment............	August 8, 1798
Mitchell, Thomas..........	Ensign, 18th Regiment...........	September 27, 1797
Peynton (Pennington?), Samuel...	Ensign, 18th Regiment.....	September 27, 1797
Randolph, William.........	Ensign, 18th Regiment............	January 1, 1798
Rees, Thomas T.	Ensign of Infantry, 18th Regiment	January 1, 1798
Roberts, Benjamin........	Surgeon's Mate, 18th Regiment....	November 5, 1798
Robins, Vincent...........	Lieutenant, 18th Regiment........	December 1, 1796
Robins, Vincent...........	Captain, 18th Regiment...........	September 27, 1797
Ryker, Gerardis...........	Ensign, 18th Regiment............	December 1, 1796
Ryker, John...............	Captain, 18th Regiment...........	December 1, 1796
Simpson, Joseph...........	Captain, 18th Regiment...........	May 21, 1798
Simpson, Robert...........	Ensign, 18th Regiment............	May 21, 1798
Spencer, Spear............	Lieutenant, 18th Regiment........	May 21, 1798
Steele, Adam..............	Captain of Artillery, 18th Regiment......................	April 17, 1798
Stout, James..............	Cornet of Cavalry, 18th Regiment.	April 17, 1798
Ulrey, Jacob..............	Ensign, 18th Regiment............	December 4, 1796
Veal, William.............	Captain, 18th Regiment...........	June 16, 1798
Watkins, Isaac............	Paymaster, 18th Regiment.........	November 5, 1798
Whitaker, Elijah..........	Lieutenant, 18th Regiment........	November 1, 1796
Winkfield, Henry..........	Ensign, 18th Regiment............	December 8, 1796

Warren County Regiment

[Laid off February 23, 1797]

Amos, James...............	Captain, 1st Battalion, 25th Regiment......................	June 7, 1797
Anderson, John............	Ensign, 2nd Battalion, 25th Regiment......................	July 7, 1797
Anderson, Vincent........	Captain, 1st Battalion, 25th Regiment......................	July 7, 1797
Bateman, Simon............	Lieutenant, 1st Battalion, 25th Regiment......................	July 7, 1797
Berrey, James.............	Ensign, 1st Battalion, 25th Regiment......................	July 7, 1797
Black, James..............	Lieutenant, 1st Battalion, 25th Regiment......................	July 7, 1797
Brannon, Edward..........	Ensign, 2nd Battalion, 25th Regiment......................	July 7, 1797
Chapman, George...........	Lieutenant, 25th Regiment........	November 1, 1797
Coker, Samuel.............	Cornet, 25th Regiment............	July 7, 1797

COMMISSIONED OFFICERS, 1797 - 1798

Coveington, Elijah.......	Lieutenant of Cavalry, 25th Regiment......................	July 7, 1797
Cox, John...............	Captain, 2nd Battalion, 25th Regiment......................	July 7, 1797
Cox, Phenis..............	Major, 25th Regiment............	February 23, 1797
Cox, Solomon............	Ensign, 2nd Battalion, 25th Regiment......................	July 7, 1797
Crump, Havilah..........	Adjutant, 25th Regiment..........	February 8, 1798
Curd, Daniel............	Quartermaster, 25th Regiment.....	February 8, 1798
Curd, John..............	Major, 25th Regiment............	February 23, 1797
Donham, John............	Ensign, 25th Regiment...........	November 1, 1797
English, Joseph.........	Lieutenant, 2nd Battalion, 25th Regiment......................	July 7, 1797
Estis, John.............	Captain, 2nd Battalion, 25th Regiment......................	July 7, 1797
Gorin, Gladin...........	Captain, 25th Regiment...........	November 1, 1797
Hall, James.............	Lieutenant, 2nd Battalion, 25th Regiment......................	July 7, 1797
Harlow, Clayton.........	Lieutenant, 1st Battalion, 25th Regiment......................	July 7, 1797
Harris, Edwin L.	Captain of Cavalry, 25th Regiment......................	July 7, 1797
Harris, Edwin L.	Major, 25th Regiment............	March 14, 1798
Holcomb, Joel...........	Ensign, 1st Battalion, 25th Regiment......................	July 7, 1797
Jackson, Burwell........	Lieutenant Colonel, Commandant 25th Regiment.................	February 23, 1797
Kelley, Dennis..........	Lieutenant, 1st Battalion, 25th Regiment......................	July 7, 1797
McFagen, Andrew.........	Major, 25th Regiment............	February 8, 1798
McHenry, William........	Lieutenant, 1st Battalion, 25th Regiment......................	July 7, 1797
Mobley, James...........	Captain, 2nd Battalion, 25th Regiment......................	July 7, 1797
Moss, John..............	Captain, 1st Battalion, 25th Regiment......................	July 7, 1797
Painter, John...........	Ensign, 1st Battalion, 25th Regiment......................	July 7, 1797
Rennick, Henry..........	Captain, 1st Battalion, 25th Regiment......................	July 7, 1797
Robertson, David........	Captain, 2nd Battalion, 25th Regiment......................	July 7, 1797
Stringfield, John.......	Captain, 1st Battalion, 25th Regiment......................	July 7, 1797
Taylor, James...........	Lieutenant, 2nd Battalion, 25th Regiment......................	July 7, 1797
Taylor, John............	Lieutenant, 2nd Battalion, 25th Regiment......................	July 7, 1797
Taylor, William.........	Ensign, 2nd Battalion, 25th Regiment......................	July 7, 1797

COMMISSIONED OFFICERS, 1797 - 1798

Tinsley, William.........	Ensign, 1st Battalion, 25th Regiment.....................	July 7, 1797
Walker, James...........	Ensign, 1st Battalion, 25th Regiment.....................	July 7, 1797

Washington County Regiment

Barnett, Solomon.........	Ensign, 4th Regiment.............	August 14, 1797
Berry, Richard...........	Captain, 4th Regiment............	November 6, 1797
Brumfield, Robert........	Ensign, 4th Regiment.............	August 28, 1797
Catlin, James............	Lieutenant, 4th Regiment.........	January 1, 1797
Creiger, George..........	Ensign, 4th Regiment.............	October 4, 1798
Davis, James.............	Ensign, 4th Regiment.............	January 1, 1797
Edland, George...........	Lieutenant, 4th Regiment.........	June 26, 1798
Faris, Elijah............	Captain, 4th Regiment............	August 14, 1797
Funk, Joseph.............	Lieutenant, 4th Regiment.........	June 26, 1798
Hagar, James.............	Ensign, 4th Regiment.............	November 6, 1797
Hammett, John............	Captain, 4th Regiment............	January 1, 1797
Hardin, Henry............	Lieutenant, 4th Regiment.........	November 6, 1797
Hayden, John.............	Captain, 4th Regiment............	November 6, 1797
Hayes, John..............	Ensign, 4th Regiment.............	November 6, 1797
Hayes, Justin............	Ensign, 4th Regiment.............	June 26, 1798
McAffee, William.........	Lieutenant, 4th Regiment.........	November 6, 1797
McIntire, Thomas.........	Lieutenant, 4th Regiment.........	August 14, 1797
McKay, George............	Ensign, 4th Regiment.............	February 8, 1797
Mock, Daniel.............	Major, 1st Battalion, 4th Regiment.....................	June 5, 1797
Nall, John...............	Captain, 4th Regiment............	April 22, 1797
Phillips, Benjamin.......	Lieutenant, 4th Regiment.........	April 22, 1797
Purdy, William...........	Lieutenant, 4th Regiment.........	February 8, 1797
Rice, Jesse..............	Ensign, 4th Regiment.............	April 22, 1797
Smith, Nicholas..........	Ensign, 4th Regiment.............	June 26, 1798
Watts, George............	Captain, 4th Regiment............	June 26, 1798

Woodford County Regiment

Ballard, George..........	Ensign, 11th Regiment............	March 29, 1797
Bartlett, Anthony........	Major, 1st Battalion, 11th Regiment.....................	January 16, 1797
Bohannon, Larkin.........	Ensign, 11th Regiment............	February 1, 1798
Brooke, George...........	Quartermaster, 11th Regiment.....	December 23, 1798
Brookens, Samuel.........	Lieutenant, 11th Regiment........	March 29, 1797
Brookens, Samuel.........	Adjutant, 11th Regiment..........	January 19, 1798
Burton, Zachariah........	Ensign, 11th Regiment............	March 29, 1797
Campbell, William........	Lieutenant, 11th Regiment........	May 11, 1798
Claggett, Thomas.........	Ensign, 11th Regiment............	February 1, 1798
Cowin, Alexander.........	Ensign, 11th Regiment............	May 11, 1798
Craig, Lewis.............	Lieutenant, Rifle Company, 11th Regiment.................	December 23, 1798

COMMISSIONED OFFICERS, 1797 - 1798

Dickton, Richard.........	Ensign, Rifle Company, 11th Regiment......................	December 23, 1798
Furnes, James............	Captain, 11th Regiment...........	May 11, 1798
Goodridge, Elisha........	Lieutenant, 11th Regiment........	May 11, 1798
Hall, William............	Ensign, 11th Regiment............	May 11, 1798
Hammilton, John..........	Ensign, 11th Regiment............	May 11, 1798
Harrison, William........	Lieutenant, 11th Regiment........	May 11, 1798
Holman, Isaac............	Lieutenant, 11th Regiment........	April 10, 1798
Lealand, Leonard.........	Surgeon's Mate, 11th Regiment....	January 19, 1798
McCrackin, Virgil........	Captain, 11th Regiment...........	July 9, 1798
McMillion, James.........	Lieutenant, 11th Regiment........	May 11, 1798
Morreson, Daniel.........	Ensign, 11th Regiment............	May 11, 1798
Nayler, John.............	Ensign, 11th Regiment............	May 11, 1798
O'Bannon, William........	Lieutenant, 11th Regiment........	April 25, 1797
Preston, Daniel..........	Surgeon, 11th Regiment...........	January 19, 1798
Pryor, Samuel............	Captain, 11th Regiment...........	June 6, 1797
Rankin, Simeon...........	Lieutenant, 11th Regiment........	May 11, 1798
Robertson, John..........	Captain, 11th Regiment...........	May 11, 1798
Rollings, Michael........	Captain, 11th Regiment...........	May 11, 1798
Scarce, Robert...........	Lieutenant, 11th Regiment........	August 1, 1797
Scearce, Robert..........	Captain, 11th Regiment...........	April 10, 1798
Stucker, Jacob...........	Ensign, 11th Regiment............	July 9, 1798
Thomas, Richard Moore....	Lieutenant, 11th Regiment........	January 1, 1797
Thompson, Anthony........	Captain, 11th Regiment...........	March 29, 1797
Trabue, Edward...........	Ensign, 11th Regiment............	April 10, 1798
Vawters, William.........	Major, 2nd Battalion, 11th Regiment......................	January 16, 1797
Young, Lewis.............	Captain, Rifle Company, 11th Regiment......................	December 23, 1798

COMMISSIONED OFFICERS, 1799 - 1804   55

General Officers

Adair, John.............	Major General, 2nd Division......	December 16, 1799
Barbee, Elias...........	Brigadier General, 10th Brigade..	December 18, 1799
Caldwell, William.......	Brigade Inspector, 6th Brigade...	June 1, 1799
Caldwell, William.......	Brigade Inspector, 1st Brigade...	November 9, 1801
Clay, Green.............	Brigadier General, 9th Brigade...	December 21, 1799
Crump, Havilah..........	Brigade Inspector, 10th Brigade..	October 2, 1800
Ewing, Robert...........	Brigadier General, 11th Brigade..	December 19, 1799
Gaines, Richard.........	Brigade Inspector, 6th Brigade...	December 17, 1799
Grant, Squire...........	Brigadier General, 4th Brigade...	December 20, 1804
Harrison, Hezekiah......	Brigade Inspector, 5th Brigade...	September 20, 1800
Henry, William..........	Brigadier General, 6th Brigade...	December 23, 1799
Hopkins, Samuel.........	Major General, 1st Division......	December 14, 1799
Huston, Nathan..........	Brigadier General, 8th Brigade...	December 17, 1799
Huston, Nathan..........	Major General, 2nd Division......	December 24, 1803
Lee, Henry..............	Major General, 3rd Division......	December 17, 1799
Lewis, Joseph...........	Brigadier General, 1st Brigade...	April 12, 1799
Logan, David............	Brigade Inspector, 8th Brigade...	No date
McDowell, Samuel........	Brigade Inspector, 8th Brigade...	August 13, 1804
Payne, Duval............	Brigade Inspector, 5th Brigade...	February 26, 1799
Pemberton, Bennett......	Brigadier General, 4th Brigade...	May 27, 1800
Ray, James..............	Brigadier General, 8th Brigade...	December 24, 1803
Russell, William........	Brigadier General, 3rd Brigade...	December 14, 1799
South, John.............	Brigadier General, 5th Brigade...	December 24, 1799
Thomas, John............	Brigadier General, 12th Brigade..	December 14, 1804
Thomas, Philemon........	Brigadier General, 7th Brigade...	December 20, 1799
Todd, Levi..............	Brigadier General, 3rd Brigade...	April 1, 1799
Todd, Levi..............	Brigadier General, 5th Division..	December 19, 1799
Voorhies, Peter G.	Brigade Inspector, 4th Brigade...	September 20, 1800
Walton, Matthew.........	Brigadier General, 6th Brigade...	April 11, 1799
Walton, Matthew.........	Major General, 4th Division......	December 18, 1799
Wells, Samuel...........	Brigadier General, 2nd Brigade...	December 16, 1799
Wells, Samuel...........	Major General, 6th Division......	December 20, 1804
Winlock, Joseph.........	Brigadier General, 2nd Brigade...	December 20, 1804

Company Officers

Adair County Regiment

[Laid off December 17, 1801]

Atkinson, Isiah.........	Ensign, 52nd Regiment............	March 20, 1802
Atkinson, Thomas........	Paymaster, 52nd Regiment.........	October 25, 1802
Barnard, Peter..........	Lieutenant, 52nd Regiment........	October 25, 1802
Beard, John.............	Cornet of Cavalry, 52nd Regiment.	December 2, 1803
Beliew, Absalom.........	Lieutenant, 52nd Regiment........	May 27, 1803
Bradley, Zion...........	Major, 2nd Battalion, 52nd Regiment......................	December 19, 1801
Bristow, Thomas.........	Ensign, 52nd Regiment Recommissioned.................	March 20, 1802
Bristow, Thomas.........	Lieutenant, 52nd Regiment........	October 25, 1802

COMMISSIONED OFFICERS, 1799 - 1804

Bryant, John G.	Quartermaster, 52nd Regiment	March 20, 1802
Buckhannon, Nathaniel	Captain, 52nd Regiment	October 25, 1802
Buckingham, Peter	Lieutenant, 52nd Regiment	March 20, 1802
Creel, John	Ensign, 52nd Regiment	March 20, 1802
Damron, George	Captain, 52nd Regiment Recommissioned	March 20, 1802
Doake, David	Captain, 52nd Regiment	March 20, 1802
Douglas, Nathan	Lieutenant, 52nd Regiment	March 20, 1802
Ewing, Andrew	Ensign, 52nd Regiment Recommissioned	March 20, 1802
Ewing, Andrew	Adjutant, 52nd Regiment	March 20, 1802
Fox, John	Ensign, 52nd Regiment	March 20, 1802 and May 27, 1803
Hardin, Joseph	Lieutenant, 52nd Regiment	October 25, 1802
Haskins, Creed	Captain, 52nd Regiment	March 20, 1802
Hays, Joseph	Ensign, 52nd Regiment	October 25, 1802
Kearns, Thomas	Ensign, 52nd Regiment	March 20, 1802
Lampton, Benjamin	Captain, 52nd Regiment	March 20, 1802
Lawson, William	Major, 1st Battalion, 52nd Regiment	December 18, 1801
McNealy, William	Lieutenant, 52nd Regiment Recommissioned	March 20, 1802
Miex (Meeks), James	Lieutenant, 52nd Regiment	March 20, 1802
Morrison, James	Ensign, 52nd Regiment	May 27, 1803
Perkins, Nicholas	1st Lieutenant of Cavalry, 52nd Regiment	December 2, 1803
Pope, Humphrey	Captain of Cavalry, 52nd Regiment	October 25, 1802
Rutherford, John, Jr.	Ensign, 52nd Regiment	March 20, 1802
Thomas, Robert	Lieutenant, 52nd Regiment Recommissioned	March 20, 1802
Trabue, Daniel	Colonel, 52nd Regiment	December 18, 1801
Trabue, Robert	Lieutenant, 52nd Regiment	March 20, 1802
Trabue, Stephen	Paymaster, 52nd Regiment	March 20, 1802
Tucker, William	Ensign, 52nd Regiment	October 25, 1802
Warren, Martin	Captain, 52nd Regiment	March 20, 1802
White (no first name)	Captain, 52nd Regiment Recommissioned	March 20, 1802
White, Jesse	Lieutenant, 52nd Regiment	March 20, 1802
White, Jesse	2nd Lieutenant of Cavalry, 52nd Regiment	December 2, 1803
Winfrey, John	Lieutenant, 52nd Regiment	May 27, 1803
Winfrey, William	Ensign, 52nd Regiment	May 27, 1803
Woolford, John	Captain, 52nd Regiment	March 20, 1802
Young, Samuel	Ensign, 52nd Regiment	October 25, 1802
Young, William	Captain, 52nd Regiment Recommissioned	March 20, 1802

Barren County Regiment

[Laid off December 22, 1799]

Akers, George............	Lieutenant, 45th Regiment........	September 1, 1802
Akers, George............	Captain, 45th Regiment...........	August 1, 1804
Akers, Thomas............	Lieutenant, 45th Regiment........	March 26, 1800
Allen, John..............	Lieutenant, 45th Regiment........	March 28, 1800
Amos, Charles............	Ensign, 45th Regiment............	November 1, 1801
Amos, Charles............	Captain, 45th Regiment...........	June 25, 1803
Bates, Robert............	Ensign, 45th Regiment............	September 1, 1802
Beck, Daniel.............	Ensign, 45th Regiment............	September 1, 1802
Bennett, William.........	Ensign, 45th Regiment............	March 30, 1801
Bibee, Sherod............	Ensign, 45th Regiment............	September 1, 1802
Bishop, Lowrey...........	Ensign, 45th Regiment............	August 1, 1804
Blakey, Thomas...........	Ensign, 45th Regiment............	March 30, 1801
Blakey, Thomas...........	Lieutenant, 45th Regiment........	November 1, 1801
Blakey, Thomas...........	Captain, 45th Regiment...........	September 1, 1802
Brook, John..............	Lieutenant, 45th Regiment........	March 29, 1800
Brooks, Miles............	Lieutenant, 45th Regiment........	June 25, 1803
Brown, Hugh..............	Lieutenant, 45th Regiment........	March 25, 1800
Brown, Hugh..............	Captain, 45th Regiment...........	November 27, 1800
Buford, John.............	Captain, 45th Regiment...........	November 27, 1800
Burks, John..............	Lieutenant, 45th Regiment........	June 25, 1803
Bush, John...............	Captain, 45th Regiment...........	September 1, 1802
Bybee, Sherod............	Lieutenant, 45th Regiment........	June 25, 1803
Carter, James............	Lieutenant, 45th Regiment........	May 20, 1800
Carter, James............	Captain, 45th Regiment...........	November 27, 1800
Celsey (Kelsey, Kelso?), John....	Ensign, 45th Regiment.....	March 25, 1800
Chapman, William.........	Lieutenant, 45th Regiment........	November 27, 1800
Clarke, George...........	Captain, 45th Regiment...........	December 22, 1802
Courts, William..........	Captain, 45th Regiment...........	December 22, 1802
Crews, James.............	Ensign, 45th Regiment............	March 29, 1800
Crump, Joshua............	Lieutenant, 45th Regiment........	November 1, 1801
Curd, Daniel.............	Ensign, 45th Regiment............	June 25, 1803
Curd, Daniel.............	Quartermaster, 45th Regiment.....	May 20, 1800
Damewood, Henry..........	Ensign, 45th Regiment............	June 25, 1803
Dickerson, John..........	Ensign, 45th Regiment............	August 1, 1804
Dooley, George...........	Lieutenant, 45th Regiment........	June 25, 1803
Emmerson, Walter.........	Lieutenant, 45th Regiment........	June 25, 1803
Fields, John.............	Ensign, 45th Regiment............	March 30, 1801
Fisher, James............	Ensign, 45th Regiment............	June 25, 1803
Flippin, William.........	Lieutenant, 45th Regiment........	May 20, 1800
Forbis, James............	Captain, 45th Regiment...........	November 1, 1801
Forbis, Robert...........	Ensign, 45th Regiment............	November 1, 1801
Forbis, Robert...........	Lieutenant, 45th Regiment........	September 1, 1802
Francis, Joseph..........	Ensign, 45th Regiment............	June 25, 1803
Franklin, John...........	Ensign, 45th Regiment............	March 27, 1800
Franklin, John, Jr.	Lieutenant, 45th Regiment........	March 30, 1801
Franklin, Martin.........	Ensign, 45th Regiment............	March 6, 1802

COMMISSIONED OFFICERS, 1799 - 1804

Gist, William	2nd Lieutenant, Light Horse, 45th Regiment	August 1, 1804
Glover, Job	Lieutenant, 45th Regiment	August 1, 1804
Gorin, John	Major, 1st Battalion, 45th Regiment	December 23, 1799
Gray, John	Captain, 45th Regiment	March 28, 1800
Hardin, David	Captain, 45th Regiment	September 1, 1802
Hardin, George	Ensign, 45th Regiment	September 1, 1802
Hardy, Benjamin	Ensign, 45th Regiment	November 27, 1800
Harris, John	Ensign, 45th Regiment	June 25, 1803
Hill, Robert	Captain, 45th Regiment	May 20, 1800
Hindman, Robert	Lieutenant, 45th Regiment	March 27, 1800
Johnson, Absolem	Cornet, Light Horse, 45th Regiment	August 1, 1804
Johnson, Forgus	Ensign, 45th Regiment	March 26, 1800
Kelsoe, John	Lieutenant, 45th Regiment	November 27, 1800
King, William	Captain, Light Horse, 45th Regiment	August 1, 1804
Kirkendole, Matthew	Ensign, 45th Regiment	June 25, 1803
Leir, Matthew	Ensign, 45th Regiment	March 28, 1800
Logan, William	Paymaster, 45th Regiment	May 20, 1800
Logue, William	Ensign, 45th Regiment	November 1, 1801
McGary, William	Ensign, 45th Regiment	March 30, 1801
McMurtry, James	Lieutenant, 45th Regiment	August 1, 1804
Martin, Joseph	Ensign, 45th Regiment	May 20, 1800
Martin, Joseph	Adjutant, 45th Regiment	May 20, 1800
Matthews, James	Lieutenant, 45th Regiment	August 1, 1804
Mayfield, John, Jr.	Ensign, 45th Regiment	June 25, 1803
Means, Thomas	Lieutenant, 45th Regiment	November 27, 1800
Mercer, Howard	Captain, 45th Regiment	June 25, 1803
Middleton, Matthew	Lieutenant, 45th Regiment	September 1, 1802
Middleton, Matthew	Captain, 45th Regiment	June 25, 1803
Moss, John	Captain, 45th Regiment	March 27, 1800
Neville, Joseph	Lieutenant, 45th Regiment	August 1, 1804
Parks, Samuel	Lieutenant, 45th Regiment	November 27, 1800
Parks, Samuel	1st Lieutenant, Light Horse, 45th Regiment	August 1, 1804
Perkins, William	Ensign, 45th Regiment	December 22, 1802
Pullem, William	Lieutenant, 45th Regiment	March 30, 1801
Pullem, William	Captain, 45th Regiment	November 1, 1801
Putman, Simeon	Captain, 45th Regiment	September 1, 1802
Renick, William	Captain, 45th Regiment	November 1, 1801
Rennic, James	Lieutenant, 45th Regiment	February 27, 1800
Rennic, William	Ensign, 45th Regiment	February 27, 1800
Rennick, Henry	Colonel, 45th Regiment	December 23, 1799
Rennick, William	Lieutenant, 45th Regiment	December 22, 1802
Rhea, Daniel	Ensign, 45th Regiment	September 1, 1802
Richardson, William	Captain, 45th Regiment	March 28, 1800
Rogers, Bird	Lieutenant, 45th Regiment	June 25, 1803
Rogers, Lewis	Ensign, 45th Regiment	June 25, 1803
Rolston, Joseph	Captain, 45th Regiment	May 20, 1800

COMMISSIONED OFFICERS, 1799 - 1804

Russel, William	Captain, 45th Regiment	March 25, 1800
Sanders, William	Ensign, 45th Regiment	March 30, 1801
Saunders, John	Lieutenant, 45th Regiment	November 1, 1801
Semple, George	Paymaster, 45th Regiment	September 1, 1802
Simpson, Thomas	Ensign, 45th Regiment	November 27, 1800
Smith, George	Ensign, 45th Regiment	August 1, 1804
Smith, Hugh	Captain, 45th Regiment	February 27, 1800
Smith, John	Captain, 45th Regiment	June 25, 1803
Smith, William	Captain, 45th Regiment	February 27, 1800
Steenburgen, Robert P.	Adjutant, 45th Regiment	March 6, 1802
Steenburgen, William	Captain, 45th Regiment	March 26, 1800
Stockdon, Robert	Major, 2nd Battalion, 45th Regiment	December 24, 1799
Tedder, John	Ensign, 45th Regiment	December 22, 1802
Tedder, Kinsey	Lieutenant, 45th Regiment	June 25, 1803
Thompson, William	Ensign, 45th Regiment	May 20, 1800
Tudor, Kinsey	Captain, 45th Regiment	August 1, 1804
Walker, John	Ensign, 45th Regiment	November 1, 1801
Walker, John	Lieutenant, 45th Regiment	September 1, 1802
Ward, Nathaniel	Ensign, 45th Regiment	November 27, 1800
Ward, Nathan	Lieutenant, 45th Regiment	September 1, 1802
Williams, Daniel	Lieutenant, 45th Regiment	November 27, 1800
Willis, Matthew	Ensign, 45th Regiment	November 1, 1801
Wood, William J.	Captain, 45th Regiment	November 27, 1800

Bourbon County Regiments

[47th Regiment laid off April 10, 1800]

Alfree, John	Ensign, 47th Regiment	October 4, 1800
Allen, John	Lieutenant, 13th Regiment	January 1, 1801
Allen, John	Captain, 13th Regiment	September 17, 1804
Amos, Abram	Lieutenant, 47th Regiment	May 22, 1801
Amos, Thomas	Captain, 13th Regiment	June 17, 1799
Anderson, Gilmore	Lieutenant, 47th Regiment	May 22, 1801
Anderson, Thomas	Ensign, 14th Regiment	April 4, 1799
Archer, John	Lieutenant, 47th Regiment	January 22, 1802
Archer, Sampson	Ensign, 47th Regiment	May 8, 1801
Ashert, Josiah	Ensign, 14th Regiment	June 15, 1801
Ashert, Josiah	Lieutenant, 14th Regiment	May 6, 1803
Austin, Obadiah	Ensign, 47th Regiment	May 8, 1801
Bailey, Thomas	Ensign, 13th Regiment	January 1, 1801
Bailey, Thomas	Lieutenant, 13th Regiment	December 28, 1801
Baird, James	Lieutenant, 14th Regiment	January 16, 1804
Baker, John	Captain, 13th Regiment	July 25, 1801
Baker, John, Jr.	Lieutenant, 13th Regiment	March 1, 1800
Barley, John	Ensign, 13th Regiment	December 28, 1801
Barnett, George	Ensign, 47th Regiment	October 4, 1800
Barnett, George	Lieutenant, 47th Regiment	December 24, 1802
Barnett, John	Ensign, 14th Regiment	May 6, 1803

COMMISSIONED OFFICERS, 1799 - 1804

Barr, Hugh	Lieutenant, 47th Regiment	October 4, 1800
Barton, William	Ensign, 13th Regiment	October 20, 1803
Barton, William	Lieutenant, 13th Regiment	May 17, 1804
Baskett, Jesse	Captain, 13th Regiment	March 1, 1800
Batterton, Henry	Ensign, Infantry Company, 14th Regiment	June 21, 1802
Batterton, Henry	Ensign, 14th Regiment	January 16, 1804
Batterton, Henry	Lieutenant, 14th Regiment	May 25, 1804
Becket, William	Lieutenant, 13th Regiment	July 15, 1799
Bedford, Benjamin	Paymaster, 14th Regiment	May 12, 1800
Berry, Robert	Captain, 47th Regiment	March 20, 1801
Black, Alexander	Major, 14th Regiment	April 30, 1799
Black, Alexander	Colonel, 14th Regiment	December 19, 1800
Black, Samuel	Major, 47th Regiment	February 21, 1801
Black, Samuel	Lieutenant, 14th Regiment	June 15, 1801
Blackburn, William	Captain, 13th Regiment	October 3, 1801
Blain, John	Ensign, 13th Regiment	December 28, 1801
Board, George	Ensign, 14th Regiment	June 21, 1802
Board, George	Lieutenant, 14th Regiment	May 6, 1803
Bowles, Nelson	Ensign, Rifle Company, 47th Regiment	May 22, 1801
Bradford, Garland	Lieutenant, 14th Regiment	October 3, 1799
Braham, William	Lieutenant, 14th Regiment	May 6, 1803
Brand, Richard	Captain, 14th Regiment	May 25, 1804
Branham, William B.	Adjutant, 14th Regiment	July 18, 1803
Bristoe, James	Lieutenant, 14th Regiment	June 21, 1802
Brown, John	Ensign, 14th Regiment	June 28, 1799
Brown, John	Ensign, 14th Regiment	December 28, 1801
Browning, Jesse	Captain, 13th Regiment	April 1, 1800
Browning, John	Ensign, 13th Regiment	May 22, 1802
Bruges, Edmond	Lieutenant, 13th Regiment	April 6, 1800
Bryan, James	Ensign, 14th Regiment	April 1, 1800
Bryan, James	Ensign, 47th Regiment	May 25, 1803
Buchanan, Henry	Lieutenant, 14th Regiment	May 12, 1800
Buchannan, Henry	Captain, 14th Regiment	June 21, 1802
Buford, Amb.	Ensign, 14th Regiment	May 6, 1803
Butler, Francis	Ensign, 13th Regiment	December 6, 1804
Byrom, Edward	Ensign, 47th Regiment	July 2, 1802
Calderwood, Adam	Captain of Infantry, 14th Regiment	June 15, 1801
Caldwell, James	Ensign, 47th Regiment	October 4, 1800
Caldwell, James	Lieutenant, 47th Regiment	May 8, 1801
Canterhill, Joseph	Ensign, 13th Regiment	May 12, 1803
Cantrill, Joseph	Lieutenant, 13th Regiment	December 6, 1804
Carter, John	Lieutenant, 47th Regiment	January 22, 1802
Carter, John	Captain, 47th Regiment	May 25, 1803
Clarkson, Charles	Colonel, 13th Regiment	May 12, 1800
Clay, Henry, Jr.	Captain, 14th Regiment	December 28, 1801
Collier, Coleman	Lieutenant, 13th Regiment	July 25, 1801
Collier, Franklin	Captain, 47th Regiment	May 25, 1803
Collins, Edward	Lieutenant, 13th Regiment	December 6, 1804

COMMISSIONED OFFICERS, 1799 - 1804

Congleton, James.........	Captain, 14th Regiment...........	June 28, 1799
Congleton, James.........	Captain, 47th Regiment Recommissioned................	August 7, 1801
Cook, Isaac.............	Lieutenant, 13th Regiment........	May 24, 1800
Cook, Isaac.............	Captain, 13th Regiment...........	July 25, 1801
Crose, Michael..........	Lieutenant, 14th Regiment........	April 1, 1800
Crouch, William.........	Ensign, 47th Regiment............	May 25, 1804
Culp, George............	Captain, Rifle Company, 13th Regiment......................	January 1, 1801
Culp, Josiah............	Lieutenant, 13th Regiment........	July 25, 1801
Dallas, William.........	Ensign, 14th Regiment............	May 6, 1803
Darnell, Thomas.........	Ensign, 14th Regiment............	January 16, 1804
Dawson, Samuel Jones....	Captain, 14th Regiment...........	May 6, 1803
Delay, James............	Ensign, 47th Regiment............	December 24, 1802
Demmit, Joshua..........	Lieutenant, 13th Regiment........	September 17, 1804
Dennison, James.........	Captain, 14th Regiment...........	February 27, 1801
Dennison, Thomas........	Lieutenant, 14th Regiment........	February 27, 1801
Donnel, James...........	Lieutenant, 14th Regiment........	June 28, 1799
Duckett, John...........	Ensign, Rifle Company, 47th Regiment......................	October 4, 1800
Duncan, James, Jr.	Ensign, 14th Regiment............	May 6, 1803
Eastin, Zachariah.......	Lieutenant, 13th Regiment........	September 17, 1804
Edwards, John...........	Captain, 13th Regiment...........	May 22, 1802
Ellis, Henry............	Ensign, 47th Regiment............	May 25, 1804
Ellis, William..........	Lieutenant, Rifle Company, 47th Regiment..................	March 20, 1801
Enlowes, Henry..........	Lieutenant, 14th Regiment........	March 4, 1801
Field, John, Jr.	Ensign, 13th Regiment............	June 17, 1799
Field, Willis...........	Ensign, Infantry Company, 14th Regiment......................	April 4, 1799
Fields, Philemon........	Ensign, 13th Regiment............	May 22, 1802
Fleming, John...........	Lieutenant, 47th Regiment........	May 22, 1801
Fleming, Peter..........	Colonel, 47th Regiment...........	February 21, 1801
Forman, Aron............	Captain, 14th Regiment...........	August 29, 1800
Friend, Andrew..........	Captain, 14th Regiment...........	October 3, 1799
Friend, Charles.........	Colonel, 14th Regiment...........	August 13, 1800
Garrard, Daniel.........	Captain, 13th Regiment...........	January 1, 1801
Garrard, James..........	Adjutant, 13th Regiment..........	April 8, 1800
Garrard, John...........	Captain of Cavalry, 13th Regiment......................	July 7, 1802
Garrard, William........	Captain, 14th Regiment...........	April 4, 1799
Gorrel, John............	Ensign, 14th Regiment............	August 29, 1800
Graves, David...........	Ensign, 47th Regiment............	May 25, 1804
Griffin, Aaron..........	Lieutenant, 14th Regiment........	June 15, 1801
Griffin, Aaron..........	2nd Lieutenant of Cavalry, 13th Regiment..................	July 7, 1802
Griffith, William.......	Ensign, 13th Regiment............	July 25, 1801
Groom, Jacob............	Ensign, 14th Regiment............	May 6, 1803
Grooms, Isaac...........	Ensign, 14th Regiment............	June 15, 1801
Hall, Benjamin..........	Captain, 14th Regiment...........	June 28, 1799
Hall, Cornelius.........	Captain, 47th Regiment...........	October 4, 1800

COMMISSIONED OFFICERS, 1799 - 1804

Hall, Cornelius, Jr.	Ensign, 47th Regiment	May 8, 1801
Hall, Isaac	Lieutenant of Infantry, 13th Regiment	June 17, 1799
Hall, Isaac W.	Ensign, 13th Regiment	May 17, 1804
Hall, John	Ensign, 13th Regiment	August 7, 1800
Hall, John	Lieutenant, 13th Regiment	July 25, 1801
Hall, John	Captain, 13th Regiment	December 28, 1801
Hall, Mahleen	Ensign, 47th Regiment	May 25, 1804
Hall, Sylvester	Lieutenant, 14th Regiment	June 28, 1799
Haman, Huston	Lieutenant, 13th Regiment	October 20, 1803
Hamilton, John	Lieutenant, 47th Regiment	October 4, 1800
Hamilton, William	Ensign, 13th Regiment	December 6, 1804
Harcourt, John	2nd Lieutenant of Infantry, 14th Regiment	June 15, 1801
Harcourt, John	Lieutenant, 14th Regiment	June 21, 1802
Hardesty, William	Ensign, 14th Regiment	March 4, 1801
Hardesty, William	Lieutenant, 14th Regiment	May 6, 1803
Harris, Samuel	Lieutenant, 14th Regiment	June 21, 1802
Harrod, Samuel	Ensign, 14th Regiment	February 27, 1801
Harrod, Samuel	Captain, 14th Regiment	January 16, 1804
Hedge, James	Ensign, 14th Regiment	May 6, 1803
Henderson, John	Ensign, 13th Regiment	May 17, 1804
Henderson, Samuel	Paymaster, 47th Regiment	July 21, 1801
Hibbler, Joseph	Lieutenant, 14th Regiment	April 1, 1800
Hicklane, Thomas	Cornet, 14th Regiment	October 3, 1799
Hook, Thomas	Ensign, 47th Regiment	January 18, 1800
Hornbeck, Michael	Lieutenant, 47th Regiment	May 25, 1803
Howell, David	Lieutenant, 14th Regiment	May 12, 1800
Hoy, Thomas	Captain, 14th Regiment	March 4, 1801
Hughes, George	Captain, 13th Regiment	April 6, 1800
Hughes, John	Captain, Rifle Company, 14th Regiment	June 28, 1799
Hughes, Robert	1st Lieutenant, 14th Regiment	October 3, 1799
Hunn, Anthony	Surgeon, 13th Regiment	April 16, 1800
Indicut, John	Ensign, 13th Regiment	May 12, 1803
Indicut, William	Lieutenant, 13th Regiment	May 17, 1804
Ireland, John	Ensign, 14th Regiment	March 4, 1801
Irvin, Stephen	Ensign, 47th Regiment	May 25, 1803
Jackson, Thomas	Lieutenant, 14th Regiment	May 25, 1804
Jackson, William Duffield	Ensign, 14th Regiment	June 15, 1801
Jacoby, Ralph	Lieutenant, 13th Regiment	December 5, 1802
Johnson, Jonathan	Captain, 13th Regiment	December 6, 1804
Johnson, William	Ensign, Rifle Company, 13th Regiment	May 22, 1802
Jones, Dumas	Lieutenant, 13th Regiment	May 22, 1802
Jones, Dumas	Captain, 13th Regiment	May 12, 1803
Kellar, Abner	Captain, 13th Regiment	July 15, 1799
Kellar, Abraham	Lieutenant, 13th Regiment	April 16, 1799
Keller, Abraham	Ensign, 13th Regiment	December 6, 1804
Kenderick, William	Lieutenant, 13th Regiment	February 12, 1799
Kenny, James	Lieutenant, 14th Regiment	August 29, 1800

Kincart, James...........	Ensign, 47th Regiment............	January 22, 1802
Kirby, Richard...........	Ensign, 13th Regiment............	May 20, 1799
Ladd, Jacob..............	Lieutenant, 14th Regiment........	December 28, 1801
Ladd, Robert.............	Ensign, 14th Regiment............	December 28, 1801
Lampton, Samuel..........	Ensign, 14th Regiment............	January 16, 1804
Laughlin, William........	Captain, 14th Regiment...........	June 15, 1801
Liter, John..............	Ensign, 13th Regiment............	December 5, 1802
Litton, Caleb............	Lieutenant, 47th Regiment........	January 22, 1802
Litton, Caleb............	Captain, 47th Regiment...........	December 24, 1802
Loaran (Lowring), Frederick...	Ensign, 13th Regiment........	July 25, 1801
Lodler, Jesse............	Ensign, 13th Regiment............	June 17, 1799
Lucky, Joseph............	Ensign, 47th Regiment............	January 22, 1802
McClanahan, Thomas.......	Captain, 13th Regiment...........	June 18, 1799
McCleland, William, Jr...	Cornet, Cavalry, 13th Regiment...	July 7, 1802
McClelland, James........	Lieutenant, 47th Regiment........	May 8, 1801
McClelland, James........	Captain, 47th Regiment...........	January 22, 1802
McConicha (McConnahy), David ...	Lieutenant, 14th Regiment..	March 4, 1801
McConnel, Edward.........	Major, 2nd Battalion, 13th Regiment......................	May 12, 1800
McConnel, John...........	Lieutenant, 13th Regiment........	August 7, 1800
McConnel, William........	Lieutenant, 13th Regiment........	December 28, 1801
McConnell, William.......	Captain, 13th Regiment...........	December 6, 1804
McCoun, George...........	Major, 14th Regiment.............	August 29, 1800
McCoun, George...........	Colonel, 14th Regiment...........	December 13, 1802
McCoy, Martin............	Ensign, 13th Regiment............	December 5, 1801
McCune, John.............	Lieutenant, 13th Regiment........	December 6, 1804
McDole, James............	Ensign, 13th Regiment............	December 6, 1804
McIntire, Robert.........	Colonel, 13th Regiment...........	July 27, 1801
McIntire, W.	Major, 13th Regiment.............	December 24, 1799
Mahan, Henry.............	Lieutenant, 13th Regiment........	May 12, 1803
Mahan, Rany	Ensign, 13th Regiment............	December 5, 1802
Markham, William.........	Lieutenant, 13th Regiment........	June 18, 1799
Marshall, Archibald......	Lieutenant, 47th Regiment........	May 25, 1803
Martin, William..........	Captain, 14th Regiment...........	April 1, 1800
Mitchel, David...........	Ensign, 14th Regiment............	May 12, 1800
Mitchel, Elijah..........	Captain, 47th Regiment...........	October 4, 1800
Mitchel, William.........	Captain, 47th Regiment...........	May 25, 1803
Montjoy, George..........	Captain, 13th Regiment...........	September 17, 1804
Moore, James.............	Ensign, 14th Regiment............	October 3, 1799
Moore, James.............	Ensign, 13th Regiment............	September 17, 1804
Moore, Samuel............	Captain, 47th Regiment. (Formerly of 14th Regiment).............	November 6, 1801
Moore, Samuel............	Major, 2nd Battalion, 47th Regiment......................	October 6, 1804
Morrow, Winn.............	Lieutenant of Infantry, 14th Regiment......................	May 30, 1799
Mosea (Mouzey?), George..	Lieutenant, 13th Regiment........	June 17, 1799
Mountjoy, George.........	Ensign, 13th Regiment............	July 25, 1801
Mountjoy, George.........	Lieutenant, 13th Regiment........	May 22, 1802
Myers, John..............	Ensign, 47th Regiment............	May 25, 1803

COMMISSIONED OFFICERS, 1799 - 1804

Neal, Jacob	Lieutenant, Rifle Company, 47th Regiment	December 24, 1802
Nisbitt, Jeremiah	Ensign, 13th Regiment	May 17, 1804
Northcutt, Hosea	Lieutenant, 14th Regiment	March 4, 1801
Orton, Joseph	Lieutenant, 47th Regiment	January 22, 1802
Parker, Aquilla	Adjutant, 47th Regiment	July 4, 1798
	Recommissioned	August 7, 1801
Parker, John	Lieutenant, 47th Regiment	October 4, 1800
Parker, John	Captain, 47th Regiment	January 22, 1802
Parker, Rowland Thomas	Ensign, 13th Regiment	December 6, 1804
Pastor, Samuel	Ensign, 14th Regiment	June 15, 1801
Payne, Jessie	Lieutenant, 14th Regiment	May 25, 1804
Phelps, John	Captain of Cavalry, 14th Regiment	June 28, 1799
Pollock, James	Lieutenant, 13th Regiment	May 22, 1802
Porter, Charles	Ensign, 13th Regiment	July 15, 1799
Porter, Charles	Captain, 13th Regiment	December 5, 1801
Porter, John	Lieutenant, 14th Regiment	May 6, 1803
Porther (Porter), Charles	Lieutenant, 13th Regiment	July 25, 1801
Potts, William	Lieutenant, 47th Regiment	March 20, 1801
Potts, William H.	Captain, 13th Regiment	July 25, 1801
Powel, Zenos	Ensign, 47th Regiment	May 22, 1801
Price, William	Ensign, Rifle Company, 13th Regiment	January 15, 1800
Ray, Francis	Lieutenant, 47th Regiment	July 4, 1798
	Recommissioned	August 7, 1801
Riggs, Erasmus	Lieutenant, 47th Regiment	January 22, 1802
Right, Jacob	Ensign, 13th Regiment	May 12, 1803
Riley, Leven	Captain, 47th Regiment	May 8, 1801
Roberts, Niely	Lieutenant of Cavalry, 14th Regiment	June 28, 1799
Robinson, Zephaniah	Lieutenant, 14th Regiment	December 28, 1801
Rule, Andrew	Captain, 47th Regiment	January 18, 1800
Rule, Matthew	Ensign, 47th Regiment	July 2, 1802
Rule, Samuel	Lieutenant, 47th Regiment	January 18, 1800
Rule, Thomas	Lieutenant Colonel, Commandant 47th Regiment	October 5, 1804
Ryley, Leven	Lieutenant, 14th Regiment	April 1, 1800
Sadler, Jesse	Captain, 13th Regiment	October 19, 1803
Scott, John	Captain, 14th Regiment	May 14, 1799
Scott, John	Captain, 14th Regiment	October 3, 1799
Scott, John	Major, 14th Regiment	December 19, 1800
Scott, John	Lieutenant Colonel, Commandant 14th Regiment	October 6, 1804
Scott, Robert	Lieutenant, 14th Regiment	October 3, 1799
Scott, Samuel	Lieutenant, 14th Regiment	June 21, 1802
Scott, Samuel	Captain, 14th Regiment	May 6, 1803
Scroggin, George	Ensign, 13th Regiment	July 25, 1801
Scrogin, Robert	Ensign, 13th Regiment	May 23, 1799
Scrogin, Robert	Lieutenant, 13th Regiment	January 15, 1801
Seever, Henry	Ensign, 14th Regiment	October 3, 1799

COMMISSIONED OFFICERS, 1799 - 1804

Selden, George	Surgeon, 13th Regiment	May 17, 1804
Shaughon (Shawhan), John	Captain, 13th Regiment	January 1, 1801
Shaw, William	Ensign, 13th Regiment	December 5, 1802
Shepherd, Abraham	Captain, 47th Regiment	March 20, 1801
Shortridge, George	Colonel, 14th Regiment	April 30, 1799
Shortridge, William	Ensign, 14th Regiment	January 16, 1804
Sites, John	Lieutenant, 14th Regiment	June 21, 1802
Smiser, John	Ensign, 14th Regiment	January 16, 1804
Smith, George	Captain, 13th Regiment	December 5, 1802
Smith, Jacob	Captain, 14th Regiment	April 1, 1800
Smith, Jacob J.	Captain, 14th Regiment	June 15, 1801
Smith, James	Lieutenant, 14th Regiment	March 4, 1801
Smith, Nathan	Captain, 13th Regiment	February 12, 1799
Smith, Weldon	2nd Lieutenant, 14th Regiment	October 3, 1799
Snap (?), George	Ensign, 13th Regiment	March 1, 1800
Snoddy, Abner	Ensign, 47th Regiment	May 25, 1804
Snodgrass, Benjamin	Captain, 47th Regiment	May 22, 1801
South, Weldon	Captain, Rifle Company, 47th Regiment	March 20, 1801
Spencer, John	Lieutenant, 14th Regiment	May 6, 1803
Spicer, Rawser	Lieutenant, 47th Regiment	January 18, 1800
Spicer, Rawser	Captain, 47th Regiment	May 22, 1801
Spurgen, David	Ensign, 14th Regiment	October 3, 1799
Spurgen, Zephan	Ensign, 14th Regiment	August 29, 1800
Starke, John, Jr.	Ensign, 14th Regiment	May 6, 1803
Stat, Robert	Captain, 14th Regiment	March 4, 1801
Stewart, John	Ensign, 14th Regiment	June 21, 1802
Stone, James	Ensign, 14th Regiment	March 4, 1801
Stone, James	Lieutenant, 14th Regiment	June 15, 1801
Strawder, George	Ensign, 13th Regiment	June 25, 1799
Strother, George	Captain, 13th Regiment	August 7, 1800
Stuart, John	Lieutenant, 14th Regiment	May 6, 1803
Summers, Daniel	Ensign, 13th Regiment	May 24, 1800
Sutton, William	1st Lieutenant of Cavalry, 13th Regiment	July 7, 1802
Talbot, Hugh	Major, 2nd Battalion, 13th Regiment	July 27, 1801
Talbot, John	Lieutenant, 14th Regiment	July 16, 1804
Tandy, Gabriel	Lieutenant, 14th Regiment	April 4, 1799
Taylor, Septim.	Lieutenant, Rifle Company, 13th Regiment	January 1, 1801
Thomas, Joseph	Lieutenant, 14th Regiment	October 3, 1799
Thompson, Daniel	Lieutenant, 13th Regiment	December 6, 1804
Thornton, Henry	Ensign, 47th Regiment	May 25, 1804
Todd, John	Ensign, 13th Regiment	June 18, 1799
Todd, John	Surgeon, 14th Regiment	May 30, 1800
Tolbert, Hugh	Captain, 13th Regiment	June 17, 1799
Tomkins, Tartin	Ensign of Infantry, 13th Regiment	June 17, 1799
Trotter, James	Captain, 14th Regiment	June 28, 1799
Trunnel, Basil	Ensign, 13th Regiment	January 1, 1801

Tucker, Elias.............	Lieutenant, 13th Regiment........	December 5, 1801
Turner, Richard..........	Ensign, 14th Regiment............	May 25, 1804
Tyra, Isom...............	Ensign, 13th Regiment............	July 25, 1801
Varnon, John.............	Lieutenant, 13th Regiment........	May 12, 1803
Vernon, John.............	Ensign, 13th Regiment............	May 22, 1802
Vimont, Lewis............	Ensign, Rifle Company, 13th Regiment.......................	May 22, 1802
Waggoner, John...........	Ensign, 13th Regiment............	December 6, 1804
Wallace, John............	Major, 14th Regiment.............	December 13, 1802
Waller, Thomas...........	Captain, 13th Regiment...........	June 17, 1799
Walls, John..............	Captain, 14th Regiment...........	June 21, 1802
Ward, Benjamin...........	Colonel, 47th Regiment...........	April 10, 1800
Ward, Thompson...........	Lieutenant, 47th Regiment........	May 25, 1804
Ware, James..............	Ensign, 47th Regiment............	July 2, 1802
Ware, James..............	Lieutenant, 47th Regiment........	May 25, 1803
Ware, Thompson...........	Captain, 13th Regiment...........	December 6, 1804
Washburn, Benjamin.......	Ensign, 13th Regiment............	July 25, 1801
Wells, Benjamin..........	Captain, 14th Regiment...........	April 1, 1800
Wells, John..............	Ensign, 13th Regiment............	February 12, 1799
West, Alvan..............	Lieutenant, 13th Regiment........	October 20, 1803
Whalley, Edward..........	Captain, 14th Regiment...........	March 4, 1801
Whaly, Edward............	Lieutenant, 14th Regiment........	August 29, 1800
Wiggs, Richard...........	Lieutenant, 14th Regiment........	January 16, 1804
Williams, John...........	Ensign, 47th Regiment............	October 4, 1800
Williams, Pope...........	Captain, 13th Regiment...........	December 28, 1801
Williams, Roger..........	Captain, 13th Regiment...........	January 15, 1800
Williams, Samuel.........	Captain, 14th Regiment...........	May 25, 1804
Wilson, Jacob............	Ensign, 13th Regiment............	May 17, 1804
Wright, Andrew...........	Ensign, 14th Regiment............	April 1, 1800
Wright, James............	Lieutenant, 14th Regiment........	April 1, 1800
Wright, James............	Captain, 14th Regiment...........	May 12, 1800
Wright, James............	Major, 2nd Battalion, 14th Regiment.......................	October 6, 1804
Wright, William..........	Ensign, 47th Regiment............	May 25, 1803
Yathey, Hen. (Henry Yeaky?)...	Ensign, 14th Regiment.......	April 1, 1800
Young, David.............	Ensign, 47th Regiment............	May 22, 1801
Young, David.............	Lieutenant, 47th Regiment........	May 25, 1803

Breckinridge County Regiment

[Laid off December 10, 1804]

Kincheloe, Thomas........	Major, 2nd Battalion, 59th Regiment.......................	December 13, 1804
Pate, John...............	Major, 1st Battalion, 59th Regiment.......................	December 13, 1804
Walker, John.............	Lieutenant Colonel, Commandant 59th Regiment.................	December 13, 1804

COMMISSIONED OFFICERS, 1799 - 1804

Bullitt County Regiment

[First commissions July 12, 1799]

Alexander, James.........	Lieutenant, 32nd Regiment........	September 1, 1803
Anderson, Thomas.........	Ensign, 32nd Regiment............	August 7, 1800
Bishop, Laurence.........	Ensign, 32nd Regiment............	August 7, 1800
Blanford, Walter.........	Lieutenant, 32nd Regiment........	September 1, 1803
Brashear, Nicholas.......	Major, 1st Battalion, 32nd Regiment......................	July 12, 1799
Brashear, Thomas C.	Major, 2nd Battalion, 32nd Regiment......................	July 13, 1799
Brown, Joseph............	Adjutant, 32nd Regiment..........	September 1, 1803
Campbell, Johnson........	Ensign, 32nd Regiment............	August 7, 1800
Chalfant, Abner..........	Captain, 32nd Regiment...........	September 1, 1803
Crist, Henry.............	Colonel, 32nd Regiment...........	July 12, 1799
Drake, Charles...........	Captain, 32nd Regiment...........	August 7, 1800
Gabriel, David...........	Lieutenant, 32nd Regiment........	August 7, 1800
Grable, David............	Captain, 32nd Regiment...........	November 23, 1803
Grayson, Frederick W. S..	Ensign, 32nd Regiment............	September 1, 1803
Griffin, Jesse...........	Ensign, 32nd Regiment............	September 1, 1803
Gunterman, Henry.........	Ensign, 32nd Regiment............	August 7, 1800
Hall, Austin.............	Ensign, 32nd Regiment............	September 1, 1803
Hall, John...............	Lieutenant, 32nd Regiment........	September 1, 1803
Hall, William............	Ensign, 32nd Regiment............	September 1, 1803
Harris, Zedekiah.........	Captain, 32nd Regiment...........	August 7, 1800
Hatfield, Thomas.........	Lieutenant, 32nd Regiment........	August 7, 1800
Hornback, John...........	Captain, 32nd Regiment...........	August 7, 1800
Huston, James............	Adjutant, 32nd Regiment..........	December 17, 1801
Lucas, Abraham...........	Lieutenant, 32nd Regiment........	August 7, 1800
Marquis, James...........	Captain, 32nd Regiment...........	August 7, 1800
Middleton, Thomas........	Ensign, 32nd Regiment............	November 23, 1803
Miles, Richard...........	Ensign, 32nd Regiment............	November 23, 1803
Nagerley, Peter..........	Lieutenant, 32nd Regiment........	November 23, 1803
Newkirk, William.........	Lieutenant, 32nd Regiment........	August 7, 1800
Orme, Moses..............	Lieutenant, 32nd Regiment........	August 7, 1800
Phelps, Guy..............	Captain, 32nd Regiment...........	September 1, 1803
Price, Isaac.............	Ensign, 32nd Regiment............	August 7, 1800
Price, Isaac.............	Lieutenant, 32nd Regiment........	November 23, 1803
Quick, Benjamin..........	Lieutenant, 32nd Regiment........	August 7, 1800
Quick, Benjamin..........	Captain, 32nd Regiment...........	September 1, 1803
Robards, Lewis...........	Quartermaster, 32nd Regiment.....	December 17, 1801
Scott, John..............	Ensign, 32nd Regiment............	August 7, 1800
Shain, Francis...........	Captain, 32nd Regiment...........	August 7, 1800
Shanklin, William........	Ensign, 32nd Regiment............	August 7, 1800
Sheppard, Adam...........	Paymaster, 32nd Regiment.........	December 16, 1800
Simmons, Griffith........	Ensign, 32nd Regiment............	August 7, 1800
Simmons, William.........	Captain, 32nd Regiment...........	August 7, 1800
Sparkes, Daniel..........	Major, 2nd Battalion, 32nd Regiment......................	December 18, 1799
Starks, William..........	Lieutenant, 32nd Regiment........	August 7, 1800

COMMISSIONED OFFICERS, 1799 - 1804

Summers, Benjamin........	Captain, 32nd Regiment...........	November 23, 1803
Waters, William..........	Captain, 32nd Regiment...........	August 7, 1800
Wilcox, Josiah...........	Lieutenant, 32nd Regiment........	August 7, 1800
Yorcum (Yocum), Matthias.	Captain, 32nd Regiment...........	August 7, 1800

Campbell County Regiment

Allen, Nesbit............	Ensign, 21st Regiment............	September 21, 1802
Beall, Benjamin..........	Lieutenant, 21st Regiment........	January 19, 1801
Boner, Charles...........	Ensign, 21st Regiment............	October 3, 1803
Brackin, Jesse...........	Lieutenant, 21st Regiment........	January 19, 1801
Burch, Darius............	Ensign, 21st Regiment............	April 30, 1800
Cave, John...............	Ensign, 21st Regiment............	August 15, 1799
Childers, Henry..........	Ensign, 21st Regiment............	May 30, 1800
Christie, George.........	Captain, 21st Regiment...........	April 30, 1800
Coleman, Daniel..........	Ensign, 21st Regiment............	January 19, and May 30, 1801
Coleman, Thomas..........	Lieutenant, 21st Regiment........	September 21, 1802
Craig, Philip............	Lieutenant, 21st Regiment........	April 30, 1800
Creal, John..............	Ensign, 21st Regiment............	May 31, 1800
Daniel, Charles, Jr.	Quartermaster, 21st Regiment.....	December 19, 1801
Daniel, Vivian...........	Ensign, 21st Regiment............	January 19, 1801
Daniel, Vivian...........	Captain, 21st Regiment...........	September 21, 1802
Dehart, William..........	Captain, 21st Regiment...........	March 5, 1804
Depew, Abraham...........	Lieutenant, 21st Regiment........	August 15, 1799
Depew, Abraham...........	Captain, 21st Regiment...........	April 30, 1800
Depew, Abraham...........	Adjutant, 21st Regiment..........	December 22, 1803
Doty, Moses..............	Captain, 21st Regiment...........	May 30, 1800 and June 27, 1804
Duncan, Elias............	Lieutenant, 21st Regiment........	October 3, 1803
Duncan, Seth.............	Adjutant, 21st Regiment..........	November 4, 1801
Duncan, Willis...........	Ensign, 21st Regiment............	March 5, 1804
Ellis, James.............	Ensign, 21st Regiment............	October 8, 1801
Ellis, James.............	Lieutenant, 21st Regiment........	October 3, 1803
Flournoy, Francis........	Paymaster, 21st Regiment.........	November 20, 1801
Glenn, John..............	Ensign, 21st Regiment............	October 3, 1803
Glenn, Joseph............	Lieutenant, 21st Regiment........	January 19, 1801
Glenn, Joseph K.	Captain, 21st Regiment...........	October 8, 1801
Goodwin, James C.	Major, 2nd Battalion, 21st Regiment......................	December 19, 1800
Goodwin, James Coleman...	Lieutenant Colonel, Commandant 21st Regiment..................	December 20, 1804
Graves, Bartlett.........	Major, 1st Battalion, 21st Regiment......................	November 12, 1802
Griffin, Jeremiah........	Ensign, 21st Regiment............	October 3, 1803
Hawkins, Zadic...........	Ensign, 21st Regiment............	March 5, 1804
Highfield, Jeremiah......	Ensign, 21st Regiment............	March 5, 1804
Hume, Stripling..........	Lieutenant, 21st Regiment........	November 19, 1804
Johnson, Nelson..........	Ensign, 21st Regiment............	October 3, 1803
Johnson, Nelson..........	Captain, 21st Regiment...........	March 5, 1804

COMMISSIONED OFFICERS, 1799 - 1804   69

Landcaster, William......	Lieutenant, 21st Regiment........	March 5, 1804
Laneir, Alexander C. ...	Ensign, 21st Regiment............	June 27, 1804
Lynn, Nathan.............	Ensign, 21st Regiment............	October 3, 1803
McClanahan, Elijah.......	Lieutenant, 21st Regiment........	January 19, 1801
McClanahan, Elijah.......	Captain, 21st Regiment...........	October 3, 1803
McCray, William..........	Lieutenant, 21st Regiment........	October 8, 1801
McCray, William..........	Captain, 21st Regiment...........	October 3, 1803
McKay, Jacob.............	Lieutenant, 21st Regiment........	August 15, 1799
McLain, Daniel...........	Lieutenant, 21st Regiment........	January 19, 1801
Mann, John...............	Lieutenant, 21st Regiment........	September 21, 1802
Minor, Waller............	Ensign, 21st Regiment............	September 21, 1802
Mize, William............	Lieutenant, 21st Regiment........	May 30, 1801
Montjoy, William.........	Major, 2nd Battalion, 21st Regiment......................	December 20, 1804
Moore, Zachariah.........	Captain, 21st Regiment...........	January 19, 1801
Morgan, John.............	Captain, 21st Regiment...........	August 15, 1799
Morris, James............	Ensign, 21st Regiment............	August 8, 1804
Morris, James............	Lieutenant, 21st Regiment........	May 31, 1800
Mountjoy, William........	Captain, 21st Regiment...........	January 19, 1801
Moyars, Andrew...........	Ensign, 21st Regiment............	October 3, 1803
Mullen, Reuben...........	Ensign, 21st Regiment............	June 27, 1804
Nelson, Richard..........	Ensign, 21st Regiment............	March 5, 1804
Pettet, Amos.............	Ensign, 21st Regiment............	September 21, 1802
Porter, George...........	Lieutenant, 21st Regiment........	August 15, 1799
Robertson, William.......	Captain, 21st Regiment...........	January 19, 1801
Robertson, Zachariah.....	Lieutenant, 21st Regiment........	March 5, 1804
Sanders, William.........	Lieutenant, 21st Regiment........	September 21, 1802
Seward, Daniel...........	Captain, 21st Regiment...........	September 21, 1802
Sharp, John..............	Ensign, 21st Regiment............	January 19, 1801
Sharp, Richard...........	Captain, 21st Regiment...........	January 19, 1801
Shaw, John...............	Ensign, 21st Regiment............	January 19, 1801
Stewart, Jesse...........	Ensign, 21st Regiment............	January 19, 1801
Swart, John..............	Ensign, 21st Regiment............	October 3, 1803
Swords, Daniel...........	Lieutenant, 21st Regiment........	May 30, 1800
Thomison, John...........	Lieutenant, 21st Regiment........	October 3, 1803
Thrasher, Stephen........	Captain, 21st Regiment...........	May 31, 1800 and August 8, 1804
Thrasher, William........	Captain, 21st Regiment...........	October 8, 1801
Toomy, John..............	Adjutant, 21st Regiment..........	August 15, 1799
Van Horn, Thomas.........	Lieutenant, 21st Regiment........	August 8, 1804
White, John..............	Ensign, 21st Regiment............	August 15, 1799
Wilson, Samuel...........	Captain, 21st Regiment...........	October 3, 1803

Campbell and Boone Regiment

[Laid off December 13, 1800]

Alley, Samuel............	Lieutenant, 48th Regiment........	October 1, 1803
Baker, Henry.............	Captain, 48th Regiment...........	October 1, 1803
Berry, Washington........	Paymaster, 48th Regiment.........	September 23, 1801

COMMISSIONED OFFICERS, 1799 - 1804

Brasher, Charles.........	Ensign, 48th Regiment............	February 21, 1801
Bush, John...............	Quartermaster, 48th Regiment.....	June 14, 1801
Cain, Asael..............	Lieutenant, 48th Regiment........	September 23, 1801
Cave, John...............	Lieutenant, 48th Regiment........	June 14, 1801
Cleveland, Levi..........	Lieutenant, 48th Regiment........	February 21, 1801
Cleveland, Levi..........	Captain, 48th Regiment...........	September 23, 1801
Conner, Tristham.........	Lieutenant, 48th Regiment........	September 6, 1802
Cooper, John.............	Ensign, 48th Regiment............	September 23, 1801
Cooper, John.............	Lieutenant, 48th Regiment........	October 1, 1803
Crisler, Allen...........	Ensign, 48th Regiment............	September 23, 1801
Finnell, Robert..........	Lieutenant, 48th Regiment........	February 21, 1801
Garnet, Robert...........	Ensign, 48th Regiment............	February 21, 1801
Graves, Bartlett.........	Major, 1st Battalion, 48th Regiment (formerly of 21st Regiment).....................	December, 1806
Graves, Joseph...........	Ensign, 48th Regiment............	June 14, 1801
Hawkins, Jameson.........	Ensign, 48th Regiment............	June 14, 1801
Hogan, Elijah............	Ensign, 48th Regiment............	September 23, 1801
Hume, John...............	Ensign, 48th Regiment............	June 14, 1801
Johnson, Cave............	Major, 2nd Battalion, 48th Regiment.......................	December 19, 1800
Kennedy, Joseph..........	Ensign, 48th Regiment............	September 6, 1802
Lindsey, John............	Captain, 48th Regiment...........	October 16, 1801
Lowrie, William..........	Lieutenant, 48th Regiment........	February 21, 1801
Lowrie, William..........	Captain, 48th Regiment...........	October 16, 1801
Noble, James.............	Ensign, 48th Regiment............	October 1, 1803
Norman, Caleb............	Ensign, 48th Regiment............	September 23, 1801
Perry, David.............	Ensign, 48th Regiment............	February 28, 1801
Rees, David..............	Ensign, 48th Regiment............	October 1, 1803
Robinson, Stephen........	Ensign, 48th Regiment............	October 16, 1801
Rogers, William..........	Lieutenant, 48th Regiment........	February 21, 1801
Sandford, Thomas.........	Colonel, 48th Regiment...........	December 18, 1800
Seabury (Sebree), Uriel..	Captain, 48th Regiment...........	February 21, 1801
Sleet, Weeden............	Captain, 48th Regiment...........	February 21, 1801
Stewart, Christian P. ..	Captain, 48th Regiment...........	February 21, 1801
Talbot, James............	Captain, 48th Regiment...........	February 21, 1801
Taylor, Edmund...........	Lieutenant, 48th Regiment........	September 23, 1801
Taylor, James............	Major, 1st Battalion, 48th Regiment.......................	December 18, 1800
Thatcher, Daniel.........	Lieutenant, 48th Regiment........	June 14, 1801
Weaver, John.............	Ensign, 48th Regiment............	September 23, 1801
Weaver, John.............	Lieutenant, 48th Regiment........	October 16, 1801
Weaver, John.............	Captain, 48th Regiment...........	September 6, 1802

Christian County Regiment

[Laid off December 13, 1799]

Adams, James, Jr.	Captain, 39th Regiment...........	October 2, 1801
Adams, Jesse............	Lieutenant, 39th Regiment........	October 2, 1801

COMMISSIONED OFFICERS, 1799 - 1804 71

Adams, Matthew...........	Captain of Cavalry, 39th Regiment......................	April 16, 1802
Arthur, Thomas...........	Major, 2nd Battalion, 39th Regiment......................	December 13, 1802
Barnett, Thomas..........	Captain, 39th Regiment..........	April 16, 1802
Black, David.............	Cornet of Cavalry, 39th Regiment......................	April 16, 1802
Blackburn, William B. ...	Adjutant, 39th Regiment..........	December 17, 1800
Brown, George............	Adjutant, 39th Regiment..........	December 12, 1803
Campbell, Angus..........	Ensign, 39th Regiment............	October 2, 1801
Campbell, Benjamin.......	Ensign, 39th Regiment............	October 2, 1801
Campbell, Samuel.........	Ensign, 39th Regiment............	April 16, 1802
Castlebury, Paul.........	Ensign, 39th Regiment............	April 16, 1802
Cavenaugh, Charles.......	Lieutenant, 39th Regiment........	January 1, 1800
Cavenaugh, William.......	Ensign, 39th Regiment............	January 1, 1800
Cavenaugh, William.......	Lieutenant, 39th Regiment........	April 16, 1802
Cook, James..............	Ensign, 39th Regiment............	October 2, 1801
Cornelius, Jesse.........	Captain, 39th Regiment...........	October 2, 1801
Cornelius, Jesse.........	Major, 1st Battalion, 39th Regiment......................	December 20, 1803
Cotton, Benjamin.........	Ensign, 39th Regiment............	April 16, 1802
Dunlap, Benjamin.........	Lieutenant, 39th Regiment........	April 16, 1802
Edwards, Edward..........	Ensign, 39th Regiment............	December 12, 1803
Estes, Asa...............	Captain, 39th Regiment...........	December 12, 1803
Ewing, Young.............	Colonel, 39th Regiment...........	December 13, 1799
Ferguson, Peter..........	Quartermaster, 39th Regiment.....	December 17, 1800
Fort, Jesse..............	Ensign, 39th Regiment............	December 12, 1803
Gillehan, William........	Major, 2nd Battalion, 39th Regiment......................	December 13, 1799
Gray, John...............	Lieutenant of Cavalry, 39th Regiment......................	April 16, 1802
Grubbs, Isaac............	Lieutenant, 39th Regiment........	April 16, 1802
Hickman, Elijah..........	Lieutenant, 39th Regiment........	April 16, 1802
Hicks, Absolem...........	Ensign, 39th Regiment............	October 2, 1801
Hicks, Absolem...........	Captain, 39th Regiment...........	April 16, 1802
Hicks, Henry.............	Lieutenant, 39th Regiment........	April 16, 1802
Hicks, Willis............	Captain, 39th Regiment...........	April 16, 1802
Jameson, Andrew..........	Ensign, 39th Regiment............	April 16, 1802
Linn, Joseph.............	Lieutenant, 39th Regiment........	April 16, 1802
Means, Robert............	Ensign, 39th Regiment............	October 2, 1801
Neeley, Andrew...........	Paymaster, 39th Regiment.........	December 17, 1800
Park, Samuel.............	Lieutenant, 39th Regiment........	April 16, 1802
Pyle, William............	Surgeon, 39th Regiment...........	March 20, 1800
Reeves, James............	Ensign, 39th Regiment............	April 16, 1802
Skinner, Theopolis.......	Lieutenant, 39th Regiment........	December 12, 1803
Skinner, William.........	Captain, 39th Regiment...........	December, 1802
Smiley, Hugh.............	Captain, 39th Regiment...........	April 16, 1802
Stewart, Abraham.........	Major, 1st Battalion, 39th Regiment......................	December 13, 1799
Stewart, Abraham.........	Colonel, 39th Regiment...........	December 13, 1802
Thompson, John...........	Captain, 39th Regiment...........	January 1, 1800

COMMISSIONED OFFICERS, 1799 - 1804

Wadlington, Ferdinand....	Captain, 39th Regiment..........	April 16, 1802
Wallace, John............	Ensign, 39th Regiment............	April 16, 1802
Waller, Pleasant.........	Lieutenant, 39th Regiment........	January 1, 1800
Willis, Wilson...........	Ensign, 39th Regiment............	April 16, 1802
Woolf, Lewis.............	Lieutenant, 39th Regiment........	October 2, 1801

Clark County Regiments

[36th Regiment laid off December 5, 1799]

Anderson, Matthew........	Lieutenant, 17th Regiment........	April 30, 1800
Bean, John...............	Ensign, 36th Regiment............	January 27, 1801
Bean, John...............	Lieutenant, 36th Regiment........	December 31, 1802
Bean, John...............	Captain, 36th Regiment...........	October 17, 1803
Blackwell, Benjamin......	Lieutenant, 36th Regiment........	May 12, 1800
Boks (Box), James........	Ensign, 17th Regiment............	January 21, 1800
Box, James...............	Lieutenant, 17th Regiment........	October 26, 1802
Brasfield, Wiley.........	Captain, 36th Regiment...........	May 29, 1800
Bristoe, Archibald.......	Ensign, 36th Regiment............	October 17, 1803
Browning, James..........	Captain, 17th Regiment...........	April 12, 1799
Bryan, Jonathan..........	Ensign, 36th Regiment............	December 31, 1802
Burges, Nicholas.........	Lieutenant, 17th Regiment........	May 20, 1800
Bush, Gholsen............	Ensign, 17th Regiment............	November 17, 1804
Bush, Philip.............	Captain, 17th Regiment...........	August 9, 1792
	Recommissioned	December 1, 1803
Chiles, Henry............	Captain, 17th Regiment...........	February 10, 1800
Chiles, Henry............	Captain, 36th Regiment...........	May 30, 1800
Christy, Ambrose.........	Captain, 17th Regiment...........	June 14, 1798
Christy, John............	Lieutenant, 17th Regiment........	October 26, 1802
Clark, Joseph............	Lieutenant, 17th Regiment........	August 2, 1802
Clarke, Robert, Jr.	Major, 1st Battalion, 36th Regiment......................	December 5, 1799
Collins, Dillard.........	Captain, 17th Regiment...........	November 12, 1799
Cornum, John.............	Lieutenant, 17th Regiment........	January 21, 1800
Crabtree, Isaac..........	Captain, 17th Regiment...........	January 1, 1798
		(Elected August 10, 1795)
Crump, Hally.............	Lieutenant, 17th Regiment........	November 12, 1799
Cunningham, Robert.......	Captain, 36th Regiment...........	May 5, 1800
Daniel, Archibald........	Ensign, 17th Regiment............	November 26, 1799
Daniel, Beverly..........	Captain, 17th Regiment...........	November 26, 1799
Daniel, James............	Ensign, 17th Regiment............	September 15, 1804
Daniel, Peter............	Quartermaster, 17th Regiment.....	April 26, 1800
Deal, John...............	Lieutenant, 17th Regiment........	August 3, 1803
Denton, David............	Ensign, 17th Regiment............	January 30, 1800
Donaldson, John..........	Major, 2nd Battalion, 36th Regiment......................	December 6, 1799
Dooley, John.............	Captain, 17th Regiment...........	August 7, 1798
Douglas, John............	Ensign, 36th Regiment............	January 27, 1801
Embre, Thomas............	Lieutenant, 17th Regiment........	May 20, 1800
Embry, Caleb.............	Lieutenant, 17th Regiment........	May 18, 1803

COMMISSIONED OFFICERS, 1799 - 1804 73

Eubank, Achilles.........	Major, 17th Regiment.............	December 5, 1799
Eubank, Ambrose..........	Lieutenant, 17th Regiment........	August 2, 1802
Frame, William...........	Captain, 17th Regiment...........	January 30, 1800
Garner, Churchill........	Lieutenant, 17th Regiment........	September 15, 1804
Goosey, Peter............	Ensign, 17th Regiment............	August 7, 1798
Grant, Robert............	Ensign, 36th Regiment............	May 5, 1800
Grigsby, Lewis...........	Quartermaster, 17th Regiment.....	May 24, 1802
Hally, William...........	Ensign, 17th Regiment............	April 30, 1800
Halsey (Halsell), Reason.	Ensign, 17th Regiment............	August 2, 1802
Haney, Henry.............	Ensign, 17th Regiment............	September 27, 1799
Haney, Henry.............	Ensign, 36th Regiment Recommissioned................	September 16, 1800
Hanks, Absolem...........	Ensign, 36th Regiment............	October 17, 1803
Hardy, Andrew............	Lieutenant, 17th Regiment........	August 7, 1798
Hickman, Joel............	Paymaster, 17th Regiment.........	November 21, 1800
Hickman, Richard.........	Colonel, 17th Regiment...........	April 12, 1799
Holliday, John...........	Adjutant, 17th Regiment..........	April 26, 1800
Holly, William...........	Ensign, 36th Regiment............	May 30, 1800
	(Originally commissioned for 17th Regiment)	
Hood, Lucas..............	Ensign, 36th Regiment............	May 29, 1802
Hood, Luke...............	Lieutenant, 36th Regiment........	October 17, 1803
Hoy, Jones...............	Ensign, 17th Regiment............	September 15, 1804
Kelly, Joseph............	Ensign, 36th Regiment............ Recommissioned................	October 29, 1798 August 16, 1800
Kelly, Joseph............	Lieutenant, 36th Regiment........	January 27, 1801
Kincaid, James...........	Ensign, 17th Regiment............	November 17, 1804
Kishner, Jacob...........	Ensign, 17th Regiment............	May 20, 1800
Lyle, Daniel.............	Ensign, Rifle Company, 17th Regiment......................	June 14, 1798
McCargo, Radford.........	Captain, 17th Regiment...........	October 14, 1796
	(Issued September, 1800)	
McCargo, Radford.........	Captain, 36th Regiment........... Recommissioned................	October 14, 1796 September 16, 1800
McCrary, Andrew..........	Lieutenant, 17th Regiment........	September 15, 1804
McGuire, William.........	Captain, 17th Regiment...........	March 4, 1803
McMahan, Joseph..........	Ensign, 17th Regiment............	September 15, 1804
McMillen, William........	Major, 1st Battalion, 36th Regiment......................	October 9, 1804
McMillion, William.......	Captain, 36th Regiment........... Recommissioned................	May 5, 1795 August 16, 1800
Martin, Job..............	Lieutenant, 17th Regiment........	June 14, 1798
Martin, John.............	Captain, 17th Regiment...........	August 3, 1803
Merrel, Andrew...........	Lieutenant, 17th Regiment........	September 27, 1799
Merton, Jonathan.........	Ensign, Rifle Company, 17th Regiment......................	November 12, 1799
Moore, Henry.............	Lieutenant, 17th Regiment........	October 26, 1802
Morgan, William..........	Ensign, 17th Regiment............	November 17, 1804
Morrow, John.............	Ensign, 17th Regiment............	April 12, 1799
Morton, Jonathan.........	Ensign, 17th Regiment............	October 26, 1802
Murrell, Andrew..........	Lieutenant, 36th Regiment........ Recommissioned................	October 14, 1796 September 16, 1800

COMMISSIONED OFFICERS, 1799 - 1804

Oldham, John..............	Captain, 17th Regiment............	January 21, 1800
Oldham, William..........	Ensign, 17th Regiment............	October 26, 1802
Pendleton, Curtis........	Ensign, 17th Regiment............	May 20, 1800
Railsback, Daniel........	Ensign, 17th Regiment............	November 17, 1804
Rankin, Benjamin.........	Lieutenant, 17th Regiment........	November 26, 1799
Rennick, George..........	Lieutenant, 36th Regiment........	May 5, 1800
Ritchea, Alexander.......	Lieutenant, 36th Regiment........	May 5, 1795
	Recommissioned.................	August 16, 1800
Ritchea, George..........	Ensign, 36th Regiment............	May 5, 1795
	Recommissioned.................	August 16, 1800
Rogers, Ezekiel..........	Lieutenant, 17th Regiment........	February 10, 1800
Rogers, Ezekiel..........	Lieutenant, 36th Regiment........	May 30, 1800
Rusk, William............	Ensign, 17th Regiment............	October 26, 1802
Scoby, Stephen...........	Ensign, 36th Regiment............	December 25, 1801
Scott, Moses.............	Lieutenant, 17th Regiment........	August 2, 1802
Sharp, George............	Captain, 17th Regiment............	May 20, 1800
Skinner, Cornelius.......	Captain, 17th Regiment............	April 30, 1800
Skinner, Cornelius.......	Captain, 36th Regiment............	May 30, 1800
Stephens, James..........	Major, 17th Regiment.............	June 15, 1803
Stroud, Stephen..........	Lieutenant, 36th Regiment........	October 29, 1798
	Recommissioned.................	August 16, 1800
Sudduth, William.........	Colonel, 36th Regiment...........	December 5, 1799
Taylor, George G.	Paymaster, 36th Regiment........	December 20, 1800
Taylor, Hubbard..........	Quartermaster, 36th Regiment.....	December 20, 1800
Thompson, David..........	Ensign, 17th Regiment............	February 10, 1800
Thompson, David..........	Ensign, 36th Regiment............	May 30, 1800
Thompson, David..........	Lieutenant, 36th Regiment........	December 25, 1801
Thompson, Neil...........	Lieutenant, 17th Regiment........	January 30, 1800
Watts, Julius............	Ensign, 17th Regiment............	September 15, 1804
Webb, George.............	Adjutant, 36th Regiment..........	December 20, 1800
White, William...........	Ensign, 17th Regiment............	August 3, 1803
Wilson, Matthew..........	Ensign, 36th Regiment............	December 31, 1802
Wilson, Matthew..........	Lieutenant, 36th Regiment........	October 17, 1803
Worker (?), Robert.......	Ensign, 17th Regiment............	March 4, 1803

Cumberland County Regiment

[Laid off December 24, 1799]

Acrey, David.............	Ensign, 46th Regiment............	September 12, 1803
Allen, John..............	Captain, 2nd Battalion, 46th Regiment......................	May 16, 1800
Allen, John..............	Major, 2nd Battalion, 46th Regiment......................	December 19, 1801
Allen, Nathan............	Lieutenant, 46th Regiment........	May 28, 1803
Anthill, Henry...........	Ensign, 1st Battalion, 46th Regiment......................	May 20, 1800
Bec(k), Edward...........	Ensign, 46th Regiment............	December 8, 1801
Brunts, Peter............	Ensign, 1st Battalion, 46th Regiment......................	May 20, 1800

COMMISSIONED OFFICERS, 1799 - 1804   75

Burks, Charles............	Ensign, 2nd Battalion, 46th Regiment......................	May 16, 1800
Burks, Charles...........	Lieutenant, 46th Regiment........	June 1, 1802
Burriss, David...........	Captain, 2nd Battalion, 46th Regiment......................	May 16, 1800
Butler, Thomas...........	Ensign, 2nd Battalion, 46th Regiment......................	May 16, 1800
Campbell, James..........	Ensign, 46th Regiment............	September 5, 1802
Campbell, James..........	Lieutenant, 46th Regiment........	April 12, 1804
Carpenter, Jesse.........	Ensign, 46th Regiment............	April 12, 1804
Chrisman, Joseph.........	Adjutant, 46th Regiment..........	June 1, 1802
Clift, Daniel............	Lieutenant, 46th Regiment........	September 5, 1802
Cloyd, Thomas............	Captain, 46th Regiment...........	February 21, 1801
Cloyd, Thomas............	Major, 2nd Battalion, 46th Regiment......................	April 7, 1803
Cope, John...............	Captain, 46th Regiment...........	September 5, 1802
Cope, John...............	Major, 1st Battalion, 46th Regiment......................	December 21, 1803
Cowan, John..............	Lieutenant, 46th Regiment........	March 31, 1803
Davis, John..............	Ensign, 1st Battalion, 46th Regiment......................	May 20, 1800
Dean, Robert.............	Ensign, 46th Regiment............	September 5, 1802
Enyart, Abraham..........	Ensign, 46th Regiment............	April 12, 1804
Evans, William...........	Ensign, 2nd Battalion, 46th Regiment......................	May 16, 1800
Fergus, James............	Quartermaster, 46th Regiment.....	September 5, 1802
Frogg, Arthur............	Lieutenant, 46th Regiment........	April 12, 1804
Frogg, Arthur............	Captain, 46th Regiment...........	September 5, 1802
Gee, John................	Lieutenant, 46th Regiment........	September 5, 1802
Gibbons, James...........	Captain, 1st Battalion, 46th Regiment......................	May 20, 1800
Glascock, Charnal........	Lieutenant, 46th Regiment........	February 21, 1801
Goodson, William.........	Captain, 46th Regiment...........	December 8, 1801
Goodson, William, Jr. ..	Ensign, 46th Regiment............	March 14, 1803
Graves, Thomas...........	Captain, 46th Regiment...........	April 12, 1804
Hall, James..............	Lieutenant, 46th Regiment........	April 12, 1804
Hall, William............	Lieutenant, 2nd Battalion, 46th Regiment......................	May 16, 1800
Heard, John..............	Ensign, 46th Regiment............	September 5, 1802
Huff, Daniel.............	Lieutenant, 1st Battalion, 46th Regiment......................	May 20, 1800
Huff, Daniel.............	Captain, 46th Regiment...........	September 5, 1802
Hull, James..............	Ensign, 46th Regiment............	May 28, 1803
Johnson, Thomas..........	Captain, 1st Battalion, 46th Regiment......................	May 20, 1800
Jones, David.............	Captain, 1st Battalion, 46th Regiment......................	May 20, 1800
Journey, Nathaniel.......	Lieutenant, 2nd Battalion, 46th Regiment......................	May 16, 1800
Journey, Nathaniel.......	Captain, 46th Regiment...........	June 1, 1802

COMMISSIONED OFFICERS, 1799 - 1804

Jump, Peter	Captain, 2nd Battalion, 46th Regiment	May 16, 1800
Jurney, John	Ensign, 46th Regiment	June 1, 1802
Jurney, John	Lieutenant, 46th Regiment	September 12, 1803
King, John E.	Colonel, 46th Regiment	December 14, 1801
Kirkpatrick, Elihu	Lieutenant, 2nd Battalion, 46th Regiment	May 16, 1800
Kirkpatrick, Elihu	Captain, 46th Regiment	February 27, 1801
Lincoln, Thomas	Ensign, 46th Regiment	September 5, 1802
Long, John	Ensign, 1st Battalion, 46th Regiment	May 20, 1800
Long, John	Lieutenant, 46th Regiment	September 5, 1802
Long, John	Captain, 46th Regiment	April 12, 1804
Long, Solomon	Lieutenant, 46th Regiment	April 12, 1804
McConnel, James	Captain, 46th Regiment	September 5, 1802
McDonnald, John	Captain, 46th Regiment	September 5, 1802
McFarland, Alexander	Colonel, 46th Regiment	July 13, 1801
Martin, Nathaniel	Adjutant, 46th Regiment	May 20, 1800
Miller, Person	Ensign, 46th Regiment	September 5, 1802
Nichols, Edward	Ensign, 46th Regiment	April 12, 1804
Obannon, John	Ensign, 2nd Battalion, 46th Regiment	May 16, 1800
Philips, John	Lieutenant, 1st Battalion, 46th Regiment	May 20, 1800
Phillips, John, Jr	Captain, 46th Regiment	March 14, 1803
Pickens, Samuel	Captain, 1st Battalion, 46th Regiment	May 20, 1800
Pickens, Samuel	Major, 46th Regiment	July 13, 1801
Poague, Robert	Lieutenant, 46th Regiment	December 8, 1801
Preas (Priest), William	Lieutenant, 1st Battalion, 46th Regiment	May 20, 1800
Ray, Thomas	Ensign, 46th Regiment	February 21, 1801
Richardson, Isaac	Ensign, 46th Regiment	September 5, 1802
Ritchey, John	Captain, 46th Regiment	May 28, 1803
Robinson, John	Ensign, 1st Battalion, 46th Regiment	May 20, 1800
Semple, John W.	Surgeon, 46th Regiment	April 12, 1804
Smith, William	Lieutenant, 2nd Battalion, 46th Regiment	May 16, 1800
Stepenson, Andrew	Lieutenant, 1st Battalion, 46th Regiment	May 20, 1800
Stephens, Peter	Captain, 2nd Battalion, 46th Regiment	May 16, 1800
Swope, George	Captain, 46th Regiment	April 12, 1804
Taylor, Isaac	Paymaster, 46th Regiment	September 5, 1802
Thomas, Henry	Ensign, 46th Regiment	April 12, 1804
Turney, John	Captain, 1st Battalion, 46th Regiment	May 20, 1800
Wallace, Jonathan	Lieutenant, 46th Regiment	May 28, 1803
Wells, William	Lieutenant, 1st Battalion, 46th Regiment	May 20, 1800

COMMISSIONED OFFICERS, 1799 - 1804   77

Williams, Ezekiel........	Captain, 46th Regiment...........	July 9, 1804
Williams, James..........	Ensign, 46th Regiment............	May 28, 1803
Wilson, James............	Ensign, 46th Regiment............	May 28, 1803
Wilson, Samuel...........	Captain, 46th Regiment...........	June 1, 1802
Wisdom, Francis..........	Lieutenant, 46th Regiment........	February 27, 1801

Fayette County Regiments

[42nd Regiment laid off December 16, 1799]

Abernethy, Blackston....	Ensign, 8th Regiment.............	November 20, 1799
Abernethy, Blackston.....	Lieutenant, 8th Regiment.........	April 1, 1800
Abernethy, Braxton.......	Captain, 8th Regiment............	September 15, 1800
Adams, Absalom...........	Captain, 8th Regiment............	March 1, 1800
Anderson, William........	Ensign, 10th Regiment............	May 22, 1800
Anderson, William........	Lieutenant, 10th Regiment........	September 29, 1800
Andrews, George..........	Lieutenant, 8th Regiment.........	September 15, 1800
Atcheson, John...........	Ensign, 42nd Regiment............	May 15, 1802
Ayres, Burton............	Lieutenant, Rifle Company, 42nd Regiment..................	March 22, 1804
Ayres, Samuel............	Captain, 42nd Regiment...........	July 2, 1800
Banks, Cuthbert..........	Captain, 42nd Regiment...........	June 21, 1799
	Recommissioned..................	July 2, 1800
Barnes, Neariah..........	Ensign, 42nd Regiment............	December 3, 1798
	Recommissioned..................	May 12, 1800
Barnes, Uriah............	Ensign, 42nd Regiment............	May 15, 1802
Barr, Thomas T.	Ensign, 8th Regiment.............	May 25, 1804
Bass, George.............	Lieutenant, 42nd Regiment........	December 4, 1803
Baxter, James............	Ensign, 8th Regiment.............	July 20, 1804
Beatty, Adam.............	Quartermaster, 42nd Regiment.....	May 11, 1801
Beatty, Cornelius........	Colonel, 42nd Regiment...........	December 16, 1799
Beatty, Edward...........	Lieutenant, 10th Regiment........	June 28, 1799
Bell, John, Sr.	Captain, Rifle Company, 42nd Regiment.......................	April 3, 1800
Benning, Levi............	Lieutenant, 8th Regiment.........	September 12, 1804
Berry, Benjamin..........	Captain, 42nd Regiment...........	July 2, 1800
Berry, James.............	Lieutenant, 42nd Regiment........	April 3, 1800
Biggs, Andrew............	Ensign, 42nd Regiment............	September 9, 1800
Bledsoe, Richard.........	Ensign, 8th Regiment.............	June 16, 1803
Bobb, John...............	Lieutenant, 42nd Regiment........	July 2, 1800
Bodley, Thomas...........	Ensign, Infantry Company, 42nd Regiment..................	May 11, 1801
Bodley, Thomas...........	Captain, 42nd Regiment...........	December 17, 1803
Bohannon, William........	Ensign, 10th Regiment............	September 19, 1802
Boswell, Joseph..........	Surgeon's Mate, 8th Regiment.....	April 9, 1799
Boswell, Joseph..........	Surgeon, 42nd Regiment...........	April 1, 1800
Bradley, Hezekiah........	Lieutenant, 8th Regiment.........	October 2, 1800
Brooke, William..........	Ensign, 10th Regiment............	March 15, 1801
Brown, John..............	Ensign, Rifle Company, 42nd Regiment.......................	March 22, 1804

COMMISSIONED OFFICERS, 1799 - 1804

Bryan, Enoch	Ensign, 8th Regiment	May 12, 1804
Bryan, Ezekiel	2nd Lieutenant, 8th Regiment	May 12, 1804
Bryan, Ezekiel	1st Lieutenant of Cavalry, 8th Regiment	July 20, 1804
Caldwell, George	Captain, 10th Regiment	November 12, 1799
Campbell, John	Ensign, Rifle Company, 42nd Regiment	March 22, 1804
Carr, Charles	Lieutenant, 8th Regiment	July 24, 1802
Cassel, Jacob	Ensign, 10th Regiment	March 15, 1801
Chinn, William	Captain, 10th Regiment	March 3, 1799
Chinn, William	Major, 1st Battalion, 10th Regiment	December 18, 1799
Christian, William	Ensign, 8th Regiment	July 4, 1801
Clarke, William	Ensign, 42nd Regiment	September 12, 1803
Cockerhill, Joseph	Ensign, 8th Regiment	July 20, 1804
Coons, Frederick	Ensign, 8th Regiment	December 5, 1800
Cord, James	Ensign, 10th Regiment	April 9, 1804
Crockett, Newbold	Ensign, 10th Regiment	October 2, 1804
Curd, Price	Ensign, 42nd Regiment	May 15, 1802
Curd, Price	Lieutenant, 42nd Regiment	December 17, 1803
Curtner, Henry	Captain, 42nd Regiment	September 12, 1803
Darnaby, Edward	Captain, 8th Regiment	September 15, 1800
Darnaby, John	Adjutant, 8th Regiment	September 20, 1802
Daunton, Richard	Lieutenant, 10th Regiment	March 16, 1800
Davenport, William	Major, 8th Regiment	October 4, 1799
Deadmon, Richard	Colonel, 42nd Regiment	December 9, 1803
Dedmon, Richmond	Major, 2nd Battalion, 42nd Regiment	December 17, 1799
Dickenson, Thomas	Lieutenant, 10th Regiment	November 12, 1799
Dickerson, Thomas J.	Lieutenant, 10th Regiment	March 15, 1801
Dohorty, John	Ensign, 10th Regiment	September 29, 1800
Dorsey, William	Ensign, 42nd Regiment	July 2, 1800
Dudley, Benjamin	Surgeon's Mate, 8th Regiment	July 16, 1803
Dudley, Robert	Captain, 8th Regiment	October 2, 1800
Dudley, William	Ensign, 8th Regiment	December 1, 1800
Dudley, William	Colonel, 8th Regiment	December 24, 1799
Dudley, William E.	Lieutenant, 8th Regiment	May 12, 1804
Dunn, Bartemus	Ensign, 8th Regiment	September 12, 1804
Elder, Matthew	Ensign, 42nd Regiment	May 12, 1800
Elder, Matthew	Lieutenant, 42nd Regiment	September 12, 1803
Ellis, Hezekiah	Ensign, 8th Regiment	June 16, 1803
Ellis, Hezekiah	Lieutenant, 8th Regiment	September 3, 1803
Ellis, Littlebury	Captain, 8th Regiment	May 20, 1799
Epperson, Robert	Ensign, 8th Regiment	July 24, 1802
Ewing, Andrew	Ensign, Rifle Company, 10th Regiment	June 28, 1799
Farguson, John	Lieutenant, 8th Regiment	September 12, 1804
Fauntleroy, John	Lieutenant, 42nd Regiment	December 4, 1803
Fishback, Dr. James	Surgeon, 8th Regiment	July 16, 1803
Foley, Elijah	Lieutenant, 42nd Regiment	April 3, 1800
Franks, John	Ensign, 8th Regiment	August 14, 1800

COMMISSIONED OFFICERS, 1799 - 1804

Frary, James..............	Cornet, 8th Regiment.............	October 13, 1802
Frye, Joseph..............	Ensign, 10th Regiment............	March 15, 1801
Garrett, Thomas...........	Ensign, 10th Regiment............	May 18, 1802
Gatewood, John............	Lieutenant, 42nd Regiment........	November 10, 1796
	Recommissioned................	May 12, 1800
Gowdy, Andrew.............	Ensign, 10th Regiment............	March 15, 1801
Graves, Benjamin..........	Major, 2nd Battalion, 8th Regiment......................	July 10, 1804
Graves, John..............	Ensign, 10th Regiment............	November 12, 1799
Graves, John..............	Lieutenant, 10th Regiment........	October 31, 1801
Greenwood, Nimrod.........	Ensign, 42nd Regiment............	December 4, 1800
Grimes, Charles...........	Captain, 8th Regiment............	July 20, 1804
Hamilton, Robert..........	Ensign, 10th Regiment............	June 28, 1799
Hanback, William..........	Lieutenant, 8th Regiment.........	September 15, 1800
Harris, Archibald.........	Ensign, 10th Regiment............	December 6, 1804
Hart, John................	Lieutenant, 8th Regiment.........	September 3, 1803
Hayes, William............	Captain, 42nd Regiment...........	September 12, 1803
Heddington, Joshua........	Ensign, 42nd Regiment............	December 7, 1802
Higgins, Stout............	Ensign, 10th Regiment............	May 18, 1802
Higgins, Stout............	Lieutenant, 10th Regiment........	August 23, 1803
Hodg, Nathan..............	Ensign, Rifle Company, 8th Regiment......................	September 12, 1804
Holeman, John.............	Ensign, 10th Regiment............	May 28, 1804
Hudson, Joseph............	Ensign, Rifle Company, 42nd Regiment......................	September 9, 1800
Hudson, Joseph............	Lieutenant, 42nd Regiment........	December 17, 1803
Hundly, Nelson............	Lieutenant, 8th Regiment.........	May 9, 1799
Hunly, Nelson.............	Lieutenant, 8th Regiment.........	May 20, 1799
Hunt, John W.	Quartermaster, 42nd Regiment.....	July 16, 1803
Hutcheson, Archibald......	Lieutenant, 10th Regiment........	April 9, 1804
January, James B.	Cornet, 42nd Regiment............	June 21, 1799
	Recommissioned................	August 18, 1800
January, James B.	Ensign, 10th Regiment............	October 31, 1801
January, James B.	Lieutenant, 10th Regiment........	May 18, 1802
Johnson, James W.	Lieutenant, 8th Regiment.........	May 25, 1804
Johnson, James W.	Captain, 8th Regiment............	July 20, 1804
Johnson, Oralea...........	Ensign, 8th Regiment.............	April 1, 1800
Jones, John...............	Captain, 8th Regiment............	August 14, 1800
Keen, John................	Lieutenant, 10th Regiment........	March 15, 1801
Keene, Oliver.............	Lieutenant, 42nd Regiment........	May 14, 1804
Keizer, Christopher.......	Captain, 42nd Regiment...........	December 17, 1803
Kenny, James..............	Cornet of Cavalry, 8th Regiment..	July 20, 1804
Kizer, Jacob..............	Lieutenant, 10th Regiment........	October 31, 1801
Kyle, Samuel..............	Ensign, 10th Regiment............	June 28, 1799
Kyser, Christopher........	Lieutenant, Rifle Company, 42nd Regiment.................	July 2, 1800
Lamm, Jesse...............	Ensign, 42nd Regiment............	March 22, 1804
Laughland, John...........	2nd Lieutenant of Cavalry, 8th Regiment...................	July 20, 1804
Ledford, James............	Ensign, 42nd Regiment............	December 4, 1803
Lemon, James..............	Lieutenant, 10th Regiment........	October 2, 1804

COMMISSIONED OFFICERS, 1799 - 1804

Linginfelter, Jacob......	Lieutenant, 42nd Regiment........	May 11, 1801
Lock, Richard S.	Lieutenant, 8th Regiment.........	July 20, 1804
Longan, Thomas...........	Captain, 10th Regiment...........	June 28, 1799
Loughland, John..........	Cornet, 8th Regiment.............	May 12, 1804
Lowry, John..............	Ensign, Rifle Company, 42nd Regiment......................	July 2, 1800
McAnn (McCann), Neal.....	Ensign, 8th Regiment.............	March 1, 1800
McCall, John.............	2nd Lieutenant of Cavalry, 8th Regiment......................	August 14, 1800
McCall, John.............	1st Lieutenant of Cavalry, 8th Regiment......................	October 13, 1802
McCall, John.............	Captain of Artillery, 8th Regiment......................	July 20, 1804
McCann, Neal.............	Lieutenant, 8th Regiment.........	December 1, 1800
McConnel, James..........	Lieutenant, 10th Regiment........	March 1, 1800
McFeters, William........	Lieutenant, 42nd Regiment........	May 14, 1804
Mason, Pet.	Ensign, 8th Regiment.............	May 20, 1800
Masterson, Aaron.........	Ensign, 10th Regiment............	October 31, 1801
Montgomery, Elijah.......	Ensign, 8th Regiment.............	September 3, 1803
Montgomery, Robinson.....	2nd Lieutenant of Cavalry, 8th Regiment...................:......	October 13, 1802
Moore, James.............	Chaplain, 42nd Regiment..........	July 16, 1803
Moore, William...........	Ensign, 10th Regiment............	October 31, 1801
Moore, William...........	Lieutenant, William Stephenson's Company, 10th Regiment.........	April 9, 1804
Morfult (Moffett?), George	Captain, 10th Regiment.........	May 28, 1804
Morris, John.............	Lieutenant, George Caldwell's Company, 10th Regiment.........	April 9, 1804
Morrison, Archibald......	Lieutenant, Rifle Company, 8th Regiment......................	September 12, 1804
Morrison, Robert.........	Ensign, 42nd Regiment............	May 14, 1804
Morton, William..........	Paymaster, 42nd Regiment.........	June 1, 1801
Muldrough, Hugh..........	Major, 1st Battalion, 10th Regiment......................	August 2, 1799
Nancarrow, Benjamin......	Ensign, 42nd Regiment............	December 17, 1803
Oliver, Joseph...........	Lieutenant, 42nd Regiment........	December 17, 1803
Orr, James...............	Ensign, 10th Regiment............	September 23, 1800
Orr, James...............	Lieutenant, 10th Regiment........	October 31, 1801
Overton, Archibald.......	Captain, 8th Regiment............	May 25, 1804
Oxley, Micajah...........	Ensign, 10th Regiment............	September 19, 1802
Oxley, Micajah...........	Lieutenant, 10th Regiment........	October 2, 1804
Parker, Alexander........	Major, 1st Battalion, 42nd Regiment......................	July 2, 1800
Patterson, George........	Ensign, 10th Regiment............	September 19, 1802
Porter, Ephraim..........	Captain, 42nd Regiment...........	December 3, 1798
	Recommissioned.................	May 12, 1800
Porter, John.............	Ensign, 10th Regiment............	August 23, 1803
Porter, William..........	Major, 2nd Battalion, 8th Regiment......................	September 25, 1800
Postlethwait, John.......	Captain, 42nd Regiment...........	May 15, 1793
	Recommissioned.................	July 2, 1800

COMMISSIONED OFFICERS, 1799 - 1804

Postlethwait, John.......	Major, 1st Battalion, 42nd Regiment......................	December 16, 1799
Postlethwait, Samuel.....	Captain, Rifle Company, 42nd Regiment......................	July 2, 1800
Prewitt, Robert..........	Ensign, 8th Regiment............	September 15, 1800
Prewitt, Robert..........	Lieutenant, 8th Regiment.........	July 4, 1801
Price, William...........	Ensign, 42nd Regiment............	May 11, 1801
Quarles, Roger...........	Captain, 10th Regiment...........	April 9, 1804
Ransdale, Elie...........	Captain, 10th Regiment...........	June 28, 1799
Ransdale, Wharton........	Ensign, Rifle Company, 10th Regiment......................	August 14, 1800
Ransdale, Wharton........	Lieutenant, 10th Regiment........	March 15, 1801
Redman, Benjamin.........	Ensign, 10th Regiment............	October 31, 1801
Robb, Joseph.............	Captain, 42nd Regiment...........	January 1, 1800
Robb, Joseph.............	Major, 1st Battalion, 42nd Regiment......................	December 10, 1803
Ross, William............	Captain, 42nd Regiment...........	July 2, 1800
Rouse, William...........	Lieutenant, 10th Regiment........	June 28, 1799
Rule, Ninian.............	Ensign, 8th Regiment.............	June 8, 1804
Russell, Robert..........	Major, 2nd Battalion, 10th Regiment......................	August 3, 1799
Russell, Robert..........	Colonel, 10th Regiment...........	December 19, 1801
Sanders, Mibird..........	Lieutenant, 10th Regiment........	December 6, 1804
Saterthwait (Satterwhite).	Mann.... Lieutenant, John Shock's Company, 10th Regiment.........	April 9, 1804
Satterwhite, Mann........	Captain, 10th Regiment...........	December 6, 1804
Scott, Samuel............	Ensign, 10th Regiment............	January 1, 1800
Scott, Samuel............	Lieutenant, 10th Regiment........	March 15, 1801
Scott, William...........	Ensign, 42nd Regiment............	December 4, 1800
Scroggin, Joseph.........	Ensign, 8th Regiment.............	December 1, 1800
Scrogham, Joseph.........	Lieutenant, 8th Regiment.........	July 20, 1804
Seitz, J. A.	2nd Lieutenant, 42nd Regiment....	June 21, 1799
	Recommissioned................	August 18, 1800
Shealy, William..........	Lieutenant, 10th Regiment........	September 29, 1800
Shock, John..............	Captain, 10th Regiment...........	September 23, 1800
Shryock, Matthias........	Ensign, 42nd Regiment............	December 17, 1803
Shryock, Matthias........	Lieutenant, 42nd Regiment........	May 14, 1804
Simpson, William.........	Ensign, 10th Regiment............	June 28, 1799
Simpson, William.........	Captain, 10th Regiment...........	March 1, 1800
Smith, George............	Ensign, 42nd Regiment............	January 1, 1800
Smith, James.............	Captain, Rifle Company, 8th Regiment......................	July 20, 1804
Smith, James.............	Paymaster, 8th Regiment..........	October 10, 1803
Smith, Martin............	Lieutenant, 8th Regiment.........	May 20, 1800
South, John..............	Colonel, 8th Regiment............	October 4, 1799
Spears, John.............	Captain, 8th Regiment............	April 1, 1800
Spur, William............	Lieutenant, 8th Regiment.........	September 3, 1803
Sqires, Cal. (Caleb Squires?)...	Ensign, 10th Regiment......	October 31, 1801
Steele, James............	Ensign, 10th Regiment............	March 16, 1800
Stevens, Thomas..........	Ensign, 10th Regiment............	October 2, 1804
Stevenson, William.......	Captain, 10th Regiment...........	October 28, 1800

COMMISSIONED OFFICERS, 1799 - 1804

Stewart, James H.	Lieutenant, 42nd Regiment........	August 11, 1794
	Recommissioned.................	July 2, 1800
Stewart, John............	Ensign, 10th Regiment............	September 29, 1800
Stewart, John............	Captain, 10th Regiment...........	October 31, 1801
Sthreshly, Thomas G. ...	Lieutenant, 10th Regiment........	May 28, 1804
Sthreshly, William.......	Captain, 10th Regiment...........	March 16, 1800
Stout, Benjamin..........	Lieutenant, 42nd Regiment........	July 2, 1800
Stout, Benjamin..........	Captain, 42nd Regiment...........	May 11, 1801
Swigert, John............	Ensign, 8th Regiment.............	September 12, 1804
Tilton, Peter............	Ensign, 10th Regiment............	December 6, 1804
Todd, Davis..............	Lieutenant, 8th Regiment.........	May 25, 1804
Todd, John...............	Cornet, 8th Regiment.............	October 13, 1802
Trotter, George, Jr. ...	Captain, Rifle Company, 42nd Regiment......................	September 9, 1800
Trotter, George, Jr. ...	Major, 42nd Regiment.............	September 13, 1803
True, William............	Ensign, 8th Regiment.............	December 1, 1800
Turner, Fielding L.	Adjutant, 42nd Regiment..........	March 21, 1804
Turner, Samuel...........	Ensign, 8th Regiment.............	June 16, 1803
Tylor, Charles...........	Lieutenant, 10th Regiment........	June 28, 1799
Vanpelt, Samuel..........	Captain, 42nd Regiment...........	December 17, 1803
Wallace, Thomas..........	Adjutant, 42nd Regiment..........	April 1, 1801
Wardlaw, John............	Lieutenant, 42nd Regiment........	January 1, 1800
Wartlow, John............	Captain, 42nd Regiment...........	December 17, 1803
Welsh, Benjamin..........	Lieutenant, 8th Regiment.........	March 1, 1800
West, Edward.............	Lieutenant, 42nd Regiment........	May 11, 1801
Whiat (Wyatt), John......	Captain, 42nd Regiment...........	September 12, 1803
Whyat (Wyatt), John.....	Ensign, 42nd Regiment............	July 2, 1800
Wiley, Matthew...........	Ensign, 10th Regiment............	October 31, 1801
Wiley, Moses.............	Ensign, 10th Regiment............	March 15, 1801
Wilgus, Asa..............	Ensign, 10th Regiment............	December 6, 1804
Wilkins, Stewart.........	Lieutenant, 42nd Regiment........	June 21, 1799
	Recommissioned.................	July 2, 1800
Williams, Henson.........	Ensign, George Caldwell's Company, 10th Regiment.........	April 9, 1804
Williams, Henson.........	Captain, 10th Regiment...........	December 6, 1804
Williams, Husin (Henson?)	Lieutenant, 10th Regiment........	May 28, 1804
Williams, Thomas.........	Lieutenant, 10th Regiment........	January 1, 1800
Wimer, Martin............	Ensign, 42nd Regiment............	April 3, 1800
Winn, John...............	Lieutenant, 8th Regiment.........	August 14, 1800
Winn, John...............	Captain, 8th Regiment............	September 3, 1803
Wood, James..............	Captain, 42nd Regiment...........	December 4, 1803
Wood, James..............	Major, 2nd Battalion, 10th Regiment......................	December 19, 1801
Wright, William..........	Lieutenant, 10th Regiment........	December 6, 1804
Wyatt, John..............	Lieutenant, 42nd Regiment........	May 15, 1802
Yeizer, Englehart........	Lieutenant, 42nd Regiment........	December 7, 1802

COMMISSIONED OFFICERS, 1799 - 1804

Fleming County Regiments

[58th Regiment laid off December 9, 1803]

Alexander, Robert	Ensign, 30th Regiment	March 16, 1801
Alexander, Robert	Lieutenant, 30th Regiment	May 21, 1802
Andrews, Robert	Captain, 30th Regiment	December 25, 1802
Armstrong, William	Ensign, 30th Regiment	December 25, 1802
Barnes, Joseph	Captain, Light Infantry, 30th Regiment	June 10, 1801
Barnes, Robert	Lieutenant, Light Infantry, 30th Regiment	June 10, 1801
Barnes, Robert	2nd Lieutenant, Light Horse Company, 30th Regiment	September 12, 1804
Barnes, Robert, Jr.	2nd Lieutenant, Troop of Horse, 30th Regiment	May 25, 1804
Beaird, John	Cornet, 30th Regiment	December 25, 1802
Beavers, Abraham	Captain, 30th Regiment	March 16, 1801
Belt, Fielding	Ensign, Rifle Company, 30th Regiment	1803
Belt, Fielding	Captain, Rifle Company, 30th Regiment	May 25, 1804
Belt, Joseph	1st Lieutenant of Cavalry, 30th Regiment	March 16, 1801
Bravard, Adam	Captain, 30th Regiment	May 29, 1800
Bright, Edward	Lieutenant, 30th Regiment	December 3, 1803
Brown, James	Lieutenant, 30th Regiment	March 16, 1801
Brown, John	Captain, 30th Regiment	March 16, 1801
Brown, Robert	Lieutenant, 30th Regiment	March 16, 1801
Browning, Albert	Lieutenant, 30th Regiment	May 25 and September 12, 1804
Bunton, Andrew	Lieutenant, 30th Regiment	September 25, 1801
Caldwell, William	Captain, 30th Regiment	April 1, 1800
Carpenter, Simon	Ensign, 30th Regiment	May 21, 1802
Carpenter, Simon	Lieutenant, 58th Regiment	May 19, 1804
Cassady, Thomas	Captain, 30th Regiment	1803
Cassady, Thomas	Captain, 58th Regiment	May 19, 1804
Chapman, William	Ensign, 30th Regiment	December 25, 1802
Christel, William	Captain, 30th Regiment	May 20, 1800
Christel, William	Adjutant, 58th Regiment	May 19, 1804
Constant, Jacob	Captain, 30th Regiment	December 3, 1803
Courtney, Robert	Lieutenant, 30th Regiment	March 16, 1801
Crain, Joseph	Ensign, 58th Regiment Recommissioned	May 19, 1804
Crane, Joseph	Ensign, 30th Regiment	September 25, 1801
Dameron, Moses	Lieutenant, 30th Regiment	March 16, 1801
Davis, John	Lieutenant, 30th Regiment	May 21, 1802
Davis, Joseph	Lieutenant, 30th Regiment	May 30, 1800
Davis, Joseph	Ensign, Rifle Company, 30th Regiment	December 25, 1802

COMMISSIONED OFFICERS, 1799 - 1804

Davis, Joseph	Captain, Rifle Company, 30th Regiment	1803
Day, Trueman	Paymaster, 58th Regiment	May 19, 1804
Deal, Ira	Ensign, 30th Regiment	May 20, 1800
Debell, John	Captain, 30th Regiment	December 5, 1799
Denton, Joseph	Captain, 30th Regiment	May 21, 1802
Denton, Joseph	Captain, 58th Regiment Recommissioned	May 19, 1804
Dinsmore, John	Ensign, 30th Regiment	April 1, 1800
Ditterow, Jacob	Captain, 30th Regiment	May 20, 1800
Drinning, Hugh	Captain, 30th Regiment	December 6, 1801
Dunlap, James	Captain, 30th Regiment	March 16, 1801
Evans, Gabriel	Major, 1st Battalion, 30th Regiment	April 1, 1800
Evans, Gabriel	Colonel, 58th Regiment	December 21, 1803
Faris, John	Paymaster, 30th Regiment	November 22, 1800
Finch, Josiah R.	Lieutenant, 30th Regiment	May 20, 1800
Fitch, Salathiel	Lieutenant, 30th Regiment	May 20, 1800
Fitch, Salathiel	Captain, 30th Regiment	May 30, 1800
Ford, Joseph	Ensign, 58th Regiment	May 19, 1804
Foster, Nathaniel	Captain, 30th Regiment	September 25, 1801
Fulton, Hugh	Major, 1st Battalion, 30th Regiment	December 5, 1799
Galascock (Glasscock), George	Lieutenant, 30th Regiment	May 30, 1800
Goodwin, David	Ensign, 58th Regiment	May 19, 1804
Graham, James	Ensign, Rifle Company, 30th Regiment	May 30, 1800
Graham, John	Lieutenant, Rifle Company, 30th Regiment	1803
Graham, John	Lieutenant, 58th Regiment Recommissioned	May 19, 1804
Gray, Isaac	Captain, 30th Regiment	September 25, 1801
Gray, Isaac	Captain, 58th Regiment Recommissioned	May 19, 1804
Green, Fielding	Ensign, 58th Regiment Recommissioned	May 19, 1804
Green, Thomas	Lieutenant, 30th Regiment	1803
Hamilton, Archibald	Lieutenant, 30th Regiment	May 30, 1800
Hart, Daniel	Captain, 30th Regiment	December 3, 1803
Hart, David	Ensign, 30th Regiment	December 5, 1799
Hart, David	Adjutant, 30th Regiment	May 21, 1800
Hart, Samuel	Cornet, Cavalry, 30th Regiment	December 6, 1801
Haslett, Samuel	Lieutenant, 30th Regiment	May 30, 1800
Hastings, Simeon	Lieutenant, 30th Regiment	May 29, 1800
Hastings, Simon	Captain, 30th Regiment	1803
Hazlitt, Samuel	Captain, Rifle Company, 30th Regiment	1803
Hazlitt, Samuel	Captain, 58th Regiment Recommissioned	May 19, 1804
Heflin, Gustias	Lieutenant, 30th Regiment	1803
Hilicost, John	Lieutenant, Rifle Company, 30th Regiment	1803

COMMISSIONED OFFICERS, 1799 - 1804

Hinton, Benonai..........	Ensign, 30th Regiment............	May 24, and September 12, 1804
Hinton, Eli..............	Ensign, 30th Regiment............	December 3, 1803
Howe, Joseph.............	Ensign, 30th Regiment............	May 21, 1802
Hunt, John...............	Major, 2nd Battalion, 30th Regiment......................	August 15, 1799
Hunt, John...............	Major, 1st Battalion, 58th Regiment......................	December 21, 1803
Hutton, Benjamin.........	Lieutenant, 30th Regiment........	December 5, 1799
Johnson, Jesse...........	Lieutenant, 30th Regiment........	May 20, 1800
Jones, Thomas............	Colonel, 30th Regiment...........	August 15, 1799
Kincaid, Andrew..........	2nd Lieutenant of Cavalry, 30th Regiment......................	December 6, 1801
Kincaid, Andrew..........	Captain, Troop of Horse, 30th Regiment......................	May 25, 1804
Kinkead, Andrew..........	Captain, Horse Company, 30th Regiment......................	September 12, 1804
Kirtly, Benjamin.........	Lieutenant, 30th Regiment........	June 10, 1801
Lamery, William..........	Lieutenant, 30th Regiment........	1803
Litton, Caleb............	Captain, 30th Regiment...........	March 16, 1801
Lowery, William..........	Captain, 30th Regiment...........	September 12, 1804
Lytle, Nathaniel.........	Lieutenant, 58th Regiment Recommissioned................	May 19, 1804
McGowan, James Strode....	Captain, Rifle Company, 30th Regiment......................	May 21, 1802
McIntire, Daniel.........	Quartermaster, 58th Regiment.....	May 19, 1804
McIntire, Joseph.........	Major, 1st Battalion, 30th Regiment......................	December 22, 1803
McRoberts, John..........	Lieutenant, Rifle Company, 30th Regiment......................	May 30, 1800
McRoberts, John..........	Captain, 58th Regiment...........	May 19, 1804
Mahan, John..............	Lieutenant, 30th Regiment........	May 30, 1800
Miles, John..............	Ensign, 30th Regiment............	May 20, 1800
Miller, Benjamin.........	Lieutenant, 58th Regiment........	May 19, 1804
Miller, Thomas...........	Ensign, 30th Regiment............	May 30, 1800
Miller, Thomas...........	Ensign, 58th Regiment Recommissioned................	May 19, 1804
Mills, Evan..............	Ensign, 30th Regiment............	June 10, 1801
Mills, John..............	Lieutenant, 30th Regiment........	June 10, 1801
Minor, Gideon............	Ensign, 30th Regiment............	March 16, 1801
Mooney, John.............	Captain, 30th Regiment...........	May 30, 1800
Moore, Richard...........	Ensign, 30th Regiment............	May 21, 1802
Murphy, Neil.............	2nd Lieutenant, 30th Regiment....	December 25, 1802
Newcombe, Daniel.........	Ensign, 30th Regiment............	May 25, and September 12, 1804
Palmer, John.............	Ensign, 58th Regiment............	May 19, 1804
Parish, Joel.............	Lieutenant, 30th Regiment........	December 25, 1802
Parks, Arthur............	Lieutenant, 30th Regiment........	April 1, 1800
Parks, Arthur............	Captain, Rifle Company, 30th Regiment......................	May 30, 1800
Patten, William..........	1st Lieutenant, 30th Regiment....	December 25, 1802

COMMISSIONED OFFICERS, 1799 - 1804

Patton, Thomas...........	Cornet, Troop of Horse, 30th Regiment......................	May 24, and September 12, 1804
Pepper, William..........	Ensign, 30th Regiment............	May 21, 1802
Pepper, William..........	Lieutenant, 30th Regiment........	December 25, 1802
Plummer, Abraham.........	Captain, 30th Regiment...........	May 30, 1800
Plummer, Benjamin........	Lieutenant, 30th Regiment........	September 25, 1801
Plummer, Benjamin........	Captain, 58th Regiment...........	May 19, 1804
Plummer, Jacob...........	Lieutenant, 30th Regiment........	September 12, 1804
Plummer, Joseph..........	Lieutenant, 30th Regiment........	May 25, 1804
Prather, John............	Lieutenant, 30th Regiment........	December 25, 1802
Price, Thomas............	Lieutenant, 30th Regiment........	May 21, 1802
Ratcliffe, Silas.........	Ensign, 30th Regiment............	March 16, 1801
Reed, Joseph.............	Ensign, 30th Regiment............	May 24, and September 12, 1804
Remey, William Page......	Lieutenant, 30th Regiment........	June 10, 1801
Rose, Joseph.............	Lieutenant, 30th Regiment........	May 25, and September 12, 1804
Sanders, James...........	Captain, 30th Regiment...........	May 30, 1800
Saylor (?), John.........	Ensign, 30th Regiment............	September 25, 1801
Scholefield, Henry.......	Captain, 58th Regiment...........	May 19, 1804
Scott, James.............	Ensign, 30th Regiment............	May 29, 1800
Shackleford, William.....	Captain, 30th Regiment...........	June 10, 1801
Smith, Joseph............	Lieutenant, 30th Regiment........	May 20, 1800
Smith, Simeon............	Ensign, 30th Regiment............	May 20, 1800
Smith, Simeon............	Adjutant, 30th Regiment..........	October 5, 1803
Sparks, George...........	Ensign, 30th Regiment............	1803
Sparks, George...........	Lieutenant, 58th Regiment Recommissioned................	May 19, 1804
Steel, Solomon...........	Ensign, 30th Regiment............	May 30, 1800
Stockdon, Edward.........	Ensign, Light Infantry, 30th Regiment......................	June 10, 1801
Stratton, Tandy..........	Ensign, 30th Regiment............	March 16, 1801
Summers, William.........	Ensign, 30th Regiment............	December 25, 1802
Talmage, Thomas..........	Lieutenant, 30th Regiment........	December 25, 1802
Taull, Bazil.............	Lieutenant, 30th Regiment........	May 24, 1804
Taylor, George...........	Captain, 30th Regiment...........	June 10, 1801
Taylor, John.............	Captain, 30th Regiment...........	May 25, and September 12, 1804
Terhoon, Jacob...........	Ensign, Rifle Company, 30th Regiment......................	1803
Terhune, Jacob...........	Ensign, Rifle Company, 58th Regiment......................	May 19, 1804
Toutt, Basil.............	Lieutenant, 30th Regiment........	September 12, 1804
Triplet, Greensbury......	Ensign, 30th Regiment............	May 2, 1800
Tully, Israel............	Captain, 30th Regiment...........	May 20, 1800
Tully, Israel............	Major, 2nd Battalion, 30th Regiment......................	December 23, 1803
Walton, John.............	Lieutenant, 30th Regiment........	March 16, 1801
Warwick, John............	Lieutenant, 30th Regiment........	December 3, 1803

COMMISSIONED OFFICERS, 1799 - 1804

Warwick, John............	Lieutenant, 58th Regiment Recommissioned................	May 19, 1804
Weaver, Philip...........	Captain, 30th Regiment...........	May 20, 1800
Weaver, Philip...........	Major, 2nd Battalion, 58th Regiment......................	December 23, 1803
Wilson, Daniel...........	Lieutenant, 30th Regiment.......	December 25, 1802
Wyatt, Joseph............	Ensign, 30th Regiment............	1803
Yates, Joseph............	Lieutenant, 30th Regiment.......	May 21, 1802
Yates, Joseph............	Captain, 58th Regiment...........	May 19, 1804
Young, James.............	Ensign, 30th Regiment............	March 16, 1801

Floyd County Regiment

[Laid off December 17, 1802]

Allen, William...........	Ensign, 56th Regiment............	April 6, 1803
Auxier, Michael..........	Ensign, 56th Regiment............	December 1, 1803
Beaver, Abraham..........	Captain, 56th Regiment...........	April 6, 1803
Beck, John...............	Paymaster, 56th Regiment.........	February 27, 1804
Berry, George............	Lieutenant, 56th Regiment.......	April 6, 1803
Bonjay, George...........	Lieutenant, 56th Regiment.......	December 1, 1803
Brown, James.............	1st Lieutenant of Horse, 56th Regiment......................	April 6, 1803
Brown, Thomas............	Ensign, 56th Regiment............	April 6, 1803
Brown, Thomas C.	Captain, 56th Regiment...........	December 1, 1803
Brumly, John.............	Ensign, 56th Regiment............	April 6, 1803
Calleham (Callahan?), William...	Ensign, 56th Regiment......	December 1, 1803
Cope, Wiley..............	Captain, 56th Regiment...........	April 6, 1803
Fugate, Benjamin.........	Ensign, 56th Regiment............	April 6, 1803
Hackwith, John...........	Captain, 56th Regiment...........	September 15, 1803
Haddix, John.............	Lieutenant, 56th Regiment.......	December 1, 1803
Haddocks, Coleby.........	Lieutenant, 56th Regiment.......	April 6, 1803
Hays, Adern..............	Captain, 56th Regiment...........	April 6, 1803
Hogg, James..............	Lieutenant, 56th Regiment.......	December 1, 1803
Lycan, Jacob Goodwin.....	Colonel, 56th Regiment...........	December 18, 1802
Lycan, John..............	Lieutenant, 56th Regiment.......	April 6, 1803
Lycan, John..............	Captain, 56th Regiment...........	December 1, 1803
Lytton, Caleb............	Captain, 56th Regiment...........	April 6, 1803
Mallett, William.........	Ensign, 56th Regiment............	December 1, 1803
Meade, Rhodes............	Ensign, 56th Regiment............	September 15, 1803
Morgan, David............	Major, 1st Battalion, 56th Regiment......................	December 18, 1802
Morgan, William..........	Captain, 56th Regiment...........	April 6, 1803
Morris, John.............	Ensign, 56th Regiment............	April 6, 1803
Patton, Felix............	Ensign, 56th Regiment............	January 16, 1804
Pierce, Benjamin.........	Ensign, 56th Regiment............	December 1, 1803
Pinson, Henry............	Lieutenant, 56th Regiment.......	December 1, 1803
Power, Holloway..........	Cornet of Horse, 56th Regiment...	April 6, 1803
Power, Holloway..........	Quartermaster, 56th Regiment.....	February 27, 1804
Ratcliffe, Silas.........	Captain, 56th Regiment...........	April 6, 1803

COMMISSIONED OFFICERS, 1799 - 1804

Shatton, John............	Lieutenant, 56th Regiment........	September 15, 1803
Spurlock, David..........	Lieutenant, 56th Regiment........	April 6, 1803
Stratton, Harry..........	Major, 2nd Battalion, 56th Regiment......................	December 20, 1802
Stratton, Tandy..........	Ensign, 56th Regiment............	April 6, 1803
Strong, William..........	Lieutenant, 56th Regiment........	April 6, 1803
Wilson, James............	Captain of Horse, 56th Regiment..	April 6, 1803
Young, Alexander.........	Adjutant, 56th Regiment..........	September 15, 1803
Young, James.............	2nd Lieutenant of Horse, 56th Regiment......................	April 6, 1803

Franklin County Regiment

Adams, William...........	Ensign, 22nd Regiment............	August 17, 1804
Arnel, John..............	Lieutenant, 22nd Regiment........	July 10, 1800
Bell, Clement............	Lieutenant, 22nd Regiment........	September 24, 1803
Blackwell, Robert........	Captain, 22nd Regiment...........	April 9, 1801
Blunt, Henry.............	Ensign, 22nd Regiment............	July 10, 1800
Bradford, James..........	Lieutenant of Infantry, 22nd Regiment......................	April 5, 1802 (?)
Bradford, James M.	Captain, Infantry Company, 22nd Regiment......................	October 16, 1802
Brock, Henry.............	Adjutant, 22nd Regiment..........	May 23, 1803
Brown, George............	Ensign, 22nd Regiment............	April 9, and August 1, 1801
Brown, William...........	Ensign, 22nd Regiment............	April 29, 1800
Buckner, Nicholas........	Quartermaster, 22nd Regiment.....	April 5, 1802
Burch, Cheadle...........	Ensign, Rifle Company, 22nd Regiment......................	May 31, 1800
Caldwell, Phillip........	Major, 2nd Battalion, 22nd Regiment......................	March 17, 1801
Carr (also Kerr), Peter..	Captain, 22nd Regiment...........	October 16, 1802
Carter, Abraham..........	Ensign, 22nd Regiment............	August 17, 1804
Clinton, Moses...........	Lieutenant, 22nd Regiment........	April 4, 1800
Combs, John..............	Ensign, 22nd Regiment............	April 15, 1799
Craig, Elijah............	1st Lieutenant, 22nd Regiment....	April 30, 1799
Craig, Lewis.............	Captain, 22nd Regiment...........	September 24, 1803
Crockett, Anthony........	Colonel, 22nd Regiment...........	May 27, 1800
Davis, James.............	Ensign, 22nd Regiment............	September 24, 1803
Davis, John..............	Lieutenant, 22nd Regiment........	July 10, 1800
Demint, Gart.	Ensign, 22nd Regiment............	April 25, 1800
Duvall, Zachariah........	Ensign, 22nd Regiment............	September 24, 1803
Fauntleroy, William......	Captain, 22nd Regiment...........	April 27, 1800
Gale, James..............	Lieutenant, Rifle Company, 22nd Regiment......................	May 31, 1800
Gale, James..............	Captain, 22nd Regiment...........	August 17, 1804
Gatewood, Hugh...........	Lieutenant, 22nd Regiment........	July 10, 1800
Gibson, William..........	Ensign, 22nd Regiment............	May 1, 1802
Gray, Prestley...........	Captain, 22nd Regiment...........	July 10, 1800
Gullion, Jeremiah........	Captain, 22nd Regiment...........	April 25, 1800

COMMISSIONED OFFICERS, 1799 - 1804

Handcock, Thomas.........	Ensign, 22nd Regiment............	September 24, 1803
Hardin, Enos.............	Captain, 22nd Regiment...........	March 25, 1800
Hawkins, Moses...........	Lieutenant, 22nd Regiment........	May 1, 1802
Hickman, Paschal.........	Ensign, 22nd Regiment............	April 5, 1802 (?)
Hickman, Paschal.........	Lieutenant, 22nd Regiment........	September 24, 1803
Hough, Joseph............	Lieutenant, 22nd Regiment........	April 27, 1800
How, Edward..............	Lieutenant, 22nd Regiment........	March 25, 1800
Hutton, Joseph...........	Captain, 22nd Regiment...........	August 1, 1801
Jameson, John............	Adjutant, 22nd Regiment..........	April 1, 1801
Jeffries, Ambrose........	Ensign, 22nd Regiment............	August 1, 1801
Jennings, Jonathan.......	Captain, 22nd Regiment...........	July 10, 1800
Keaton, Hezekiah.........	Lieutenant, 22nd Regiment........	October 16, 1802
Kerr, Peter..............	Lieutenant, 22nd Regiment........	August 1, 1801
King (no first name).....	Lieutenant, 22nd Regiment........	July 10, 1800
Lamb, Jacob..............	Lieutenant, 22nd Regiment........	April 1, 1801
Lee, Willis..............	Captain, 22nd Regiment...........	April 15, 1799
Lee, Willis A.	Adjutant, 22nd Regiment..........	September 23, 1800
Lightfoot, John..........	Captain, Rifle Company, 22nd Regiment......................	October 17, 1802
Lillard, Thomas..........	Major, 1st Battalion, 22nd Regiment......................	May 27, 1800
Long, Thomas.............	Ensign of Infantry, 22nd Regiment	April 5, 1802 (?)
Long, Thomas.............	Lieutenant, Infantry Company, 22nd Regiment..................	October 16, 1802
Long, Thomas.............	Ensign, 22nd Regiment............	September 24, 1803
Long, Thomas.............	Lieutenant, 22nd Regiment........	August 17, 1804
Loughberry, Thomas V. ..	Lieutenant, 22nd Regiment........	April 8, 1801
Loughborrough, Thomas....	Ensign, 22nd Regiment............	April 26, 1800
McBrayer, Andrew.........	Ensign, 22nd Regiment............	October 16, 1802
McBrayer, James..........	Ensign, 22nd Regiment............	October 16, 1802
Martin, John L.	Captain of Infantry, 22nd Regiment	April 5, 1802 (?)
Mears, Samuel............	Lieutenant, 22nd Regiment........	April 8, 1801
Mitchel, Samuel..........	Ensign, 22nd Regiment............	October 17, 1802
Morris, John.............	Ensign, 22nd Regiment............	July 10, 1800
Munday, Stephen..........	Lieutenant, Rifle Company, 22nd Regiment..................	October 17, 1802
Pace, William............	Ensign, 22nd Regiment............	September 24, 1803
Patterson, Peter.........	Lieutenant, 22nd Regiment........	April 5, 1802 (?)
Pemberton, John..........	Ensign, 22nd Regiment............	April 5, 1802 (?)
Price, Richard...........	2nd Lieutenant, 22nd Regiment....	April 30, 1799
Price, Richard...........	Adjutant, 22nd Regiment..........	March 1, 1802
Quarles, Ambrose.........	Captain, 22nd Regiment...........	October 16, 1802
Ray, John................	Ensign, 22nd Regiment............	July 10, 1800
Rennick, John............	Captain, 22nd Regiment...........	April 8, 1801
Richardson, John.........	Lieutenant, 22nd Regiment........	April 15, 1799
Rowland, William.........	Ensign of Infantry, 22nd Regiment	March 25, 1800
Samuel, William..........	Ensign, 22nd Regiment............	August 17, 1804
Sanders, John, Jr.	Captain, 22nd Regiment...........	July 10, 1800
Saunders, Hugh...........	Captain, Rifle Company, 22nd Regiment......................	May 31, 1800
Scott, John M.	Colonel, 22nd Regiment...........	March 3, 1801

Sharp, Abraham	Ensign, 22nd Regiment	August 1, 1801
Sharp, Abraham	Lieutenant, 22nd Regiment	October 16, 1802
Sheets, Henry	Captain, 22nd Regiment	September 24, 1803
Smither, John	Ensign, 22nd Regiment	September 24, 1803
Staat, Stephen	Ensign, 22nd Regiment	April 9, 1801
Stephens, Wilford	Ensign, 22nd Regiment	March 25, 1800
Tandy, John	Lieutenant, 22nd Regiment	August 17, 1804
Thomas, Joseph	Ensign, 22nd Regiment	July 10, 1800
Tinsley, Archibald	Ensign, 22nd Regiment	October 17, 1802
Trigg, William	Quartermaster, 22nd Regiment	January 12, 1803
Tunstall, Henry	Lieutenant, 22nd Regiment	April 9, 1801
Tunstall, Henry	Captain, 22nd Regiment	September 24, 1803
Vawter, John	Ensign, 22nd Regiment	July 10, 1800
West, J.	Ensign, 22nd Regiment	April 4, 1800
West, James	Ensign, 22nd Regiment	March 20, 1799
White, Philip	Captain, 22nd Regiment	July 10, 1800
White, William	Lieutenant, 22nd Regiment	September 24, 1803
Williams, Charles	Lieutenant, 22nd Regiment	October 17, 1802
Williams, Charles	Captain, 22nd Regiment	August 16, 1804
Wilson, Isaac	Lieutenant, 22nd Regiment	August 16, 1804
Wingate, Thomas	Ensign, 22nd Regiment	August 16, 1804

Gallatin County Regiment

[Laid off December 20, 1800]

Arnold, John	Lieutenant, 51st Regiment	May 13, 1801
Blount, Henry	Lieutenant, 51st Regiment	May 13, 1801 and May 4, 1804
Blount, Henry	Paymaster, 51st Regiment	June 28, 1802
Brockman, Job	Ensign, 51st Regiment	March 28, 1803
Craig, Benjamin	Captain, 51st Regiment	March 28, 1803
Craig, Elijah	Major, 2nd Battalion, 51st Regiment	December 23, 1800
Davis, John	Captain, 51st Regiment	May 13, 1801
Dean, William	Ensign, 51st Regiment	March 28, 1803
Dean, William	Lieutenant, 51st Regiment	May 4, 1804
DeMint, Jared	Ensign, 51st Regiment Recommissioned	May 13, 1801
DeMint, Jared	Lieutenant, 51st Regiment	March 28, 1803
Gatewood, Hugh L.	Paymaster, 51st Regiment	December 5, 1803
Gray, Jesse	Ensign, 51st Regiment	May 13, 1801 and March 28, 1803
Gray, Jesse	Lieutenant, 51st Regiment	March 28, 1803
Gray, Prestley	Major, 1st Battalion, 51st Regiment	December 22, 1800
Gray, Prestley	Colonel, 51st Regiment	December 13, 1802
Grimes, John	Colonel, 51st Regiment	December 22, 1800
Gullion, Jeremiah	Captain, 51st Regiment Recommissioned	May 13, 1801

Holt, Zila...............	Lieutenant, 51st Regiment........	March 28, 1803
Jennings, Jonathan.......	Captain, 51st Regiment...........	May 13, 1801
Jennings, Jonathan.......	Major, 2nd Battalion, 51st Regiment.......................	September 13, 1803
Johnson, Daniel..........	Lieutenant, 51st Regiment........	May 20, 1803
Jones, Joshua............	Ensign, 51st Regiment............	May 4, 1804
Jones, Thomas............	Ensign, 51st Regiment............	May 4, 1804
King, Thomas.............	Captain, 51st Regiment...........	May 13, 1801
Lamb, Jacob..............	Lieutenant, 51st Regiment........	May 13, 1801
Larue, Jacob.............	Quartermaster, 51st Regiment.....	June 28, 1802
Lee, Gersham, Jr.	Ensign, 51st Regiment............	May 13, 1801
Morris, John.............	Lieutenant, 51st Regiment........	May 13, 1801
Morris, John.............	Major, 1st Battalion, 51st Regiment.......................	March 12, 1803
Owens, David.............	Adjutant, 51st Regiment..........	June 28, 1802
Payne, Enoch.............	Ensign, 51st Regiment............	May 20, 1803
Ray, John................	Lieutenant, 51st Regiment........	May 13, 1801
Ray, John................	Captain, 51st Regiment...........	May 4, 1804
Restine, Henry...........	Ensign, 51st Regiment............	May 4, 1804
Sale, Robert.............	Captain, 51st Regiment...........	December 5, 1803
Sanders, John, Jr.	Captain, 51st Regiment Recommissioned.................	May 13, 1801
Sanders, Samuel..........	Ensign, 51st Regiment............	May 13, 1801
Taylor, Benjamin.........	Ensign, 51st Regiment............	March 28, 1803
Thomas, Joshua...........	Ensign, 51st Regiment Recommissioned.................	May 13, 1801
Weigley (Weekly), Abraham...	Adjutant, 51st Regiment........	May 13, 1801
Whitehead, John..........	Lieutenant, 51st Regiment........	March 28, 1803

Garrard County Regiments

[57th Regiment laid off March 3, 1803]

Aldrige, James...........	Captain, 57th Regiment...........	April 30, 1803
Anderson, James..........	Lieutenant, 26th Regiment........	July 9, 1799
Anderson, James..........	Captain, 26th Regiment...........	April 18, 1803
Anderson, William........	Ensign, 26th Regiment............	April 15, 1799
Anderson, William........	Lieutenant, 26th Regiment........	April 18, 1803
Baker, Abner.............	Captain of Infantry, 26th Regiment.......................	August 1, 1799
Ballinger, Achilles......	Captain, 26th Regiment...........	June 15 and June 30, 1799
Barbour, Richard.........	Adjutant, 26th Regiment..........	February 11, 1801
Barnard, John............	Ensign, 26th Regiment............	May 10, 1800
Bledsoe, Benjamin........	Ensign, 26th Regiment............	March 12, 1799
Bledsoe, Joseph..........	Captain, 26th Regiment...........	March 12, 1799
Bledsoe, William M.	Paymaster, 26th Regiment.........	April 18, 1803
Bowman, John.............	Adjutant, 57th Regiment..........	April 30, 1803
Boys, Robert.............	Captain, 57th Regiment...........	April 30, 1803
Brown, Arabia J.	Ensign, 57th Regiment............	April 30, 1803

COMMISSIONED OFFICERS, 1799 - 1804

Brown, Arabia J.	Captain, 57th Regiment	May 11, 1804
Brown, Stephen	Ensign, 26th Regiment	March 15, 1800
Bruce, John	Lieutenant, 26th Regiment	May 10, 1800
Bryant, John	Paymaster, 57th Regiment	April 30, 1803
Buford, Henry	Lieutenant of Infantry, 26th Regiment	October 17, 1799
Buford, Thomas	Adjutant, 26th Regiment	October 17, 1799
Buford, Thomas	Lieutenant, 26th Regiment	June 22, 1802
Buford, Thomas	Captain, 57th Regiment	April 30, 1803
Buford, Thomas	Major, 1st Battalion, 57th Regiment	October 5, 1804
Bunton, John	Quartermaster, 57th Regiment	April 30, 1803
Burnside, Robert	Ensign, 26th Regiment	June 22, 1802
Burnside, Robert	Ensign, 57th Regiment	April 30, 1803
Cole, Ebenezer	Ensign, 26th Regiment	June 2, 1802
Cole, Ebenezer	Lieutenant, 57th Regiment	April 30, 1803
Collier, James	Captain, 26th Regiment	October 17, 1799
Cummins, Daniel	Ensign, 26th Regiment	April 18, 1803
Denton, John	Ensign, 26th Regiment	May 10, 1800
Dismukes, William	Ensign, 26th Regiment	June 15 and June 30, 1799
Doty, Jesse	Ensign, 26th Regiment	June 22, 1802 and April 18, 1803
Duff, William	Lieutenant, 26th Regiment	June 18, 1804
Dunn, Benjamin	Ensign, 57th Regiment	April 30, 1803
Edmonson, John	Captain, 26th Regiment	June 22, 1802
Faulkner, John	Lieutenant, 26th Regiment	June 22, 1802
Faulkner, John	Captain, 26th Regiment	April 18, 1803
Faulkner, John	Major, 1st Battalion, 26th Regiment	December 8, 1804
Finnel, James	Major, 1st Battalion, 26th Regiment	December 19, 1800
Finnell, Achilles	Cornet, 26th Regiment	April 15, 1799
Finnell, Achilles	Lieutenant, 26th Regiment	June 18, 1804
Finnell, James	Ensign, 26th Regiment	June 18, 1804
George, James	Lieutenant, 57th Regiment	April 30, 1803
Gibbs, Ezekiel	Lieutenant, 26th Regiment	April 15, 1799
Grider, Tobias	Captain, 26th Regiment	June 15 and June 30, 1799
Guthrie, James	Ensign, 26th Regiment	June 22, 1802
Guthrie, James	Lieutenant, 26th Regiment	April 18, 1803
Harris, Robert	Lieutenant, 26th Regiment	April 15, 1799
Harrison, John	Colonel, 57th Regiment	March 3, 1803
Hawkins, Weedon	Lieutenant, 26th Regiment	June 15 and June 30, 1799
Hedrick, Joseph	Lieutenant, 26th Regiment	June 15 and June 30, 1799
Hicks, Daniel	Lieutenant, 26th Regiment	March 12, 1799
Hicks, Daniel	Captain, 26th Regiment	May 10, 1800
Huffman, Frederick	Lieutenant, 26th Regiment	June 15 and July 30, 1799

COMMISSIONED OFFICERS, 1799 - 1804

Jeffries, Daniel.........	Captain, 26th Regiment...........	March 15, 1800
Jennings, August(ine)....	Lieutenant, 26th Regiment........	April 15, 1799 and February 11, 1801
Jennings, Augustine......	Quartermaster, 26th Regiment.....	April 18, 1803
Jennings, William........	Major, 2nd Battalion, 26th Regiment........................	March 3, 1803
Jennings, William........	Lieutenant Colonel, Commandant 26th Regiment..................	December 8, 1804
Kennedy, David...........	Major, 1st Battalion, 26th Regiment........................	November 5, 1802
Lackey, Gabriel..........	Ensign, 26th Regiment............	June 18, 1804
Lackey, William..........	Captain, 26th Regiment...........	June 18, 1804
Letcher, Benjamin........	Major, 1st Battalion, 57th Regiment........................	March 3, 1803
Letcher, Benjamin........	Lieutenant Colonel, Commandant 57th Regiment..................	October 5, 1804
Littlepage, Epps.........	Ensign, 26th Regiment............	July 9, 1799
Lobb, William............	Lieutenant, 26th Regiment........	June 15 and July 30, 1799
McLaughlin, John.........	Lieutenant, 26th Regiment........	June 18, 1804
Marksberry, Isaac........	Lieutenant, 26th Regiment........	June 22, 1802
Marksberry, Isaac........	Lieutenant, 57th Regiment........	April 30, 1803
Marksberry, John.........	Ensign, 26th Regiment............	June 15, 1799
Maxberry, John...........	Ensign, 26th Regiment............	July 30, 1799
Maxbury, Isaac...........	Ensign, 26th Regiment............	October 17, 1799
Mitchell, James..........	Lieutenant, 26th Regiment........	June 18, 1804
Morrison, John...........	Lieutenant, 57th Regiment........	April 30, 1803
Mounce, Smith............	Captain, 26th Regiment...........	June 15 and June 30, 1799
Mounts, Henry............	Lieutenant, 26th Regiment........	August 20, 1800
Nelson, Matthew..........	Ensign of Infantry, 26th Regiment........................	October 17, 1799
Nelson, Matthew..........	Ensign, 57th Regiment............	April 30, 1803
Nicholson, William.......	Captain, 26th Regiment...........	April 15, 1799
Nicholson, William.......	Major, 2nd Battalion, 26th Regiment........................	December 8, 1804
O'Bannion, William B. ...	Captain, 57th Regiment...........	April 30, 1803
O'Bannon, William........	Ensign, 26th Regiment............	August 20, 1800
Owsley, William..........	Adjutant, 26th Regiment..........	March 30, 1802
Patterson, Thomas........	Captain, 26th Regiment...........	April 18, 1803
Perkins, Edmond..........	Captain, 26th Regiment...........	June 22, 1802
Perkins, Edmond..........	Captain, 57th Regiment...........	April 30, 1803
Perkins, Stephen.........	Captain, 26th Regiment...........	March 15, 1800
Perkins, Stephen.........	Adjutant, 26th Regiment..........	April 6, 1802
Perkins, Stephen.........	Captain, 57th Regiment...........	April 30, 1803
Posey, Thomas............	Ensign, 26th Regiment............	June 2, 1802
Price, William...........	Captain, 26th Regiment...........	June 22, 1802
Proctor, Jeremiah........	Ensign, 26th Regiment............	June 18, 1804
Reynolds, William........	Lieutenant, 26th Regiment........	March 15, 1800 and June 22, 1802
Reynolds, William........	Lieutenant, 57th Regiment........	April 30, 1803

COMMISSIONED OFFICERS, 1799 - 1804

Roberts, James............	Ensign, 26th Regiment............	February 11, 1801
Rogers, Charles..........	Ensign, 57th Regiment............	May 11, 1804
Rout, John...............	Ensign, 26th Regiment............	June 15 and July 30, 1799
Rout, John...............	Captain, 26th Regiment...........	August 20, 1800
Sasseen, Francis.........	Ensign, 26th Regiment............	June 22, 1802
Sasseen, Francis.........	Ensign, 57th Regiment............	April 30, 1803
Sasseen, Louis...........	Ensign, 57th Regiment............	May 11, 1804
Saylers, Dunn............	Lieutenant, 57th Regiment........	April 30, 1803
Smith, Edmund............	Ensign, 26th Regiment............	June 22, 1802
Smith, Edmund............	Lieutenant, 26th Regiment........	March 15, 1800
Smith, Edmund............	Lieutenant, 57th Regiment........	April 30, 1803
Smith, James.............	Lieutenant, 26th Regiment........	February 11, 1801
Smith, John..............	Ensign, 57th Regiment............	April 30, 1803
Smith, Weeden............	Captain, 57th Regiment...........	April 30, 1803
Smith, William...........	Captain, 26th Regiment...........	April 15, 1799
Smith, William...........	Major, 2nd Battalion, 57th Regiment......................	March 4, 1803
Spelman, Charles.........	Lieutenant, 26th Regiment........	February 11, 1801
Swope, Charles...........	Ensign, 26th Regiment............	February 11, 1801
Whitehead, John..........	Ensign, 26th Regiment............	June 18, 1804
Williams, Walter.........	Captain, 26th Regiment...........	April 18, 1803
Withrow, James...........	Ensign, 26th Regiment............	June 18, 1804
Wood, William............	Ensign, 26th Regiment............	June 18, 1804
Woods, John..............	Lieutenant of Cavalry, 26th Regiment......................	April 15, 1799
Yantis, John.............	Cornet of Cavalry, 57th Regiment......................	April 30, 1803

Green County Regiment

Allen, David.............	Captain, 16th Regiment...........	March 11, 1803
Allen, James.............	Major, 16th Regiment.............	December 18, 1802
Allen, James.............	Lieutenant Colonel, Commandant 16th Regiment.................	December 13, 1804
Andrews, John............	Lieutenant, 16th Regiment........	August 28, 1799
Ball, James..............	Ensign, 16th Regiment............	May 28, 1803
Barnett, Andrew..........	Captain, 16th Regiment...........	October 23, 1801
Barnett, William.........	Colonel, 16th Regiment...........	December 18, 1799
Barringer, Jonathan......	Ensign, 16th Regiment............	December 3, 1803
Bass. Peter..............	Ensign, 16th Regiment............	June 25, 1802
Bell, Robert.............	Lieutenant, 16th Regiment........	June 25, 1802
Billen, Absolam..........	Ensign, 16th Regiment............	October 28, 1801
Blane, James.............	Major, 2nd Battalion, 16th Regiment......................	July 20, 1799
Bottoms, Robert..........	Lieutenant, 16th Regiment........	October 28, 1801
Bristow, Thomas..........	Ensign, 16th Regiment............	November 5, 1799
Brownlee, Charles........	Ensign, 16th Regiment............	October 1, 1802
Burton, Joseph...........	Ensign, 16th Regiment............	June 25, 1802
Cabel, Joseph............	Captain, 16th Regiment...........	March 11, 1803

COMMISSIONED OFFICERS, 1799 - 1804

Cain, Charles............	Captain, 16th Regiment...........	October 28, 1801
Caldwell, Beverly........	Lieutenant, 16th Regiment........	October 28, 1801
Caldwell, David..........	Ensign, 16th Regiment............	March 11, 1803
Compton, Joel............	Ensign, 16th Regiment............	November 5, 1799
Cowherd, James...........	Paymaster, 16th Regiment.........	June 25, 1802
Cowherd, James...........	Captain, 16th Regiment...........	May 28, 1803
Cumpton, Joel............	Captain, 16th Regiment...........	December 3, 1803
Damron, George...........	Captain, 16th Regiment...........	May 21, 1799
Day, Middleton...........	Lieutenant, 16th Regiment........	December 11, 1802
Dixon, Henry.............	Captain, 16th Regiment...........	August 28, 1799
Doake, David.............	Lieutenant, 16th Regiment........	November 1, 1799
Douglass, Charles........	Lieutenant, 16th Regiment........	October 1, 1802
Durham, James............	Lieutenant, 16th Regiment........	May 28, 1803
Durham, James............	Captain, 16th Regiment...........	November 5, 1799
Dyal, James..............	Ensign, 16th Regiment............	August 28, 1799
Eastland, Thomas.........	Adjutant, 16th Regiment..........	August 16, 1802
Edrington, Thomas........	Ensign, 16th Regiment............	May 28, 1803
Elliott, William.........	Captain, 16th Regiment...........	November 10, 1799
Ewing, Andrew............	Ensign, 16th Regiment............	November 5, 1799
Ford, Luke...............	Captain, 16th Regiment...........	May 28, 1803
Gist, Thomas.............	Captain, 16th Regiment...........	August 28, 1799
Goffey, James............	Captain, 16th Regiment...........	May 21, 1799
Gupton, Stephen..........	Lieutenant, 16th Regiment........	August 28, 1799
Hardin, Aaron.............	Ensign, 16th Regiment............	October 28, 1801
Harding, John............	Captain, 16th Regiment...........	November 6, 1799
Harrard (Harrod), John...	Ensign, 16th Regiment............	October 1, 1802
Harris, Alexander........	Ensign, 16th Regiment............	November 5, 1799
Harrod, John.............	Captain, 16th Regiment...........	December 11, 1802
Hunt, Robison............	Lieutenant, 16th Regiment........	October 23, 1801
Husk, John...............	Ensign, 16th Regiment............	November 1, 1799
Hutcheson, David.........	Lieutenant, 16th Regiment........	March 11, 1803
Jameson, John............	Ensign, 16th Regiment............	June 25, 1802
Johnson, William.........	Ensign, 16th Regiment............	October 15, 1799
Johnston, William........	Lieutenant, 16th Regiment........	November 5, 1799
Jones, John..............	Ensign, 16th Regiment............	June 25, 1802
Kaen (Cain), Charles.....	Lieutenant, 16th Regiment........	May 21, 1799
Latimar, Samuel..........	Ensign, 16th Regiment............	October 1, 1802
Latimer, Jacob...........	Lieutenant, 16th Regiment........	December 10, 1799
Latimore, Jacob..........	Captain, 16th Regiment...........	October 28, 1801
Lawson, William..........	Captain, 16th Regiment...........	November 1, 1799
Lee, William.............	Lieutenant, 16th Regiment........	October 28, 1801
McLain, John.............	Ensign, 16th Regiment............	May 21, 1799
McMurtry, Joseph.........	Ensign, 16th Regiment............	December 11, 1802
McNabb, William..........	Lieutenant, 16th Regiment........	October 15, 1799
McNabb, William..........	Captain, 16th Regiment...........	November 5, 1799
McNeeley, William........	Lieutenant, 16th Regiment........	November 5, 1799
Malone, Bannister........	Ensign, 16th Regiment............	November 5, 1799
Marshall, Robert.........	Ensign, 16th Regiment............	November 5, 1799
Mitchel, John............	Lieutenant, 16th Regiment........	November 5, 1799
Mitchell, James..........	Major, 16th Regiment.............	December 19, 1801
Mitchell, James..........	Colonel, 16th Regiment...........	December 14, 1802

COMMISSIONED OFFICERS, 1799 - 1804

Moore, Samuel	Ensign, 16th Regiment	October 1, 1802
Morrison, James	Captain, 16th Regiment	November 5, 1799
Nailor, Benjamin	Captain, 16th Regiment	November 20, 1799
Owens, John	Ensign, 16th Regiment	August 28, 1799
Patton, Alexander	Lieutenant, 16th Regiment	May 28, 1803
Patton, Thomas	Captain, 16th Regiment	November 5, 1799
Prigmore, Benjamin	Ensign, 16th Regiment	October 28, 1801
Prigmore, Benjamin	Lieutenant, 16th Regiment	May 28, 1803
Ray, Joseph	Captain, 16th Regiment	October 1, 1802
Reaves, James	Major, 1st Battalion, 16th Regiment	August 29, 1802
Rice, James	Lieutenant, 16th Regiment	June 25, 1802
Rice, John	Lieutenant, 16th Regiment	November 6, 1799
Richeson, John	Ensign, 16th Regiment	October 28, 1801
Richeson, John	Lieutenant, 16th Regiment	October 1, 1802
Richeson, Joseph	Lieutenant, 16th Regiment	May 20, 1799
Richeson, Joseph, Jr.	Captain, 16th Regiment	October 1, 1802
Rogers, John	Ensign, 16th Regiment	May 20, 1799
Russel, William	Lieutenant, 16th Regiment	May 20, 1799
Rutledge, Isaac	Ensign, 16th Regiment	November 20, 1799
Skaggs, James	Ensign, 16th Regiment	October 23, 1801
Smith, Thomas	Captain, 16th Regiment	October 28, 1801
Spears, George	Captain, 16th Regiment	October 15, 1799 and December 3, 1803
Sublett, Abraham	Captain, 16th Regiment	October 28, 1801
Sutton, William	Lieutenant, 16th Regiment	October 28, 1801
Thomas, Robert	Lieutenant, 16th Regiment	May 21, 1799
Trabue, Daniel	Major, 16th Regiment	December 28, 1799
Trabue, Robert	Ensign, 16th Regiment	October 23, 1801
Walker, Alexander	Lieutenant, 16th Regiment	November 10, 1799
Walker, Joseph	Ensign, 16th Regiment	October 23, 1801
West, Alexander	Ensign, 16th Regiment	May 21, 1799
White, Andrew, Sr.	Lieutenant, 16th Regiment	May 28, 1803
White, Jesse	Lieutenant, 16th Regiment	November 20, 1799
White, Samuel	Ensign, 16th Regiment	May 28, 1803
White, Thomas	Captain, 16th Regiment	October 23, 1801
Whiteson, Andrew	Ensign, 16th Regiment	March 11, 1803
William, Thomas	Ensign, 16th Regiment	October 1, 1802
Williams, Ezekiel	Captain, 16th Regiment	August 28, 1799
Wood, Jesse	Lieutenant, 16th Regiment	August 28, 1799
Workman, Benjamin	Lieutenant, 16th Regiment	November 5, 1799
Young, William	Captain, 16th Regiment	November 5, 1799

Hardin County Regiments

[60th Regiment laid off December 10, 1804]

Ashby, Bladen	Captain, 3rd Regiment	February 26, 1799
Ashby, Thompson	Lieutenant, 3rd Regiment	February 26, 1799
Ashcraft, Abijah	Lieutenant, 3rd Regiment	June 13, 1801

COMMISSIONED OFFICERS, 1799 - 1804

Ashcraft, Daniel	Lieutenant, 3rd Regiment	October 14, 1803
Carr, Thomas	Ensign, 3rd Regiment	October 3, 1799
Chaffin, John	Ensign, 3rd Regiment	June 29, 1802
Coe, James	Ensign, 3rd Regiment	May 31, 1802
Coombs, Eden	Captain, 3rd Regiment	October 14, 1803
Cooprider, Peter	Ensign, 3rd Regiment	November 17, 1804
Cready, David	Lieutenant, 3rd Regiment	June 29, 1802
Custard, Conrad	Ensign, 3rd Regiment	June 13, 1801
Ditto, Henry, Jr.	Ensign, 3rd Regiment	June 13, 1801
Dunn, Vincent	Captain, 3rd Regiment	November 9, 1801
Dunn, Vincent	Major, 2nd Battalion, 60th Regiment	December 13, 1804
Enlow, Isham	Captain, 3rd Regiment	April 2, 1799
Enlow, Isham	Major, 1st Battalion, 60th Regiment	December 13, 1804
Enlow, Jacob	Lieutenant, 3rd Regiment	June 13, 1801
Enlow, Joseph	Captain, 3rd Regiment	October 3, 1799
Ewing, Henry	Captain, 3rd Regiment	June 29, 1802
Farmer, James	Ensign, 3rd Regiment	June 29, 1802
Gibson, Daniel	Lieutenant, 3rd Regiment	June 9, 1804
Hardin, William, Jr.	Lieutenant, 3rd Regiment	August 27, 1799
Helm, Benjamin	Adjutant, 3rd Regiment	May 31, 1802
Hinton, John	Lieutenant, 3rd Regiment	June 18, 1803
Hodgen, Isaac	Ensign, 3rd Regiment	June 13, 1801
Hornback, James	Lieutenant, 3rd Regiment	May 31, 1802
Hornback, James	Captain, 3rd Regiment	October 14, 1803
Howard, George H.	Ensign, 3rd Regiment	June 13, 1801
Hudspeth, Thomas	Captain, 3rd Regiment	May 31, 1802
Irvine, Benjamin	Lieutenant, 3rd Regiment	May 29, 1802
Jenkins, John	Lieutenant, 3rd Regiment	November 9, 1801
Jenkins, John	Captain, 3rd Regiment	May 31, 1802
Keisinger, Joseph	Ensign, 3rd Regiment	November 9, 1801
Larue, James	Ensign, 3rd Regiment	April 2, 1799
Larue, James	Lieutenant, 3rd Regiment	June 13, 1801
Linder, Daniel, Jr.	Ensign, 3rd Regiment	May 31, 1802
McAllister, Edward	Captain, 3rd Regiment	June 9, 1804
McGrady, Samuel	Captain, 3rd Regiment	May 2, 1799
McIntire, Thomas	Major, 3rd Regiment	February 25, 1801
McIntire, Thomas	Lieutenant Colonel, Commandant 60th Regiment	December 13, 1804
McWilliams, James	Captain, 3rd Regiment	November 17, 1804
Miller, Nicholas	Major, 3rd Regiment	December 19, 1800
Miller, Nicholas	Lieutenant Colonel, Commandant 3rd Regiment	December 13, 1804
Money, Joseph	Captain, 3rd Regiment	June 13, 1801
Morrison, Daniel L.	Adjutant, 3rd Regiment	July 25, 1801
Munford, William	Captain, 3rd Regiment	June 9, 1804
New, James	Ensign, 3rd Regiment	May 2, 1799
Owens, Benjamin	Ensign, 3rd Regiment	October 14, 1803
Painter, John	Ensign, 3rd Regiment	June 29, 1802
Pate, John	Captain, 3rd Regiment	April 1, 1799

COMMISSIONED OFFICERS, 1799 - 1804

Pearpoint, Francis.......	Major, 1st Battalion, 3rd Regiment......................	December 13, 1804
Pepper, Daniel...........	Ensign, 3rd Regiment.............	June 9, 1804
Pierpoint, Francis.......	Captain, 3rd Regiment............	April 3, 1799
Rawlings, Edward.........	Lieutenant, 3rd Regiment.........	November 9, 1801
Read, Hensley............	Lieutenant, 3rd Regiment.........	May 31, 1802
Rentch, Michael..........	Captain, 3rd Regiment............	June 13, 1801
Riley, James.............	Ensign, 3rd Regiment.............	June 29, 1802
Shacklett, Benjamin......	Major, 2nd Battalion, 3rd Regiment......................	December 13, 1804
Shanklett, Benjamin......	Captain, 3rd Regiment............	November 9, 1801
Slaughter, Robert C. ...	Ensign, 3rd Regiment.............	November 9, 1801
Smith, James.............	Ensign, 3rd Regiment.............	October 14, 1803
Swank, Jacob.............	Ensign, 3rd Regiment.............	November 17, 1804
Syhneider (Snider), Samuel...	Ensign, 3rd Regiment.............	June 9, 1804
Thomas, Hardin...........	Captain, 3rd Regiment............	November 9, 1801
Thomas, Massey...........	Lieutenant, 3rd Regiment.........	May 2, 1799
Tichnor, Timothy.........	Lieutenant, 3rd Regiment.........	May 31, 1802
Travis, Charles..........	Captain, 3rd Regiment............	August 27, 1799
Vanvacter, Benjamin......	Ensign, 3rd Regiment.............	May 31, 1802
Wade, Daniel.............	Lieutenant, 3rd Regiment.........	April 1, 1799
Wadkins, Josiah..........	Lieutenant, 3rd Regiment.........	November 9, 1801
Walters, James...........	Lieutenant, 3rd Regiment.........	June 18, 1803
Weedman, Jacob...........	Lieutenant, 3rd Regiment.........	October 3, 1799
Westfall, Cornelius......	Ensign, 3rd Regiment.............	February 26, 1799
Wilkerson, James.........	Lieutenant, 3rd Regiment.........	June 9, 1804
Wright, Benjamin.........	Captain, 3rd Regiment............	October 14, 1803

Harrison County Regiment

Anderson, Francis........	Captain, 20th Regiment...........	November 24, 1801
Barnes, Abraham..........	Lieutenant, 20th Regiment........	May 26, 1800
Barrett, Peter...........	Lieutenant, 20th Regiment........	April 6, 1801
Beauvrie, Matthew........	Ensign, 20th Regiment............	December 16, 1799
Berry, John..............	Lieutenant, 20th Regiment........	October 1, 1801
Blackburn, David.........	Captain, 20th Regiment...........	October 1, 1801
Bodkin, Richard..........	Captain, 20th Regiment...........	May 26, 1800
Bodkin, William..........	Captain, 20th Regiment...........	July 1, 1799
Boswell, William E.	Colonel, 20th Regiment...........	March 2, 1801
Brown, Samuel............	Lieutenant, 20th Regiment........	October 1, 1801
Bryant, John.............	Adjutant, 20th Regiment..........	April 9, 1799
Caldwell, James..........	Paymaster, 20th Regiment.........	December 3, 1799
Caldwell, James..........	1st Lieutenant, 20th Regiment....	December 26, 1803
Campbell, Alexander......	Surgeon, 20th Regiment...........	November 30, 1801
Carnagant, John..........	Lieutenant, 20th Regiment........	March 10, 1803
Clary, Vachel............	Lieutenant, 20th Regiment........	July 4, 1803
Cokendofer, John.........	Ensign, 20th Regiment............	November 4, 1800
Craig, James.............	Lieutenant, Rifle Company, 20th Regiment......................	August 1, 1799
Craig, Thomas............	Captain, 20th Regiment...........	May 25, 1804

COMMISSIONED OFFICERS, 1799 - 1804

Davis, George............	Ensign, 20th Regiment............	April 6, 1801
Dunn, Benajah............	Ensign, 20th Regiment............	February 1, 1802
Dunn, Benjamin...........	Ensign, 20th Regiment............	May 25, 1804
Edds, William Gibson.....	Lieutenant, 20th Regiment........	March 31, 1800
Ellison, Robert..........	Ensign, Rifle Company, 20th Regiment.......................	March 10, 1803
Fitzwaters, John.........	Captain, 20th Regiment...........	March 10, 1803
Franklin, James..........	Lieutenant, 20th Regiment........	November 4, 1800
Garnett, Leonard.........	Lieutenant, 20th Regiment........	July 20, 1799
Gray, Francis............	Ensign, Rifle Company, 20th Regiment.......................	October 1, 1801
Gray, Francis............	Lieutenant, Rifle Company, 20th Regiment..................	March 10, 1803
Hail, Robert.............	Ensign, 20th Regiment............	May 26, 1800
Hampton, John............	Captain, 20th Regiment...........	April 1, 1800
Hampton, Lewis...........	Lieutenant, 20th Regiment........	May 25, 1804
Hayden, John.............	Lieutenant, 20th Regiment........	July 4, 1803
Hedger, Jonathan.........	Captain, 20th Regiment...........	May 25, 1804
Hickman, Benjamin........	Ensign, 20th Regiment............	October 1, 1801
Hindershot, John.........	Ensign, 20th Regiment............	April 6, 1801
Hindershot, John.........	Lieutenant, 20th Regiment........	November 24, 1801
Hiron, Samuel............	Ensign, 20th Regiment............	February 19, 1800
Hufford, David...........	Lieutenant, 20th Regiment........	April 1, 1800
Johnston, Jacob..........	Lieutenant, 20th Regiment........	October 1, 1801
Johnston, John...........	Ensign, 20th Regiment............	May 25, 1804
Jones, John..............	Lieutenant, 20th Regiment........	June 20, 1799
King, Richard............	Lieutenant, 20th Regiment........	April 6, 1801
King, Richard............	Captain, 20th Regiment...........	March 10, 1803
Lewis, Alexander.........	Lieutenant, 20th Regiment........	April 6, 1801
McClure, James...........	Ensign, Rifle Company, 20th Regiment.......................	April 6, 1801
McClure, Nathaniel.......	Captain, 20th Regiment...........	December 16, 1799
McCord, James............	Ensign, 20th Regiment............	March 10, 1803
McIlvain, Moses..........	Captain, 20th Regiment...........	February 19, 1800
McIlvain, Samuel.........	Captain, 20th Regiment...........	March 28, 1800
McKitrick, Robert........	Captain, 20th Regiment...........	April 6, 1801
Martin, William..........	Ensign, Rifle Company, 20th Regiment.......................	May 25, 1803
Miller, Hugh.............	Cornet, 20th Regiment............	December 26, 1803
Miller, Isaac............	2nd Lieutenant, 20th Regiment....	December 26, 1803
Miller, James............	Major, 2nd Battalion, 20th Regiment.......................	December 26, 1799
Miller, John.............	Lieutenant, 20th Regiment........	May 25, 1804
Miller, John.............	Captain, 20th Regiment...........	March 29, 1800
Minter, William..........	Lieutenant, Rifle Company, 20th Regiment..................	March 10, 1803
Mith, Jacob..............	Ensign, 20th Regiment............	July 4, 1803
Moore, William...........	Adjutant, 20th Regiment..........	April 1, 1800
Moore, William...........	Captain, 20th Regiment...........	December 26, 1803
Naylor, Thomas...........	Lieutenant, 20th Regiment........	March 16, 1799
Naylor, Thomas...........	Captain, 20th Regiment...........	October 1, 1801

Nelson, Hayden............	Captain, 20th Regiment............	February 1, 1802
Newel, William............	Lieutenant, 20th Regiment.........	March 28, 1800
Perrin, Josephus..........	Captain, 20th Regiment............	October 1, 1801
Porter, Andrew............	Major, 1st Battalion, 20th Regiment........................	August 4, 1801
Rankin, Robert............	Ensign, 20th Regiment.............	July 4, 1803
Rankin, Robert............	Lieutenant, 20th Regiment.........	May 25, 1804
Rees, George..............	Captain, 20th Regiment............	May 5, 1800
Richards, Arnold..........	Ensign, 20th Regiment.............	October 1, 1801
Robinson, Joseph..........	Ensign, 20th Regiment.............	March 16, 1799
Rowland, Jacob............	Ensign, 20th Regiment.............	October 1, 1801
Scott, John...............	Ensign, 20th Regiment.............	March 10, 1803
Scott, Robert.............	Lieutenant, 20th Regiment.........	November 24, 1801
Scott, Thomas.............	Lieutenant, 20th Regiment.........	February 1, 1802
Scrogin, Thomas...........	Ensign, Rifle Company, 20th Regiment...................	August 1, 1799
Scrogin, Thomas...........	Lieutenant, Rifle Company, 20th Regiment...................	April 6, 1801
Shields, John.............	Lieutenant, 20th Regiment.........	February 19, 1800
Shipp, Jacob..............	Ensign, 20th Regiment.............	July 4, 1803
Smith, John...............	Ensign, 20th Regiment.............	April 1, 1800
Stephenson, Robert........	Quartermaster, 20th Regiment......	December 19, 1799
Stephenson, William.......	Ensign, 20th Regiment.............	November 24, 1801
Stowers, William..........	Captain, 20th Regiment............	March 31, 1800
Thompson, James...........	Ensign, 20th Regiment.............	March 29, 1800
Thompson, Thomas..........	Ensign, 20th Regiment.............	November 24, 1801
Veach, Jeremiah...........	Lieutenant, Rifle Company, 20th Regiment...................	October 1, 1801
Veach, Jeremiah...........	Captain, Rifle Company, 20th Regiment...................	March 10, 1803
Vineyard, Absolam.........	Ensign, 20th Regiment.............	March 31, 1800
Walker, Alexander.........	Ensign, 20th Regiment.............	April 6, 1801
Walker, Alexander.........	Lieutenant, 20th Regiment.........	November 24, 1801
Wall, Garrett.............	Captain, 20th Regiment............	March 16, 1799
Ward, James...............	Captain, Rifle Company, 20th Regiment........................	August 1, 1799
Ward, John................	Ensign, 20th Regiment.............	November 24, 1801
Wigglesworth, Thompson....	Lieutenant, 20th Regiment.........	March 10, 1803
Woods, Archibald..........	Lieutenant, 20th Regiment.........	July 4, 1803
Worrell, Atteway..........	Lieutenant, 20th Regiment.........	March 29, 1800

Henderson County Regiment

[Laid off December 16, 1799]

Ashby, Daniel.............	Colonel, 41st Regiment............	December 16, 1799
Ashby, Stephen............	Captain, 41st Regiment............	November 23, 1803
Barnett, Jacob............	Adjutant, 41st Regiment...........	December 18, 1800
Berry, Benjamin...........	Captain, 41st Regiment............	November 20, 1803
Boles, James..............	Ensign, 41st Regiment.............	November 19, 1803

COMMISSIONED OFFICERS, 1799 - 1804

Christian, John..........	Major, 1st Battalion, 41st Regiment......................	December 16, 1799
Davenport, Marmaduke S...	Ensign, 41st Regiment............	November 21, 1803
Fugate, Vincent..........	Ensign, 41st Regiment............	November 23, 1803
Gordon, John.............	Lieutenant, 41st Regiment........	November 24, 1803
Gwatkin, Horatio.........	Major, 1st Battalion, 41st Regiment......................	March 31, 1802
Jones, Fielding..........	Captain, 41st Regiment...........	November 19, 1803
Kilgore, John............	Ensign, 41st Regiment............	November 22, 1803
Lindsey, Nevil...........	Lieutenant, 41st Regiment........	November 21, 1803
McBee, Silas.............	Quartermaster, 41st Regiment.....	December 18, 1800
McBride, Daniel..........	Captain, 41st Regiment...........	November 22, 1803
Martin, Abner............	Captain, 41st Regiment...........	November 24, 1803
Newman, Jacob............	Paymaster, 41st Regiment.........	December 18, 1800
Owens, Reubin............	Lieutenant, 41st Regiment........	November 20, 1803
Ruby, John...............	Ensign, 41st Regiment............	November 20, 1803
Sibley, Isaac............	Lieutenant, 41st Regiment........	November 19, 1803
Smith, Daniel............	Lieutenant, 41st Regiment........	November 22, 1803
Stewart, William.........	Major, 2nd Battalion, 41st Regiment......................	December 17, 1799
Talbot, Edmond...........	Captain, 41st Regiment...........	November 21, 1803
Timmons, George..........	Lieutenant, 41st Regiment........	November 23, 1803
Wagoner, John............	Lieutenant Colonel, Commandant 41st Regiment.................	March 31, 1802
Weir, Bazaliel...........	Major, 2nd Battalion, 41st Regiment......................	March 31, 1802
Wilson, John.............	Ensign, 41st Regiment............	November 24, 1803

Henry County Regiment

[Laid off December 11, 1799]

Admyre, Henry............	Ensign, 38th Regiment............	September 15, 1802
Bain, Lewis..............	Lieutenant, Rifle Company, 38th Regiment.................	September 20, 1800
Bain, Lewis..............	Lieutenant, 38th Regiment........	September 15, 1802
Baker, John..............	Captain, 1st Battalion, 38th Regiment......................	April 7, 1800
Bane, LeRoy..............	Lieutenant, 2nd Battalion, 38th Regiment.................	April 7, 1800
Banta, Daniel............	Captain, 38th Regiment...........	March 24, 1804
Bartlett, Edmund.........	Colonel, 38th Regiment...........	December 12, 1799
Bartlett, James..........	Paymaster, 38th Regiment.........	December 18, 1799
Bryan, Morgan............	Quartermaster, 38th Regiment.....	December 18, 1799
Butler, William..........	Major, 2nd Battalion, 38th Regiment......................	December 13, 1799
Calloway, John...........	Captain, 38th Regiment...........	September 20, 1800
Cammeron, Robert.........	Captain, 1st Battalion, 38th Regiment......................	April 11, 1800
Combs, Jonah.............	Captain, 38th Regiment...........	May 22, 1802

COMMISSIONED OFFICERS, 1799 - 1804

Crawford, James	Lieutenant, 2nd Battalion, 38th Regiment	April 9, 1800
Crawford, James	Captain, 38th Regiment	March 23, 1801
Dale, Reuben	Ensign, 38th Regiment	September 20, 1800
Degarnet, Bird	Ensign, 38th Regiment	March 8, 1800
Dougherty, Samuel	Lieutenant, 38th Regiment	March 23, 1801
Dunn, George	Lieutenant, 38th Regiment	August 21, 1800
Elston, William	Lieutenant, 38th Regiment	May 22, 1802
Farley, Daniel	Captain, Rifle Company, 38th Regiment	September 20, 1800
Ford, James	Lieutenant, 38th Regiment	September 20, 1800
Fore, Augustus	Surgeon's Mate, 38th Regiment	September 24, 1801
Gerald, Joseph F.	Lieutenant, 38th Regiment	March 23, 1801
Green, Stephen	Ensign, 38th Regiment	September 15, 1802
Hall, Squire	Captain, 38th Regiment	May 22, 1802
Hammon, William	Ensign, 1st Battalion, 38th Regiment	April 9, 1800
Hickerson, Thomas	Ensign, 38th Regiment	September 20, 1800
Hilman, Benjamin	Ensign, 38th Regiment	August 21, 1801
Holecraft, Richard	Ensign, 38th Regiment	May 21, 1804
Holley, Samuel	Lieutenant, 38th Regiment	December 10, 1802
Hoskins, Achilles	Captain, 38th Regiment	August 21, 1800
Ireland, Samuel	Paymaster, 38th Regiment	March 24, 1804
Irwin, Robert	Captain, 2nd Battalion, 38th Regiment	April 10, 1800
Jackson, Joel	Ensign, 38th Regiment	May 21, 1803
Jenkins, John	Ensign, 2nd Battalion, 38th Regiment	April 9, 1800
Johes (Joyes?), William	Captain, 1st Battalion, 38th Regiment	April 9, 1800
Jones, Peter	Lieutenant, 38th Regiment	May 22, 1802
Lagoe, Wilson	Captain, 38th Regiment	September 24, 1801
Lancaster, James	Lieutenant, 38th Regiment	September 20, 1800
Lawson, John	Lieutenant, 1st Battalion, 38th Regiment	April 7, 1800
Lee, Moses	Lieutenant, 1st Battalion, 38th Regiment	April 11, 1800
Lemasters, James	Lieutenant, 38th Regiment	May 22, 1802
Louden, Thomas	Captain, 2nd Battalion, 38th Regiment	April 7, 1800
Lowden, John	Ensign, 38th Regiment	December 10, 1802
McAllister, Colister	Lieutenant, 38th Regiment	May 22, 1802
McAndre, Bunyan	Ensign, 1st Battalion, 38th Regiment	April 11, 1800
McCollister, Collister	Ensign, 38th Regiment	August 21, 1800
McCray, William	Ensign, 38th Regiment	May 22, 1802
McGrew, Moses	Ensign, 38th Regiment	May 21, 1803
McGuyer, Jesse	Ensign, 38th Regiment	August 21, 1801
McKinly, Samuel	Captain, 1st Battalion, 38th Regiment	April 10, 1800
Marshall, George	Lieutenant, 38th Regiment	May 21, 1804

COMMISSIONED OFFICERS, 1799 - 1804

Miller, Abraham..........	Lieutenant, 1st Battalion, 38th Regiment......................	April 9, 1800
Miller, Jacob............	Ensign, 1st Battalion, 38th Regiment......................	April 10, 1800
Moore, William...........	Lieutenant, 1st Battalion, 38th Regiment......................	April 8, 1800
Neale, George............	Ensign, 38th Regiment............	August 21, 1801
Neale, George............	Lieutenant, 38th Regiment........	December 10, 1802
Neale, William...........	Major, 1st Battalion, 38th Regiment......................	December 12, 1799
Neavill, George..........	Ensign, 38th Regiment............	May 21, 1804
Osburn, Michael..........	Lieutenant, 38th Regiment........	May 22, 1802
Osburn, Michael..........	Captain, 38th Regiment...........	May 21, 1804
Owen, David..............	Captain, 2nd Battalion, 38th Regiment......................	April 8, 1800
Pemberton, Reuben........	Captain, 38th Regiment...........	March 8, 1800
Perry, James.............	Lieutenant, 38th Regiment........	May 21, 1804
Piles, John..............	Lieutenant, 38th Regiment........	May 21, 1803
Pringle, Alexander.......	Paymaster, 38th Regiment.........	September 24, 1801
Pringle, William.........	Lieutenant, 2nd Battalion, 38th Regiment..................	April 10, 1800
Rayls, William...........	Ensign, 38th Regiment............	March 23, 1801
Rees, Thomas T.	Lieutenant, 38th Regiment........	September 15, 1802
Rice, William............	Captain, 1st Battalion, 38th Regiment......................	April 8, 1800
Rice, William M.	Major, 1st Battalion, 38th Regiment......................	December 15, 1803
Riley, Rasmus............	Lieutenant, 38th Regiment........	December 10, 1803
Roberts, Joseph..........	Ensign, 1st Battalion, 38th Regiment......................	April 8, 1800
Robertson, Littleton.....	Lieutenant, 38th Regiment........	March 8, 1800
Robinson, Littleton......	Captain, 38th Regiment...........	May 22, 1802
Rumjul (Romjeu), John....	Surgeon, 38th Regiment...........	September 24, 1801
Samuel, John.............	Lieutenant, 38th Regiment........	December 10, 1803
Samuel, William..........	Captain, 2nd Battalion, 38th Regiment......................	April 9, 1800
Sanders, John............	Ensign, 38th Regiment............	May 22, 1802
Scott, Elijah............	Captain, 38th Regiment...........	March 23, 1801
Shaw, Michael............	Ensign, 38th Regiment............	September 24, 1801
Smith, David.............	Ensign, 2nd Battalion, 38th Regiment......................	April 10, 1800
Smith, Nicholas..........	Ensign, 1st Battalion, 38th Regiment......................	April 7, 1800
Smith, Nicholas..........	Captain, 38th Regiment...........	August 21, 1801
Smith, Samuel............	Lieutenant, 1st Battalion, 38th Regiment.................	April 10, 1800
Tanner, Matthew..........	Ensign, 2nd Battalion, 38th Regiment......................	April 8, 1800
Thomas, Robert...........	Lieutenant, 38th Regiment........	August 21, 1801
White, Archibald.........	Lieutenant, 2nd Battalion, 38th Regiment......................	April 8, 1800

COMMISSIONED OFFICERS, 1799 - 1804

White, Thomas............	Adjutant, 38th Regiment..........	December 18, 1799
Williams, Isaac..........	Ensign, 38th Regiment............	August 21, 1801
Williams, John...........	Lieutenant, 38th Regiment........	August 21, 1801
Winkfield, Henry.........	Ensign, 2nd Battalion, 38th Regiment.......................	April 7, 1800
Winkfield, Henry.........	Ensign, 38th Regiment............	May 22, 1802
Wood, William............	Ensign, Rifle Company, 38th Regiment.......................	September 20, 1800
Wyman, Adam..............	Lieutenant, 38th Regiment........	September 20, 1800

Jefferson County Regiments

[33rd Regiment laid off November 21, 1799]

Allison, William.........	Lieutenant, 1st Regiment.........	February 4, 1800
Applegate, Benjamin......	Lieutenant, 33rd Regiment........ (Formerly in 1st Regiment)	March 14, 1800
Applegate, Benjamin......	Captain, 33rd Regiment...........	November 15, 1800
Ashby, Edward............	Ensign, 33rd Regiment............	February 23, 1802
Baggerly, Isaac..........	Ensign, 33rd Regiment............	July 30, 1803
Bartlett, Frederick......	Major, 2nd Battalion, 1st Regiment.......................	December 7, 1799
Bateman, Henry...........	Ensign, 33rd Regiment............ (Formerly in 1st Regiment)	March 14, 1800
Bates, John..............	Lieutenant, 1st Regiment.........	November 28, 1803
Batts, John..............	Ensign, 1st Regiment.............	June 12, 1799
Beverley, John...........	Ensign, 1st Regiment.............	September 24, 1799
Bohannon, George.........	Captain, 33rd Regiment...........	July 1, 1802
Brindley, John...........	Ensign, 33rd Regiment............	September 27, 1802
Bringman, Martin.........	Lieutenant, Rifle Company, 33rd Regiment (Formerly in 1st Regiment)	April 30, 1800
Brinkman, Martin.........	Captain, Rifle Company, 33rd Regiment.......................	November 15, 1800
Brown, David.............	Lieutenant, 1st Regiment.........	October 5, 1802
Brown, David.............	Captain, 1st Regiment............	November 28, 1803
Brown, John..............	Lieutenant, 33rd Regiment........ (Formerly in 1st Regiment)	March 14, 1800
Buckner, N(icholas)......	Lieutenant, 33rd Regiment........ (Formerly in 1st Regiment)	March 14, 1800
Burton, Zachariah........	Ensign, 33rd Regiment............	October 23, 1802
Campbell, Allan..........	2nd Lieutenant of Cavalry, 1st Regiment..................	January 5, 1804
Chambers, William........	Captain, 33rd Regiment........... (Formerly in 1st Regiment)	April 30, 1800
Chenoweth, James.........	Ensign, 33rd Regiment............ (Formerly in 1st Regiment)	March 14, 1800
Chenoweth, James.........	Lieutenant, 33rd Regiment........	November 15, 1800
Churchill, Samuel........	Ensign, 1st Regiment.............	March 25, 1802
Clark, William...........	Captain of Cavalry, 1st Regiment.	May 28, 1800
Clarke, Ludlow...........	Lieutenant, 1st Regiment.........	March 25, 1802

COMMISSIONED OFFICERS, 1799 - 1804 105

Clayton, William..........	2nd Lieutenant of Artillery, 33rd Regiment..................	July 1, 1802
Coons, John...............	Lieutenant, 33rd Regiment........	July 30, 1803
Cummins, William..........	Lieutenant, 1st Regiment.........	November 28, 1803
Curry, Edward.............	Lieutenant, 33rd Regiment........	October 23, 1802
Dorsey, Edward............	Captain, Rifle Company, 33rd Regiment......................	January 7, 1804
Duncan, Charles...........	Lieutenant, 1st Regiment.........	April 6, 1801
Edwards, James M.	Lieutenant, 33rd Regiment........	December 19, 1802
Edwards, William..........	Captain, 1st Regiment............	February 12, 1799
Edwards, William..........	Captain, 33rd Regiment........... (Formerly in 1st Regiment)	March 14, 1800
Edwards, William..........	Major, 2nd Battalion, 33rd Regiment......................	April 29, 1801
Ellis, Daniel.............	Ensign, 33rd Regiment............	February 23, 1802
Evans, John...............	Ensign, Rifle Company, 33rd Regiment......................	November 15, 1800
Finley, John..............	Ensign, 33rd Regiment............	December 19, 1802
Finley, Richard...........	Captain, 33rd Regiment...........	December 19, 1802
Finley, Richard, Jr. ...	Lieutenant, 33rd Regiment........	February 23, 1802
Floyd, George G. C.	Captain of Artillery, 33rd Regiment......................	May 23, 1801
Floyd, John...............	Ensign, 33rd Regiment............	November 15, 1800
Forsythe, James...........	Ensign, 33rd Regiment............	November 15, 1800
Forsythe, James...........	Lieutenant, 33rd Regiment........	February 23, 1802
Fowler, Joshua............	Captain, 33rd Regiment...........	March 14, 1800
Funk, John................	Ensign, 33rd Regiment............ (Formerly in 1st Regiment)	March 14, 1800
Funk, John................	Captain, 33rd Regiment...........	December 19, 1802
Funk, John, Jr.	Lieutenant, 33rd Regiment........	February 23, 1802
Funk, Joseph..............	Ensign, 33rd Regiment............	September 27, 1802
Geiger, Jacob.............	Lieutenant, 33rd Regiment........	March 14, 1800
Geiger, Jacob.............	Captain, 33rd Regiment...........	May 23, 1801
Harbolt, Leonard..........	Ensign, 33rd Regiment............	July 1, 1802
Harris, Hezekiah P.	Ensign, 1st Regiment.............	April 6, 1801
Hatfield, Thomas..........	Lieutenant, 1st Regiment.........	October 5, 1802
Hawes, John...............	Ensign, 1st Regiment.............	April 6, 1801
Hinch, Samuel.............	Ensign, 1st Regiment.............	October 5, 1802
Hoke, Leonard.............	Ensign, 33rd Regiment............	February 23, 1802
Hord, Willis..............	Adjutant, 33rd Regiment..........	November 24, 1801
Horn, Thomas..............	Ensign, 33rd Regiment............	March 14, 1800
Hughes, John..............	2nd Lieutenant of Cavalry, 1st Regiment...................	September 2, 1800
Hughes, John..............	Captain, 1st Regiment............	November 1, 1801
Hykes, Jacob..............	Ensign, 1st Regiment.............	March 25, 1802
Hykes, Jacob..............	Lieutenant, 1st Regiment.........	January 21, 1804
Johnson, Gabriel J.	Major, 1st Battalion, 1st Regiment......................	December 21, 1799
Kellar, Abraham...........	Ensign, 1st Regiment.............	January 21, 1804
Kendal, R.	Ensign, 1st Regiment.............	April 6, 1801
Kendal (Rawleigh)........	Captain, 1st Regiment............	March 25, 1802

COMMISSIONED OFFICERS, 1799 - 1804

Lacey, Isiah............	Captain, 1st Regiment............	April 6, 1801
Lacy, Isiah.............	Lieutenant, 1st Regiment........	November 28, 1799
Lane, Daniel............	Captain, 1st Regiment............	November 28, 1799
Lightfoot, Edmund.......	Lieutenant, 33rd Regiment.......	November 15, 1800
Linn, Asahel............	Captain, 1st Regiment............	April 8, 1800
Linn, William...........	Colonel, 1st Regiment............	December 17, 1799
Lockrey, Jeremiah.......	Ensign, 1st Regiment............	November 28, 1799
Lockrey, Jeremiah.......	Lieutenant, 1st Regiment........	April 6, 1801
Love, James.............	Ensign, 33rd Regiment............	November 15, 1800
Love, James.............	Lieutenant, 33rd Regiment.......	February 23, 1802
Luckett, Samuel.........	1st Lieutenant, Artillery Company, 33rd Regiment........	May 30, 1800
McCachley (McCauley?), Joshua...	Lieutenant, 1st Regiment...	September 24, 1799
Martin, James...........	Ensign, 1st Regiment............	November 28, 1803
Murphy, John............	Captain, 1st Regiment............	June 12, 1799
Nash, Harman............	Captain, 33rd Regiment........... (Formerly in 1st Regiment)	March 14, 1800
Nash, Harman............	Major, 33rd Regiment............	August 26, 1800
Oglesby, Elias..........	Lieutenant, 33rd Regiment.......	November 15, 1800
Oglesby, Ellis (Elias?)..	Captain, 33rd Regiment...........	February 23, 1802
Oglesby, Joseph.........	Captain, 33rd Regiment...........	November 15, 1800
Parker, Joshua..........	Ensign, 1st Regiment............	May 14, 1800
Parker, Samuel..........	Lieutenant, 1st Regiment........	May 14, 1800
Parker, Samuel..........	Captain, 1st Regiment............	April 6, 1801
Parker, Samuel..........	Ensign, 1st Regiment............	March 25, 1802
Pearce, Richard.........	Lieutenant, 33rd Regiment.......	May 23, 1801
Pearce, Walter..........	Ensign, Rifle Company, 33rd Regiment......................	January 7, 1804
Pearce, William.........	Ensign, 33rd Regiment............	September 27, 1802
Peck, Major.............	2nd Lieutenant, Artillery Company, 33rd Regiment........	May 30, 1800
Peyton, Phillip.........	Ensign, Rifle Company, 33rd Regiment.....................	July 30, 1803
Phillips, Samuel........	Paymaster, 33rd Regiment........	August 12, 1804
Philps (Phillips), Samuel...	Captain, 33rd Regiment...........	July 1, 1802
Pickett, John...........	Captain, Artillery Company, 33rd Regiment.....................	May 30, 1800
Pomeroy, Francis........	Lieutenant, 33rd Regiment.......	November 15, 1800
Pottorff, Henry.........	Ensign, 1st Regiment............	February 4, 1800
Pottorff, Henry.........	Captain, 1st Regiment............	April 6, 1801
Prather, Thomas.........	Paymaster, 1st Regiment.........	March 25, 1802
Prince, Thomas..........	Captain, 1st Regiment............	February 4, 1800
Pumeroy, Frank..........	Captain, 33rd Regiment...........	July 30, 1803
Querry, Charles.........	Major, 1st Battalion, 33rd Regiment......................	November 19, 1802
Query, Charles..........	Captain, 33rd Regiment...........	July 1, 1802
Quirry, Charles.........	Captain, 33rd Regiment........... (Formerly in 1st Regiment)	March 14, 1800
Quotermus, James........	Captain, 1st Regiment............	September 24, 1799
Ray, Samuel.............	Ensign, 33rd Regiment............	November 15, 1800
Read, Mordecai..........	Lieutenant, 33rd Regiment.......	July 1, 1802

COMMISSIONED OFFICERS, 1799 - 1804

Ross, Charles............	Ensign, 33rd Regiment............	July 30, 1803
Ross, Philip.............	Lieutenant, 33rd Regiment........	July 1, 1802
Ross, Stephen............	Ensign, 33rd Regiment............	July 1, 1802
Rudy, Daniel.............	Ensign, 33rd Regiment............	February 23, 1802
Rudy, George.............	Ensign, 33rd Regiment............	February 23, 1802
Rudy, George.............	Lieutenant, Rifle Company, 33rd Regiment.......................	July 30, 1803
Sale, Lewis..............	Lieutenant, 33rd Regiment........	September 27, 1802
Scott, William...........	Ensign, 33rd Regiment............	October 23, 1802
Seaton, George...........	Ensign, 1st Regiment.............	April 6, 1801
Seaton, George...........	Lieutenant, 1st Regiment.........	November 28, 1803
Seaton, James............	Ensign, 1st Regiment.............	October 5, 1802
Shivley, Philip..........	Lieutenant, 1st Regiment.........	November 1, 1801
Shreader, Christopher....	Ensign, 33rd Regiment............	February 23, 1802
Simrall, William F.	Captain, 1st Regiment............	January 5, 1804
Spangler, David..........	Ensign, 1st Regiment.............	February 12, 1799
Spangler, David..........	Ensign, 33rd Regiment............ (Formerly in 1st Regiment)	March 14, 1800
Spear, James E.	Adjutant, 33rd Regiment..........	July 1, 1802
Spear, James G.	Captain, Rifle Company, 33rd Regiment.......................	July 30, 1803
Spurr, James G.	Lieutenant, Rifle Company, 33rd Regiment.......................	November 15, 1800
Standeford, Elisha.......	Ensign, 1st Regiment.............	November 28, 1803
Strawther, John..........	Lieutenant, 1st Regiment.........	February 12, 1799
Strawther, John..........	Lieutenant, 33rd Regiment........ (Formerly in 1st Regiment)	March 18, 1800
Strother, Joseph, Jr. ..	Captain, 33rd Regiment...........	February 23, 1802
Sullivan, William........	Quartermaster, 1st Regiment......	March 25, 1802
Swearingen, Abijah.......	Captain, 1st Regiment............	October 5, 1802
Taylor, Colby............	Captain, 33rd Regiment...........	September 27, 1802
Taylor, Francis..........	Lieutenant, Light Infantry Company, 33rd Regiment.........	January 7, 1804
Taylor, Jonathan.........	Captain, Infantry Company, 33rd Regiment.......................	January 7, 1804
Taylor, Nathaniel........	Lieutenant, 1st Regiment.........	June 12, 1799
Taylor, Thompson.........	Captain, 1st Regiment............	May 14, 1800
Taylor, Thompson.........	Captain, 33rd Regiment...........	September 27, 1802
Tully, Wyatt P.	Lieutenant, Rifle Company, 33rd Regiment.......................	January 7, 1804
Wade, James..............	Ensign, 33rd Regiment............	July 1, 1802
Walford, Adam............	Ensign, 1st Regiment.............	April 8, 1800
Washburn, Samuel.........	Ensign, Light Infantry Company, 33rd Regiment.................	January 7, 1804
Washburne, Delany........	Lieutenant, 33rd Regiment........	December 19, 1802
Wells, Yelverton P.	Colonel, 33rd Regiment...........	August 26, 1800
White, Thomas............	Captain, 1st Regiment............	September 24, 1799
White, Thomas............	Captain, 33rd Regiment...........	September 24, 1799
White, William...........	Cornet, 1st Regiment.............	May 28, 1800
Wilkes, Daniel...........	Lieutenant, 1st Regiment.........	April 6, 1801

COMMISSIONED OFFICERS, 1799 - 1804

Wise, David.............. Captain, 33rd Regiment........... March 14, 1800
                          (Formerly in 1st Regiment)
Young, Christopher....... Ensign, 33rd Regiment............ July 30, 1803

Jessamine County Regiment

[First commissions June 21, 1799]

Akers, Peter............. Ensign, 9th Regiment............. May 25, 1800
Alcorn, George........... Captain, 9th Regiment............ November 1, 1800
Amy, William............. Ensign, 9th Regiment............. September 3, 1800
Amy, William............. Lieutenant, 9th Regiment......... April 10, 1804
Banks, Cuthbert.......... Captain, 9th Regiment............ June 21, 1799
Barr, George............. Lieutenant, 9th Regiment......... April 10, 1804
Barr, William............ Ensign, 9th Regiment............. May 27, 1803
Bartley, John............ Lieutenant, 9th Regiment......... June 28, 1802
Boatman, John............ Lieutenant, 9th Regiment......... November 1, 1800
Bowen, Elijah............ Lieutenant, 9th Regiment......... May 27, 1803
Bowling, William......... Captain, 9th Regiment............ July 29, 1799
Caldwell, William........ Lieutenant, Rifle Company, 9th
                          Regiment....................... April 15, 1800
Crowder, Starling........ Ensign, 9th Regiment............. May 20, 1801
Crowder, Starling........ Lieutenant, 9th Regiment......... October 9, 1802
Crowder, Sterling........ Captain, 9th Regiment............ April 10, 1804
Curd, Woodford........... Captain, 9th Regiment............ July 29, 1799
Drake, Nathaniel......... Ensign, 9th Regiment............. November 1, 1800
Drake, Nathaniel......... Lieutenant, 9th Regiment......... October 9, 1802
Duncan, Charles.......... Ensign, 9th Regiment............. April 25, 1800
Duncan, Charles.......... Lieutenant, 9th Regiment......... November 1, 1800
Dunn, James.............. Captain, 9th Regiment............ April 1, 1800
Ellege, Benjamin......... Lieutenant, 9th Regiment......... April 10, 1804
Ellige, Thomas........... Ensign, 9th Regiment............. May 27, 1803
Evans, John.............. Ensign, 9th Regiment............. July 29, 1799
Freeman, John............ Captain, 9th Regiment............ March 25, 1801
Gates, John.............. Ensign, 9th Regiment............. April 10, 1804
Gatewood, Richard........ Ensign, 9th Regiment............. April 10, 1804
Gatewood, Thomas......... Captain, 9th Regiment............ July 29, 1799
Greenwood, John.......... Ensign, 9th Regiment............. April 10, 1804
Hawkins, James........... Ensign, 9th Regiment............. October 9, 1802
Hawkins, James........... Lieutenant, 9th Regiment......... April 10, 1804
Hickman, Thomas.......... Ensign, 9th Regiment............. October 9, 1802
Highbee, Joseph.......... Ensign, 9th Regiment............. December 10, 1803
Hightower, Richard....... Captain, Rifle Company, 9th
                          Regiment....................... April 15, 1800
January, James B. ...... Cornet, 9th Regiment............. June 21, 1799
Kersey, Claiborne........ Lieutenant, 9th Regiment......... July 20, 1801
Kindred, Bartholomew..... Lieutenant, 9th Regiment......... July 29, 1799
Kindred, Bartholomew..... Adjutant, 9th Regiment........... June 28, 1802
Kirly, Francis........... Ensign, 9th Regiment............. February 19, 1800
Lafon, Richard........... Lieutenant, 9th Regiment......... April 25, 1800

COMMISSIONED OFFICERS, 1799 - 1804

Lewis, Joshua............	Paymaster, 9th Regiment..........	March 25, 1801
Lewis, Stephen...........	Ensign of Cavalry, 9th Regiment..	September 18, 1801
Lewis, Stephen...........	2nd Lieutenant of Cavalry, 9th Regiment...................	April 10, 1804
Lewis, Thomas............	Paymaster, 9th Regiment..........	June 28, 1802
Lewis, Thomas............	Captain, 9th Regiment............	May 27, 1803
Lockett, James...........	Ensign, 9th Regiment.............	July 29, 1799
Lockhart, James..........	Lieutenant, 9th Regiment.........	April 1, 1800
Lowry, John..............	Ensign, 9th Regiment.............	April 10, 1804
Lusk, Hugh...............	Captain, 9th Regiment............	October 9, 1802
McGrath, Terrence........	Ensign, 9th Regiment.............	April 10, 1804
McKee, David.............	Lieutenant, 9th Regiment.........	June 1, 1800
McKinney, John...........	Captain, 9th Regiment............	October 9, 1802
Mosley, John.............	Ensign, 9th Regiment.............	April 1, 1800
Mosley, John.............	Lieutenant, 9th Regiment.........	April 10, 1804
Moss, William............	Ensign, Rifle Company, 9th Regiment......................	April 15, 1800
Moss, William............	Lieutenant, 9th Regiment.........	April 10, 1804
Oliver, Thomas...........	Lieutenant, 9th Regiment.........	September 3, 1800
Oliver, Thomas...........	Captain, 9th Regiment............	June 28, 1802
Owens, James.............	Captain, 9th Regiment............	May 25, 1800
Peneston, Thomas.........	Ensign, 9th Regiment.............	October 9, 1802
Pilcher, Fielding........	Lieutenant, 9th Regiment.........	July 29, 1799
Poindexter, Peter........	Captain, 9th Regiment............	May 20, 1801 and June 28, 1802
Price, James.............	Cornet, Cavalry Company, 9th Regiment......................	April 10, 1804
Ramsay, George...........	Major, 1st Battalion, 9th Regiment......................	February 19, 1800
Scott, Thomas............	Ensign, 9th Regiment.............	April 10, 1804
Seitz, John A.	2nd Lieutenant, 9th Regiment.....	June 21, 1799
Shanklin, Gordon.........	Ensign, 9th Regiment.............	November 1, 1800
Singleton, Mason.........	Ensign, 9th Regiment.............	October 1, 1801
Spires, Solom............	Lieutenant, 9th Regiment.........	May 25, 1800
Stonestreet, John D. ...	Ensign, 9th Regiment.............	April 10, 1804
Talbot, George...........	Lieutenant, 9th Regiment.........	September 18, 1801
Thruston, Seth...........	Captain, 9th Regiment............	July 29, 1799
Walker, George...........	Quartermaster, 9th Regiment......	June 28, 1802
Webber, Philip...........	Adjutant, 9th Regiment...........	March 25, 1801
West, Richard............	Ensign, 9th Regiment.............	October 9, 1802
Wilkins, Stewart.........	1st Lieutenant, 9th Regiment.....	June 21, 1799
Williams, James..........	Major, 2nd Battalion, 9th Regiment......................	December 15, 1804
Woodson, Samuel H.	Captain, 9th Regiment............	September 18, 1801
Yeizer, Jacob............	Ensign, 9th Regiment.............	May 27, 1803
Yeizer, Jacob............	Lieutenant, 9th Regiment.........	April 10, 1804

Knox County Regiment

[Laid off December 10, 1802]

Arthur, Ambrose..........	Paymaster, 54th Regiment..........	January 3, 1803
Arthur, Ambrose..........	Lieutenant, Rifle Company, 54th Regiment..................	May 28, 1803
Arthur, Thomas, Jr.	Ensign, Rifle Company, 54th Regiment......................	May 26, 1804
Asher, Dillon............	Ensign, Rifle Company, 54th Regiment......................	January 3, 1803
Ayres, Moses.............	Captain, 54th Regiment..........	May 26, 1804
Baker, Brice.............	Lieutenant, 54th Regiment........	May 26, 1804
Ballinger, Eastham.......	Captain, 54th Regiment..........	January 3, 1803
Ballinger, Eastham.......	Adjutant, 54th Regiment..........	December 1, 1803
Ballinger, John..........	Colonel, 54th Regiment..........	December 14, 1802
Ballinger, Richard.......	Captain, Rifle Company, 54th Regiment......................	January 3, 1803
Brittain, James..........	Captain, 54th Regiment..........	January 3, 1803
Britton, George..........	Major, 2nd Battalion, 54th Regiment......................	December 15, 1802
Bunch, George............	Lieutenant, 54th Regiment........	May 28, 1803
Burns, James.............	Lieutenant, 54th Regiment........	December 1, 1803
Chestnut, Abram..........	Ensign, 54th Regiment............	May 28, 1803
Comer, Martin............	Ensign, 54th Regiment............	January 3, 1803
Craig, George W.	Captain, 54th Regiment..........	January 3, 1803
Duncan, Joseph...........	Ensign, Rifle Company, 54th Regiment......................	January 3, 1803
Duncan, Joseph...........	Lieutenant, Rifle Company, 54th Regiment......................	May 26, 1804
Eaton, John..............	Ensign, 54th Regiment............	May 26, 1804
Farris, George...........	Lieutenant, 54th Regiment........	January 3, 1803
Farris, George...........	Captain, 54th Regiment..........	May 28, 1803
Farris, John.............	Ensign, 54th Regiment............	December 1, 1803
Farris, William..........	Captain, 54th Regiment..........	January 3, 1803
Ferguson, Andrew.........	Ensign, 54th Regiment............	January 3, 1803
Ferguson, Andrew.........	Lieutenant, 54th Regiment........	May 26, 1804
Gray, Andrew.............	Paymaster, 54th Regiment..........	December 1, 1803
Herndon, Richard.........	Captain, 54th Regiment..........	January 3, 1803
Hogan, David.............	Lieutenant, 54th Regiment........	January 3, 1803
Hogan, David.............	Quartermaster, 54th Regiment.....	January 3, 1803
Hogan, David.............	Captain, 54th Regiment..........	May 28, 1803
Howard, Benjamin.........	Ensign, 54th Regiment............	May 28, 1803
Ingle, Peter.............	Lieutenant, 54th Regiment........	January 3, 1803
Johnson, Joseph..........	Lieutenant, Rifle Company, 54th Regiment..................	January 3, 1803
Jones, Elijah............	Ensign, 54th Regiment............	December 1, 1803
Jones, Ezekiel...........	Ensign, 54th Regiment............	May 28, 1803
Killam, Gilbert..........	Ensign, 54th Regiment............	December 1, 1803
Laughlin, Thomas.........	Captain, Rifle Company, 54th Regiment......................	January 3, 1803

Laughlin, Thomas.........	Major, 1st Battalion, 54th Regiment......................	December 15, 1804
McNeil, James............	Ensign, 54th Regiment............	January 3, 1803
McNeil, James............	Lieutenant, 54th Regiment........	May 28, 1803
Mahan, Thomas............	Ensign, 54th Regiment............	January 3, 1803
Miller, Daniel...........	Lieutenant, Rifle Company, 54th Regiment......................	January 3, 1803
Moore, Thomas............	Major, 1st Battalion, 54th Regiment......................	December 14, 1802
Moore, William...........	Lieutenant, 54th Regiment........	December 1, 1803
Muncey, John.............	Lieutenant, 54th Regiment........	May 28, 1804
Neil, Arthur.............	Lieutenant, 54th Regiment........	May 28, 1803
Shoemaker, Leonard C. ..	Captain, 54th Regiment...........	January 3, 1803
Smith, Gideon............	Quartermaster, 54th Regiment.....	December 1, 1803
Stinson, Robert..........	Ensign, Rifle Company, 54th Regiment......................	May 26, 1804
Stotts, James............	Lieutenant, 54th Regiment........	January 3, 1803
Stotts, James............	Adjutant, 54th Regiment..........	January 3, 1803
Stotts, James............	Captain, 54th Regiment...........	May 26, 1804
Willburn, Edward.........	Lieutenant, 54th Regiment........	January 3, 1803
Willburn, Edward.........	Captain, 54th Regiment...........	May 26, 1804
Woodson, Henry...........	Ensign, 54th Regiment............	January 3, 1803

Lincoln County Regiment

Alcorn, George...........	Lieutenant, 6th Regiment.........	February 2, 1799
Asher, John..............	Lieutenant, 6th Regiment.........	September 10, 1799
Bailey, John.............	Lieutenant, 6th Regiment.........	April 6, 1800
Ball, William............	Ensign, 6th Regiment.............	November 21, 1801
Ballinger, John..........	Captain, 6th Regiment............	September 10, 1799
Bethuram, William........	Lieutenant, 6th Regiment.........	March 21, 1803
Bingerman, Henry.........	Captain, 6th Regiment............	April 26, 1800
Blane, John..............	Major, 1st Battalion, 6th Regiment......................	December 17, 1799
Blane, John..............	Lieutenant Colonel, Commandant 6th Regiment...................	December 15, 1804
Bockman, Hr. (Baughman, Henry?)...	Ensign, 6th Regiment....	December 14, 1803
Briggs, Benjamin.........	Captain, 6th Regiment............	March 21, 1803
Bryant, Robert...........	Captain, 6th Regiment............	September 13, 1802
Cabbel, Joseph...........	Lieutenant, 6th Regiment.........	May 4, 1800
Campbell, John...........	Lieutenant, 6th Regiment.........	November 21, 1801
Carr, Armstrong..........	Lieutenant, 6th Regiment.........	May 5, 1800
Collier, Moses...........	Lieutenant, 6th Regiment.........	November 21, 1801
Collins, Joel............	Captain, 6th Regiment............	November 3, 1799
Cook, Anthony............	Lieutenant, 6th Regiment.........	December 14, 1803
Coulter, Morris..........	Ensign, 6th Regiment.............	March 21, 1803
Cox, William.............	Ensign, 6th Regiment.............	September 13, 1802
Crow, Walter.............	Lieutenant, 6th Regiment.........	September 13, 1802
Cumings, Daniel..........	Ensign, 6th Regiment.............	November 21, 1801
Dawson, Benjamin.........	Captain, 6th Regiment............	May 12, 1803

COMMISSIONED OFFICERS, 1799 - 1804

Denton, Robert...........	Lieutenant, 6th Regiment.........	May 12, 1800
Denton, Robert...........	Captain, 6th Regiment............	March 21, 1803
Dismuke, Joseph..........	Captain, 6th Regiment............	December 14, 1803
Edgeman, Kimberland......	Captain, 6th Regiment............	January 21, 1799
Embrie, Moses............	Ensign, 6th Regiment.............	November 21, 1801
Feland, Joseph...........	Lieutenant, 6th Regiment.........	May 12, 1803
Forbis, Jonathan.........	Paymaster, 6th Regiment..........	September 13, 1802
Gay, John................	Lieutenant, 6th Regiment.........	April 29, 1800
Gay, Thomas..............	Captain, 6th Regiment............	November 21, 1801
Glover, John.............	Ensign, 6th Regiment.............	September 19, 1803
Good, Fleming............	Ensign, 6th Regiment.............	September 13, 1802
Gum, Norton..............	Captain, 6th Regiment............	September 13, 1802
Hall, Andrew.............	Ensign, 6th Regiment.............	November 21, 1801
Hamen (Harman?), George..	Ensign, 6th Regiment.............	April 26, 1800
Hartgrove, William.......	Captain, 6th Regiment............	February 2, 1799
Hill, William............	Ensign, 6th Regiment.............	November 21, 1801
Hutchins, Gabriel........	Lieutenant, 6th Regiment.........	March 21, 1803
Jasper, John.............	Ensign, 6th Regiment.............	February 2, 1799
Jenkins, William.........	Ensign, 6th Regiment.............	December 14, 1803
Johnson, Joseph..........	Lieutenant, 6th Regiment.........	November 3, 1799
Johnston, Jacob..........	Lieutenant, 6th Regiment.........	May 29, 1800
Kirkland, Charles........	Captain, 6th Regiment............	May 12, 1800
Lewis, Joseph............	Major, 2nd Battalion, 6th Regiment...................	December 18, 1799
Lewis, Samuel............	Lieutenant, 6th Regiment.........	April 26, 1800
Linebarger, Frederick....	Ensign, 6th Regiment.............	September 13, 1802
Lithill, Lott (Lott Luttrell?)...	Ensign, 6th Regiment......	May 4, 1800
Lithill, Roadshah (Rodham Luttrell?)...	Captain, 6th Regiment......................	May 4, 1800
McKinney, James..........	Captain, 6th Regiment............	September 13, 1802
McKinsey, David..........	Captain, 6th Regiment............	January 24, 1799
Magil, William...........	Ensign, 6th Regiment.............	April 6, 1800
Manifee, John............	Lieutenant, 6th Regiment.........	November 21, 1801
Martin, William..........	Ensign, 6th Regiment.............	November 3, 1799
Mason, Richard...........	Ensign, 6th Regiment.............	May 5, 1800
May, John................	Ensign, 6th Regiment.............	April 29, 1800
Miller, Daniel...........	Ensign, 6th Regiment.............	September 10, 1799
Murrel, George...........	Colonel, 6th Regiment............	December 17, 1799
Nash, John...............	Ensign, 6th Regiment.............	May 29, 1800
Nash, Marvel.............	Ensign, 6th Regiment.............	May 5, 1800
Nash, William............	Captain, 6th Regiment............	May 29, 1800
Nichols, George..........	Lieutenant, 6th Regiment.........	January 21, 1799
Paris, Johnston..........	Captain, 6th Regiment............	January 17, 1799
Paris, William...........	Lieutenant, 6th Regiment.........	January 17, 1799
Perry, Jeremiah..........	Captain, 6th Regiment............	January 14, 1800
Potts, Hep.	Ensign, 6th Regiment.............	November 21, 1801
Ratcliffe, Harper........	Ensign, 6th Regiment.............	January 21, 1799
Renfrow, Lewis...........	Ensign, 6th Regiment.............	March 21, 1803
Sapp, Caleb..............	Ensign, 6th Regiment.............	May 12, 1803
Sapp, Caleb..............	Lieutenant, 6th Regiment.........	December 14, 1803
Scholefield, John........	Ensign, 6th Regiment.............	May 12, 1803

COMMISSIONED OFFICERS, 1799 - 1804   113

Shackleford, Bennet......	Ensign, 6th Regiment.............	November 21, 1801
Shackleford, James.......	Lieutenant, 6th Regiment.........	September 13, 1802
Shackleford, James.......	Captain, 6th Regiment............	April 29, 1800
Shackleford, John........	Adjutant, 6th Regiment...........	September 13, 1802
Skidmore, Joseph.........	Lieutenant, 6th Regiment.........	November 21, 1801
Smith, Abraham...........	Lieutenant, 6th Regiment.........	March 21, 1803
Smith, John..............	Lieutenant, 6th Regiment.........	May 26, 1799
Smith, William...........	Captain, 6th Regiment............	March 21, 1803
Spragens, Nathaniel......	Ensign, 6th Regiment.............	September 13, 1802
Spragin, William.........	Ensign, 6th Regiment.............	November 21, 1801
Stephens, Jac.	Ensign, 6th Regiment.............	September 13, 1802
Steward, Charles.........	Lieutenant, 6th Regiment.........	January 24, 1799
Sutton, James............	Captain, 6th Regiment............	April 30, 1799
Swinney, Shepherd........	Ensign, 6th Regiment.............	December 14, 1803
Tanner, William..........	Ensign, 6th Regiment.............	January 17, 1799
Thomas, John.............	Ensign, 6th Regiment.............	March 21, 1803
Trap, John...............	Ensign, 6th Regiment.............	January 24, 1799
Umphers (Humphries), John	Lieutenant, 6th Regiment.........	September 13, 1802
Vandiver, Asbury.........	Lieutenant, 6th Regiment.........	May 5, 1800
Wade, William............	Lieutenant, 6th Regiment.........	November 21, 1801
Warren, John.............	Captain, 6th Regiment............	November 21, 1801
Weathers, James..........	Lieutenant, 6th Regiment.........	January 10, 1799
Webster, William.........	Ensign, 6th Regiment.............	May 12, 1800
Whittle, John............	Lieutenant, 6th Regiment.........	March 21, 1803
Williams, Samuel.........	Ensign, 6th Regiment.............	May 26, 1799
Williams, Walter.........	Captain, 6th Regiment............	November 21, 1801
Wood, John...............	Captain, 6th Regiment............	May 5, 1800

Livingston County Regiments

[24th Regiment first commissions July 1, 1799]

[55th Regiment laid off December 15, 1802]

Anderson, John...........	Ensign, 24th Regiment............	May 31, 1800
Anderson, John...........	Lieutenant, 24th Regiment........	April 1, 1801
Anderson, John...........	Captain, 55th Regiment...........	February 12, 1803
Barker, Lewis............	Captain, 24th Regiment...........	January 8, 1802
Barker, Lewis............	Captain, 55th Regiment Recommissioned.................	April 7, 1803
Barnes, Joseph...........	Ensign, 24th Regiment............	August 4, 1800
Bearden, John............	Captain, 24th Regiment...........	January 8, 1802
Bearden, John............	Captain, 55th Regiment Recommissioned.................	April 7, 1803
Bearden, Winn	Lieutenant, 24th Regiment........	April 1, 1801
Birdsong, William........	Captain, 24th Regiment...........	April 1, 1801
Birdsong, William........	Major, 2nd Battalion, 55th Regiment......................	December 16, 1802
Blackburn, William B. ..	Adjutant, 24th Regiment..........	August 15, 1799
Bradford, William........	Captain, 24th Regiment...........	August 2, 1799

COMMISSIONED OFFICERS, 1799 - 1804

Brown, Joseph	Ensign, 24th Regiment	October 5, 1803
Campbell, John	Lieutenant, 24th Regiment	March 10, 1803
Clarke, Gideon	Ensign, 24th Regiment	April 1, 1801
Cole, John	Captain, 24th Regiment	April 10, 1800
Corn, Aaron	Lieutenant, 24th Regiment	November 20, 1804
Davis, Levi	Lieutenant, 55th Regiment	February 12, 1803
	Recommissioned	April 7, 1803
Davis, Nathan	Captain, 24th Regiment	March 10, 1803
Dobbins, James	Ensign, 24th Regiment	April 1, 1801
Dobbins, Robert	Ensign, 24th Regiment	April 1, 1801
Dobbins, Robert	Lieutenant, 24th Regiment	January 8, 1802
Dodd, Francis	Lieutenant, 24th Regiment	January 8, 1802
Dodd, James	Ensign, 24th Regiment	November 20, 1804
Dodds, John	Ensign, 24th Regiment	March 10, 1803
Downing, William	Lieutenant, 24th Regiment	August 2, 1799
Elder, James	Lieutenant, 24th Regiment	April 10, 1800
Elder, James	Captain, 24th Regiment	October 5, 1803
Elder, Thomas	Lieutenant, 24th Regiment	October 5, 1803
Farguson, Hamlett	Captain, 24th Regiment	March 3, 1800
Ferguson, Hamlett	Major, 2nd Battalion, 24th Regiment	December 15, 1802
Ferguson, Peter	Quartermaster, 24th Regiment	August 15, 1799
Ferguson, Richard	Captain, 24th Regiment	March 10, 1803
Fletcher, Peter	Lieutenant, 24th Regiment	March 2, 1800
Ford, James	Captain of Cavalry, 24th Regiment	April 1, 1801
Gaskins, John	Ensign, 24th Regiment	March 10, 1803
George, James	Ensign, 24th Regiment	April 1, 1801
Givins, Joseph	Lieutenant, 24th Regiment	August 4, 1800
Greer, James	Ensign, 55th Regiment	February 12, 1803
Grier, Isaac	Lieutenant, 55th Regiment	February 12, 1803
Hamilton, John	Captain, 24th Regiment	March 1, 1800
Hamilton, John	Major, 1st Battalion, 24th Regiment	December 14, 1802
Hardin, John	Ensign, 24th Regiment	November 20, 1804
Haskins, Joshua	Captain, 24th Regiment	March 10, 1803
Hathorn, Andrew	Ensign, 24th Regiment	October 5, 1803
Hibbs, Jonah	Lieutenant, 24th Regiment	March 3, 1800
Hodges, Robert	Captain, 24th Regiment	March 10, 1803
Hodges, Thomas	Ensign, 24th Regiment	November 20, 1804
Hooper, Enoch	Captain, 24th Regiment	April 1, 1801
Jones, Benjamin	Adjutant, 24th Regiment	November 20, 1800
Jones, Benjamin	Adjutant, 55th Regiment	December 17, 1802
Jones, John	Captain, 24th Regiment	June 26, 1801
Jones, John	Captain, 55th Regiment Recommissioned	April 7, 1803
Kilgore, William	Captain, 24th Regiment	July 1, 1799
Kivell, Benjamin	Quartermaster, 55th Regiment	December 17, 1802
Lacy, Edward, Jr.	Captain, 24th Regiment	August 4, 1800
Lacy, Edward, Jr.	Major, 2nd Battalion, 24th Regiment	April 6, 1804

COMMISSIONED OFFICERS, 1799 - 1804

Lamkin, Samuel...........	Lieutenant, 24th Regiment........	March 1, 1800
Logan, Robert A.	Lieutenant, 24th Regiment........	August 2, 1799
Lusk, Vance.............	1st Lieutenant of Cavalry, 24th Regiment......................	April 1, 1801
McElmurray, John........	Major, 1st Battalion, 24th Regiment......................	April 5, 1804
McElmury, John..........	Captain, 24th Regiment..........	March 2, 1800
McLain, Alney...........	Ensign, 24th Regiment...........	August 2, 1799
McLendon, Benjamin......	Ensign, 24th Regiment...........	August 2, 1799
McNab, James............	Captain, 24th Regiment..........	April 1, 1801
McNab, James............	Captain, 55th Regiment..........	February 12, 1803
	Recommissioned.................	April 7, 1803
McWilliams, David.......	Ensign, 24th Regiment...........	March 3, 1800
Michuson, John..........	2nd Lieutenant of Cavalry, 24th Regiment......................	April 1, 1801
Miles, Charles..........	Captain, 24th Regiment..........	November 20, 1804
Miles, James............	Cornet of Cavalry, 24th Regiment......................	April 1, 1801
Mitcheson, Edward.......	Captain, 24th Regiment..........	May 31, 1800
Mitchuson, Edward.......	Major, 1st Battalion, 55th Regiment......................	December 15, 1802
Mitchuson, William......	Colonel, 55th Regiment..........	December 15, 1802
Mitchusson, John........	Captain of Cavalry, 55th Regiment......................	February 12, 1803
Mitchusson, William.....	Major, 2nd Battalion, 24th Regiment......................	December 14, 1799
Montgomery, John........	Ensign, 24th Regiment...........	March 2, 1800
Neely, Andrew...........	Paymaster, 24th Regiment........	August 15, 1799
Parker, Isaac...........	Lieutenant, 24th Regiment.......	June 26, 1801
Parsons, Joseph.........	Lieutenant, 24th Regiment.......	November 20, 1804
Peal, Richard...........	Captain, 24th Regiment..........	March 10, 1803
Pennington, Isaac.......	Captain, 24th Regiment..........	August 2, 1799
Phelps, Micajah.........	Lieutenant, 24th Regiment.......	October 5, 1803
Pounds, John............	Lieutenant, 24th Regiment.......	May 31, 1800
Pounds, John............	Captain, 24th Regiment..........	January 8, 1802
Pounds, John............	Captain, 55th Regiment Recommissioned.................	April 7, 1803
Rammage, Jess...........	Lieutenant, 24th Regiment.......	March 10, 1803
Ramsay, Jonathan........	Major, 1st Battalion, 24th Regiment......................	December 13, 1799
Ramsay, Jonathan........	Colonel, 24th Regiment..........	December 14, 1802
Richey, James...........	Ensign, 24th Regiment...........	April 10, 1800
Richey, James, Jr.	Lieutenant, 24th Regiment.......	March 10, 1803
Richey, James, Jr.	Captain, 24th Regiment..........	October 5, 1803
Ritchey, Adam...........	Quartermaster, 24th Regiment.....	January 8, 1802
Roach, Matthew..........	Ensign, 24th Regiment...........	March 10, 1803
Rounseval, Josiah.......	Ensign, 24th Regiment...........	March 1, 1800
Rounseval, Josiah.......	Lieutenant, 24th Regiment.......	March 10, 1803
Shaw, William...........	Captain, 24th Regiment..........	January 8, 1802
Shaw, William...........	Captain, 55th Regiment Recommissioned.................	April 7, 1803

Shelby, Moses, Jr.	Captain, 24th Regiment	August 4, 1800
Shetford, William	Ensign, 55th Regiment	February 12, 1803
	Recommissioned	April 7, 1803
Simpson, Benjamin	Ensign, 24th Regiment	April 1, 1801
Simpson, William	Lieutenant, 24th Regiment	April 1, 1801
Sons, Abraham	Captain, 24th Regiment	April 1, 1801
Stephens, Elijah	Paymaster, 24th Regiment	January 8, 1802
Stephens, Elijah	Paymaster, 55th Regiment	December 17, 1802
Stewart, Abraham	Major, 2nd Battalion, 24th Regiment	August 2, 1799
Stokes, Absalom	Ensign, 24th Regiment	May 31, 1800
Talbot, Joshua	Ensign, 24th Regiment	March 10, 1803
Thompson, John	Lieutenant, 24th Regiment	May 31, 1800
Travis, Daniel	Lieutenant, 24th Regiment	January 8, 1802
Trimble, George	Ensign, 24th Regiment	March 10, 1803
Trimble, Walter	Lieutenant, 24th Regiment	March 10, 1803
Wadlington, James	Lieutenant, 24th Regiment	April 1, 1801
Wadlington, James	Captain, 55th Regiment	February 12, 1803
Wadlington, William	Lieutenant, 55th Regiment	February 12, 1803
Welch, William	Ensign, 24th Regiment	November 20, 1804
Wheeler, Henry	Ensign, 24th Regiment	January 8, 1802
Wing, Charles	Lieutenant, 24th Regiment	August 2, 1799
Wyatt, John	Ensign, 24th Regiment	January 8, 1802

Logan County Regiment

Adams, Matthew	Captain, 23rd Regiment	August 20, 1799
Bailey, Thomas	Lieutenant, 23rd Regiment	November 5, 1800
Butler, Thomas	Ensign, 23rd Regiment	November 5, 1800
Butler, Thomas	Captain, 23rd Regiment	April 16, 1804
Collins, Edward	Ensign, Rifle Company, 23rd Regiment	October 16, 1801
Dickey, John	Major, 2nd Battalion, 23rd Regiment	December 10, 1803
Edwards, Ninian	Major, 2nd Battalion, 23rd Regiment	December 13, 1802
Ewing, John	Ensign, 23rd Regiment	November 5, 1800
Ewing, Reubin	Paymaster, 23rd Regiment	April 15, 1801
Ewing, Samuel	Ensign, 23rd Regiment	November 5, 1800
Ewing, Samuel	Lieutenant, 23rd Regiment	November 5, 1800
Fike, John	Lieutenant, 23rd Regiment	April 16, 1804
Fursith (Forsythe), William	Lieutenant, 23rd Regiment	May 4, 1800
Goreham, Thomas	Captain, 23rd Regiment	October 31, 1802
Graham, James	Ensign, 23rd Regiment	October 31, 1802
Hargraves, Willis	Captain, 23rd Regiment	November 5, 1800
Harrison, Burr	Cornet, 23rd Regiment	November 5, 1800
Harrison, William	Adjutant, 23rd Regiment	March 24, 1799
Hawes, Jacob	Lieutenant, 23rd Regiment	November 5, 1800
Hawes, John	Ensign, 23rd Regiment	November 5, 1800
Hay, Daniel	Ensign, 23rd Regiment	November 5, 1800

COMMISSIONED OFFICERS, 1799 - 1804

Hay, Daniel...............	Lieutenant, 23rd Regiment........	October 31, 1802
Hay, John G.	Captain, 23rd Regiment...........	November 5, 1800
Hill, James...............	Ensign, 23rd Regiment............	October 31, 1802
Hill, Richard.............	Captain, 23rd Regiment...........	December 1, 1798
Hill, William.............	Ensign, 23rd Regiment............	May 4, 1800
Hopkins, Samuel...........	Ensign, 23rd Regiment............	November 5, 1800
Houston, Robert...........	Ensign, 23rd Regiment............	April 30, 1798
Houston, Robert...........	Lieutenant, 23rd Regiment........	November 5, 1800
Hunter, William...........	Captain, 23rd Regiment...........	October 31, 1802
Keith, Abraham............	Lieutenant, 23rd Regiment........	August 20, 1799
Keith, William............	Ensign, 23rd Regiment............	August 20, 1799
Latham, John..............	Lieutenant, 23rd Regiment........	April 16, 1804
Lee, Miller...............	Lieutenant, Rifle Company, 23rd Regiment......................	April 16, 1804
McDaniel, Daniel..........	Ensign, 23rd Regiment............	April 16, 1804
McGoodwin, Daniel.........	Captain, 23rd Regiment...........	November 5, 1800
McGrady, Israel...........	Captain, 23rd Regiment...........	November 5, 1800
McLaughlin, Robert........	Lieutenant, 23rd Regiment........	October 16, 1801
McLean, Samuel............	Lieutenant, 23rd Regiment........	December 1, 1798
Marrs, Isaac (?)..........	Ensign, 23rd Regiment............	October 16, 1801
Maulden, Morton...........	Colonel, 23rd Regiment...........	December 19, 1799
Neal, Andrew..............	Ensign, 23rd Regiment............	August 8, 1799
Nowlin, Bryan Ward........	Lieutenant, 23rd Regiment........	August 8, 1799
Nowlin, Payton............	Captain, 23rd Regiment...........	December 1, 1798
Patterson, Robert.........	Lieutenant, 23rd Regiment........	April 16, 1804
Porter, John..............	Captain, 23rd Regiment...........	May 4, 1800
Prewitt, George...........	Lieutenant, 23rd Regiment........	October 31, 1802
Proctor, Thomas...........	Captain, 23rd Regiment...........	April 1, 1800
Redman, Thomas............	Ensign, 23rd Regiment............	April 16, 1804
Rhodes, Solom.............	Ensign, 23rd Regiment............	August 20, 1799
Rice, Joshua..............	Lieutenant, 23rd Regiment........	October 31, 1802
Robertson, John...........	Captain, 23rd Regiment...........	April 16, 1804
Rogers, John..............	Ensign, 23rd Regiment............	October 16, 1801
Rotramell, John...........	Captain, 23rd Regiment...........	November 5, 1800
Shannon, Joseph...........	Lieutenant, 23rd Regiment........	October 16, 1801
Sharp, Maxwell............	Lieutenant, 23rd Regiment........	October 16, 1801
Simons, Peter.............	Lieutenant, 23rd Regiment........	December 1, 1798
Snodgrass, David..........	Lieutenant, Rifle Company, 23rd Regiment......................	October 31, 1802
Townsend, Lite............	Captain, 23rd Regiment...........	October 31, 1802
Tramel, Philip............	Lieutenant, 23rd Regiment........	December 1, 1798
Tramel, Philip............	Captain, 23rd Regiment...........	October 16, 1801
Turnbo, Isaac.............	Ensign, 23rd Regiment............	October 16, 1801
Tyler, John...............	Lieutenant, 23rd Regiment........	October 16, 1801
Tyler, John...............	Captain, 23rd Regiment...........	October 31, 1802
Ward, Jonathan............	Lieutenant, 23rd Regiment........	October 16, 1801
White, Alexander..........	Cornet, 23rd Regiment............	December 1, 1798

COMMISSIONED OFFICERS, 1799 - 1804

Madison County Regiments

[35th Regiment laid off November 29, 1799]

Alcorn, William..........	Ensign, 19th Regiment............	April 6, 1804
Allcorn, Thomas..........	Captain, 19th Regiment.......	October 9, 1802
Anderson, John...........	Lieutenant, 19th Regiment........	December 2, 1803
Anderson, William........	Ensign, 19th Regiment............	November 7, 1804
Bacon (?), Robert........	Ensign, 35th Regiment............	July 7, 1804
Baker, Joseph............	Lieutenant, 7th Regiment.........	January 9, 1799
Ball, John...............	Lieutenant, 7th Regiment.........	May 31, 1800
Barnett, Alexander.......	Lieutenant, 19th Regiment........	November 7, 1804
Barnett, Skiller.........	Ensign, Light Infantry Company, 19th Regiment..................	April 6, 1804
Barnett, William.........	Captain, 19th Regiment...........	October 29, 1803
Baxter, Edward...........	Major, 2nd Battalion, 35th Regiment........................	March 14, 1800
Beck, William............	Captain, 7th Regiment............	August 18, 1799
Blackwell, William.......	Lieutenant, 7th Regiment.........	April 29, 1800
Boone, William...........	Captain, 19th Regiment...........	April 23, 1799
Bredwell, Fielding.......	Ensign, 19th Regiment............	November 29, 1799
Briscoe, Andrew..........	Captain, 35th Regiment...........	November, 1801
Brown, James.............	Lieutenant, 7th Regiment.........	September 3, 1799
Brown, James.............	Lieutenant, 35th Regiment........	November 20, 1800
	First commissioned.............	September 3, 1799
Brown, Nicholas..........	Lieutenant, 35th Regiment........	May 12, 1800
Bullock, Edward..........	Adjutant, 35th Regiment..........	July 16, 1800
Burgain, Thomas..........	Captain, 7th Regiment............	July 2, 1799
Burnham, Henry...........	Ensign, 35th Regiment............	August 20, 1800
Caldwell, Robert.........	Major, 19th Regiment.............	December 19, 1801
Callaway, Richard........	Colonel, 7th Regiment............	December 21, 1799
Campbell, John...........	Major, 2nd Battalion, 35th Regiment........................	November 29, 1799
Caperton, John...........	Ensign, 35th Regiment............	October 12, 1802
Caperton, William........	Lieutenant, 35th Regiment........	August 20, 1800
Carpenter, William.......	Ensign, 7th Regiment.............	July 24, 1801
Cloyd, John..............	Captain, 19th Regiment...........	April 6, 1804
Cochran, Samuel..........	Major, 19th Regiment.............	November 20, 1799
Cook, William............	Lieutenant, 19th Regiment........	September 16, 1801
Cooper, Benjamin.........	Captain, 7th Regiment............	January 11, 1799
Cooper, Francis..........	Lieutenant, 35th Regiment........	June 22, 1802
Cooper, Richard..........	Ensign, 19th Regiment............	October 9, 1802
Corum, John..............	Quartermaster, 35th Regiment.....	July 7, 1804
Crook, John..............	Ensign, 7th Regiment.............	July 1, 1799
Crook, John..............	Lieutenant, 19th Regiment........	April 3, 1802
Crooke, Hezekiah.........	Ensign, 35th Regiment............	November 20, 1800
	First commissioned.............	November 15, 1799
Crooke, John.............	Captain, 35th Regiment...........	November 20, 1800
Davis, Joshua............	Lieutenant, 7th Regiment.........	April 4, 1800
Deatheridge, George......	Lieutenant, 7th Regiment.........	April 15, 1800
DeGarnett, James.........	Ensign, 7th Regiment.............	July 24, 1801

COMMISSIONED OFFICERS, 1799 - 1804

DeGarnett, James.........	Captain, 7th Regiment............	January 1, 1804
DeJarnet, John...........	Lieutenant, 7th Regiment.........	November 5, 1804
Dinwiddie, William.......	Lieutenant, 7th Regiment.........	September 19, 1801
Divers, Samuel...........	Ensign, 19th Regiment............	January 30, 1801
Dollard, John............	Lieutenant, 35th Regiment........	November 20, 1800
	First commissioned.............	December 23, 1799
Dougherty, Alexander.....	Captain, 19th Regiment...........	April 3, 1802
Duncan, John.............	Lieutenant, 19th Regiment........	October 1, 1802
Duncan, Robert...........	Ensign, 19th Regiment............	September 16, 1801
Dunken, Robert...........	Ensign, 19th Regiment............	October 29, 1803
Dunwiddie, William.......	Ensign, 7th Regiment.............	May 7, 1800
Dunwiddie, William.......	Paymaster, 7th Regiment..........	May 22, 1800
Durbin, Christian........	Ensign, 7th Regiment.............	June 18, 1799
Elliott, David...........	Lieutenant, 19th Regiment........	February 23, 1799
Ellison, James...........	Ensign, 35th Regiment............	July 7, 1804
Estill, James............	Quartermaster, 7th Regiment......	May 22, 1800
Estill, James............	Ensign, 19th Regiment............	October 29, 1803
Estill, James............	Lieutenant, 19th Regiment........	April 6, 1804
Estill, James............	Captain, 19th Regiment...........	November 7, 1804
Estill, Samuel...........	Lieutenant, 19th Regiment........	November 7, 1804
Faris, Dudley............	Captain, 19th Regiment...........	November 7, 1804
Faris, George............	Ensign, 19th Regiment............	September 16, 1801
Faris, George............	Lieutenant, 19th Regiment........	November 7, 1804
Ferril, John.............	Ensign, 35th Regiment............	January 1, 1800
Fish, William............	Ensign, 19th Regiment............	November 7, 1804
Garvin, John.............	Adjutant, 19th Regiment..........	(April 6, 1804?)
Gass, James..............	Captain, 19th Regiment...........	December 2, 1803
Gentry, Rubin............	Lieutenant, 19th Regiment........	November 7, 1804
George, Richard..........	Ensign, 19th Regiment............	December 2, 1803
Gilbard (Gilbert?), John.	Lieutenant, 35th Regiment........	July 7, 1804
Glasgow, Samuel..........	Ensign, 35th Regiment............	October 2, 1801
Glenn, Hugh..............	Captain, 19th Regiment...........	February 25, 1799
Glenn, Hugh..............	Major, 19th Regiment.............	February 7, 1803
Goe, John................	Ensign, 7th Regiment.............	April 15, 1800
Goodrich, Samuel.........	Lieutenant, 19th Regiment........	April 3, 1802
Green, William...........	Lieutenant, 19th Regiment........	December 2, 1803
Griffith, Patterson......	Lieutenant, 35th Regiment........	July 7, 1804
Grubbs, Thomas...........	Lieutenant, 7th Regiment.........	May 22, 1800
Grubbs, Thomas...........	Captain, 7th Regiment............	March 14, 1803
Hackett, Peter...........	Captain, 35th Regiment...........	May 12, 1800
Hall, Elisha.............	Lieutenant, 19th Regiment........	July 29, 1799
Ham, John................	Lieutenant, 19th Regiment........	May 6, 1799
Harper, Turner...........	Ensign, 19th Regiment............	March 1, 1799
Harris, Henry............	Ensign, 7th Regiment.............	July 24, 1801
Harris, John.............	Major, 1st Battalion, 35th Regiment......................	November 29, 1799
Harris, William..........	Ensign, 19th Regiment............	November 7, 1804
Harris, William..........	Lieutenant, 35th Regiment........	July 7, 1804
Harvey, Norris...........	Captain, 19th Regiment...........	December 2, 1803
Harvey, William..........	Lieutenant, 19th Regiment........	April 23, 1799
Harvey, William..........	Captain, 19th Regiment...........	January 30, 1801

Haskins, Phil.	Ensign, 35th Regiment	June 22, 1802
Hawkins, John	Ensign, 35th Regiment	July 7, 1804
Hogan, John	Ensign, 19th Regiment	February 25, 1799
Hogan, John	Lieutenant, 19th Regiment	October 29, 1803
Houston, William	Lieutenant, 19th Regiment	August 2, 1799
Howard, Josh.	Ensign, 7th Regiment	December 9, 1799
Huston, Simon	Ensign, 35th Regiment	July 7, 1804
Jameson, Robert	Captain, 35th Regiment	November 20, 1800
Johnson, Richard, Jr.	Ensign, 7th Regiment	March 14, 1803
Johnson, Richard, Sr.	Lieutenant, 7th Regiment	March 14, 1803
Jones, Humphrey	Major, 2nd Battalion, 7th Regiment	January 27, 1803
Jones, James	Captain, 7th Regiment	January 1, 1804
Kellian, Jacob	Ensign, 19th Regiment	April 23, 1799
Kelly, Giles	Lieutenant, 19th Regiment	November 29, 1799
Kennedy, Andrew	Colonel, 19th Regiment	November 20, 1799
Kennedy, Joseph	Paymaster, 19th Regiment	March 15, 1800
Killing, Jacob	Ensign, 19th Regiment	January 28, 1799
Kincaid, David	Captain, 19th Regiment	October 29, 1803
Kincaid, James	Captain, 35th Regiment	July 7, 1804
Lackey, William	Ensign, 19th Regiment	February 24, 1799
McCollum, William	Ensign, 19th Regiment	September 16, 1801
McCrary, William	Lieutenant, 35th Regiment	August 20, 1800
McCreery, William	Ensign, 7th Regiment	January 11, 1799
McDaniel, James	Ensign, 7th Regiment	April 4, 1800
McGee, Humphrey	Ensign, 7th Regiment	August 18, 1799
McMullen, James	Ensign, 19th Regiment	October 9, 1802
McWilliams, James	Lieutenant, 19th Regiment	October 29, 1803
Mallott, Joseph	Ensign, 7th Regiment	March 14, 1803
March, Rudolph	Ensign, 19th Regiment	November 7, 1804
Mason, John	Ensign, 19th Regiment	November 7, 1804
Massey, Sylvanus	Ensign, 35th Regiment	June 22, 1802
Massey, Sylvanus	Lieutenant, 35th Regiment	July 7, 1804
Maupin, Thomas	Lieutenant, 19th Regiment	October 29, 1803
Maupine, John	Ensign, 35th Regiment	August 20, 1800
Milam, Jarvis	Ensign, 7th Regiment	May 22, 1800
Miller, Daniel	Quartermaster, 35th Regiment	July 16, 1800
Miller, Robert	Captain, 7th Regiment	June 5, 1799
Mills, Robert	Ensign, 19th Regiment	October 29, 1803
Mobley, John	Lieutenant, 35th Regiment	October 12, 1802
Moor, David	Ensign, 19th Regiment	November 7, 1804
Moore, David	Captain, 19th Regiment	February 25, 1799
Moore, James	Lieutenant, 19th Regiment	March 29, 1799
Moore, James	Captain, 19th Regiment	October 29, 1803
Moppen (Maupin), Thomas	Lieutenant, 19th Regiment	November 29, 1799
Morrison, George	Captain, 19th Regiment	March 6, 1803
Noland, William	Lieutenant, 35th Regiment	November 20, 1800
Norcutt, John	Captain, 19th Regiment	January 30, 1801
Northcutt, John	Lieutenant, 19th Regiment	April 30, 1799
Parks, Nathaniel	Lieutenant, 7th Regiment	July 2, 1799
Parks, Nathan(iel)	Captain, 35th Regiment	August 20, 1800

Pasley, James............	Lieutenant, 7th Regiment.........	June 5, 1799
Patrick, Alexander.......	Surgeon, 7th Regiment............	December 3, 1804
Patton, James............	Ensign, 7th Regiment.............	September 19, 1801
Petterson, Thomas........	Captain, 19th Regiment...........	October 9, 1802
Phillips, William........	Lieutenant, 19th Regiment........	December 2, 1803
Poague, Jonathan.........	Lieutenant, 19th Regiment........	October 9, 1802
Poge, John...............	Ensign, 19th Regiment............	October 29, 1803
Prater, Phil.	Lieutenant, 7th Regiment.........	July 24, 1801
Pryor, Abraham...........	Lieutenant, 19th Regiment........	February 24, 1799
Quick, Aron..............	Ensign, 35th Regiment............	August 20, 1800
Reed, William............	Ensign, 19th Regiment............	February 13, 1799
Reid, John...............	Ensign, 7th Regiment.............	July 1, 1799
Reid, John...............	Lieutenant, 7th Regiment.........	May 7, 1800
Reid, John...............	Captain, 7th Regiment............	September 19, 1801
Reid, William............	Ensign, 7th Regiment.............	June 5, 1799
Reilly, William..........	Ensign, 7th Regiment.............	November 5, 1804
Richardson, Daniel.......	Captain, 35th Regiment...........	May 31, 1800
Richardson, John, Jr. ...	Lieutenant, 35th Regiment........	May 31, 1800
Riley, John..............	Ensign, 7th Regiment.............	July 24, 1801
Runyon, Martin...........	Ensign, 35th Regiment............	May 12, 1800
Sampson, Benjamin........	Ensign, 19th Regiment............	November 29, 1799
Sampson, Benjamin........	Lieutenant, 19th Regiment........	January 30, 1801
Sappington, Richard......	Lieutenant, 7th Regiment.........	July 24, 1801
Searcy, Samuel...........	Paymaster, 35th Regiment.........	July 16, 1800
Seburn, Jacob............	Adjutant, 7th Regiment...........	December 16, 1800
Self, John...............	Captain, 19th Regiment...........	November 29, 1799
Shelton, Thomas..........	Lieutenant, 19th Regiment........	October 9, 1802
Simpson, Benjamin........	Lieutenant, 19th Regiment........	January 30, 1801
Smith, Samuel............	Ensign, 19th Regiment............	April 6, 1804
Smith, Thomas............	Captain, 19th Regiment...........	May 6, 1799
Snoddy, John.............	Captain, 19th Regiment...........	October 9, 1802
Snoddy, Samuel...........	Captain, 19th Regiment...........	February 13, 1799
Snoddy, Samuel...........	Major, 2nd Battalion, 19th Regiment......................	April 5, 1802
Snow, Aquila.............	Ensign, 19th Regiment............	December 2, 1803
South, Samuel............	Colonel, 35th Regiment...........	November 29, 1799
Stevenson, John..........	Ensign, 19th Regiment............	December 2, 1803
Strawhan, Benjamin.......	Lieutenant, 7th Regiment.........	October 2, 1804
Strowhorn, Joseph........	Ensign, 7th Regiment.............	October 27, 1802
Tharp, Josiah............	Ensign, 35th Regiment............	July 7, 1804
Thomas, James............	Ensign, 7th Regiment.............	July 29, 1799
Thomas, James............	Ensign, 35th Regiment............	November 20, 1800
	First commissioned.............	February 10, 1797
Thomas, James....,......	Lieutenant, 35th Regiment........	July 7, 1804
Thomas, Zachariah........	Ensign, 35th Regiment............	July 7, 1804
Titus, John..............	Ensign, 19th Regiment............	April 3, 1802
Tivis, Robert............	Captain, 7th Regiment............	May 31, 1800
Towns, Oswald............	Major, 1st Battalion, 7th Regiment......................	December 21, 1799
Townsend, Thomas.........	Captain, 35th Regiment...........	November 20, 1800
	First commissioned.............	July 9, 1798

COMMISSIONED OFFICERS, 1799 - 1804

Trigg, Stephen............	Lieutenant, 7th Regiment.........	January 11, 1799
Trigg, Stephen............	Captain, 35th Regiment...........	August 20, 1800
Tunstall, Richard........	Ensign, 7th Regiment.............	October 2, 1804
Turley, Samuel............	Ensign, 35th Regiment............	May 31, 1800
Turley, Samuel............	Lieutenant, 35th Regiment........	November, 1801
Walker, James.............	Captain, 19th Regiment...........	September 16, 1801
Walker, Stephen...........	Captain, 19th Regiment...........	February 24, 1799
Wallace, John.............	Lieutenant, 19th Regiment........	April 6, 1804
Wells, Joseph.............	Lieutenant, 35th Regiment........	August 20, 1800
Wheeler, Leven............	Ensign, 7th Regiment.............	April 29, 1800
White, James..............	Captain, 35th Regiment...........	January 1, 1800
White, James..............	Ensign, 35th Regiment............	October 2, 1801
White, James..............	Lieutenant, 35th Regiment........	June 22, 1802
White, Joel...............	Ensign, 19th Regiment............	September 7, 1799
White, Joel...............	Captain, 19th Regiment...........	April 3, 1802
Wilkerson, John...........	Major, 2nd Battalion, 7th Regiment.......................	November 29, 1799
Williams, Caleb...........	Ensign, 19th Regiment............	March 2, 1799
Williams, Daniel..........	Captain, 7th Regiment............	April 15, 1800
Williams, William.........	Captain, 7th Regiment............	December 9, 1799
Willis, Edward............	Captain, 19th Regiment...........	April 3, 1802
Winscutt (no first name).	Ensign, 7th Regiment.............	January 1, 1804
Witt, William.............	Ensign, 35th Regiment............	June 22, 1802
Wood, William.............	Captain, 19th Regiment...........	September 16, 1801
Woods, Adam...............	Ensign, 7th Regiment.............	January 1, 1804
Woods, Adam...............	Lieutenant, 7th Regiment.........	October 2, 1804
Woods, John...............	Ensign, 19th Regiment............	April 6, 1804
Woods, John...............	Lieutenant, 19th Regiment........	April 3, 1802
Woods, Patrick............	Lieutenant, 7th Regiment.........	December 9, 1799
Woods, William............	Captain, 35th Regiment...........	July 7, 1804

Mason County Regiments

Adams, James..............	Lieutenant, 29th Regiment........	November, 1800
Adams, Jesse..............	Ensign, 29th Regiment............	November, 1800
Allinson (Allison), John.	Captain, 29th Regiment...........	October 2, 1801
Ashcraft, Jacob...........	Captain, 29th Regiment...........	November 3, 1800
Baldwin, Samuel...........	Captain, 15th Regiment...........	June 26, 1802
Barclay, James............	Captain, 15th Regiment...........	May 21, 1803
Baylis, Benjamin..........	Captain of Cavalry, 15th Regiment.......................	August 13, 1801
Bennett, Titus............	Ensign, 15th Regiment............	September 15, 1800
Bennett, Titus............	Lieutenant, 15th Regiment........	August 13, 1801
Berry, Henry..............	Captain, 29th Regiment...........	April 1, 1800
Berry, Reuben.............	Lieutenant, 29th Regiment........	November 17, 1804
Boyd, John................	Lieutenant, 29th Regiment........	May 15, 1798
Bronaugh, William.........	Ensign, 15th Regiment............	September 15, 1801
Bronaugh, William.........	Captain, 15th Regiment...........	January 7, 1804
Brown, John...............	Captain, 15th Regiment...........	August 15, 1799
Brown, Joseph.............	Lieutenant, 15th Regiment........	December 4, 1800

Bullock, Lewis	Major, 2nd Battalion, 15th Regiment	August 15, 1799
Byram, William	Lieutenant, 15th Regiment	August 13, 1801
Byram, William	Captain, 15th Regiment	May 21, 1803
Cameron, John	Lieutenant, 29th Regiment	April 25, 1800
Carman, Caleb	Ensign, 29th Regiment	November 17, 1804
Cleneay, Joseph	Lieutenant, 15th Regiment	June 26, 1802
Colbert, Jesse	Ensign, 29th Regiment	October 12, 1802
Colbert, Jesse	Lieutenant, 29th Regiment	October 12, 1802
Cook, Jacob	Ensign, 29th Regiment	November, 1800
Cornelius, Jesse	Ensign, 29th Regiment	November, 1800
Cravens, Jeremiah	Captain, 29th Regiment	November, 1800
Cravens, William	Captain, 29th Regiment	November, 1800
Cravens, William, Jr.	Lieutenant, 29th Regiment	November, 1800
Curtis, John	Captain, 15th Regiment	October 3, 1799
Daugherty, Armstrong	Ensign, 15th Regiment	May 21, 1803
Davis, George N.	Lieutenant, 15th Regiment	January 7, 1804
Dayton, Garrat	Ensign, 29th Regiment	January 26, 1800
Deason, Michael	Lieutenant, 29th Regiment	November, 1800
Dempsey, Jeptha	Lieutenant, 29th Regiment	November, 1800
Dempsey, John	Captain, 29th Regiment	November, 1800
Desha, John	Lieutenant, 15th Regiment	October 3, 1799
Desha, John	Captain, 15th Regiment	December 4, 1800
Desha, Joseph	Colonel, 29th Regiment	March 23, 1799
Dillen, William	Ensign, 29th Regiment	November 17, 1804
Donovan, Joseph	Lieutenant, 15th Regiment	May 21, 1803
Dougherty, Robert	Ensign, Rifle Company, 15th Regiment	August 5, 1799
Downing, Ellis	Captain, 15th Regiment	October 3, 1799
Downing, James	Lieutenant, Rifle Company, 15th Regiment	August 13, 1801
Downing, James	Captain, 15th Regiment	May 21, 1803
Downing, Joseph	Ensign, Rifle Company, 15th Regiment	October 3, 1799
Downing, Thomas	Lieutenant, Rifle Company, 15th Regiment	June 26, 1802
Downing, Timothy	Lieutenant Colonel, Commandant 15th Regiment	December 18, 1802
Drake, Jacob	Captain, 29th Regiment	September 17, 1799
Drake, John	Surgeon, 29th Regiment	December 3, 1800
Dupuy, David	Ensign, 29th Regiment	November, 1800
Dyer, John	Ensign, 29th Regiment	November, 1800
Earley, David	Ensign, 29th Regiment	May 15, 1798
Ebbert, Philip	Captain, 15th Regiment	September 15, 1800
Estis, Asa	Captain, 29th Regiment	November, 1800
Evans, John	Captain, 29th Regiment	March 15, 1799
Forman, Joseph	Lieutenant, 15th Regiment	September 15, 1801
Franklin, Zepheniah	Captain, 29th Regiment	November 17, 1804
Glenn, Isaac	Ensign, 29th Regiment	May 8, 1802
Glenn, Robert	Quartermaster, 29th Regiment	December 3, 1800
Gordon, Lewis	Captain, 15th Regiment	May 21, 1803

Gow, William..............	Ensign, 15th Regiment............	October 3, 1799
Gow, William..............	Lieutenant, 15th Regiment........	December 4, 1800
Grant, Charles............	Lieutenant, 29th Regiment........	November, 1800
Gray, David...............	Lieutenant, 29th Regiment........	October 12, 1802
Hall, Thomas..............	Captain, 29th Regiment...........	April 25, 1800
Hardin, James.............	Ensign, 29th Regiment............	October 2, 1801
Harper, James.............	Lieutenant, 29th Regiment........	October 2, 1801
Hart, Zephaniah...........	Ensign, 29th Regiment............	November 3, 1800
Hart, Zephaniah...........	Lieutenant, 15th Regiment........	September 15, 1801
Hawison (Houston?), John.	Paymaster, 29th Regiment.........	December 17, 1801
Hoard, Edward.............	Lieutenant, 29th Regiment........	April 26, 1800
Hoard, Edward.............	Captain, 29th Regiment...........	October 2, 1801
House, John...............	Lieutenant, 29th Regiment........	March 15, 1799
Houston, Aron.............	Captain, 15th Regiment...........	October 3, 1799
Irvin, Thompson...........	Ensign, 15th Regiment............	January 7, 1804
Jackson, Dempsey..........	Ensign, Rifle Company, 29th Regiment.....................	May 24, 1799
Johnson, Samuel...........	Ensign, 15th Regiment............	August 13, 1801
Jonston, Aaron............	Ensign, 29th Regiment............	June 11, 1799
Kercheval, John...........	Adjutant, 29th Regiment..........	July 21, 1799
Kinsor, George............	Lieutenant, 15th Regiment........	September 15, 1800
Lee, Barton...............	Ensign, 15th Regiment............	May 21, 1803
Logan, Joseph.............	Ensign, 15th Regiment............	January 7, 1804
McClain, James............	Ensign, 15th Regiment............	May 21, 1803
McCord, Michael...........	Ensign, 29th Regiment............	October 2, 1801
McCord, Michael...........	Lieutenant, 29th Regiment........	November 17, 1804
McCord, William...........	Lieutenant, 29th Regiment........	January 26, 1800
McDonald, Samuel..........	Ensign, 15th Regiment............	January 7, 1804
McGinnes, William.........	Ensign, 29th Regiment............	November 3, 1800
McKenny, Daniel...........	Captain, 15th Regiment...........	August 5, 1799
McMullin, Daniel..........	Lieutenant, 29th Regiment........	July 1, 1799
McNary, John..............	Lieutenant, 15th Regiment........	May 21, 1803
Maddan, Levi..............	Ensign, 29th Regiment............	October 2, 1801
Martin, Elijah............	Lieutenant, 15th Regiment........	May 21, 1803
Martin, Jeremiah..........	Ensign, 15th Regiment............	June 26, 1802
Martin, Jeremiah..........	Captain, 15th Regiment...........	January 7, 1804
Martin, Micajah...........	Ensign, 15th Regiment............	January 7, 1804
Mayhall, Timothy..........	Lieutenant, 15th Regiment........	October 3, 1799
Mayhall, Timothy..........	Captain, Rifle Company, 15th Regiment......................	August 13, 1801
Metcalf, Eli..............	Captain, Infantry Company, 29th Regiment.................	May 24, 1799
Metcalf, Thomas...........	Lieutenant, 29th Regiment........	October 2, 1801
Metcalf, Thomas...........	Captain, 29th Regiment...........	October 12, 1802
Miller, Alexander.........	Ensign, 15th Regiment............	September 15, 1801
Miller, Alexander.........	Lieutenant, 15th Regiment........	May 21, 1803
Miller, Robert............	Captain, 15th Regiment...........	September 15, 1800
Miller, William...........	Lieutenant, 29th Regiment........	January 2, 1799
Miller, William...........	Captain, 29th Regiment...........	January 26, 1800
Moffard, Thomas...........	Ensign, 15th Regiment............	May 21, 1803
Murphy, Wallace...........	Ensign, Cavalry, 15th Regiment...	August 13, 1801

COMMISSIONED OFFICERS, 1799 - 1804 125

Nichols, John............	Captain, 29th Regiment...........	May 27, 1799
Norris, Abraham..........	Lieutenant, 15th Regiment........	June 26, 1802
Oliver, Thomas...........	Ensign, 29th Regiment............	April 25, 1800
Painter, John............	Ensign, 15th Regiment............	December 4, 1800
Parker, William..........	Ensign, 29th Regiment............	November 17, 1804
Parker, Winslow..........	Lieutenant, Rifle Company, 15th Regiment......................	August 5, 1799
Parry, Thomas............	Ensign, 15th Regiment............	June 26, 1802
Pepper, Samuel...........	Lieutenant, 29th Regiment........	November 17, 1804
Pepper, William..........	Captain, 29th Regiment...........	April 26, 1800
Perrill (Pearl), William.	Lieutenant, 15th Regiment........	August 5, 1799
Phillips, John...........	Ensign, 15th Regiment............	May 21, 1803
Phillips, John...........	Lieutenant, 15th Regiment........	January 7, 1804
Pickett, John............	Major, 1st Battalion, 15th Regiment......................	December 19, 1802
Plummer, Thomas..........	Ensign, 29th Regiment............	March 15, 1799
Poague, Robert...........	Captain, 29th Regiment...........	May 15, 1798
Poague, Robert...........	Major, 1st Battalion, 29th Regiment......................	December 18, 1802
Prather, Jeremiah........	Lieutenant, Infantry Company, 29th Regiment..................	May 24, 1799
Proctor, Jeremiah........	Ensign, 15th Regiment............	May 21, 1803
Ragsdale, John...........	Ensign, 29th Regiment............	January 2, 1799
Reaves, Samuel...........	Ensign, 15th Regiment............	December 4, 1800
Reaves, Tabes............	Ensign, 29th Regiment............	April 4, 1799
Reaves, William..........	Captain, 29th Regiment...........	April 4, 1799
Reese, Daniel............	Lieutenant, 29th Regiment........	November 3, 1800
Reeves, Samuel...........	Captain, 15th Regiment...........	May 21, 1803
Roberts, John............	Captain, 29th Regiment...........	November, 1800
Roberts, Joshua..........	Lieutenant, 29th Regiment........	November, 1800
Ross, Joseph.............	Ensign, 29th Regiment............	May 8, 1802
Sargent, John............	Ensign, 15th Regiment............	October 3, 1799
Schofield, Henry.........	Captain, 15th Regiment...........	October 3, 1799
Scott, Solomon...........	Lieutenant, 29th Regiment........	October 12, 1802
Shackleford, John........	Major, 1st Battalion, 29th Regiment......................	October 3, 1799
Sharp, Solomon...........	Ensign, 15th Regiment............	June 26, 1802
Small, Henry.............	Lieutenant, 29th Regiment........	May 8, 1802
Small, James.............	Captain, 29th Regiment...........	November 4, 1800
Smith, John..............	Ensign, 29th Regiment............	November 17, 1804
Standeford, Nathaniel C..	Captain, 29th Regiment...........	January 2, 1799
Stephenson, Richard......	Captain, 15th Regiment...........	June 26, 1802
Stewart, William.........	Lieutenant, 15th Regiment........	September 15, 1800
Stewart, Willoughby......	Lieutenant, 29th Regiment........	May 27, 1799
Stublefield, William.....	Captain, Rifle Company, 15th Regiment......................	August 5, 1799
Taylor, Edward...........	Ensign, 29th Regiment............	October 1, 1802
Taylor, James............	Lieutenant, 29th Regiment........	September 17, 1799
Taylor, James............	Captain, 29th Regiment...........	October 1, 1802
Thomas, Phenis...........	Ensign, 15th Regiment............	October 3, 1799
Trussell, John...........	Lieutenant, 15th Regiment........	May 21, 1803

Vowshel, Daniel	Captain, 15th Regiment	October 3, 1799
Walker, James	Lieutenant, 15th Regiment	May 21, 1803
Walker, William	Captain, 15th Regiment	May 21, 1803
Wallace, William	Lieutenant, 15th Regiment	August 15, 1799
Ward, Charles	Captain, 15th Regiment	June 26, 1802
Waring, Clement	Ensign, 15th Regiment	August 13, 1801
Waring, Clement	Captain, 15th Regiment	June 26, 1802
Waring, Francis	Lieutenant, 15th Regiment	June 26, 1802
Welsh, Abraham	Captain, 29th Regiment	November 3, 1800
Willett, George	Ensign, 15th Regiment	June 26, 1802
Wilson, James	Paymaster, 29th Regiment	December 3, 1800
Wise, Abraham	Ensign, 29th Regiment	October 2, 1801
Wise, Abraham	Lieutenant, 29th Regiment	October 1, 1802

Mason and Bracken Regiment

Abrahams, Benjamin	Ensign, 28th Regiment	April 11, 1801
Anderson, Charles	Ensign, 28th Regiment	December 26, 1801
Applegate, George	Captain, 28th Regiment	May 14, 1803
Asbury, William	Ensign, 28th Regiment	April 29, 1800
Asbury, William	Lieutenant, 28th Regiment	November 9, 1800
Asbury, William	Captain, 28th Regiment	September 25, 1801
Baker, Abraham	Lieutenant, 28th Regiment	March 20, 1799
Bruce, Alexander	Lieutenant, Rifle Company, 28th Regiment	June 3, 1799
Chiles, David	Colonel, 28th Regiment	December 20, 1799
Craig, Elijah	Ensign, 28th Regiment	December 26, 1800
Craig, Lewis	Lieutenant, 28th Regiment	September 25, 1801
Craig, Lewis	Captain, Infantry Company, 28th Regiment	December 24, 1803
Critcald (Critchfield?), William	Ensign, 28th Regiment	December 26, 1800
Cummins, David	Cornet, 28th Regiment	December 18, 1799
Davison, John	Captain, 28th Regiment	May 4, 1799
Dowden, John	Captain, 28th Regiment	December 26, 1800
Fee, James	Ensign, Rifle Company, 28th Regiment	June 3, 1799
Hale, John	Ensign, 28th Regiment	September 25, 1801
Hardin, Amos	Ensign, 28th Regiment	May 14, 1803
Hart, William	Captain, 28th Regiment	December 26, 1801
Hawkins, Lewis	Ensign, 28th Regiment	September 25, 1801
Hawkins, Lewis	Ensign, Rifle Company, 28th Regiment	December 24, 1803
Hollin, William	Ensign, 28th Regiment	February 12, 1799 and December 3, 1798
Hook, John	Captain, Rifle Company, 28th Regiment	June 3, 1799
Hook, John	Major, 1st Battalion, 28th Regiment	December 19, 1799
Hunt, John	Adjutant, 28th Regiment	December 24, 1803
Keith, Thomas	Ensign, 28th Regiment	May 14, 1803

COMMISSIONED OFFICERS, 1799 - 1804

Key, Peyton R.	Lieutenant, 28th Regiment	May 4, 1799
Lewis, Joseph	Ensign, 28th Regiment	September 17, 1803
McMahan, James	Ensign, 28th Regiment	September 17, 1803
Manhan, John	Major, 2nd Battalion, 28th Regiment	December 20, 1799
Mastin, Elijah	Ensign, 28th Regiment	November 9, 1800
Mastin, Elijah	Lieutenant, 28th Regiment	September 25, 1801
Mastin, Elijah	Captain, 28th Regiment	October 22, 1802
Mattox, John	Ensign, 28th Regiment	October 22, 1802
Mills, Thomas	Lieutenant of Infantry, 28th Regiment	July 1, 1799
Norris, Joseph	Lieutenant, 28th Regiment	April 11, 1801
Norris, Joseph	Captain, 28th Regiment	September 25, 1801
Norris, Joseph	Lieutenant, 28th Regiment	May 14, 1803
O'Bannon, William	Ensign, 28th Regiment	May 4, 1799
Overturf, Conrad	Ensign, 28th Regiment	October 22, 1802
Patterson, Edward	Ensign, Rifle Company, 28th Regiment	November 9, 1800
Pattie, Sylvester	Lieutenant, 28th Regiment	October 22, 1802
Pollock, James	2nd Lieutenant, 28th Regiment	December 18, 1799
Ringland, Joseph	Lieutenant, 28th Regiment	December 26, 1801
Robertson, Andy	Captain, 28th Regiment	December 18, 1799
Smalley, Andrew	Ensign, Rifle Company, 28th Regiment	December 24, 1803
Smith, Robert	1st Lieutenant, 28th Regiment	December 18, 1799
Sroufe, Adam	Lieutenant, 28th Regiment	September 25, 1801
Thomas, Jesse B.	Captain, Rifle Company, 28th Regiment	December 26, 1801
Wallis, Michael	Lieutenant, 28th Regiment	September 25, 1801
Walton, Robert	Ensign, 28th Regiment	September 25, 1801
Watson, William	Ensign, 28th Regiment	March 8, 1800
Watson, William	Lieutenant, 28th Regiment	December 26, 1800
Wells, Solomon	Lieutenant, 28th Regiment	October 22, 1802
Whips, James	Captain, 28th Regiment	March 8, 1800
Whips, John	Ensign, 28th Regiment	February 12, 1799
Whips, John	Lieutenant, 28th Regiment	March 8, 1800
Wood, Thomas	Ensign, 28th Regiment	March 20, 1799
Worthington, Joseph	Lieutenant, 28th Regiment	April 11, 1801

Mercer County Regiments

[43rd Regiment laid off December 17, 1799]

Adams, James	Ensign, 5th Regiment	September 8, 1800
Adams, William	Lieutenant, 5th Regiment	September 8, 1800
Adams, William	Captain, 5th Regiment	November 26, 1801
Anderson, Benjamin	Lieutenant, 43rd Regiment	April 10, 1799
Anderson, John	Ensign, 43rd Regiment	April 10, 1799
Anderson, Samuel	Ensign, 5th Regiment	May 7, 1802
Armstrong, Lanty	Ensign, 5th Regiment	September 8, 1800

COMMISSIONED OFFICERS, 1799 - 1804

Armstrong, Lanty..........	Captain, 5th Regiment............	May 7, 1802
Armstrong, Lanty..........	Major, 2nd Battalion, 5th Regiment......................	March 6, 1804
Barbee, Joshua...........	Major, 1st Battalion, 43rd Regiment.......................	December 17, 1799
Bohon, John..............	Ensign, 5th Regiment............	July 12, 1804
Bohon, Thomas............	Lieutenant, 5th Regiment........	July 12, 1804
Bridges, John L.	Ensign, 43rd Regiment............	October 15, 1801
Brown, William...........	Lieutenant, 43rd Regiment........	October 29, 1802
Buckhanan, James.........	Lieutenant, 5th Regiment........	September 8, 1800
Buckhannan, Alexander....	Major, 2nd Battalion, 5th Regiment......................	December 18, 1799
Burton, May..............	Ensign, 5th Regiment............	September 8, 1800
Burton, May..............	Lieutenant, 5th Regiment........	September 11, 1801
Burton, Robert...........	Lieutenant, 43rd Regiment........	April 30, 1799
Burton, Robert...........	Captain, 43rd Regiment...........	October 15, 1801
Cary, Ebenezer...........	Lieutenant, 43rd Regiment........	October 15, 1801
Cassady, Andrew..........	Ensign, 43rd Regiment............	October 29, 1802
Chamberlain, Pearce......	Ensign, 5th Regiment............	May 7, 1802
Cockran, John............	Captain, Infantry Company, 43rd Regiment.................	May 19, 1800
Conner, Henry............	Ensign, 5th Regiment............	September 17, 1802
Copeland, John...........	Ensign, 43rd Regiment...........	April 30, 1799
Coulter, Mark............	Lieutenant, 5th Regiment........	May 6, 1803
Crutchfield, Richard.....	Lieutenant, 43rd Regiment........	October 29, 1802
Crutchfield, William.....	Ensign, 43rd Regiment............	February 22, 1800
Cummingore, Abraham......	Ensign, 5th Regiment............	May 6, 1803
Curry, Robert............	Adjutant, 5th Regiment...........	April 8, 1800
Curry, William...........	Ensign, 5th Regiment............	September 11, 1801
Darnaby, Cornelius.......	Ensign, 5th Regiment............	September 11, 1801
Daveiss, Samuel..........	Captain, 43rd Regiment...........	April 1, 1800
Davenport, Richard.......	2nd Lieutenant, 5th Regiment.....	June 24, 1799
Davenport, Richard.......	Lieutenant, 43rd Regiment........	April 21, 1800
Davenport, Richard.......	Major, 1st Battalion, 43rd Regiment......................	August 13, 1800
Day, Edmond..............	Ensign, 43rd Regiment............	October 27, 1801
Day, Edmond..............	Lieutenant, 43rd Regiment........	October 29, 1802
Demmitt, William Sinclair	Quartermaster, 5th Regiment......	June 20, 1803
Eccles, John.............	Lieutenant, 5th Regiment........	November 26, 1801
Edgerton, William........	Ensign, 5th Regiment............	May 20, 1800
Fisher, Stephen, Jr. ...	Captain, 43rd Regiment...........	October 29, 1802
Gibson, John.............	Captain, 5th Regiment............	May 6, 1803
Gowdy, Samuel............	Ensign, 5th Regiment............	September 8, 1800
Gowdy, Samuel............	Lieutenant, 5th Regiment........	September 11, 1801
Grahan, Benjamin.........	Ensign, 5th Regiment............	September 11, 1801
Grant, John..............	Ensign, 43rd Regiment............	April 1, 1800
Grayham, Joseph..........	Captain, 5th Regiment............	May 7, 1802
Greay (Gray), Samuel.....	Captain, 5th Regiment............	September 8, 1800
Hale, John...............	Captain, 5th Regiment............	May 7, 1802
Hale, Thomas.............	Ensign, 5th Regiment............	May 6, 1803
Hanes, Josiah............	Ensign, 5th Regiment............	January 3, 1800

COMMISSIONED OFFICERS, 1799 - 1804

Hanna, Thomas............	Captain, 5th Regiment............	December 9, 1799
Harbeson, Arthur.........	Captain, 43rd Regiment..........	April 30, 1799
Harris, Frederick........	Lieutenant, 5th Regiment.........	May 6, 1803
Humphries, Charles.......	Paymaster, 5th Regiment..........	June 20, 1803
Irvine, William D.	Ensign, 43rd Regiment............	October 15, 1801
Jourden, John............	Ensign, 5th Regiment.............	May 6, 1803
Jourden, Peter...........	Lieutenant, 5th Regiment.........	May 6, 1803
Latimore, John...........	Captain, 43rd Regiment...........	October 29, 1802
Lee, Samuel..............	Lieutenant, 5th Regiment.........	January 3, 1800
Lee, Samuel..............	Captain, 5th Regiment............	May 6, 1803
McAffee, George..........	Lieutenant, 5th Regiment.........	May 7, 1802
McAffee, George..........	Captain, 5th Regiment............	November 26, 1801
McAffee, George..........	Captain, 5th Regiment............	July 12, 1804
McAffee, George..........	Major, 2nd Battalion, 5th Regiment......................	February 28, 1804
McAffee, John............	Captain, 5th Regiment............	September 8, 1800
McAffee, Robert..........	Ensign, 5th Regiment.............	September 11, 1801
McAffee, Robert..........	Lieutenant, 5th Regiment.........	May 7, 1802
McAffee, Robert..........	Captain, 5th Regiment............	July 12, 1804
McAffee, Samuel..........	Ensign, 5th Regiment.............	May 7, 1802
McAffee, Samuel..........	Lieutenant, 5th Regiment.........	July 12, 1804
McAmy (McKamey), Robert..	Ensign, 5th Regiment.............	July 12, 1804
McClure, Nathaniel.......	Lieutenant, 5th Regiment.........	May 20, 1800
McCormic, Abraham........	Ensign, 5th Regiment.............	May 6, 1803
McDonnald, William.......	Major, 1st Battalion, 5th Regiment......................	December 23, 1802
McDowell, Ephraim........	Paymaster, 43rd Regiment.........	October 27, 1801 and June 1, 1802
McDowell, William........	Colonel, 43rd Regiment...........	December 17, 1799
McGinnis, Samuel.........	Lieutenant, 43rd Regiment........	February 22, 1802
Mahan, John..............	Major, 2nd Battalion, 43rd Regiment......................	December 18, 1799
Marr, George.............	Paymaster, 5th Regiment..........	September 11, 1801
Martin, William..........	Ensign, 43rd Regiment............	October 29, 1802
Moore, James.............	Captain, 43rd Regiment...........	April 21, 1800
Moore, Josiah............	Lieutenant, Infantry Company, 43rd Regiment.................	May 19, 1800
Mundy, Harrison..........	Lieutenant, 5th Regiment.........	September 17, 1802
Nield, Robert............	Lieutenant, 5th Regiment.........	December 9, 1799
Palmer, Henry............	Captain, 5th Regiment............	May 20, 1800
Prather, Thomas..........	Lieutenant, 43rd Regiment........	October 15, 1801
Prather, William.........	Ensign, 5th Regiment.............	December 14, 1803
Randal, Wharton..........	Captain, 5th Regiment............	September 8, 1800
Riley, Robert............	Lieutenant, 43rd Regiment........	October 15, 1801
Ripperton, John..........	Ensign, 43rd Regiment............	October 29, 1802
Roberts, William.........	Ensign, 43rd Regiment............	April 30, 1799
Ryan, Solomon............	Ensign, 5th Regiment.............	May 20, 1800
Ryan, Solomon............	Lieutenant, 5th Regiment.........	May 6, 1803
Sea (Seay), Leonard......	Adjutant, 5th Regiment...........	September 11, 1801
Sevier, Enoch............	Lieutenant, 43rd Regiment........	April 1, 1800
Silvertooth, John........	Ensign, 43rd Regiment............	October 15, 1801

COMMISSIONED OFFICERS, 1799 - 1804

Simpson, Robert..........	Lieutenant, 5th Regiment.........	September 8, 1800
Simpson, Robert..........	Captain, 5th Regiment............	September 11, 1801
Slaughter, Gabriel.......	Major, 1st Battalion, 5th Regiment........................	December 17, 1802
Slaughter, Gabriel.......	Colonel, 5th Regiment............	December 24, 1803
Stephenson, John..........	Ensign, 5th Regiment.............	May 6, 1803
Thomas, Joseph...........	Lieutenant, 5th Regiment.........	December 4, 1801
Thomas, Joseph...........	Captain, 5th Regiment............	September 17, 1802
Thompson, George.........	Lieutenant, 5th Regiment.........	December 14, 1803
Thompson, George.........	Captain, 5th Regiment............	November 26, 1801
Thompson, Samuel.........	Lieutenant, 5th Regiment.........	September 8, 1800
Thompson, Samuel.........	Lieutenant, 5th Regiment.........	September 17, 1802
Thompson, Samuel.........	Captain, 5th Regiment............	May 6, 1803
Timberlake, William......	Cornet, 5th Regiment.............	June 24, 1799
Vanasdal, Cornelius O. ..	Ensign, 5th Regiment.............	December 9, 1799
Wood, James..............	Ensign, 43rd Regiment............	October 29, 1802
Wood, William............	Ensign, 5th Regiment.............	December 14, 1803
Yeiser, Jacob............	Ensign, Rifle Company, 43rd Regiment........................	May 19, 1800

Montgomery County Regiments

[34th Regiment laid off November 28, 1799]

Adams, Elijah............	Lieutenant, 34th Regiment........	December 2, 1799
Alchire, John............	Ensign, 34th Regiment............	December 1, 1799
Alexander, John..........	Paymaster, 31st Regiment.........	April 24, 1801
Allen, Joseph............	Captain, 31st Regiment...........	April 29, 1800
Anderson, James..........	Ensign, 31st Regiment............	September 5, 1801
Atcheson, William........	Lieutenant, 34th Regiment........	November 9, 1802
Barnes, Noble............	Lieutenant, 34th Regiment........	November 9, 1802
Bilbo, Archibald.........	Captain, 34th Regiment...........	August 13, 1800
Black, George............	Ensign, 31st Regiment............	May 30, 1801
Black, George............	Lieutenant, 31st Regiment........	October 19, 1803
Blair, James.............	Ensign, 34th Regiment............	November 9, 1802
Boyd, John...............	Ensign, 34th Regiment............	December 2, 1799
Boyd, John...............	Lieutenant, 34th Regiment........	May 8, 1802
Bomfield (Bromfield), Robert...	Ensign, 34th Regiment.......	August 13, 1800
Burchem, Samuel..........	Major, 2nd Battalion, 34th Regiment........................	December 13, 1802
Caldwell, Robert.........	Ensign, Rifle Company, 34th Regiment........................	May 8, 1802
Cantrel, William.........	Ensign, 34th Regiment............	November 9, 1802
Cash, Caleb..............	Ensign, 31st Regiment............	October 21, 1802
Clark, John..............	Ensign, 34th Regiment............	May 8, 1802
Colvin, Joseph...........	Captain, Rifle Company, 31st Regiment........................	January 1, 1800
Cook, William W.	Captain of Cavalry, 31st Regiment........................	October 19, 1803
Copeland, John...........	Lieutenant, 34th Regiment........	August 13, 1800

COMMISSIONED OFFICERS, 1799 - 1804

Creason, John	Lieutenant, 31st Regiment	May 5, 1800
Daniel, Jesse	Captain, 31st Regiment	October 19, 1803
Davis, Jeremiah	Paymaster, 31st Regiment	February 28, 1804
Diskins, Daniel	Adjutant, 34th Regiment	October 29, 1802
Donaldson, William	Lieutenant, 34th Regiment	May 12, 1800
Donaldson, William	Captain, 34th Regiment	November 9, 1802
Downing, Samuel	Major, 1st Battalion, 34th Regiment	November 28, 1799
Dun, James	Ensign, 34th Regiment	August 13, 1800
Durham, Thomas	Captain, 34th Regiment	August 13, 1800
Evans, Francis	Lieutenant, Troop of Horse, 34th Regiment	May 8, 1802
Evans, Samuel	Lieutenant, 34th Regiment	December 3, 1799
Evans, Samuel	Captain, 34th Regiment	April 29, 1800
Farrow, William	Major, 1st Battalion, 31st Regiment	December 6, 1804
Fleming, George	Lieutenant, 34th Regiment	December 13, 1803
Gelaspy, Simon	Lieutenant, 31st Regiment	May 30, 1801
Gradey, Samuel	Cornet, Troop of Horse, 34th Regiment	February 15, 1800
Graham, Forgy	Ensign, 34th Regiment	March 22, 1800
Graham, James M.	Captain, Rifle Company, 34th Regiment	April 29, 1800
Haggin, Robert	Ensign, Rifle Company, 31st Regiment	January 1, 1800
Hall, Richmond	Lieutenant, 31st Regiment	May 4, 1800
Hammon, John	Ensign, 31st Regiment	May 30, 1801
Hatcher, Samuel	Captain, 31st Regiment	May 30, 1801
Hawkins, William	Lieutenant, 34th Regiment	December 13, 1803
Hayes, Richard	Lieutenant, Rifle Company, 31st Regiment	January 1, 1800
Higgins, James	Captain, 31st Regiment	May 5, 1800
Hode (Hodge), Andrew	Captain, 31st Regiment	May 30, 1801
Hodge, Andrew	Lieutenant, 31st Regiment	November 30, 1800
Hughes, David	Major, 1st Battalion, 34th Regiment	September 8, 1800
Hughes, William	Ensign, Troop of Horse, 34th Regiment	May 8, 1802
Jameson, John	Lieutenant, Rifle Company, 34th Regiment	March 22, 1800
Jameson, John	Captain, Rifle Company, 34th Regiment	May 8, 1802
Kennedy, James	Captain, 34th Regiment	December 2, 1799
Lane, James H.	Major, 1st Battalion, 34th Regiment	December 18, 1800
Lane, James H.	Lieutenant Colonel, Commandant 34th Regiment	October 9, 1804
Latimore, John	Lieutenant, 34th Regiment	August 13, 1800
Linney, George	Lieutenant, Troop of Horse, 34th Regiment	February 15, 1800
McCleanay, Micajah	Ensign, 31st Regiment	October 19, 1803

COMMISSIONED OFFICERS, 1799 - 1804

McClure, Matthew	Ensign, Rifle Company, 34th Regiment	April 29, 1800
McGuire, John	Lieutenant, 34th Regiment	December 13, 1803
McIllhaney, James	Major, 2nd Battalion, 34th Regiment	November 28, 1799
McIllhaney, James	Colonel, 34th Regiment	June 22, 1802
Maberry, Joel	Ensign, 31st Regiment	April 29, 1800
Mauks, Randolph	Ensign, 34th Regiment	August 13, 1800
Metier, Thomas	Lieutenant, 31st Regiment	May 30, 1801
Metter, Thomas	Ensign, 31st Regiment	April 29, 1800
Morrow, Robert	Paymaster, 34th Regiment	October 29, 1802
Mosley, Thomas	Captain, Rifle Company, 34th Regiment	March 22, 1800
Murphy, Zephaniah	Lieutenant, 34th Regiment	December 1, 1799
Nickoll, Thomas	Major, 2nd Battalion, 31st Regiment	December 6, 1804
Offil, Samuel	Lieutenant, 34th Regiment	November 9, 1802
Parrish, Joseph	Ensign, 31st Regiment	May 30, 1801
Paul, Michael	Lieutenant, 31st Regiment	October 21, 1802
Payne, Jilston	Major, 1st Battalion, 31st Regiment	November 28, 1799
Richards, Josiah	Captain, 34th Regiment	November 9, 1802
Richards, William	Ensign, 34th Regiment	November 9, 1802
Ringo, Joseph	Quartermaster, 34th Regiment	October 29, 1802
Robinson, John	Lieutenant, Rifle Company, 34th Regiment	April 29, 1800
Rogers, Thomas	Captain, 34th Regiment	May 8, 1802
Rogers, William	Major, 31st Regiment	March 10, 1800
Sharp, Stephen	Lieutenant, Rifle Company, 34th Regiment	May 8, 1802
South, Benjamin	Captain, Troop of Horse, 34th Regiment	February 15, 1800
South, Benjamin	Major, 1st Battalion, 34th Regiment	October 9, 1804
Spradlin, Obediah	Captain, 31st Regiment	May 4, 1800
Stone, Robert	Ensign, 34th Regiment	December 13, 1803
Swearengen, Andrew	Colonel, 34th Regiment	November 29, 1799
Swim, Alexander	Captain, 34th Regiment	December 1, 1799
Thompson, Abraham	Adjutant, 34th Regiment	February 10, 1800
Thompson, Thomas	Lieutenant, 31st Regiment	April 29, 1800
Trumbo, John	Lieutenant, 34th Regiment	December 1, 1799
Trumbo, John	Captain, 34th Regiment	November 9, 1802
Wade, Dawson	Captain, 34th Regiment	May 8, 1802
Ward, James	Quartermaster, 31st Regiment	April 24, 1802
Warren, James	Lieutenant, 34th Regiment	August 13, 1800
Wells, Edward	Lieutenant of Cavalry, 34th Regiment	December 13, 1803
Wiatt, Emanuel	Ensign, 31st Regiment	October 21, 1802
Wilcox, David	Major, 2nd Battalion, 31st Regiment	November 29, 1799
Wyatt, John	Ensign, 31st Regiment	November 30, 1800
Yosom (Yocum), George	Ensign, 31st Regiment	October 21, 1802

Muhlenberg County Regiment

[Laid off December 15, 1799]

Adams, John, Jr.	Lieutenant, 40th Regiment	May 24, 1802
Arnold, Joseph, Jr.	Ensign, 40th Regiment	May 24, 1802
Bell, Robert	Captain, 40th Regiment	May 24, 1802
Bell, William	Paymaster, 40th Regiment	February 9, 1801
Boggus, William	Captain, 40th Regiment	April 5, 1800
Bradford, William	Major, 1st Battalion, 40th Regiment	September 30, 1800
Bradley, John	Lieutenant, 40th Regiment	May 24, 1802
Campbell, William	Colonel, 40th Regiment	December 15, 1799
Canoy, Jacob	Cornet, 40th Regiment	May 20, 1800
Cargle, John	Lieutenant, 40th Regiment	March 22, 1803
Casibier, David	Lieutenant, 40th Regiment	April 5, 1800
Coffer, Henry	Adjutant, 40th Regiment	February 9, 1801
Craig, Jacob	Ensign, 40th Regiment	May 24, 1802
Craig, Thomas	Ensign, 40th Regiment	May 24, 1802
Dennis, John, Jr.	Ensign, 40th Regiment	March 22, 1803
Dobyns, John	Captain, 40th Regiment	March 22, 1803
Glenn, Robert	Lieutenant, 40th Regiment	August 15, 1803
Graves, John Sanders	Ensign, 40th Regiment	May 24, 1802
Ham, Matthew	Lieutenant of Cavalry, 40th Regiment	May 24, 1802
Hamm, Jacob	Lieutenant, L. H. (Light Horse), 40th Regiment	May 20, 1800
Hynes, William	Major, 2nd Battalion, 40th Regiment	December 16, 1799
Keith, Abner	Captain, 40th Regiment	August 15, 1803
Kinchaloe, Lewis	Major, 1st Battalion, 40th Regiment	December 13, 1799
Kinchaloe, Louis	Colonel, 40th Regiment	September 30, 1800
Kinchaloe, Stephen	Lieutenant, 40th Regiment	September 17, 1800
Langley, Jeremiah	Ensign, 40th Regiment	April 7, 1801
Langley, Jeremiah	Lieutenant, 40th Regiment	March 22, 1803
Littlepage, Eppes	Lieutenant, 40th Regiment	August 15, 1803
Littlepage, Thomas	Ensign, 40th Regiment	March 22, 1803
McCommon, William	Captain, 40th Regiment	September 17, 1800
Matthews, Job.	Lieutenant, 40th Regiment	August 15, 1803
Morgan, John	Adjutant, 40th Regiment	February 15, 1802
Morgan, Willis	Captain, 40th Regiment	August 15, 1803
Oyler, Jonathan	Captain, 40th Regiment	May 24, 1802
Patton, William	Captain, 40th Regiment	August 15, 1803
Penrod, Samuel	Lieutenant, 40th Regiment	September 17, 1800
Randal, Robert	Ensign, 40th Regiment	September 17, 1800
Randolph, Robert	Lieutenant, 40th Regiment	May 24, 1802
Randolph, Thomas	Captain, 40th Regiment	March 22, 1803
Renno, Jesse	Captain, 40th Regiment	May 24, 1802
Renno, Lewis	Ensign, 40th Regiment	May 24, 1802
Rhoads, Henry	Lieutenant, 40th Regiment	September 17, 1800

COMMISSIONED OFFICERS, 1799 - 1804

Russel, Samuel............	Lieutenant, 40th Regiment........	April 7, 1801
Russel, Samuel............	Captain, 40th Regiment..........	March 22, 1803
Smith, John B.	Ensign, 40th Regiment............	April 5, 1803
Studebaker, Jacob........	Captain, 40th Regiment...........	September 17, 1800
Tennille, John...........	Captain, 40th Regiment...........	September 17, 1800
Weir, James..............	Captain, L. H. (Light Horse Troop), 40th Regiment..........	May 20, 1800
Whittaker, Alexander.....	Ensign, 40th Regiment............	September 17, 1800
Wing, Charles............	Captain, 40th Regiment...........	April 7, 1801
Worthington, William.....	Quartermaster, 40th Regiment.....	February 9, 1801

Nelson County Regiments

Alban, John..............	Ensign, 27th Regiment............	July 3, 1799
Anderson, Josiah.........	Ensign, 27th Regiment............	May 12, 1804
Atherton, David..........	Ensign, 2nd Regiment.............	December 10, 1799
Baird, James.............	Ensign, 2nd Regiment.............	May 10, 1802
Beauchamp, Stephen.......	Ensign, 27th Regiment............	May 1, 1802
Beauchamp, Thomas........	Ensign, 27th Regiment............	May 21, 1803
Bell, Peter..............	Captain, 2nd Regiment............	December 12, 1799
Bibb, George.............	Ensign, 2nd Regiment.............	July 27, 1801
Bissett, Thomas..........	Lieutenant, 2nd Regiment.........	May 25, 1804
Blinker (Blincoe), Benjamin...	Ensign, 27th Regiment........	February 18, 1800
Blinko (Blincoe), Benjamin....	Captain, 27th Regiment.......	July 25, 1801
Bodine, John.............	Ensign, 27th Regiment............	January 1, 1799
Bodine, John.............	Lieutenant, 27th Regiment........	July 8, 1799
Bowles, Ignatius.........	Lieutenant, 27th Regiment........	July 25, 1801
Bowling, Thomas..........	Lieutenant, 2nd Regiment.........	May 10, 1802
Brashear, Dennis.........	Ensign, Infantry Company, 2nd Regiment......................	May 25, 1804
Brashear, Walter.........	Captain, 2nd Regiment............	May 25, 1804
Brooner, John............	Lieutenant, 27th Regiment........	August 3, 1802
Brown, Nathaniel.........	Lieutenant, 27th Regiment........	February 18, 1800
Brown, William...........	Lieutenant, 2nd Regiment.........	April 29, 1800
Burton, Wilson...........	Ensign, 2nd Regiment.............	December 6, 1802
Calvert, Richard.........	Ensign, 27th Regiment............	July 25 1801
Carr, Ichabod............	Ensign, 27th Regiment............	May 12, 1804
Carter, Peter............	Ensign, 27th Regiment............	January 1, 1800
Cartmel, Jacob...........	Lieutenant, 27th Regiment........	July 1, 1799
Case, James..............	Ensign, 27th Regiment............	September 2, 1800
Chinoweth, William.......	Major, 2nd Regiment..............	November 16, 1801
Colbert, Thomas..........	Captain, 27th Regiment...........	January 29, 1799
Coleman, James...........	Ensign, Light Infantry Company, 2nd Regiment...................	May 10, 1802
Colvert, Richard.........	Lieutenant, 27th Regiment........	May 1, 1802
Cox, Isaac...............	Ensign, 27th Regiment............	May 21, 1803
Cox, Isaac...............	Lieutenant, 27th Regiment........	February 25, 1804
Crawford, Hugh...........	Ensign, 2nd Regiment.............	July 27, 1801
Creamer, Moses...........	Ensign, 27th Regiment............	July 2, 1799
Crist, Jacob.............	Captain, 27th Regiment...........	July 1, 1799

COMMISSIONED OFFICERS, 1799 - 1804

Crutcher, Isaac..........	Captain, 2nd Regiment............	May 10, 1802
Crutcher, William........	Adjutant, 2nd Regiment...........	August 3, 1803
Davis, Amos..............	Adjutant, 27th Regiment..........	July 25, 1801
Davis, James Dozer.......	Lieutenant of Infantry, 27th Regiment.......................	November 20, 1800
Davis, Vincent...........	Quartermaster, 27th Regiment.....	December 24, 1803
Davis, William...........	Lieutenant, 27th Regiment........	July 4, 1799
Dawson, John.............	Ensign, 2nd Regiment.............	December 6, 1802
Decker, Luke.............	Lieutenant, 27th Regiment........	April 9, 1800
Dorsey, Charles, Jr. ...	Adjutant, 2nd Regiment...........	June 4, 1802
Dozer, John..............	Captain of Infantry, 27th Regiment.......................	November 20, 1800
Dunim, Benjamin..........	Lieutenant, 27th Regiment........	January 29, 1799
Duval, John L.	Lieutenant, 2nd Regiment.........	April 10, 1799
Duval, John Lewis........	Captain, 2nd Regiment............	March 21, 1800
Edwards, Elisha..........	Captain, 27th Regiment...........	October 18, 1804
Elder, Thomas............	Ensign, 27th Regiment............	May 21, 1803
Enlow, Henry.............	Ensign, 27th Regiment............	July 1, 1799
Foster, John.............	Ensign, 2nd Regiment.............	April 29, 1800
Fryrar (Fryrear), Jeremiah...	Lieutenant, 2nd Regiment......	December 6, 1802
Gardiner, Joseph J.	Captain, Infantry Company, 27th Regiment.......................	January 31, 1801
Glascock, John...........	Captain, 27th Regiment...........	July 3, 1799
Glasscock, Thomas........	Ensign, 27th Regiment............	August 3, 1802
Grant, John..............	Ensign, 27th Regiment............	July 8, 1799
Grayson, Benjamin........	Captain, 2nd Regiment............	July 27, 1801
Grigsby, Joseph..........	Ensign, 27th Regiment............	September 2, 1800
Grimes, Andrew...........	Ensign, 2nd Regiment.............	July 27, 1801
Hagan, Caleb.............	Ensign, 2nd Regiment.............	May 31, 1800
Hagan, Caleb.............	Lieutenant, 2nd Regiment.........	May 10, 1802
Hagan, Caleb.............	Captain, 2nd Regiment............	December 6, 1802
Hagan, Ignatius..........	Captain, 2nd Regiment............	July 14, 1800
Hahn, Charles............	Adjutant, 2nd Regiment...........	November 20, 1800
Hardesty, Caleb..........	Captain, 27th Regiment...........	May 21, 1803
Harned, Edward...........	Captain, 2nd Regiment............	April 10, 1799
Harrison, Burr...........	Lieutenant, 2nd Regiment.........	July 27, 1801
Havenhill, John..........	Lieutenant, 27th Regiment........	May 1, 1802
Hedgdon (Higdon), Thomas.	Lieutenant, 27th Regiment........	May 21, 1803
Higdon, Leonard..........	Ensign, 27th Regiment............	May 21, 1803
Higdon, Thomas...........	Ensign, Rifle Company, 27th Regiment.......................	January 31, 1801
Hubbard, Armistead.......	Captain, 2nd Regiment............	July 27, 1801
Ise, Jesse...............	Ensign, 2nd Regiment.............	July 14, 1800
James, Joseph............	Lieutenant, 27th Regiment........	March 25, 1800
Johnson, John............	Lieutenant, 2nd Regiment.........	May 31, 1800
Johnson, John............	Captain, 2nd Regiment............	May 10, 1802
Kendal, Hebe.............	Ensign, 2nd Regiment.............	May 19, 1800
Kendal, Henry............	Lieutenant, 2nd Regiment.........	July 27, 1801
Kincheloe, Elias.........	Ensign of Infantry, 27th Regiment.......................	November 20, 1800
King, Abner..............	Captain, 27th Regiment...........	May 12, 1804

COMMISSIONED OFFICERS, 1799 - 1804

Leslie, Solomon	Ensign, 2nd Regiment	December 6, 1802
Love, William	Lieutenant, 2nd Regiment	July 27, 1801
McClasky, Joseph	Ensign, 27th Regiment	May 12, 1804
McCowan, James	Lieutenant, 2nd Regiment	December 6, 1802
McLean, Samuel	Ensign, 27th Regiment	February 25, 1804
McLean, Samuel	Lieutenant, 27th Regiment	May 12, 1804
McMahon, Friend	Lieutenant, 27th Regiment	July 3, 1799
Marshall, William	Ensign, 27th Regiment	July 25, 1801
Mason, Benjamin	Ensign, 27th Regiment	May 1, 1802
Mason, William	Captain, 27th Regiment	April 4, 1799
Masterson, Hugh	Lieutenant, 2nd Regiment	December 10, 1799
May, Edmund	Captain, 27th Regiment	May 1, 1802
May, Humphrey	Lieutenant, 27th Regiment	August 3, 1802
May, John W.	Captain, 27th Regiment	February 25, 1804
Minor, William	Lieutenant, Rifle Company, 27th Regiment	January 31, 1801
Morehead, Charles	Major, 2nd Regiment	December 6, 1799
Nall, Martin	Lieutenant, 27th Regiment	October 18, 1804
Neafus, George	Ensign, 2nd Regiment	May 25, 1804
Neal, Samuel	Ensign, 2nd Regiment	April 10, 1799
Neal, William	Lieutenant, 27th Regiment	May 12, 1804
Nevitt, Joseph	Captain, 2nd Regiment	December 10, 1799
Nevitt, Matthew	Ensign, 2nd Regiment	May 10, 1802
Nevitt, Matthew	Lieutenant, 2nd Regiment	December 6, 1802
O'Neil, Charles	Ensign, 27th Regiment	August 3, 1802
Park, George	Lieutenant, 2nd Regiment	July 14, 1800
Parks, George	Ensign, 2nd Regiment	May 1, 1800
Paul, James	Ensign, 2nd Regiment	May 10, 1802
Paul, James	Lieutenant, 2nd Regiment	May 25, 1804
Polke, Edmund	Ensign, 27th Regiment	July 25, 1801
Polke, Samuel	Captain, 27th Regiment	February 18, 1800
Poole, William	Ensign, 27th Regiment	April 15, 1800
Pottinger, Samuel, Jr.	Lieutenant, 2nd Regiment	July 19, 1804
Rapir (Rapier), William	Ensign, 2nd Regiment	December 6, 1802
Robertson, Joseph	Ensign, 27th Regiment	August 3, 1802
Roby, Barton	Ensign, 2nd Regiment	July 14, 1800
Rogers, Jonathan	Captain, 2nd Regiment	May 10, 1802
Rogers, William	Colonel, 2nd Regiment	November 19, 1799
Samuels, James	Captain, 2nd Regiment	May 10, 1802
Samuels, William	Lieutenant, 2nd Regiment	May 10, 1802
Scissell (Cissell), James	Ensign, 2nd Regiment	July 19, 1804
Scott, Daniel	Lieutenant, 2nd Regiment	May 20, 1800
Seissel (Cissell), Ignatius	Captain, 2nd Regiment	May 10, 1802
Shockency, Elijah	Lieutenant, 27th Regiment	July 25, 1801
Shockency, Elijah	Captain, 27th Regiment	February 25, 1804
Skaggs, Stephen	Ensign, 2nd Regiment	May 20, 1800
Slaughter, Robert, Sr.	Paymaster, 2nd Regiment	December 6, 1800
Sneid, John	Ensign, 2nd Regiment	July 19, 1804
Spencer, Sharp	Captain, 27th Regiment	July 2, 1799
Stewart, Charles	Lieutenant, 2nd Regiment	July 19, 1804
Stone, Elijah	Lieutenant, 27th Regiment	February 25, 1804

COMMISSIONED OFFICERS, 1799 - 1804   137

Sweets, Thomas............	Captain, 2nd Regiment............	May 1, 1800
Sweets, Thomas............	Captain, 2nd Regiment............	May 10, 1802
Tutt, Thomas..............	Captain, 2nd Regiment............	December 11, 1799
Vittetow, William.........	Ensign, 2nd Regiment.............	July 27, 1801
Wakefield, William........	Captain, 27th Regiment...........	April 4, 1799
Washer, George............	Lieutenant, 2nd Regiment.........	March 21, 1800
Washer, George............	Captain, 2nd Regiment............	July 27, 1801
Weller, Henry.............	Ensign, 2nd Regiment.............	July 14, 1800
Weller, Henry.............	Lieutenant, 2nd Regiment.........	July 27, 1801
White, Jacob..............	Lieutenant, 2nd Regiment.........	May 10, 1802
Wickliff, Robert..........	Lieutenant, 2nd Regiment.........	May 25, 1804
Wilhoit, Abraham..........	Lieutenant, 27th Regiment........	July 2, 1799
Wilson, Isaac.............	Captain, 27th Regiment...........	May 12, 1804
Wilson, Vance.............	Lieutenant, 27th Regiment........	September 2, 1800
Worthum, Charles..........	Captain, 2nd Regiment............	April 29, 1800
Worthum, Henry............	Ensign, 2nd Regiment.............	May 10, 1802

Ohio and Breckinridge Regiment

[Laid off December 13, 1800]

[Designated as Ohio County Regiment December 10, 1804]

Allen, Samuel.............	Captain, 49th Regiment...........	October 11, 1803
Anderson, Ethel (Athel)..	Captain, 49th Regiment...........	August 3, 1802
Baird, James..............	Lieutenant, 49th Regiment........	May 15, 1804
Bare, Adam................	Ensign, 49th Regiment............	April 16, 1801
Barnard, Joshua...........	Lieutenant, 49th Regiment........	October 10, 1802
Barnes, John..............	Ensign, 49th Regiment............	October 10, 1802
Barnett, Joshua...........	Ensign, 49th Regiment............	February 14, 1801
Bennett, John.............	Lieutenant, 49th Regiment........	February 14, 1801
Bennett, John.............	Captain, 49th Regiment...........	October 4, 1802
Bond, James...............	Ensign, 49th Regiment............	October 4, 1802
Brothers, John............	Captain, 49th Regiment...........	April 16, 1801
Claycomb, John............	Lieutenant, 49th Regiment........	October 10, 1802
Cleaver, Stephen..........	Colonel, 49th Regiment...........	December 18, 1800
Conner, Samuel............	Ensign, 49th Regiment............	October 11, 1803
Cooper, Robert............	Ensign, 49th Regiment............	August 3, 1802
Cooper, Robert............	Lieutenant, 49th Regiment........	May 15, 1804
Craven, Jesse.............	Paymaster, 49th Regiment.........	February 14, 1801
Crawford, Mason...........	Ensign, 49th Regiment............	August 3, 1802
Crawford, Samuel..........	Lieutenant, 49th Regiment........	October 10, 1802
Crow, John................	Major, 1st Battalion, 49th Regiment......................	December 18, 1800
Cummins, Presley..........	Ensign, 49th Regiment............	October 11, 1803
Dooling, Daniel...........	Captain, 49th Regiment...........	February 14, 1801
Dye, James................	Ensign, 49th Regiment............	May 15, 1804
Edwards, Elijah...........	Adjutant, 49th Regiment..........	November 22, 1802
Ferry, James..............	Lieutenant, 49th Regiment........	April 16, 1801
Field, Henry..............	Lieutenant, 49th Regiment........	October 10, 1802

COMMISSIONED OFFICERS, 1799 - 1804

Gentry, Joseph............	Ensign, 49th Regiment............	November 22, 1802
Gentry, William..........	Ensign, 49th Regiment............	May 15, 1804
Gibson, John.............	Ensign, 49th Regiment............	July 8, 1801, December 30, 1803, and May 15, 1804
Gilbert, Benjamin........	Captain, 49th Regiment...........	February 14, 1801
Glenn, William...........	Ensign, 49th Regiment............	April 26, 1803
Glenn, William...........	Lieutenant, 49th Regiment........	May 15, 1804
Hardin, Henry............	Ensign, 49th Regiment............	April 16, 1801
Hardin, William, Jr. ...	Captain, 49th Regiment...........	October 10, 1802
Huff, R(eubin)...........	Ensign, 49th Regiment............	October 10, 1802
Huff, Reubin.............	Lieutenant, 49th Regiment........	August 3, 1802
Jackson, Christopher, Jr.	Quartermaster, 49th Regiment.....	February 14, 1801
James, William...........	Lieutenant, 49th Regiment........	February 14, 1801
James, William...........	Captain, 49th Regiment...........	October 10, 1802
Kinchaloe, Thomas........	Captain, 49th Regiment...........	April 16, 1801
McGrady, Samuel..........	Major, 2nd Battalion, 49th Regiment.......................	December 13, 1804
Meadows, John............	Ensign, 49th Regiment............	October 10, 1802
Meeks, William...........	Lieutenant, 49th Regiment........	August 3, 1802
Morgan, Thomas...........	Ensign, 49th Regiment............	May 15, 1804
Mosley, John.............	Ensign, 49th Regiment............	February 14, 1801
Mosley, John.............	Lieutenant, 49th Regiment........	October 4, 1802
Myers, Elijah............	Lieutenant, 49th Regiment........	May 15, 1804
New, Jacob...............	Ensign, 49th Regiment............	April 26, 1803
Parker, Thomas...........	Captain, 49th Regiment...........	July 8, 1801
Perigoe, Romey...........	Ensign, 49th Regiment............	May 15, 1804
Rice, Jacob..............	Ensign, 49th Regiment............	August 3, 1802
Risley, John.............	Ensign, 49th Regiment............	October 10, 1802
Risley, John.............	Lieutenant, 49th Regiment........	April 26, 1803
Rizley, John.............	Captain, 49th Regiment...........	December 30, 1803
Smithers, William........	Ensign, 49th Regiment............	October 11, 1803
Smithers, William........	Lieutenant, 49th Regiment........	December 30, 1803
Taylor, Richard..........	Captain, 49th Regiment...........	October 4, 1802
Vertrees, John...........	Captain, 49th Regiment...........	April 26, 1803
Walker, John.............	Major, 2nd Battalion, 49th Regiment.......................	December 19, 1800
Walker, William..........	Ensign, 49th Regiment............	April 16, 1801
Walker, William..........	Lieutenant, 49th Regiment........	October 10, 1802
Work, Samuel.............	Adjutant, 49th Regiment..........	February 14, 1801

Pulaski County Regiment

[Laid off December 20, 1799]

Alcorn, George...........	Lieutenant, 44th Regiment........ (Formerly of 6th Regiment)	December 6, 1800
Alcorn, George...........	Captain, 44th Regiment...........	August 8, 1803
Alderson, James..........	Captain, 44th Regiment...........	August 8, 1803
Alexander, Nicholas......	Lieutenant, 44th Regiment........	February 23, 1801
Alexander, Nicholas......	Captain, 44th Regiment...........	July 10, 1802

COMMISSIONED OFFICERS, 1799 - 1804

Atkins, Andrew...........	Ensign, 44th Regiment............	August 8, 1803
Bebare (Baber), Robert...	Captain, 44th Regiment...........	July 10, 1802
Blevens, Elisha..........	Ensign, 44th Regiment............	July 10, 1802
Brutin, George...........	Lieutenant, 44th Regiment........	February 23, 1801
Burnham, Thomas..........	Lieutenant, 44th Regiment........	August 8, 1803
Carlock, Joseph..........	Ensign, 44th Regiment............	July 10, 1802
Carr, James..............	Lieutenant, 44th Regiment........	July 10, 1802
Clarke, Stewart..........	Ensign, 44th Regiment............	August 8, 1803
Coffie, John.............	Ensign, 44th Regiment............	July 10, 1802
Cowen, John..............	2nd Lieutenant, 44th Regiment....	December 19, 1801
Davis, John..............	Lieutenant, 44th Regiment........	July 10, 1802
Davis, Samuel............	Ensign, 44th Regiment............	February 23, 1801
Dean, Michael............	Ensign, 44th Regiment............	July 10, 1802
Deane, Michael...........	Ensign, 44th Regiment............	February 23, 1801
Debrel, Charles..........	Major, 1st Battalion, 44th Regiment......................	December 20, 1799
Dodson, Asa..............	Ensign, 44th Regiment............	August 8, 1803
Edgeman, Thomas K.	Captain, 44th Regiment........... (Formerly of 6th Regiment)	December 6, 1800
Emerson, Walter..........	Cornet, 44th Regiment............	December 19, 1801
Forbis, Nathaniel........	Lieutenant, 44th Regiment........	August 8, 1803
Fox, William.............	Major, 2nd Battalion, 44th Regiment......................	December 22, 1799
Francis, Henry...........	Captain, 44th Regiment...........	December 6, 1800
Francis, Henry...........	Major, 1st Battalion, 44th Regiment......................	December 13, 1802
Gill, John...............	Ensign, 44th Regiment............	December 6, 1800
Goodwin, Richard.........	Ensign, 44th Regiment............	February 23, 1801
Goodwin, Richard.........	Lieutenant, 44th Regiment........	July 10, 1802
Griffin, John............	Captain, 44th Regiment...........	December 6, 1800
Halfacre, Christian......	Captain, 44th Regiment...........	July 10, 1802
Hardgrove, William.......	Captain, 44th Regiment........... (Formerly of 6th Regiment)	December 6, 1800
Harril, James............	Ensign, 44th Regiment............	December 6, 1800
Hess, Henry..............	Lieutenant, 44th Regiment........	December 6, 1800
Hill, William............	Captain, 44th Regiment...........	February 23, 1801
Hines, Joseph............	Captain, 44th Regiment...........	February 23, 1801
Isball, Godfrey..........	Captain, 44th Regiment...........	February 23, 1801
Jackson, Joel............	Ensign, 44th Regiment............	July 10, 1802
James, Henry.............	Lieutenant, 44th Regiment........	July 10, 1802
James, Henry.............	Captain, 44th Regiment...........	August 8, 1803
Jasper, John.............	Ensign, 44th Regiment............ (Formerly of 6th Regiment)	December 6, 1800
Jasper, John.............	Lieutenant, 44th Regiment........	July 23, 1801
Johnson, James...........	Ensign, 44th Regiment............	July 23, 1801
Johnson, Thomas..........	Captain, 44th Regiment...........	February 23, 1801
Jones, William...........	Lieutenant, 44th Regiment........	July 10, 1802
Keaney, Michael..........	Captain, 44th Regiment........... (Formerly of 6th Regiment)	December 6, 1800
Kesiah, James............	Ensign, 44th Regiment............	July 23, 1801
Kitchens, James..........	Ensign, 44th Regiment............	December 6, 1800

COMMISSIONED OFFICERS, 1799 - 1804

Long, John..............	Captain, 44th Regiment..........	December 19, 1801
Lynch, William..........	Lieutenant, 44th Regiment.......	February 23, 1801
McFall, John............	Ensign, 44th Regiment...........	August 8, 1803
McKinsey, David.........	Captain, 44th Regiment.......... (Formerly of 6th Regiment)	December 6, 1800
McWaters, John..........	Lieutenant, 44th Regiment.......	December 6, 1800
Martin, John............	Lieutenant, 44th Regiment.......	December 19, 1801
Meadows, Isaac..........	Lieutenant, 44th Regiment.......	February 23, 1801
Meadows, Isaac..........	Captain, 44th Regiment..........	July 10, 1802
Miller, Andrew..........	Captain, 44th Regiment..........	February 23, 1801
Modrel, Robert..........	Ensign, 44th Regiment...........	July 23, 1801
Modrell, Robert, Sr. ...	Major, 2nd Battalion, 44th Regiment.....................	May 16, 1800
Moore, Alexander........	Ensign, 44th Regiment...........	February 23, 1801
Nicholas, (George?).....	Lieutenant, 44th Regiment....... (Formerly of 6th Regiment)	December 6, 1800
Nicholas, James.........	Ensign, 44th Regiment...........	February 23, 1801
Patterson, William......	Ensign, 44th Regiment...........	August 8, 1803
Press, William..........	Lieutenant, 44th Regiment.......	July 23, 1801
Prewitt, William........	Lieutenant, 44th Regiment.......	February 23, 1801
Richardson, David.......	Ensign, 44th Regiment...........	July 10, 1802
Richardson, David.......	Captain, 44th Regiment..........	August 8, 1803
Richardson, Jesse.......	Colonel, 44th Regiment..........	December 20, 1799
Runnard, Benjamin.......	Lieutenant, 44th Regiment.......	August 8, 1803
Salisbury, Nathaniel....	Ensign, 44th Regiment...........	December 6, 1800
Singleton, Louis........	Captain, 44th Regiment..........	July 10, 1802
Smith, John.............	Lieutenant, 44th Regiment....... (Formerly of 6th Regiment)	December 6, 1800
Smith, John.............	Captain, 44th Regiment..........	February 23, 1801
Smith, Robert...........	Lieutenant, 44th Regiment.......	August 8, 1803
Stewart, Charles........	Lieutenant, 44th Regiment....... (Formerly of 6th Regiment)	December 6, 1800
Sublett, Phil. A.	Lieutenant, 44th Regiment.......	February 23, 1801
Thompson, Thomas........	Ensign, 44th Regiment...........	July 10, 1802
Trapp, John.............	Ensign, 44th Regiment........... (Formerly of 6th Regiment)	December 6, 1800
Trapp, John.............	Lieutenant, 44th Regiment.......	July 23, 1801
Ussery, William.........	Captain, 44th Regiment..........	August 8, 1803
Vanwinckle, Abraham.....	Ensign, 44th Regiment...........	February 23, 1801
Wade, Joseph............	Lieutenant, 44th Regiment.......	July 10, 1802
Wilds, Thomas...........	Paymaster, 44th Regiment........	December 16, 1800
Wiles, Thomas...........	Adjutant, 44th Regiment.........	March 25, 1803
Williams, John..........	Lieutenant, 44th Regiment.......	August 8, 1803
Williams, Samuel........	Ensign, 44th Regiment........... (Formerly of 6th Regiment)	December 6, 1800
Willis, Thomas..........	Captain, 44th Regiment..........	December 6, 1800
Wyatt, William..........	Captain, 44th Regiment..........	July 10, 1802

COMMISSIONED OFFICERS, 1799 - 1804 141

Scott County Regiment

Acoff, Christopher	Ensign, 12th Regiment	May 25, 1804
Acoff, Christopher	Lieutenant, 12th Regiment	September 12, 1804
Adams, Nathan	Lieutenant, 12th Regiment	May 28, 1801
Ballad, George	Lieutenant, 12th Regiment	September 12, 1804
Bellows, John	Ensign, 12th Regiment	June 25, 1804
Berriman, Josias	Ensign, 12th Regiment	March 3, 1801
Bond, William	Ensign, 12th Regiment	June 28, 1802
Bond, William	Lieutenant, 12th Regiment	December 24, 1802
Bradford, Fielding	Ensign, 12th Regiment	December 10, 1800
Bradford, Fielding	Captain, 12th Regiment	December 11, 1801
Branham, John	Ensign, 12th Regiment	May 23, 1802
Branham, John	Lieutenant, 12th Regiment	June 28, 1802
Branham, William	Lieutenant, 12th Regiment	March 3, 1801
Branham, William	Captain, 12th Regiment	May 23, 1802
Brookes, James	Ensign, 12th Regiment	December 11, 1801
Burbridge, George	Captain, 12th Regiment	December 10, 1800
Burch, Joseph	Ensign, 12th Regiment	December 11, 1801
Burch, Joseph	Lieutenant, 12th Regiment	May 23, 1802
Campbell, William	Lieutenant, 12th Regiment	March 29, 1800
Campbell, William	Captain, 12th Regiment	May 21, 1803
Collins, Richard	Ensign, 12th Regiment	December 11, 1801
Craig, Nathaniel	Ensign, Rifle Company, 12th Regiment	March 3, 1801
Crouch, John	Ensign, 12th Regiment	May 23, 1802
Curry, John	Ensign, 12th Regiment	September 1, 1800
Dehaven, Samuel	Lieutenant, 12th Regiment	August 1, 1800
Denny, Fielding	Lieutenant, 12th Regiment	May 21, 1803
Elliott, Benjamin	Ensign, 12th Regiment	May 21, 1803
Elliott, John	Ensign, 12th Regiment	May 23, 1802
Faukener, Nicholas	Ensign, 12th Regiment	December 11, 1801
Ficklin, John	Lieutenant, 12th Regiment	March 3, 1801
Foster, Thomas	Ensign, 12th Regiment	May 25, 1804
Gano, Richard M.	Captain, Infantry Company, Georgetown Blues, 12th Regiment	October 26, 1801
Gass, Samuel	Ensign, 12th Regiment	May 21, 1803
Gibson, James	Ensign, 12th Regiment	December 11, 1801
Grant, James	Lieutenant, 12th Regiment	June 25, 1804
Hamond, James	Ensign, 12th Regiment	December 30, 1803
Herndon, Henry	Lieutenant, Infantry Company, Georgetown Blues, 12th Regiment	October 26, 1801
Holland, Ephraim	Ensign, 12th Regiment	May 21, 1803
Hopkins, James	Ensign, 12th Regiment	May 23, 1802
Hurst, John	Captain, 12th Regiment	April 8, 1799
Hutcheson, Alexander	Lieutenant, 12th Regiment	April 8, 1799
Johnson, Adam	Captain, 12th Regiment	March 21, 1800
Johnson, Richard	Lieutenant, 12th Regiment	December 11, 1801
Johnson, William	Captain, 12th Regiment	March 3, 1801
Johnson, William G.	Ensign, 12th Regiment	June 4, 1804
Kelly, Griffin	Captain, 12th Regiment	April 29, 1800

COMMISSIONED OFFICERS, 1799 - 1804

Kirtley, Larkin	Ensign, 12th Regiment	June 25, 1804
Lindsey, Anthony	Lieutenant, 12th Regiment	May 25, 1804
Lindsey, Henry	Captain, 12th Regiment	April 11, 1800
McAlla (McCalla), Robert	Ensign, 12th Regiment	December 24, 1802
McCormic, William	Lieutenant, 12th Regiment	December 30, 1803
McCoy, Alexander	Ensign, 12th Regiment	December 24, 1802
Massey, William	Ensign, 12th Regiment	April 11, 1800
Miller, Jac.	Cornet, Troop of Horse, 6th Brigade (12th Regiment)	September 24, 1803
Miller, John	Captain, 12th Regiment	August 1, 1800
Moody, Thomas	Lieutenant, 12th Regiment	April 29, 1800
Moody, Thomas	Captain, 12th Regiment	December 11, 1801
Moody, William	Lieutenant, 12th Regiment	December 11, 1801
Nall, Charles	Ensign, 12th Regiment	March 3, 1801
Nall, Charles L.	Lieutenant, 12th Regiment	May 23, 1802
Nall, Charles L.	Captain, 12th Regiment	June 28, 1802
Neale, Daniel	Ensign, 12th Regiment	March 29, 1800
Neale, Daniel	Lieutenant, 12th Regiment	March 3, 1801
Oldham, George	Ensign, 12th Regiment	August 2, 1799
Oldham, George, Jr.	Lieutenant, 12th Regiment	June 4, 1804
Oldham, George, Jr.	Captain, 12th Regiment	June 25, 1804
Orsburn, James	Lieutenant, 12th Regiment	May 25, 1804
Payne, John	Colonel, 12th Regiment	December 17, 1799
Payne, Zadock	Lieutenant, 12th Regiment	April 1, 1800
Pitts, Younger	Ensign, 12th Regiment	May 21, 1803
Richey, Stephen	Ensign, 12th Regiment	December 10, 1800
Robinson, George	Ensign, 12th Regiment	December 30, 1803
Robinson, George	Lieutenant, 12th Regiment	May 25, 1804
Rodes, Waller	Lieutenant, 12th Regiment	December 24, 1802
Royal, Stephen	Lieutenant, 12th Regiment	December 11, 1801
Samuel, Thomas	Ensign, 12th Regiment	December 30, 1803
Scott, Abraham	Ensign, Infantry Company, Georgetown Blues, 12th Regiment	October 26, 1801
Scott, Joel	Lieutenant, 12th Regiment	November 8, 1804
Scraggs, Thomas	Lieutenant, 12th Regiment	December 30, 1803
Shelton, Medley	Ensign, 12th Regiment	September 12, 1804
Short, Obed	Ensign, 12th Regiment	April 1, 1800
Shortridge, Daniel	Ensign, 12th Regiment	March 21, 1800
Shortridge, Daniel	Lieutenant, 12th Regiment	September 28, 1801
Stephenson, James	Ensign, 12th Regiment	May 25, 1804
Stone, Asa	Ensign, 12th Regiment	August 1, 1800
Stone, Asa	Lieutenant, 12th Regiment	May 21, 1803
Stone, John	Ensign, 12th Regiment	June 4, 1804
Sutton, William	Captain, 12th Regiment	September 24, 1803 and May 25, 1804
Sweetnum, George	Ensign, 12th Regiment	September 28, 1801
Swetman, George	Lieutenant, 12th Regiment	September 12, 1804
Tarleton, Caleb	Lieutenant, 12th Regiment	December 11, 1801
Thomas, Solomon	Ensign, 12th Regiment	April 29, 1800 and December 30, 1803
Thomas, Solomon	Lieutenant, 12th Regiment	May 25, 1804

COMMISSIONED OFFICERS, 1799 - 1804

Thompson, David..........	Captain, 12th Regiment...........	March 21, 1800
Thompson, Gilbert........	Ensign, 12th Regiment............	September 28, 1801
Triplett, Hedgeman.......	Major, 1st Battalion, 12th Regiment......................	May 24, 1802
Webb, John V.	Captain, 12th Regiment...........	April 1, 1800
White, John..............	Captain, 12th Regiment...........	December 30, 1803
Willson, John............	Ensign, 12th Regiment............	November 8, 1804
Woolf, Jacob.............	Ensign, 12th Regiment............	September 12, 1804
Woolfolk, Elijah.........	Lieutenant, 12th Regiment........	December 30, 1803

Shelby County Regiments

[37th Regiment laid off December 5, 1799]

Adams, Simon.............	Major, 2nd Battalion, 18th Regiment......................	May 18, 1804
Allen, Stephen...........	Ensign, 18th Regiment............	September 12, 1803
Archer, John.............	Ensign, 37th Regiment............	December 5, 1801
Ashby, Beady.............	Ensign, 37th Regiment............	October 5, 1798
	Recommissioned..................	December 18, 1800
Ashby, Landin............	Lieutenant, 18th Regiment........	August 21, 1802
Ashby, Silas.............	Captain, 18th Regiment...........	August 21, 1802
Ashby, Stinson...........	Ensign, Rifle Company, 37th Regiment......................	November 4, 1800
Ballard, James...........	Major, 1st Battalion, 37th Regiment......................	December 5, 1799
Ballard, James...........	Lieutenant Colonel, Commandant 37th Regiment..................	December 20, 1804
Banks, James.............	Lieutenant, 37th Regiment........	May 26, 1800
Bartlett, Edmond.........	Captain, Rifle Company, 18th Regiment......................	June 11, 1799
Bedle, Jonathan..........	Captain, 37th Regiment...........	September 5, 1801
Beedle, Jonathan.........	Lieutenant, 37th Regiment........	September 1, 1797
	Recommissioned..................	December 18, 1800
Bell, John...............	Lieutenant, 18th Regiment........	April 7, 1801
Booker, Richard..........	Ensign of Infantry, 18th Regiment......................	May 10, 1800
Booker, Richard..........	Lieutenant, 18th Regiment........	February 20, 1802
Booker, Richard..........	Captain, 18th Regiment...........	May 14, 1804
Bradshaw, John...........	Captain, 18th Regiment...........	January 1, 1800
Brady, William...........	Ensign, 37th Regiment............	July 29, 1799
	Recommissioned..................	December 18, 1800
Brady, William...........	Captain, 37th Regiment...........	April 21, 1800
Breeding, William........	Ensign, 37th Regiment............	May 19, 1804
Brenton, John............	Lieutenant, 18th Regiment........	September 12, 1803
Brinton, John............	Lieutenant, 18th Regiment........	March 2, 1800
Brody, William...........	Ensign, 18th Regiment............	July 29, 1799
Cardwell, Isaac..........	Ensign, Rifle Company, 18th Regiment......................	June 22, 1802
Cardwell, William........	Ensign, 18th Regiment............	September 26, 1801

Carlin, Thomas............	Lieutenant, 37th Regiment........	May 27, 1802
Carr, Absalom.............	Major, 2nd Battalion, 37th Regiment......................	December 6, 1799
Castleman, Jacob..........	Captain, 18th Regiment...........	June 5, 1801
Clark, Obadiah............	Captain, 37th Regiment...........	May 26, 1800
Clarke, Zachariah.........	Lieutenant, 37th Regiment........	December 5, 1801
Clayton, James............	Ensign, 37th Regiment............	March 14, 1803
Clayton, James............	Lieutenant, 37th Regiment........	September 3, 1803
Clemmons, James...........	Captain, 37th Regiment...........	May 19, 1804
Connelly, James...........	Lieutenant, 37th Regiment........	March 14, 1803
Conolly, Jesse............	Ensign, 37th Regiment............	September 3, 1803
Cooper, Eliab.............	Lieutenant, 37th Regiment........	September 3, 1803
Crabb, Jeremiah...........	Lieutenant, 18th Regiment........	May 14, 1804
Crist, William............	Ensign, 37th Regiment............	May 19, 1804
Eakin, John...............	Lieutenant, 18th Regiment........	February 26, 1799
Elam, Richard.............	Ensign, 18th Regiment............	September 8, 1800
Ellin (Allen), Thomas....	Ensign, 37th Regiment............	March 14, 1803
Fisher, Zachariah.........	Ensign; 18th Regiment............	March 2, 1800
Fisher, Zachariah.........	Lieutenant, 18th Regiment........	February 20, 1802
Fore, John................	Lieutenant, 18th Regiment........	May 14, 1804
Fuqua, Joseph.............	Ensign, 18th Regiment............	February 20, 1802
Gill, George..............	Lieutenant, 37th Regiment........	May 19, 1804
Glover, Uriah.............	Ensign, 37th Regiment............	December 3, 1803
Gragg, David..............	Captain, 37th Regiment...........	April 25, 1797
	Recommissioned.................	December 18, 1800
Graham, Thomas............	Ensign, 18th Regiment............	February 26, 1799
Graham, Thomas............	Captain, 18th Regiment...........	April 22, 1800
Gullion, Jeremiah.........	Captain, 18th Regiment...........	November 4, 1799
Hackett, James............	Ensign, 18th Regiment............	April 7, 1801
Hackett, James............	Captain, 18th Regiment...........	February 20, 1802
Harson (Harrison?), John.	Ensign, 37th Regiment............	December 7, 1799
Henderson, James L.	Captain, 37th Regiment...........	May 27, 1802
Hensly, Jonathan..........	Ensign, 37th Regiment............	May 19, 1804
Hill, Isaac...............	Lieutenant, 37th Regiment........	May 19, 1804
Hinton, William...........	Lieutenant, 18th Regiment........	February 20, 1802
Hinton, William...........	Captain, 18th Regiment...........	March 14, 1803
Holmes, Jesse.............	Lieutenant, 18th Regiment........	June 22, 1802
Holmes, Jesse.............	Captain, 18th Regiment...........	March 14, 1803
Hornsby, Joseph, Jr. ...	Paymaster, 37th Regiment.........	December 18, 1800
Hornsby, Thomas...........	Adjutant, 37th Regiment..........	September 26, 1800
Hunter, William...........	Ensign, 18th Regiment............	April 8, 1800
Hunter, William...........	Lieutenant, 18th Regiment........	February 20, 1802
Johnson, George...........	Ensign, 37th Regiment............	May 27, 1802
Johnson, James............	Ensign, 37th Regiment............	April 28, 1800
Johnson, James............	Lieutenant, Rifle Company, 37th Regiment.............January 1 and November 4, 1800	
Johnson, James............	Lieutenant, 37th Regiment........	September 5, 1801
Johnson, Larkin...........	Ensign, 37th Regiment............	September 3, 1803
Johnson, Thomas...........	Ensign, 18th Regiment............	July 29, 1799
Johnson, Thomas...........	Adjutant, 18th Regiment..........	August 5, 1801
Johnson, William..........	Ensign, 37th Regiment............	September 5, 1801

COMMISSIONED OFFICERS, 1799 - 1804

Johnstone, John	Captain, 18th Regiment	September 12, 1803
Jones, Joshua	Lieutenant, 18th Regiment	November 4, 1799
Kendal, William	Lieutenant, 37th Regiment	March 10, 1802
Kerr (Carr), Elijah	Captain, 18th Regiment	February 20, 1802
Ketcham, John	Ensign, 18th Regiment	August 21, 1802
Kindle, William	Ensign, 37th Regiment	September 5, 1801
King, Nathaniel	2nd Lieutenant, 18th Regiment	January 1, 1800
Knight, George B.	Ensign, 37th Regiment	May 19, 1804
Knight, John	Surgeon, 37th Regiment	December 18, 1800
Kykendol, Peter	Lieutenant, 37th Regiment	April 29, 1800
Lamb, Jacob	Ensign, 18th Regiment	November 4, 1799
Lain (Lane), Thomas	Ensign, 37th Regiment	April 21, 1800
Lane, Thomas	Lieutenant, 37th Regiment	September 5, 1801
Leatherman, Christopher	Lieutenant, 37th Regiment	September 3, 1803
Lindsey, William	Lieutenant, 37th Regiment	September 5, 1801
Love, James	Captain, 18th Regiment	August 21, 1802
McCambel, James	Lieutenant, 18th Regiment	May 28, 1800
McClure, William	Major, 2nd Battalion, 18th Regiment	May 1, 1800
McCormic, Peter P.	Captain, 37th Regiment	September 1, 1797
	Recommissioned	December 18, 1800
McCormic, William	Captain, 37th Regiment	May 26, 1800
McDavid, James	Ensign, 18th Regiment	May 27, 1799
McDavid, James	Ensign, 37th Regiment	May 27, 1799
	Recommissioned	December 18, 1800
McDavid, James	Ensign, Rifle Company, 37th Regiment	May 27, 1802
McDavitt, James	Captain, 37th Regiment	March 14, 1803
McGaughey, John	Major, 1st Battalion, 18th Regiment	April 8, 1800
McGaughey, John	Colonel, 18th Regiment	December 23, 1801
Mahorney, James	Ensign, 18th Regiment	January 9, 1801
Mahorney, James	Lieutenant, 18th Regiment	June 5, 1801
Martin, Edward	Ensign, 37th Regiment	May 19, 1804
Martin, Thomas	Captain, 18th Regiment	July 15, 1799
Martin, Thomas	Captain, 37th Regiment	July 15, 1799
	Recommissioned	December 18, 1800
Martin, Thomas	Major, 1st Battalion, 37th Regiment	December 20, 1804
Matthews, John	Lieutenant, 37th Regiment	September 5, 1801
Matthews, John	Captain, 37th Regiment	May 27, 1802
Mattox, Absalom	Captain, 18th Regiment	May 28, 1800
Meddox, John W.	Captain, 18th Regiment	June 22, 1802
Minor, Thomas	Ensign, 18th Regiment	April 22, 1800
Mitchel, Thomas	Captain, 18th Regiment	January 9, 1801
Moore, Robert	Lieutenant, 18th Regiment	August 21, 1802
Moore, Robert M.	Captain, 18th Regiment	May 14, 1804
Mulliken, William	Ensign, 18th Regiment	August 21, 1802
Nash, John	Ensign, 18th Regiment	March 14, 1803
Nash, Noble	Captain, 18th Regiment	April 7, 1801
Ogden, Masterson	Captain, 18th Regiment	February 20, 1802

COMMISSIONED OFFICERS, 1799 - 1804

Owen, William............	Lieutenant, 18th Regiment........	September 26, 1801
Owens, Abraham...........	Captain, 18th Regiment..........	September 26, 1801
Owens, Abraham...........	Major, 1st Battalion, 18th Regiment......................	May 18, 1804
Owens, William...........	Ensign, 18th Regiment............	November 14, 1800
Patterson, William.......	Captain, 37th Regiment...........	March 28, 1800
Payne, Jilston...........	Colonel, 37th Regiment...........	June 15, 1803
Payton, Daniel...........	Major, 1st Battalion, 37th Regiment......................	June 15, 1803
Pearcy, George...........	Lieutenant, 18th Regiment........	August 21, 1802
Perry, Franklin..........	Ensign, 18th Regiment............	March 14, 1803
Perry, Randolph..........	Lieutenant, 18th Regiment........	March 14, 1803
Phillips, John H.	Lieutenant, 37th Regiment........	May 19, 1804
Piercy, George...........	Ensign, 18th Regiment............	February 20, 1802
Polk, William............	Lieutenant, 18th Regiment........	July 8, 1799
Polke, William...........	Lieutenant, 37th Regiment........	March 14, 1803
Porter, Samuel...........	Lieutenant, 18th Regiment........	July 29, 1799 and September 8, 1800
Poulke, William..........	Lieutenant, Rifle Company, 37th Regiment.................	August, 1799
	Recommissioned..............	December 18, 1800
Prewitt, Beverly.........	Ensign, 37th Regiment............	September 5, 1801
Prewitt, Elisha..........	Ensign, 37th Regiment............	May 19, 1804
Prewitt, Joshua..........	Lieutenant, 18th Regiment........	March 14, 1803
Price, James.............	Ensign, 37th Regiment............	March 28, 1800
Price, Josiah............	Lieutenant, 37th Regiment........	March 28, 1800
Pruet, Beverly...........	Lieutenant, 37th Regiment........	May 27, 1802
Randolph, William........	Ensign, 37th Regiment............	April 4, 1798
	Recommissioned.................	December 18, 1800
Ray, Aaron...............	Ensign, 37th Regiment............	March 10, 1802
Redman, Washington.......	Ensign, 18th Regiment............	May 14, 1804
Reid, Alexander..........	Captain, 18th Regiment...........	January 9, 1801
Reid, Caleb..............	Captain, 37th Regiment...........	November 4, 1800
Reid, James..............	Adjutant, 18th Regiment..........	September 17, 1799
Robinson, George.........	Captain, 18th Regiment...........	February 28, 1800
Robinson, Joshua.........	Lieutenant, 18th Regiment........	March 14, 1803
Ruble, Isaac.............	Lieutenant, 37th Regiment........	December 18, 1800
Ruble, Jacob.............	Lieutenant, 18th Regiment........	July 15, 1799
Rycar (Ryker), John......	Colonel, 18th Regiment...........	April 9, 1800
Ryland, Nicholas.........	Captain, 18th Regiment...........	April 25, 1800
Scisars (Scifrass), Mathias...	Ensign, 37th Regiment........	May 26, 1800
Scott, John..............	Ensign, 37th Regiment............	September 5, 1801
Scott, Martin............	Ensign, 37th Regiment............	May 26, 1800
Searce, Henry............	Lieutenant, 18th Regiment........	February 20, 1802
Shank, John..............	Lieutenant, 18th Regiment........	September 12, 1803
Shannon, James...........	Lieutenant, 18th Regiment........	April 25, 1800
Sharp, Anthony...........	Ensign, 37th Regiment............	September 5, 1801
Shaver, David............	Lieutenant, 37th Regiment........	April 21, 1800
Shaver, David............	Captain, 37th Regiment...........	September 5, 1801
Shelady, George..........	Lieutenant, 18th Regiment........	April 22, 1800
Shipman, William.........	Ensign, 18th Regiment............	February 20, 1802

COMMISSIONED OFFICERS, 1799 - 1804

Sill, Adam...............	Captain, 18th Regiment...........	February 26, 1799
Simpson, Joseph..........	Captain, 37th Regiment...........	August 2, 1802
Smith, Abraham...........	1st Lieutenant, 18th Regiment....	January 1, 1800
Smith, Nicholas..........	Ensign, 18th Regiment............	May 6, 1799
Spencer, Spear...........	Captain, Rifle Company, 18th Regiment......................	July 8, 1799
Spencer, Spear...........	Captain, Rifle Company, 37th Regiment......................	July 8, 1799
	Recommissioned...............	December 18, 1800
Staundeford, Israel......	Ensign, 37th Regiment............	May 27, 1802
Steele, Adam.............	Quartermaster, 18th Regiment.....	December 16, 1801
Steele, Richard..........	Quartermaster, 18th Regiment.....	June 10, 1799
Stillwell, John..........	Captain, 37th Regiment...........	March 14, 1803
Sturgis, James...........	Ensign, 18th Regiment............	April 25, 1800
Swaney, Henry............	Ensign, 18th Regiment............	August 21, 1802
Taylor, Richard..........	Captain, 37th Regiment...........	September 3, 1803
Threlkeld, John, Jr. ...	Ensign, 18th Regiment............	June 11, 1804
Tilley, Aaron............	Ensign, 37th Regiment............	September 3, 1803
Tinsley, Samuel..........	Lieutenant, 37th Regiment........	April 3, 1801
Tinsley, William.........	Ensign, 37th Regiment............	December 3, 1803
Trammel, John............	Ensign, 18th Regiment............	June 5, 1801
Trammel, John............	Lieutenant, 18th Regiment........	February 20, 1802
Tunstal, James...........	Cornet, 18th Regiment............	January 1, 1800
Tunstall, William........	Captain, 18th Regiment...........	May 20, 1800
Tunstall, William........	Major, 1st Battalion, 18th Regiment......................	December 23, 1801
Tunstall, William J. ...	Lieutenant Colonel, Commandant 18th Regiment.................	May 18, 1804
Waddy, Samuel............	Captain, 37th Regiment...........	May 19, 1804
Walker, George...........	Adjutant, 37th Regiment..........	December 18, 1800
Waller, Stephen..........	Quartermaster, 37th Regiment.....	December 18, 1800
Walls, William...........	Lieutenant, 37th Regiment........	April 22, 1800
Walls, William...........	Captain, 37th Regiment...........	September 5, 1801
Watkins, Isaac...........	Adjutant, 18th Regiment..........	June 5, 1801
Webb, Samuel.............	Lieutenant, 37th Regiment........	December 7, 1799
Wells, John..............	Ensign, 18th Regiment............	February 20, 1802
White, Archibald.........	Ensign, Rifle Company, 18th Regiment......................	June 11, 1799
White, David.............	Ensign, 18th Regiment............	May 28, 1800
White, Thomas............	Lieutenant, Rifle Company, 18th Regiment......................	June 11, 1799
Whitesides, Isaac........	Lieutenant, 37th Regiment........	December 3, 1803
Whittaker, Elijah........	Lieutenant, 37th Regiment........	November 1, 1796
	Recommissioned................	December 18, 1800
Whittaker, Elijah........	Captain, 37th Regiment...........	April 22, 1800
Whittaker, Isaac.........	Ensign, 37th Regiment............	April 22, 1800
Wilcox, George...........	Captain, 18th Regiment...........	May 28, 1800
Wilcox, Joseph...........	Ensign, 18th Regiment............	February 20, 1802
Williamson, John.........	Lieutenant, 18th Regiment........	May 14, 1804
Winlock, Joseph..........	Colonel, 37th Regiment...........	December 5, 1799
Woods, John..............	Lieutenant, 18th Regiment........	July 15, 1799

COMMISSIONED OFFICERS, 1799 - 1804

Woods, John..............	Captain, 37th Regiment...........	December 7, 1799
Woodside, William........	Ensign, Light Infantry Company, 18th Regiment..................	February 20, 1802
Woodside, William........	Lieutenant, 18th Regiment.......	June 11, 1804
Young, James.............	Lieutenant, 18th Regiment.......	May 14, 1804

Warren County Regiments

[61st Regiment created December 10, 1804]

Abshaw, John.............	Lieutenant, 25th Regiment.......	July 4, 1803
Anderson, Andrew.........	Ensign, 25th Regiment...........	July 4, 1804
Anderson, William........	Captain, 25th Regiment..........	July 4, 1803
Anthony, Joseph..........	Lieutenant, 25th Regiment.......	November 1, 1801
Anthony, Joseph..........	Captain, 25th Regiment..........	July 4, 1803
Armstrong, Joshua........	Ensign, 25th Regiment...........	November 1, 1801
Berryman, William........	Lieutenant, 25th Regiment.......	July 4, 1804
Boteman, Simon...........	Captain, 25th Regiment..........	November 1, 1801
Briggs, Robert...........	Lieutenant, 25th Regiment.......	November 19, 1804
Caldwell, James..........	Ensign, 25th Regiment...........	July 4, 1803
Campbell, John...........	Lieutenant, 25th Regiment.......	November 1, 1801
Chapman, George..........	Captain, 25th Regiment..........	July 4, 1803
Clack, Sterling..........	Lieutenant, 25th Regiment.......	November 1, 1801
Coher, Samuel............	2nd Lieutenant, Light Horse Company, 25th Regiment........	May 14, 1798
	Recommissioned..............	February 15, 1799
Cole, Andrew.............	Ensign, 25th Regiment...........	July 4, 1804
Cole, James..............	Lieutenant, 25th Regiment.......	July 4, 1804
Covington, Elijah M. ...	Major, 1st Battalion, 25th Regiment......................	December 18, 1802
Covington, Elijah M. ...	Colonel, 25th Regiment..........	December 12, 1803
Covington, Thomas A. ...	1st Lieutenant, 25th Regiment....	June 1, 1803
Cox, Phenehas............	Lieutenant Colonel, Commandant 61st Regiment.................	December 13, 1804
Crawford, Anthony........	Lieutenant, 25th Regiment.......	July 4, 1804
Crouch, Daniel...........	Ensign, 25th Regiment...........	November 19, 1804
Douglas, John............	Lieutenant, 25th Regiment.......	November 1, 1801
Doyle, Gregory...........	Ensign, 25th Regiment...........	November 19, 1804
Elam, Andrew.............	Ensign, 25th Regiment...........	November 19, 1804
Furgerson, John..........	Lieutenant, 25th Regiment.......	November 1, 1801
Gatewood, William........	Ensign, 25th Regiment...........	July 4, 1803
Gorin, Henry.............	Captain, 25th Regiment..........	June 1, 1803
Goring, Glading..........	Major, 1st Battalion, 61st Regiment......................	December 13, 1804
Gorrin, Henry............	Cornet, Light Horse Company, 25th Regiment..................	May 14, 1798
	Recommissioned..............	February 15, 1799
Green, George............	Ensign, 25th Regiment...........	November 1, 1801
Grider, Martin...........	Captain, 25th Regiment..........	November 1, 1801
Hall, James..............	Captain, 25th Regiment..........	November 1, 1801

COMMISSIONED OFFICERS, 1799 - 1804

Hammett, Elijah	Lieutenant, 25th Regiment	November 1, 1801
Hampton, Benjamin	Captain, Light Horse Company, 25th Regiment	May 14, 1798
	Recommissioned	February 15, 1799
Harman, Lewis	Ensign, 25th Regiment	July 4, 1804
Harrington, Charles	Ensign, 25th Regiment	July 4, 1803 and July 4, 1804
Hatfield, Henry	Ensign, 25th Regiment	November 1, 1801
Henson, Jessey	Lieutenant, 25th Regiment	November 1, 1801
Henson, John	Ensign, 25th Regiment	November 1, 1801
Higgarson, George	Captain, 25th Regiment	November 1, 1801
Higginson, James, Jr.	Ensign, 25th Regiment	November 19, 1804
Hines, John	Lieutenant, 25th Regiment	November 19, 1804
Hopson, Zach.	Captain, 25th Regiment	November 1, 1801
Hubbard, Simon Miller	2nd Lieutenant, 25th Regiment	June 1, 1803
Hudspeth, David	Major, 2nd Battalion, 25th Regiment	December 19, 1799
Hudspeth, David	Colonel, 25th Regiment	December 18, 1802
Hudspeth, George	Captain, 25th Regiment	November 1, 1801
Hudspeth, George	Major, 2nd Battalion, 25th Regiment	December 13, 1804
Isbell, Jasen	Captain, 25th Regiment	November 1, 1801
Janos, William	Lieutenant, 25th Regiment	July 4, 1803
Jones, John	Ensign, 25th Regiment	November 1, 1801
Key, Elijah	Captain, 25th Regiment	July 4, 1804
Key, William	Lieutenant, 25th Regiment	July 4, 1804
Kirby, Samuel	Captain, 25th Regiment	July 4, 1804
Kirkum, Henry	Captain, 25th Regiment	July 4, 1804
Langston, John	Captain, 25th Regiment	November 1, 1801
Lenier, Collins	Ensign, 25th Regiment	November 1, 1801
Lewis, Josiah	Captain, 25th Regiment	July 4, 1804
Melton, John	Ensign, 25th Regiment	July 4, 1803
Mitchel, Samuel	Lieutenant, 25th Regiment	July 4, 1803
Moberly, John	Ensign, 25th Regiment	July 4, 1803
Mobley, Charles	Ensign, 25th Regiment	November 1, 1801
Moore, Robert	Paymaster, 25th Regiment	July 4, 1804
Oliver, William	Lieutenant, 25th Regiment	November 1, 1801
Payne, William R.	Cornet, 25th Regiment	June 1, 1803
Potter, Lewis	Captain, 25th Regiment	November 1, 1801
Potter, Lewis	Major, 2nd Battalion, 61st Regiment	December 13, 1804
Potter, Royal	Lieutenant, 25th Regiment	November 1, 1801
Potts, Jonathan	Ensign, 25th Regiment	July 4, 1803
Pullam, Benjamin	Lieutenant, 25th Regiment	November 1, 1801
Putman, Daniel	Captain, 25th Regiment	November 19, 1804
Richey, James	Ensign, 25th Regiment	November 1, 1801
Riley, Daniel	Lieutenant, 25th Regiment	November 1, 1801
Sayling, William	Lieutenant, 25th Regiment	November 1, 1801
Shipley, Robert	Lieutenant, 25th Regiment	July 4, 1803
Smith, Richard	Captain, 25th Regiment	November 1, 1801
Stagner, William	Lieutenant, 25th Regiment	November 19, 1804

COMMISSIONED OFFICERS, 1799 - 1804

Swearingen, William......	Captain, 25th Regiment...........	November 1, 1801
Swearingen, William D. ...	Major, 1st Battalion, 25th Regiment......................	December 12, 1803
Turnbel (Trimble), Moses.	Ensign, 25th Regiment...........	November 1, 1801
Tyler, James.............	Captain, 25th Regiment...........	November 19, 1804
Walker, James............	Ensign, 25th Regiment...........	November 1, 1801
Warren, James............	Ensign, 25th Regiment...........	November 1, 1801
Watson, Joab.............	Captain, 25th Regiment...........	November 1, 1801
Wren, James..............	Lieutenant, 25th Regiment........	July 4, 1803
Wright, Elijah...........	Ensign, 25th Regiment...........	November 1, 1801
Young, Glading...........	Major, 1st Battalion, 61st Regiment......................	December 11, 1804

Washington County Regiments

[50th Regiment laid off December 18, 1800]

Austin, (James?).........	Ensign, Light Infantry Company, 4th Regiment...................	December 8, 1801
Beauchamp, Jeroboam......	Captain, 4th Regiment............	December 3, 1803
Berry, Francis...........	Lieutenant, 50th Regiment........	June 24, 1801
Beswell, Jeremiah........	Captain, 50th Regiment...........	April 5 and June 12, 1804
Biswell, Jeremiah........	Lieutenant, 50th Regiment........	June 24, 1801
Brothers, Jeremiah.......	Captain, 4th Regiment............	December 3, 1802
Catlin, Seth.............	Captain, 50th Regiment...........	September 12, 1803
Cissel, William..........	Ensign, 4th Regiment.............	December 3, 1803
Cleaver, David...........	Major, 4th Regiment..............	December 9, 1803
Clever, David............	Captain, 4th Regiment............	February 10, 1801
Colter, John.............	Ensign, 4th Regiment.............	September 30, 1800
Davis, John..............	Captain, 50th Regiment...........	June 24, 1801
Dean, Thomas.............	Captain, 4th Regiment............	July 4, 1801
Edland, George...........	Captain, 4th Regiment............	May 12, 1800
Evans, James.............	Ensign, 4th Regiment.............	May 12, 1800
Ewing, George............	Major, 4th Regiment..............	April 15, 1799 and April 15, 1802
Ewing, George............	Colonel, 4th Regiment............	July 12, 1803
Graham, George...........	Ensign, 4th Regiment.............	July 4, 1801
Gray, Joseph.............	Captain, 4th Regiment............	April 1, 1800
Grey, John...............	Lieutenant, 50th Regiment........	June 24, 1801
Hagan, Ignatius..........	Captain, 50th Regiment...........	March 1, 1803
Hager, James.............	Captain, 4th Regiment............	December 20, 1800
Hamilton, Clement........	Lieutenant, 4th Regiment.........	December 20, 1800
Harbeson, John...........	Captain, 50th Regiment...........	August 11, 1802
Hardin, Harry............	Captain, 4th Regiment............	December 3, 1799
Hayden, George...........	Ensign, 4th Regiment.............	July 4, 1801
Hayden, George...........	Lieutenant, 4th Regiment.........	December 20, 1800
Hayden, George...........	Captain, 50th Regiment...........	June 24, 1801
Hayden, John.............	Ensign, 50th Regiment............	May 15, 1802
Herbert, Jeremiah........	Lieutenant, 4th Regiment.........	December 8, 1801

Hog, Milbourn	Ensign, 50th Regiment	March 1, 1803
Holly, Samuel	Ensign, 4th Regiment	February 10, 1801
Hoskins, David	Ensign, 4th Regiment	December 3, 1803
Hundley, Charles	Ensign, 50th Regiment	December 20, 1800
Hundley, Charles	Lieutenant, 50th Regiment	March 1, 1803
Hungate, John	Captain, 4th Regiment	September 30, 1800
Hungate, John	Major, 1st Battalion, 50th Regiment	June 1, 1804
Kellow, Daniel	Lieutenant, Infantry Company, 50th Regiment	April 5, 1804
Lancaster, John	Captain, 4th Regiment	July 4, 1801
Lincoln, Mordecai	Major, 2nd Battalion, 50th Regiment	December 22, 1800
McDonald, Richard	Major, 1st Battalion, 50th Regiment	December 20, 1800
McKittrick, John	Captain, 4th Regiment	December 20, 1800
McKneff, John	Adjutant, 50th Regiment	June 24, 1801
McLaughlin, John	Ensign, 50th Regiment	June 24, 1801
Miles, John	Ensign, 4th Regiment	December 3, 1802
Mock, Daniel	Colonel, 50th Regiment	December 20, 1800
Monroe, Charles	Lieutenant, 4th Regiment	September 30, 1800
Mudd, Richard	Captain, 4th Regiment	December 8, 1801
Myor, Daniel	Ensign, 50th Regiment	June 12, 1804
Nall, John	Ensign, 50th Regiment	April 5 and June 12, 1804
Neibors, Abraham	Lieutenant, 4th Regiment	December 3, 1803
Parrott, William	Ensign, 4th Regiment	May 28, 1803
Parsons, James	Captain, 4th Regiment	August 1, 1800
Peterson, Garret	Lieutenant, 4th Regiment	December 3, 1802
Pierce, Jacob	Ensign, 50th Regiment	March 1, 1803
Pierce, Jacob	Lieutenant, 50th Regiment	April 5 and June 12, 1804
Pyle, Benjamin	Captain, 50th Regiment	April 5 and June 12, 1804
Quigley, John	Lieutenant, 50th Regiment	August 11, 1802
Quigley, Lewis	Ensign, 50th Regiment	August 11, 1802
Ray, Absalom	Ensign, 4th Regiment	December 3, 1802
Ray, Joseph	Captain, 4th Regiment	December 8, 1801
Ray, Nicholas	Lieutenant, 4th Regiment	December 3, 1803
Rice, Jesse	Lieutenant, 4th Regiment	May 28, 1803
Rice, Larkin	Ensign, 4th Regiment	December 20, 1800
Right, John	Captain, 50th Regiment	May 15, 1802
Robertson, Fleming	Lieutenant, 4th Regiment	December 3, 1799
Robertson, James	Ensign, 50th Regiment	September 12, 1803
Rogers, William	Ensign, 50th Regiment	December 20, 1800
Rutter, Ed(mund?)	Ensign, 4th Regiment	December 20, 1800
Scott, Robert	Lieutenant, 4th Regiment	July 4, 1801
Seay, Jacob	Paymaster, 50th Regiment	March 17, 1804
Seay, Samuel	Ensign, 4th Regiment	December 20, 1800
Seay, Samuel	Captain, 4th Regiment	May 28, 1803
Sibert, Peter	Ensign, Infantry, 50th Regiment	April 5, 1804

COMMISSIONED OFFICERS, 1799 - 1804

Simpson, James............	Ensign, 50th Regiment............	March 1, 1803
Smith, Nicholas..........	Lieutenant, 4th Regiment.........	December 20, 1800
Smith, Thomas............	Ensign, 50th Regiment............	June 12, 1804
Smock, Henry.............	Major, 4th Regiment..............	December 22, 1800
Spalding, Thomas.........	Ensign, 4th Regiment.............	December 20, 1800
Spinks, Ignatius.........	Captain, Infantry Company, 50th Regiment.......................	April 5, 1804
Springer, Charles........	Ensign, 4th Regiment.............	May 15, 1800
Springer, Charles........	Lieutenant, 50th Regiment........	December 20, 1800
Springer, Charles........	Captain, 50th Regiment...........	March 1, 1803
Taylor, Zachariah........	Lieutenant, 50th Regiment........	June 12, 1804
Thompson, Austin.........	Lieutenant, 50th Regiment........	May 15, 1802
Thompson, Thomas.........	Lieutenant, 50th Regiment........	September 12, 1803
Turnham, John............	Captain, 50th Regiment...........	April 5 and June 12, 1804
Walker, John.............	Lieutenant, 50th Regiment........	April 5 and June 12, 1804
Wapshot, Graves..........	Colonel, 4th Regiment............	April 15, 1799 and April 15, 1802
Watkins, George..........	Lieutenant, 4th Regiment.........	December 20, 1800
Weaver, George...........	Captain, 4th Regiment............	May 15, 1800
Whitehead, Joseph........	Lieutenant, 4th Regiment.........	July 4, 1801
Wickliffe, Martin........	Captain, 4th Regiment............	December 20, 1800

Wayne County Regiment

[Laid off December 10, 1802]

Allcorn, John............	Lieutenant, 53rd Regiment........	April 9, 1803
Beason, Isaac............	Ensign, 53rd Regiment............	April 9, 1803
Blevens, Elisha..........	Ensign, 53rd Regiment............	No date. (1802?)
Christman, Isaac.........	Major, 1st Battalion, 53rd Regiment.......................	December 13, 1802
Coffee, John W.	Lieutenant, 53rd Regiment........	April 9, 1803
Davis, John..............	Captain, 53rd Regiment...........	April 9, 1803
Deane, Michael...........	Ensign, 53rd Regiment............	No date. (1802?)
Debrel, Charles..........	Colonel, 53rd Regiment...........	December 13, 1802
Edgeman, Thomas K.	Major, 2nd Battalion, 53rd Regiment.......................	December 14, 1802
Goading, James...........	2nd Lieutenant, 53rd Regiment....	April 9, 1803
Goodwin, Richard.........	Ensign, 53rd Regiment............	No date. (1802?)
Halfacre, Christopher....	Captain, 53rd Regiment...........	No date. (1802?)
Harbert, Matthew.........	Ensign, 53rd Regiment............	April 9, 1803
Huffaker, Jacob..........	Cornet, 53rd Regiment............	April 9, 1803
James, John..............	Lieutenant, 53rd Regiment........	April 9, 1803
Johnson, James...........	Ensign, 53rd Regiment............	No date. (1802?)
Johnson, Thomas..........	Captain, 53rd Regiment...........	No date. (1802?)
Jones, William...........	Lieutenant, 53rd Regiment........	No date. (1802?)
Long, John...............	Captain of Cavalry, 53rd Regiment.......................	April 9, 1803

COMMISSIONED OFFICERS, 1799 - 1804   153

Martin, John.............	1st Lieutenant of Cavalry, 53rd Regiment..................	April 9, 1803
Meadows, Isaac...........	Captain, 53rd Regiment...........	No date. (1802?)
Mercer, James............	Lieutenant, 53rd Regiment........	April 9, 1803
Mullins, William.........	Captain, 53rd Regiment...........	April 9, 1803
Owens, Reuben............	Ensign, 53rd Regiment............	April 9, 1803
Payne, Philemon..........	Captain, 53rd Regiment...........	April 9, 1803
Sanders, Zachariah.......	Adjutant, 53rd Regiment..........	August 5, 1803
Simpson, Moses...........	Ensign, 53rd Regiment............	April 9, 1803
Smilie, Thomas...........	Captain, 53rd Regiment...........	April 9, 1803
Sutton, William..........	Ensign, 53rd Regiment............	April 9, 1803
Taul, Micajah............	Adjutant, 53rd Regiment..........	June 20, 1803
Trixall, Jacob...........	Lieutenant, 53rd Regiment........	April 9, 1803
Vandiver, Thomas.........	Ensign, 53rd Regiment............	April 9, 1803
Vanwinkle, Abraham.......	Ensign, 53rd Regiment............	No date. (1802?)
Wade, Joseph.............	Lieutenant, Captain Halfacre's Company, 53rd Regiment.........	April 9, 1803
West, Alexander..........	Captain, 53rd Regiment...........	April 9, 1803

Woodford County Regiment

Allen, John..............	Lieutenant, 11th Regiment........	March 21, 1802
Ashford, Thomas..........	Ensign, 11th Regiment............	May 4, 1804
Bain, George.............	Ensign, 11th Regiment............	May 11, 1801
Bain, George.............	Lieutenant, 11th Regiment........	May 15, 1800
Berry, Allen.............	Ensign, 11th Regiment............	May 11, 1801
Berry, Samuel............	Ensign, 11th Regiment............	May 4, 1804
Blackmore, John..........	Adjutant, 11th Regiment..........	August 7, 1799
Brown, Benjamin..........	Ensign, 11th Regiment............	February 25, 1800
Brown, Preston...........	Adjutant, 11th Regiment..........	September 1, 1800
Burbridge, Benjamin......	Captain, 11th Regiment...........	May 20, 1803
Cellars, Joseph..........	Ensign, 11th Regiment............	May 20, 1803
Christopher, William, Jr.	Lieutenant, 11th Regiment........	May 4, 1804
Claggett, Thomas.........	Lieutenant, 11th Regiment........	July 27, 1799
Delano, A(masa?).........	Surgeon's Mate, 11th Regiment....	April 11, 1804
Dictum, Richard..........	Lieutenant, Rifle Company, 11th Regiment..................	May 15, 1800
Eastland, Thomas.........	Captain of Cavalry, 11th Regiment.......................	May 4, 1804
Francisco, George........	1st Lieutenant of Cavalry, 11th Regiment.................	May 4, 1804
Francisco, John..........	Major, 1st Battalion, 11th Regiment.......................	October 22, 1799
Gay, James...............	Ensign, 11th Regiment............	May 4, 1804
Gay, Robert..............	Ensign, 11th Regiment............	May 15, 1800
Gay, Robert..............	Lieutenant, 11th Regiment........	May 4, 1804
Guthrie, James...........	Ensign, 11th Regiment............	April 27, 1800
Hiter, Charles...........	Ensign, 11th Regiment............	May 11, 1801
Hiter, Charles...........	Captain, 11th Regiment...........	May 20, 1803
Holman, James............	Lieutenant, 11th Regiment........	April 8, 1800

COMMISSIONED OFFICERS, 1799 - 1804

Holmes, Hugh.............	Lieutenant, 11th Regiment........	November 22, 1799
Houghland, Cornelius.....	Major, 1st Battalion, 11th Regiment......................	December 13, 1802
Howard, Isaac............	Lieutenant, 11th Regiment........	May 11, 1801
Hunter, William..........	2nd Lieutenant of Artillery, 11th Regiment.................	May 4, 1804
Kincaid, Archibald.......	Captain, 11th Regiment...........	December 16, 1799
Kinkead, James...........	Cornet of Cavalry, 11th Regiment.	May 4, 1804
Kyle, Thomas.............	Ensign, 11th Regiment............	December 2, 1803
Martin, Hudson...........	Ensign, 11th Regiment............	May 20, 1803
Mileham (Milam), Archibald...	Ensign, 11th Regiment........	March 21, 1802
Morton, Jonathan.........	Ensign, 11th Regiment............	March 21, 1802
Peters, James............	Ensign, 11th Regiment............	May 11, 1801
Quarles, Tunstal.........	Lieutenant, 11th Regiment........	May 15, 1800
Rearden, Henry...........	Lieutenant, 11th Regiment........	July 1, 1799
Reed, William............	Ensign, 11th Regiment............	December 31, 1800
Smith, Humphrey..........	Lieutenant, 11th Regiment........	May 20, 1803
Sullinger, Thomas........	Ensign, 11th Regiment............	May 20, 1803
Sullinger, Thomas........	Lieutenant, 11th Regiment........	December 2, 1803
Taylor, Joseph...........	Captain, 11th Regiment...........	September 17, 1799
Trabue, Edward...........	Lieutenant, 11th Regiment........	March 21, 1802
Wallace, Samuel..........	Captain, 11th Regiment...........	September 27, 1799
Watkins, Benjamin........	Ensign, 11th Regiment............	March 21, 1802
Weisager, John K.	Ensign, Rifle Company, 11th Regiment......................	May 15, 1800
Williams, John...........	Ensign, 11th Regiment............	May 30, 1800
Williams, John...........	Lieutenant, 11th Regiment........	March 21, 1802
Wilson, John.............	Ensign, 11th Regiment............	July 27, 1799
Young, Lewis.............	Paymaster, 11th Regiment.........	April 11, 1804
Young, William...........	Ensign, 11th Regiment............	March 21, 1802

COMMISSIONED OFFICERS, 1805 - 1811   155

General Officers

Allen, James............	Brigadier General, 10th Brigade..	January 17, 1811
Barry, William T.	Aide-de-Camp to Major General Marquis Calmes, 5th Division...	February 1, 1809
Boswell, William E.	Brigadier General, 4th Brigade...	January 27, 1809
Caldwell, Samuel........	Brigadier General, 11th Brigade..	January 31, 1811
Calmes, Marquis.........	Brigadier General, 3rd Brigade...	December 18, 1806
Calmes, Marquis.........	Major General, 5th Division......	February 3, 1809
Campbell, John..........	Aide-de-Camp to Major General Samuel Hopkins.................	December 5, 1805
Campbell, John B.	Brigadier General, 11th Brigade..	December 7, 1810
Campbell, John B.	Quartermaster General............	January 25, 1811
Chiles, David...........	Brigadier General, 7th Brigade...	December 29, 1806
Clay, Green.............	Major General, 2nd Division......	December 16, 1805
Cleaver, Stephen........	Brigadier General, 12th Brigade..	February 20, 1808
Covington, Elijah M. ...	Brigadier General, 20th Brigade..	January 17, 1811
Crist, Henry...........	Brigadier General, 1st Brigade...	January 17, 1811
Crittenden, John J.	Aide-de-Camp, 1st Division.......	January 9, 1811
Davis, Amos.............	Brigade Inspector, 1st Brigade...	February 12, 1808
Desha, Joseph...........	Brigadier General, 7th Brigade...	September 5, 1805
Desha, Joseph...........	Major General, 7th Division......	December 29, 1806
Dunlap, John, Jr.	Aide-de-Camp to General Charles Scott, Governor and Commander in Chief of the Militia of Kentucky. (The First Kentucky Colonel?)....................	October 20, 1809
Edwards, Amos...........	Quartermaster, 11th Brigade......	January 26, 1811
Evans, Gabriel..........	Brigadier General, 14th Brigade..	December 29, 1806
Fleming, William P.	1st Aide-de-Camp, 7th Division...	May 23, 1807
Flournoy, Matthews......	2nd Aide-de-Camp, 5th Division...	March 6, 1807
Floyd, George R. C.	2nd Aide-de-Camp to Major General (Samuel) Wells.................	May 12, 1805
Garrard, James..........	Brigade Major, 6th Brigade.......	February 10, 1809
Gist, Henry C.	Aide-de-Camp to Major General Thomas Posey, 1st Division.....	December 22, 1808
Grayson, Alfred W.	1st Aide-de-Camp, 5th Division...	March 6, 1807
Guthrie, Adam...........	Brigadier General, 1st Brigade...	July 11, 1805
Hawkins, Jamison........	Brigade Inspector, 4th Brigade...	February 23, 1808
Helm, Benjamin..........	Brigade Inspector, 12th Brigade..	February 11, 1805
Helm, George............	Aide-de-Camp to Major General John Thomas...................	September 22, 1810
Henry, Robert P.	Aide-de-Camp, 3rd Brigade........	January 31, 1810
Henry, William..........	Major General, 3rd Division......	July 16, 1806
Hickman, Richard........	Brigadier General, 5th Brigade...	December 10, 1810
Hopkins, Samuel G.	Aide-de-Camp to Major General Thomas Posey, 1st Division.....	December 22, 1808
Hord, Edward............	2nd Aide-de-Camp, 7th Division...	May 23, 1807
Jones, Moses............	Brigade Inspector, 15th Brigade..	September 15, 1807
Kennedy, Andrew.........	Brigadier General, 9th Brigade...	December 16, 1805
Kerley, William.........	Brigade Inspector, 13th Brigade..	March 10, 1807

COMMISSIONED OFFICERS, 1805 - 1811

Kincheloe, Lewis	Brigadier General, 17th Brigade	February 19, 1808
King, John E.	Brigadier General, 10th Brigade	January 26, 1809
King, John E.	Major General, 9th Division	January 17, 1811
Letcher, Benjamin	Brigadier General, 9th Brigade	December 13, 1809
Lewis, Joseph	Major General, 4th Division	July 11, 1805
Logan, David	1st Aide-de-Camp to Major General (Nathan) Huston	July 3, 1805
Logan, William	1st Aide-de-Camp, 2nd Division	August 27, 1807
McCormick, James	Brigade Inspector, 9th Brigade	November 5, 1807
McDowell, Joseph	Brigade Inspector, 8th Brigade	March 4, 1805
McDowell, Joseph	Aide-de-Camp to Major General (James) Ray, 8th Division	February 3, 1809
McDowell, Samuel	2nd Aide-de-Camp to Major General (Nathan) Huston	July 3, 1805
McDowell, Samuel	2nd Aide-de-Camp, 2nd Division	September 15, 1807
McDowell, William	Brigadier General, 8th Brigade	February 17, 1808
McIntire, Daniel	Brigade Inspector, 14th Brigade	April 18, 1807
McIntire, Robert	Brigadier General, 15th Brigade	December 29, 1806
McKinney, John	Aide-de-Camp to Major General Marquis Calmes	December 15, 1810
Marshall, Lewis	Aide-de-Camp to Major General (Marquis) Calmes, 5th Division	February 1, 1809
Miller, David	1st Aide-de-Camp, 2nd Division	February 23, 1808
Mock, Daniel	Brigadier General, 8th Brigade	December 10, 1810
Morton, John H.	Quartermaster, 5th Brigade	January 25, 1811
Payne, John	Brigadier General, 6th Brigade	July 16, 1806
Posey, Fayette	Aide-de-Camp, 1st Division	March 15, 1811
Posey, John	Quartermaster, 17th Brigade	January 26, 1811
Posey, Thomas	Major General, 1st Division	February 3, 1809
Preston, Walter	Brigade Inspector, 5th Brigade	July 16, 1810
Ramsey, Jonathan	Brigadier General, 19th Brigade	January 17, 1811
Ray, James	Major General, 8th Division	February 17, 1808
Richardson, Jesse	Brigadier General, 16th Brigade	February 18, 1808
Robinson, Isaac	1st Aide-de-Camp, 6th Division	December 4, 1811
Rogers, Coleman	Aide-de-Camp to Major General (James) Ray, 8th Division	February 3, 1809
Russell, Robert	Brigadier General, 3rd Brigade	February 3, 1809
Russell, William	Major General, 5th Division	December 18, 1806
Sandford, Thomas	Brigadier General, 4th Brigade	July 17, 1806
Sharp, Phidelio C.	Brigade Quartermaster, 19th Brigade	January 25, 1811
South, Samuel	Brigadier General, 13th Brigade	December 24, 1806
Taylor, Edmund	1st Aide to Major General (Samuel) Wells	May 12, 1805
Thomas, John	Major General, 4th Division	August 8, 1807
Warren, William	2nd Aide-de-Camp, 3rd Division	July 30, 1806
Wells, Levi	2nd Aide-de-Camp, 6th Division	December 4, 1811
White, Hugh	Brigadier General, 18th Brigade	January 17, 1811
Wilcox, George	Brigade Inspector, 2nd Brigade	February 5, 1805
Williams, Roger	1st Aide-de-Camp, 3rd Division	July 30, 1806

COMMISSIONED OFFICERS, 1805 - 1811

Company Officers*

Abell, Jesse.............	Ensign, 4th Regiment.............	June 23, 1806
Adair, William J.........	Captain, Cavalry Company, 16th Regiment.......................	November 5, 1807
Adair, William J.........	Major, 1st Battalion, 16th Regiment......................	January 17, 1811
Adair, William J.........	Major, 2nd Battalion, 16th Regiment.......................	December 10, 1811
Adam, Nathan.............	Captain, 12th Regiment..........	October 2, 1806
Adams, Elijah............	Captain, 16th Regiment..........	August 20, 1808
Adams, W.	Lieutenant, 22nd Regiment.......	March 24, 1806
Adams, William..........	2nd Lieutenant, Light Horse Company, 18th Regiment........	July 11, 1806
Adamson, Henry...........	Ensign, 28th Regiment............	November 19, 1805
Agan, Michael............	Ensign, 4th Regiment............	June 23, 1806
Akin, John...............	Lieutenant, 18th Regiment.......	February 4, 1805
Akin, John...............	Captain, 18th Regiment..........	October 6, 1807
Allcorn, James...........	Lieutenant, 6th Regiment........	December 8, 1806
Allen, David.............	Major, 16th Regiment............	February 23, 1808
Allen, David.............	Lieutenant Colonel, Commandant 16th Regiment.................	January 17, 1811
Allen, Granvil...........	Ensign, 14th Regiment...........	June 11, 1806
Allen, John..............	Captain, 13th Regiment..........	July 8, 1805
Allen, Joseph............	Major, 1st Battalion, 31st Regiment......................	February 19, 1808
Allentharp, Benjamin.....	Ensign, Rifle Company, 12th Regiment......................	September 17, 1805
Allison, James...........	Lieutenant, 23rd Regiment.......	November 4, 1806
Allison, James...........	Captain, Rifle Company, 23rd Regiment......................	December 22, 1807
Allison, John............	Major, 2nd Battalion, 13th Regiment......................	December 29, 1806
Ambrose, William.........	Lieutenant, Rifle Company, 28th Regiment......................	November 19, 1805
Amment, John.............	Ensign, 3rd Regiment............	February 3, 1807
Anderson, Hugh...........	Ensign, 9th Regiment............	November 7, 1807
Anderson, John...........	Captain, 19th Regiment..........	November 19, 1805
Anderson, Nicholas M. ..	Lieutenant, 16th Regiment.......	November 5, 1807
Anderson, Reuben.........	Lieutenant, 16th Regiment.......	November 25, 1805

---

* Records for this period of company officers in all grades exist only for the years 1805 - 1808, and for the first - thirtieth regiments only. Only records of commissions for Lieutenant Colonels and Majors exist for the remaining years of the period, 1809 - 1811. It was thought best, therefore, to group these incomplete records in one alphabetical sequence rather than to separate them sparsely by county, as in preceding sections. For county designations of the various regiments see Preface.

COMMISSIONED OFFICERS, 1805 - 1811

Anderson, Vincent.........	Major, 2nd Battalion, 84th Regiment.........................	January 15, 1811
Anderson, Walter..........	Ensign, 6th Regiment..............	August 20, 1808
Anderson, William.........	Major, 1st Battalion, 25th Regiment.........................	December 13, 1810
Andrews, George...........	Captain, 8th Regiment.............	August 14, 1806
Angel, John...............	Lieutenant, 21st Regiment.........	April 18, 1807
Ansley, William...........	Ensign, 30th Regiment.............	January 30, 1808
Applegate, Richard........	Ensign, 28th Regiment.............	June 17, 1805
Applegate, Richard........	Ensign, 15th Regiment............. (Formerly of 28th Regiment)	September 12, 1807
Archer, James.............	Lieutenant, 13th Regiment.........	May 23, 1807 and March 27, 1808
Archer, John..............	Quartermaster, 13th Regiment......	July 2, 1808
Ardery, Robert............	Lieutenant, 13th Regiment.........	May 23, 1807
Arnold, David.............	Ensign, 9th Regiment..............	May 26, 1807
Arthur, Thomas............	Lieutenant Colonel, Commandant 39th Regiment...................	December 16, 1805
Ashby, Silas..............	Major, 2nd Battalion, 18th Regiment.........................	May 6, 1806
Ashby, Stephen............	Colonel, Commandant, 76th Regiment.........................	February 2, 1809
Ashert, Josiah............	Captain, 14th Regiment............	January 29, 1805
Ashert, Josiah............	Major, 2nd Battalion, 14th Regiment.........................	September 15, 1807
Ashford, Thomas...........	Lieutenant, 11th Regiment.........	July 10, 1806
Ashford, William..........	Ensign, 11th Regiment.............	July 10, 1806
Atwood, William...........	Quartermaster, 11th Regiment......	March 17, 1807
Augustus, John............	Ensign, Rifle Company, 1st Regiment.........................	June 18, 1807
Baber, Isham..............	Lieutenant, 17th Regiment.........	January 30, 1808
Bacon, Edmund.............	Ensign, Light Infantry Company, 22nd Regiment...................	April 25, 1806
Bacon, Edmund.............	Lieutenant, 22nd Regiment.........	July 14, 1807
Bacon, Edmund.............	Captain, Light Infantry Company, 22nd Regiment...................	December 1, 1807
Bacon, Liddale............	Ensign, 22nd Regiment.............	June 1, 1808
Bailey, James.............	Ensign, 18th Regiment.............	October 6, 1807
Bailey, John..............	Captain, 23rd Regiment............	August 11, 1806
Bailey, Joseph............	Lieutenant, 18th Regiment.........	May 26, 1808
Bailey, Reubin............	Lieutenant, 6th Regiment..........	December 8, 1806
Bailey, Thomas............	Captain, 12th Regiment............	December 5, 1807
Baird, James..............	Major, 1st Battalion, 49th Regiment.........................	January 18, 1809
Baird, Thomas.............	Major, 2nd Battalion, 85th Regiment.........................	January 26, 1811
Baker, Amos...............	Lieutenant, 8th Regiment..........	May 16, 1808
Baker, George.............	2nd Lieutenant, 17th Regiment.... Approved......................	January 30, 1808 June 25, 1807
Baker, James..............	Lieutenant, 21st Regiment.........	April 20, 1805
Baker, James..............	Captain, 13th Regiment............	July 8, 1805

COMMISSIONED OFFICERS, 1805 - 1811 159

Baker (John?)............	Cornet, Troop of Horse, 17th Regiment.......................	November 4, 1806
Baker, John..............	Ensign, 29th Regiment............	May 6, 1806
Baker, John..............	Captain, 29th Regiment...........	May 26, 1808
Baker, Robert............	Major, 2nd Battalion, 68th Regiment.......................	January 17, 1811
Baldock, James...........	Lieutenant, 12th Regiment........	October 2, 1806
Baldwin, Samuel..........	Captain, 15th Regiment...........	June 17, 1805
Ballad, George...........	Captain, 12th Regiment...........	April 9, 1805
Ballenger, Richard.......	Major, 1st Battalion, 54th Regiment......................,.	January 26, 1809
Ballenger, Richard.......	Major, 1st Battalion, 75th Regiment.......................	February 1, 1809
Ballenger, Richard.......	Lieutenant Colonel, Commandant 75th Regiment..................	January 23, 1810
Ballew, Fleming..........	Ensign, 19th Regiment............	September 12, 1807
Baltzell, George.........	Ensign, 22nd Regiment............	March 24, 1806
Baltzell, George.........	Lieutenant, 22nd Regiment........	May 3, 1806
Banks, James.............	Ensign, 26th Regiment............	July 1, 1808
Barbour, Philip..........	Major, 2nd Battalion, 41st Regiment.......................	February 2, 1809
Barbour, Philip..........	Lieutenant Colonel, Commandant 41st Regiment..................	January 17, 1811
Barclay, John............	Captain, 9th Regiment............	August 28, 1805
Barker, John H.	Ensign, 21st Regiment............	April 18, 1807
Barker, Neely............	Ensign, 23rd Regiment............	December 22, 1807
Barker, Thomas...........	Ensign, 27th Regiment............	October 14, 1805
Barkley, James...........	Lieutenant, 12th Regiment........	September 17, 1805
Barnard, Valentine.......	Captain, 16th Regiment...........	November 5, 1807
Barnet, John.............	Lieutenant, 13th Regiment........	July 2, 1808
Barnett, John............	Captain, 23rd Regiment...........	November 4, 1806
Barnett, John............	Major, 2nd Battalion, 23rd Regiment.......................	January 18, 1809
Barnett, Schyler.........	Lieutenant, 19th Regiment........	September 12, 1807
Barnhill, Samuel.........	Lieutenant, Infantry Company, 12th Regiment..................	September 17, 1805
Barns, Philip............	Ensign, 7th Regiment.............	July 2, 1807
Barr, John...............	Lieutenant, 9th Regiment.........	November 7, 1807
Barret, Robert...........	Lieutenant, 16th Regiment........	December 8, 1806 and November 5, 1807
Barret, Robert...........	Captain, 16th Regiment...........	August 20, 1808
Barrett, Robert..........	Ensign, 16th Regiment............	March 14, 1806
Bartlett, Frederick......	Lieutenant Colonel, Commandant 1st Regiment...................	August 31, 1805
Bartley, James...........	Captain, Rifle Company, 12th Regiment.......................	September 12, 1807
Baxter, Edward...........	Lieutenant Colonel, Commandant 35th Regiment..................	December 24, 1806 and January 8, 1810
Baxter, James............	Lieutenant, 8th Regiment.........	June 11, 1805 and September 11, 1806

COMMISSIONED OFFICERS, 1805 - 1811

Bayles, Stephen	Lieutenant, 15th Regiment	December 24, 1806
Bayles, Stephen	Captain, 15th Regiment	September 12, 1807
Baylis, Stephen	Major, 1st Battalion, 15th Regiment	December 10, 1811
Baylor, George W.	Captain, Paris Company, 14th Regiment	July 20, 1808
Beachem, William	Lieutenant, 20th Regiment	June 22, 1805
Bealer, John	Lieutenant, 2nd Regiment	May 26, 1805
Beall (also Bell), Paterson	Ensign, 1st Regiment	April 21, 1808
Beardin, John	Major, 1st Battalion, 55th Regiment	January 17, 1811
Beauchamp, Jeroboam	Major, 1st Battalion, 4th Regiment	December 10, 1811
Beauchamp, Samuel	Ensign, 10th Regiment	December 6, 1805
Beaufort, William	Lieutenant, 11th Regiment	July 10, 1806
Beck, Jeremiah	Ensign, 30th Regiment	March 25, 1806
Beck, William	Major, 2nd Battalion, 7th Regiment	March 9, 1807
Beckerly, Henry	Captain, 18th Regiment	June 12, 1807
Beckerly, Levy	Ensign, 18th Regiment	October 6, 1807
Beckett, Anthony	Ensign, 4th Regiment	January 9, 1808
Beckett, Joseph	Ensign, 20th Regiment	August 28, 1806
Beckett, Joseph	Lieutenant, 20th Regiment	July 29, 1807
Been (Bean), Benjamin	Ensign, 15th Regiment	October 2, 1806
Been (Bean), John	Major, 2nd Battalion, 36th Regiment	June 12, 1806
Bell, Henry	Ensign, 2nd Regiment	December 16, 1807
Bell, Joseph	Major, 2nd Battalion, 38th Regiment	January 10, 1811
Bell, Robert	Captain, 16th Regiment	November 25, 1805
Bell, Thomas	Ensign, 2nd Regiment	May 15, 1806
Bell, Thomas	Major, 2nd Battalion, 41st Regiment	January 17, 1811
Bell, Thomas	Major, 1st Battalion, 82nd Regiment	January 17, 1811
Belt, Joseph	Adjutant, 30th Regiment	March 7, 1806
Belt, Marsham	Lieutenant, 30th Regiment	March 25, 1806
Belt, William	Lieutenant, 9th Regiment	February 5, 1805
Bennett, John	Major, 2nd Battalion, 23rd Regiment	January 31, 1809
Bennett, John	Major, 1st Battalion, 49th Regiment	August 31, 1805
Bennett, John	Lieutenant Colonel, Commandant 49th Regiment	January 31, 1809
Benton, Erasmus	Ensign, 12th Regiment	June 12, 1805
Benton, Erasmus	Lieutenant, 12th Regiment	December 13, 1805
Berry, Benjamin	Lieutenant, 3rd Regiment	September 17, 1805 and March 14, 1806
Berry, Benjamin	Major, 2nd Battalion, 41st Regiment	July 29, 1807
Berry, Benjamin	Major, 76th Regiment	February 2, 1809

COMMISSIONED OFFICERS, 1805 - 1811

Berry, Henry.............	Major, 1st Battalion, 29th Regiment......................	December 16, 1805
Berry, Reubin............	Captain, 29th Regiment...........	May 6, 1806
Berry, Robert............	Major, 1st Battalion, 13th Regiment......................	December 29, 1806
Berry, Robert............	Lieutenant Colonel, Commandant 13th Regiment.................	January 26, 1810
Berry, Samuel, Jr.	Lieutenant, 11th Regiment........	August 5, 1808
Berryman, William........	Captain, 25th Regiment...........	March 2, 1808
Best, James..............	Lieutenant, 20th Regiment........	April 14, 1805
Best, James..............	Captain, 20th Regiment...........	February 22, 1806
Biers, Jacob.............	Lieutenant, 20th Regiment........	June 22, 1805
Biggerstaff, Hiram.......	Captain, 7th Regiment............	June 18, 1807
Biram, Joseph............	Lieutenant, 19th Regiment........	July 19, 1805
Bird, Abraham............	Ensign, 10th Regiment............	July 8, 1805
Birdsong, William........	Lieutenant Colonel, Commandant 84th Regiment.................	January 15, 1811
Bishop, George...........	Lieutenant, 30th Regiment........	March 27, 1805
Bishop, George...........	Captain, 30th Regiment...........	April 18, 1807
Biswell, Jeremiah........	Major, 1st Battalion, 50th Regiment......................	December 7, 1810
Black, George............	Major, 2nd Battalion, 31st Regiment......................	January 28, 1811
Black, John..............	Captain, Rifle Company, 28th Regiment......................	November 19, 1805
Blackburn, George........	Ensign, 11th Regiment............	June 17, 1805
Blackburn, Robert........	Lieutenant, 20th Regiment........	February 22, 1806
Blackwood, Joseph........	Adjutant, 5th Regiment...........	April 25, 1808
Blair, Alexander.........	Captain, 13th Regiment...........	March 27, 1808
Blake, James.............	Ensign, 18th Regiment............	June 12, 1807
Blanton, James...........	Ensign, 11th Regiment............	June 17, 1805
Bledsoe, Richard.........	Lieutenant, 8th Regiment.........	June 2, 1806
Bledsoe, Richard.........	Captain, 8th Regiment............	May 11, 1807
Bodley, Thomas...........	Major, 2nd Battalion, 42nd Regiment......................	January 7, 1811
Boggess, Vincent.........	Lieutenant, 14th Regiment........	January 29, 1805
Bohannon, Abraham........	Lieutenant, 18th Regiment........	February 4, 1805 and February 9, 1807
Bohannon, German.........	Cornet, Troop of Horse, 11th Regiment.................	August 8, 1807
Bohon, John..............	Lieutenant, 5th Regiment.........	April 14, 1805
Bolin, Daniel............	Ensign, 7th Regiment.............	June 28, 1808
Bonwell, John............	Ensign, 28th Regiment............	November 19, 1805
Booker, Richard..........	Major, 1st Battalion, 85th Regiment......................	January 26, 1811
Boon, Ratliff............	Ensign, 25th Regiment............	March 2, 1808
Boone, George............	Ensign, 18th Regiment............	February 4, 1805
Boone, George............	Lieutenant, 18th Regiment........	July 11, 1806
Boone, George............	Captain, 18th Regiment...........	May 20, 1807
Boss, John...............	Lieutenant, 23rd Regiment........	December 22, 1807
Bostwick, Truman.........	Captain, 1st Regiment............	May 31, 1806

Bows, Jacob...............	Ensign, 12th Regiment............	December 5, 1807
Boyd, Joseph..............	Paymaster, 20th Regiment.........	April 16, 1807
Boyd, William.............	Major, 2nd Battalion, 37th Regiment......................	December 13, 1810 and January 5, 1811
Brackenridge, John.......	Lieutenant, 14th Regiment........	January 30, 1808
Braconriedg, John........	Ensign, 14th Regiment............	June 11, 1806
Bradford, Henry..........	Lieutenant, Rifle Company, 12th Regiment.................	July 13, 1807
Bradford, James..........	Major, 1st Battalion, 49th Regiment.....................	January 31, 1809
Bradford, William........	Lieutenant Colonel, Commandant 40th Regiment..................	February 19, 1808
Bradley, Sion............	Lieutenant Colonel, Commandant 52nd Regiment..................	February 23, 1808
Bradley, Terry...........	Ensign, 8th Regiment.............	June 2, 1806
Bradshaw, John...........	1st Lieutenant, Light Horse Company, 18th Regiment.........	July 11, 1806
Bradshaw, Robert.........	Ensign, 13th Regiment............	May 23, 1807
Brandenburgh, Solomon....	Captain, 3rd Regiment............	March 10, 1805
Branham, Benjamin........	Captain, Rifle Company, 12th Regiment......................	July 13, 1807
Branham, Harbin..........	Ensign, 14th Regiment............	January 24, 1807
Brashear, Walter.........	Lieutenant Colonel, Commandant 2nd Regiment...................	December 13, 1809
Bray, John...............	Ensign, 19th Regiment............	February 3, 1807
Brenham, Robert..........	Ensign, 22nd Regiment............	July 14, 1807
Brenham, Robert..........	Lieutenant, 22nd Regiment........	December 1, 1807
Briggs, George...........	Ensign, Infantry Company, 23rd Regiment..................	August 11, 1806
Briscoe, Philip..........	Ensign, Rifle Company, 7th Regiment......................	September 23, 1805
Bristoe, James...........	Major, 1st Battalion, 37th Regiment......................	December 10, 1811
Brite, Henry.............	Ensign, 10th Regiment............	September 30, 1807
Britton, George..........	Lieutenant Colonel, Commandant 54th Regiment..................	December 22, 1808
Brookhart, Jacob.........	Lieutenant, 1st Regiment.........	June 18, 1807
Brookhart, Jacob.........	Captain, 1st Regiment............	December 16, 1807
Brooking, John...........	Ensign, 11th Regiment............	August 8, 1807
Brooking, John...........	Lieutenant, 11th Regiment........	September 15, 1807
Brown, Elisha............	Lieutenant, 18th Regiment........	June 12, 1807
Brown, George, Jr........	Lieutenant, 22nd Regiment........	May 3, 1806
Brown, Henry.............	Lieutenant, 24th Regiment........	March 25, 1807
Brown, Hugh..............	Lieutenant Colonel, Commandant 64th Regiment..................	May 9, 1806
Brown, James.............	Ensign, 10th Regiment............	March 2, 1807
Brown, James.............	Lieutenant, 10th Regiment........	October 4, 1808
Brown, James, Jr.	Lieutenant, 3rd Regiment.........	September 17, 1805
Brown, John..............	Captain, 14th Regiment...........	June 11, 1806
Brown, John P.	Lieutenant, 4th Regiment.........	January 24, 1807

COMMISSIONED OFFICERS, 1805 - 1811   163

Brown, William	Lieutenant, Rifle Company, 12th Regiment	September 12, 1807
Brown, William	Ensign, 17th Regiment	August 20, 1808
Browning, James	Major, 2nd Battalion, 17th Regiment	February 23, 1808
Browning, James	Lieutenant Colonel, Commandant 17th Regiment	March 14 and December 10, 1811
Browning, Thomas	Ensign, 15th Regiment	November 4, 1805
Brownlee, Charles	Lieutenant, 16th Regiment	November 25, 1805
Bruce, John	Lieutenant, 28th Regiment	June 18, 1807
Bruice, John	Lieutenant, 28th Regiment	January 9, 1808
Bryan, George	2nd Lieutenant, Troop of Horse, 8th Regiment	June 11, 1805
Bryan, George	1st Lieutenant, Troop of Horse, 8th Regiment	June 2, 1806
Bryant, Enoch	Lieutenant, 8th Regiment	February 3, 1806
Buchanan, Thomas	Ensign, 23rd Regiment	February 5, 1805
Buckner, Nicholas	Major, 1st Battalion, 33rd Regiment	January 30, 1809
Buckner, William	Lieutenant, 28th Regiment	November 4, 1806
Buford, Abram	Ensign, 14th Regiment	January 24, 1807
Buford, Thomas	Lieutenant Colonel, Commandant 57th Regiment	December 13, 1809
Bullock, Edward	Captain, Infantry Company, 16th Regiment	December 8, 1806
Bullock, John	Lieutenant Colonel, Commandant 62nd Regiment	December 22, 1805
Bullock, Thomas	Ensign, 4th Regiment	January 9, 1808
Burbridge, Benjamin	Captain, Rifle Company, 11th Regiment	September 15, 1807
Burbridge, Thomas	Ensign, 12th Regiment	February 3, 1807
Burbridge, Thomas	Lieutenant, 12th Regiment	July 13, 1807
Burcham, Samuel	Lieutenant Colonel, Commandant 65th Regiment	December 18, 1806
Burgan, Thomas	Major, 1st Battalion, 71st Regiment	December 13, 1809
Burkhart, Joshua H.	Ensign, 1st Regiment	April 21, 1808
Burks, Roland	Captain, 6th Regiment	December 8, 1806
Burks, Rowland	Major, 2nd Battalion, 74th Regiment	January 29, 1811
Burnett, James C.	Lieutenant, 5th Regiment	November 4, 1806
Burnett, James C.	Captain, 5th Regiment	October 15, 1807
Burnsides, Robert	Major, 1st Battalion, 57th Regiment	December 13, 1809
Burris, Zadock	Lieutenant, 30th Regiment	August 28, 1806
Burton, Archibald	Captain, 6th Regiment	August 20, 1808
Burton (?), Samuel	Captain, 24th Regiment	August 28, 1805
Busey, Jacob	Ensign, 18th Regiment	May 26, 1808
Busey, Jacob	Lieutenant, 18th Regiment	July 20, 1808
Bush, Isaac	Lieutenant, 3rd Regiment	September 17, 1805

COMMISSIONED OFFICERS, 1805 - 1811

Bush, J. Gholston........	Lieutenant, 17th Regiment........	October 2, 1806
Bush, John V.	Lieutenant, 17th Regiment........	April 26, 1808
Bush, Philip.............	Captain, Light Infantry Company, 22nd Regiment................	April 25, 1806
Bush, Philip.............	Major, 1st Battalion, 17th Regiment......................	June 12, 1806
Butler, Francis..........	Ensign, 13th Regiment...........	July 8, 1805
Byram, William...........	Major, 1st Battalion, 69th Regiment......................	December 29, 1806
Cabbell, William.........	Captain, 6th Regiment..........	August 20, 1808
Caffin, William..........	Major, 2nd Battalion, 28th Regiment......................	December 19, 1810
Caldwell, Robert.........	Captain, 24th Regiment..........	September 12, 1807
Caldwell, Robert S.	Ensign, 24th Regiment...........	March 25, 1807
Caldwell, Samuel.........	Lieutenant Colonel, Commandant 23rd Regiment................	June 27, 1806
Caldwell, Waller.........	Captain, 13th Regiment..........	May 23, 1807 and March 27, 1808
Caldwell, Walter (Waller?)	Major, 1st Battalion, 13th Regiment......................	January 26, 1810
Caldwell, William........	Ensign, 21st Regiment...........	April 14, 1808
Call, William............	Lieutenant, 14th Regiment........	June 28, 1808
Callaway, John...........	Major, 2nd Battalion, 38th Regiment......................	May 25, 1807
Calloway, John...........	Lieutenant Colonel, Commandant 38th Regiment................	December 7, 1810 and January 5, 1811
Calvert, Thomas..........	Major, 1st Battalion, 62nd Regiment......................	December 22, 1805
Cambell, William.........	Ensign, 19th Regiment...........	September 13, 1805
Campbell, George.........	Ensign, 23rd Regiment...........	November 4, 1806
Campbell, Hugh...........	Lieutenant, 29th Regiment........	November 22, 1805
Campbell, James..........	Major, 2nd Battalion, 81st Regiment......................	January 17, 1811
Campbell, Matthew........	Lieutenant, 21st Regiment........	August 18, 1806
Camron, Bazel............	Lieutenant, 4th Regiment.........	June 23, 1806
Canthill (Canterhill), Joseph...	Lieutenant, 13th Regiment..	July 8, 1805
Cape, John...............	Lieutenant Colonel, Commandant 46th Regiment................	February 1, 1809
Cape, John...............	Lieutenant Colonel, Commandant 81st Regiment................	January 17, 1811
Cardwell, Jacob..........	Lieutenant, 18th Regiment........	February 4, 1805
Cardwell, John...........	Lieutenant, 5th Regiment.........	November 4, 1806
Carmon, Caleb............	Lieutenant, 29th Regiment........	October 8, 1807
Carna, Pleasant..........	Lieutenant, 12th Regiment........	June 12, 1805
Carnahan, Robert.........	Lieutenant, 13th Regiment........	July 2, 1808
Carpenter, John..........	Ensign, 19th Regiment...........	July 19, 1805
Carr, Absalom............	Lieutenant Colonel, Commandant 37th Regiment................	March 12, 1807
Carr, Charles............	Paymaster, 8th Regiment..........	December 13, 1808
Carr, David..............	Lieutenant, 3rd Regiment.........	March 10, 1805

COMMISSIONED OFFICERS, 1805 - 1811   165

Carr, David..............	Captain, 3rd Regiment............	November 5, 1807
Carr, James..............	Ensign, 14th Regiment............	October 10, 1808
Carter, Charles..........	Major, 1st Battalion, 6th Regiment......................	May 9, 1806
Carter, Elisha...........	Captain, 14th Regiment...........	January 30, 1808
Carter, Jesse............	Captain, 6th Regiment............	December 8, 1806
Carter, John.............	Lieutenant, 28th Regiment........	November 19, 1805
Carter, John.............	Captain, 15th Regiment........... (Originally in 28th Regiment)	September 12, 1807
Carter, Joseph...........	Ensign, 28th Regiment............	November 19, 1805
Cartmell, Jacob..........	Captain, 27th Regiment...........	April 1, 1806
Cartmell, William........	Lieutenant, Rifle Company, 20th Regiment.................	August 20, 1808
Castleman, David.........	Lieutenant, 11th Regiment........	June 17, 1805
Castleman, David.........	Captain, Rifle Company, 11th Regiment......................	September 15, 1807
Castleman, Jacob.........	Major, 1st Battalion, 18th Regiment......................	March 10, 1808 and January 31, 1809
Castleman, Jacob.........	Lieutenant Colonel, Commandant 18th Regiment.................	December 11, 1811
Cavell, Joseph...........	Lieutenant, 6th Regiment.........	February 3, 1806
Cessell, William.........	Lieutenant, 4th Regiment.........	June 23, 1806
Chaffin, John............	Captain, 3rd Regiment............	September 17, 1805
Chaffin, William.........	Major, 2nd Battalion, 28th Regiment......................	January 26, 1811
Chalfan, John............	Captain, 3rd Regiment............	March 14, 1806
Chalfant, Robert.........	Lieutenant, 28th Regiment........	June 18, 1807
Chenoweth, Jacob.........	Captain, 2nd Regiment............	May 26, 1805
Cherry, William..........	Lieutenant, 24th Regiment........	March 25, 1807
Chiles, Henry............	Major, 2nd Battalion, 36th Regiment......................	April 24, 1805
Chiles, Thomas...........	Captain, 18th Regiment...........	February 9, 1807
Chinn, William...........	Lieutenant Colonel, Commandant 10th Regiment.................	January 30, 1809
Chinoweth, John..........	Ensign, 1st Regiment.............	February 2, 1805
Christopher, John........	Ensign, 11th Regiment............	July 10, 1806
Christopher, John........	Lieutenant, 11th Regiment........	August 8, 1807
Christopher, John........	Captain, 11th Regiment...........	August 5, 1808
Christopher, William.....	Captain, 11th Regiment...........	April 13, 1807
Churchill, John..........	Quartermaster, 3rd Regiment......	March 14, 1806
Churchill, Samuel........	Quartermaster, 1st Regiment......	May 31, 1806
Clark, Benjamin..........	Ensign, 2nd Regiment.............	December 16, 1807
Clark, Bolin.............	Lieutenant, 25th Regiment........	March 2, 1808
Clark, James.............	Ensign, 17th Regiment............ Approved......................	January 30, 1808 June 25, 1807
Clark, Joseph............	Captain, 17th Regiment........... Approved......................	January 30, 1808 June 25, 1807
Clark, Septimus D.	Ensign, 29th Regiment............	October 8, 1807
Clay, Henry..............	Major, 1st Battalion, 14th Regiment......................	June 11, 1806

COMMISSIONED OFFICERS, 1805 - 1811

Clay, Henry..............	Lieutenant Colonel, Commandant 14th Regiment...................	February 19, 1808
Clay, Samuel.............	Ensign, 9th Regiment.............	August 28, 1805
Cleaveland, George.......	Captain, 14th Regiment...........	June 11, 1806
Cleaver, David...........	Colonel, Commandant, 4th Regiment.......................	February 10, 1809
Clement, James...........	Major, 1st Battalion, 37th Regiment......................	May 25, 1807
Cleveland, George........	Ensign, 14th Regiment............	January 29, 1805
Cleveland, George........	Major, 2nd Battalion, 14th Regiment......................	January 31, 1809
Cloyd, John..............	Major, 2nd Battalion, 19th Regiment......................	January 18, 1809
Cochran, George..........	Ensign, 24th Regiment............	February 22, 1806
Cochren, James...........	Captain, 30th Regiment...........	August 8, 1805
Cockeral, Joseph.........	Lieutenant, 8th Regiment.........	June 2, 1806
Coffee, Jesse............	Ensign, 6th Regiment.............	December 8, 1806
Coffee, Osburn...........	Adjutant, 6th Regiment...........	June 10, 1806
Colbert, Burwell.........	Lieutenant (?), 29th Regiment....	May 6, 1806
Colbert, Jesse...........	Ensign, 10th Regiment............	December 6, 1805
Colbert, Jesse...........	Lieutenant, 10th Regiment........	December 4, 1806
Coleman, Daniel..........	1st Lieutenant, Troop of Horse, 17th Regiment....................	November 4, 1806
Coleman, James...........	2nd Lieutenant, "Choir" of Light Horse, 20th Regiment.............	November 5, 1807
Coleman, John............	Ensign, 24th Regiment............	September 12, 1807
Coleman, Thomas..........	Captain, 21st Regiment...........	April 20, 1805
Collier, Coleman.........	Lieutenant, 13th Regiment........	March 27, 1808
Collier, Isaac...........	Ensign, 18th Regiment............	February 9, 1807
Collier, Isaac...........	Lieutenant, 18th Regiment........	May 20, 1807
Collier, Solomon.........	Lieutenant, 6th Regiment.........	February 3, 1806
Collins, Edmond..........	Ensign, 13th Regiment............	May 23, 1807
Collins, Edward..........	Captain, Rifle Company, 23rd Regiment......................	December 22, 1807
Collins, Isaac...........	Lieutenant, 15th Regiment........	June 17, 1805
Collins, Lewis...........	Lieutenant, 10th Regiment........	October 4, 1808
Colman, James............	Lieutenant, 2nd Regiment.........	March 3, 1807
Colman, James............	Captain, 2nd Regiment............	December 16, 1807
Colvert, Landon..........	Lieutenant, 15th Regiment........	October 2, 1806
Colvin, Charles, Jr. ...	Lieutenant, 21st Regiment........	April 18, 1807
Colvin, George...........	Ensign, 9th Regiment.............	April 9, 1805
Colvin, George...........	Ensign, 21st Regiment............	March 14, 1806
Colvin, George...........	Captain, 21st Regiment...........	April 18, 1807
Combs, Adin..............	Major, 2nd Battalion, 60th Regiment......................	January 25, 1811
Combs, Elijah............	Major, 2nd Battalion, 80th Regiment......................	January 17, 1811
Combs, Samuel............	Lieutenant, 16th Regiment........	August 20, 1808
Combs, Samuel R.	2nd Lieutenant, Troop of Horse, 17th Regiment..................	November 4, 1806
Comley, Absolem..........	Ensign, 26th Regiment............	March 22, 1805

COMMISSIONED OFFICERS, 1805 - 1811 167

Compton, Joel............	Lieutenant, 16th Regiment........	March 14, 1806
Congleton, James.........	Major, 2nd Battalion, 47th Regiment.......................	January 31, 1809
Connady (Kennedy), Washington...	Ensign, 14th Regiment......	June 11, 1806
Connell, James...........	Ensign, 18th Regiment............	March 14, 1806
Cooke, Giles.............	Ensign, Infantry Company, 25th Regiment......................	December 24, 1806
Cooley, Charles..........	Ensign, 6th Regiment.............	February 3, 1806
Coombs, Andrew...........	Lieutenant, Rifle Company, 11th Regiment......................	September 15, 1807
Coon, Aron...............	Lieutenant, 24th Regiment........	December 8, 1806
Cooper, Jeconias.........	Captain, 28th Regiment...........	June 17, 1805
Corbin, Elija............	Ensign, 28th Regiment............	January 9, 1808
Corbin, Thomas...........	Captain, 17th Regiment...........	July 1, 1805
Cord, Zachus.............	Lieutenant, 30th Regiment........	April 18, 1807
Corn, Jesse..............	Ensign, 5th Regiment.............	October 15, 1807
Cornelius, Abner.........	Lieutenant, 7th Regiment.........	June 28, 1808
Corwine, Samuel..........	Ensign, 15th Regiment............	December 24, 1806
Cotton, Charles..........	Ensign, 1st Regiment.............	December 16, 1807
Cotton, Daniel...........	Ensign, 2nd Regiment.............	May 15, 1806
Cotton, Daniel...........	Lieutenant, 2nd Regiment.........	September 12, 1807
Cotton, John.............	Ensign, 11th Regiment............'	September 15, 1807
Coun (Cowan), James......	Ensign, 13th Regiment............	January 11, 1806
Covenhover, Peter........	Major, 1st Battalion, 11th Regiment......................	December 13, 1809
Covington, Thomas A. ...	Captain, Horse Company, 25th Regiment......................	July 19, 1805
Covington, Thomas A. ..	Major, 1st Battalion, 25th Regiment......................	January 17, 1811
Cowherd, James...........	Major, 16th Regiment.............	September 5, 1805
Cowherd, Simeon..........	Ensign, 16th Regiment............	November 25, 1805
Cox, James...............	Lieutenant Colonel, Commandant 27th Regiment..................	July 11, 1805
Cox, John................	Ensign, 1st Regiment.............	June 18, 1807
Crab, Jeremiah...........	Captain, 18th Regiment...........	March 14, 1806
Craig, David.............	Ensign, 18th Regiment............	December 21, 1807
Craig, Lewis.............	Major, 2nd Battalion, 15th Regiment......................	December 29, 1806
Craighead, Robert........	Ensign, 15th Regiment............	September 12, 1807
Cranmore, George.........	Ensign, 12th Regiment............	October 2, 1806
Craycraft, Samuel........	Lieutenant, 29th Regiment........	May 26, 1808
Crenshaw, Thompson.......	Major, 2nd Battalion, 45th Regiment......................	December 7, 1810
Crist, Jacob.............	Major, 2nd Battalion, 27th Regiment......................	December 22, 1805
Cristman, Isaac..........	Lieutenant Colonel, Commandant 53rd Regiment.................	January 31, 1809
Crofford, Oliver.........	Captain, 17th Regiment...........	July 1, 1805
Crooke, John.............	Major, 1st Battalion, 35th Regiment......................	December 16, 1805
Crowder, Burwell.........	Ensign, 25th Regiment............	December 24, 1806

COMMISSIONED OFFICERS, 1805 - 1811

Crutcher, Robert.........	Ensign, 9th Regiment.............	February 22, 1806
Crutcher, Robert.........	Lieutenant, 9th Regiment.........	November 7, 1807
Culbertson, Alexander....	Cornet, Cavalry Company, 25th Regiment......................	March 2, 1808
Cullum, Francis..........	Ensign, 17th Regiment............	June 11, 1806
Culm (Cullum), Francis...	Captain, 17th Regiment...........	October 2, 1806
Culp, Josiah.............	Ensign, 13th Regiment............	September 24, 1806
Culp, Thomas.............	Ensign, 13th Regiment............	July 2, 1808
Culver, Benjamin.........	Captain, 17th Regiment...........	January 30, 1808
	Approved......................	June 25, 1807
Cummings, Abraham........	Lieutenant, 5th Regiment.........	October 15, 1807
Cummins, Robert..........	Ensign, 27th Regiment............	October 14, 1805
Cummins, William.........	Captain, 1st Regiment............	May 31, 1806
Cumpton, Rochard (Richard ?)...	Captain, 16th Regiment......	August 20, 1808
Cupp, Henry..............	Lieutenant, 24th Regiment........	August 28, 1805
Curry, Robert............	Ensign, 5th Regiment.............	November 21, 1805
Damrell, George..........	Major, 2nd Battalion, 52nd Regiment......................	February 23, 1808
Daniel, James............	Lieutenant, 17th Regiment........	August 20, 1808
Daniel, Jesse............	Major, 2nd Battalion, 31st Regiment......................	February 19, 1808
Daniel, John.............	Ensign, 8th Regiment.............	June 11, 1805
Darnaby, William.........	Ensign, Rifle Company, 8th Regiment......................	May 16, 1808
Daugherty, James.........	Ensign, 29th Regiment............	October 8, 1807
Daveiss, John............	Major, 2nd Battalion, 73rd Regiment......................	February 19, 1808
Daveiss, John............	Lieutenant Colonel, Commandant 73rd Regiment.................	January 23, 1810
Daveiss, Joseph H.	Lieutenant Colonel, Commandant 73rd Regiment.................	February 19, 1808
Davenport, Richard.......	Lieutenant Colonel, Commandant 43rd Regiment.................	December 13, 1809
Davenport, Samuel........	Ensign, 17th Regiment............	October 2, 1806
Davidson, Samuel.........	Major, 1st Battalion, 63rd Regiment......................	May 9, 1806
Davis, Arthur............	Major, 1st Battalion, 55th Regiment......................	December 10, 1811
Davis, Arthur............	Major, 2nd Battalion, 55th Regiment......................	January 17, 1811
Davis, Benjamin..........	Ensign, 24th Regiment............	December 8, 1806
Davis, George N.	Captain, 15th Regiment...........	October 2, 1806
Davis, Humphrey..........	Ensign, 17th Regiment............	August 20, 1808
Davis, John..............	Major, 2nd Battalion, 51st Regiment......................	December 7, 1805
Davis, Joseph............	Ensign, Rifle Company in Flemingsburg, 30th Regiment...........	August 8, 1805
Davis, Joseph............	Ensign, Rifle Company, 30th Regiment......................	August 28, 1806
Davis, Thomas............	Ensign, 11th Regiment............	June 17, 1805
Davis, Thomas............	Lieutenant, 11th Regiment........	January 24, 1807

COMMISSIONED OFFICERS, 1805 - 1811

Davis, William...........	Lieutenant, Rifle Company, 23rd Regiment.................	February 5, 1805
Davis, William...........	Adjutant, 6th Regiment...........	February 3, 1806
Dawson, Peter............	Lieutenant, 20th Regiment........	July 29, 1807
Dawson, Samuel J.	Major, 14th Regiment............	April 30, 1808
Dawson, Samuel Jones.....	Major, 1st Battalion, 14th Regiment.....................	February 19, 1808
Dawson, Samuel Jones.....	Lieutenant Colonel, Commandant 14th Regiment.................	December 10, 1811
Dean, Thomas.............	Major, 2nd Battalion, 4th Regiment.....................	December 13, 1809
Deatherage, Amos.........	Lieutenant, 7th Regiment........	June 28, 1808
Debon, Samuel............	Lieutenant, 5th Regiment........	November 21, 1805
Dehaven, Isaac...........	Ensign, 12th Regiment...........	July 7, 1806
Delany, William..........	Ensign, 7th Regiment............	June 28, 1808
Demaree, David...........	Lieutenant, 18th Regiment.......	December 21, 1807
Denton, Robert...........	Major, 1st Battalion, 74th Regiment.....................	February 1, 1809
Depauw, John.............	Lieutenant, 6th Regiment........	February 3, 1806
Depauw, John.............	Captain, 6th Regiment...........	August 20, 1808
Depauw, Peter............	Ensign, 6th Regiment............	August 20, 1808
Depew, Abraham...........	Lieutenant Colonel, Commandant. 67th Regiment.................	December 10, 1811
Dever, John..............	Ensign, 19th Regiment...........	November 19, 1805
Devere, John.............	Lieutenant, 19th Regiment.......	April 18, 1807
Dickey, Elisha...........	Ensign, 7th Regiment............	June 18, 1807
Dickey, John.............	Lieutenant Colonel, Commandant 66th Regiment.................	December 18, 1806
Dickey, Joseph...........	Ensign, 16th Regiment...........	November 25, 1805
Dickey, William..........	Ensign, 10th Regiment...........	December 6, 1805
Dickinson, William.......	Captain, 21st Regiment..........	March 14, 1806
Dismukes, Joseph.........	Major, 2nd Battalion, 74th Regiment.....................	February 1, 1809
Ditto, William...........	Ensign, 3rd Regiment............	February 3, 1807
Dixon, Henry.............	Major, 2nd Battalion, 61st Regiment.⟨....................	December 13, 1809
Dobbins, Charles.........	Lieutenant, 29th Regiment.......	May 26, 1808
Dobbins, John............	Lieutenant Colonel, Commandant 82nd Regiment.................	January 17, 1811
Dobings, Edward..........	Lieutenant, 30th Regiment.......	August 28, 1806
Dobyns, John.............	Major, 2nd Battalion, 40th Regiment.....................	December 14, 1805
Dodd, James..............	Lieutenant, 24th Regiment.......	August 28, 1805
Dodd, John...............	Captain, 24th Regiment..........	December 8, 1806
Donaldson, William.......	Lieutenant Colonel, Commandant 65th Regiment.................	January 26, 1810
Donan, David C.	1st Lieutenant of Cavalry, 16th Regiment.....................	November 5, 1807
Donnaldson, William......	Major, 1st Battalion, 65th Regiment.....................	December 18, 1806

COMMISSIONED OFFICERS, 1805 - 1811

Donnelson, John..........	Lieutenant Colonel, Commandant 36th Regiment.................	April 24, 1805
Doogan, Jeremiah.........	Ensign, 20th Regiment............	June 28, 1808
Dorsey, Azle.............	Ensign, 3rd Regiment............	May 24, 1806
Dougherty, James.........	Ensign, 10th Regiment............	July 2, 1807
Douglass, Hezekiah.......	Lieutenant, Rifle Company, 11th Regiment......................	September 15, 1807
Downard, Adam............	Ensign, 21st Regiment............	June 25, 1807
Downing, William.........	Captain, 16th Regiment...........	November 25, 1805
Draine, Stephen..........	Ensign, 18th Regiment............	November 19, 1805
Drake, Enoch.............	Ensign, 10th Regiment............	September 30, 1807
Drake, Josiah............	Ensign, 28th Regiment............	June 17, 1805
Drake, Josiah............	Captain, 28th Regiment...........	October 2, 1806
Drake, Josiah............	Captain, 15th Regiment........... (Originally in 28th Regiment)	September 12, 1807
Drane, Stephen...........	Lieutenant, 18th Regiment........	March 14, 1806
Draper, John.............	Ensign, 20th Regiment............	March 5, 1807
Draper, John.............	Lieutenant, 20th Regiment........	July 29, 1807
Dudley, James............	Captain, 8th Regiment............	June 6, 1808
Dudley, William E.	Captain, 8th Regiment............	June 11, 1805
Duncan, Benjamin.........	Captain, 6th Regiment............	February 3, 1806
Duncan, Benjamin.........	Major, 1st Battalion, 73rd Regiment......................	January 23, 1810
Duncan, Charles..........	Captain, 1st Regiment............	May 26, 1808
Duncan, Coleman..........	Ensign, 1st Regiment.............	December 16, 1807
Duncan, Coleman..........	Lieutenant, 1st Regiment.........	April 21, 1808
Duncan, Elias............	Captain, 21st Regiment...........	June 25, 1807
Duncan, James............	Captain, 14th Regiment...........	January 30, 1808
Duncan, James, Jr.	Lieutenant, 14th Regiment........	January 29, 1805
Duncan, James, Jr.	Major, 2nd Battalion, 14th Regiment......................	March 14, 1811
Duncan, Joseph...........	Lieutenant, 6th Regiment.........	August 20, 1808
Duncan, Thomas...........	Lieutenant, 25th Regiment........	July 19, 1805
Duncan, Willis...........	Lieutenant, 21st Regiment........	March 14, 1806
Dunham, Timothy..........	Ensign, 25th Regiment............	July 19, 1805
Dunn, Benajah............	Lieutenant, 20th Regiment........	February 22, 1806
Dupey, Samuel............	Cornet, Troop of Cavalry, 18th Regiment......................	December 21, 1807
Dupuy, Abraham...........	Major, 1st Battalion, 67th Regiment......................	December 18, 1806
Dupuy, Alexander.........	Ensign, 14th Regiment............	January 30, 1808
Durbin, John.............	Lieutenant, 13th Regiment........	January 11, 1806
Durbin, John.............	Captain, 13th Regiment...........	September 24, 1806
Durham, James............	Captain, Infantry Company, 16th Regiment.................	November 25, 1805
Durham, James............	Major, 2nd Battalion, 16th Regiment......................	February 22, 1811
Durham, James............	Major, 1st Battalion, 16th Regiment......................	April 4, 1811
Duval, Thompson..........	Ensign, 8th Regiment............	June 2, 1806
Duvall, John.............	Lieutenant, 12th Regiment........	April 9, 1805

COMMISSIONED OFFICERS, 1805 - 1811   171

Duvall, John.............	Captain, 12th Regiment...........	July 13, 1807
Duvall, William P.	Lieutenant, Rifle Company, 2nd Regiment.......................	September 11, 1806
Duvall, Zachariah.......	Lieutenant, 12th Regiment........	July 13, 1807
Dye, James..............	Lieutenant, 25th Regiment........	July 1, 1808
Dye, John...............	Lieutenant, 29th Regiment........	May 6, 1806
East, Isaac.............	Ensign, 6th Regiment.............	September 12, 1807
Easten, Charles.........	Ensign, 18th Regiment............	July 23, 1808
Easten, Charles..........	Lieutenant, 18th Regiment........	September 3, 1808
Eastin, Zachariah.......	Lieutenant, 13th Regiment........	July 8, 1805
Eastin, Zachariah.......	Captain, 13th Regiment...........	January 11, 1806
Eastis, Fielding........	Ensign, 12th Regiment............	September 17, 1805
Ebert, Philip...........	Cornet, Troop of Horse, 15th Regiment.......................	September 12, 1807
Edwards, Amos...........	Captain, Light Infantry, Town Company, 23rd Regiment.........	February 5, 1805
Edwards, Cornelius......	Ensign, Rifle Company, 11th Regiment.......................	September 15, 1807
Elder, James............	Major, 1st Battalion, 24th Regiment.......................	December 13, 1809
Elder, James............	Lieutenant Colonel, Commandant 24th Regiment.................	January 26, 1811
Elliet, Edward..........	Lieutenant, 30th Regiment........	February 3, 1807
Elliott, David..........	Adjutant, 19th Regiment..........	March 27, 1808
Elliott, Elijah.........	Lieutenant, 28th Regiment........	June 18, 1807
		and January 9, 1808
Ellis, Daniel...........	Ensign, 18th Regiment............	February 4, 1805
Ellis, Daniel...........	Lieutenant, 18th Regiment........	October 6, 1807
Ellis, Israel...........	Ensign, 22nd Regiment............	July 14, 1807
Ellis, Israel...........	Lieutenant, 22nd Regiment........	June 1, 1808
Ellis, James............	Captain, 21st Regiment...........	March 14, 1806
Emison, Thomas..........	Captain, 12th Regiment...........	September 17, 1805
Engles, Joseph..........	Captain, 20th Regiment...........	February 22, 1806
Epperson, David.........	Ensign, 6th Regiment.............	December 8, 1806
Epperson, Robert........	Lieutenant, 7th Regiment.........	June 18, 1807
Estes, Asa..............	Lieutenant Colonel, Commandant 72nd Regiment.................	February 19, 1808
Estill, Samuel..........	Captain, 19th Regiment...........	July 19, 1805
	and	February 3, 1807
Eubank, Ambrose.........	Captain, 17th Regiment...........	October 2, 1806
Eubank, Ambrose.........	Major, 2nd Battalion, 17th Regiment.......................	December 10, 1811
Eubanks, Thomas.........	Captain, 25th Regiment...........	July 1, 1808
Evans, Bennet...........	Lieutenant, Rifle Company in Flemingsburg, 30th Regiment....	August 8, 1805
Evans, Bennet H.	Lieutenant, Rifle Company, 30th Regiment.......................	August 28, 1806
Evans, Hugh.............	Ensign, 5th Regiment.............	November 4, 1806
Evans, Samuel...........	Ensign, 30th Regiment............	March 27, 1805
Evans, Silas............	Lieutenant, 17th Regiment........	January 30, 1808
	Approved.....................	June 25, 1807

COMMISSIONED OFFICERS, 1805 - 1811

Evans, William..........	Lieutenant, Rifle Company, 7th Regiment.................	September 23, 1805
Eve, Joseph.............	Major, 1st Battalion, 75th Regiment.....................	December 10, 1811
Ewen, Robert............	2nd Lieutenant, Troop of Horse, 30th Regiment.................	August 8, 1805
Ewin, Henry.............	Major, 3rd Regiment...........	September 17, 1805
Ewing, Putnam...........	Major, 1st Battalion, 34th Regiment.....................	January 10, 1811
Ewing, William..........	Lieutenant, Rifle Company, 23rd Regiment.....................	November 4, 1806
Fare, Absalom...........	Ensign, 6th Regiment...........	December 8, 1806
Farguson, Robert........	Lieutenant, 8th Regiment.......	July 2, 1806
Farguson, Vivian........	Ensign, 8th Regiment...........	September 11, 1806
Farguson, Vivion........	Lieutenant, 8th Regiment.......	May 11, 1807
Faris, George...........	Captain, 19th Regiment.........	September 12, 1807
Farris, William.........	Captain, 6th Regiment..........	February 3, 1806
Farrow, Joseph M.	Captain, 30th Regiment.........	April 18, 1807
Farrow, William.........	Lieutenant Colonel, Commandant 31st Regiment.................	February 19, 1808
Fauntleroy, John........	Major, 2nd Battalion, 43rd Regiment.....................	February 23, 1808
Feilder, John...........	Ensign, 17th Regiment..........	October 2, 1806
Fenwick, Ignatius.......	Ensign, 22nd Regiment..........	July 14, 1807
Ferguson, Richard.......	Surgeon, 1st Regiment..........	August 20, 1806
Ferguson, Richard.......	Major, 1st Battalion, 24th Regiment.....................	March 19, 1807
Ferril, Robert..........	Major, 1st Battalion, 40th Regiment.....................	December 13, 1809
Field, Benjamin.........	Major, 1st Battalion, 73rd Regiment.....................	February 19, 1808
Field, John.............	Ensign, 14th Regiment..........	January 29, 1805
Field, John.............	Lieutenant, 1st Regiment.......	June 18, 1807
Field, Joseph...........	Ensign, 18th Regiment..........	May 16, 1805
Fields, William.........	Lieutenant, 28th Regiment......	November 4, 1806
Fields, William.........	Captain, 28th Regiment.........	June 18, 1807
Finch, Samuel...........	Ensign, 14th Regiment..........	January 24, 1807
Finley, James...........	Lieutenant, 28th Regiment......	November 19, 1805
Finley, Richard.........	Major, 2nd Battalion, 33rd Regiment.....................	December 13, 1810
Finnell, Achilles.......	Captain, 26th Regiment.........	January 29, 1805
Finnell, James..........	Lieutenant, 26th Regiment......	January 29, 1805
Fips, John..............	Ensign, 1st Regiment...........	June 18, 1807
Fish, William...........	Lieutenant, 19th Regiment......	February 3, 1807
Fishback, George........	Lieutenant, 13th Regiment......	July 8, 1805
Fishback, Martin........	Ensign, 28th Regiment..........	June 18, 1807
Fisher, Samuel..........	Ensign, 10th Regiment..........	December 6, 1805
Fisher, Stephen.........	Major, 1st Battalion, 43rd Regiment.....................	December 13, 1809
Fissor (Fisher?), Shaderic...	Lieutenant, 23rd Regiment.....	February 5, 1805
Fitch, Salathiel........	Major, 30th Regiment...........	December 16, 1805

COMMISSIONED OFFICERS, 1805 - 1811 173

Fleming, John D.	Captain, 30th Regiment...........	March 16, 1808
Fletcher, Thomas.........	Major, 2nd Battalion, 65th Regiment......................	December 18, 1806
Flippo, John............	Ensign, 23rd Regiment...........	December 22, 1807
Floyd, Alexander........	Captain, 25th Regiment..........	December 24, 1806
Floyd, Nathaniel........	Major, 2nd Battalion, 83rd Regiment......................	January 17, 1811
Floyd, R. C.	Captain, 1st Regiment............	June 18, 1807
Foley, James............	Ensign, 19th Regiment...........	June 18, 1807
Forbis, Morgan...........	Lieutenant, 16th Regiment........	November 5, 1807
Ford, Benjamin...........	Ensign, 10th Regiment...........	October 4, 1808
Fore, John..............	Captain, 18th Regiment..........	July 11, 1806
Foster, John.............	Ensign, 20th Regiment...........	February 22, 1806
Fowler, Stephan..........	Ensign, 24th Regiment...........	December 8, 1806
Fraizer, Joel............	Paymaster, 20th Regiment........	June 22, 1805
Frame, William...........	Major, 1st Battalion, 17th Regiment......................	May 27, 1807
Frame, William...........	Lieutenant Colonel, Commandant 17th Regiment.................	July 16, 1810
Francisco, George........	Captain, Troop of Horse, 11th Regiment......................	August 8, 1807
Francisco, John..........	Lieutenant Colonel, Commandant 11th Regiment.................	December 13, 1809
Frazer, James............	Ensign, 13th Regiment...........	May 23, 1807
Frazer, Thomas...........	Ensign, 23rd Regiment...........	November 4, 1806
Frederick, John..........	Ensign, 1st Regiment............	February 2 and November 9, 1805
Frier, John.............	Lieutenant, 21st Regiment........	April 18, 1807
Fuget, Martin............	Captain, Rifle Company, 21st Regiment......................	August 18, 1806
Fulton, James............	Ensign, 18th Regiment...........	February 9, 1807
Fulton, Samuel...........	Captain, 13th Regiment..........	May 23, 1807
Fulton, Samuel...........	Major, 1st Battalion, 13th Regiment......................	December 10, 1811
Furgason, John...........	Lieutenant, 23rd Regiment........	November 4, 1806
Furgeson, Richard........	2nd Major, 1st Battalion, 24th Regiment.................	March 19, 1807
Furnish, William.........	Ensign, Rifle Company, 20th Regiment......................	August 28, 1806
Gaddy, James.............	Captain, 16th Regiment..........	November 25, 1805
Gaither, Thomas..........	Major, 1st Battalion, 18th Regiment......................	December 11, 1811
Gale, John..............	Ensign, 20th Regiment...........	July 29, 1807
Gale, John..............	Lieutenant, 20th Regiment........	June 28, 1808
Gano, Richard M.	Major, 1st Battalion, 77th Regiment......................	February 11, 1809
Garrard, Daniel..........	Lieutenant Colonel, Commandant 68th Regiment.................	December 6, 1811
Gary, James.............	Ensign, 19th Regiment...........	March 27, 1808
Gather, Thomas...........	Ensign, 18th Regiment...........	February 9, 1807
Gather, Thomas...........	Captain, 18th Regiment..........	May 26, 1808

Gathright, John	Ensign, 18th Regiment	May 16, 1805
Gathright, John	Lieutenant, 18th Regiment	July 11, 1806
Gault, Edward	Ensign, 29th Regiment	June 9, 1806
Gawslin, Rubin	Ensign, 30th Regiment	February 3, 1807
Gay, Thomas	Major, 2nd Battalion, 6th Regiment	February 1, 1809
Gedians, John	Captain, 13th Regiment	May 23, 1807
Gentry, David	Lieutenant, 19th Regiment	July 19, 1805
Gentry, Richard	Lieutenant, 19th Regiment	March 27, 1808
George, Abner	Lieutenant, 20th Regiment	June 22, 1805
Gibson, James	Ensign, 17th Regiment	July 1, 1805
Gidins, Isham	Lieutenant, 17th Regiment	August 20, 1808
Gilaspie, James	Ensign, 13th Regiment	July 2, 1808
Gilbert, John	Major, 1st Battalion, 68th Regiment	February 2, 1808
Gilbert, John	Lieutenant Colonel, Commandant 68th Regiment	January 17, 1811
Gilmore, James, Jr.	Lieutenant, 6th Regiment	June 10, 1806
Giltner, Michel	Ensign, 14th Regiment	June 11, 1806
Giltner, Micah	Lieutenant, 14th Regiment	January 24, 1807
Glaves, Michael	Captain, 21st Regiment	April 18, 1807
Glenn, Samuel	Major, 1st Battalion, 84th Regiment	January 15, 1811
Glenn, William	Major, 2nd Battalion, 73rd Regiment	December 10, 1811
Glover, John	Lieutenant, 29th Regiment	October 8, 1807
Gogins, Stephen	Lieutenant, 19th Regiment	June 18, 1807
Gohagan, John	Lieutenant, 13th Regiment	May 23, 1807
Goheen, James	Lieutenant, 23rd Regiment	August 11, 1806
Golson, Samuel	Cornet, Cavalry Company, 16th Regiment	November 5, 1807
Gooch, John A.	Captain, 24th Regiment	March 25, 1807
Goode, William	Captain, 6th Regiment	February 3, 1806
Goolsby, James	Captain, 16th Regiment	March 14, 1806
Gorden, Samuel	Captain, 23rd Regiment	August 11, 1806
Gorden, Samuel	Major, 2nd Battalion, 23rd Regiment	January 31, 1811
Gordon, Lewis	Major, 1st Battalion, 15th Regiment	August 28, 1806
Gorham, William	Captain, 23rd Regiment	December 22, 1807
Gorin, Gladen	Lieutenant Colonel, Commandant 61st Regiment	January 26, 1809
Gosney, Frederick	Ensign, 21st Regiment	April 20, 1805
Grable, David	Major, 1st Battalion, 32nd Regiment	September 2, 1807
Grable, David	Lieutenant Colonel, Commandant 32nd Regiment	December 11, 1811
Graham, Francis	Lieutenant, 22nd Regiment	September 12, 1807
Graham, Francis, Jr.	Ensign, 22nd Regiment	October 30, 1806
Graham, George	Lieutenant, 4th Regiment	January 9, 1808
Graham, James	Lieutenant, 15th Regiment	June 17, 1805

COMMISSIONED OFFICERS, 1805 - 1811　　　　　175

Graham, Samuel............	Captain, 5th Regiment............	April 27, 1807
Graham, William..........	Major, 2nd Battalion, 22nd Regiment......................	February 19, 1808
Grant, James.............	Captain, 12th Regiment............	December 5, 1807
Grant, Robert............	Major, 1st Battalion, 14th Regiment......................	December 10, 1811
	Robert Grant in pro tem commission dated................	October 5, 1811
Graves, John.............	Captain, 10th Regiment...........	December 6, 1805
Graves, Joseph...........	Major, 1st Battalion, 67th Regiment......................	December 10, 1811
Graves, Thomas...........	Ensign, 10th Regiment...........	May 2, 1807
Gray, David..............	Ensign, 9th Regiment............	May 26, 1807
Gray, David..............	Lieutenant, 9th Regiment.........	November 7, 1807
Gray, David..............	Captain, 13th Regiment............	May 23, 1807, March 27 and July 2, 1808
Gray, Francis............	Adjutant, 20th Regiment..........	June 19, 1806
Gray, Isaac..............	Major, 1st Battalion, 58th Regiment......................	December 29, 1806
Gray, Patrick...........	Major, 1st Battalion, 9th Regiment......................	February 10, 1809
Grayson, Robert H.	Captain, 15th Regiment............	October 2, 1806
Green, George............	Ensign, 2nd Regiment............	December 16, 1807
Green, Liberty..........	Ensign, Infantry Company, 16th Regiment......................	November 25, 1805
Greer, George............	Captain, Troop of Cavalry, 22nd Regiment......................	December 1, 1807
Griffin, Jasper..........	Ensign, 9th Regiment............	February 22, 1806
Griffin, John............	Major, 2nd Battalion, 44th Regiment......................	February 19, 1808
Griffin, Thomas..........	Lieutenant, 25th Regiment.......	December 24, 1806
Griffin, William.........	Major, 2nd Battalion, 72nd Regiment......................	December 19, 1810
Griffith, John...........	Lieutenant, 21st Regiment........	March 14, 1806
Griffith, Robert.........	Captain, 20th Regiment............	April 14, 1805
Griffith, William........	Major, 2nd Battalion, 72nd Regiment......................	January 25, 1811
Griffith, William........	Major, 1st Battalion, 47th Regiment......................	December 10, 1811
Grigg, Clem..............	Lieutenant, 17th Regiment........	October 2, 1806
Grove, Henry.............	Ensign, 16th Regiment...........	November 25, 1805
Grugett, John............	Captain, 7th Regiment............	February 3, 1807
Grundy, Felix............	Captain, 2nd Regiment............	September 11, 1806
Guardiner, Ralph.........	Lieutenant, 4th Regiment.........	January 9, 1808
Guiwn, James.............	Ensign, 2nd Regiment............	May 26, 1805
Guthrey, Dempsey.........	Ensign, 16th Regiment...........	August 20, 1808
Guy, Robert..............	Lieutenant, 9th Regiment.........	February 22, 1806
Guy, Robert..............	Captain, 9th Regiment............	May 26, 1807
Hackett, James...........	Captain, 18th Regiment............	June 12, 1807
Hackley, John............	Ensign, Light Infantry Company, 22nd Regiment.................	May 3, 1806

COMMISSIONED OFFICERS, 1805 - 1811

Hackley, John............	Lieutenant (?), 22nd Regiment....	December 1, 1807
Hackley, Robert..........	Ensign, 2nd Regiment............	May 15, 1806
Haddicks, John...........	Major, 2nd Battalion, 68th Regiment......................	December 18, 1806
Haddix, John.............	Lieutenant Colonel, Commandant 80th Regiment.................	January 17, 1811
Halbert, James...........	Lieutenant, 1st Regiment.........	February 2, 1805
Halbert, John............	Ensign, 27th Regiment............	June 11, 1805
Hale, Hezekiah...........	Ensign, 24th Regiment............	September 12, 1807
Hale, John...............	Captain, 5th Regiment............	April 14, 1805
Hale (or Hall?), Samuel..	Ensign, 8th Regiment.............	August 14, 1806
Hale, Thomas.............	Lieutenant, 5th Regiment.........	April 14, 1805
Halffield, John..........	Ensign, 28th Regiment............	November 4, 1806
Hall, George.............	Ensign, 6th Regiment.............	February 3, 1806
Hall, Jeremiah...........	Ensign, 22nd Regiment............	June 1, 1808
Hall, Philip.............	Lieutenant, 20th Regiment........	April 14, 1805
Hallard, John............	Captain, Light Horse Company, 17th Regiment..................	October 2, 1806
Ham, George..............	Lieutenant, 19th Regiment........	July 19, 1805
Hambleton, Charles.......	Cornet, 6th Regiment.............	August 20, 1808
Hambleton, Clement.......	Captain, 2nd Regiment............	September 12, 1807
Hamilton, John...........	Ensign, 11th Regiment............	January 24, 1807
Hamilton, John...........	Captain, 10th Regiment...........	December 4, 1806
Hamilton, Samuel.........	Ensign, 13th Regiment............	July 8, 1805
Hamilton, William........	Ensign, 13th Regiment............	July 8, 1805
Hamton, Thomas (G.?).....	Ensign, 28th Regiment............	January 9, 1808
Handcock, John...........	Ensign, 22nd Regiment............	September 12, 1807
Handcock, Thomas.........	Lieutenant, 22nd Regiment........	April 4, 1805
Handcock, Thomas G.	Captain, 22nd Regiment...........	July 14, 1807
Handley, John............	Paymaster, 4th Regiment..........	January 24, 1807
Hannah, John H.	2nd Lieutenant, Troop of Cavalry, 22nd Regiment.................	December 1, 1807
Hanson, John.............	Ensign, 21st Regiment............	April 18, 1807
Hardesty, Caleb..........	Major, 1st Battalion, 62nd Regiment......................	February 3, 1807
Hardin, Davis............	Ensign, 7th Regiment.............	November 4, 1806 and February 3, 1807
Hardin, Davis............	Lieutenant, 7th Regiment.........	June 18, 1807
Hardin, Davis (or David?)	Major, 1st Battalion, 64th Regiment......................	May 9, 1806
Hardin, John.............	Captain, 24th Regiment...........	February 22, 1806
Harding, Aaron...........	Captain, 16th Regiment...........	December 8, 1806
Harges, Thomas...........	Lieutenant, 3rd Regiment.........	February 3, 1807
Hargrave, Willis.........	Captain, 23rd Regiment...........	August 11, 1806
Harkins, Isaac...........	Lieutenant, 18th Regiment........	May 16, 1805
Harper, Joseph...........	Ensign, 6th Regiment.............	August 20, 1808
Harris, Archibald........	Lieutenant, 10th Regiment........	August 8, 1805
Harris, John.............	Ensign, 11th Regiment............	August 8, 1807
Harris, Samuel...........	Captain, 19th Regiment...........	July 19, 1805
Harris, William..........	Ensign, 19th Regiment............	July 19, 1805
Harrison, Reuben.........	Major, 39th Regiment.............	January 25, 1811

COMMISSIONED OFFICERS, 1805 - 1811

Harrison, Samuel	Cornet, 30th Regiment	January 30, 1808
Harrison, Thomas G.	Lieutenant, 4th Regiment	January 9, 1808
Harrod, Samuel	Major, 2nd Battalion, 14th Regiment	February 19, 1808
Hart, David	Major, 1st Battalion, 30th Regiment	December 6, 1811
Hartgrove, Valentine	Ensign, 6th Regiment	June 10, 1806
Hartley, George	Ensign, 30th Regiment	February 3, 1807
Hatcher, Robert	Lieutenant, 16th Regiment	November 25, 1805
Hatfield, Thomas	Captain, 1st Regiment	November 9, 1805
Hawkins, William	Ensign, 19th Regiment	September 12, 1807
Hay, Daniel	Major, 1st Battalion, 66th Regiment	December 29, 1806
Hayden, John	Captain, 20th Regiment	June 22, 1805
Hayden, Samuel	Ensign, 5th Regiment	April 14, 1805
Haynes, Joseph	Lieutenant, 5th Regiment	April 27, 1807
Head, Edward	Major, 2nd Battalion, 24th Regiment	January 26, 1811
Heck, John	Ensign, 28th Regiment	June 17, 1805
Hedges, Samuel P.	Captain, 28th Regiment	June 18, 1807
Henderson, Alexander	Ensign, 12th Regiment	December 5, 1807
Henderson, James	Ensign, 26th Regiment	January 29, 1805
Henderson, James	Lieutenant, 26th Regiment	September 23, 1805
Hendricks, James	Ensign, 7th Regiment	September 23, 1805
Hendricks, James	Ensign, 25th Regiment	July 1, 1808
Hendson, Enos	Ensign, 19th Regiment	March 27, 1808
Henrix, Joseph	Ensign, 20th Regiment	March 5, 1807
Henry, Belfield	Ensign, 16th Regiment	March 14, 1806
Henry, Belfield	Lieutenant, 16th Regiment	August 20, 1808
Henry, Joel	Lieutenant, 11th Regiment	January 19, 1808
Henry, Joel	Captain, 11th Regiment	August 5, 1808
Henry, Vincent	Ensign, 12th Regiment	July 20, 1808
Henson, Benjamin H.	Ensign, 28th Regiment	November 19, 1805
Herndon, Richard	Major, 2nd Battalion, 54th Regiment	January 26, 1809
Herndon, Richardson	Major, 2nd Battalion, 75th Regiment	February 1, 1809
Hesler, Jacob	Ensign, 18th Regiment	May 16, 1805
Hiatt, Elijah	Ensign, 26th Regiment	June 14, 1806
Hibbs, Jonah	Captain, 24th Regiment	February 22, 1806
Hibbs, Jonah	Major, 2nd Battalion, 24th Regiment	December 24, 1809
Hibler, Daniel	Ensign, 14th Regiment	January 29, 1805
Hickinbottom, James	Lieutenant, 9th Regiment	February 22, 1806
Hickland, James	Ensign, 22nd Regiment	December 1, 1807
Hickman, P(aschal?)	Captain, 22nd Regiment	March 24, 1806
Hickman, Thomas	Ensign, 9th Regiment	February 5, 1805
Hicks, Isaac	Captain, 24th Regiment	September 12, 1807
Hicks, John	Ensign, 26th Regiment	July 1, 1808
Higbee, Vincent	Ensign, 9th Regiment	May 26, 1807
Higdon, Thomas, Jr.	Captain, Infantry, 27th Regiment	June 11, 1805

COMMISSIONED OFFICERS, 1805 - 1811

Higdon, Zachariah........	Lieutenant of Infantry, 27th Regiment......................	June 11, 1805
Hill, Ezekiel............	Lieutenant, 13th Regiment........	September 24, 1806
Hill, Joel...............	Ensign, 7th Regiment.............	September 23, 1805
Hill, William............	Ensign, 25th Regiment............	July 1, 1808
Hill, William............	Adjutant, 19th Regiment..........	February 3, 1807
Hilless, James...........	Ensign, 14th Regiment............	June 11, 1806
Hillhouse, George........	Lieutenant, 24th Regiment........	August 28, 1805
Hinck, Samuel............	1st Lieutenant in Cavalry, 1st Regiment...................	November 9, 1805
Hinton, William..........	Major, 2nd Battalion, 18th Regiment.......................	March 12, 1807
Hite, Lewis..............	Captain, 1st Regiment............	December 16, 1807
Hites, Jacob.............	Major, 2nd Battalion, 1st Regiment.......................	December 13, 1809
Hoagland, Dorsey.........	Lieutenant, 27th Regiment........	April 1, 1806
Hobdy, John..............	Adjutant, 21st Regiment..........	June 25, 1807
Hockersmith, John........	Ensign, 19th Regiment............	February 3, 1807
Hodge, Andrew............	Major, 2nd Battalion, 31st Regiment.......................	April 14, 1806
Hodge, William...........	Ensign, 6th Regiment.............	August 20, 1808
Hodge, William...........	Ensign, 30th Regiment............	January 30, 1808
Hodges, Thomas...........	Captain, 24th Regiment...........	August 28, 1805
Hogan, David.............	Major, 1st Battalion, 54th Regiment.......................	February 4, 1809
Holbert, John............	Lieutenant, 27th Regiment........	October 14, 1805
Holding, James...........	Ensign, Infantry Company, 12th Regiment.......................	July 13, 1807
Holding, James...........	Lieutenant, 12th Regiment........	December 5, 1807
Holeman, Isaac...........	Captain, 20th Regiment...........	August 28, 1806
Holland, Alland..........	Ensign, 19th Regiment............	February 3, 1807
Hollandsworth, John......	Ensign, 26th Regiment............	September 23, 1805
Hollandsworth, John......	Lieutenant, 26th Regiment........	June 14, 1806
Holliday, John...........	Ensign, 17th Regiment...........	August 20, 1808
Holliday, William........	Lieutenant, Rifle Company, 20th Regiment.......................	August 28, 1806
Holliday, William........	Captain, 20th Regiment...........	June 28, 1808
Holman, Isaac............	Major, 2nd Battalion, 20th Regiment.......................	January 31, 1811
Holmes, James............	Ensign, 18th Regiment............	February 4, 1805
Holmes, Samuel...........	Ensign, 26th Regiment............	June 14, 1806
Holmes, Samuel...........	Captain, 26th Regiment...........	September 12, 1807
Holt, Isaac..............	Ensign, 1st Regiment.............	June 18, 1807
Holt, Isaac..............	Lieutenant, 1st Regiment.........	December 16, 1807
Holton, John.............	Ensign, 22nd Regiment...........	April 4, 1805
Homes, Robert............	Ensign, 1st Regiment.............	June 18, 1807
Homes, Robert M.	Lieutenant, 1st Regiment.........	December 16, 1807
Hook, John...............	Lieutenant Colonel, Commandant 28th Regiment.................	December 29, 1806
Hooten, John.............	Ensign, 19th Regiment............	February 3, 1807
Hooten, John.............	Lieutenant, 19th Regiment........	April 18, 1807

COMMISSIONED OFFICERS, 1805 - 1811

Hopkins, Samuel G.	Major, 1st Battalion, 41st Regiment......................	January 17, 1811
Hopwood, John............	Captain, 19th Regiment...........	February 3, 1807
Hornbeck, John...........	Major, 2nd Battalion, 32nd Regiment......................	December 11, 1811
Hornbeck, John...........	Lieutenant Colonel, Commandant 32nd Regiment.................	December 6, 1811
Hornbeck, Solomon........	Ensign, 14th Regiment............	January 29, 1805
Hosick, William..........	Lieutenant, 19th Regiment........	March 27, 1808
Houston, James...........	Ensign, 2nd Regiment.............	December 16, 1807
Howard, William..........	Lieutenant, 8th Regiment.........	September 17, 1805
Howe, Ezra...............	Ensign, 13th Regiment............	July 2, 1808
Howe, James..............	Major, 1st Battalion, 70th Regiment......................	January 31, 1811
Howel, Charles...........	Lieutenant, 2nd Regiment.........	December 16, 1807
Howell, William..........	Ensign, 20th Regiment............	June 28, 1808
Hoy, Jones...............	Lieutenant, 17th Regiment........	August 20, 1808
Hubbard, Armistead.......	Major, 2nd Battalion, 2nd Regiment......................	February 12, 1806
Hudspeth, George.........	Lieutenant Colonel, Commandant 25th Regiment.................	January 17, 1811
Huff, John...............	Ensign, 28th Regiment............	November 4, 1806
Huff, Jonathan...........	Captain, 5th Regiment............	November 21, 1805
Huffaker, Christopher....	Major, 1st Battalion, 53rd Regiment......................	January 31, 1809
Hughs, John..............	Major, 1st Battalion, 1st Regiment......................	March 30, 1807
Hulse, John..............	Lieutenant, 17th Regiment........	January 30, 1808
	Approved........................	June 25, 1807
Hume, Stripling..........	Lieutenant, Rifle Company, 21st Regiment......................	August 18, 1806
Humes, Prue.	Lieutenant, 21st Regiment........	April 20, 1805
Humes, Pru B.	Captain, 21st Regiment...........	March 14, 1806
Humphres, Thomas.........	Ensign, 3rd Regiment.............	August 8, 1805
Hund, Anthony............	Sergeant, 6th Regiment...........	February 3, 1806
Hungate, John............	Lieutenant Colonel, Commandant 50th Regiment.................	December 7, 1810
Hunt, John...............	Lieutenant Colonel, Commandant 58th Regiment.................	December 29, 1806
Hunter, James............	Cornet, Cavalry, 1st Regiment....	November 9, 1805
Hunter, John.............	Ensign, 10th Regiment............	December 4, 1806
Hunter, John.............	Ensign, 29th Regiment............	June 9, 1806
Hunter, John.............	Lieutenant, 13th Regiment........	May 23, 1807 and March 27, 1808
Hunter, William..........	1st Lieutenant, Troop of Horse, 11th Regiment.................	August 8, 1807
Hunter, William..........	Major, 2nd Battalion, 66th Regiment......................	December 18, 1806
Huston, Robert...........	Adjutant, 3rd Regiment...........	February 5, 1805
Hutchings, John..........	Lieutenant, 6th Regiment.........	September 12, 1807
Hutton, Samuel...........	Captain, 22nd Regiment...........	March 24, 1806

COMMISSIONED OFFICERS, 1805 - 1811

Hyatt, Shadrach..........	Ensign, 13th Regiment............	July 2, 1808
Hykes, Jacob.............	Captain, Rifle Company, 1st Regiment......................	November 4, 1806
Inlow, Isham.............	Lieutenant Colonel, Commandant 60th Regiment.................	February 19, 1808
Innes, Hugh..............	Ensign, 22nd Regiment............	April 4, 1805
Innes, Hugh..............	Lieutenant, 22nd Regiment........	March 24, 1806
Innes, James.............	Lieutenant, 10th Regiment........	September 19, 1806
Ireland, John R.	Captain, 12th Regiment...........	June 12, 1805
Ireland, John R.	Captain, Rifle Company, 12th Regiment......................	December 5, 1807
Ireland, Samuel..........	Major, 1st Battalion, 38th Regiment......................	January 31, 1809
Irvin, John..............	Ensign, 9th Regiment.............	November 7, 1807
Irvine, David C.	Paymaster, 7th Regiment..........	September 24, 1805
Irwin, Benjamin..........	Captain, 3rd Regiment............	March 10, 1805
Irwin, Benjamin..........	Major, 1st Battalion, 3rd Regiment......................	February 19, 1808
Irwin, John..............	Surgeon, 17th Regiment...........	July 1, 1805
Irwine, Benjamin.........	Major, 3rd Regiment..............	November 5, 1807
Isles, Thomas............	Major, 1st Battalion, 65th Regiment......................	January 26, 1810
Jack, James..............	Ensign, 2nd Regiment.............	May 26, 1805
Jackson, David...........	Ensign, 19th Regiment............	November 19, 1805
Jackson, David...........	Lieutenant, 19th Regiment........	February 3, 1807
Jackson, James...........	Captain, 17th Regiment...........	June 11, 1806
James, Ellzey L.	Ensign, 22nd Regiment............	May 3, 1806
Jamison, John............	Major, 2nd Battalion, 34th Regiment......................	December 18, 1806
Jamison, Robert..........	Major, 2nd Battalion, 35th Regiment......................	December 24, 1806
Jecoby (Jacobus), John...	Lieutenant, 13th Regiment........	July 8, 1805
Jecoby (Jacobus), Ralph..	Captain, 13th Regiment...........	July 8, 1805
Jenkins, Hambleton.......	Ensign, 8th Regiment.............	June 2, 1806
Jenkins, Hamilton........	Lieutenant, 8th Regiment.........	May 11, 1807
Jenkins, John............	Ensign, 20th Regiment............	April 14, 1805
Jennings, Daniel.........	Ensign, 9th Regiment.............	November 7, 1807
John, Jonathan...........	Ensign, 12th Regiment............	September 12, 1807
Johnson, Cave............	Lieutenant Colonel, Commandant 67th Regiment.................	December 18, 1806
Johnson, Gabriel J.	Lieutenant Colonel, Commandant 1st Regiment..................	March 9, 1807
Johnson, James...........	Major, 2nd Battalion, 49th Regiment......................	January 31, 1809
Johnson, James...........	Adjutant, 12th Regiment..........	February 11, 1809
Johnson, John............	Ensign, 3rd Regiment.............	June 27, 1806
Johnson, John............	Ensign, 6th Regiment.............	September 12, 1807
Johnson, John............	Ensign, 7th Regiment.............	January 30, 1808
Johnson, John............	Lieutenant, 3rd Regiment.........	November 5, 1807
Johnson, John............	Lieutenant, 6th Regiment.........	August 20, 1808
Johnson, John S.	Ensign, 12th Regiment............	September 12, 1807

COMMISSIONED OFFICERS, 1805 - 1811   181

Johnson, Jonathan........	Captain, 13th Regiment...........	July 8, 1805
Johnson, Richard.........	Captain, 7th Regiment............	July 2, 1807
Johnson, Samuel..........	Major, 1st Battalion, 57th Regiment.......................	December 10, 1811
Johnson, William.........	Major, 2nd Battalion, 12th Regiment.......................	February 11, 1809
Johnson, William.........	Major, 2nd Battalion, 86th Regiment.......................	January 31, 1811
Johnston, Edward.........	Ensign, 26th Regiment............	January 29, 1805
Johnston, Nelson.........	Ensign, Rifle Company, 21st Regiment.......................	August 18, 1806
Johnston, Peter..........	Ensign, 30th Regiment............	March 27, 1805
Johnston, Philip.........	Major, 1st Battalion, 32nd Regiment.......................	December 11, 1811
Johnston, Thomas.........	Cornet, Light Horse Company, 18th Regiment..................	July 11, 1806
Johnston, Thomas.........	2nd Lieutenant, Troop of Cavalry, 18 Regiment....................	December 21, 1807
Jones, Dumas..............	Major, 1st Battalion, 71st Regiment.......................	December 29, 1806
Jones, Dumas..............	Major, 1st Battalion, 86th Regiment.......................	January 31, 1811
Jones, Fielding..........	Major, 1st Battalion, 41st Regiment.......................	July 29, 1807
Jones, Fielding..........	Major, 1st Battalion, 83rd Regiment.......................	January 17, 1811
Jones, Humphrey..........	Lieutenant Colonel, Commandant 7th Regiment...................	September 8, 1806
Jones, James.............	Captain, Rifle Company, 7th Regiment.......................	October 8, 1807
Jones, John..............	Lieutenant, 16th Regiment........	November 25, 1805
Jones, John..............	Captain, 1st Regiment............	June 18, 1807
Jones, Richard...........	Lieutenant, 24th Regiment........	December 8, 1806
Jones, Strother..........	Ensign, 14th Regiment............	October 10, 1808
Jones, William...........	Ensign, Rifle Company, 12th Regiment.......................	December 5, 1807
Jonston, Thomas..........	Lieutenant, 14th Regiment........	January 29, 1805
Jordan, Peter............	Captain, 5th Regiment............	November 4, 1806
Jorden, William..........	Captain, 3rd Regiment............	August 8, 1805
Journey, Nathaniel.......	Major, 2nd Battalion, 46th Regiment.......................	March 6, 1806
Joyes, Thomas............	Ensign, 1st Regiment.............	June 18, 1807
Joyes, Thomas............	Lieutenant, 1st Regiment.........	April 21, 1808
Kauns (Kounce), John.....	Major, 1st Battalion, 70th Regiment.......................	December 13, 1809
Keaton, Hezekiah.........	Captain, 22nd Regiment...........	April 4, 1805
Keith, Thomas............	Lieutenant, 28th Regiment........	June 17, 1805
Keith, Thomas............	Captain, 28th Regiment...........	November 19, 1805
Keith, Thomas............	Captain, 15th Regiment........... (Formerly in 28th Regiment)	September 12, 1807
Keith, Thomas............	Major, 15th Regiment.............	December 13, 1809

Keller, Abraham..........	Ensign, 13th Regiment............	January 11, 1806
Keller, Abraham..........	Lieutenant,1st Regiment..........	May 26, 1808
Keller, Isaac............	Lieutenant, 22nd Regiment........	July 14, 1807
Kelley, Joseph...........	Ensign, 30th Regiment............	August 28, 1806 and February 3, 1807
Kelly, William...........	Ensign, 15th Regiment............	June 17, 1805
Kemp, Edward.............	Lieutenant, 21st Regiment........	August 20, 1808
Kemper, Thomas...........	Lieutenant, 20th Regiment........	August 28, 1806
Kenady, Eli..............	Lieutenant, 14th Regiment........	June 23, 1806
Kenard, William..........	Ensign, 29th Regiment............	October 8, 1807
Kenard, William..........	Lieutenant, 29th Regiment........	July 20, 1808
Kendall, Jacob...........	Ensign, 2nd Regiment.............	May 26, 1805
Kendrick, Alexander......	Captain, 6th Regiment............	August 20, 1808
Kennady, James...........	Lieutenant, 6th Regiment.........	September 12, 1807
Kennard, William.........	Captain, 15th Regiment...........	June 17, 1805
Kennedy, Eli.............	Lieutenant, 14th Regiment........	January 24, 1807
Kennedy, John............	Ensign, 21st Regiment............	August 20, 1808
Kennedy, John............	Captain, 26th Regiment...........	September 23, 1805
Kenyan, Henry............	Ensign, 15th Regiment............	September 12, 1807
Kenyan, Henry............	Adjutant, 15th Regiment..........	September 12, 1807
Kertly, Pleasant.........	Major, 1st Battalion, 16th Regiment......................	December 11, 1811
Key, Marshall............	Lieutenant, 15th Regiment........	June 17, 1805
Kincaid, James...........	Lieutenant Colonel, Commandant 68th Regiment.................	December 18, 1806
Kindred, Bartholemy......	Lieutenant, 9th Regiment.........	August 28, 1805
King, Abner..............	Adjutant, 27th Regiment..........	May 2, 1808
King, Ibzan..............	Ensign, 5th Regiment.............	October 15, 1807
King, John...............	Captain, 20th Regiment...........	April 14, 1805
King, Robert.............	Ensign, 6th Regiment.............	August 20, 1808
King, Robert.............	Ensign, 20th Regiment............	February 22, 1806
Kinkead, James...........	2nd Lieutenant, Troop of Horse, 11th Regiment...................	August 8, 1807
Kinon, John..............	Ensign, 26th Regiment............	June 14, 1806
Kircheval, Thomas........	Ensign, 29th Regiment............	May 6, 1806
Kirtley, Elliott.........	Lieutenant, 11th Regiment........	August 8, 1807
Kirtly, Elliott..........	Captain, 11th Regiment...........	September 15, 1807
Kirtly, Pleasant.........	Lieutenant, 16th Regiment........	December 8, 1806
Kirtly, Pleasant.........	Captain, 16th Regiment...........	November 5, 1807
Kiser, Adam..............	Ensign, 8th Regiment.............	June 2, 1806
Kounce, Jacob............	Major, 1st Battalion, 70th Regiment.........................	December 29, 1806
Kutch, John..............	Ensign, 6th Regiment.............	February 3, 1806
Lacey, Edward, Jr.	1st Major, 24th Regiment.........	December 8, 1806
Lacey, Joshua............	Paymaster, 24th Regiment.........	August 28, 1805
Lackey, Alexander........	Major, 1st Battalion, 56th Regiment......................	December 16, 1805
Lacy, Thomas.............	Lieutenant, Infantry Company, 25th Regiment...................	December 24, 1806
Laird, Samuel............	Lieutenant, 10th Regiment........	December 6, 1805
Lamb, Basil..............	Lieutenant, 29th Regiment........	October 8, 1807

COMMISSIONED OFFICERS, 1805 - 1811

Lancaster, John..........	Ensign, 9th Regiment.............	February 5, 1805
Lancaster, Ralph.........	Lieutenant, 27th Regiment........	November 5, 1807
Lander, Henry............	Ensign, 14th Regiment............	January 30, 1808
Landers, John............	Ensign, 4th Regiment.............	June 23, 1806
Landrith, James..........	Ensign, 23rd Regiment............	February 5, 1805
Lane, Moses..............	Captain, 27th Regiment...........	April 1, 1806
Langhorn, Maurice........	Captain, 14th Regiment...........	June 11, 1806
Langhorn, Maurice........	(Captain) to command the Paris Light Infantry Company, 14th Regiment......................	October 10, 1808
Lanham, Stephen..........	Ensign, 7th Regiment.............	June 18, 1807
Lanier, Alexander........	Captain, 21st Regiment...........	March 14, 1806
Lanier, Alexander C. ...	Lieutenant, 21st Regiment........	April 20, 1805
Lapsley, John............	Lieutenant, 26th Regiment........	September 12, 1807
Larue, Samuel............	Major, 1st Battalion, 60th Regiment......................	January 25, 1811
Lastley, John............	Ensign, 17th Regiment............	August 20, 1808
Latham, Phillip..........	Lieutenant, Infantry Company, 23rd Regiment.................	August 11, 1806
Laton, James.............	Ensign, 26th Regiment............	January 29, 1805
Laughlin, John W.	Captain, Troop of Horse, 8th Regiment......................	June 2, 1806
Laughlin, Thomas.........	Lieutenant Colonel, Commandant 75th Regiment.................	February 1, 1809
Laws, William............	Ensign, 12th Regiment............	December 5, 1807
Lawson, William..........	Lieutenant Colonel, Commandant 52nd Regiment.................	September 19, 1805
Lawyers, John............	Major, 1st Battalion, 79th Regiment......................	January 23, 1810
Lay, George..............	Ensign, 10th Regiment............	December 4, 1806
Leace, George............	Ensign, 18th Regiment............	February 9, 1807
Leace, George............	Lieutenant, 18th Regiment........	May 20, 1807
Leathers, John...........	Major, 1st Battalion, 48th Regiment......................	December 10, 1811
Lee, Ambrose.............	Quartermaster, 6th Regiment......	June 10, 1806
Lee, John................	Ensign, 27th Regiment............	June 11, 1805
Lee, John................	Captain, 15 Regiment.............	November 4, 1805
Lee, Samuel..............	Captain, 5th Regiment............	April 14, 1805
Lemon, David.............	Ensign, 20th Regiment............	June 22, 1805
Lemon, John..............	Captain, 2nd Regiment............	May 26, 1805
Lenear, Collins..........	Captain, 25th Regiment...........	July 19, 1805
Leright, Minor...........	Ensign, 3rd Regiment.............	August 20, 1806
Levil, James.............	Ensign, 7th Regiment.............	June 18, 1807
Levil, James.............	Lieutenant, 7th Regiment.........	July 2, 1807
Lewis, Andrew P.	Ensign, 5th Regiment.............	November 4, 1806
Lewis, Daniel............	Captain, 27th Regiment...........	October 14, 1805
Lewis, Joseph............	Lieutenant Colonel, Commandant 63rd Regiment.................	May 9, 1806
Lewis, Joshua............	Lieutenant, Rifle Company, 9th Regiment......................	February 5, 1805
Lewis, Robert............	Lieutenant, 6th Regiment.........	February 3, 1806

COMMISSIONED OFFICERS, 1805 - 1811

Lewis, Robert T.	Captain, 6th Regiment	August 20, 1808
Lewis, William	Colonel, Commandant, 9th Regiment	February 10, 1809
Lincoln, Thomas	Ensign, 3rd Regiment	September 17, 1805
Lindsay, Anthony	Captain, 12th Regiment	February 3, 1807
Lindsey, Elisha	Ensign, 18th Regiment	February 4, 1805
Lindsey, Joshua	Major, 1st Battalion, 72nd Regiment	December 31, 1811
Linsey, Thomas	Ensign, 14th Regiment	October 10, 1808
Linsy, James	Ensign, 20th Regiment	August 28, 1806
Lipscomb, Nathan	Major, 2nd Battalion, 35th Regiment	December 10, 1811
Littlepage, Eppes	Major, 1st Battalion, 40th Regiment	December 13, 1809
Lockridge, James	Captain, 13th Regiment	May 23, 1807
Logan, Alexander	Ensign, 12th Regiment	December 13, 1805
Logan, John	Ensign, 13th Regiment	May 23, 1807 and March 27, 1808
Loofbouron, Thomas V.	Ensign, 22nd Regiment	December 1, 1807
Love, Arthur	Lieutenant, 24th Regiment	September 12, 1807
Love, Joseph	Ensign, 18th Regiment	February 9, 1807
Love, William	Ensign, 24th Regiment	September 12, 1807
Lovelas, Archibald	Ensign, 23rd Regiment	November 4, 1806
Lowe, Barney	Lieutenant, 25th Regiment	July 1, 1808
Lowery, John	Ensign, Rifle Company, 9th Regiment	February 5, 1805
Lowery, William G.	Major, 2nd Battalion, 30th Regiment	July 13, 1807
Lowman, Joseph	Ensign, Light Infantry Company, 1st Regiment	November 9, 1805
Lowry, Samuel	Major, 1st Battalion, 12th Regiment	February 28, 1805
Lowry, William G.	Major, 2nd Battalion, 30th Regiment	August 7, 1807
Lucas, Charles	Cornet, 8th Regiment	July 2, 1806
Lurty, William	Ensign, 15th Regiment	September 12, 1807
Luves (Love), Thomas	Lieutenant, 23rd Regiment	August 11, 1806
McAfee, Clark	Ensign, 5th Regiment	April 14, 1805
McAfee, Clark	Lieutenant, 5th Regiment	November 21, 1805
McAfee, George	Captain, 5th Regiment	April 14, 1805
McAfee, Robert	Captain, 5th Regiment	April 14, 1805
McAfee, Robert B.	Captain, 5th Regiment	November 21, 1805
McAfee, Robert B.	Judge Advocate, 5th Regiment	October 15, 1807
McBride, William	Paymaster, 5th Regiment	December 11, 1806
McCalla, Thomas	Ensign, 1st Regiment	May 31, 1806
McCallen, Haze	Lieutenant, 30th Regiment	August 8, 1805
McCambell, Andrew	Ensign, 18th Regiment	November 19, 1805
McCann, Neal	Captain, 8th Regiment	June 2, 1806
McCarty, James	Captain, 3rd Regiment	November 5, 1807
McClanahan, Elijah	Major, 1st Battalion, 21st Regiment	December 22, 1806

McCleland, James.........	Lieutenant Colonel, Commandant 47th Regiment..................	December 10, 1811
McClelland, James........	Major, 1st Battalion, 47th Regiment......................	December 13, 1809
McClenahan, William......	Lieutenant, 13th Regiment........	March 27, 1808
McClure, James...........	Ensign, 20th Regiment............	June 22, 1805
McColgan, James..........	Major, 2nd Battalion, 46th Regiment......................	January 17, 1811
McConnell, Edward........	Lieutenant Colonel, Commandant 71st Regiment..................	December 29, 1806
McConnell, John..........	Ensign, 27th Regiment............	April 1, 1806
McCoun, George...........	Major, 2nd Battalion, 39th Regiment......................	February 19, 1808
McCuddy, Isaac...........	Lieutenant, 11th Regiment........	June 17, 1805
McCuddy, Isaac...........	Captain, 11th Regiment...........	July 10, 1806
McDavett, James..........	Lieutenant Colonel, Commandant 37th Regiment..................	January 5, 1811
McDowel (?), James.......	Ensign, 13th Regiment............	July 8, 1805
McDowel, James...........	Lieutenant, 13th Regiment........	January 11, 1806
McDowel, Joseph..........	Lieutenant, 28th Regiment........	November 4, 1806
McDowell, John G.	Major, 2nd Battalion, 69th Regiment......................	January 18, 1811
McDowell, Samuel.........	Lieutenant, 10th Regiment........	October 4, 1808
McElroy, John............	Ensign, 25th Regiment............	July 1, 1808
McFadin, Elias...........	Cornet, Horse Company, 25th Regiment......................	July 19, 1805
McFarlane, Jonathan......	Lieutenant, 25th Regiment........ (McFadin in Warren County tax lists)	July 19, 1805
McGary, Daniel...........	Major, 1st Battalion, 76 th Regiment......................	February 2, 1809
McGary, William R.	Major, 1st Battalion, 76th Regiment......................	December 13, 1809
McGee, John..............	Ensign, 5th Regiment.............	November 21, 1805
McGoodin, Daniel.........	Lieutenant Colonel, Commandant 23rd Regiment..................	January 31, 1811
McGoodwin, Daniel........	Major, 1st Battalion, 23rd Regiment......................	December 18, 1806
McGrady, Samuel..........	Lieutenant Colonel, Commandant 49th Regiment..................	February 17, 1808
McHatton, Samuel.........	Ensign, 12th Regiment............	September 12, 1807
McIlvain, Robert.........	Ensign, 15th Regiment............	October 2, 1806
McIlvain, William........	Ensign, 11th Regiment............	July 10, 1806
McIlvain, William........	Lieutenant, 11th Regiment........	September 15, 1807
McIntire, Joseph.........	Lieutenant Colonel, Commandant 30th Regiment..................	December 16, 1805
McKee, John..............	Captain, 29th Regiment...........	November 22, 1805
McKenney, John...........	Ensign, 16th Regiment............	December 8, 1806
McKeown, Morgan..........	Lieutenant, 1st Regiment.........	February 2 and November 9, 1805
McKinney, Francis........	Lieutenant, 13th Regiment........	July 8, 1805
McKinney, James..........	Ensign, 13th Regiment............	July 8, 1805

COMMISSIONED OFFICERS, 1805 - 1811

McKinney, James..........	Major, 2nd Battalion, 63rd Regiment......................	December 31, 1811
McLaflin, John...........	Captain, 26th Regiment..........	January 29, 1805
McLaughlin, John.........	1st Lieutenant, Troop of Horse, 8th Regiment..................	June 11, 1805
McLaughlin, John.........	Captain, 21st Regiment..........	April 18, 1807
McLaughlin, Robert K. ..	Ensign, 21st Regiment...........	August 20, 1808
McLenagan (McClannahan), William ...	Captain, 13th Regiment.	July 2, 1808
McMahan, James...........	Lieutenant, 20th Regiment.......	July 29, 1807
McMahan, Joseph..........	Lieutenant, 17th Regiment.......	July 1, 1805
McMahan, William.........	Ensign, 17th Regiment...........	July 1, 1805
McMillin, John...........	Captain, 23rd Regiment..........	August 11, 1806
McMurtrey, Levi..........	Ensign, 10th Regiment...........	March 2, 1807
McMurtry, William........	Ensign, 12th Regiment...........	July 7,* 1806
McMurtry, William........	Lieutenant, 12th Regiment.......	April 18, 1807
McNeil, John.............	2nd Lieutenant, Horse Company, 25th Regiment.................	July 19, 1805
McWilliams, James........	Lieutenant, 19th Regiment.......	September 12, 1807
McWilliams, James........	Captain, 19th Regiment..........	February 3, 1807
McWilliams, John.........	Ensign, 19th Regiment...........	September 12, 1807
Macconnell, Robert.......	Lieutenant, 1st Regiment........	June 18, 1807
Mackoy, James............	Lieutenant, 15th Regiment.......	September 12, 1807
Madcalf, Thomas..........	Captain, 13th Regiment..........	March 27, 1808
Madden, John.............	Ensign, 30th Regiment...........	August 8, 1805
Maddon, Jeremiah.........	Lieutenant, 30th Regiment.......	February 3, 1807
Maginnis, William........	Lieutenant, 13th Regiment.......	January 11, 1806
Mahan, John..............	Lieutenant Colonel, Commandant 43rd Regiment.................	February 19, 1808
Malin, Jacob.............	Ensign, 27th Regiment...........	November 5, 1807
Malott, Hiram............	Lieutenant, 1st Regiment........	December 16, 1807
Malott, Hiram............	Captain, 1st Regiment...........	April 21, 1808
Mann, John...............	Ensign, 21st Regiment...........	April 18, 1807
Mann, John T.	Captain, 21st Regiment..........	April 20, 1805
Mann, Peter..............	Ensign, 28th Regiment...........	November 4, 1806
Mann, Richard............	Ensign, 21st Regiment...........	April 20, 1805
Mann, Richard Y.	Lieutenant, 21st Regiment.......	April 18, 1807
Maple, Benjamin..........	Lieutenant, 28th Regiment.......	June 17, 1805
Maple, Benjamin..........	Captain, 28th Regiment..........	October 2, 1806
Maple, Benjamin..........	Captain, 15th Regiment.......... (Originally in 28th Regiment)	September 12, 1807
Marks, George............	Captain, 27th Regiment..........	October 14, 1805
Markwell, Elias..........	Ensign, 1st Regiment............	November 4, 1806
Marshal, Joseph..........	Ensign, Rifle Company, 16th Regiment......................	November 25, 1805
Martin, Henry............	Ensign, 11th Regiment...........	June 17, 1805
Martin, Hugh.............	Ensign, Rifle Company, 28th Regiment......................	November 19, 1805
Martin, Hugh.............	Captain, 28th Regiment..........	June 18, 1807
Martin, Jeremiah.........	Major, 1st Battalion, 15th Regiment......................	December 13, 1809

COMMISSIONED OFFICERS, 1805 - 1811   187

Martin, Jeremiah.........	Lieutenant Colonel, Commandant 15th Regiment..................	December 10, 1811
Martin, John.............	Major, 1st Battalion,17th Regt...	December 7, 1810
Martin, Micajah..........	Lieutenant, 15th Regiment........	October 2, 1806
Martin, Nathan...........	Lieutenant, 7th Regiment.........	September 23, 1805
Martin, Thomas...........	Ensign, 16th Regiment............	November 25, 1805
Martin, Thomas...........	Lieutenant Colonel, Commandant 37th Regiment..................	March 18, 1808 and January 31, 1809
Martin, William..........	Captain, Rifle Company, 20th Regiment.......................	August 28, 1806
Mason, Benjamin..........	Lieutenant, 13th Regiment........	May 23, 1807
Mason, James.............	Major, 1st Battalion, 31st Regiment.......................	December 15, 1810
Mason, Richard...........	Lieutenant, 6th Regiment.........	February 3, 1806
Mason, Richard...........	1st Lieutenant, 6th Regiment.....	August 20, 1808
Mason, William...........	Major, 1st Battalion, 27th Regiment.......................	August 31, 1805
Mastin, William..........	Lieutenant, 22nd Regiment........	April 4, 1805
Mattingly, John..........	Lieutenant, 4th Regiment.........	June 23, 1806
Mattock, James...........	Ensign, 28th Regiment............	June 17, 1805
Maupin, Richard A.	Lieutenant, 1st Regiment.........	June 18, 1807
Maupin, Richard A.	Cornet, Troop of Cavalry, 1st Regiment.......................	December 16, 1807
Maupin, Thomas...........	Captain, 19th Regiment...........	April 18, 1807
May, Stephen.............	Lieutenant, 27th Regiment........	October 14, 1805
Mayberry, John...........	Major, 1st Battalion, 72nd Regiment.......................	June 7, 1811
Meadows, William.........	Lieutenant, 17th Regiment........ Approved....................	January 30, 1808 June 25, 1807
Meason, Benjamin.........	Lieutenant, 2nd Regiment.........	April 23, 1808
Medcalf, John............	Ensign, 18th Regiment............	July 20, 1808
Meeks, Sylvester.........	Ensign, 3rd Regiment.............	November 5, 1807
Menefee, Jarret..........	Ensign, 6th Regiment.............	February 3, 1806
Meranda, Thomas..........	Lieutenant, 28th Regiment........	October 2, 1806
Meredith, William P. ...	Ensign, 11th Regiment............	January 19, 1808
Meredith, William P. ...	Lieutenant, 11th Regiment........	August 5, 1808
Merrell, William.........	Ensign, 10th Regiment............	October 4, 1808
Merritt, John............	Ensign, 26th Regiment............	June 14, 1806
Metcalf, Orrick..........	Ensign, Paris Company, 14th Regiment.......................	July 20, 1808
Metcalf, Thomas..........	Major, 2nd Battalion, 13th Regiment.......................	January 25, 1811
Metts, Jacob.............	Lieutenant, 20th Regiment........	April 14, 1805
Middleton, Adam..........	Ensign, 18th Regiment............	July 20, 1808
Middleton, David.........	Ensign, 18th Regiment............	May 16, 1805
Milam, Moses.............	Ensign, 18th Regiment............	July 20, 1808
Miles, Charles...........	Ensign, 20th Regiment............	July 29, 1807
Miles, John, Jr.	Ensign, 18th Regiment............	February 9, 1807
Miles, Thomas............	Ensign, 27th Regiment............	April 1, 1806
Miles, William...........	Ensign, 18th Regiment............	September 3, 1808

COMMISSIONED OFFICERS, 1805 - 1811

Miller, Adam...............	Lieutenant, 20th Regiment........	February 22, 1806
Miller, Adam...............	Captain, 20th Regiment...........	July 29, 1807
Miller, Dr. Alexander....	Surgeon, 7th Regiment............	February 3, 1807
Miller, Henry.............	Ensign, 12th Regiment............	April 9, 1805
Miller, Isaac.............	Adjutant, 20th Regiment..........	September 19, 1805
Miller, Isaac.............	1st Lieutenant, "Choir of Light Horse," 20th Regiment..........	November 5, 1807
Miller, Jacob.............	1st Lieutenant, Cavalry Company, 12th Regiment..................	April 9, 1805
Miller, Jacob.............	Lieutenant, 2nd Regiment.........	May 26, 1805
Miller, Jacob.............	Captain, 2nd Regiment............	September 12, 1807
Miller, James.............	Cornet, "Choir of Light Horse," 20th Regiment..................	November 5, 1807
Miller, John..............	Ensign, 7th Regiment.............	September 23, 1805
Miller, John..............	Lieutenant, 7th Regiment.........	November 4, 1806 and February 3, 1807
Miller, John..............	Major, 1st Battalion, 20th Regiment.......................	January 30, 1809
Miller, John..............	Major, 2nd Battalion, 77th Regiment.......................	February 11, 1809
Miller, Peter.............	Ensign, 1st Regiment.............	April 21, 1808
Miller, Robert............	Major, 2nd Battalion, 7th Regiment.......................	December 22, 1805
Miller, Thomas............	Captain, Rifle Company, 7th Regiment.......................	September 23, 1805
Miller, William...........	Ensign, 6th Regiment.............	June 10, 1806
Miller, William...........	Lieutenant, 6th Regiment.........	August 20, 1808
Mills, Richard............	Captain, 1st Regiment............	May 31, 1806
Milspaw, Daniel G.	Ensign, 23rd Regiment............	December 22, 1807
Minor, John S.............	Lieutenant, 12th Regiment........	February 3, 1807
Mitcham, William..........	Ensign, 11th Regiment............	August 8, 1807
Mitcham, William..........	Lieutenant, 11th Regiment........	August 5, 1808
Mitchell, James...........	Captain, 26th Regiment...........	January 29, 1805
Mitchell, John A.	Adjutant, 22nd Regiment..........	February 18, 1806
Mitchell, John A.	Lieutenant, Light Infantry Company, 22nd Regiment.........	April 25, 1806
Mitchell, Richard D.	Ensign, 12th Regiment............	February 3, 1807
Mitchell, Dr. Samuel G...	Surgeon, 13th Regiment...........	February 3, 1806
Modrill, Robert...........	Lieutenant Colonel, Commandant 44th Regiment.................	February 19, 1808
Moffat, John..............	Major, 1st Battalion, 28th Regiment.......................	December 29, 1806
Monroe, William...........	Lieutenant, 9th Regiment.........	April 9, 1806
Montgomery, William.......	Ensign, 27th Regiment............	November 5, 1807
Montjoy, George...........	Captain, 13th Regiment...........	July 8, 1805
Montjoy, William..........	Lieutenant Colonel, Commandant 21st Regiment.................	December 22, 1806
Moody, William............	Ensign, 12th Regiment............	July 20, 1808
Moor, Henry...............	Captain, 17th Regiment...........	April 26, 1808
Moor, John................	Ensign, 1st Regiment.............	December 16, 1807
Moor, Levy................	Captain, 28th Regiment...........	November 4, 1806

COMMISSIONED OFFICERS, 1805 - 1811

Moore, George E.	Lieutenant, 15th Regiment	June 17, 1805
Moore, Harbin	Paymaster, 28th Regiment	May 14, 1807
Moore, Harbin	Quartermaster, 28th Regiment	January 9, 1808
Moore, James	Lieutenant, 13th Regiment	September 24, 1806
Moore, James	Quartermaster, 19th Regiment	March 27, 1808
Moore, John	Ensign, 10th Regiment	December 4, 1806
Moore, Leroy	Major, 1st Battalion, 28th Regiment	December 7, 1810
Moore, Martin	Ensign, 8th Regiment	September 17, 1805
Moore, Martin	Lieutenant, 8th Regiment	June 2, 1806
Moore, Samuel	Lieutenant Colonel, Commandant 13th Regiment	December 29, 1806
Moore, William	Ensign, 20th Regiment	April 14, 1805
Moore, Zachariah	Major, 2nd Battalion, 48th Regiment	January 31, 1809
Morfett, George	Captain, 10th Regiment	May 15, 1806
Morgan, David	Lieutenant Colonel, Commandant 56th Regiment	December 16, 1805
Morris, James	Lieutenant, 21st Regiment	April 20, 1805
Morris, James	Captain, 21st Regiment	April 18, 1807
Morris, Thomas	Lieutenant, 14th Regiment	January 24, 1807
Morris, William	Ensign, 11th Regiment	June 17, 1805
Morrison, David	Ensign, 20th Regiment	July 29, 1807
Morrow, Robert	Lieutenant, 14th Regiment	January 30, 1808
Morrow, Thomas F.	Ensign, 17th Regiment	April 26, 1808
Mosby, John	Major, 2nd Battalion, 11th Regiment	December 18, 1806
Moseby, Nicholas, Jr.	Ensign, 11th Regiment	April 13, 1807
Mosely, Daniel P.	Major, 2nd Battalion, 34th Regiment	January 10, 1811
Mountague, Thomas	Ensign, 22nd Regiment	December 1, 1807
Mountjoy, George	Major, 2nd Battalion, 71st Regiment	January 31, 1811
Mountjoy, John	Ensign, 21st Regiment	April 20, 1805
Mullins, Reuben	Lieutenant, 21st Regiment	March 14, 1806
Mullins, Reuben	Captain, 21st Regiment	April 14, 1808
Muncey, John	Major, 2nd Battalion, 54th Regiment	February 1, 1809
Munroe, William	Lieutenant, 21st Regiment	March 14, 1806
Murfey, William	Ensign, 6th Regiment	February 3, 1806
Murphree, Isaac	Ensign, 25th Regiment	July 19, 1805
Murrel, James	Lieutenant, 6th Regiment	June 10, 1806
Murry, Enoch	Lieutenant, 27th Regiment	October 14, 1805
Musick, Ephraim	Ensign, 7th Regiment	February 3, 1807
Myers, Henry	Lieutenant, Rifle Company, 23rd Regiment	December 22, 1807
Myers, Jacob	Ensign, 19th Regiment	April 18, 1807
Myres, Joseph	Lieutenant, 21st Regiment	August 20, 1808
Nafus, George	Captain, 2nd Regiment	May 26, 1805
Nagly, David	Lieutenant, 5th Regiment	April 14, 1805

Nall, John	Major, 1st Battalion, 4th Regiment	March 31, 1807
Nash, Marvell	Ensign, 6th Regiment	February 3, 1806
Neely, Edward	Captain, 23rd Regiment	August 11, 1806
Nelson, Andrew	Ensign, 26th Regiment	September 23, 1805
Nelson, Andrew	Lieutenant, 26th Regiment	September 12, 1807
Nelson, John	Lieutenant, Light Infantry Company, 1st Regiment	November 9, 1805
Nelson, Richard	Major, 2nd Battalion, 48th Regiment	December 10, 1811
Nesbet, Jeremiah	Lieutenant, 13th Regiment	January 11, 1806
Nesbet, Joseph Mc.	Ensign, 13th Regiment	September 24, 1806
Nettles (Nuttles), Price.	Captain, 18th Regiment	December 21, 1807
Nevill, Joseph	Major, 2nd Battalion, 2nd Regiment	February 4, 1809
Nevitt (Nevill?), Joseph.	Lieutenant Colonel, Commandant 2nd Regiment	December 19, 1810
New, Robert A.	Captain, Light Infantry Company, 1st Regiment	November 9, 1805
Nichols, Simon	Ensign, 21st Regiment	March 14, 1806
Nickson, John	Lieutenant, 15th Regiment	November 4, 1805
Nixon, Samuel	Lieutenant, 2nd Regiment	May 26, 1805
Nixon, Samuel	Captain, 2nd Regiment	May 15, 1806
Noland, James	Lieutenant, 17th Regiment	October 2, 1806
Nolin, (Turner?)	Captain, 17th Regiment	August 20, 1808
Norris, Benjamin	Ensign, 28th Regiment	October 2, 1806
Norris, Benjamin	Ensign, 15th Regiment (Originally in 28th Regiment)	September 12, 1807
Norris, James	Lieutenant, 28th Regiment	October 2, 1806
Norris, James	Lieutenant, 15th Regiment (Originally in 28th Regiment)	September 12, 1807
Norris, Thomas	Lieutenant, 28th Regiment	November 19, 1805
North, Henry	Ensign, 20th Regiment	July 29, 1807
Norwood, Frederick	Ensign, 11th Regiment	August 5, 1808
Nowell (Noel), Barnett	Ensign, 5th Regiment	November 4, 1806
Nowell (Noel), Barnett	Lieutenant, 5th Regiment	October 15, 1807
Nowls, William	Ensign, 15th Regiment	September 12, 1807
Nunn, Samuel	Major, 1st Battalion, 24th Regiment	January 26, 1811
Nuttles, Price	Ensign, 18th Regiment	July 11, 1806
Nuttles, Price	Lieutenant, 18th Regiment	February 9, 1807
Ogle, John	Ensign, 13th Regiment	January 11, 1806
Oldham, John P.	Quartermaster, 23rd Regiment	May 30, 1807
Oldham, Richard	Ensign, 1st Regiment	May 31, 1806
Oldham, Richard	Lieutenant, 1st Regiment	June 18, 1807
Olvy (Alvey), Bennett	Ensign, 4th Regiment	June 23, 1806
Ormsby, Peter B.	2nd Lieutenant of Cavalry, 1st Regiment	November 9, 1805
Overturf, Conrad	Captain, 28th Regiment	June 17, 1805
Overturf, Conrad	Lieutenant Colonel, Commandant 28th Regiment	January 26, 1811

COMMISSIONED OFFICERS, 1805 - 1811

Owen, John	Ensign, 17th Regiment	January 30, 1808
Owen, Reubin	Major, 2nd Battalion, 76th Regiment	December 13, 1809
Owens, Abraham	Lieutenant Colonel, Commandant 18th Regiment	March 10, 1808 and January 31, 1809
Owens, Maximilian	Surgeon, 15th Regiment	September 12, 1807
Oxen, Nathan	Major, 2nd Battalion, 56th Regiment	December 13, 1809
Oxley, Micajah	Captain, 10th Regiment	October 4, 1808
Page, John	Captain, Rifle Company, 19th Regiment	September 13, 1805
Pairpoint, Jeremiah	Captain, 3rd Regiment	May 24, 1806
Palmer, Henry	Major, 1st Battalion, 5th Regiment	December 15, 1806
Palsgrove, Henry	Ensign, 21st Regiment	August 20, 1808
Parker, Lamuel	Ensign, 14th Regiment	January 30, 1808
Parker, Rowland	Ensign, 13th Regiment	July 8, 1805
Parker, Samuel	Major, 2nd Battalion, 64th Regiment	May 9, 1806
Parker, William	Lieutenant, 29th Regiment	October 8, 1807
Parks, John	Ensign, 6th Regiment	February 3, 1806
Parks, Nathan	Major, 2nd Battalion, 78th Regiment	January 23, 1810
Parmerlee (no first name given)	Ensign, 6th Regiment	February 3, 1806
Parmerly, Samuel	Ensign, 24th Regiment	August 28, 1805
Parrish, Thompson	Lieutenant, 8th Regiment	June 11, 1805
Parrish, Woodson	Lieutenant, 21st Regiment	March 14, 1806
Parrot, Richard	Ensign, 4th Regiment	June 23, 1806
Parrot, William	Lieutenant, 4th Regiment	June 23, 1806
Parrott, William	Captain, 4th Regiment	January 9, 1808
Paton, John	Ensign, 19th Regiment	July 19, 1805
Patten, Thomas	Ensign, 3rd Regiment	November 5, 1807
Patten, William, Jr.	Ensign, 6th Regiment	February 3, 1806
Patterson, Joseph	Lieutenant, 10th Regiment	March 2, 1807
Patterson, Joseph	Captain, 10th Regiment	October 4, 1808
Patterson, William	Major, 1st Battalion, 37th Regiment	March 18, 1808 and January 31, 1809
Patton, Abraham	Lieutenant, Rifle Company, 19th Regiment	September 13, 1805
Patton, James	Captain, 30th Regiment	August 28, 1806
Patton, James	Major, 2nd Battalion, 30th Regiment	December 6, 1811
Patton, Thomas	2nd Lieutenant, 30th Regiment	January 30, 1808
Paxton, John	Major, 2nd Battalion, 63rd Regiment	May 9, 1806
Paxton, John	Lieutenant Colonel, Commandant, 63rd Regiment	December 7, 1810
Payne, Asa	Ensign, Rifle Company, 12th Regiment	July 13, 1807

COMMISSIONED OFFICERS, 1805 - 1811

Payne, Jammy	Paymaster, 10th Regiment	September 30, 1807
Payne, John	Ensign, 4th Regiment	June 23, 1806
Payne, John	Lieutenant, 4th Regiment	January 9, 1808
Payne, William R.	Captain, 25th Regiment	January 21, 1805
Payton, Bluford	Ensign, 6th Regiment	June 10, 1806
Pearce, James	Lieutenant, 6th Regiment	February 3, 1806
Peck, Jacob	Lieutenant, 30th Regiment	March 27, 1805
Pemberton, John	Ensign, 22nd Regiment	March 24, 1806
Peniston, Samuel	Ensign, 9th Regiment	May 26, 1807
Penix, Edward	Lieutenant, 6th Regiment	December 8, 1806
Penn, Ely	Ensign, 14th Regiment	October 10, 1808
Pennington, Francis P.	Lieutenant Colonel, Commandant 39th Regiment	January 25, 1811
Pennington, Tobias	Ensign, 10th Regiment	September 19, 1806
Peper, Israel	Ensign, 15th Regiment	November 4, 1805
Pepper, Elijah	Ensign, 12th Regiment	April 9, 1805
Pepper, Elijah	Lieutenant, 12th Regiment	July 7, 1806
Pepper, Elijah	Captain, 12th Regiment	April 18, 1807
Perkins, Edmond	Major, 1st Battalion, 57th Regiment	December 13, 1809
Perrin, Josephus	Major, 2nd Battalion, 20th Regiment	December 16, 1805
Perrin, Josephus	Lieutenant Colonel, Commandant 86th Regiment	January 31, 1811
Peterson, Garret	Captain, 4th Regiment	June 23, 1806
Philips, David	Ensign, 4th Regiment	January 24, 1807
Phillips, William	Lieutenant, 4th Regiment	June 23, 1806
Phillips, William	Captain, 4th Regiment	January 24, 1807
Pickett, John	Lieutenant Colonel, Commandant 15th Regiment	August 28, 1806
Pile, Thomas	2nd Lieutenant, Cavalry Company, 16th Regiment	November 5, 1807
Plummer, Benjamin	Major, 2nd Battalion, 58th Regiment	December 28, 1808
Poage, John	Lieutenant Colonel, Commandant 70th Regiment	December 29, 1806
Poage, Robert	Lieutenant Colonel, Commandant 29th Regiment	December 16, 1805
Polk, James	Lieutenant, 2nd Regiment	May 26, 1805
Pollock, James	Captain, 13th Regiment	September 24, 1806
Poole, William	Lieutenant, 27th Regiment	November 5, 1807
Poole, William	Captain, 27th Regiment	June 28, 1808
Porter, Andrew	Lieutenant Colonel, Commandant 20th Regiment	January 27, 1809
Porter, John	Major, 1st Battalion, 66th Regiment	December 18, 1806
Porter, John	Lieutenant Colonel, Commandant 66th Regiment	December 29, 1806
Porter, Roley	Ensign, 29th Regiment	October 8, 1807
Posey, John	Ensign, 23rd Regiment	December 22, 1807
Pottorff, Jacob	Ensign, 1st Regiment	November 9, 1805

COMMISSIONED OFFICERS, 1805 - 1811

Potts, Jonathan..........	Major, 2nd Battalion, 61st Regiment......................	December 13, 1809
Potts, Jonathan..........	Lieutenant Colonel, Commandant 61st Regiment..................	December 20, 1811
Powell, John.............	Ensign, 13th Regiment............	July 2, 1808
Prater, Thomas...........	Ensign, 28th Regiment............	January 9, 1808
Prather, William.........	Lieutenant, 5th Regiment.........	November 21, 1805
Preston, Francis.........	Ensign, Rifle Company, 8th Regiment......................	June 11, 1805
Prewitt, William.........	Ensign, 8th Regiment.............	September 11, 1806
Price, Andrew F.	Captain, 8th Regiment............	May 16, 1808
Price, James.............	Ensign, 20th Regiment............	June 28, 1808
Price, James C.	Captain, Rifle Company, 9th Regiment......................	February 22, 1806 and May 26, 1807
Price, Reason............	Lieutenant, 2nd Regiment.........	May 26, 1805
Price, Richard...........	Lieutenant, 22nd Regiment........	July 14, 1807
Price, Richard...........	Captain, 22nd Regiment...........	June 1, 1808
Price, William...........	Major, 2nd Battalion, 26th Regiment......................	January 25, 1811
Price, William B.	Captain, Rifle Company, 10th Regiment......................	March 2, 1807
Price, Willis............	Ensign, Rifle Company, 10th Regiment......................	July 2, 1807
Proctor, Jeremiah........	Lieutenant, 26th Regiment........	January 29, 1805
Proctor, John............	Lieutenant, 23rd Regiment........	December 22, 1807
Proctor, Thomas..........	Major, 2nd Battalion, 23rd Regiment......................	August 11, 1806
Proctor, William.........	Lieutenant, 26th Regiment........	March 22, 1805
Protzman, Jacob..........	Ensign, 2nd Regiment.............	April 23, 1808
Pullum, Benjamin.........	Captain, 25th Regiment...........	July 19, 1805
Pullum, Burwell..........	Ensign, 25th Regiment............	July 19, 1805
Putman, Daniel...........	Captain, 25th Regiment...........	March 2, 1808
Quarles, Roger...........	Major, 2nd Battalion, 10th Regiment......................	January 30, 1809
Quigley, Lewis...........	Lieutenant, 2nd Regiment.........	September 11, 1806
Quigley, Lewis...........	Captain, 2nd Regiment............	March 3, 1807
Radford, William.........	Ensign, 18th Regiment............	November 19, 1805
Railsback, Daniel........	Lieutenant, 17th Regiment........	July 1, 1805
Rankin, Simeon...........	Ensign, 20th Regiment............	June 22, 1805
Rankin, Simeon...........	Lieutenant, 20th Regiment........	August 28, 1806
Raper, Charles...........	Ensign, 2nd Regiment.............	May 26, 1805
Rapier, Charles..........	Lieutenant, 2nd Regiment.........	May 15, 1806
Ratcliff, Joseph.........	Lieutenant, 11th Regiment........	April 13, 1807
Ratliff, Joseph..........	Ensign, 11th Regiment............	January 24, 1807
Ray, Absalom.............	Lieutenant, 4th Regiment.........	June 23, 1806
Ray, Samuel..............	Captain, 4th Regiment............	June 23, 1806
Reavis, Charles..........	Captain, 25th Regiment...........	March 2, 1808
Records, William.........	Ensign, 15th Regiment............	September 12, 1807
Redd, Thomas.............	Ensign, 20th Regiment............	June 22, 1805
Redd, Thomas.............	Lieutenant, 20th Regiment........	March 5, 1807

COMMISSIONED OFFICERS, 1805 - 1811

Redding, Eli	Ensign, 11th Regiment	October 5, 1808
Redman, Thomas	Ensign, 23rd Regiment	December 22, 1807
Reed, Alexander	Ensign, 26th Regiment	July 1, 1808
Reed, Handherson, Jr.	Ensign, 11th Regiment	August 5, 1808
Reed, James	Ensign, 26th Regiment	September 12, 1807
Reed, John	Ensign, Rifle Company, 23rd Regiment	November 4, 1806
Reed, John	Lieutenant, 15th Regiment	September 12, 1807
Reed, John	Lieutenant, 26th Regiment	September 12, 1807
Reed, Thomas B.	Lieutenant, 2nd Regiment	December 16, 1807
Reed, William	Ensign, 1st Regiment	May 31, 1806
Reed, William	Lieutenant, 29th Regiment	June 9, 1806
Reed, William	Major, 2nd Battalion, 29th Regiment	December 16, 1805
Rees, David	Lieutenant, 20th Regiment	March 5, 1807
Rees, David	Captain, 20th Regiment	June 28, 1808
Reese, Jonathan	Ensign, 15th Regiment	October 2, 1806
Reeves, Joseph	Lieutenant, 30th Regiment	January 30, 1808
Reeves, William	Lieutenant, 20th Regiment	June 28, 1808
Reid, John	Ensign, 26th Regiment (Nominated)	October 9, 1808
Rennick, Henry	Lieutenant Colonel, Commandant 45th Regiment	December 9, 1806
Rentfro, Absalom	Ensign, 6th Regiment	June 10, 1806
Respass, Robert	Captain, 10th Regiment	May 15, 1806
Rhodes, Bennett	Ensign, 4th Regiment	June 23, 1806
Richards, Ambrose R.	Ensign, 25th Regiment	July 19, 1805
Richards, William	Lieutenant, 13th Regiment	July 2, 1808
Richardson, Dr. William C.	Surgeon, 12th Regiment	September 5, 1806
Richeson, Thomas	Ensign, 16th Regiment	December 8, 1806
Richey, Elijah	Lieutenant, 12th Regiment	September 12, 1807
Richey, John	Major, 1st Battalion, 46th Regiment	January 17, 1811
Richey, Stephen	Ensign, 12th Regiment	July 13, 1807
Richie, James	Lieutenant, 10th Regiment	May 15, 1806
Richie, Stephen	Captain, 12th Regiment	July 20, 1808
Rife, Christopher	Colonel, Commandant, 74th Regiment	February 2, 1809
Rigg, John	Lieutenant, 5th Regiment	November 4, 1806
Riker, Samuel	Ensign, 18th Regiment	October 6, 1807
Rinarson, Christopher	Lieutenant, 6th Regiment	February 3, 1806
Rinarson, Christopher	Captain, 6th Regiment	June 10, 1806
Ripley, Richard	Ensign, 19th Regiment	June 18, 1807
Risk, John	Ensign, 12th Regiment	February 3, 1807
Rob, Thomas	Captain, 4th Regiment	June 23, 1806
Robards, William	Ensign, 9th Regiment	August 28, 1805
Roberts, Elisha	Captain, 25th Regiment	July 19, 1805
Roberts, Handley	Lieutenant, 13th Regiment	May 23, 1807
Roberts, John	Major, 2nd Battalion, 39th Regiment	December 16, 1805
Robertson, Fleming	Major, 2nd Battalion, 50th Regiment	December 24, 1809
Robertson, Littleton	Captain, 20th Regiment	July 29, 1807

COMMISSIONED OFFICERS, 1805 - 1811　　　　　　　　　　195

Robeson, William.........	Lieutenant, 22nd Regiment........	September 12, 1807
Robinson, Edward.........	Major, 2nd Battalion, 55th Regiment......................	December 6, 1811
Robinson, George.........	Captain, 12th Regiment..........	June 12, 1805
Robinson, James..........	Ensign, 22nd Regiment...........	March 24, 1806
Robinson, William........	Ensign, 22nd Regiment...........	April 4, 1805
Rodgers, William C.	Captain, 24th Regiment..........	June 12, 1806
Roe, Thomas..............	Cornet, 17th Regiment...........	January 30, 1808
	Approved......................	June 25, 1807
Rogers, George...........	Ensign, 18th Regiment...........	February 9, 1807
Rogers, George...........	Lieutenant, 18th Regiment.......	July 23, 1808
Rogers, John.............	Lieutenant, 2nd Regiment........	May 26, 1805
Rogers, John.............	Captain, 2nd Regiment...........	May 15, 1806
Ross, James..............	Ensign, 2nd Regiment............	May 26, 1805
Ross, James..............	Lieutenant, 2nd Regiment........	May 15, 1806
Ross, Presley............	Lieutenant, Rifle Company, 1st Regiment..................	November 4, 1806
Rowland, Reuben..........	Lieutenant, 4th Regiment........	June 23, 1806
Rowlings, Edward.........	Captain, 3rd Regiment...........	September 17, 1805
Rucker, Reuben...........	Major, 2nd Battalion, 70th Regiment......................	December 29, 1806
Ruddell, Stephen.........	Ensign, 11th Regiment...........	June 17, 1805
Ruddell, Stephen.........	Lieutenant, 11th Regiment.......	July 10, 1806
Runion, David............	Lieutenant, 30th Regiment.......	August 8, 1805
Rush, Thomas.............	Ensign, 21st Regiment...........	March 14, 1806
Rush, Thomas.............	Lieutenant, 21st Regiment.......	April 14, 1808
Russell, Samuel..........	Major, 1st Battalion, 40th Regiment......................	January 31, 1809
Russell, Thomas..........	Ensign, 6th Regiment............	December 8, 1806
St. Clair, William.......	Ensign, 12th Regiment...........	July 13, 1807
Salley, William..........	Lieutenant, Rifle Company, 9th Regiment...................	February 22, 1806
Salley, William..........	Ensign, Rifle Company, 9th Regiment......................	May 26, 1807
Salley, William..........	Ensign, 19th Regiment...........	June 18, 1807
Samuel, Reubin...........	Lieutenant, 22nd Regiment.......	June 1, 1808
Sander, Henry............	Lieutenant, Infantry Company, 14th Regiment..................	January 24, 1807
Sanders, Reymon..	Ensign, 10th Regiment...........	December 4, 1806
Sanders, William.........	Captain, 21st Regiment..........	April 20, 1805
Saunders, John...........	Ensign, 22nd Regiment...........	April 4, 1805
Saunders, Rayman........,..	Lieutenant, Rifle Company, 10th Regiment......................	July 2, 1807
Sayers, John.............	Lieutenant, 6th Regiment........	February 3, 1806
Schooler, Nathan.........	Lieutenant, 19th Regiment.......	February 3, 1807
Scirvin, Clayton.........	Lieutenant, 21st Regiment.......	August 20, 1808
Scissell, James..........	Ensign, 2nd Regiment............	May 15, 1806
Scott, John..............	Lieutenant, 20th Regiment.......	July 8, 1805
Scott, Robert............	Ensign, 14th Regiment...........	April 30, 1808
Scott, Robert............	Lieutenant, 14th Regiment.......	October 10, 1808
Scott, Robert............	Captain, 4th Regiment...........	June 23, 1806

COMMISSIONED OFFICERS, 1805 - 1811

Scott, Robert............	Paymaster, 14th Regiment.........	July 20, 1808
Scott, Thomas............	Ensign, 20th Regiment............	February 22, 1806
Scott, Thomas............	Captain, 20th Regiment...........	July 29, 1807
Scott, Thomas B.	Lieutenant, 9th Regiment.........	February 5, 1805
Scott, Thomas B.	Captain, 9th Regiment............	February 22, 1806
Scott, Thomas B.	Paymaster, 9th Regiment..........	May 26, 1807
Scott, William...........	Ensign, 9th Regiment.............	August 28, 1805
Scott, William...........	Lieutenant, 14th Regiment........	June 11, 1806
Scott, William...........	2nd Lieutenant, 6th Regiment.....	August 20, 1808
Scott, William...........	Lieutenant, Paris Light Infantry Company, 14th Regiment.........	October 10, 1808
Scott, William...........	Major, 1st Battalion, 33rd Regiment.......................	January 31, 1809
Scrogham, Joseph.........	Captain, 8th Regiment............	June 2, 1806
Searcey, Berry...........	Captain, Rifle Company, 22nd Regiment.......................	December 1, 1807
Seaton, James............	Lieutenant, 1st Regiment.........	February 2 and November 9, 1805
Sebree, Uriel............	Major, 2nd Battalion, 67th Regiment.......................	December 18, 1806
Senter, James............	Ensign, 6th Regiment.............	September 12, 1807
Shackleford, James.......	Captain, 29th Regiment...........	October 8, 1807
Shackleford, Robert......	Lieutenant, 18th Regiment........	May 16, 1805
Shackleford, Samuel......	Paymaster, 6th Regiment..........	June 10, 1806
Shackleford, Thomas......	Captain, 6th Regiment............	September 12, 1807
Shadburn, William........	Ensign, 1st Regiment.............	February 2, 1805
Shadburn, William........	Lieutenant, 1st Regiment.........	June 18, 1807
Shadwell, William........	Paymaster, 29th Regiment.........	August 27, 1806
Shanacy, William.........	Lieutenant, 2nd Regiment.........	September 12, 1807
Shanklin, John...........	Captain, 30th Regiment...........	March 25, 1806
Shanks, Thomas...........	Lieutenant, 18th Regiment........	December 21, 1807
Shanucy, William.........	Ensign, 2nd Regiment.............	May 26, 1805
Sharp, James.............	Lieutenant, 16th Regiment........	November 5, 1807
Shaver, Benjamin.........	Lieutenant, 3rd Regiment.........	March 10, 1805
Shealds, William.........	Lieutenant, 28th Regiment........	November 4, 1806
Shelby, James............	Captain, 8th Regiment............	June 2, 1806
Shelby, James............	Major, 1st Battalion, 8th Regiment.......................	December 7, 1810
Shelton, Curtis..........	Ensign, 9th Regiment.............	February 5, 1805
Shelton, Liberty.........	Ensign, 6th Regiment.............	September 12, 1807
Shelton, Medley..........	Lieutenant, 12th Regiment........	April 18, 1807
Shelton, Thomas..........	Captain, 19th Regiment...........	February 3, 1807
Shelton, Thomas..........	Major, 2nd Battalion, 79th Regiment.......................	January 23, 1810
Shepard, John............	Ensign, 11th Regiment............	September 15, 1807
Shewmate, Nimrod.........	Ensign, 3rd Regiment.............	March 10, 1805
Shields, William.........	Lieutenant, 15th Regiment........ (Originally in 28th Regiment)	September 12, 1807
Shipman, William.........	Ensign, 18th Regiment............	May 16, 1805
Shipman, William.........	Captain, 18th Regiment...........	September 17, 1806
Shirley, Charles.........	Major, 80th Regiment.............	January 17, 1811

COMMISSIONED OFFICERS, 1805 - 1811   197

Shively, Philip..........	Captain, 1st Regiment............	June 18, 1807
Shoptaw, William.........	Lieutenant, 27th Regiment........	April 1, 1806
Shortridge, George.......	Lieutenant, 14th Regiment........	June 11, 1806
Shortridge, George.......	Captain, 14th Regiment...........	June 28, 1808
Simalt (Zumalt), Philip..	Ensign, 20th Regiment............	June 28, 1808
Simmons, Joseph..........	Ensign, 3rd Regiment.............	March 10, 1805
Simpson, Joseph..........	Major, 2nd Battalion, 37th Regiment......................	March 12, 1807
Simpson, Thomas..........	Ensign, 27th Regiment............	October 14, 1805
Simpson, William.........	Lieutenant, Infantry Company, 16th Regiment.................	November 25, 1805
Simpson, William.........	Lieutenant, 6th Regiment.........	June 10, 1806
Simpson, William.........	Major, 1st Battalion, 10th Regiment......................	January 30, 1809
Simrall, James...........	Captain, Light Horse Company, 18th Regiment.................	July 11, 1806
Simrall, James...........	Major, 1st Squadron of Cavalry, 2nd Brigade...................	December 10, 1811
Simrall, William F.	Major, Commandant, Squadron of Cavalry, 2nd Brigade..........	January 25, 1811
Sims, Randol.............	Ensign, Rifle Company, 7th Regiment......................	October 8, 1807
Singleton, Jechonias.....	Major, 2nd Battalion, 11th Regiment......................	January 31, 1809
Singleton, Mason.........	Lieutenant, 9th Regiment.........	February 5, 1805
Singleton, Philip........	Major, 1st Battalion, 68th Regiment......................	January 17, 1811
Singleton, Philip........	Lieutenant Colonel, Commandant 68th Regiment.................	December 31, 1811
Singleton, Richard.......	Lieutenant, 6th Regiment.........	February 3, 1806
Sinks, Jacob.............	Ensign, 21st Regiment............	April 18, 1807
Skinner, Theophelus......	Major, 1st Battalion, 72nd Regiment......................	February 19, 1808
Skinner, Theophelus......	Lieutenant Colonel, Commandant 72nd Regiment.................	December 10, 1811
Slack, Randolph..........	Lieutenant, 3rd Regiment.........	August 8, 1805
Slaughter, John H.	Cornet, Troop of Cavalry, 22nd Regiment......................	December 1, 1807
Sleet, Weeden............	Major, 2nd Battalion, 67th Regiment......................	December 10, 1811
Small, Henry.............	Captain, 29th Regiment...........	May 6, 1806
Smith, George............	Major, 1st Battalion, 71st Regiment......................	December 29, 1806
Smith, John..............	Ensign, 3rd Regiment.............	June 27, 1806
Smith, John..............	Ensign, 13th Regiment............	May 23, 1807
Smith, John..............	Ensign, 27th Regiment............	November 5, 1807 and May 2, 1808
Smith, John..............	Ensign, 30th Regiment............	January 30, 1808
Smith, John..............	Lieutenant, 1st Regiment.........	May 31, 1806
Smith, John..............	Lieutenant, 3rd Regiment.........	November 5, 1807
Smith, John..............	Lieutenant, 13th Regiment........	March 27, 1808

Smith, John..............	Captain, 1st Regiment............	June 18, 1807
Smith, John B.	Lieutenant, Horse Company, 25th Regiment......................	July 19, 1805
Smith, John B.	Captain, 25th Regiment...........	July 1, 1808
Smith, Jonathan..........	Lieutenant, 23rd Regiment........	November 4, 1806
Smith, Thomas............	Lieutenant, 24th Regiment........	September 12, 1807
Smith, Thomas............	Major, 16th Regiment.............	September 19, 1805
Smith, Weathers..........	Lieutenant, 14th Regiment........	January 24, 1807
Smith, William...........	Cornet, Cavalry Company, 12th Regiment.................	July 7, 1806
Smith, William...........	Lieutenant Colonel, Commandant 79th Regiment..................	January 23, 1810
Smithey, Fielding........	Ensign, 10th Regiment...........	July 8, 1805 and October 4, 1808
Smock, Henry.............	Lieutenant Colonel, Commandant 4th Regiment...................	April 3, 1806
Snap, Lewis..............	Ensign, 3rd Regiment.............	September 17, 1805
Sneed, John..............	Ensign, 2nd Regiment............	December 16, 1807
Sneed, John..............	Lieutenant, 2nd Regiment........	May 15, 1806
Snell, John..............	Lieutenant, 18th Regiment........	February 9, 1807
Snoddy, John.............	Major, 19th Regiment.............	June 18, 1807
Snoddy, Samuel...........	Lieutenant Colonel, Commandant 19th Regiment.................	December 16, 1805
Snodgrass, David.........	Major, 1st Battalion, 66th Regiment.................	December 10, 1811
Snodgrass, Samuel........	Ensign, 20th Regiment...........	July 8, 1805
Snodgrass, Samuel........	Lieutenant, 20th Regiment.......	July 29, 1807
South, Benjamin..........	Lieutenant Colonel, Commandant 34th Regiment.................	December 18, 1806
South, Weldon............	Major, 2nd Battalion, 47th Regiment......................	January 5, 1811
Southerland, John........	Major, 2nd Battalion, 2nd Regiment......................	December 7, 1810
Soward, Richard..........	Major, 1st Battalion, 69th Regiment......................	January 18, 1811
Spalding, Richard........	Ensign, 4th Regiment............	June 23, 1806
Spalding, Thomas.........	Lieutenant, 4th Regiment........	June 23, 1806
Sparks, Thomas...........	Ensign, 22nd Regiment...........	July 14, 1807
Spears, Samuel...........	Lieutenant, 16th Regiment.......	August 20, 1808
Speed, John..............	Lieutenant, 6th Regiment........	June 10, 1806
Spencer, Bernard.........	Ensign, 21st Regiment...........	April 20, 1805
Spencer, Bernard.........	Captain, 21st Regiment..........	March 14, 1806
Spergeon, Moses..........	Ensign, 30th Regiment...........	April 18, 1807
Spratt, William..........	Ensign, 6th Regiment............	February 3, 1806
Stafford, Thomas.........	Lieutenant, 1st Regiment........	November 4, 1806
Standeford, Elisha.......	Lieutenant, 1st Regiment........	May 31, 1806
Stapleton, George........	Ensign, 8th Regiment............	May 11, 1807
Stapp, Elijah............	Ensign, 12th Regiment...........	July 13, 1807
Stark, David.............	Ensign, 29th Regiment...........	November 22, 1805
Stark, David.............	Lieutenant, 29th Regiment.......	May 6, 1806
Stephens, Joseph.........	Lieutenant, 19th Regiment.......	November 19, 1805

COMMISSIONED OFFICERS, 1805 - 1811 199

Stephenson, Benjamin	Adjutant, 23rd Regiment	October 28, 1807
Stephenson, John	Ensign, 5th Regiment	November 21, 1805
Stephenson, John	Captain, 29th Regiment	July 20, 1808
Stephenson, Joseph H.	Captain, 19th Regiment	April 18, 1807
Stephenson, William	Lieutenant, 12th Regiment	October 2, 1806
Sterman, Thomas I.	Ensign, 7th Regiment	June 18, 1807
Stevens, John	Lieutenant, 10th Regiment	March 2, 1807
Stevenson, William	Captain, 20th Regiment	March 5, 1807
Stewart, Christopher P.	Major, 2nd Battalion, 48th Regiment	December 22, 1806
Stewart, Elijah	Major, 1st Battalion, 39th Regiment	February 19, 1808
Stewart, James	Ensign, 21st Regiment	April 20, 1805
Stewart, James	Lieutenant, 21st Regiment	March 14, 1806
Stewart (?), William	Lieutenant, 13th Regiment	July 8, 1805
Stith, Joseph	Adjutant, 3rd Regiment	November 5, 1807
Stockton, John	Captain, Rifle Company in Flemingsburg, 30th Regiment	August 8, 1805
Stockton, John	Captain, Rifle Company, 30th Regiment	August 28, 1806
Stone, Jesse	Captain, 27th Regiment	May 2, 1808
Stone, John	Lieutenant, Rifle Company, 12th Regiment	December 5, 1807
Stotts, James	Major, 1st Battalion, 75th Regiment	December 7, 1810
Stowers, William	Quartermaster, 21st Regiment	June 25, 1807
Stratton, Aron	Major, 2nd Battalion, 15th Regiment	December 16, 1805
Stratton, Aron	Lieutenant Colonel, Commandant 69th Regiment	December 29, 1806
Stratton, Henry	Lieutenant Colonel, Commandant 56th Regiment	December 28, 1808
Stroud, Thomas P.	Ensign, Rifle Company, 23rd Regiment	February 5, 1805
Sutherland, John, Jr.	Major, 2nd Battalion, 2nd Regiment	January 22, 1811
Sutherlin, John, Jr.	Captain, 2nd Regiment	December 16, 1807
Sutphin, John	Ensign, 12th Regiment	December 13, 1805
Suttles, Edward	Lieutenant, 29th Regiment	October 8, 1807
Sutton, James	Major, 1st Battalion, 63rd Regiment	December 13, 1809
Sutton, Thomas	Ensign, 23rd Regiment	December 22, 1807
Swan, John	Ensign, Rifle Company, 12th Regiment	July 13, 1807
Swank, Jacob	Captain, 3rd Regiment	November 5, 1807
Swenk, Jacob	Lieutenant, 3rd Regiment	March 10, 1805
Sweny, Job	Captain, 6th Regiment	December 8, 1806
Swetnam, George	Captain, 12th Regiment	April 18, 1807
Swiget, James	Lieutenant, 6th Regiment	December 8, 1806
Swiggitt, James	Captain, 6th Regiment	September 12, 1807
Swiney, Jobe	Ensign, 6th Regiment	February 3, 1806

COMMISSIONED OFFICERS, 1805 - 1811

Swinney, Henry	Captain, 18th Regiment	February 4, 1805
Talbert, Gazaway	Ensign, 12th Regiment	October 2, 1806
Talbot, Thomas	Ensign, 1st Regiment	November 9, 1805
Talbott, Nicholas	Lieutenant, 14th Regiment	July 20, 1808
Talbut, William	Ensign, 2nd Regiment	September 12, 1807
Taliafero, John C.	Ensign, 28th Regiment	January 9, 1808
Tandy, William	Major, 2nd Battalion, 39th Regiment	January 25, 1811
Tarlton, Ralph	Lieutenant, 12th Regiment	July 20, 1808
Tate, Isaac	Adjutant, 16th Regiment	September 5, 1805
Tatem, Seewood (?)	Ensign, 19th Regiment	July 19, 1805
Taul, Micah	Major, 2nd Battalion, 53rd Regiment	December 13, 1809
Taul, Samuel	Ensign (?), 8th Regiment	September 11, 1806
Taylor, Edmond	Major, 2nd Battalion, 48th Regiment	December 13, 1809
Taylor, George	Captain, 30th Regiment	August 8, 1805
Taylor, James	Lieutenant, Rifle Company, 12th Regiment	February 3, 1807
Taylor, James	Lieutenant Colonel, Commandant 48th Regiment	July 17, 1806
Taylor, John	Captain, 30th Regiment	March 25, 1806
Taylor, Jonathan	Major, 1st Battalion, 33rd Regiment	March 26, 1807
Taylor, Nathan	Captain, 1st Regiment	February 2 and November 9, 1805
Taylor, Robert	Ensign, 26th Regiment	September 12, 1807
Taylor, Dr. Septemus	Surgeon, 20th Regiment	June 22, 1805
Taylor, Simon	Ensign, 14th Regiment	October 10, 1808
Taylor, William	Ensign, 20th Regiment	April 14, 1805
Teeter, George	Ensign, 26th Regiment	March 22, 1805
Temple, Robert (W.?)	Ensign, 23rd Regiment	August 11, 1806
Tendley, Charles	Captain, 4th Regiment	June 23, 1806
Tensly, William	Ensign, 6th Regiment	August 20, 1808
Terrill, John	Lieutenant, 26th Regiment	June 14, 1806
Terrill, Robert L.	Major, 1st Battalion, 81st Regiment	January 17, 1811
Thomas, John	Ensign, 9th Regiment	February 22, 1806
Thomas, John	Lieutenant, 9th Regiment	May 26, 1807
Thomas, John D.	Cornet, Troop of Horse, 8th Regiment	June 11, 1805
Thomas, Joseph	Ensign, 3rd Regiment	March 10, 1805
Thomas, Joseph	Captain, 5th Regiment	April 14, 1805
Thomas, Joseph	Captain, 14th Regiment	April 30, 1808
Thomas, Notley	Lieutenant, 20th Regiment	March 5, 1807
Thomas, Obediah	Lieutenant, 6th Regiment	August 20, 1808
Thomas, Reuben	Ensign, 6th Regiment	February 3, 1806
Thompson, Daniel	Ensign, 13th Regiment	March 27, 1808
Thompson, Daniel	Ensign, Infantry Company, 28th Regiment	October 2, 1806
Thompson, David	Major, 12th Regiment	December 29, 1806

Thompson, David.........	Lieutenant Colonel, Commandant 12th Regiment.................	December 7, 1810
Thompson, George B.	Captain, 28th Regiment..........	November 4, 1806
Thompson, George B.	Major, 1st Battalion, 28th Regiment.....................	January 26, 1811
Thompson, George W.	Captain, 5th Regiment...........	October 15, 1807
Thompson, John..........	Lieutenant Colonel, Commandant 12th Regiment.................	July 16, 1806
Thompson, Samuel........	Captain, 5th Regiment...........	April 14, 1805
Thompson, Samuel........	Captain, 20th Regiment..........	April 14, 1805
Thompson, Samuel........	Major, 1st Battalion, 73rd Regiment.....................	January 31, 1809
Thomson, David..........	Lieutenant Colonel, Commandant 12th Regiment.................	March 7, 1811
Thrailkel, Daniel.......	Lieutenant, 28th Regiment.......	November 4, 1806
Thrailkell, John........	Lieutenant, 18th Regiment.......	July 20, 1808
Thrasher, Stephen.......	Major, 2nd Battalion, 21st Regiment.....................	December 22, 1806
Throckmorton, Aris......	Ensign, 13th Regiment...........	July 2, 1808
Throgmorton, Ariss......	Ensign, 13th Regiment...........	May 23, 1807
Throgmorton, Thomas.....	Adjutant, 13th Regiment.........	March 27, 1808
Timberlake, Henry.......	Ensign, 14th Regiment...........	June 23, 1806
Timberlake, Henry.......	Ensign, Paris Light Infantry Company, 14th Regiment........	October 10, 1808
Tipton, Moses...........	Ensign, 7th Regiment............	September 23, 1805
Titus, John.............	Captain, 19th Regiment..........	April 18, 1807
Todd, Benjamin..........	Captain, 13th Regiment..........	January 11, 1806
Todd, Daniel............	Ensign, 8th Regiment............	September 17, 1805
Todd, David.............	Captain, 8th Regiment...........	February 3, 1806
Todd, Davis.............	Ensign, 7th Regiment............	January 30, 1808
Tolbert, Samuel.........	Lieutenant, 14th Regiment.......	June 11, 1806
Tolbott, Nicholas.......	Lieutenant, 14th Regiment.......	October 10, 1808
Tomason, Joseph T.	Ensign, 12th Regiment...........	July 13, 1807
Trammell, John..........	Lieutenant, 18th Regiment.......	November 19, 1805
Trigg, Stephen..........	Captain, 17th Regiment..........	August 20, 1808
Trigg, Stephen..........	Lieutenant Colonel, Commandant 78th Regiment.................	January 23, 1810
Trimble, John...........	Lieutenant, Paris Militia Company, 14th Regiment........	July 20, 1808
Trotter, George, Jr. ...	Lieutenant Colonel, Commandant 42nd Regiment.................	March 2, 1805
Trotter, William........	Ensign, 22nd Regiment...........	July 14, 1807
Tucker, Ed.	Ensign, 13th Regiment...........	January 11, 1806
Tucker, Edward..........	Ensign, 28th Regiment...........	November 4, 1806
Tunstall, Henry.........	Adjutant, 22nd Regiment.........	March 7, 1806
Tunstall, William J. ...	Quartermaster, 18th Regiment....	March 11, 1808
Turner, Nelson..........	Lieutenant, 10th Regiment.......	August 8, 1805
Tuttle, William.........	Captain, 17th Regiment..........	June 11, 1806
Tylor, Levi.............	Ensign, 1st Regiment............	April 21, 1808
Uncell, Henry...........	Ensign, 2nd Regiment............	December 16, 1807
Vancleave, Benjamin.....	Ensign, 18th Regiment...........	July 3, 1805

COMMISSIONED OFFICERS, 1805 - 1811

Vancleave, Samuel	Lieutenant, 18th Regiment	July 3, 1805
Vancleve, Peter	Ensign, 18th Regiment	May 20, 1807
Vanderon, Godfrey	Captain, 20th Regiment	March 5, 1807
Vatner, Daniel	Paymaster, 15th Regiment	September 12, 1807
Vaughtier, -ehemen (Hayman Vawter)	Lieutenant, 20th Regiment	June 28, 1808
Vawter, Jameson	Lieutenant, 11th Regiment	January 19, 1808
Vawter, William	Lieutenant Colonel, Commandant 11th Regiment	December 18, 1806
Vemount, Louis	Lieutenant, 13th Regiment	September 24, 1806
Vertresse, Jacob	Lieutenant, 3rd Regiment	March 10, 1805
Vertresse, John	Captain, 3rd Regiment	March 10, 1805
Viers, Robert	Ensign, 15th Regiment	October 2, 1806
Vitetow, James	Ensign, 2nd Regiment	September 11, 1806
Vowls, Thomas	Lieutenant, 2nd Regiment	September 11, 1806
Waddle, Charles	Lieutenant, 25th Regiment	July 19, 1805
Wade, Dawson	Major, 1st Battalion, 34th Regiment	December 18, 1806
Wade, William	Captain, 6th Regiment	February 3, 1806
Waggoner, John	Lieutenant Colonel, Commandant 83rd Regiment	January 17, 1811
Wakefield, William	Major, 2nd Battalion, 62nd Regiment	December 22, 1805
Walingford, Joseph	Lieutenant, 30th Regiment	July 13, 1807
Walker, David V.	Captain, 19th Regiment	June 18, 1807
Walker, John	Lieutenant, 30th Regiment	March 27, 1805
Walker, John	Captain, 30th Regiment	August 28, 1806
Walker, John W.	Adjutant, 7th Regiment	May 2, 1808
Walker, Patterson	Ensign, 5th Regiment	November 21, 1805
Walker, Richard	Ensign, 3rd Regiment	September 17, 1805
Walker, William	Major, 2nd Battalion, 69th Regiment	December 29, 1806
Wall, Garrett	Captain, Rifle Company, 20th Regiment	August 20, 1808
Wallace, Andrew	Major, 2nd Battalion, 14th Regiment	December 10, 1811
Wallace, John	Ensign, 8th Regiment	February 3, 1806
Wallace, John	Captain, 20th Regiment	August 28, 1806
Wallace, Thomas	Lieutenant, 28th Regiment	June 17, 1805
Waller, John	Ensign, 29th Regiment	October 8, 1807
Waller, William S.	1st Lieutenant, Troop of Cavalry, 22nd Regiment	December 1, 1807
Wallingford, John	Ensign, 30th Regiment	January 30, 1808
Walton, Thomas	Ensign, 13th Regiment	January 11, 1806
Warden, John	Ensign, 23rd Regiment	February 5, 1805
Ware, Thompson	Captain, 13th Regiment	July 8, 1805
Warfield, Dr. Nicholas	Surgeon, 14th Regiment	August 11, 1806
Waters, Richard	Lieutenant, 1st Regiment	April 21, 1808
Watkins, Joseph	Ensign, 11th Regiment	October 5, 1808
Watson, David	Cornet, Troop of Horse, 8th Regiment	June 2, 1806

COMMISSIONED OFFICERS, 1805 - 1811

Weagle, John.............	Ensign, 7th Regiment.............	June 28, 1808
Weatherington, David.....	Lieutenant, 28th Regiment........	November 19, 1805
Weatherington, Joseph....	Captain, 28th Regiment...........	November 19, 1805
Weathers, Carland........	Lieutenant, 6th Regiment.........	February 3, 1806
Weathers, Gideon.........	Ensign, 3rd Regiment.............	August 20, 1806
Weathers, Gideon.........	Captain, 3rd Regiment............	February 3, 1807
Weathers, James..........	Quartermaster, 6th Regiment......	February 3, 1806
Weaver, Philip...........	Lieutenant Colonel, Commandant 58th Regiment...................	December 28, 1808
Webb, John V.	Major, 2nd Battalion, 12th Regiment.......................	July 30, 1806
Webb, John V.	Colonel, Commandant, 77th Regiment.......................	February 11, 1809
Webber, Archer...........	Lieutenant, 9th Regiment.........	May 26, 1807
Webber, William..........	Ensign, 18th Regiment............	July 11, 1806
Weller, Henry............	Ensign, Rifle Company, 2nd Regiment.......................	September 11, 1806
Weller, Henry............	Lieutenant, 2nd Regiment.........	December 16, 1807
Wells, Francis...........	Captain, 28th Regiment...........	November 4, 1806
Wells, James.............	Quartermaster, 28th Regiment.....	May 14, 1807
Wells, Micajah...........	Major, 2nd Battalion, 82nd Regiment.......................	January 17, 1811
Wells, Samuel............	Ensign, 29th Regiment............	July 20, 1808
West, Alexander..........	Major, 2nd Battalion, 53rd Regiment.......................	January 31, 1809
West, Lynn...............	Ensign, "Georgetown Blues," 12th Regiment..................	February 3, 1807
Whealer, George F.	Ensign, 21st Regiment............	March 14, 1806
Whealey, James...........	2nd Lieutenant, Troop of Horse, 8th Regiment...................	June 2, 1806
Wheeler, Hezekiah........	Captain, 21st Regiment...........	April 18, 1807
Wheeler, Ignatius........	Ensign, 21st Regiment............	March 14, 1806
Wheeler, Ignatius, Jr....	Lieutenant, 21st Regiment........	April 18, 1807
While (Wiley?), Samuel...	Captain, 18th Regiment...........	May 16, 1805
White, Hugh..............	Major, 1st Battalion, 68th Regiment.......................	December 18, 1806
White, Hugh..............	Lieutenant Colonel, Commandant 68th Regiment...................	February 1, 1808
White, John B.	Ensign, 22nd Regiment............	December 1, 1807
White, Leonard...........	Lieutenant, Light Infantry Town Company, 23rd Regiment.........	February 5, 1805
White, Philip............	Major, 2nd Battalion, 22nd Regiment.......................	January 1, 1810
White, Samuel............	Major, 2nd Battalion, 18th Regiment.......................	December 10, 1811
White, Thomas............	Ensign, 9th Regiment.............	April 9, 1806
White, Thomas............	Ensign, 21st Regiment............	March 14, 1806
White, William...........	Captain, 17th Regiment...........	January 30, 1808
White, William...........	Captain, 22nd Regiment...........	March 24, 1806
Whitecotton, Moses.......	Lieutenant, 13th Regiment........	July 2, 1808
Whitehead, John..........	Captain, 20th Regiment...........	February 22, 1806

COMMISSIONED OFFICERS, 1805 - 1811

Whitlock, Nathaniel B....	Captain, 1st Regiment	April 21, 1808
Whittinghill, David......	Ensign, 5th Regiment	October 15, 1807
Wickliff, Moses..........	Major, 2nd Battalion, 40th Regiment	January 17, 1811
Wiggins, Archibald.......	Ensign, 29th Regiment	May 26, 1808
Wigglesworth, John.......	Lieutenant, 20th Regiment	August 28, 1806
Wigglesworth, William....	Ensign, 20th Regiment	June 28, 1808
Wilcox, George...........	Lieutenant Colonel, Commandant 85th Regiment	January 26, 1811
Wilcox, Joseph...........	Ensign, 18th Regiment	May 16, 1805
Wilgus, Asa..............	Lieutenant, 10th Regiment	July 2, 1807
Wilkerson, Presley.......	Captain, 7th Regiment	June 18, 1807
Willan, Thomas...........	Captain, 16th Regiment	November 25, 1805
Williams, Benjamin.......	Ensign, Rifle Company, 9th Regiment	February 22, 1806
Williams, Benjamin.......	Lieutenant, Rifle Company, 9th Regiment	May 26, 1807
Williams, Charles........	Ensign, 3rd Regiment	March 10, 1805
Williams, Dan.	Lieutenant, Rifle Company, 7th Regiment	October 8, 1807
Williams, Daniel.........	Ensign, 21st Regiment	April 18, 1807
Williams, Daniel.........	Captain, 16th Regiment	March 14, 1806
Williams, David..........	Lieutenant, 6th Regiment	August 20, 1808
Williams, James..........	Ensign, 11th Regiment	August 5, 1808
Williams, Joel...........	Ensign, 9th Regiment	May 26, 1807
Williams, John...........	Lieutenant, 12th Regiment	June 12, 1805
Williams, John...........	Captain, 12th Regiment	December 13, 1805
Williams, John...........	Major, 1st Battalion, 12th Regiment	December 10, 1811
Williams, Jonah..........	Ensign, 11th Regiment	September 15, 1807
Williams, Joseph.........	Lieutenant, 15th Regiment	October 2, 1806
Williams, Joseph.........	Adjutant, 29th Regiment	October 8, 1807
Williams, Roger..........	Lieutenant Colonel, Commandant 71st Regiment	December 13, 1809
Williams, William........	Major, 1st Battalion, 7th Regiment	December 7, 1810
Williams, William........	Major, 2nd Battalion, 7th Regiment	March 8, 1811
Williamson, John.........	Captain, 18th Regiment	May 16, 1805
Willson, Sandford........	Ensign, 12th Regiment	December 13, 1805
Willson, Sandford........	Lieutenant, 12th Regiment	December 5, 1807
Wilson, Robert...........	Adjutant, 10th Regiment	May 2, 1807
Wilson, Samuel...........	Ensign, 24th Regiment	June 12 and and December 8, 1806
Wilson, Samuel...........	Major, 1st Battalion, 46th Regiment	February 1, 1809
Wilson, Samuel...........	Major, 2nd Battalion, 46th Regiment	December 13, 1809
Wilson, Samuel...........	Lieutenant Colonel, Commandant 46th Regiment	January 17, 1811
Wilson, Singleton........	Ensign, 18th Regiment	September 17, 1806

COMMISSIONED OFFICERS, 1805 - 1811

Wilson, Singleton........	Lieutenant, 18th Regiment........	February 9, 1807
Winfrey, James...........	Lieutenant, 25th Regiment........	July 1, 1808
Wingate, Thomas..........	Ensign, 22nd Regiment............	July 14, 1807
Winlock, George..........	Ensign, 16th Regiment............	November 25, 1805
Winlock, George..........	Lieutenant, 16th Regiment........	March 14, 1806
Winn, John...............	Major, 1st Battalion, 8th Regiment......................	March 5, 1807
Winn, Thomas M.	Lieutenant, 1st Regiment.........	November 9, 1805
Wise, Abraham............	Captain, 29th Regiment...........	October 8, 1807
Wiseheart, John..........	Lieutenant, 2nd Regiment.........	September 12, 1807
Wiseman, Abner...........	Major, 3rd Battalion, 17th Regiment......................	February 23, 1808
Witt, Charles............	Ensign, 16th Regiment............	November 5, 1807
Wolf, Lewis..............	Major, 2nd Battalion, 72nd Regiment......................	February 19, 1808
Wood, Abraham............	Lieutenant, 6th Regiment.........	September 12, 1807
Wood, David..............	Ensign, 29th Regiment............	October 8, 1807
Wood, John...............	Major, 2nd Battalion, 6th Regiment......................	May 9, 1806
Wood, William............	Captain, 5th Regiment............	November 4, 1806
Wood, William............	Captain, 26th Regiment Nominated......................	October 9, 1808
Wood, William............	Major, 2nd Battalion, 35th Regiment......................	December 7, 1810
Woods, William...........	Lieutenant, 26th Regiment........	January 29, 1805
Woods, William...........	Captain, 26th Regiment...........	September 12, 1807
Woods, William...........	Major, 2nd Battalion, 19th Regiment......................	December 16, 1805
Woods, William...........	Major, 19th Regiment.............	February 3, 1807
Woods, William...........	Major, 2nd Battalion, 35th Regiment......................	June 13, 1810 and March 15, 1811
Woolford, John...........	Major, 2nd Battalion, 52nd Regiment......................	February 4, 1809
Woolry, Jacob............	Ensign, 20th Regiment............	June 28, 1808
Worrell, James...........	Ensign, 20th Regiment............	July 29, 1807
Worthan, Thomas..........	Ensign, 2nd Regiment.............	March 3, 1807
Worthington, John........	Major, 2nd Battalion, 28th Regiment......................	December 29, 1806
Wright, Benjamin.........	Major, 1st Battalion, 60th Regiment......................	February 19, 1808
Wright, Benjamin.........	Lieutenant Colonel, Commandant 60th Regiment.................	January 25, 1811
Wright, James............	Lieutenant Colonel, Commandant 14th Regiment.................	September 15, 1807
Wright, Samuel...........	Ensign, 12th Regiment............	October 2, 1806
Wright, Samuel...........	Lieutenant, 12th Regiment........	February 3, 1807
Wright, William..........	Ensign, 14th Regiment............	January 29, 1805
Wyatt, John..............	Major, 2nd Battalion, 42nd Regiment......................	March 27, 1805
Wyatt, Joseph............	Ensign, 30th Regiment............	March 25, 1806

Yagar, Joseph	Lieutenant, 4th Regiment	January 9, 1808
Yates, Stephen	Ensign, 4th Regiment	June 23, 1806
Yeiser, Jacob	Captain, Rifle Company, 2nd Regiment	September 11, 1806
Yeizer, Jacob	Captain, Rifle Company, 9th Regiment	February 5, 1805
Yeizer, Jacob	Major, 1st Battalion, 2nd Regiment	January 21, 1811
Young, James	Captain, 18th Regiment	July 3, 1805
Young, John	Captain, 24th Regiment	August 28, 1805
Young, Nimrod	Ensign, 22nd Regiment	May 3, 1806
Young, Richard M.	Ensign, 11th Regiment	January 19, 1808
Young, Robert	Ensign, 18th Regiment	July 23, 1808
Young, William	[Rank not given], 3rd Regiment	November 5, 1807
Young, William	Major, 2nd Battalion, 1st Regiment	December 19, 1805
Young, William	Major, 1st Battalion, 52nd Regiment	September 19, 1805

INDEX

A

Abbott, Samuel, 19
Abel, Robert, 13
Abell, Jesse, 157
Abernethy, Blackston, 77
　Braxton, 77
Abrahams, Benjamin, 126
Abshaw, John, 148
Acoff, Christopher, 141
Acrey, David, 74
Adair, John, 23, 28, 55
　William J., 157
Adam, Nathan, 157
Adams, Absalom, 18, 31, 77
　Elijah, 130, 157
　James, 122, 127
　James, Jr., 70
　Jesse, 70, 122
　John, Jr., 133
　Matthew, 7, 71, 116
　Nathan, 141
　Simon, 17, 50, 143
　W., 157
　William, 88, 127, 157
Adamson, Henry, 157
Admyre, Henry, 101
Agan, Michael, 157
Aken, John, 50
Akers, George, 57
　Peter, 108
　Thomas, 57
Akin, John, 157
Akins, Josiah, 38
Alban, John, 134
Alchire, John, 130
Alcorn, George, 108, 111, 138
　John, 7, 21, 35
　William, 118
Alderson, James, 138
Aldreidge, John, 43, 45
Aldrige, James, 91
Alexander, Aaron, 15
　James, 18, 32, 67
　John, 130
　Nicholas, 138
　Robert, 83
Alfree, John, 59
Allcorn, James, 157
　John, 152
　Thomas, 118
Allen, Beverly Anthony, 40
　David, 94, 157
　Granvil, 157
　James, 5, 24, 94, 155
　John, 1,13,57,59,74,153,157
　Joseph, 130, 157
　Nathan, 74
　Nesbit, 68
　Samuel, 137
　Stephen, 143
　William, 87
Allentharp, Benjamin, 157
Alley, Samuel, 69
Allin, Thomas, 45
Allinson, John, 122
Allison, James, 157
　John, 157
　William, 3, 104
Ambrose, William, 157
Amment, John, 157
Amos, Abram, 59
　Charles, 57
　James, 51
　Thomas, 5, 59
Amy, William, 108
Anderson, Abihew, 17, 46
　Andrew, 148
　Benjamin, 127
　Charles, 126
　Ethel, 137
　Francis, 98

Anderson, cont'd.
　George, 3
　Gilmore, 59
　Hugh, 157
　James, 91, 130
　John, 21,51,113,118,127,157
　Josiah, 134
　Matthew, 43, 45, 72
　Nicholas M., 157
　Reuben, 157
　Samuel, 127
　Stokes, 45
　Thomas, 59, 67
　Vincent, 51, 158
　Walter, 158
　William, 29,41,77,91,118,
　　148,158
Andrews, George, 77, 158
　John, 94,
　Robert, 83
Angel, John, 158
Ansley, William, 158
Anthill, Henry, 74
Anthony, Joseph, 148
Applegate, Benjamin, 38, 104
　George, 126
　Richard, 43, 158
Archer, James, 28, 158
　John, 59, 143, 158
　Sampson, 59
Ardery, Robert, 158
Armstrong, Archibald, 38
　Joshua, 22, 148
　Lanty, 127, 128
　Robert, 9
　William, 83
Arnel, John, 88
Arnold, David, 158
　Humphrey, 6
　James, 13
　John, 9, 34, 90
　Joseph, Jr., 133
　Stephen, 9, 34
　William, 1
Arthur, Ambrose, 110
　Thomas, 30, 71, 158
　Thomas, Jr., 110
Artkus, Jacob, 39
Asbury, William, 126
Ash, Peter, 47
Ashby, Beacy, 50, 143
　Bladen, 96
　Daniel, 100
　Edward, 104
　Fielding, 5
　Landin, 143
　Silas, 50, 143, 158
　Stephen, 100, 158
　Stinson, 143
　Thompson, 96
Ashcraft, Abijah, 96
　Daniel, 37, 97
　Jacob, 43, 122
　Jediah, 29
Asher, Dillon, 110
　John, 111
Ashert, Josiah, 59, 158
Ashford, Thomas, 14,153,158
　William, 158
Ashmore, Samuel, 40
Atcheson, John, 77
　William, 130
Atherton, David, 134
Atkins, Andrew, 139
Atkinson, Isaiah, 55
　Thomas, 55
Atwood, William, 158
Augustus, John, 158
Austin, (James?), 150
　Obadiah, 59

Auxier, Michael, 87
Ayres, Burton, 77
　Moses, 110
　Samuel, 77

B

Baber, Isham, 158
　See also Bebare.
Bacon, Edmund, 158
　Liddale, 158
　Robert, 118
Baggerly, Isaac, 104
Bailey, Henry, 8
　James, 158
　John, 7, 111, 158
　Joseph, 158
　Reuben, 158
　Thomas, 59, 116, 158
Baily, James, 40
Bain, George, 153
　Lewis, 101
Baird, Alexander, 47
　James, 59,134,137,158
　Robert, 24
　Thomas, 158
Baker, Abner, 91
　Abraham, 126
　Amos, 158
　Brice, 110
　George, 158
　Henry, 69
　James, 28, 158
　John, 59, 101, 159
　John, Jr., 59
　Joseph, 21, 41, 118
　Joshua, 8, 43
　Robert, 159
　William, 1, 28
Baldock, James, 159
Baldwin, Samuel, 43,122,159
Bales, Alexander, 41
Ball, James, 94
　John, 118
　William, 111
Ballad, George, 141, 159
Ballard, Bland, 25
　George, 53
　James, 5, 50, 143
Ballenger, Richard, 159
Ballew, Fleming, 159
Ballinger, Achilles, 91
　Eastham, 110
　John, 110, 111
　Richard, 110
Baltimore, Philip, 8
Baltzell, George, 159
Bane, LeRoy, 101
Banks, Cuthbert, 77, 108
　James, 34, 143, 159
Banta, Daniel, 101
Banton, John, 35
Barbee, Daniel, 9
　Elias, 19, 37, 55
　Joshua, 1, 128
　Thomas, 10, 15
Barbour, Philip, 159
　Richard, 91
Barclay, James, 122
　John, 159
Bare, Adam, 137
Barker, Elias, 21
　John, H., 159
　Lewis, 113
　Neely, 159
　Thomas, 159
Barkley, James, 159
　Robert, 41
Barley, John, 59

Barlow, Aron, 45
  Cornelius, 25
Barnard, John, 91
  Joshua, 137
  Peter, 55
  Valentine, 159
Barnes, Abraham, 98
  John, 137
  Joseph, 83, 113
  Neariah, 77
  Noble, 130
  Robert, 83
  Robert, Jr., 83
  Uriah, 77
Barnet, John, 159
Barnett, -----, 19
  Alexander, 118
  Andrew, 19, 94
  George, 59
  Jacob, 100
  John, 59, 159
  Joshua, 137
  Schyler, 159
  Skiller, 118
  Solomon, 53
  Thomas, 71
  William, 37, 94, 118
Barnhill, Samuel, 159
Barns, Heriah, 32
  Philip, 159
  William, 34
Barr, George, 108
  Hugh, 60
  John, 159
  Thomas T., 77
  William, 108
Barrett, Peter, 38, 98
  Robert, 159
Barringer, Jonathan, 94
Barrow, George, 22
Barry, William T., 155
Bartel, John, 16
Bartholomew, Joseph, 5
Bartlett, Anthony, 14, 53
  Edmund, 101, 143
  Frederick, 5, 104, 159
  James, 101
  William, 1
Bartley, James, 159
  John, 108
  See also Bertly.
Barton, William, 60
Baskett, Jesse, 60
Bass, George, 77
  Peter, 94
Bateman, Henry, 104
  Simon, 51
Bates, John, 104
  Robert, 57
Batman, Henry, 38
Batterton, Henry, 60
Batts, John, 104
Baughman, Henry. See Hr.
  Bockman.
Baxter, Edmund, 21
  Edward, 118, 159
  James, 77, 159
  Thomas, 3, 18
Bayles, Stephen, 160
Baylis, Benjamin, 122
  Stephen, 160
Baylor, George W., 160
Beachem, William, 160
Beaird, John, 83
Bealer, Christopher, 10
  John, 160
Beall, Benjamin, 68
  Paterson, 160
  See also Bell.
Bean, George, 26
  John, 72
  See also Been
Beard, John, 55

Bearden, John, 113
  Winn, 113
Beardin, John, 160
Beason, Isaac, 152
Beatty, Adam, 77
  Cornelius, 77
  Edward, 77
  Otho, 26, 34
Beaty, Cornelius, 3, 18
Beauchamp, Jeroboam, 150,160
  Samuel, 160
  Stephen, 134
  Thomas, 134
Beaufort, William, 160
Beauvrie, Matthew, 98
Beaver, Abraham, 87
Beavers, Abraham, 83
Bebare, Robert, 139
  See also Baber.
Beck, Daniel, 57
  Edward, 74
  Jeremiah, 160
  John, 87
  William, 118, 160
Beckerly, Henry, 160
  Levy, 160
Becket, William, 60
Beckett, Anthony, 16-
  Joseph, 160
Beckly, Peter, 45
Bedford, Benjamin, 60
Bedle, Jonathan, 50, 143
Beedle, Jonathan, 143
Been, Benjamin, 160
  John, 160
  See also Bean.
Belcher, John, 19
Beliew, Absalom, 55
Bell, Clement, 88
  David, 43
  George, 30
  Henry, 160
  James, 12
  John, 143
  John, Sr., 77
  Joseph, 160
  Peter, 47, 134
  Robert, 40,94,133,160
  Thomas, 160
  William, 133
  See also Beall.
Bellows, John, 141
Belt, Fielding, 83
  Joseph, 83, 160
  Marsham, 160
  William, 160
Bennet, Benjamin, 13
  Hardy, 7
  William, 9
Bennett, Hardiman, 21
  John, 34,37,137,160
  Titus, 122
  William, 57
Benning, Levi, 77
Benton, Erasmus, 160
  Richard, 41
Berrey, James, 51
Berriman, Josias, 141
Berry, Allen, 153
  Benjamin, 14,77,100,160
  Francis, 150
  George, 87
  Henry, 122, 161
  James, 77
  John, 98
  Joseph, 39
  Reuben, 122, 161
  Richard, 53
  Robert, 28, 60, 161
  Samuel, 153
  Samuel, Jr., 161
  Washington, 69
  William, 3

Berryman, William, 148,161
Bertly, James, 43
  See also Bartley.
Best, James, 161
Beswell, Jeremiah, 150
Bethuram, William, 111
Beverley, John, 104
Bibb, George, 134
Bibee, Sherod, 57
Biers, Jacob, 161
Biggerstaff, Hriam, 161
Biggs, Andrew, 77
Bilbo, Archibald, 46, 130
Bilderback, Jacob, 50
Bilderbec, Ephraim, 23
Billen, Absalom, 94
Bingerman, Henry, 111
Biram, Joseph, 161
Bird, Abraham, 161
Birdsong, William, 113, 161
Bishop, George, 161
  Laurence, 67
  Lowney, 57
Bissett, Thomas, 134
Biswell, Jeremiah, 150, 161
Black, Alexander, 1, 15,60
  David, 46, 71
  George, 29,130,161
  James, 51
  John, 161
  Samuel, 28, 60
Blackberry, William, 28
Blackburn, David, 98
  George, 161
  Joseph, 17
  Robert, 161
  William, 60
  William B., 71, 113
Blackmore, John, 153
Blackwell, Benjamin, 21,72
  Robert, 88
  William, 118
Blackwood, Joseph, 161
Blain, James, 6
  John, 6, 60
  See also Blane.
Blair, Alexander, 161
  James, 130
  John, 39
Blake, James, 161
Blakey, Pleasant, 35
  Thomas, 57
Blanchard, John, 43, 45
Bland, Elijah, 47
  John, 47
Blane, James, 94
  John, 111
  See also Blain.
Blanford, Walter, 67
Blanton, James, 161
Blare, John, 1
Bledsoe, Benjamin, 14, 91
  Jacob, 34
  Joseph, 91
  Richard, 77, 161
  William M., 91
Blevens, Elisha, 139, 152
Blinker, Benjamin, 134
Blinko, Benjamin, 134
Blount, Andrew, 28
  Henry, 90
Blunt, Henry, 88
Board, George, 6-
Boatman, John, 108
Bobb, John, 77
Bockman, Hr., 111
Bodine, John, 134
Bodkin, Richard, 98
  William, 98
Bodley, Thomas, 77, 161
Boggess, Vincent, 161
Boggus, William, 133
Bohannon, Abraham, 161

Bohannon, cont'd.
  George, 26, 104
  German, 161
  Larkin, 53
  William, 77
Bohon, John, 128, 161
  Thomas, 128
Boks, James, 72
  See also Box.
Boles, James, 100
Bolin, Daniel, 161
Bomfield, Robert, 130
Bond, James, 137
  William, 141
Bone, John, 21
Boner, Charles, 68
Bonjay, George, 87
Bonwell, John, 161
Booker, Richard, 143, 161
Boon, John, 50
  Ratliff, 161
Boone, George, 161
  John, 25
  William, 5, 113
Boss, John, 161
Boston, Reuben, 18
Bostwick, Truman, 161
Boswell, George, 49
  George G., 49
  Joseph, 77
  William, 3
  William E., 38, 98, 155
Boteman, Simon, 148
Bottoms, Robert, 94
Botts, Richard, 43
Bowen, Elijah, 108
Bowles, Egnatius, 134
  Nelson, 60
  Wilfred, 47
Bowling, Thomas, 134
  William, 108
Bowman, Aron, 50
  John, 91
  William, 10, 47
Bows, Jacob, 162
Box, James, 72
  See also Boks,
Boyd, John, 122, 130
  Joseph, 24, 162
  William, 162
Boyles, Alexander, 7
  David, 24
Boys, Robert, 91
Boyston, William, 21
Boyworth, Jonathan, 37
Brackenridge, John, 162
Brackin, Jesse, 29, 68
Braconriedg, John, 162
Bradford, Fielding, 141
  Garland, 60
  Henry, 162
  James, 88, 162
  James M., 88
  William, 113, 133, 162
Bradley, Bensa, 24
  Hezekiah, 77
  John, 133
  Sion, 162
  Terry, 162
  Zion, 55
Bradly, Thomas, 12
Bradshaw, John, 50,143,162
  Robert, 162
Brady, William, 1, 28, 143
Braham, William, 60
Brand, Richard, 60
Bradenburgh, Solomon, 162
Branham, Benjamin, 162
  Harbin, 162
  John, 141
  William, 49, 141
  William B., 60
Brannon, Edward, 51

Brasfield, Wiley, 72
Brashear, Dennis, 134
  Nicholas, 67
  Thomas C., 67
  Walter, 134, 162
Brashears, Thomas, 45, 47
Brasher, Charles, 70
Bravard, Adam, 83
Bray, John, 162
Bready, William, 1
Breckinridge, Robert, 1,15,28
Bredwell, Fielding, 118
Breeding, William, 143
Brenham, Robert, 162
  Thomas, 12
Brenton, James, 23
  John, 5, 143
  William, 1
Brevard, Adam, 9
Briant, Absalom, 40
Briant, Alexander, 28
  Andrew, 28
  John, 19, 23
Bridges, John L., 128
Briggs, Benjamin, 111
  George, 162
  Robert, 148
Bright, Edward, 43, 83
Brindley, John, 104
Bringman, Martin, 38, 104
Brinkman, Martin, 104
Brinson, Thomas, 23
Brinton, John, 143
Briscoe, Andrew, 118
  Hezekiah, 26
  Jeremiah, 13
  Philip, 162
Bristoe, Archibald, 72
  James, 60, 162
Bristow, Thomas, 55, 94
Brite, Henry, 162
Brittain, James, 110
Britton, George, 110, 162
Brock, Harry, 3
  Henry, 3, 88
  Thomas, 21, 41
Brockman, Job, 90
Brody, William, 143
Bronaugh, William, 122
Brook, John, 57
Brooke, George, 53
  William, 77
Brooken, Samuel, 53
Brookens, Samuel, 53
Brookes, James, 141
Brookhart, Jacob, 162
Brooking, John, 162
  Samuel, 26
Brooks, Lynch, 21
  Miles, 57
  William, 9
Brooner, John, 134
Brothers, Jeremiah, 150
  John, 137
Brown, Arabia J., 91, 92
  Benjamin, 153
  Beverly, 21, 35
  David, 104
  Elijah, 3
  Elisha, 162
  George, 71, 88
  George, Jr., 162
  Henry, 162
  Hugh, 57, 162
  James, 83,87,118,162
  James, Jr., 162
  Jeremiah, 46
  Jesse, 34
  John, 32,38,43,60,77,83,
    104,122,162
  John P., 11, 162
  Joseph, 43,67,114,122
  Nathaniel, 47, 134

Brown, cont'd.
  Nicholas, 118
  Patrick, 11
  Preston, 153
  Robert, 83
  Samuel, 98
  Stephen, 92
  Thomas, 87
  Thomas C., 87
  William, 26,88,128,134,
    163
Brownfield, William, 10
Browning, Abner, 32
  Albert, 83
  James, 17, 72, 163
  Jesse, 15, 60
  John, 60
  Thomas, 163
Brownlee, Charles, 94, 163
Bruce, Alexander, 126
  George, 11
  John, 92, 163
Bruges, Edm., 60
Bruice, John, 163
Brumfield, Robert, 53
Brumley, John, 87
Brunts, Peter, 74
Brutin, Davis, 41
  George, 139
Bryan, Alexander, 15
  Anderson, 17
  Andrew, 15
  Enoch, 78
  Ezekiel, 78
  George, 163
  James, 60
  Jonathan, 72
  Morgan, 32, 101
Bryant, Enoch, 163
  George, 32
  John, 6,35,92,98
  John G., 56
  Robert, 111
  William, 35
Buchanan, Henry, 60
Buchanan, James, 10
  Thomas, 163
Buchannan, Alexander, 43,46
  Henry, 60
  James, 46
Buckhanan, James, 46, 128
Buckhannon, Nathaniel, 56
Buckingham, Peter, 56
Buckner, Nicholas, 20, 38,
    88, 104, 163
  William, 163
Bufford, Thomas, 35
Buford, Abram, 163
  Amb., 60
  Henry, 92
  John, 57
  Thomas, 92, 163
Bukhannan, Henry, 28
Bullock, Edmond, 32
  Edward, 118, 163
  John, 47, 163
  Lewis, 3, 43, 123
  Nathaniel, 3
  Thomas, 163
Bunch, George, 110
Bunton, Andrew, 83
  John, 92
Burbridge, Benjamin, 153,
    163
  George, 24, 141
  Rowland, 26
  Thomas, 163
Burch, Cheadle, 88
  Darius, 68
  Joseph, 141
Burcham, Samuel, 46, 163
Burchem, Samuel, 130
Burdet, Joseph, 21

Burditt, Enoch, 35
  Joseph L., 35
Burgain, Thomas, 118
Burgan, Thomas, 163
Burgen, Thomas, 41
Burges, Nicholas, 72
Burk, Richard, 49
Burkhart, Joshua H., 163
Burks, Charles, 75
  John, 5, 57
  Nicholas, 19, 37
  Roland, 163
  Rowland, 163
  Samuel, 19
Burnett, James C., 163
Burnham, Henry, 118
  Thomas, 139
Burns, James, 110
Burnside, Robert, 92
Burnsides, Robert, 163
Burris, Zadock, 163
Burriss, David, 75
Burton, Abraham, 7
  Archibald, 163
  Jeremiah, 26
  Joseph, 94
  May, 128
  Robert, 128
  Samuel, 163
  Wilson, 134
  Zachariah, 53, 104
Busey, Jacob, 163
Bush, Gholsen, 72
  Isaac, 163
  J. Gholston, 164
  John, 57, 70
  John V., 164
  Philip, 3,46,72,164
Buskirk, Thomas, 50
Butler, Francis, 60, 164
  John, 19
  Thomas, 7, 75, 116
  William, 23, 25, 101
Butts, Aron, 43
Bybee, Sherod, 57
Byram, William, 123, 164
Byrd, John, 1
Byrom, Edward, 60

C

Cabbel, Joseph, 111
Cabbell, William, 164
Cabel, Joseph, 94
Caffin, William, 164
Cain, Asael, 70
  Charles, 95
  See also Charles Kaen.
Caits, Joshua, 24
Calderwood, Adam, 60
Caldwell, Beverly, 95
  David, 13, 26, 95
  George, 78
  James, 60, 98, 148
  John, 13
  Phillips, 34, 88
  Robert, 41,118,130,164
  Robert S., 164
  Samuel, 40,155,164
  Waller, 164
  Walter, 164
  William, 28,55,83,108,164
Calhoon, George, 11
Call, Thomas, 26
  See also Thomas Cull.
  William, 164
Callaway, John, 164
  Richard, 41, 118
Callehem, William, 87
Calloway, Chesly, 24
  Edmond, 3
  John, 101, 164
  Richard, 21

Calmes, Marquis, 14, 26, 155
Calvert, Richard, 134
  Thomas, 164
Cambell, William, 40, 164
Cameron, John, 123
Cammeron, Robert, 101
Campbell, Alexander, 98
  Allan, 104
  Angus, 71
  Benajmin, 71
  George, 164
  Hugh, 164
  James, 75, 164
  John, 78,111,114,118,148,
    155
  John B., 155
  Johnson, 67
  Mathew, 164
  Robert, 3
  Samuel, 71
  William, 3,6,16,21,24,35,
    38,53,133,141
Camron, Bazel. 164
Cannon, John, 19
Canoy, Jacob, 133
Canterhill, Joseph, 60
Canthill, Joseph, 164
Cantrel, William, 130
Cantrill, Joseph, 60
Cape, John, 164
Caperton, John, 118
  William, 118
Cardwell, Isaac, 143
  Jacob, 164
  John, 164
  William, 143
Cargle, John, 133
Carlin, Thomas, 144
Carlisle, James, 13
Carlock, Joseph, 139
Carman, Caleb, 123, 164
Carna, Pleasant, 164
Carnagant, John, 98
Carnahan, Robert, 164
Carpenter, Conrod, 6
  Jesse, 75
  John, 164
  Simon, 83
  William, 118
Carr, Absalom, 50,144,164
  Armstrong, 111
  Charles, 78, 164
  David, 164, 165
  Elijah, 50
  Ichabod, 134
  James, 139, 165
  Peter, 88, 139, 165
  Thomas, 97
  See also Kerr.
Carson, Lindsey, 7
Carter, Abraham, 88
  Charles, 39, 165
  Elisha, 165
  James, 57
  Jesse, 39, 165
  John, 60, 165
  Joseph, 165
  Peter, 134
Cartes, John, 9
Cartmel, Jacob, 134
Cartmell, Jacob, 165
  William, 165
Caruthers. See Crawthers.
Cary, Ebenezer, 128
Case, James, 134
  William, 11, 48
Casey, William, 19
Cash, Caleb, 130
  Earren, 50
Casibier, David, 133
Cassady, Andrew, 128
  Michael, 33
  Thomas, 83

Cassel, Jacob, 78
Castlebury, Paul, 71
Castleman, David, 165
  Jacob, 144, 165
Catlin, James, 26, 53
  Seth, 150
Caulk, Richard, 38
Cave, John, 68, 70
Cavell, Joseph, 165
Cavenaugh, Charles, 71
  William, 71
Cellars, Joseph, 153
Celsey, John, 57
Cessell, William, 165
Chaffin, John, 97, 165
  William, 165
Chalfan, John, 165
Chalfant, Abner, 67
  Robert, 165
Chalfunt, Abner, 48
Chamberlain, Pearce, 128
Chambers, William, 39, 104
Chapman, George, 51, 148
  Thomas, 10, 24
  William, 57, 83
Cheatam, Lewis, 46
Chenoweth, Jacob, 165
  James, 39, 104
Chenowith, William, 48
Cherry, William, 165
Chestnut, Abram, 110
Childers, Henry, 68
  Robert, 29
Chiles, David, 43,45,126,
    155
  Henry, 72, 165
  James, 21
  Thomas, 165
Chinault, William, 41
Chinn, Christopher, 32
  Elijah, 3
  William, 32, 78, 165
  William Ball, 28
Chinoweth, William, 11,134
Chinowith, John, 165
Chisum, George, 37
Chrisman, Joseph, 75
Christel, William, 83
Christian, John, 101
  William, 78
Christie, George, 68
  William, 5
Christman, Isaac, 152
Christopher, John, 165
  William, 14, 165
  William, Jr., 153
Christy, Ambrose, 31, 72
  John, 72
  William, 39
Churchill, John, 165
  Samuel, 104, 165
Cisna, William, 37
Cissel, William, 150
  See also Scissell,
    Seissel.
Clack, Sterling, 148
Claggett, Thomas, 53, 153
Clark, Benjamin, 165
  Bennet, 3
  Bolin, 165
  Christopher, 21
  James, 165
  John, 130
  Joseph, 72, 165
  Obadiah, 144
  Septimus D., 165
  Thomas, 35
  William, 104
Clarke, George, 57
  Gideon, 114
  Ludlow, 104
  Robert, Jr., 72
  Stewart, 139

Clarke, cont'd.
  William, 78
  Zachariah, 144
Clarkson, Charles, 15,28,60
Clarkston, David, 28
Clary, Vachel, 98
Clay, Green, 41,55,155
  Henry, 165, 166
  Henry, Jr., 60
  Samuel, 166
Claycomb, John, 137
Clayton, James, 144
  William, 105
Cleaveland, George, 166
Cleaver, David, 150, 166
  Jacob, 48
  Stephen, 10,37,137,155
Clement, James, 166
Clements, Jeremiah, 10
Clemmons, James, 144
Cleneay, Joseph, 123
Cleveland, George, 166
  Levi, 70
Clever, David, 150
Clift, Daniel, 75
Clinton, Moses, 88
Cloyd, John, 118, 166
  Thomas, 75
Cochran, George, 166
  James, 8
  John, 10, 128
  Samuel, 22, 118
Cochren, James, 166
Cock, John, 3
Cockeral, Joseph, 166
Cockerhill, Joseph, 78
Coe, James, 97
Coffee, Jesse, 166
  John W., 152
  Osburn, 166
Coffer, Henry, 133
Coffie, John, 139
Coger, James, 18
Coher, Samuel, 148
Cokendofer, John, 98
Coker, Samuel, 51
Colbert, Burwell, 166
  Jesse, 123, 166
  Thomas, 134
Cole, Andrew, 148
  Ebenezer, 92
  James, 148
  Jesse, 49
  John, 114
  Richard, 26
Coleman, Daniel, 68, 166
  James, 134, 166
  John, 166
  Robert, 30
  Thomas, 68, 166
Colglaizer, Christopher, 43
Collier, Coleman, 60, 166
  Franklin, 60
  Isaac, 166
  James, 92
  Moses, 39, 111
  Solomon, 166
Collins, Barby, 22
  Bartlett, 12
  Dillard, 72
  Emond, 166
  Edward, 60,116,166
  Isaac, 166
  Joel, 26, 111
  Lewis, 166
  Richard, 141
  Solom, 45
  William, 24
  Zebulon, 5
Colman, James, 166
Colter, John, 150
Colvert, Landon, 166
  Richard, 134

Colvill, William, 43
Colvin, Charles, Jr., 166
  George, 166
  John, 29
  Joseph, 1, 130
  Luke, 11
Combs, Adin, 166
  Elijah, 166
  John, 88
  Jonah, 101
  Samuel, 166
  Samuel R., 166
Comer, Martin, 110
Comley, Absolem, 166
Compton, Joel, 95, 167
Congleton, James, 61, 167
Conn, John, 15
  Thomas, 1
Connady, Washington, 167
Connaway, Hugh, 50
Connell, James, 11, 167
Connelly, James, 144
Conner, Frederic, 29
  Henry, 128
  Samuel, 137
  Tristham, 70
Connolly, Arthur, 14
  James, 24
Conolly, Jesse, 144
Constant, Jacob, 83
Cook, Anthony, 39, 111
  Isaac, 61
  Jacob, 123
  James, 71
  John, 10
  William, 118
  William W., 130
Cooke, Giles, 167
Cooley, Charles, 167
Coombe, Asa, 48
  Edward, 48
Coombs, Andrew, 167
  Eden, 97
Coon, Aron, 167
Coons, Frederick, 78
  John, 105
Cooper, Benjamin, 8, 118
  Eliab, 144
  Francis, 118
  Jeconias, 167
  John, 70
  Richard, 118
  Robert, 137
Cooprider, Peter, 97
Cope, John, 75
  Wiley, 87
Copeland, John, 128, 130
Corbin, Elija, 167
  Thomas, 167
Cord, James, 78
  Zachus, 167
Corn, Aaron, 114
  George, 16
  Jesse, 167
Cornelius, Abner, 167
  Jesse, 71, 123
Cornum, John, 72
Cornwell, John, 43
Corum, John, 118
Corwine, Amos, 43
  Samuel, 167
Cotton, Benjamin, 71
  Charles, 167
  Daniel, 167
  John, 167
  Zachariah, 48
Couchman, Mely, 1
Coulter, Mark, 128
  Morris, 111
Coun, James, 167
  See also Cowan, Cowen, Cowin.
Courtney, Robert, 83

Courts, William, 57
Coveington, Elijah, 52
Covenhover, Peter, 167
Covington, Elijah M., 148, 155
  Thomas A., 148, 167
Cowan, John, 75
  See also Coun, Cowen, Cowin.
Cowen, John, 139
Cowherd, James, 3, 95, 167
  Simeon, 167
Cowin, Alexander, 53
  Hugh, 28
Cox, Isaac, 134
  James, 11,41,48,167
  John, 52, 167
  Phenehas, 148
  Phenis, 10, 52
  Phenix, 24
  Solomon, 52
  William, 111
Crab, Jeremiah, 167
Crabb, Jeremiah, 144
Crabtree, Isaac, 31, 72
Cragg, John, 15
Craig, Benjamin, 90
  David, 167
  Elijah, 34,88,90,126
  George W., 110
  Jacob, 133
  James, 98
  John, 1, 43
  John H., 16
  Lewis, 45,53,88,126,167
  Nathaniel, 141
  Philip, 67
  Thomas, 98, 133
  Toliver, Jr., 12
  Whitfield, 45
  William, 49
Craighead, Robert, 167
Crain, Joseph, 83
Crane, Joseph, 83
Cranmore, George, 167
Craven, Jeremiah, 10
  Jesse, 137
Cravens, Jeremiah, 123
  Jesse, 1
  William, 123
  William, Jr., 123
Crawford, Anthony, 148
  Edward, 22
  Hugh, 134
  James, 102
  Mason, 137
  Samuel, 137
Crawthers, William, 30
Craycraft, Samuel, 167
Cready, David, 97
Creal, John, 68
Creamer, Moses, 134
Creason, John, 131
Creel, John, 56
Creiger, George, 53
Crenshaw, Thompson, 167
Crews, James, 57
  Jeremiah, 41
  Thomas, 8, 22
Crighton, Henry, 49
Crisler, Allen, 70
Crispin, Hugh, 18
Crist, Henry, 67, 155
  Jacob, 48, 134, 167
  William, 144
Cristman, Isaac, 167
Cristy, James, 43
Critcald, William, 126
Critchlow, James, 37
Crittenden, John J., 155
Croathers, James, 32
Crockett, Anthony, 6,34,88
  Newbold, 78
  William, 34

Crofford, Oliver, 167
Croghan, William, 6
Crook, John, 118
Crooke, Hezekiah, 118
  John, 118, 167
Crookes, William, 6
Crose, Michael, 61
Crouch, Daniel, 148
  John, 141
  William, 61
Croutch, James, 28
Crow, John, 137
  Joshua, 37
  Walter, 111
Crowder, Burwell, 167
  Sterling, 108
Crump, Hally, 72
  Havilah, 52, 55
  Joshua, 57
Crutcher, Isaac, 135
  Robert, 168
  William, 135
Crutchfield, John, 34
  Richard, 128
  William, 128
Culbertson, Alexander, 168
Cull, Thomas, 26
Cullum, Francis, 168
Culm, Francis, 168
Culp, George, 61
  Josiah, 61, 168
  Thomas, 168
Culver, Benjamin, 168
Culwell, William, 41
Cumings, Daniel, 111
Cummingore, Abraham, 128
Cummings, Abraham, 168
Cummins, Daniel, 92
  David, 126
  John, 37
  Presley, 137
  Robert, 168
  William, 105, 168
Cumpton, Joel, 95
  Rochard, 168
Cunningham, John, 13
  Right, 35
  Robert, 72
Cupp, Henry, 168
Curd, Daniel, 52, 57
  John, 52
  Price, 78
  Woodford, 108
Curry, Edward, 105
  John, 141
  Robert, 46,128,168
  William, 128
Curtis, John, 123
Curtner, Henry, 3, 78
Custard, Conrad, 97
Custed, Arnold, 3
Cutright, Samuel, 1

D

Dale, John, 17
  Reuben, 102
Dallas, William, 61
Dameron, Moses, 83
Damewood, Henry, 57
Damrell, George, 168
Damron, George, 56, 95
Dangerfield, William, 18
Daniel, Archibald, 72
  Beverly, 72
  Charles, Jr., 68
  James, 72, 168
  Jesse, 131, 168
  John, 168
  Peter, 72
  Vivian, 68

Darnaby, Cornelius, 128
  Edward, 32, 78
  John, 18, 78
  William, 168
Darnell, Thomas, 61
Daugherty, Armstrong, 123
  James, 168
Daunton, Richard, 78
Davee, James, 48
Daveiss, John, 168
  Joseph H., 168
  Samuel, 128
Davenport, Marmaduke S., 101
  Richard, 128, 168
  Samuel, 168
  William, 32, 78
Davidson, David, 30
  Samuel, 39, 168
Daviess, Samuel, 46
Davis, Amos, 135, 155
  Arthur, 168
  Benjamin, 168
  David, 23, 43
  George, 99
  George N., 123, 168
  Humphrey, 168
  James, 35,53,88,135
  James D., 48
  Jeremiah, 46, 131
  John, 13,41,50,75,83,88,
     90,139,150,152,168
  Joseph, 10,83,84,168
  Joshua, 118
  Levi, 114
  Nathan, 114
  Norton, 19
  Samuel, 139
  Thomas, 6, 168
  Vincent, 135
  William, 24, 135, 169
  Zachariah, 8
Davison, John, 126
  Josiah, 43
Dawson, Benjamin, 111
  John, 135
  Peter, 169
  Samuel J., 169
  Samuel Jones, 61, 169
Day, Edmond, 128
  Middleton, 95
  Trueman, 84
Dayton, Garrat, 123
  Deadmon, Richard, 78
  Deal, Ira, 84
  John, 72
Deam, John, 38
Dean, Michael, 139
  Robert, 75
  Thomas, 150, 169
  William, 90
Deane, Michael, 139, 152
Deason, Michael, 123
Deatherage, Amos, 169
Deatheridge, George, 118
Debell, John, 84
Debon, Samuel, 169
Debrel, Charles, 139, 152
Debriel, Charles, 8
Decker, Luke, 48, 135
Dedman, Richard, 3
Dedmon, Richmond, 78
Degarnet, Bird, 102
DeGarnett, James, 118,119
Dehart, William, 68
Dehaven, Edward, 25
  Isaac, 169
  Samuel, 141
Dejarnet, John, 119
Delano, A(masa?), 153
Delany, William, 169
Delay, James, 61
Demaree, David, 169
Demint, Gart., 88

DeJared, 90
Demmit, Joshua, 61
Demmitt, William Sinclair,
  128
Dempsey, Jeptha, 123
  John, 123
Dennis, John, Jr., 133
Dennison, James, 1, 61
  Thomas, 61
  William, 18
Denny, Fielding, 141
  George, 22
  James, 6
Denton, David, 72
  John, 92
  Joseph, 84
  Robert, 112, 169
Depauw, John, 169
  Peter, 169
Depew, Abraham, 68, 169
Depriest, John, 22
Desha, John, 123
  Joseph, 43,123,155
Deshea, Joseph, 23
Dever, John, 169
Devere, John, 169
Dickenson, Thomas, 78
Dickerson, John, 57
  Thomas J., 78
Dickey, Adam, 18
  Elisha, 169
  John, 40, 116, 169
  Joseph, 169
  William, 169
Dickinson, William, 169
Dickison, Archer, 3
  Mastin, 3
Dickton, Richard, 54
Dictum, Richard, 153
Dillen, William, 123
Dillingham, Vachel, Jr., 30
Dinsmore, John, 84
Dinwiddie, William, 119
Dishay, John, 9
Diskins, Daniel, 131
Dismuke, Joseph, 112
Dismukes, Joseph, 35, 169
  William, 92
Ditterow, Jacob, 84
Ditto, Henry, Jr., 97
  William, 169
Divers, Samuel, 119
Dixon, Henry, 37, 95, 169
Doake, David, 56, 95
Dobbins, Charles, 169
  James, 114
  John, 169
  Robert, 114
Dobings, Edward, 169
Dobson, James, 19
Dobyns, John, 133, 169
Dodd, Francis, 114
  James, 114, 169
  John, 169
Dodds, John, 114
Dodson, Asa, 139
Dohorty, John, 78
Dollard, John, 119
Donan, David C., 169
Donaldson, John, 15, 72
  William, 131, 169
Donelson, Robert, 8
Donham, John, 52
Doniphan, Anderson, 45
Donnaldson, William, 169
Donnel, James, 61
Donnelson, John, 170
Donovan, Joseph, 123
Doogan, Jeremiah, 170
Dooley, George, 57
  John, 31, 72
  Moses, 8
Dooling, Daniel, 137

Doom, Jacob, 30
Dornaby, Edward, 18
Dorsey, Azle, 170
 Charles, Jr., 135
 Edward, 105
 William, 78
Dotson, William, 11
Doty, Jesse, 92
 Moses, 68
Dougherty, Alexander, 119
 James, 170
 Robert, 1, 123
 Samuel, 102
Douglas, High, 31
 John, 72, 148
 Nathan, 56
Douglass, Charles, 95
 Hezekiah, 170
Dowden, John, 126
Downard, Adam, 170
Downing, Ellis, 123
 James, 123
 Joseph, 43, 123
 Samuel, 17, 46, 131
 Thomas, 123
 Timothy, 43, 123
 William, 114, 170
Doyle, Gregory, 148
Dozer, John, 135
Dozier, John, 11, 48
Draine, Stephen, 170
Drake, Charles, 67
 Enoch, 170
 Isaac, 9
 Jacob, 23, 123
 John, 48, 123
 Josiah, 170
 Nathaniel, 108
 Reune, 23
Drane, Stephen, 170
Draper, John, 170
Drinning, Hugh, 84
Dromgoole, Alexander, 24
Drummin, Samuel, 43
Duckett, John, 61
Dudley, Benjamin, 78
 James, 170
 Robert, 78
 William, 3, 78
 William E., 78, 170
Dudly, Robert, 32
 William, 32
Duff, William, 92
Duke, Basil, 43
Dullum, Francis, 3
Dun, James, 131
Duncan, Benjamin, 170
 Charles, 105, 108, 170
 Coleman, 170
 Elias, 68, 170
 James, 1, 170
 James, Jr., 61, 170
 John, 1, 10, 119
 Joseph, 110, 170
 Robert, 41, 119
 Samuel, 11
 Seth, 68
 Thomas, 170
 Willis, 68, 170
Dunham, John, 22
 Timothy, 170
Dunim, Benjamin, 135
Dunken, Robert, 119
Dunlap, Benjamin, 71
 James, 84
 John, Jr., 155
Dunn, Bartemas, 78
 Benajah, 99, 170
 Benjamin, 92, 99
 George, 102
 James, 3, 108
 Vincent, 11, 24, 97
Dunwiddie, William, 119

Dupey, Samuel, 170
Dupuy, Abraham, 170
 Alexander, 170
 David, 123
Durbin, Christian, 119
 Edward, 22, 42
 John, 170
 Joseph, 42
Durham, James, 19, 95, 170
 Thomas, 46, 131
Duval, John L., 135
 John Lewis, 135
 Thompson, 170
Duvall, John, 170, 171
 William P., 171
 Zachariah, 88, 171
Dyal, James, 95
Dye, James, 137, 171
 John, 171
Dyer, John, 123

E

Eakin, John, 144
Earley, David, 123
Early, David, 23
East, Isaac, 171
 James, 22, 36
 North, 8
Easten, Charles, 171
Eastin, Zachariah, 61, 171
Eastis, Fielding, 171
Eastland, Thomas, 95, 153
Eaton, John, 110
Ebbert, Philip, 123
Ebert, Philip, 171
Eccles, John, 128
Edds, William Gibson, 99
Edgeman, Kimberland, 112
 Thomas K., 139, 152
Edger, William, 40
Edgerton, William, 128
Edland, George, 53, 150
Edmonson, John, 92
Edrington, Thomas, 95
Edwards, Amos, 155, 171
 Cornelius, 171
 Edward, 71
 Elijah, 137
 Elisha, 135
 James M., 105
 John, 61
 Ninian, 116
 William, 39, 105
Elam, Andrew, 148
 Richard, 144
Elder, James, 114, 171
 Matthew, 78
 Thomas, 114, 135
Elgin, Samuel, 1
Ellege, Benjamin, 108
Elliet, Edward, 171
Ellige, Thomas, 108
Ellin, Thomas, 144
Elliot, Alexander, 21
Elliott, Benjamin, 141
 David, 119, 171
 Elijah, 171
 John, 141
 William, 95
Ellis, Daniel, 105, 171
 Henry, 15, 61
 Hezekiah, 18, 78
 Israel, 171
 James, 68, 119, 171
 Littlebury, 32, 78
 William, 61
Ellison, James, 119
 Robert, 99
Elms, David, 40
 Thomas, 40
Elston, William, 102

Ely, Henry, 25
Embre, Thomas, 72
Embree, Joshua, 6
Embrie, Moses, 112
Embry, Caleb, 72
Emerson, Walter, 139
Emison, Thomas, 171
Emmerson, Thomas, 49
 Walter, 57
Emmitt, Alexander, 16
Engles, Joseph, 171
English, Joseph, 52
Enlow, Henry, 135
 Isham, 97
 Jacob, 97
 Joseph, 97
Enlowes, Henry, 61
Enyart, Abraham, 75
Epperson, David, 171
 Robert, 78, 171
Estes, Asa, 71, 171
Estill, James, 119
 Samuel, 8, 22, 119, 171
Estis, Asa, 123
 John, 52
Eubank, Achilles, 73
 Ambrose, 73, 171
Eubanks, Thomas, 171
Evans, Bennet, 171
 Bennet H., 171
 Francis, 131
 Gabriel, 23, 33, 84, 155
 Hamilton, 18
 Hugh, 171
 James, 150
 John, 105, 108, 123
 Nathan, 9
 Samuel, 131, 171
 Silas, 171
 William, 75, 172
Eve, Joseph, 172
Ewalt, Henry, 15
Ewen, Robert, 172
Ewin, Henry, 172
 John, 12
Ewing, Andrew, 56, 78, 95
 Charles, 13
 Chatham, 24, 40
 Elijah, 40
 Finis, 40
 George, 13, 150
 Henry, 97
 John, 25, 116
 Putnam, 172
 Reubin, 116
 Robert, 40, 55
 Samuel, 116
 Urban, 21, 40
 William, 172
 Young, 24, 30, 71

F

Fare, Absalom, 172
Ferguson, Hamlett, 114
 John, 78
 Robert, 172
 Vivion, 172
Faris, Dudley, 119
 Elijah, 10, 53
 George, 119, 172
 James, 6
 John, 84
 Johnston, 7, 21
Farley, Daniel, 102
Farmer, James, 97
Farris, George, 110
 John, 110
 William, 110, 172
Farrow, Joseph M., 172
 William, 46, 131, 172
Faukener, Nicholas, 141

Faulkner, John, 92
　Joseph, 3
　See also Folkner.
Fauntleroy, John, 78, 172
　William, 88
Fee, James, 43, 45, 126
　John, 45
Fegland, John, 25
　See also John Ficklin.
Feilder, John, 172
Feland, Joseph, 112
Fenwick, Ignatius, 172
　William, 34
Fergus, James, 75
Ferguson, Andrew, 110
　Hamlett, 114
　Peter, 71, 114
　Richard, 114, 172
Ferril, John, 119
　Robert, 172
Ferry, James, 137
Ficklin, John, 141
　See also John Fegland.
Field, Benjamin, 172
　Henry, 37, 137
　John, 172
　John, Jr., 61
　Joseph, 172
　Willis, 61
Fields, Henry, 26
　John, 57
　Philemon, 61
　Thomas, 43
　William, 172
Fike, John, 116
Finch, John, 9
　Josiah R., 84
　Samuel, 172
Finley, George, 6
　James, 8, 172
　John, 105
　Richard, 105, 172
　Richard, Jr., 105
Finnel, James, 36, 92
Finnell, Achilles, 92, 172
　James, 22, 92, 172
　Robert, 70
Fips, John, 172
Fish, William, 119, 172
Fishback, George, 172
　Dr. James, 78
　Martin, 172
Fisher, James, 57
　Joseph, 46
　Samuel, 172
　Solomon, 15, 28
　Stephen, Jr., 128, 172
　Zachariah, 144
Fissor, Shaderic, 172
Fitch, Elisha, 33
　Salathiel, 84, 172
Fitte, John, 2
Fitzgerald, Jesse, 32
　Thomas, 9
Fitzwaters, John, 99
Fleming, George, 131
　John, 61
　John D., 173
　Peter, 61
　William, 46
　William P., 155
Fletcher, Peter, 114
　Thomas, 2, 173
Flippin, William, 57
Flippo, John, 173
Flora, Abijah, 43
Flournoy, Daniel, 12
　Francis, 25, 68
　John J., 25, 29
　Matthew, 25, 155
Floyd, Alexander, 173
　Davis, 39

Floyd, cont'd.
　George G.C., 105, 155
　John, 24, 105
　Nathaniel, 173
　R.C., 173
　Robert, 6
Foley, Elijah, 78
　James, 173
Folkner, John, 36
　See also Faulkner.
Forbis, James, 57
　Jonathan, 112
　Morgan, 173
　Nathaniel, 139
　Robert, 57
Ford, Benjamin, 173
　Charles, 21
　James, 102, 114
　Joseph, 84
　Luke, 95
Fore, Augustus, 102
　John, 144, 173
Foreman, David, 7
　Joseph, 11
Forman, Aron, 61
　Joseph, 123
Forsythe, James, 105
　See also Fursith.
Fort, Frederick, 22
　Jesse, 71
Foster, John, 135, 173
　Nathaniel, 84
　Thomas, 141
Fotch, Nathan, 9
Fought, George, 20, 23
Fowler, Edmond, 30
　Joshua, 39, 105
　Stephan, 173
　Thomas, 22
Fox, Arthur, 9
　John, 56
　Richard, 14
　William, 139
Fraizer, Joel, 173
Frame, William, 73, 173
Francis, Henry, 139
　Joseph, 57
Francisco, George, 153, 173
　John, 14,26,153,173
Franklin, James, 99
　John, 57
　John, Jr., 57
　Martin, 57
　Zepheniah, 123
Franks, John, 78
Frary, James, 79
Frazer, George, 4
　James, 173
　Thomas, 173
Freck, Joseph, 10
Frederick, John, 173
Freeman, Elijah, 18
　John, 108
Friend, Andrew, 61
　Charles, 2, 61
　Elijah, 28
Frier, John, 173
Frogg, Arthur, 75
Froman, John, 11, 48
Fry, Jacob, 9
Frye, Joseph, 79
Fryrar, Jeremiah, 135
Fucher, Robert, 32
Fugate, Benjamin, 87
　Vincent, 101
Fuget, Martin, 173
Fuice, Joseph, 38
Fulkerson, Jacob, 48
Fulton, Hugh, 23, 43, 84
　James, 173
　Samuel, 173
Funk, Adam, 15
　Christopher, 40

Funk, cont'd.
　John, 105
　John, Jr., 20, 105
　Joseph, 53, 105
Funkhouser, Christley, 37
Fuqua, Joseph, 144
Furgason, John, 173
Furgerson, John, 148
Furgeson, Richard, 173
Furman, James, 28
Furnes, James, 54
Furnis, James, 2
Furnish, William, 173
Fursith, William, 116
　See also Forsythe.

G

Gabriel, David, 67
Gaddy, James, 173
Gaines, Richard, 55
Gaither, Thomas, 173
Gaits, William, 24
Galascock, George, 84
　See also Glasscock.
Gale, James, 88
　John, 173
Gallager, Edward, 43
Gano, Daniel, 34
　Isaac E., 34
　Richard M., 26,141,173
Gaphney, John, 39
Gardener, Thomas, 6
Gardiner, Joseph J., 135
Garner, Churchill, 73
Garnet, Robert, 70
Garnett, Edward, 16
　Leonard, 99
Garrard, Daniel, 61, 173
　James, 61, 155
　John, 61
　William, 61
Garrett, Thomas, 79
Garrison, James, 30
Garven, Isaac, 39
Garvin, John, 119
Gary, James, 173
Gaskins, John, 114
Gass, James, 119
　Samuel, 141
Gates, James, 46
　John, 108
　William, 45
Gatewood, Hugh, 88
　Hugh L., 90
　John, 79
　Richard, 108
　Thomas, 108
　William, 148
Gath, John, 12
Gather, Thomas, 173
Gathins, Henry, 2
Gathright, John, 174
Gault, Edward, 174
Gawslin, Rubin, 174
Gay, James, 153
　John, 112
　Robert, 153
　Thomas, 112, 174
Geaham, Jeremiah, 20
Gedians, John, 174
Gee, John, 75
Geiger, Frederick, 20
　Jacob, 105
Gelaspy, Simon, 131
Gentry, David, 8, 174
　Joseph, 138
　Richard, 174
　Rubin, 119
　William, 138
George, Abner, 174
　James, 92, 114
　Richard, 119

Gerald, Joseph F., 102
Gevill, John, 25
Gholson, Francis, 12, 25
　See also Golson.
Gibb, Samuel, 30
Gibbons, James, 75
Gibbs, Benjamin, 13
　Ezekiel, 92
Gibson, Daniel, 97
　James, 141, 174
　John, 32, 128, 138
　William, 88
Gidins, Isham, 174
Giger, Frederick, 6
　Jacob, 20
Gilaspie, James, 174
Gilbard, John, 119
Gilbert, Benjamin, 138
　John, 40, 174
Gilkerson, James, 43
Gilkison, William, 4
Gill, George, 144
　John, 139
Gillehan, William, 71
Gillihan, William, 30
　Gilmore, James, Jr., 174
Giltner, Francis, 15
　Micah, 174
　Micel, 174
Gist, Henry C., 155
　Thomas, 14, 34, 95
　William, 58
Givens, Robert, 7
Givins, Joseph, 114
Glascock, Charnal, 75
　John, 135
Glasgow, Samuel, 119
Glasscock, Thomas, 135
　See also Galascock.
Glave, Matthew, 30
Glaves, Michael, 174
Glen, John, 37
Glenn, Hugh, 119
　Isaac, 123
　John, 68
　Joseph, 68
　Joseph K., 68
　Robert, 123, 133
　Samuel, 174
　William, 138, 174
Glover, Abner, 39
　Job, 58
　John, 24, 112, 174
　Joseph, 7
　Uriah, 144
Goading, James, 152
Goe, John, 119
Goffey, James, 95
Goggins, John, 22, 42
Goghagan, Anthony, 48
Gogins, Stephen, 174
Gohagan, John, 174
Goheen, James, 174
Goldsby, James, 20
Golson, Samuel, 174
　See also Gholson.
Gonns, Thomas, 9
Gooch, John A., 174
Good, Fleming, 112
Goode, William, 174
Goodman, Philip, 42
　Samuel, 10
Goodnight, Peter, 32
Goodrich, Samuel, 119
Goodridge, Elisha, 38, 54
Goodson, William, 75
　William, Jr., 75
Goodwin, B., 38
　David, 84
　James C., 68
　James Coleman, 68
　Richard, 139, 152
Goolsby, James, 174

Goosey, Peter, 31, 73
Gorden, John, 30
　Samuel, 174
Gordon, John, 30, 101
　Lewis, 123, 174
　Richard, 8
　Samuel, 40
Goreham, Thomas, 40, 116
Gorham, William, 174
Gorin, Gladin, 52, 174
　Henry, 148
　John, 58
Goring, Glading, 148
Gorrel, John, 61
Gorrin, Henry, 148
Gosney, Frederick, 174
Gouch, Thomas, 38
Goudy, Samuel, 128
Gow, William, 124
Gowdy, Andrew, 79
　Samuel, 128
Grabel, David, 48
Grabell, Joseph, 11
Grable, David, 67, 174
　Joseph, 48
Gradey, Samuel, 131
Gragg, David, 50, 144
Graham, Forgy, 131
　Francis, 174
　Francis, Jr., 174
　George, 150, 174
　James, 84,116,131,174
　John, 84
　Joseph, 46
　Luke, 36
　Samuel, 175
　Thomas, 144
　William, 26, 34, 175
Grahan, Benjamin, 128
Grant, Charles, 30, 124
　James, 141, 175
　John, 12, 128, 135
　Loudovic, 34
　Robert, 73, 175
　Squire, 17, 25, 55
　William, 4
Graves, Anthony, 40
　Bartel, 17
　Bartlett, 68, 70
　Benjamin, 32, 79
　David, 61
　Dennis, 24
　John, 18, 79, 175
　John C., 32
　John Sanders, 133
　Joseph, 70, 175
　Thomas, 75, 175
　William, 17
Gray, Andrew, 110
　David, 124, 175
　Francis, 99, 175
　Isaac, 84, 175
　Jesse, 90
　John, 58, 71
　Joseph, 150
　Patrick, 18, 175
　Prestley, 11, 88, 90
　See also Greay.
Grayham, Henry R., 43
　Joseph, 128
Grayson, Alfred W., 155
　Benjamin, 135
　Frederick W.S., 67
　Reuben, 40
　Robert H., 175
　Thomas, 30
Greathouse, Herman, 48
　Isaac, 6
Greay, Samuel, 128
　See also Gray.
Green, Fielding, 84
　George, 148, 175
　John, 23

Green, cont'd.
　Liberty, 175
　Stephen, 102
　Thomas, 84
　William, 119
Greenwood, John, 108
　Nimrod, 79
Greer, George, 175
　James, 114
Gregg, James, 28
Gregor, Stephen, 12
Gregory, Richard, 6
Grey, John, 150
Grider, Henry, 24, 36
　Martin, 148
　Tobias, 36, 92
Grier, Isaac, 114
Griffin, Aaron, 61
　Jasper, 175
　Jeremiah, 68
　Jesse, 67
　John, 139, 175
　Thomas, 2, 175
　William, 175
Griffith, John, 39, 175
　Josiah, 12
　Patterson, 119
　Robert, 12, 175
　William, 61, 175
Grifhum, Uriah, 39
Grigg, Clem, 175
Grigsby, Joseph, 135
　Lewis, 31, 73
Grimes, Andrew, 135
　Charles, 79
　John, 34, 90
Grisom, Thomas, 30
Groom, Jacob, 61
Grooms, Isaac, 61
Grove, Henry, 175
Grubbs, Isaac, 71
　Thomas, 119
Grugett, John, 175
Grundy, Felix, 175
Guardiner, Ralph, 175
Guiwn, James, 175
Gullion, Jeremiah, 14,88,
　90,144
Gum, Norton, 112
Gunterman, Henry, 67
Gupton, Stephen, 95
Guthrey, Dempsy, 175
Guthrie, Adam, 10, 48, 155
　James, 92, 153
Guy, Robert, 175
Gwatkin, Horation, 101
Hackett, James, 144, 175
　Peter, 22, 42, 119
Hackley, John, 175, 176
　Robert, 176
Hackwith, John, 87
Haddicks, John, 176
Haddix, John, 87, 176
Haddocks, Coleby, 87
Hagan, Caleb, 135
　Ignatius, 135, 150
Hagar, James, 53
Hagen, Ignatius, 10
Hager, James, 150
Haggin, Robert, 131
Hahn, Charles, 135
Hail, Robert, 99
Halbert, James, 176
　John, 176
Hale, Armstrong, 46
　Frederick, 8
　Hezekiah, 176
　Job, 10
　John, 126,128,176
　Samuel, 176
　Thomas, 128, 176
Halfacre, Christian, 139
　Christopher, 152

Halffield, John, 176
Hall, Adam, 28
  Andrew, 112
  Austin, 67
  Benjamin, 61
  Cornelius, 61, 62
  David, 176
  Elisha, 119
  George, 176
  Horatio, 2, 15
  Isaac, 62
  Isaac W., 62
  James, 2,52,75,148
  Jeremiah, 176
  John, 62, 67
  John, Jr., 25
  Mahlen, 62
  Moses, 4
  Philip, 176
  Richmond, 131
  Squire, 102
  Sylvester, 62
  Thomas, 124
  William, 6,50,54,67,75
Hallard, John, 176
Hally, William, 73
Halsey, Reason, 73
Ham, George, 176
  John, 119
  Matthew, 133
Haman, Huston, 62
Hambleton, Charles, 176
  Clement, 176
  Joseph, 15
  Robert, 15
Hamen, George, 112
Hamilton, Alexander, 12
  Archibald, 84
  Clement, 150
  Ferdinand, 37
  John, 2,32,62,114,176
  Robert, 2, 79
  Samuel, 176
  Thomas, 2
  William, 62, 176
Hamm, Jacob, 133
Hammett, Elijah, 149
  John, 53
Hammilton, John, 54
Hammitt, John, 26
Hammon, John, 131
  William, 102
Hamond, James, 141
Hampton, Benjamin, 149
  David, 4
  John, 99
  Lewis, 99
Hamton, Thomas (G?), 176
Hanback, William, 32, 79
Hancock, Joseph, 9
Handcock, John, 176
  Thomas, 89, 176
  Thomas G., 176
Handley, John, 176
Hane, Drew, 8
Hanes, Josiah, 128
Haney, Henry, 73
Hanks, Absolem, 73
Hann, Christian, 48
Hanna, Thomas, 129
Hannah, John H., 176
Hans, Jacoby, 40
Hanson, John, 176
Haplittle, William, 46
Harbenson, John, 10
Harbert, Matthew, 152
Harbeson, Arthur, 129
  John, 150
Harbolt, Leonard, 105
Harcourt, John, 62
Hardesty, Uriah, 23
Hardesty, Caleb, 135, 176
  William, 62
Hardgrove, James, 7

Hardgrove, cont'd.
  William, 139
Hardin, Aaron, 95
  Abraham, 24
  Amos, 126
  David, 58, 176
  David, 176
  Enos, 89
  George, 58
  Henry, 53, 138, 150
  James, 124
  John, 1,13,32,114,176
  Joseph, 56
  William, Jr., 97, 138
  See also Harding.
Harding, Aaron, 176
  John, 95
  See also Hardin.
Hardy, Andrew, 31, 73
  Benjamin, 58
  John D., 18
Harges, Isaac, 37
  Thomas, 176
Hargraves, Willis, 116, 176
Hargrove, Willis, 40
Harkins, Isaac, 176
Harling, George, 21, 25
Harlow, Clayton, 52
Harman, Abraham, 26
  James, 9
  Lewis, 149
  Mathias, 23
  Samuel, 45
Harned, Edward, 48, 135
Harper, James, 124
  Joseph, 176
  Turner, 119
Harrard, John, 95
  See also Harrod.
Harrell, Moses, 11
Harril, James, 139
Harrington, Charles, 149
Harris, Alexander, 95
  Archibald, 79, 176
  Edward, 43, 44
  Edward, Jr., 44
  Edwin L., 52
  Frederick, 129
  George, 44
  Henry, 119
  Hezekiah P., 105
  Hosea, 38
  John, 58, 119, 176
  Jordan, 14
  Robert, 92
  Samuel, 62, 176
  William, 119, 176
  Zedekiah, 67
Harrison, Benjamin, 1, 15
  Burr, 116, 135
  Cuthbert, 10
  Hezekiah, 55
  John, 6,10,23,36,92
  Micajah, 47
  Reuben, 176
  Robert, 2, 15
  Samuel, 177
  Thomas G., 177
  William, 38, 40, 54, 116
Harrod, John, 95
  Samuel, 62, 177
  See also Harrard.
Harsley, Elijah, 17
Harson, John, 144
Hart, Daniel, 84
  David, 84, 177
  John, 79
  Samuel, 84
  William, 126
  Zephaniah, 124
Hartgrove, Valentine, 177
  William, 112
Hartley, George, 177

Harvey, Norris, 119
  William, 119
Harwood, John, 25
Haskin, George, 44
Haskins, Creed, 56
  Joshua, 114
  Phil, 120
Haslett, Samuel, 84
Hastings, Simeon, 84
  Simon, 84
Hatcher, Robert, 177
  Samuel, 131
Hatfield, Henry, 149
  Thomas, 67, 105, 177
Hathaway, David, 17, 47
Hathorn, Andrew, 114
Hattey, Samuel, 50
Hatton, Robert, 34
Havenhill, John, 135
Hawes, Jacob, 116
  John, 105, 116
Hawison, John, 124
Hawkins, (no first name),2
  James, 108
  Jameson, 70, 155
  John, 4, 120
  Josiah, 30
  Lewis, 126
  Moses, 89
  Samuel, 28
  Weedon, 92
  William, 131, 177
  Zadic, 68
Hay, Daniel, 116,117,177
  John G., 117
Hayden, Charles, 13
  Ezekiel, 26
  George, 150
  James, 40
  John, 13,53,99,150,177
  Samuel, 177
  Wilford, 13
Haydon, Benjamin, 14, 26
  Ezekiel, 14
  James, 14
Hayes, John, 53
  Justin, 53
  Richard, 131
  Robert, 30
  William, 79
Haynes, Joseph, 177
Hays, Adern, 87
  Joseph, 56
Hazlitt, Samuel, 84
Head, Edward, 177
Headspeath, Charles, 20
Heady, James, 11
Jeard, John, 75
Heck, John, 177
Heddington, Joshua, 79
Hedgdon, Thomas, 135
Hedge, James, 62
Hedger, Jonathan, 99
Hedges, Jonathan, 14
  Samuel P., 177
Hedrick, Joseph, 92
Heflin, Gustias, 84
Helm, Benjamin, 97, 155
  George, 24, 155
  Meredith, 9
  William, 9
Helms, John, 13
  William, 44
Henderson, Alexander, 177
  James L., 144, 177
  John, 49, 62
  Samuel, 62
Hendricks, James, 177
Hendrickson, John, 42
Hendson, Enos, 177
Henrix, Joseph, 177
Henry, Belfield, 177
  Joel, 177

Henry, cont'd.
  Robert P., 155
  Vincent, 177
  William, 1,12,25,49,55,155
Hensly, Jonathan, 144
Henson, Benjamin H., 177
  Jessey, 149
  John, 149
Herbert, Jeremiah, 150
Herndon, Henry, 141
  Richard, 110, 177
  Richardson, 177
Herriford, John, 47
Hesler, Jacob, 177
Hess, Henry, 139
Hiat, Benjamin, 36
Hiatt, Elijah, 177
Hibbler, Joseph, 62
Hibbs, Jonah, 114, 177
Hibler, Daniel, 177
  Samuel, 28
Hickerson, Thomas, 102
Hickinbottom, James, 177
Hickland, James, 177
Hicklane, Thomas, 62
Hickman, Benjamin, 99
  Elijah, 71
  James, 4
  Joel, 73
  Paschal, 89, 177
  Richard, 4, 73, 155
  Thomas, 108, 177
Hicks, Absolem, 71
  Daniel, 92
  Henry, 71
  Isaac, 177
  John, 177
  Willis, 71
Higbee, Vincent, 177
Higdon, Leonard, 135
  Thomas, 135
  Thomas, Jr., 177
  Zachariah, 178
Higgarson, George, 149
Higgins, James, 131
  Robert, 31
  Stout, 79
Higginson, James, Jr., 149
Highat, William, 22
Highbee, Joseph, 108
Highfield, Jeremiah, 68
Hightower, Richard, 108
Hildreth, Joseph, 15
Hilicost, John, 84
Hill, Ezekiel, 178
  Hardy, 6
  Isaac, 144
  James, 117
  Joel, 178
  Richard, 117
  Robert, 10, 58
  William, 7,112,117,139, 178
Hilless, James, 178
Hillhouse, George, 178
Hilman, Benjamin, 102
Hinch, Samuel, 105, 179
Hindershot, John, 99
Hindman, Robert, 58
Hines, John, 149
  Joseph, 139
Hinkson, William, 20
Hinkston, William, 38
Hinton, Benonai, 85
  Eli, 85
  John, 97
  William, 144, 178
Hiron, Samuel, 99
Hite, Lewis, 178
  Thomas, 39
Hiter, Charles, 153
Hites, Jacob, 178
Hoagland, Dorsey, 178

Hoard, Edward, 124
  Elias, 23
Hobdy, John, 49, 178
Hockersmith, John, 178
Hode, Andrew, 131
Hodg, Nathan, 79
Hodge, Andrew, 131, 178
  Samuel, 30
  William, 178
Hodgen, Isaac, 97
Hodges, Robert, 114
  Thomas, 114, 178
Hog, Milbourn, 151
Hogan, David, 110, 178
  Elijah, 70
  James, 4
  John, 120
Hogg, James, 87
Hogland, Moses, 50
Hoke, Leonard, 105
Holbert, John, 178
Holcomb, Joel, 52
Holder, John, 17
Holding, James, 178
Holecraft, Richard, 102
Holeman, Isaac, 178
  John, 79
Holland, Alland, 178
  Ephraim, 141
Hollandsworth, John, 178
Holley, Samuel, 102
Holliday, John, 73, 178
  William, 178
Hollin, William, 126
Holly, Samuel, 151
  William, 73
Holman, Isaac, 26, 54, 178
  James, 153
Holmes, Andrew, 50
  Elias, 24
  Hugh, 154
  James, 178
  Jesse, 144
  Samuel, 178
Holt, Isaac, 178
  Zila, 91
Holton, John, 178
Homes, Robert, 178
  Robert M., 178
Hood, Lucas, 73
  Luke, 73
Hook, John, 45, 126, 178
  Thomas, 62
Hooper, Enoch, 114
Hooten, John, 178
Hopkins, James, 141
  Samuel, 55, 117
  Samuel G., 155, 179
Hopson, Zach., 149
Hopwood, John, 179
Hord, Edward, 155
  Willis, 105
Horine, George, 7
  Jacob, 21, 39
  Michael, 21
Horn, Elijah, 44
  Thomas, 105
Hornback, James, 97
  John, 2, 67
Hornbeck, John, 179
  Michael, 62
  Solomon, 179
Hornsby, Joseph, Jr., 144
  Thomas, 144
Hosick, William, 179
Hoskins, Achilles, 102
  David, 151
Hough, Joseph, 89
Houghland, Cornelius, 154
Houghman, True, 36
House, John, 124
Houston, Aron, 124
  David, 42

Houston, cont'd.
  James, 179
  John, 42
  Robert, 117
  William, 120
How, Edward, 89
Howard, Benjamin, 4, 110
  Edwin, 14
  Elisha, 24
  George H., 97
  Isaac, 154
  Josh., 120
  Thomas, 45
  William, 179
Howe, Ezra, 179
  James, 179
  John, 50
  Joseph, 85
Howel, Charles, 179
Howell, David, 62
  William, 179
Howson, John, 33
Howston, John, 48
Hoy, Jones, 73, 179
  Thomas, 62
Hubbard, Armistead, 135,179
  Dirrett, 42
  Simon Miller, 149
Hubbs, Jacob, 50
Hudson, Joseph, 79
Hudspeth, David, 149
  George, 149, 179
  Thomas, 97
Huff, Daniel, 75
  John, 4, 179
  Jonathan, 179
  Reuben, 138
Huffaker, Christopher, 179
  Jacob, 152
Huffman, Frederick, 92
Hufford, David, 99
Hughes, David, 2, 17, 131
  George, 62
  John, 62, 105
  Robert, 62
  William, 28, 131
Hughs, John, 179
Hull, James, 75
Hulse, John, 179
Humble, Uriah, 17
Hume, Gerard, 30
  Gerrand, 4
  John, 70
  Stripling, 68, 179
Humes, Pru B., 179
  Prue, 179
Humphres, Thomas, 179
Humphries, Charles, 129
Hund, Anthony, 179
Hundley, Charles, 151
Hundly, Nelson, 79
Hungate, Charles, 46
  John, 151, 179
Hunly, Nelson, 79
Hunn, Anthony, 62
Hunt, John, 44,85,126,179
  John W., 79
  John William, 18
  Robison, 95
Hunter, James, 179
  John, 12,22,25,49,179
  Joseph, 6
  Robert, 25
  William, 117,144,154,179
Hurst, John, 141
Husk, John, 95
Huston, (no first name),48
  Anthony, 25
  James, 48, 67
  Nathan, 7, 21, 55
  Robert, 179
  Simon, 120
Hutcheson, Alexander, 141

Hutcheson, cont'd.
  Archibald, 38, 79
  David, 95
  John, 38
  Lawrence, 22, 36
Hutchin, John, 39
Hutchings, John, 179
Hutchins, Gabriel, 112
Hutton, Benjamin, 85
  Joseph, 34, 89
  Samuel, 10, 179
Hyatt, Shadrach, 180
Hykes, Jacob, 105, 180
Hynes, William, 133

I

Indicut, John, 62
  William, 62
Ingle, Peter, 110
Inlow, Isham, 10, 180
Innes, Hugh, 180
  James, 180
Ireland, David, 28
  John, 62
  John R., 180
  Samuel, 102, 180
Irvin, John, 180
  Stephen, 62
  Thompson, 124
Irvine, Benjamin, 97
  David C., 180
  William D., 129
Irwin, Benjamin, 180
  James, 45, 48
  John, 180
  Robert, 32, 102
  William, 2
Irwine, Benjamin, 180
Isball, Godfrey, 139
Isbell, Jasen, 149
Ise, Jesse, 135
Isles, Thomas, 180

J

Jack, James, 180
Jackson, Burwell, 52
  Christopher, Jr., 138
  David, 180
  Dempsey, 124
  James, 180
  Joel, 102, 139
  Thomas, 28, 62
  William Duffield, 62
Jacobs, Samuel, 50
Jacoby, Ralph, 62
  See also Jecoby.
James, Ellzey L., 180
  Henry, 139
  John, 162
  Joseph, 135
  William, 138
Jameson, Andrew, 71
  John, 89, 95, 131
  Joseph, 42
  Robert, 22, 42, 120
Jamison, John, 180
  Robert, 180
Janos, William, 149
January, James B., 79, 108
Jarvis, Franklin, 26
Jasper, John, 39, 112, 139
Jay, Francis, 28
Jecoby, John, 180
  Ralph, 180
  See also Jacoby.
Jeffries, Ambrose, 89
  Daniel, 93
Jenkins, Hamilton, 180
  John, 97, 102, 180

Jenkins, cont'd.
  William, 112
Jenney, Nathaniel, 39
Jennings, Augustine, 36,93
  Daniel, 180
  Jonathan, 89, 91
  William, 7, 21, 36, 93
Johes, William, 102
  See also Joyes.
  John, Jonathan, 180
Johns, Henry, 50
Johnson, Absolem, 58
  Adam, 49, 141
  Cave, 70, 180
  Daniel, 91
  Forgus, 58
  Gabriel J., 105, 180
  George, 144
  Hugh, 30
  James, 49,139,144,152,180
  James W., 79
  Jesse, 85
  John, 50, 135, 180
  John S., 180
  Jonathan, 62, 181
  Joseph, 110, 112
  Larkin, 144
  Matthew, 42
  Nelson, 68
  Oralea, 79
  Richard, 141, 181
  Richard, Sr., 120
  Richard, Jr., 120
  Robert, 12
  Samuel, 124, 181
  Thomas, 75, 139,144,152
  William, 62,95,141,144,181
  William,G., 141
Johnston, David, 44
  Edward, 181
  Ephraim, 11
  Gabriel J., 39
  Jacob, 99, 112
  James, 17, 22
  John, 99
  Martin, 4, 17
  Nelson, 181
  Peter, 181
  Philip, 181
  Silas, 4
  Thomas, 181
  William, 15, 95
Johnstone, John, 145
Jones, Benjamin, 23, 114
  David, 75
  Dumas, 62, 181
  Elijah, 110
  Ezekiel, 110
  Fielding, 101, 181
  Humphrey, 42, 120, 181
  Jacob, 44
  James, 12, 120, 181
  John, 2,32,79,95,99,114,
    149,181
  Joseph, 18
  Joshua, 91, 145
  Moses, 28, 155
  Peter, 102
  Richard, 181
  Robert, 18
  Strother, 181
  Thomas, 2,4,23,33,85,91
  William, 41,139,152,181
Jonston, Aaron, 124
  Thomas, 181
Jordan, Peter, 181
Jorden, William, 181
Jourden, John, 129
  Peter, 129
  William, 48
Journey, Nathaniel, 75, 181
Joyes, Thomas, 181
  See also Johes.

Judy, John, 17, 47
Jump, Peter, 23, 76
Junifer, John, 28
Junip, Peter, 20
Jurney, John, 76

K

Kaen, Charles, 95
  See also Charles Cain.
Kauns, John, 181
  See also Kounce.
Kavanaugh, William, 8,22,42
Keaney, Michael, 139
Kearns, Thomas, 56
Keaton, Hezekiah, 89,181
Keen, John, 79
Keene, Oliver, 79
Keisinger, Joseph, 97
Keith, Abner, 133
  Abraham, 117
  John, 33
  Thomas, 126, 181
  William, 11, 117
Keizer, Christopher, 79
Kellar, Abner, 62
  Abraham, 62, 105
Keller, Abraham, 62, 182
  Isaac, 182
Kelley, Dennis, 52
  George, 17
  Joseph, 182
Kellian, Jacob, 120
Kellow, Daniel, 151
Kelly,(no first name), 31
  Giles, 120
  Griffin, 12, 141
  Joseph, 73
  Nathaniel, 17, 23
  William, 12, 182
Kelso, Henry, 17
Kelsoe, John, 58
Kemp, Edward, 182
  Reuben, 15
Kemper, Thomas, 182
Kenady, Eli, 182
Kenard, William, 182
Kendal, Hebe, 135
  Henry, 135
  R., 105
  Rawleigh, 105
  William, 145
Kendall, Jacob, 182
Kenderick, William, 62
Kendrick, Alexander, 182
Kennady, David, 36
  James, 182
Kennard, William, 182
Kennedy, Andrew, 8,42,120,
    155
  Benjamin, 34
  Charles, 11
  David, 8, 93
  Eli, 182
  James, 131
  John, 182
  Joseph, 2,8,70,120
  Thomas, 1
Kenney, John, 28
Kennon, William, 33
Kenny, James, 62, 79
Kenton, Simon, 9, 23
Kenyan, Henry, 182
Kercheval, John, 124
Kerley, William, 8,42,155
Kerns, Alexander, 36
Kerr, Armstrong, 21
  Elijah, 145
  Peter, 34, 89
  See also Carr.
Kersey, Claiborne, 108
Kertly, Pleasant, 182

Kesiah, James, 139
Ketcham, John, 145
Key, Elijah, 149
  Marshall, 182
  Peyton R., 127
  William, 149
Kilger, Robert, 30
Kilgore, John, 101
  William, 114
Killam, Gilbert, 110
Killing, Jacob, 120
Kincaid, Andrew, 85
  Archibald, 154
  David, 120
  James, 73, 120, 182
Kincart, James, 63
Kinchaloe, Lewis, 133
  Louis, 133
  Stephen, 133
  Thomas, 138
Kincheloe, Elias, 135
  Lewis, 156
  Thomas, 66
Kinchloe, Lewis, 30
Kindle, William, 145
Kindred, Bartholomew, 32,108, 182
Kiney, Michael, 39
King, (no first name), 89
  Abner, 135, 182
  Ibzan, 182
  John, 182
  John E., 37, 76, 156
  Nathaniel, 145
  Richard, 99
  Robert, 182
  Thomas, 91
  William, 58
Kinkhead, Andrew, 85
  James, 154, 182
Kinnason, John, 39
Kinon, John, 182
Kinsor, George, 124
Kirby, Richard, 63
  Samuel, 149
Kircheval, Thomas, 182
Kirk, Vincent, 2
Kirkendole, Matthew, 58
Kirkland, Charles, 112
Kirkly, Beverly, 47
Kirkpatrick, Elihu, 76
  Joseph, 2, 11
  Moses, 10, 23
Kirkum, Henry, 149
Kirling, Thomas, 9
Kirly, Francis, 108
Kirtley, Elliott, 182
  Larkin, 142
Kirtly, Benjamin, 85
  Elliott, 182
  Pleasant, 182
Kirtner, Christopher, 4
Kiser, Adam, 182
Kishner, Jacob, 73
Kitchens, James, 139
Kivell, Benjamin, 114
Kizer, Jacob, 2, 4, 79
Knight, George B., 145
  John, 31, 50, 145
Knox, Robert, 8
Kounce, Jacob, 182
  See also Kauns.
Kutch, John, 182
Kuykendal, Moses, 20
Kykendol, Peter, 145
Kyle, Samuel, 79
  Thomas, 154
Kyser, Christopher, 79

L

Lacey, Edward, Jr., 182

Lacey, cont'd.
  Isiah, 106
  Joshua, 182
Lackey, Alexander, 182
  Gabriel, 93
  William, 93, 120
Lacy, Edward, Jr., 114
  Isiah, 106
  Thomas, 182
Ladd, Jacob, 63
  Robert, 63
Lafon, Nicholas, 34
  Richard, 108
Lagoe, Wilson, 102
Lain, Thomas, 145
Laird, Samuel, 182
Lamb, Basil, 182
  Jacob, 89, 91, 145
  William, 10
Lambert, Daniel, 25
Lamery, William, 85
Lamkin, Samuel, 115
Lamm, Jesse, 79
Lampton, Benjamin, 56
  Samuel, 63
Lancaster, Henry, 45
  James, 102
  John, 151, 183
  Ralph, 183
Landcaster, William, 69
Lander, Henry, 183
Landers, Jacob, 4
  John, 183
Landham, Thomas, 8
Landrith, James, 183
Lane, Daniel, 106
  James H., 131
  Moses, 183
  Thomas, 145
Laneir, Alexander C., 69
Langhorn, Maurice, 183
Langley, Jeremiah, 133
Langston, Jacob, 47
  John, 149
Lanham, Stephen, 183
Lanier, Alexander, 183
  Alexander C., 183
Lansdale, James, 44
Lapsley, John, 183
Larue, Jacob, 91
  James, 97
  Samuel, 183
Lasey, James, 47
Lastley, John, 183
Latham, John, 117
  Phillip, 183
Latimar, Samuel, 95
Latimore, David, 49
  Jacob, 95
  John, 129, 131
Laton, James, 183
Laughland, John, 79
Laughlin, John W., 183
  Thomas, 110, 111, 183
  William, 15, 63
Law, Laurence, 46
Lawding, Thomas, 50
Laws, William, 183
Lawson, David, 21
  John, 50, 102
  William, 56, 95, 183
Lawyers, John, 183
Lay, George, 183
Leace, George, 183
Lealand, Leonard, 54
Leaman, Robert, 48
Leatherman, Christopher, 145
Leathers, John, 183
Ledford, James, 79
Lee, Ambrose, 12, 183
  Barton, 124
  Gersham, Jr., 91
  Henry, 9, 28, 55

Lee, cont'd.
  John, 183
  Miller, 117
  Moses, 102
  Samuel, 129, 183
  William, 95
  Willis, 26, 34, 89
  Willis A., 89
Leech, Benjamin, 44
Leir, Matthew, 58
Lemasters, James, 102
Lemon, David, 183
  James, 1, 15, 79
  John, 183
Lenear, Collins, 183
Lenier, Collins, 149
Leright, Minor, 183
Leslie, Solomon, 136
Letcher, Benjamin, 36, 93, 156
Levil, James, 183
Lewis, Alexander, 99
  Andrew P., 183
  Daniel, 183
  George, 9
  Jasper, 11
  John, 36
  Joseph, 7, 39, 55, 112, 127, 156, 183
  Joshua, 109, 183
  Josiah, 149
  Robert, 183
  Robert T., 184
  Samuel, 112
  Stephen, 109
  Thomas, 109
  William, 4, 184
Lightfoot, Edmund, 106
  John, 89
Lillard, Thomas, 34, 89
Lincoln, Mordacai, 13, 26, 151
  Thomas, 76, 184
Linder, Daniel, Jr., 97
  Isaac, 37
  Jacob, 24
Lindsay, Anthony, 184
  Henry, 25
  John V., 12
Lindsey, Anthony, 142
  Elisha, 184
  George, 28
  Henry, 142
  John, 70
  Joseph, 25
  Joshua, 184
  Nevil, 101
  William, 145
Linebarger, Frederick, 112
Linginfelter, Jacob, 80
Linn, Asahel, 39, 106
  Joseph, 71
  Nathan, 30
  William, 6, 106
Linney, George, 131
Linsey, Thomas, 184
Linsy, James, 184
Lips, Jacob, 38
Lipscomb, Nathan, 184
Liter, John, 63
Lithill, Lott, 112
  Roadshah, 112
Litten, Caleb, 47
Little, James, 17
  John, 46
Littlepage, Epps, 36, 93, 133, 184
  Thomas, 133
Litton, Caleb, 63, 85
  John, 28
Lizenbry, William, 26
Loaran, Frederick, 63
Lobb, William, 93

Lock, Richard S., 80
Lockett, James, 109
Lockhart, James, 109
Lockrey, Jeremiah, 106
Lockridge, James, 184
Lodler, Jesse, 63
Logan, Alexander, 184
  Benjamin, 1
  David, 55, 156
  Hugh, 18, 39
  John, 184
  Jonathan, 7
  Joseph, 124
  Robert A., 30, 115
  William, 58, 156
Logsdon, Joseph, 8
  Thomas, 37
Logue, William, 58
Long, Anderson, 51
  John, 76, 140, 152
  Solomon, 76
  Thomas, 89
Longan, Thomas, 80
Loofbouron, Thomas V., 184
Looney, David, 44
Louden, Thomas, 102
Loughberry, Thomas V., 89
Loughborrough, Thomas, 89
Loughland, John, 80
Louir, Christian, 28
Love, Arthur, 184
  James, 41,48,106,145
  Joseph, 184
  Thomas, 18
  William, 136, 184
Lovelas, Archibald, 184
Lowden, John, 102
Lowe, Barney, 184
Lowery, John, 184
  William, 85
  William G., 184
Lowman, Joseph, 184
Lowrie, William, 70
Lowry, John, 80, 109
  Samuel, 49, 184
  William G., 184
Lucas, Abraham, 67
  Charles, 184
Luckett, Samuel, 106
Lucky, Joseph, 63
Lucust, Jesse, 17
Lurty, William, 184
Lusk, Hugh, 109
  Vance, 115
Luttrell, Lott,
  See Lott Lithill
  Rodham. See Roadshah
    Lithill.
Luves, Thomas, 184
Lycan, Jacob, 87
  John, 87
Lyle, Daniel, 31, 73
Lynch, David, 22, 42
  William, 140
Lynn, Nathan, 69
  William, 20, 140
Lyon, Hezekiah, 16
  John, 28
Lytle, Nathaniel, 85
Lytton, Caleb, 87

Mc

McAfee, Clark, 184
  George, 184
  John, 10
  Robert, 184
  Robert B., 184
MaAffee, George, 129
  John, 46, 129
  Robert, 129
  Samuel, 129
  William, 53

McAlister, James, 8
McAlla, Robert, 142
  See also McCalla.
McAllister, Colister, 102
  Edward, 97
McAmy, Robert, 129
McAndre, Bunyan, 102
McAnn, Neal, 80
  See also Neal McCann.
McArty, Jonathan, 48
  See also McCarty.
McBee, Silas, 101
McBrayer, Andrew, 89
  James, 89
McBride, Daniel, 101
  William, 184
McCachley, Joshua, 106
McCall, John, 80
McCalla, Thomas, 184
  See also McAlla.
McCallen, Haze, 184
McCambel, James, 145
McCambell, Andrew, 184
McCambron, James, 48
McCandles, John, 37
  William, 38
McCann, Neal, 80, 184
  See also McAnn.
McCargo, Radford, 73
McCartey, Elijah, 20
McCarty, James, 184
  See also McArty.
McClain, James, 124
McClanahan, Elijah, 30,69,184
  Thomas, 63
McClane, Duncan, 48
McClasky, Joseph, 136
McCleland, James, 185
  William, Jr., 63
McClelland, Abram, 12
  James, 63, 185
McClenahan, William, 185
McClenay, Micajah, 131
McClenehan, Thomas, 2
McClung, Matthew, 17, 47
McClure, (no first name)38
  James, 12, 99, 185
  Matthew, 132
  Nathaniel, 99, 129
  William, 7, 51, 145
McColgan, James, 185
McCollister, Collister, 102
McCollum, William, 120
McCombs, John, 24
McCommon, William, 133
McConicha, David, 63
McConnel, Edward, 16, 63
  James, 76, 80
  John, 63
  William, 63
McConnell, Edward, 185
  John, 4, 18, 185
  William, 63
McCord, James, 99
  Michael, 124
  William, 124
McCormic, Abraham, 129
  James, 42
  Peter P., 51, 145
  William, 142, 145
McCormick, James, 156
McCoun, George, 63, 185
McCowan, Alexander, 11
  James, 136
McCoy, Alexander, 142
  Kenneth, 4
  Martin, 63
McCrackin, Virgil, 54
McCrary, Andrew, 73
  William, 120
McCray, William, 30, 69, 102
McCreery, William, 120
McCressky, James, 25

McCuddy, Isaac, 185
McCulloch, Alexander, 33
McCullough, John, 23
McCune, George, 16
  John, 63
McCutchen, Hugh, 41
McDaniel, Daniel, 117
  Francis, 2
  James, 41, 120
  John, 29
  Richard, 26
  Rowland, 29
  William, 46
McDanniel, John, 2
McDavid, James, 145
McDavitt, James, 51,145,185
McDole, James, 63
  John, 9
McDonald, James, 16
  Richard, 151
  Samuel, 124
McDonnald, John, 76
  William, 129
McDowel, James, 185
  Joseph, 185
McDowell, Ephraim, 129
  James, 4, 18
  John, 4, 18
  John G., 185
  Joseph, 156
  Samuel, 55,156,185
  William, 46, 129, 156
McElhatten, William, 13
McElmurray, John, 115
McElmury, John, 115
McElroy, John, 185
McFaddin, Samuel, 30
McFadin, Elias, 185
McFagen, Andrew, 52
McFall, John, 140
McFarland, Alexander,20,76
McFarlane, Jonathan, 185
McFarlin, John, 23
McFeran, James, 39
McFeters, William, 80
McGary, Daniel, 185
  Robert, 17
  William, 58
  William R., 185
McGaughey, John, 51, 145
McGee, Humphrey, 120
  John, 185
McGinnis, Samuel, 129
  William, 124
McGlaughlin, George, 16
McGoodin, Daniel, 185
McGoodwin, Daniel, 41,117, 185
McGowan, James Strode, 85
McGrady, Israel, 117
  Samuel, 97,138,185
McGrath, Terrence, 109
McGrew, Moses, 102
McGuire, John, 132
  William, 73
McGuyer, Jesse, 102
McHatton, Samuel, 185
McHenry, Isaac, 20
  William, 52
McIllhaney, James, 132
McIlvain, Moses, 99
  Robert, 185
  Samuel, 99
  William, 185
McIntire, Da-iel, 85, 156
  John, 2
  Joseph, 33, 85, 185
  Robert, 29, 63, 156
  Thomas, 53, 97
  W., 63
McKay, George, 53
  Jacob, 69
McKee, (no first name, 18

McKee, cont'd.
　Archibald, 18
　David, 109
　John, 185
McKenney, John, 185
McKenny, Daniel, 124
McKeown, Morgan, 185
McKiney, John, 18
McKinly, Samuel, 102
McKinney, Francis, 185
　James, 112, 185, 186
　John, 21, 109, 156
McKinny, John, 4, 7
McKinsey, David, 112, 140
McKinzy, Colin, 39
McKitrick, James, 16
　Robert, 99
McKittrick, John, 151
McKneff, John, 151
McLaflin, John, 186
McLain, Alney, 115
　Daniel, 69
　John, 95
McLane, Thomas, 39
McLaughlin, Charles, 30
　John, 93, 151, 186
　Robert, 117
　Robert K., 186
　Thomas, 39
McLean, Charles, 41
　Ephraim, 41
　Samuel, 117, 136
McLenagan, William, 186
McLendon, Benjamin, 115
McMahan, James, 127, 186
　Joseph, 73, 186
　William, 186
McMahon, Friend, 136
McMilian, William, 17
McMillen, William, 73
McMillian, William, 4
McMi-lin, John, 186
McMillion, James, 4, 22, 54
　Robert, 4
　William, 73
McMullen, James, 36, 120
McMullin, Daniel, 124
McMurdie, Francis, 4
McMurtrey, Levi, 186
McMurtry, James, 4, 58
　Joseph, 32, 95
　William, 186
McNab, James, 115
McNabb, William, 95
McNary, John, 124
McNealy, William, 56
McNeeley, William, 95
McNeil, James, 111
　John, 186
McNeley, George, 22
McQueen, John, 22, 42
McRoberts, John, 85
McWaters, John, 140
McWilliams, David, 115
　James, 97, 120, 186
　John, 186

M

Maberry, Joel, 132
Macconnell, Robert, 186
Mackoy, James, 186
Madcalf, Thomas, 186
　See also Metcalfe.
Maddan, Levi, 124
Madden, John, 186
Maddox, Jeremiah, 186
Magil, William, 112
Magill, James, 17
Maginnis, William, 186
Mahan, Henry, 63

Mahan, cont'd.
　John, 46,85,129,186
　Rany, 63
　Thomas, 111
Mahorney, James, 145
Mais, Mathew, 23
Malin, Jacob, 186
Mallett, William, 87
Mallott, Joseph, 120
Malone, Bannister, 95
Malott, Hiram, 186
Manhan, John, 127
Manifee, John, 112
　See also Menefee.
Mann, John, 69, 186
　John T., 186
　Peter, 186
　Richard, 186
　Richard Y., 186
Mannon, John, 44, 45
Maple, Benjamin, 186
March, Rudolph, 120
Markham, William, 63
Marklin, Thomas, 17
Marks, George, 12, 48, 186
Marksberry, Isaac, 93
　John, 93
Markwell, Elias, 186
Marquis, James, 67
Marr, George, 129
Marrs, Isaac, 117
Marshal, Joseph, 186
Marshall, Archibald, 63
　George, 102
　Henry, 4, 18
　James, 26
　Lewis, 156
　Robert, 95
　William, 26, 136
Marshon, Daniel, 33
Martin, Abner, 101
　Azariah, 8
　Edward, 145
　Elijah, 124
　Henry, 2, 186
　Hudson, 154
　Hugh, 186
　James, 4, 106
　Jeremiah, 124,186,187
　Job, 31, 73
　John, 4,26,31,73,140,153,
　　187
　John L., 89
　Joseph, 58
　Micajah, 124, 187
　Nathaniel, 76, 187
　Thomas, 51, 145, 187
　William, 29,30,63,99,112,
　　129,187
Mason, Benjamin, 136, 187
　James, 187
　John, 120
　Pet., 80
　Richard, 112, 187
　William, 136, 187
Massey, John, 38
　Sylvanus, 120
　William, 142
Masterson, Aaron, 80
　Charles, 11
　Hugh, 136
　Jeremiah, 11
　Moses, 32
Mastin, Elijah, 127
　William, 187
Mastison, John, 11
Matlock, Absolem, 25
Matthews, James, 58
　Job, 133
　John, 145
　William, 2
Mattingly, John, 187
Mattock, James, 187

Mattox, Absalom, 145
　John, 127
Mauks, Randolph, 132
Maulden, Morton, 117
Mauldin, Morton, 12
Maulding, Moreton, 41
　Richard, 41
Maupin, Daniel, 42
　James, 17
　Richard A., 187
　Thomas, 120, 187
　See also Moppen.
Maupine, John, 120
　Maxberry, John, 93
　Maxbury, Isaac, 93
　Maxfield, David, 8
May, Edmond, 48, 136
　Humphrey, 136
　John, 112
　John W., 136
　Stephen, 187
Mayberry, John, 187
Mayfield, John, Jr., 58
Mayhall, Timothy, 124
Mays, Robert, 32
Meade, Rhodes, 87
Meadows, Isaac, 140, 153
　John, 138
　William, 187
Means, Robert, 71
　Thomas, 58
Mears, Samuel, 34, 89
Meason, Benjamin, 187
Medcalf, John, 187
　See also Madcalf,
　　Metcalfe.
Meddox, John W., 145
Meek, Jeremiah, 51
Meeks, Sylvester, 187
　William, 138
Melton, John, 149
Menefee, Jarret, 187
　See also Manifee.
Meranda, George, 44
　Isaac, 44
　Thomas, 187
Mercer, Howard, 58
　James, 153
Meredith, Samuel, 4, 32
　William P., 187
Merefield, Alexander, 51
Merrel, Andrew, 73
Merrell, William, 187
Merritt, John, 187
Merton, Jonathan, 73
Meshawn, Daniel, 23
Metcalf, Eli, 124
　Orrick, 187
　Thomas, 124, 187
　See also Madcalf,
　　Medcalf.
Metier, Thomas, 132
Metter, Thomas, 132
Metts, Jacob, 187
Michie, Daniel, 9
Michuson, John, 115
Middleton, Adam, 187
　David, 187
　Matthew, 58
　Thomas, 67
Miex, James, 56
Milam, Jarvis, 120
　Moses, 187
Mileham, Archibald, 154
Miles, Charles, 115, 187
　James, 115
　John, 10, 85, 151
　John, Jr., 187
　Richard, 67
　Thomas, 187
　William, 187
Miliken, James, 37
Miller, Abraham, 7, 103

Miller, cont'd.
  Adam, 11, 12, 188
  Alexander, 124
  Dr. Alexander, 188
  Andrew, 140
  Benjamin, 85
  Daniel, 111, 112, 120
  David, 156
  Henry, 188
  Hugh, 99
  Isaac, 99, 188
  Jac., 142
  Jacob, 103, 188
  James, 4,38,99,188
  John, 2,8,99,142,188
  Nicholas, 37, 97
  Person, 76
  Peter, 188
  Robert, 42,44,120,124,188
  Samuel, 11, 20, 48
  Thomas, 85, 188
  William, 11,27,124,188
Milligan, Joseph, 12
Mills, Evan, 85
  John, 85
  Richard, 188
  Robert, 120
  Thomas, 127
Milspaw, Daniel G., 188
Minor, Gideon, 85
  Jo-n S., 188
  Nicholas, 48
  Thomas, 17, 145
  Waller, 69
  William, 136
Minter, William, 99
Mitcham, William, 188
Mitchel, Adam, 20, 37
  David, 63
  Elijah, 63
  John, 20, 95
  Joseph F., 26
  Samuel, 89, 149
  Thomas, 29, 51, 145
  William, 63
Mitchell, Daniel, 4
  James, 93, 95, 188
  John A., 188
  Moses, 16
  Richard, 4, 18
  Richard D., 188
  Dr. Samuel G., 188
  William, 4, 16
Mitchem, Dudley, 18
Mitcheson, Edward, 115
Mitchuson, Edward, 115
  William, 115
Mitchusson, John, 115
  William, 115
Mith, Jacob, 99
Mize, William, 69
Moberly, John, 149
Mobley, Charles, 149
  James, 52
  John, 120
Mock, Daniel, 13,53,151,156
Mockabee, John, 47
Modrel, Robert, 140
Modrell, Robert, Sr., 140
Modrill, Robert, 188
Moffard, Thomas, 124
Moffat, John, 188
Moffett, George, 14
Money, Joseph, 37, 97
Monroe, Charles, 151
  William, 188
Montgomery, Elijah, 80
  Isaac, 47
  John, 115
  Nathan, 20
  Robert, 7
  Robinson, 80
  Samuel, 7
  William, 14, 188

Montjoy, George, 63, 188
  William, 69, 188
Montur, Robert, 2
Moody, Thomas, 142
  William, 142, 188
Mooney, John, 16, 85
Moor, Benjamin, 45
  David, 120
  Henry, 188
  John, 188
  Levy, 188
Moore, Alexander, 140
  David, 22, 120
  George E., 189
  Harbin, 189
  Harry, 31
  Henry, 73
  James, 63,80,120,129,189
  John, 189
  Jonathan, 40
  Josiah, 129
  Leroy, 189
  Martin, 189
  Peter, 1
  Richard, 85
  Robert, 145, 149
  Robert M., 145
  Samuel, 7,29,63,96,189
  Thomas, 47, 111
  William, 2,4,16,32,80,99,
    103,111,189
  Williams, 8
  Zachariah, 69, 189
Moppen, Thomas, 120
  See also Maupin.
Moreen, John, 42
Morehead, Charles, 11,48,136
Morfett, George, 189
Morford, John, 45
Morfult, George, 80
Morgan, David, 87, 189
  John, 69, 133
  Thomas, 138
  William, 73, 87
  Willis, 30, 133
Morreson, Daniel, 54
Morris, Adam, 40
  James, 69, 189
  John, 80, 87, 89, 91
  Nathaniel G., 45
  Thomas, 189
  William, 189
Morrison, Archibald, 80
  Daniel L., 97
  David, 189
  George, 120
  James, 56, 96
  John, 4, 93
  Robert, 80
  William, 8, 22, 42
  William Mitchell, 42
Morrow, John, 73
  Robert, 132, 189
  Thomas F., 189
  Winn, 63
Morton, Francis, 48
  John, 17
  John H., 156
  Jonathan, 73, 154
  Samuel, 12
  William, 80
Mosby, John, 14, 26, 189
Mosea, George, 63
Moseby, Nicholas, Jr., 189
Mosely, Daniel P. 189
Mosley, John, 109, 138
  Thomas, 132
Moss, James W., 44
  John, 4, 18, 52, 58
  William, 109
Mounce, Smith, 93
Mountague, Thomas, 189
Mountjoy, George, 63, 189

Mountjoy, cont'd.
  John, 189
  William, 69
Mounts, Henry, 93
  Thomas, 38
Moyars, Andrew, 69
Mudd, Francis, 26
  Richard, 151
Muldrough, Hugh, 4, 80
  John, 13
Muldrow, Hugh, 32
Mullen, Reuben, 69
Mullens, Gabriel, 22
Mulliken, William, 145
Mullins, Gabriel, 42
  Reuben, 189
  William, 153
Muncey, John, 111, 189
Munday, Stephen, 89
Mundy, Harrison, 129
Munford, William, 97
Munroe, William, 189
Murfey, William, 189
Murphree, Isaac, 189
Murphy, John, 106
  Neil, 85
  Wallace, 124
  Zaphaniah, 132
Murrel, George, 112
  James, 189
Murrell, Andrew, 73
  George, 7
Murry, Enoch, 189
Musick, Ephraim, 189
Myers, Elijah, 138
  Henry, 189
  Jacob, 189
  John, 63
  William, 13
Myor, Daniel, 151
Myres, Joseph, 189

N

Nafus, George, 189
Nagerley, Peter, 67
Nagly, Davie, 189
Nailor, Benjamin, 96
Nall, Charles, 142
  Charles L., 142
  John, 12,53,151,190
  Martin, 136
Nalle, John, 48
  John, Jr., 48
Nancarrow, Benjamin, 80
Nash, Harmon, 6, 39, 106
  John, 112, 145
  Marvel, 112, 190
  Noble, 145
  William, 21, 112
Nayler, John, 54
Naylor, Thomas, 99
Neafus, George, 136
Neal, Andrew, 117
  Archibald, 19
  Jacob, 64
  John, 24
  Samuel, 136
  William, 136
Neale, Daniel, 142
  George, 103
  William, 103
Neasbit, Robert, 29
Neavill, George, 103
Neeley, Andrew, 71
Neely, Andrew, 115
  Edward, 190
Neibors, Abraham, 151
Neil, Arthur, 111
Neisbit, Robert, 38
Nellis, William, 16
Nelson, Andrew, 190

Nelson, cont'd.
  Hayden, 100
  John, 29, 39, 190
  Matthew, 93
  Richard, 69, 190
Nesbet, Jeremiah, 190
  Joseph Mc., 190
Nettles, Price, 190
  See also Nuttles
Nevill, Joseph, 190
Neville, Joseph, 58
Nevitt, Joseph, 136, 190
  Matthew, 136
New, Jacob, 138
  James, 97
  Robert A., 190
Newberry, Henry, 34
Newcombe, Daniel, 85
Newel, William, 100
Newkirk, William, 67
Newman, Isaac, 41
  Jacob, 101
Nicholas, (George?), 140
  James, 140
Nichols, Edward, 76
  George, 112
  John, 125
  Simon, 190
  Thomas, 44
  William, 25
Nicholson, William, 36, 93
Nickel, John, 47
  Thomas, 47
Nickleson, William, 22
Nickoll, Thomas, 132
Nickson, John, 190
Nield, Robert, 129
Nisbitt, Jeremiah, 64
Nixon, Samuel, 190
Noble, James, 70
Noel. See Nowell.
Noland, James, 190
  William, 42, 120
Nolin, (Tuner?), 190
Norcutt, John, 120
Norman, Caleb, 70
  Ezekiel, 29
Norris, Abraham, 135
  Benjamin, 190
  James, 190
  Joseph, 127
  Thomas, 190
North, Henry, 190
Northcut, Hosea, 64
  John, 120
Norton, James, 16
Norwood, Frederick, 190
Nowell, Barnett, 190
Nowlin, Bryan Ward, 117
  Payton, 117
Nowls, William, 190
Nuckles, Lewis, 49
Nunn, Samuel, 190
Nuttles, Price, 190
  See also Nettles.

O

Oakly, William, 17
O'Bannion, William B., 93
Obannon, John, 76
  William, 54, 93, 127
Odum, Willis, 37
Offil, Samuel, 132
Ogden, Masterson, 145
Ogle, John, 190
Oglesby, Elias, 106
  Ellis (Elias?), 106
  Joseph, 106
Oldham, George, 142
  George, Jr., 142
  John, 74

Oldham, cont'd.
  John P., 190
  Richard, 190
  William, 74
Oliver, Joseph, 32, 80
  Thomas, 109, 125
  William, 149
Olvy, Bennett, 190
O'Neal, George, 48
O'Neil, Charles, 136
Orme, Moses, 67
Ormsby, Peter B., 190
  Stephen, 1
Orr, James, 80
Orsburn, James, 142
Orton, Joseph, 64
Osburn, Michael, 103
Overton, Archibald, 80
  Waller, 4
Overturf, Conrad, 127, 190
Owen, David, 103
  John, 191
  Reubin, 191
  William, 146
Owens, Abraham, 146, 191
  Benjamin, 97
  David, 91
  James, 109
  John, 96
  Maximilian, 191
  Reubin, 101, 153
  William, 146
Owsley, Thomas, 40
  William, 93
Oxen, Nathan, 191
Oxley, Micajah, 80, 191
Oyler, Jonathan, 133

P

Pace, William, 89
Page, John, 191
Painter, John, 52, 97, 125
Pairpoint, Jeremiah, 191
Paisley, James, 22
Palmer, Henry, 46, 129, 191
  John, 85
Palsgrove, Henry, 191
Paris, Johnston, 112
  William, 112
Parish, Joel, 85
Park, George, 136
  Samuel, 71
Parker, Alexander, 1, 80
  Aquilla, 64
  Henry, 44
  Isaac, 115
  John, 64
  Joshua, 106
  Lamuel, 191
  Rowland, 64, 191
  Samuel, 106, 191
  Thomas, 19, 138
  William, 125, 191
  Winslow, 125
Parks, Arthur, 44, 85
  George, 136
  John, 191
  Nathaniel, 120, 191
  Samuel, 58
Parmerlee, (no first name), 191
Parmerly, Samuel, 191
Parrish, James, 19
  Joseph, 132
  Thompson, 191
  Woodson, 191
Parrot, Richard, 191
  William, 191
Parrott, William, 151, 191
Parry, Thomas, 125
Parsons, James, 151

Parsons, cont'd.
  Joseph, 115
Pasley, James, 121
Pastor, Samuel, 64
Pate, John, 66, 97
Paton, Daniel, 47
  John, 191
Patrick, Alexander, 121
Patten, James, 44
  Thomas, 191
  William, 85
  William, Jr., 191
Patterson, Edward, 127
  Ezekiel, 4, 32
  George, 80
  Joseph, 191
  Peter, 89
  Robert, 32, 117
  Samuel, 32
  Thomas, 93
  William, 140, 146, 191
Pattie, Sylvester, 127
Patton, Abraham, 191
  Alexander, 96
  Felix, 87
  James, 7, 121, 191
  Thomas, 86, 96, 191
  William, 133
Paul, James, 136
  Michael, 47, 132
Paxton, John, 40, 191
Payne, Asa, 191
  Duvall, 23, 33, 55
  Edward, 4, 32
  Enoch, 91
  Jammy, 192
  Jessie, 64
  Jilston, 132, 146
  John, 13,25,142,156,192
  Philemon, 153
  Reuben, 21, 40
  William R., 149, 192
  Zadock, 142
Payton, Bluford, 192
  Daniel, 146
Peal, Richard, 115
Pearce, James, 192
  Richard, 106
  Walter, 106
  William, 22, 106
Pearcy, George, 146
Pearpoint, Francis, 98
Peary, William, 30
Peck, Jacob, 192
  Major, 106
Pemberton, Bennett,14,34,55
  John, 89, 192
  Reuben, 103
Pendleton, Curtis, 74
Peneston, Thomas, 109
Peniston, Samuel, 192
Penix, Edward, 192
Penn, Ely, 192
Pennington, Francis P.,192
  Isaac, 115
  Tobias, 192
Penrod, Samuel, 133
Peper, Israel, 192
Pepper, Daniel, 98
  Elijah, 192
  Jesse, 23, 45
  Samuel, 125
  William, 23, 86, 125
Perigoe, Romey, 138
Perkins, Edmond, 93, 192
  Nicholas, 56
  Stephen, 93
  William, 58
Perrill, William, 125
Perrin, Josephus, 100,192
Perry, David, 70
  Franklin, 146
  James, 103

Perry, cont'd.
  Jeremiah, 112
  Randolph, 146
Peters, James, 154
Peterson, Garret, 151, 192
Petterson, Thomas, 121
Pettet, Amos, 69
Petty, Ebenezer, 16
Peynton, Samuel, 51
Peyton, Phillip, 106
Phelps, Guy, 67
  John, 22, 29, 64
  Micajah, 115
Philips, David, 6, 192
  Elijah, 2
  John, 76
  William, 13
Phillips, Benjamin, 53
  Elijah, 29
  John, 125
  John, Jr., 76
  John H., 146
  Richard, 39
  Samuel, 106
  William, 121, 192
Philps, Samuel, 106
  See also Samuel Phillips.
Pickens, Aaron, 2
  Samuel, 76
Pickett, John, 44,106,125,192
Pierce, Benjamin, 87
  Jacob, 151
  William, 8
Piercy, George, 146
Pierpoint, Francis, 98
Pilcher, Fielding, 109
Pile, Thomas, 192
Piles, John, 103
Pinson, Henry, 87
Pitts, Younger, 142
Plummer, Abraham, 33, 86
  Benjamin, 86, 192
  Jacob, 86
  Joseph, 86
  Thomas, 125
  William, 33
Poage, James, 47
  John, 192
  Robert, 192
Poague, Jonathan, 121
  Robert, 76, 125
Poge, John, 121
Poindexter, Peter, 109
Polk, William, 146
Polke, Charles, 12, 48
  Edmund, 136
  James, 192
  Samuel, 136
  William, 146
Pollard, Absolem, 7
  Bland Williams, 6
  Braxton, 32
Pollock, James, 64, 127,192
Pomeroy, Francis, 106
Poole, William, 136, 192
Pope, Alexander, 36
  Elemander, 7, 21
  Humphrey, 56
Porter, Andrew, 29,38,100, 192
  Charles, 64
  Ephraim, 32, 80
  George, 69
  John, 64,80,117,192
  Nathaniel, 4
  Roley, 192
  Samuel, 146
  William, 19, 32, 80
  William, Jr., 32
Porther, Charles, 64
  See also Porter.
Portman, John, 40
Portwood, Page, 8

Posey, Fayette, 156
  John, 156, 192
  Thomas, 93, 156
Postlethwait, John, 80, 81
  Samuel, 81
Potter, Lewis, 149
  Royal, 149
Pottinger, Samuel, Jr., 136
Pottorff, Henry, 106
  Jacob, 192
Potts, Hep., 112
  Jonathan, 149, 193
  William, 64
  William, H., 64
Poulke, William, 146
Pounds, John, 115
Powel, Zenos, 64
Powell, John, 193
Power, Holloway, 87
Prater, Phil., 121
  Thomas, 193
Prather, Jeremiah, 125
  John, 86
  Thomas, 106, 129
  William, 129, 193
Pratter, Enos, 44
Preas, William, 76
Press, William, 140
Preston, Daniel, 54
  Francis, 193
  Walter, 156
Prewitt, Beverly, 146
  Elisha, 146
  George, 117
  Joshua, 146
  Robert, 81
  William, 140, 193
Price, Andrew F., 193
  Bird, 4
  Evan, 4
  Francis, 31
  Isaac, 67
  James, 109, 146, 193
  James C., 193
  John, 4
  Josiah, 146
  Reason, 193
  Richard, 89, 193
  Samuel, 19
  Thomas, 86
  William, 5,19,64,81,93, 193
  William B., 193
  Willis, 193
Prigmore, Benjamin, 96
Prince, Thomas, 39, 106
Pringle, Alexander, 103
  William, 103
Pritchett, John, 47
Proctor, Jeremiah, 93,125,193
  John, 42, 193
  Nicholas, 22
  Paige, 42
  Thomas, 117, 193
  William, 193
Protzman, Jacob, 193
Pruet, Beverly, 146
Pryor, Abraham, 121
  Samuel, 54
Puits, John, 17
Pullam, Benjamin, 149
Pullem, William, 58
Pullen, James, 16
Pullers, Lofty, 22
Pullon, John, 2
Pullum, Benjamin, 193
  Burwell, 193
Pumeroy, Frank, 106
Pumroy, Thomas, 39
Purcell, James, 12
Purdy, Edmund, 26
  William, 53
Putman, Daniel, 149, 193

Putman, cont'd.
  James, 44
  Simeon, 58
Pyle, Benjamin, 151
  William, 71

Q

Quarles, Ambrose, 89
  Roger, 81, 193
  Tunstal, 154
Querey, Charles, 20
Querry, Charles, 106
Quertermus, Elisha, 6
Query, Charles, 106
Quick, Alexander, 42
  Aron, 121
  Benjamin, 67
Quigley, John, 151
  Lewis, 151, 193
Quirry, Charles, 106
Quotermus, James, 106

R

Radford, William, 193
Ragsdale, John, 125
Railsback, Daniel, 74, 193
Rains, James, 10, 46
  John, 9
Ralls, Hardy, 40
Rammage, Jess, 115
Ramsay, George, 109
  Jonathan, 115
Ramsey, George, 5
  Jonathan, 156
Randal, Robert, 133
  Wharton, 129
Randolph, Moses, 32
  Robert, 133
  Thomas, 133
  William, 51, 146
Rankin, Benjamin, 74
  David, 38
  Robert, 100
  Simeon, 54, 193
Rankins, Benjamin, 44
Ransdale, Elie, 81
  Wharton, 81
Raper, Charles, 193
Rapier, Charles, 193
Rapir, William, 136
Rardon, Moses, 38
Ratcliff, Joseph, 193
Ratcliffe, Harper, 112
  Silas, 86, 87
Ratliff, Joseph, 193
Rawlings, Edward, 98
  Nathan, 2, 20
Ray, Aaron, 146
  Absalom, 151, 193
  Francis, 64
  James, 7,41,46,55,156
  John, 5, 17, 89, 91
  Joseph, 20, 96, 151
  Nicholas, 151
  Samuel, 106, 193
  Thomas, 76
Raybourn, James, 26
Rayburn, Joseph, 32
Rayls, William, 103
Rayman, William, 44
Read, Hensley, 98
  Mordecai, 106
Reader, Thomas, 2
Rearden, Henry, 154
Reaves, James, 33, 96
  Samuel, 125
  Tabes, 125
  William, 125
Reavis, Charles, 193

Records, Spencer, 9
  William, 193
Redd, Thomas, 193
Redding, Eli, 194
Redman, Benjamin, 81
  George, 22
  Thomas, 117, 194
  Washington, 146
Reed, Alexander, 194
  Archibald H., 30
  Handherson, Jr., 194
  James, 194
  John, 194
  Joseph, 86
  Thomas B., 194
  William, 44,121,154,194
Rees, David, 70, 194
  George, 100
  Thomas T., 51, 103
Reese, Daniel, 125
  Jonathan, 194
Reeves, James, 71
  Joseph, 194
  Samuel, 125
  William, 194
Reid, Alexander, 146
  Caleb, 146
  James, 146
  John, 121, 194
  William, 121
Reilly, William, 121
Remey, William Page, 86
Renfrow, Lewis, 112
Renick, William, 58
Rennic, James, 58
  William, 58
Rennick, George, 74
  Henry, 52, 58, 194
  Jo-n, 89
  William, 58
Renno, Jesse, 133
  Lewis, 133
Renshaw, Samuel, 36
Rentch, Michael, 98
Rentfro, Absalom, 194
Renwick, John, 35
Respass, Robert, 194
Restine, Henry, 91
Reybourn, Robert, 21
Reynick, Henry, 20
Reynolds, Charles, 7
  John, 20
  William, 93
Rhea, Daniel, 58
  Robert, 37
Rhoads, Henry, 133
Rhodes, Bennett, 194
  David, 41
  Solom, 117
Rice, Jacob, 138
  James, 96
  Jesse, 53, 151
  John, 19, 96
  Joshua, 117
  Larkin, 151
  William, 103
  William M., 103
Richards, Ambrose R., 194
  Arnold, 100
  Josiah, 132
  Phillip, 26
  William, 132, 194
Richardson, Daniel, 121
  David, 140
  Isaac, 76
  Jesse, 7,21,40,140,156
  John, 35, 89
  John, Jr., 121
  Joseph, 33
  William, 58
  Dr. William C., 194
Richerson, Daniel, 42
Richeson, John, 96

Richeson, cont'd.
  Joseph, 96
  Joseph, Jr., 96
  Thomas, 194
Richey, Elijah, 194
  James, 115, 149
  James, Jr., 115
  John, 194
  Stephen, 142, 194
Richie, James, 194
  Stephen, 194
Rickar, John, 6
Ricketts, Richard, 9
Ridgley, Frederick, 33
Rife, Christopher, 194
Rifle, John, 30
Rigdon, John, 23
Rigg, John, 194
Riggs, Erasmus, 64
Right, Jacob, 64
  John, 151
  William, 13
Riker, Samuel, 194
Riley, Daniel, 149
  James, 98
  John, 121
  Leven, 64
  Rasmus, 103
  Robert, 129
Rinarson, Christopher, 194
Ring, William, 33
Ringland, Joseph, 127
Ringo, Joseph, 132
Ripley, Richard, 194
Ripperton, John, 129
Risk, John, 194
Risley, John, 138
Ritchea, Alexander, 74
  George, 74
Ritcher, Alexander, 17
  George, 17
Ritchey, Adam, 115
  John, 76
Ritchie, John, 5
Ritter, Richard, 44
Rizley, John, 138
Roach, Matthew, 115
Robards, Joseph, 10
  Lewis, 67
  William, 194
Robb, Joseph, 81
  Robert, 44
  Thomas, 194
Roberts, Benjamin, 51
  Elisha, 42, 194
  Handley, 194
  James, 94
  John, 44, 125, 194
  Joseph, 31, 103
  Joshua, 125
  Niely, 64
  William, 29, 129
Robertson, Andey, 127
  David, 52
  Fleming, 151, 194
  George, 31, 46
  James, 41, 151
  Jesse, 17
  John, 10,11,31,54,117
  Joseph, 2, 136
  Littleton, 103, 194
  Robert, 16
  William, 69
  Zachariah, 69
Robeson, William, 195
Robins, Aron, 26
  Thomas, 35
  Vincent, 51
Robinson, Edward, 195
  George, 142, 146, 195
  Isaac, 156
  James, 195
  John, 11, 76, 132

Robinson, cont'd.
  Joseph, 2, 100
  Joshua, 146
  Littleton, 103
  Stephen, 70
  William, 195
  Zaphaniah, 64
Roby, Barton, 136
Rodes, Waller, 142
Rodgers, George, 33
  William, 17, 47
  William C., 195
Roe, Thomas, 195
Rogers, Bird, 58
  Charles, 94
  Coleman, 156
  Ezekiel, 74
  George, 195
  John, 96, 117, 195
  Jonathan, 136
  Lewis, 58
  Thomas, 2, 132
  William, 12,47,70,132, 136,151
Rollings, Michael, 54
Rollins, Stephen, 12
Rolston, Joseph, 58
Romjeu. See Rumjul.
Rose, Joseph, 86
  Lewis, 10
  Mathias, 6
Ross, Charles, 107
  Henry, 41
  James, 195
  Joseh, 125
  Philip, 20, 107
  Presley, 195
  Stephen, 107
  William, 9, 81
  Zachariah, 26, 35
Rotramell, John, 117
Rounseval, Josiah, 115
Rouse, William, 81
Rout, John, 94
Rowland, Jacob, 100
  Reuben, 195
  Robert, 46
  William, 89
Rowlings, Edward, 195
Royal, Stephen, 142
Rozel, Stephen, 49
Rub, John (?), 6
Ruble, Isaac, 146
  Jacob, 146
Ruby, John, 101
Rucker, Reuben, 195
Ruddell, Stephen, 195
Ruddle, John, 29
Rudy, Daniel, 107
  George, 107
Rule, Andrew, 64
  Matthew, 64
  Ninian, 81
  Samuel, 64
  Thomas, 64
Rumjul, John, 103
Runion, David, 195
Runnard, Benjamin, 140
Runyon, Martin, 121
Rush, Peter, 30
  Thomas, 195
Rusk, William, 74
Russel, Andrew, 40
  Robert, 33
  Samuel, 134
  William, 59, 96
Russell, Charles, 13
  Handly, 41
  Robert, 81, 156
  Samuel, 195
  Thomas, 195
  William, 5, 19, 55, 156
Rutherford, John, Jr., 56

Rutledge, Isaac, 96
Rutter, Ed(mund?), 151
Ryan, Solomon, 129
Rycar, John, 146
  See also Riker, Ryker.
Ryker, Gerardis, 51
  John, 51
Ryland, Nicholas, 25, 146
Ryley, Leven, 64

S

Sadler, Jesse, 64
St. Clair, William, 195
Sale, Lewis, 107
  Robert, 91
Salisbury, Nathaniel, 140
Salley, William, 195
Sample, John, 14
Sampson, Benjamin, 121
Samuel, James, 12
  John, 103
  Reubin, 195
  Robert, 12
  Thomas, 142
  William, 89, 103
Samuels, James, 136
  William, 136
Sander, Henry, 195
Sanders, Charles, 5
  Hanary, 20
  James, 86
  John, 103
  John, Jr., 89, 91
  Mibird, 81
  Reymon, 195
  Robert, 25
  Samuel, 91
  William, 59, 69, 195
  Zachariah, 153
Sandford, Thomas, 30, 70, 156
Sandusky, John, 13
Sapp, Caleb, 112
Sappington, Richard, 121
Sargeant, William, 35
Sargent, John, 125
Sasseen, Francis, 94
  Louis, 94
Satterwhite, Mann, 81
Saunders, Hugh, 89
  John, 59, 195
  Nathaniel, 5
  Rayman, 195
Sayers, John, 195
Saylers, Dunn, 94
Sayling, William, 149
Saylor (?), John, 86
Scaggs, William, 20
Scandland, Benjamin, 49
Scarce, Robert, 54
Scearce, Robert, 54
Schofield, Henry, 125
Scholefield, Henry, 86
  John, 112
Scholl, Isaac, 19
  Joseph, 5
Schooler, Nathan, 195
Scirvin, Clayton, 195
Scisars, Mathias, 146
Scissell, James, 136, 195
  See also Cissel, Seissel
Scoby, Stephen, 74
Scott, Abraham, 142
  Andrew, 6
  Benjamin, 19
  Charles, 1, 15
  Daniel, 136
  Elijah, 29, 103
  George, 2, 16
  James, 2, 86
  Joel, 142
  John, 23,29,35,64,67,100, 146,195

Scott, cont'd.
  John M., 35, 89
  Martin, 146
  Moses, 34, 74
  Robert, 29,64,100,151,195, 196
  Samuel, 33, 64, 81
  Solomon, 125
  Thomas, 30,100,109,196
  Thomas B., 196
  William, 81, 107, 196
Scraggs, Thomas, 142
Scroggin, George, 64
Scroggins, John, 29
  Joseph, 81
Scrogham, Joseph, 81, 196
Scrogin, Robert, 64
  Thomas, 100
Sea, Leonard, 129
Seabury, Uriel, 70
  See also Uriel Sebree.
Searce, Henry, 146
Searcey, Berry, 196
Searcy, Asa, 8
  Berry, 35
  Edmund, 27
  Samuel, 121
Seaton, George, 107
  James, 107, 196
Seay, Jacob, 151
  Samuel, 151
Sebastian, William, 42
Sebree, Uriel, 196
  See also Uriel Seabury.
Seburn, Jacob, 121
Seever, Henry, 64
Seisam, Benjamin, 23
Seissel, Ignatius, 136
Seitz, J.A., 81
  John A., 109
Selden, George, 65
Self, John, 121
Selby, Thomas, 20
Selfe, John, 42
Semple, George, 59
  John W., 76
Senter, James, 196
Sevier, Enoch, 129
Seward, Daniel, 69
Shackleford, Bennet, 113
  Edward, 7, 22, 36
  James, 8, 113, 196
  John, 23,34,113,125
  Richard, 21
  Robert, 196
  Samuel, 196
  Thomas, 196
  William, 40, 86
  Zachariah, 7
Shacklett, Benjamin, 98
Shadburn, William, 196
Shadwell, William, 196
Shain, Francis, 48, 67
Shanacy, William, 196
Shank, John, 146
Shanklett, Benjamin, 98
Shanklin, Gordon, 109
  John, 196
  William, 67
Shanks, Thomas, 196
Shannon, George, 13
  James, 146
  Joseph, 117
Shanucy, William, 196
Sharp, Abraham, 90
  Anthony, 146
  George, 74
  James, 196
  John, 69
  Maxwell, 117
  Phidelio C., 156
  Richard, 30, 69
  Solomon, 125

Sharp, cont'd.
  Stephen, 132
Shatton, John, 88
Shaughton, John, 65
Shaver, Benjamin, 196
  David, 146
Shaw, John, 69
  Michael, 103
  William, 65, 115
Shealds, William, 196
Shealy, William, 81
Shears, Charles, 5
Sheats, Henry, 35
Sheets, Henry, 90
Shelady, George, 146
Shelby, James, 196
  Moses, 31
  Moses, Jr., 116
Sheley, David, 5
Shelton, Curtis, 196
  Liberty, 196
  Medley, 142, 196
  Thomas, 121, 196
Shepard, John, 196
Shepherd, Abraham, 65
  Samuel, 13
Sheppard, Adam, 67
Sherron, Peter, 2
Shetford, William, 116
Shewmate, Nimrod, 196
Shields, James, 20
  John, 100
  William, 196
Shipley, Robert, 149
Shipman, William, 146, 196
Shipp, Jacob, 100
Shirley, Charles, 196
Shivley, Philip, 107, 197
Shivly, Jacob, 20
Shock, John, 33, 81
Shockency, Elijah, 136
Shoemaker, Leonard C., 111
Shook, John, 7
Shoptaw, William, 197
Shores, Richard, 5, 19
Short, Obed, 142
Shortridge, Daniel, 142
  George, 2,16,65,197
  William, 65
Shrader, Jacob, 6
Shreader, Christopher, 107
Shroud, William, 48
Shryock, Matthias, 81
Sibert, Peter, 151
Sibley, Isaac, 101
Sidner, Peter, 33
Sill, Adam, 147
Silvertooth, John, 129
Simalt, Philip, 197
Simmons, Griffith, 67
  Joseph, 197
  William, 12, 67
Simons, Peter, 117
Simpson, Benjamin,116,121
  James, 152
  John, 19
  Joseph, 47,51,147,197
  Moses, 153
  Robert, 51, 130
  Samuel, 5
  Thomas, 59, 197
  William, 81, 116, 197
Simrall, James, 197
  William F., 107, 197
Sims, Randol, 197
Singleton, Jaconiar, 27
  Jechonias, 197
  Louis, 140
  Mason, 109, 197
  Philip, 197
  Richard, 197
Sinks, Jacob, 197
Sites, John, 2, 65

Skaggs, David, 20, 37
  Frederick, 20
  James, 11, 96
  Solomon, 37
  Stephen, 136
  William, 11
Skidmore, Joseph, 113
Skinner, Cornelius, 74
  Theopolis, 71, 197
  William, 71
Slack, Jacob, 45
  Randolph, 197
Slaughter, Gabriel, 130
  George, 35
  James, Jr., 49
  John H., 197
  Robert, Sr., 49, 136
  Robert C., 98
Sleet, Weeden, 70, 197
Slegar, David, 39
Sloane, Thomas, 38
Small, Henry, 125, 197
  James, 44, 125
  John, 22
Smalley, Andrew, 127
Smiley, Hugh, 71
Smilie, Thomas, 153
Smiser, John, 65
Smith, Abraham, 113, 147
  Charles, 2
  Daniel, 37, 101
  David, 31, 103
  Edmund, 94
  Enoch, 47
  George, 59,65,81,197
  Gideon, 111
  Hugh, 59
  Humphrey, 154
  Jacob, 6, 65
  Jacob J., 65
  James, 35,36,65,81,94,98
  Jesse, 10
  John, 5,29,59.94,100,113,
    125,140,197,198
  John B., 134, 198
  Jonathan, 198
  Joseph, 86
  Lawrence, 20
  Martin, 33, 81
  Nathan, 65
  Nicholas, 53,103,147,152
  Rhodes, 25
  Richard, 149
  Robert, 127, 140
  Samuel, 9,44,103,121
  Simeon, 86
  Thomas, 42,96,121,152,198
  Weathers, 198
  Weeden, 94
  Weldon, 65
  William, 36,37,39,59,76,
    94,113,198
Smither, John, 90
Smithers, William, 138
Smithey, Fielding, 198
Smock, Henry, 13, 152, 198
Smyth, Samuel, 33
Snap (?), George, 65
  Lewis, 198
Sneed, John, 198
Sneid, John, 136
Snell, John, 198
Snellen, William, 49
Snider, Jacob, 11
  See also Syhneider.
Snoddy, Abner, 65
  John, 121, 198
  Samuel, 121, 198
Snodgrass, Benjamin, 65
  David, 117, 198
  Samuel, 198
Snow, Aquila, 121
Snyder, John, 24

Sons, Abraham, 116
Soreney, (no first name), 2
South, Benjamin, 132, 198
  John, 5, 55, 81
  Samuel, 8,22,121,156
  Weldon, 65, 198
Southerland, John, 198
Soward, Richard, 44, 198
Spalding, Richard, 198
  Thomas, 152, 198
Spangler, David, 107
  John, 33
Sparkes, Daniel, 67
Sparks, Daniel, 6
  George, 86
  James, 20
  Thomas, 198
Spear, James E., 107
  James G., 107
Spears, George, 37, 96
  Jacob, 3
  John, 81
  Samuel, 198
Speed, John, 198
Spelman, Charles, 94
Spencer, Barnard, 198
  Edward, 14, 27
  John, 23, 65
  Sharp, 49, 136
  Spear, 12, 51, 147
Spergeon, Moses, 198
Spicer, Rawser, 65
Spilman, Charles, 10
  James, 23
Spinks, Ignatius, 152
Spires, Solom, 109
Spradlin, Obediah, 132
Spragens, Nathaniel, 113
Spragin, William, 113
Spratt, William, 198
Springer, Charles, 152
Spur, William, 81
Spurgen, David, 65
  Isaac, 17
  Zephan, 65
Spurlock, David, 88
Spurr, James G., 107
Sqires, Cal., 81
Squires, Caleb. See Cal.
  Sqires.
Sroufe, Adam, 127
Staat, Stephen, 90
Stafford, Thomas, 198
  William, 47
Stagner, William, 149
Standeford, Elisha, 107,198
  Nathaniel C., 125
Stansel, Henry, 44
Stapleton, George, 198
Stapp, Elijah, 198
Stark, David, 198
Starke, John, Jr., 65
Starks, William, 67
Stat, Robert, 65
Staundeford, Israel, 147
Steel, Jacob, 34
  Solomon, 86
  William, 14
Steele, Jacob, 34
  Solomon, 86
  William, 14
Steele, Adam, 51, 147
  James, 81
  Richard, 147
Steen, John, 24
Steenburgen, Robert P., 59
  William, 59
Steene, William, 7
Stepenson, Andrew, 76
Stephens, Elijah, 116
  Jac., 113
  James, 5, 74
  Joseph, 198

Stephens, cont'd.
  Peter, 76
  Richard, 11, 49
  Seth, 33
  Wilford, 90
Stephenson, Benjamin, 199
  David, 40
  James, 142
  John, 130, 199
  Joseph H., 199
  Mills, 9
  Richard, 125
  Robert, 7, 100
  William, 29,33,100,199
Stepp, Elijah, 22
Sterman, Thomas I., 199
Stevens, John, 199
  Thomas, 81
Stevenson, John, 121
  William, 81, 199
Steward, Charles, 113
  Robert, 23
  William, 199
Stewart, Abraham,31,71,116
  Charles, 41, 136, 140
  Christian P., 70
  Christopher P., 199
  Elijah, 199
  James, 14, 27, 199
  James H., 19, 82
  Jesse, 38, 69
  John, 65, 82
  Robert, 44
  William, 44,101,125
  Willoughby, 125
Sthreshly, Thomas G., 82
  William, 82
Stillwell, John, 147
Stinson, John, 3
  Robert, 111
Stith, Baldwin, 44
  Baldwin B., 44
  Joseph, 199
Stockdon, Edward, 86
  George, 9
  Robert, 59
Stockton, John, 199
Stokes, Absalom, 116
Stone, Asa, 142
  Elijah, 136
  James, 33, 65
  Jesse, 199
  John, 142, 199
  Robert, 132
Stonestreet, John D., 109
Stotts, James, 111, 199
Stout, Benjamin, 82
  David, 5
  James, 51
Stowers, William, 100,199
Stratton, Aaron, 44, 199
  Harry, 88
  Henry, 199
  Tandy, 86, 88
Strawder, George, 65
Strawhan, Benjamin, 121
Strawther, John, 107
Strickling, David, 9
Stringfield, John, 52
Strode, Jeremiah, 17
  Stephen, 31
Strong, Waller Edward, 10
  Walter E., 10, 46
  William, 88
Strother, George, 65
  Joseph, Jr., 107
Stroud, Stephen, 74
  Thomas P., 199
Strowhorn, Joseph, 121
Strutten, Solomon, 23
Stuart, John, 65
Stublefield, William, 125
Stucker, Jacob, 13, 54
  Philip, 27

Studebaker, Jacob, 134
Sturgis, James, 147
Sublett, Abraham, 96
  Phil. A., 140
Sudduth, William, 17, 74
Sugget, James, 49
Sullinger, Thomas, 154
Sullivan, William, 6, 107
Summers, Benjamin, 68
  Daniel, 65
  William, 86
Summit, George, 3
Survell, Benjamin, 9
Sutherland, John, Jr., 199
Sutherlin, John, Jr., 199
Sutphin, John, 199
Suttles, Edward, 199
Sutton, James, 7, 113, 199
  Thomas, 199
  William, 65,96,142,153
Swan, John, 199
Swaney, Henry, 147
Swank, Jacob, 98, 199
Swart, John, 69
Sweaney, James, 29
  John, 29
Swearengen, Andrew, 132
  William D., 150
Swearingen, Abijah, 107
  Charles, 13
  William, 150
Swearingham, Andrew, 47
  Joseph, 16
Sweet, Benjamin, 23
Sweetnum, George, 142
Sweets, Thomas, 49, 137
Swenk, Jacob, 199
Sweny, Job, 199
Swetman, George, 142
Swetnam, George, 199
Swift, John, 41
Swigert, John, 82
Swiget, James, 199
Swiggitt, James, 199
Swim, Alexander, 132
Swiney, Jobe, 199
Swinney, Henry, 200
  James, 29
  John, 33
  Shepherd, 113
Swope, Charles, 94
  George, 76
Swords, Daniel, 69
  Donald, 30
Syhneider, Samuel, 98
  See also Snider.
Symes, Randall, 8
Sypoald, Jasper, 23

T

Talbert, Gazaway, 200
Talbot, Edmond, 101
  George, 109
  Hugh, 29, 65
  James, 70
  John, 65
  Joshua, 116
  Thomas, 200
Talbott, Nicholas, 200
Talbut, William, 200
Taliafero, John C., 200
Talmage, Thomas, 86
Tandy, Gabriel, 65
  John, 90
  William, 200
Tanner, Matthew, 103
  William, 113
Tarleton, Caleb, 142
Tarlton, Ralph, 200
Tate, Isaac, 200
  Stephen, 41

Tatem, Seewood(?), 200
Taul, Micajah, 153, 200
  Samuel, 200
Taull, Bazil, 86
Taurence, David, 49
Taylor, Benjamin, 91
  Colby, 107
  Edmund, 70, 156, 200
  Edward, 125
  Francis, 9, 107
  George, 5, 86, 200
  George G., 74
  Hubbard, 74
  Isaac, 49, 76
  James, 52,70,125,200
  John, 24,36,52,86,200
  Jonathan, 107, 200
  Joseph, 27, 154
  Nathaniel, 107, 200
  Richard, 14, 138, 147
  Robert, 200
  Dr. Septemus, 200
  Septim, 65
  Simon, 200
  Tekler, 41
  Thompson, 20, 107
  William, 52, 200
  Zachariah, 152
Tedder, John, 59
  Kinsey, 59
Teder, Valentine, 42
Teeter, George, 200
Temple, Robert (W.?), 200
Tendley, Charles, 200
Tennille, John, 134
Tensly, William, 200
Terhoon, Jacob, 86
Terhune, Jacob, 86
Terrel, John, 47
Terrell, Edmund, 8
Terrill, Edmund, 8, 22,36
  John, 200
  Robert L., 200
Tharp, Josiah, 121
  Samuel, 3
Thatcher, Daniel, 70
Thomas, Edward, 1
  Elisha, 25, 37
  Hardin, 13, 98
  Henry, 76
  Jacob, 44
  James, 121
  Jesse B., 127
  John, 11,12,24,45,55,113, 156,200
  John D., 200
  Joseph, 65,90,130,200
  Joshua, 91
  Massey, 98
  Notley, 200
  Obediah, 200
  Phenis, 125
  Philemon, 45, 55
  Reuben, 200
  Richard Moore, 54
  Robert, 56, 96, 103
  Rowland, 45
  Solomon, 142
  Thruston, 44
  William, 14
  Zachariah, 121
Thomison, John, 69
Thompson, Abraham, 38, 132
  Andrew, 34
  Anthony, 27, 54
  Austin, 152
  Clifton, 5
  Daniel, 65, 200
  David, 74,143,200,201
  George, 130
  George B., 201
  George W., 201
  Gilbert, 143

Thompson, cont'd.
  Hugh, 5, 33
  James, 100
  John, 49,71,116,201
  Neil, 74
  Rhodes, 13
  Samuel, 130, 201
  Thomas, 100,132,140,152
  Thomas A., 29
  William, 3, 5, 59
  William, Jr., 7
Thomson, David, 201
Thornton, Henry, 65
Thorpe, Zach., 42
Thrailkel, Daniel, 201
Thrailkell, John, 201
Thrasher, Stephen,25,69,201
  William, 30, 69
Threlkeld, John, Jr., 147
Throckmorton, Aris, 201
Throgmorton, Ariss, 201
  Thomas, 201
Thruston, John, 6
  Seth, 109
Thurman, Fielding, 19
  Richard, 20
Tichnor, Timothy, 98
Tilford, David, 49
Tillett, Giles, 29
  James, 16, 29
Tilley, Aaron, 147
Tilton, Peter, 82
Timberlake, Henry, 201
  William, 130
Timmerson, John, 29
Timmons, George, 101
Tincle, George, 7
Tinsley, Archibald, 90
  Samuel, 147
  William, 18, 53, 147
Tipton, Moses, 201
Tittle, John, 38
Titus, John, 121, 201
Tivis, Robert, 121
Todd, Benjamin, 201
  Daniel, 201
  David, 201
  Davis, 82, 201
  John, 65, 82
  Levi, 5, 55
  Robert, 1, 15
  Thomas, 7
Tolbert, Hugh, 65
  Samuel, 201
Tolbott, Nicholas, 201
Tomason, Joseph T., 201
Tomkins, Tartin, 65
Toomy, John, 69
Toutt, Basil, 86
Towns, Oswald, 42, 121
Townsend, Lite, 117
  Thomas, 42, 121
Trabue, Daniel, 14,27,56, 96
  Edward, 54, 154
  Robert, 56, 96
  Stephen, 56
Tramcand, William, 6
Tramel, Philip, 117
Trammel, John, 147
Trammell, John, 201
Trapp, John, 113, 140
Travis, Charles, 98
  Daniel, 116
Trigg, Stephen, 122, 201
  William, 90
Trimble, George, 116
  James, 29
  John, 3, 201
  Robert, 16
  Walter, 116
Triplet, Greensbury, 86
Triplett, Hedgeman, 50,143

Trixall, Jacob, 153
Trotter, George, Jr., 82,201
  James, 5, 50, 65
  Joseph, 16
  William, 13, 201
Troutman, Jacob, 12
True, William, 82
Trumbo, John, 132
Trunnel, Basil, 65
Trussell, John, 125
Tucker, Edward, 201
  Elias, 66
  Leonard, 16, 29
  William, 56
Tuder, Valentine, 8
Tudor, Kinsey, 59
Tully, Israel, 86
  Wyatt P., 107
Tuly, Charles, 6
Tunstal, James, 147
Tunstall, Henry, 90, 201
  Richard, 122
  William, 147
  William J., 147, 201
Turley, Samuel, 122
Turnbel, Moses, 150
Turnbo, Isaac, 117
Turner, Charles, 46
  Edward, 8
  Fielding Lewis, 19,82
  John, 8
  Nelson, 201
  Richard, 66
  Samuel, 82
  Thomas, 42
Turney, John, 76
Turnham, John, 152
Turpin, Champion, 42
Tutt, Thomas, 137
Tuttle, William, 201
Twyman, Reuben, 14
Tyler, Charles, 33
  James, 150
  John, 117
  Robert, 20
Tylor, Charles, 82
  Levi, 201
Tyra, Isom, 66

U

Ulrey, Jacob, 51
Umphers, John, 113
Uncell, Henry, 201
Ussery, William, 140
Utterback, Lewis, 27

V

Valandingham, George, 19
Valindingham, George, 19
Vanarsdall, Lucas, 46
Vanasdal, Cornelius O., 130
Vancleave, Benjamin, 201
  Samuel, 202
Vancleve, Peter, 202
Vanderon, Godfrey, 202
Vandiver, Asbury, 113
  Thomas, 153
VanHook, Samuel, 38
VanHorn, Thomas, 69
Vanmetre, Morgan, 3
Vanpelt, Samuel, 82
Vanvacter, Benjamin, 98
Vanwinckle, Abraham, 140
Vanwinkle, Abraham, 153
Varnon, John, 66
Vatner, Daniel, 202
Vaughan, George, 31
  John, 6, 14
  Joseph, 31
Vaughter, William, 12

Vaughtier, -ehemen, 202
Vawter, Hayman. See
  -ehemen
Vaughtier.
  Jameson, 202
  John, 90
  William, 202
Vawters, William, 54
Veach, Jeremiah, 100
  Thomas, 38
Veal, William, 51
Veanoy, Anderson, 10
Vemount, Louis, 202
Venable, Abraham, 5
Vernon, John, 66
Vertress, John, 138
Vertresse, Jacob, 202
  John, 202
Vertrice, Joseph, 11
Viers, Robert, 202
Vimont, Lewis, 66
Vineyard, Absolam, 100
Vitetow, James, 202
Vitito, Samuel, 11
Vittetow, William, 137
Voorheis, Peter G., 35,55
Voress, Cornelius, 10
Voshell, Daniel, 44
Vowls, Thomas, 202
Vowshel, Daniel, 126

W

Waddle, Charles, 202
Waddy, Samuel, 147
Wade, Daniel, 98
  Dawson, 132, 202
  James, 18, 107
  Joseph, 140, 153
  Pierce, 7
  See also Pearce Waid.
  William, 113, 202
Wadkins, Josiah, 98
Wsdlington, Ferdinand, 72
  James, 116
  William, 116
Waggoner, John, 66, 202
Wagoner, John, 101
Waid, Pearce, 40
  See also Pierce Wade.
Wakefield, John, 12
  William, 137, 202
Walford, Adam, 107
Walingford, Joseph, 202
Walker, Alexander, 9,96,100
  Charles, 19
  David V., 202
  George, 109, 147
  James, 44,53,122,126,150
  John, 37,59,66,138,152,202
  John W., 202
  Joseph, 96
  Patterson, 202
  Philip, 10, 46
  Richard, 202
  Stephen, 122
  William, 126,138,202
Wall, Garrett, 100, 202
Wallace, Andrew, 202
  John, 3,5,16,66,72,122,202
  Jonathan, 76
  Samuel, 154
  Thomas, 82, 202
  William, 126
Waller, John, 202
  Mathias, 49
  Pleasant, 72
  Stephen, 147
  Thomas, 66
  William S., 202
Wallingford, John, 202
Wallis, Michael, 127
  William, 31

Walls, John, 20, 66
  William, 13, 147
Walters, James, 98
Walton, John, 86
  Matthew, 13, 55
  Robert, 127
  Thomas, 202
Wapshot, Graves, 13, 152
  James, 26
Ward, Andrew, 38
  Benjamin, 3, 16, 66
  Charles, 126
  George, 5, 19
  James, 9, 100, 132
  John, 100
  Jonathan, 117
  Nathaniel, 59
  Thomas, 31
  Thompson, 66
  William, 28, 50
Warden, John, 202
Wardlaw, John, 82
Ware, James, 66
  Thompson, 66, 202
Warfield, Dr. Nicholas, 202
  Walter, 33
Warfoed, David, 6
Waring, Clement, 126
  Francis, 126
Warney, Jonathan, 9
Warren, James, 132, 150
  John, 113
  Martin, 56
  Thomas, 40
  William, 156
Wartlow, John, 82
Warwick, John, 86, 87
Washburn, Benjamin, 66
  John, 13
  Phillip, 26
  Samuel, 107
Washburne, Delany, 107
Washer, Joseph, 137
Waters, Conrad, 11
  John, 11
  Richard, 202
  William, 68
Watkins, Benjamin, 154
  George, 152
  Isaac, 51, 147
  Joseph, 202
Watson, David, 202
  James, 49
  Joab, 150
  John, 44
  William, 127
Watts, George, 53
  Julius, 74
  Peter, 10, 46
Weagle, John, 203
Weagly, Abraham, 33
Weas, Philip, 37
Weatherington, David, 203
  John, 45
  Joseph, 203
Weathers, Carland, 203
  Gideon, 203
  James, 113, 203
  John, 50
Weaver, George, 152
  John, 70
  Philip, 87, 203
Webb, Charles, 33
  Edward, 17
  George, 74
  Jesse, 41
  John V., 143, 203
  Samuel, 147
Webber, Archer, 203
  Philip, 109
  William, 203
Webster, William, 113
Weedman, Jacob, 98

Weekly. See Weigley.
Weid, Peace, 21
Weigley, Abraham, 91
Weir, Bazaliel, 101
  James, 134
Weisager, John K., 154
Weiseger, Daniel, 35
Welch, William, 116
Weldon, John, 8
Weller, Henry, 137, 203
Wells, Benjamin, 66
  Edward, 132
  Francis, 3, 203
  James, 203
  John, 66, 147
  Joseph, 122
  Levi, 156
  Micajah, 203
  Samuel, 6,20,55,203
  Solomon, 127
  William, 76
  Yelverton Peyton, 20,107
Welsh, Abraham, 126
  Benjamin, 82
West, Alexander, 96,153,203
  Alvan, 66
  Edward, 82
  J., 90
  James, 90
  Joseph, 36
  Lewis, 19
  Lynn, 50, 203
  Richard, 109
  William, 33
Westfall, Cornelius, 37, 98
Whalley, Edward, 66
Whaly, Edward, 66
Whealer, George F., 203
Whealey, James, 203
Whealy, John, 29
Wheat, Jacob, 6
Wheeler, Henry, 116
  Hezekiah, 203
  Ignatius, 203
  Ignatius, Jr., 203
  Leven, 122
Whetherson, John, 49
Whiat, John, 82
  See also John Whyat, Wyatt.
While, Samuel, 203
  See also Wiley.
Whiles, Thomas, 21
Whips, James, 44, 45, 127
  John, 127
Whitacre, Aquilla, 6
Whitaker, Elijah, 51
White, (no first name), 56
  Alexander, 41, 117
  Andrew, Sr., 96
  Archibald, 103, 147
  David, 147
  Hugh, 156, 203
  Jacob, 49, 137
  James, 22, 122
  Jeremiah, 33
  Jesse, 56, 96
  Joel, 122
  John, 42,50,69,143
  John B., 203
  Leonard, 203
  Philip, 90, 203
  Samuel, 96, 203
  Thomas, 96,104,107,147,203
  William, 74, 90, 107, 203
Whitecotton, Moses, 203
Whitehead, John, 91, 94, 203
  Joseph, 152
Whiteman, Benjamin 9, 23
Whiteside, William, 5
Whitesides, Isaac, 147
Whiteson, Andrew, 96
Whitley, Elijah, 31
  William, 7, 21
Whitlock, Nathaniel B., 204

Whittaker, Alexander, 134
  Aquilla, 25
  Elijah, 147
  Isaac, 147
Whittinghill, David, 204
Whittle, John, 113
Whyat, John, 82
  See also John Whiat, Wyatt.
Wiatt, Emanuel, 132
Wickliff, Moses, 204
  Robert, 137
Wickliffe, Martin, 152
Wiggins, Archibald, 204
Wigglesworth, John, 204
  Thompson, 100
  William, 204
Wiggs, Richard, 66
Wilcox, David, 47, 132
  George, 147, 156, 204
  Joseph, 147, 204
  Josiah, 68
Wilds Thomas, 140
Wiles, Thomas, 140
Wiley, Matthew, 82
  Moses, 82
  See also While.
Wilgus, Asa, 82, 204
Wilhoit, Abraham, 137
Wilkerson, James, 98
  John, 122
  Presley, 204
Wilkes, Daniel, 107
Wilkins, Charles, 5
  Stewart, 82, 109
Wilkinson, Abner, 30
  John, 7, 21, 22
Willan, Thomas, 204
Willburn, Edward, 111
Willett, George, 126
  William, Thomas, 96
Williams, Benjamin, 204
  Caleb, 122
  Charles, 90, 204
  Daniel, 8,59,122,204
  David, 204
  Edward, 11
  Ezekiel, 77, 96
  Frederick, 22
  Henson, 82
  Husin, 82
  Isaac, 104
  James, 77, 109, 204
  Jarrod, 12
  Joel, 204
  John, 8,12,31,42,66,104,
    140,154,204
  Jonah, 204
  Joseph, 204
  Lawrence, 9
  Pope, 66
  Roger, 29,66,156,204
  Samuel, 66, 113, 140
  Thomas, 82
  Walter, 94,113
  William, 122, 204
Williamson, John, 147, 204
Willis, Edward, 122
  Matthew, 59
  Thomas, 140
  Wilson, 72
Wills, Alexander, 42
Willson, John, 143
  Sandford, 204
Wilmot, Robert, 3
Wilson, Charles, 33
  Daniel, 18, 87
  George, 11, 24
  Isaac, 90, 137
  Israel, 3, 22
  Jacob, 66
  James, 9, 77, 88, 126
  John, 8,9,12,47,49,101,154
  Matthew, 74
  Nathaniel, 5

Wilson, cont'd.
  Robert, 204
  Samuel, 19,24,69,77,204
  Singleton, 204, 205
  Uriah, 47
  Vance, 137
Wimer, Martin, 82
Winchester, William, 6
Winfrey, James, 205
  John, 56
  William, 56
Wing, Charles, 116, 134
Wingate, Thomas, 90, 205
Winkfield, Henry, 51, 104
Winlock, George, 205
  Joseph, 6,25,55,147
Winn, John, 82, 205
  Thomas, 19, 33
  Thomas M., 205
Winscutt, (no first name)122
Wisdom, Francis, 77
Wise, Abraham, 126, 205
  David, 39, 108
Wisehart, John, 205
Wiseman, Abner, 205
Withrons, John, 24
Withrow, James, 94
Witt, Charles, 205
  William, 122
Witterbach, Martin, 27
Wolf, Lewis, 205
Wood, Abner, 23, 44
  Abraham, 205
  Andrew, 45
  David, 23, 205
  Edmund, 50
  James, 33, 82, 130
  Jesse, 96
  John, 23,40,113,205
  Thomas, 13, 127
  William, 94,104,122,130,
    205
  William J., 59
Woods, Adam, 122
  Archibald, 100
  James, 12
  John, 94,122,147,148
  Moses, 9
  Patrick, 122
  Samuel, 10, 46
  William, 122, 205
Woodside, William, 148
Woodson, Henry, 111
  Samuel H., 109
Woodward, Joel, 45
Wooldridge, Elisha, 27
Wooldrige, Jonah, 14
Woolf, Jacob, 143
  Lewis, 72
Woolfolk, Elijah, 143
  Sowell, 14
Woolford, John, 56, 205
Woolry, Jacob, 205
Work, Samuel, 138
Worker (?), Robert, 74
Workman, Benjamin, 96
Worly, A., 3
Worrell, Atteway, 100
  James, 205
Wortham, Charles, 49
Worthan, Thomas, 205
Worthington, Edward, 7
  John, 205
  Joseph, 127
  William, 134
Worthum, Charles, 137
  Henry, 137
Wren, James, 150
Wright, Andrew, 66
  Benjamin, 98, 205
  Elijah, 150
  Israel, 5
  James, 29, 66, 205

Wright, cont'd.
  John, 40
  Samuel, 205
  William, 66, 82, 205
Wyatt, John, 82, 116, 132, 205
  See also John Whiat, Whyat.
  Joseph, 87, 205
  William, 140
Wyman, Adam, 104

Y

Yagar, Joseph, 206
Yantis, John, 94
Yarborrough, John, 47
Yarbrough, John, 18
Yates, Benjamin, 18
  Joseph, 87
  Stephen, 206
Yathey, Hen., 66
Yeaky. See Yathey.
Yeiser, Jacob, 130, 206
Yeizer, Englehart, 82
  Jacob, 109, 206
Yocum, Jesse, 10
Yorcum, Matthias, 68
Yosom, George, 132
Young, Alexander, 88
  Christopher, 108
  David, 66
  Ezekiel, 31
  Glading, 150
  Henry, 10
  James, 31,87,88,148,206
  John, 206
  Lewis, 54, 154
  Minor, 19
  Nimrod, 206
  Richard, 14
  Richard M., 206
  Robert, 206
  Samuel, 56
  William, 39,56,96,154,206

Z

Zimerman, Frederick, 5
Zumalt. See Simalt.

****

www.ingramcontent.com/pod-product-compliance
Lightning Source LLC
Chambersburg PA
CBHW051424290426
44109CB00016B/1423